PRAISE FOR
The Savage City

"It's an absolute great piece of work."

—Jon Stewart, *The Daily Show*

"T.J. English, who chronicled Irish gangsters in *The Westies*, Vietnamese gangs in Chinatown in *Born to Kill*, and the Mafia's pre-Castro Cuba, returns with a swashbuckling, racially charged nightmare about New York City in the 1960s. This is one nightmare worth reliving because Mr. English so vividly recreates an era. . . . He graphically reconstructs a rampaging decade through three lives."

—*New York Times*

"It's dripping with the kind of detail that's too good to make up."

—*Mother Jones*

"A searing profile of an ugly New York. . . . *The Savage City* is meant to make us look back in anger and sorrow, perhaps to reflect upon what stayed the same as things changed."

—*New York Daily News*

"Epic new history. . . . English has found iconic characters for a particular time and place—New York in the 1960s and 1970s."

—*The Village Voice*

"A brutal reminder that New York was not always such a welcoming place."

—*New York Post*

"*The Savage City* is spellbinding and suspenseful. . . . The author masterfully recreates [an] urban underworld. . . . [His] sympathy for his subjects and his decision to let them speak for themselves gives the narrative immediacy and power."

—*Pittsburgh Post-Gazette*

"A comprehensive, still-shocking exhumation of racial discord in America."

—*Kirkus Reviews*

"An epic look at the racial animus, fear, and hatred that characterized [a] troubled decade. Drawing on interviews with former police and prosecutors, activists, hustlers, and journalists, English recounts a time of growing and visceral hostility between a police department steeped in corruption and a besieged black community that exploded in violence. . . . Through the lives of three ostensibly unrelated men, English peels back the underlying turmoil that led to the violent period and the unaddressed social ills that remain to this day."

—*Booklist* (starred review)

"Forget Vietnam—New York City in the 1960s and 1970s hosted its own civil war between a racist police force and a newly militant black underclass, according to this bare-knuckled true-crime saga. . . . English paints a vivid, gritty panorama of a city wracked by racial insurgency, showing us precinct house backrooms where black suspects are beaten and white perps let off with a bribe, seething ghettos ready to riot at the next police shooting, and mean streets where the cops themselves face machine-gun fire. . . . A gripping, noirish retrospective of an era when brutal misrule sparked desperate rage."

—*Publishers Weekly*

"*The Savage City* is a necessary examination of the people, passions, and maligned principles by which New York City once lived and died. English has a magnificent sense of the manner in which people, landscape, and history are bound together. Every world is a corner and every corner is a world."

—Colum McCann, author of *Let the Great World Spin*

"T.J. English has mastered the hybrid narrative art form of social history and underworld thriller. *The Savage City* is a truly gripping read filled with unexpected twists and turns. Highly recommended."

—Douglas Brinkley,
author of *The Wilderness Warrior* and *The Great Deluge*

"T.J. English's magisterial history of New York City in the 1960s and '70s deals with race and corruption within the New York Police Department and the so-called justice system."

—Leonard Levitt, author of *NYPD Confidential*

THE SAVAGE CITY

Also by T.J. English

Havana Nocturne

Paddy Whacked

Born to Kill

The Westies

THE
SAVAGE

CITY

Race, Murder, and a
Generation on the Edge

T.J. English

WILLIAM MORROW
An Imprint of HarperCollins*Publishers*

Grateful acknowledgment is made for permission to reprint the following:

"The Payback," words and music by James Brown, Fred Wesley, and John Starks, © 1973 (renewed) Dynatone Publishing Company. All rights administered by Unichappell Music, Inc. All rights reserved. Used by permission of Alfred Music Publishing Co., Inc.

A hardcover edition of this book was published in 2011 by William Morrow, an imprint of HarperCollins Publishers.

HarperCollins books may be purchased for educational, business, or sales promotional use. For information please write: Special Markets Department, HarperCollins Publishers, 10 East 53rd Street, New York, NY 10022.

FIRST WILLIAM MORROW PAPERBACK EDITION PUBLISHED 2012.

The Library of Congress has catalogued the hardcover edition as follows:

English, T. J., 1957–
    The savage city : race, murder, and a generation on the edge / by T. J. English.
        p.   cm.
    Includes bibliographical references and index.
    ISBN 978-0-06-182455-5
    1. Murder—New York (State)—New York. 2. Violence—New York (State)—New York. 3. Police corruption—New York (State)—New York. 4. New York (N.Y.)—Race relations. I. Title.
HV6534.N5E54   2011
364.109747'1—dc22
                                                                                    2010052270

ISBN 978-0-06-182458-6 (pbk.)

12 13 14 15 16   OV/RRD   10 9 8 7 6 5 4 3 2 1

For George Whitmore

CONTENTS

INTRODUCTION

THE STREETS OF New York City are saturated with blood.

This is more than a metaphor. In the largest city in the United States, generations of inhabitants have given their lives to the wheels of progress. They have been struck and killed by taxis, buses, or subway trains; thrown off buildings onto the sidewalk below; trapped in burning tenements and charred to death; blown up by exploding manhole covers; electrocuted by falling telephone wires; mugged, stabbed, or shot by depraved and desperate criminals; shot dead in the street by family members or other loved ones; shot dead by police officers; even incinerated by terrorists flying jetliners into the side of a building.

Untold thousands, perhaps millions, have fallen prey to the perils of municipal dysfunction, to the growing pains of a city forced to adjust to violent demographic shifts, internal hostilities, wrenching social changes anticipated by no one.

In recent years, New York has been promoted as the Safest Big City in America. This claim is made without irony, as if the previous fifty years of the city's existence were nothing more than a bad dream.

Yet it was not so long ago that the city was perched on the brink of self-immolation. Beginning in the early 1960s, a mood of uncertainty and menace entered the bloodstream of the great metropolis. The result was a spiraling crime rate unlike anything the city had seen before. For the first time since the years of the Great Depression, the violence became a daily reality throughout the five boroughs, something you could reach out and touch. Citizens walking to the corner deli after dark were mugged or shanked for the change in their pockets. Dope fiends, armed and danger-ous, climbed over rooftops and down fire escapes to steal valuables from apartments, offices, and cars. Rapists walked around with their dicks hanging out. There was all manner of homicide, the plaintive sound of sirens in the night, the rancid smell of a city that had begun to rot.

This book covers the ten-year period when New York City began its now-legendary descent into mayhem. From 1963 to 1973, crime became a viral infection that gripped the body politic. The shocking upsurge in predatory violence led to fear, and that fear led to more violence. Free-flowing hostility among the city's inhabitants fueled the paranoiac mood. Longtime residents sensed that the city was entering a period of transition and were troubled by the prospect. The best that could be said was that New York was going through some kind of evolution, pushing itself toward something—but what? Urban hell on earth? Armageddon? Better days in the afterlife?

The city had always been a complex organism. It had endured its share of growing pains before, often involving the cycles of violence and fear that were the consequence of an evolutionary process. A city could attempt to manage and control the potential for crime and danger within its city limits, but no municipal government, no citizens action group, can fully foresee the larger trends that shape an urban universe from the outside. The era of turmoil that began in 1963 had many internal factors—some of which will be detailed in this book—but one event that would reshape the city in surprising ways occurred hundreds of miles away, in a dusty hamlet outside the town of Clarksdale, Mississippi.

On October 2, 1944, just outside town on Highway 49, a crowd of people gathered on a modest plantation to see the very first public dem-onstration of a working, production-ready mechanical cotton picker. At that moment, in Mississippi, a demographic bomb exploded that sent seismic waves out across the United States. Every region and most cities would be affected, but none more so than northern industrial centers like New York.

For generations, cotton picking in the South had been a source of employment and servitude for the descendants of slaves, who had sur-vived all manner of human horror to find themselves at the mercy of the system known as sharecropping. The workers who spent long, back-breaking days in the fields, picking cotton by hand, received abysmal pay—sometimes as low as five dollars a week—but it was a means of subsistence for those whose forebearers had been denied the forty acres and a mule promised to them after Emancipation.

The mechanical cotton picker was a godsend to the planters. An efficient field hand could pick twenty pounds of cotton in an hour. A mechanical cotton picker harvested as much as a thousand pounds—two bales—in that same time. One Mississippi plantation owner estimated that picking a bale of cotton by machine cost him $5.26, while picking it by hand cost $39.41. Each machine did the work of fifty people.

The mechanical cotton picker made sharecropping obsolete. With their primary form of livelihood eliminated virtually overnight, rural African Americans in the South had little choice but to head out into the great unknown in search of a new life. Most headed north to the Promised Land of industry and factory employment. This great black migration, since chronicled and studied in countless works of history, was one of the largest and most rapid internal movements of people in history—perhaps *the* greatest such shift not caused by a natural catastrophe or immediate threat of disease or starvation.

In New York City, the waves of black migrants from the South began flooding in by the late 1940s. New York had Harlem, the preeminent African American neighborhood and cultural center in the United States. But the infusion of migrants over the next twenty-five years was far too vast for any one neighborhood to absorb. Blacks began settling on the fringes of white working-class neighborhoods throughout the city's five boroughs, but nowhere was the transformation more startling than in Brooklyn.

The Borough of Churches—which had been its own city until its incorporation into New York City in 1898—had been home to generations of Irish, Italians, and Eastern European Jews. Now, older residents who had lived in Brooklyn since the 1920s, 1930s, or 1940s were shocked to find their neighborhoods on the receiving end of a massive migration of poor, desperate Negroes from the South—along with a significant migration of Puerto Ricans, who were fleeing the impoverished Caribbean island, part of the U.S. commonwealth. Some lower-middle-class white communities in Brooklyn already suffered from poverty and municipal neglect; the latent, free-floating bitterness among their residents soon turned to aggressive anger toward the alien horde of "niggers" and "spics" who were—seemingly—being dumped onto their streets by the thousands each month.

Some whites stayed and resisted the tides of change, but most fled. In three Brooklyn neighborhoods—Brownsville, Bushwick, and East New York—the transition was catastrophic. Over a five-year period in the early 1960s, the neighborhood of East New York went from being 80 percent white to 80 percent black and Puerto Rican. There were no social programs to deal with this unprecedented shift in the community's racial composition. The new arrivals were met mostly with a potent mixture of fear, hostility, and outright racism—a combination the Negroes found all too familiar.

There was no Ku Klux Klan in New York. There was something more overt: the New York City Police Department. By the early 1960s, the NYPD had evolved into a largely autonomous institution, whose officers and beat cops did things their own way. For generations, when it came to dealing with black people, that way generally involved brute force. Over the next ten years, hostilities between blacks and the police in New York would finally come to a head, with casualties on both sides and severe repercussions for the city as a whole.

The overwhelming majority of the police department was composed of working-class white men who lived in Brooklyn and elsewhere in the boroughs. Some officers shared the common sense of fear and displacement at the growing influx of desperate, often illiterate Negroes arriving in huge numbers. Beyond race, there was the issue of poverty: filthy living conditions, large groups of unemployed teens hanging out on the streets, lewd public behavior, and, of course, all manner of crime.

In the book *My Father's Gun*, Brian McDonald traces three generations of cops in his own family and how they were affected by the city's shifting racial landscape. The McDonald family had lived in the mostly Irish Catholic Fordham Road section of the Bronx for two generations—until 1956, when they picked up and moved to the suburban bedroom community of Pearl River, in Rockland County, sixty miles north of the city. The road to Rockland County was well worn: between 1950 and 1960, more than fifty thousand people moved north from the city. The overwhelming majority were white, many of them police officers who had concluded that the urban jungle, increasingly overrun by blacks and Puerto Ricans and rising crime, was no longer for them.

At the time, New York City cops were still required to live within city limits. This law dated back to the Great Depression, when it had been championed by James J. Lyons, the Bronx borough president, under a rallying cry of "Local jobs for local boys." Before long, however, many cops and firemen were flouting the so-called Lyons Law by establishing fake residences in the city. Brian McDonald's father, a first-grade detective stationed back in the old neighborhood, got around the law by using his sister-in-law's Bronx address on tax returns and other official papers. Later, the law was changed to accommodate the growing number of cops—many of them high-ranking members of the department—who chose not to live in the city where they worked.

McDonald describes witnessing his father come home from work each day more and more disgusted and alienated by the city he once loved. He would pour himself a stiff drink, sit in a chair, and grumble angrily about the "Mau Maus" and "goddamn junkies" who had turned his precinct into a "jungle." Lieutenant McDonald's disgust was hardened by his own isolation: in the upstate community where he now lived, he was surrounded largely by other white cop families who'd fled the city just as he had. Bitterness seethed among these exiled cops: to them, the city seemed more alien and unsalvageable with each passing day.

Relations between cops and blacks in the city had always been tense. New York was a place of extreme wealth and dire poverty, of glittering Manhattan financial centers and teeming slums. It was the job of the NYPD to make sure these two universes did not overlap. There were no Jim Crow segregation laws in New York, as there still were in the South, but unofficial segregation was a fact of life. A significant aspect of policing in relation to blacks and Puerto Ricans was to make sure they "stayed in their place," both figuratively and literally. There were few black officers on the force, and even they were viewed with suspicion by residents.

The reality of police repression was stark. African Americans suffered disproportionately from a wide range of abuses, including indiscriminate searches, station house beatings, and coerced "confessions." They knew that a cop could stop them anytime, and there was little they could do about it. Nothing filled black citizens with dread more than being led into a police station house, and by the late 1950s those stations were increasingly run by suburban white men, long since estranged from the city they policed.

Black citizens knew what most whites were unaware of or chose not to know: in police custody, black men were beaten with phone books and rubber hoses. Police violence and malevolence against black people were business as usual.

As far back as the 1920s, the National Association for the Advancement of Colored People (NAACP) had begun lodging complaints of police brutality against the NYPD. These complaints increased greatly in the post–World War II years, when a number of black servicemen were shot and killed by New York police. To see veterans victimized after serving their country in the war was particularly galling to black advocacy groups, but the violence did not end there. From 1947 to 1952, forty-six unarmed African Americans were killed by police officers in the state of New York. Only two whites were killed by police in the same period. When it came to black people, the policy seemed to be to shoot first and ask questions later.

This rampant police violence did not escape public notice, but with complaints came consequences. After one of the city's few Negro councilmen referred to police brutality in New York as "lynching, Northern style," he was accused of being a Communist by white political leaders and newspaper editorialists. Throughout the 1950s, white supremacists sought to undermine the struggle for civil rights by interpreting it through the prism of the cold war. There must be some foreign element, the thinking went, behind these Negroes and white liberals who were agitating for civil rights. Most blacks saw these accusations for what they were: racism by another name.

Despite this widespread abuse, by the mid-1950s there was an almost eerie complacency among the city's black population. With the neighborhood of Harlem as its African American center, New York had always been able to put forth the image of a thriving black middle class. Many black business leaders and politicians had a vested interest in maintaining this image. A full-scale riot occurred in Harlem in 1943, which was instigated by a police officer's mistreatment and arrest of a black female in the street, but since then black protest had been muted. The promise of prosperity in the postwar years seemed real enough to stave off social protest in the big city.

Yet there were signs of subterranean strain within the city's underclass, rumblings that grew louder and more destabilizing as the Great Migration burgeoned. Southern blacks brought news of unprecedented civil rights protests in places like Mississippi and Alabama. An unassuming black woman named Rosa Parks had refused to sit in the back of a city bus in Montgomery, which led to an organized boycott by black preachers and civil rights workers. Something was happening down

South: blacks were standing up for themselves, engaging in nonviolent confrontation as a way to expose the basic inhumanity and moral corruptibility of white supremacy.

Most white residents of New York City knew little of the civil rights movement in the South. Reports about it in the city's newspapers were limited, and television had not yet emerged as the instant communicator it would become. Images of police fire hoses, billy clubs, and attack dogs being unleashed on peaceful protesters were just beginning to penetrate the national consciousness. But the city's black residents—especially those recently arrived from the Deep South, with family still there— had begun to feel the earliest inklings of righteous indignation. And these emotions informed an incident on April 14, 1957, that initiated New York City into the modern struggle for civil rights. It was the kind of encounter that would become all too commonplace in the years ahead, but in the year 1957 it was an unusual situation.

On that day, near the intersection of 125th Street and Seventh Avenue in the heart of Harlem, a crowd gathered to watch a fight between two black men. Several police units were dispatched to quell the disturbance. When the cops arrived, following their usual practice when dealing with disturbances of this size in the ghetto, they began indiscriminately clubbing onlookers who were slow to disperse.

One Harlem resident, Johnson Hinton, was horrified to see the police beating one innocent bystander. "You are not in Alabama," he reportedly told a cop. "This is New York." The cop turned on Hinton, clubbing him over the head, cracking his skull and knocking him unconscious.

More cops arrived on the scene, but as the crowd of residents grew more hostile, the police retreated to the Twenty-eighth Precinct station house—where they were startled to find a menacing mob gathering in front of the building.

Johnson Hinton, age thirty-two, was a black Muslim, known to his congregates as Johnson X. Many of the Irish Catholic cops in the fray that afternoon probably didn't even know what a Muslim was, much less that a group calling itself the Nation of Islam had taken root in Harlem. Johnson X was a member of Mosque Number Seven, the largest Muslim mosque in the country, located in a building at 116th Street and Seventh Avenue, not far from where the police beating had occurred.

The leader of the mosque was a young Muslim preacher named Malcolm X. When Malcolm received word of the beating—and learned that Johnson X had been transferred to the station house, bleeding and unconscious—he set off to find him.

Within minutes, Malcolm X arrived at the Twenty-eighth Precinct to serve as a negotiator between the police and the community. The cops were demanding that the protesters disperse from around the station house, but the angry residents were refusing to budge. A member of the police negotiating team, Walter Arm, the NYPD's public relations officer, opened the meeting by saying that the presence of both the captain of the precinct and a deputy commissioner "indicates how much concern the police department has for this situation. However, I'd like to say that the police of the city of New York can handle any situation that arises in Harlem, and we're not here to ask anybody's help."

The police spokespeople had never heard of Malcolm X. Thirty-one years old at the time, dressed in the Nation of Islam uniform of a bow tie, white shirt, and brown suit, the Muslim leader listened quietly as the police made their statement. Then he looked at the cops, stood up, and proceeded to leave the room.

When the cops realized that their hard-line tactic had failed, they immediately sent a reporter from the *Amsterdam News*, Harlem's black newspaper, to find Malcolm X and bring him back to the negotiating table.

When Malcolm returned, he made his position clear. "I have no respect for you or your police department," he told Walter Arm and the other police representatives. If the police wanted the crowd to disperse, he announced, they must transfer Johnson X to Harlem Hospital at once. The police agreed. After making a series of further demands, Malcolm filled out an incident report that noted that Johnson X had been an innocent bystander who was attacked on account of brute viciousness by city police officers.

Johnson X was escorted out of the station house by a phalanx of Muslims. Then, with a simple hand gesture, Malcolm X motioned the group of protesters to disperse, which they did in an orderly fashion.

"No man should have that much power over that many people," one police captain reportedly said.

It was the beginning of a new kind of relationship between blacks and the police in the city of New York.

IN RETROSPECT, the hostilities that ravaged New York City in the 1960s may have been inevitable. With such dramatic shifts in the city's social makeup, the fault line between black and white residents could no longer hold. Blacks felt aggrieved; many whites felt a mounting sense of terror. As one political operative put it, "A boiler that is allowed to get too hot will eventually explode."

It is a testament to the resilience of the city that this explosion did not occur all at once. The social upheaval that occurred was contained within the fabric of everyday life; though it would continue to fester for more than a decade, the city still functioned. Yet the precipitous decline in quality of life and peace of mind was almost beyond calculation.

The worst clashes between blacks and the police took place in the streets and within the police precincts. But they often played out within the bounds of the criminal justice system. The courts and prisons were an extension of policing at the street level; they reflected the common attitudes of the day. Beginning in 1963, untold numbers of citizens, police officers, criminal defense lawyers, prosecutors, district attorneys, judges, bail bondsmen, and social activists would get drawn into the maelstrom.

This book traces the parallel lives of three people whose personal journeys were central to the era—three men who never met, but whose exploits, taken together, would have a revolutionary effect on the nature of criminal justice in New York City.

GEORGE WHITMORE

As a young Negro subsisting on the margins of society in the early 1960s, Whitmore found himself the target of a type of injustice that was both typical and extraordinary. While being held in custody at a Brooklyn police station, he was coerced into signing a confession to a series of horrific crimes. His struggle to free himself from false prosecution at the hands of a compromised criminal justice system would become one of the defining narratives of the entire era.

WILLIAM "BILL" PHILLIPS

As a boy, Phillips—the son of a twenty-year NYPD veteran—listened to his pop and fellow officers regale one another with stories from the days of Prohibition, when a precinct cop received one dollar for every barrel of illegal bootleg beer delivered to a speakeasy. By the time Bill Jr. joined the NYPD, corruption had become so rife within the department—with officers looking to "score" and spread the money around to commanders and supervisors—that few even thought of it as corruption. Phillips was a more aggressive hustler than most, but he was also a classic product of a diseased system—which made it all the more devastating when he turned snitch and exposed the NYPD to the most devastating scandal in its history.

DHORUBA BIN WAHAD

For every George Whitmore—simple, compliant, looking to get along—there was a Dhoruba Bin Wahad, who would come to be viewed by many cops as the prototypical black militant. Dhoruba was a product of 1950s gang life and various penal institutions in and around New York City; by the time he was released into the political and racial tumult of the late 1960s, he was ripe to assume the role of the Black Avenger. His position as one of the key founders of the Black Panther Party in New York would lead to his being targeted by virtually every level of law enforcement, from the NYPD's Bureau of Special Services to the highest levels of the Federal Bureau of Investigation.

THESE THREE MEN—WHITMORE, Phillips, and Bin Wahad—represent three points of a triangle: Whitmore, the hapless victim of a repressive law enforcement system; Phillips, foot soldier for that system, which saw its mandate as stemming an incipient racial revolution; and Bin Wahad, inheritor of a new age of militancy inspired and defined by the likes of Malcolm X. Though their stories would unfold independent of one another, all three men became enmeshed in a similar matrix of forces—political, social, and racial—that would alter the direction of the city. Their lives, chronicled closely at the time but largely forgotten today, cast a refracted glow on one another and on an entire generation of contemporaries caught up in the turmoil of the times.

In the struggle for racial equality, the road to the Promised Land was strewn with land mines and strafed by sniper fire. There were 563 murders in New York City in 1963. By 1973 there were more than one thousand—a 95 percent increase. Rape was up 120 percent, robberies up 82 percent, assaults up 90 percent. Homes and places of business were violated and burglarized at a staggering rate. The city's descent into criminal pathology seemed to have no narrative thread and no purpose. Urban life became synonymous with a state of chaos.

There was no disputing that crime was out of control. But the mood of fear and paranoia in the city was also a product of the social agitation of the postwar years—and that, in turn, was a reaction to decades of oppression and abuse. As the civil rights movement moved northward from the South, its tactics changed. The concept of nonviolent resistance gave way to Black Power; the dream of integration was subsumed by the demand for black liberation. The NYPD was assigned the task of containing a revolution. The violence that resulted must have seemed pointless, an expression of hatred and self-destruction in its purest form. But within the conflict there was also hope—the pain and anxiety of a city yearning to be something better than it was, with a criminal justice system that deserved the trust of its citizens.

THE PAST IS not past: a city's identity is composed not just of events in the present moment but also of all that came before. If New York City today is a place of prosperity, safety, and good times, as its civic leaders and financial developers contend, it is useful to remember that these things have come at a price. Forty-five years ago, a generation of New Yorkers—motivated by chutzpah, fear, an instinct for survival, and a sense of righteous indignation—changed their city forever. The process was long, agonizing, and ugly, but if we are to understand the city that thrives today, we must first come to understand the past, when the struggle for fairness, respect, and personal security was literally a matter of life and death.

So let us lift the rock and sift through the detritus of a time, not so long ago, when no one in their right mind would have called New York the Safest Big City in America. Let us revisit an era when the great metropolis was struggling to define itself in the modern age, when crime was on the rise and dread and hostility entwined the citizenry in what seemed to be a dance to the death. It was a time of hope and desperation, a time of reckoning, a time when the nation's greatest experiment in democracy earned the right to be called the Savage City.

| PART I |

I have a dream that one day . . . the rough places will be
made plain and the crooked places will be made straight.

—*Martin Luther King Jr.*
August 28, 1963

| PART II |

[one]

BLOOD OF THE LAMB

WHEN MARTIN LUTHER King Jr. visited the great city of New York, he was greeted with a silver letter opener plunged swiftly and unceremoniously into his chest.

It happened at Blumstein's department store in Harlem. King was in town to promote *Stride Toward Freedom*, his new book about the Negro rights struggle. At Blumstein's, he sat at a table signing books and making small talk with Harlem residents. King was young—just twenty-nine—but he was already a preacher and civil rights leader of note, a survivor of the 1955 Montgomery bus boycotts, and a man known for his skills as a speaker. He was famous for his rapturous oratorical style and basso profundo voice, which sounded like the instrument of a much older man and seemed to carry the very wisdom of the ages.

At one point during the signing, King was approached by a harmless-looking black woman, age forty-two. "Is this Martin Luther King?" she asked.

"Yes, it is," he replied cheerily.

That's when the woman lunged at the good reverend with something metallic. King tried to block the attack with his left arm; the razor-sharp opener sliced his hand before sinking into his chest a few inches below and to the left of the knot in his tie. Without removing the weapon, the woman stepped back and declared, "I've been after him for six years! I'm glad I done it."

The woman was easily apprehended, and King was rushed to Harlem Hospital with the eight-inch letter opener still stuck in his chest. Daylong surgery extracted the implement, which had penetrated his chest just a few centimeters from the heart. A surgeon later told King that, given the critical position of the opener, even a sneeze from King could have punctured the aorta and killed him.

The assailant, a domestic originally from Georgia, delivered a largely incoherent diatribe about the evils of communism and how King's movement had diminished her Catholic faith. The woman was committed to the Matteawan State Hospital for the Criminally Insane in upstate New York.

The incident left a lasting impression. From that point on, Martin Luther King would capture the attention of locals, in part because he had visited the city and paid the price: he had been baptized in his own blood. Only the coldest-hearted racist could refuse to acknowledge that King deserved respect—or at least an expression of regret—for enduring such an attack, in broad daylight, in a city that should have welcomed him with open arms.

FIVE YEARS AFTER the stabbing—in the early-morning hours of Wednesday, August 28, 1963—the name of Martin Luther King Jr. was once again on local minds. In the predawn darkness that morning, hordes of New Yorkers gathered together in preparation to travel to a massive public event where King and other civil rights leaders were scheduled to appear. The event itself was occurring two hundred forty miles to the south, yet preparations for it had occupied the city's most engaged citizens for months. After dozens of strategy sessions, heated arguments, leaflet campaigns, and exhortations to rally the troops, the time had arrived for what was being billed as the March on Washington. It promised to be an unprecedented event, one that would alter the trajectory of race relations throughout the United States—and in New York City itself.

It was a sight to behold, the throngs of activists gathered together before dawn like algae in a vast pond. In Harlem, Greenwich Village, and Brooklyn, church groups, civil rights workers, students, and community activists piled into automobiles. At the commuter terminals of Penn Station and Port Authority, thousands waited patiently in line to board buses and trains. Many carried a sack lunch that had been prepared for them by nuns and volunteers at Riverside Church on the Upper West Side: a cheese sandwich with mustard, a piece of marble cake, and an apple, price fifty cents. On 125th Street in Harlem, dozens of buses had been chartered for the occasion. A huge crowd spilled out into the street. Some were there to board the buses; others, who couldn't make the trip to Washington themselves, had come to wish the marchers well.

"They look just like soldiers going off," said an elderly woman as the travelers boarded the buses, lined up along the curb past the Apollo Theater as far as the eye could see.

"Tell them I want a job," a man shouted to no one in particular.

The main headquarters for the march was just a few blocks away, in a four-story tenement building on 130th Street and Seventh Avenue. For months a banner had hung below the headquarters' third-story window: MARCH ON WASHINGTON FOR JOBS AND FREEDOM—AUGUST 28. Hundreds of community and church organizations had pledged to deliver high numbers of participants—pledges that seemed overly optimistic at the time but now were proving true.

As dawn approached, the buses kicked into gear and departed for tunnels and bridges out of the city, a vast civilian army—black, white, young, and old—headed toward the nation's capital. Later reports estimated that 917 chartered buses, thirteen special trains, and untold numbers of vans and cars—carrying roughly fifty-five thousand people in all—left New York for Washington that morning. It was the largest self-generated evacuation in the city's history.

As the morning wore on, those who remained in town caught snippets of the march on television. At 11:30 A.M., all three major networks interrupted their regular programming to begin live coverage of the event. By then, the estimated two hundred thousand people who had arrived in Washington from all over the country had already assembled at the Washington Monument. They began to march along Constitution and Independence avenues in the direction of the Lincoln Memorial. Television cameras captured the procession, beaming the black-and-white images across the nation.

In New York City, these images appeared on TV screens in diners, barbershops, beauty salons, homes and apartments, in newsrooms, and in the front windows of electronics stores. Pedestrians stopped to catch a glimpse of the marchers, a sea of humanity, heads bobbing as they walked, placards hoisted with slogans and demands: THE TIME HAS COME!; DECENT HOUSING NOW!; END POLICE BRUTALITY!

The initial news reports hardly slowed the hustle of life in the big city. Regardless of how many people had left that morning, it was still a city of nearly eight million inhabitants with people to see, places to go, bills to pay. It wasn't until a couple hours later—after dozens of marchers and celebrities had been interviewed by TV reporters; after poets and singers had done their thing; after the preliminary speakers had variously excited and taxed the patience of the demonstrators in D.C. and the estimated ten million TV watchers nationwide—that the city of New York was riveted to attention. The day's keynote speaker had finally arrived at the podium, his face in close-up in living rooms everywhere.

The voice was piercing, a mellifluous baritone that emanated from the TVs and radios and swept out over New York City like a sweet summer breeze.

"I am happy to join with you today in what will go down in history as the greatest demonstration for freedom in the history of this nation," King told the crowd, to applause that was eager but restrained. As he began his speech in earnest, the telecast cut from the podium to tight shots of the crowd—and, from a camera mounted high on the Lincoln Memorial, to a breathtaking overhead panorama of the massive gathering of people on the steps of the monument and all around the Reflecting Pool.

King's voice filled the air with the certitude of a small-town preacher speaking to his personal congregation. "We have come to this hallowed spot to remind America of the fierce urgency of now," he declared. "The Negro is not free. The Negro lives on a lonely island of poverty in the midst of a vast ocean of prosperity. . . . We can never be satisfied as long as the Negro is the victim of unspeakable horrors of police brutality. . . . Nineteen sixty-three is not an end, but a beginning. And those who hope that the Negro needed to blow off steam and will now be content will have a rude awakening if the nation returns to business as usual. . . . We cannot be satisfied as long as a Negro in Mississippi cannot vote and a Negro in New York believes he has nothing for which to vote."

All around New York City, people stopped to listen, or at least to acknowledge the voice. As his voice grew in timbre, his vocal inflections more biting and precise, it became clear that King was laying down a gauntlet, challenging all Americans to demand a society that lived up to "the true meaning of its creed: We hold these truths to be self-evident, that all men are created equal."

The speech was short, but it maintained an inner rhythm that swelled to a rousing finale, the preacher's voice echoing across the city from taxi stands, restaurant kitchens, tenement apartments, and car radios.

"When we allow freedom's ring, when we let it ring from every village and every hamlet, from every state and every city, we will be able to speed up the day when all God's children, black men and white men, Jews and Gentiles, Protestants and Catholics, will be able to join hands and sing the words of the old Negro spiritual: Free at last, free at last, thank God Almighty, we are free at last!"

NOT LONG AFTER the speech was over, and before the dust had settled on the March on Washington, a phone rang at the Twenty-third Precinct station house on East 104th Street in Manhattan. Detective Martin J. Zinkand was on duty, having just returned to the station house with his partner after investigating a burglary. He had just sat down at his desk when the police switchboard operator told him there was a call on the line. He picked up the phone. "Zinkand, two-three detective squad. How can I help you?"

A young woman's voice responded. "My name is Patricia Tolles. I live at Fifty-seven East Eighty-eighth Street, number three C. I think something bad happened in my apartment. I don't know if anything has been stolen, but the whole place is a mess—and we can't find my roommate." The woman was distressed, if only mildly.

"Okay," said Zinkand. "Wait there and we'll be right over."

The detective hung up. He straightened the mess on his desk. The address, on East Eighty-eighth near Madison Avenue, was in one of the most exclusive neighborhoods in the city. Burglaries and purse snatchings were not uncommon in the area, but violent felonies were rare compared with most other areas of Manhattan and the outer boroughs. Zinkand figured it was likely a missing persons case. Twenty years on the job had conditioned him to react with an even keel to even the most hysterical cries for help. He alerted his partner, Detective John J. Lynch, but neither of them was in a rush. Twenty minutes later, after they had checked their phone messages and had a cup of coffee, they headed out the front door.

As they were getting into their car in front of the precinct, a sergeant emerged from the front door. "Hey, fellas, it's a double homicide," he shouted.

"What?" asked Lynch.

"Eighty-eighth Street. We just got another call. Double homicide."

The detectives nodded at each other and got in the car. "Double homicide, hell," said Zinkand while starting the ignition. "I'll bet you it's a murder and suicide."

They drove the short distance—less than a mile—from the precinct to the apartment building. Nice place. Doorman. Well-kept lobby, smooth-running elevator, and clean, well-lit hallways.

The mood inside apartment 3C was dark. There was a gathering of people, most of them probably family members. A man, early sixties, introduced himself to the cops as Max Wylie. He pointed out the others in the room: his wife, seated on a sofa staring into space, seemingly in a state of shock; Patricia Tolles, the woman who'd called the precinct, now hunched over, sobbing hysterically; and her boyfriend, who was trying to console her. Wylie led the detectives into the bedroom. The room looked like a tornado had hit it: clothes and other personal belongings were strewn around the room, chairs and bedside lamps overturned. And one other thing: blood, splattered around the room, and especially on one of the two single beds, so saturated with blood it was almost black.

Wylie led the detectives over to a space between the bed and the wall. On the floor were the bodies of two young women bound together, partially covered by a blanket. One of the bodies was nude, with curlers in the woman's hair. The other body was fully clothed. Both women had been hacked to death, with something sharp and powerful.

The man spoke in a monotone, his words so brittle they seemed as though they might break into pieces. "The one on the right is my daughter, Janice Wylie. The other is her roommate Emily Hoffert."

Wylie explained to the cops that Patricia Tolles, the third of three roommates who lived in the apartment, had called him immediately after she telephoned the precinct. He and his wife had rushed right over from their home, just three blocks away on East Eighty-fifth Street. When they got to the apartment, Wylie told his wife and Patricia and her boyfriend to wait in the front room while he searched the apartment. It was then that he discovered the ghastly scene in the bedroom.

Detectives Zinkand and Lynch steeled themselves for the brutality that confronted them. This was the kind of moment they talked about at the police academy; veteran cops are supposed to be immune to even the worst of tragedies, but this was one for the books. Max Wylie began to stutter; the facade he'd constructed to calm his wife, the roommate, and himself crumbling as he spoke. Zinkand pulled the father aside and began gently asking questions—simple queries designed to calm his nerves and distract him from the ugly reality that lay at their feet.

Detective Lynch hunched down and looked over the bodies. As Zinkand led the stunned Wylie out of the bedroom into the other room, Lynch pulled out a pad and began jotting down notes:

You could see these feet jutting out behind the bed here. And looking between the bed and the window you could observe two legs coming out from under a blue blanket. These two legs were tied at the ankles with white cloth. At the top end of the blanket you could see a head of a female which was completely covered with blood.

When I lifted the blanket up I could see the bodies of two dead girls. One girl was nude. That was Janice Wylie. [She] was on her back with her head turned towards the windows a bit. The other girl who had clothes on was Emily Hoffert. [She] was slightly on her side and her legs doubled up under her body from the knees on.

Janice Wylie's ankles were bound together with white cloth. There was blood on her legs, particularly the upper portion of her legs, and her intestines were out of her stomach. They were on top of her stomach.

Her wrists were bound together with cloth. There was blood on her chest, on her neck, on her face and she had what appeared to be a stab wound in her chest. Her arms were bent, tied together across her chest. Her fists were not clenched, limp. Her hand was limp.

I could partially see the body of Emily Hoffert. She had on a green skirt, on which there was blood, and the upper portion of her body that I could see was just completely covered with blood. . . . You could see large gaping wounds in the neck of Emily Hoffert and her neck was coated with blood as her head also. There was blood on the floor.

Lynch emerged from the bedroom ashen and sweaty. He whispered to his partner, "There's a slaughterhouse in there."

Zinkand put out a call, and within minutes other police officials began to arrive. It was a reality of police work that the address of a crime tended to dictate the response it received. This one was a doozy: Upper East Side, two white females, an incident of shocking savagery in the heart of one of the city's most privileged—and protected—neighborhoods.

The first to arrive was a patrolman, Michael J. McAleer, who had been driving by when the call went out over the police radio. Then came the police brass: Assistant Chief Inspector Joseph Coyle, who would be in charge of the case; Chief of Detectives Lawrence J. McKearney and his aide, Lieutenant Cyril Regan; and the deputy commissioner in charge of public relations, Walter Arm, who would deal with the community and the press. Other high-ranking officers whose duties were not directly linked to the murder investigation flocked to the scene out of professional curiosity. Flashing police lights and sirens created a cluster in front of the building, which had to be redirected to make room for arriving forensics detectives and the medical examiner.

By the time Dr. Bela K. Der arrived at the murder scene, the investigators had already begun to apply their trade. Behind the police rope that cordoned off the apartment, technicians dusted for fingerprints, gathered blood samples, hunted for fibers and other clues. The detectives inventoried everything in the apartment. A police photographer snapped shots of the bodies in the bedroom and the rest of the apartment from every conceivable angle. In the front room, Zinkand and Lynch continued their questioning of Max Wylie, Patricia Tolles, and the others, all under the watchful eye of the assistant chief and chief of detectives.

In the bedroom, Dr. Der looked over the murder scene. Judging from the warmth of the bodies and the viscosity of the blood, the crime had happened within the last four hours or so—which meant, quite possibly, that Janice Wylie and Emily Hoffert were being brutally hacked to death even as much of the city was listening to Martin Luther King's speech in Washington.

The doctor donned plastic surgical gloves and moved in closer to the bodies. As an assistant medical examiner for the city of New York, he had conducted nearly two thousand autopsies over the course of twenty-one years. There wasn't much he hadn't seen, but he knew at a glance that this was one of the most violent double killings he would ever encounter. The gashes on Emily Hoffert's neck were so severe that the assailant seemed to have tried to saw off her head. There were scratches and cuts on Hoffert's wrists and palms, suggesting that she had desperately tried to defend herself from the attack. On Janice Wylie's nude torso the doctor counted seven stab wounds over her heart, where the killer had apparently plunged a knife over and over again. She had been disemboweled, her innards spilled out on the floor. Janice Wylie's anus and vagina were smeared with Vaseline or cream, suggesting sexual assault and possibly rape.

The doctor stood and removed his gloves. In a voice that still bore traces of his Hungarian ancestry, he said to a nearby group of police officials, "This is not the way humans should die. This is the way chickens are executed."

IT WOULD BE hours before the New York Police Department first released details about the Wylie-Hoffert murders to the press, but by the morning of August 29 it was a major story. The front page of the *New York Times* was dominated by two articles.

Above the fold, a headline told of the historic March on Washington, which had transfixed the nation: "Gentle Army Occupies Capitol; Politeness Is Order of the Day."

At the bottom of the front page, a different headline: "2 Girls Murdered in E. 88th St. Flat."

To anyone reading the *Times* that morning, the juxtaposition of these two stories must have struck a discordant note. Aside from the fact that they happened on the same day, there was little to suggest that the events were related in any way.

Within a few days, the March on Washington quietly faded from the headlines. The march had been an unprecedented event, but it offered little in the way of follow-up stories for reporters. Reasonable people agreed that the time was long overdue for the nation to commit itself to improving the plight of the Negro—but now what? It would take weeks, months, maybe even years for such a protest to lead to tangible results.

The Wylie-Hoffert story, on the other hand, was a gold-star murder investigation. New York had seven daily newspapers, three of them tabloids that feasted on crimes of violence, the more sensationalistic the better. Some led with headlines of a size usually reserved for presidential elections and declarations of war. The *New York Daily News* bumped the civil rights march in Washington to page three, leading with the headline "2 Career Girls Savagely Slain" above smiling photos of Janice Wylie and Emily Hoffert. Every good newspaperman knew that a prominent murder case needed a catchy moniker, and the *Daily News* got there first: Wylie and Hoffert were young women with professional jobs in the city, and their double homicide would now be known as the Career Girls Murders.

The next few days brought more big headlines but few tangible leads. Initial police reports revealed little beyond the forensic details of the crime. There were no immediate or obvious clues to set investigators off in any one direction. Speaking about the killer, or killers, Chief of Detectives McKearney told the *Daily News*, "We don't even know how he, or they, got into the apartment."

With no clear suspects, reporters spent much of their time speculating that the key to the case might be found in the personal histories of the victims. Janice Wylie, who worked as a copy girl for *Newsweek* and had maintained an active social life in Manhattan, swiftly became a source of scrutiny and fascination—including a decided interest in her "promiscuous" dating habits. The implications were not subtle: *Maybe she was a slut? Murdered by someone she knew? An old boyfriend or a one-night stand?* And there were other theories: *What was the father doing there? Maybe he had something to do with it.* Or, worst of all: maybe there was no sense whatsoever to this horrific attack. Maybe it was just a random act of evil, the work of a homicidal sex maniac loose on the streets of Manhattan.

In the newspaper business, speculation was a narcotic. While the rest of the city sought to bend their minds around the depravity of the Career Girls Murders, eager newshounds popped a vein and shot a load. Like a good fix, the tingling sensation of a lead story worked its way into their bloodstreams, the irresistible commingling of hemoglobin and printer's ink, with juicy quotes and banner headlines sure to follow.

ACROSS THE RIVER from New York, in the small coastal town of Wildwood, New Jersey, George Whitmore Jr. knew nothing of the Wylie-

Hoffert murders—despite the blanket coverage they had received in the TV, radio, and tabloid news throughout the New York–New Jersey area. Whitmore's obliviousness to the story was not unusual for him. At nineteen, he was a high-school dropout who lived with his family in a shack on the outskirts of an automobile scrap yard. George Whitmore was the proverbial invisible Negro. Living not far from the most exalted city in the world, he was anonymous to all but a handful of family and friends—and even they sometimes wondered if George was really there at all, or if he was really a figment of their imaginations.

He was thought to have a low IQ. In truth, Whitmore's problem was his vision. At the age of sixteen he'd been tested and shown to have 20/200 eyesight, making him near-clinically blind. In recent years he had acquired a pair of glasses, but he'd misplaced or broken them and was too ashamed to tell his parents. Even if he had, the Whitmores didn't have the money to buy a new pair. And so George walked through life in a blur, his literal lack of focus leading friends and teachers to write him off as dim-witted.

On the day of the murders, George Whitmore had been working at a restaurant and entertainment hall inside the Ivy Hotel, in Wildwood, where he had a part-time job. He was able to catch bits and pieces of the March on Washington on TV. When Reverend King stepped to the microphone to give his speech, George was sitting alone in the restaurant's large catering hall in front of a black-and-white Motorola TV. In the emptiness of the room, with King's voice echoing to the rafters, the young Negro absorbed the historical moment in solitude, with a mixture of wonderment and awe.

In the days and weeks that followed, Whitmore plodded on as always. He showed up for work on time and performed his duties, which sometimes involved cleaning toilets and picking up trash on the Jersey boardwalk with a spiked pole, and collected his pay: twenty dollars a week.

To those who knew him, George was a good-natured kid, five foot five, skinny, with an easy smile—something of a miracle given the life Whitmore had led. He came from poverty and had known nothing else. Sometimes his personal circumstances weighed heavily on his shoulders; pain and disappointment became a daily fact of life for him, though he usually kept them hidden. He tried to maintain a veneer of anonymity, ducking his head and averting his eyes as if he were trying to disappear.

Generations earlier, long before Martin Luther King Jr.'s stirring calls for change, the predicament faced by Whitmore and others like him had been detailed by another great African American leader. "The Negro is a sort of seventh son . . . shut out from the world by a vast veil," wrote W. E. B. Du Bois in *The Souls of Black Folk*. "The shades of the prison-house are closed round about us all: walls straight and stubborn to the whitest, but relentlessly narrow, tall, and unscalable to sons of night who must plod darkly on in resignation, or beat unavailing palms against the stone, or steadily, half hopelessly, watch the streak of blue above."

Whitmore was born on May 26, 1944, in Philadelphia. The location was more or less an accident: George's father was an itinerant laborer whose family had come up from the South along with tens of thousands of other Negroes in the 1930s, years before the Great Migration. Memories of the Ku Klux Klan and segregationist Jim Crow laws were part of the family inheritance. Having settled briefly in Philadelphia, the babies came fast and furious. First Shelley, the oldest, then George Jr., then Gerald and Geraldine.

"I never did like big cities," Whitmore Sr. would say years later. "Always wanted to move out to the country. Things kept getting in the way. Birdine, my wife, was a frail sort, sick a lot. Little George got sick, too. Was not but eight months old an' he had a terrible attack of diarrhea. Spent seventeen days in the hospital. All his veins were closed up, kept givin' him blood in his chin an' his head. Oh, we thought it was bad for George. He's still got some of those scars."

The Whitmores did eventually get out of Philadelphia. In 1947, when George was three years old, the family packed up their meager belongings and headed toward the Garden State. "I remember the night, that summer," George Whitmore's mother recalled. "We were all crowded, all six of us, in this car we borrowed and we drove over the Camden bridge into New Jersey. It was very funny. On the Philadelphia side, it was very hot, we were all perspiring. The minute we crossed over into Jersey it was freezin'. It was like we were goin' into a different world."

New Jersey *was* a different world; the Whitmore family bounced from home to home in Cape May County. There wasn't much money, which turned George Sr. into a bitter man. "He was mean," recalled Birdine. "He would just walk in the door and slap me for no reason. So mean. He has so much hate in him. Somethin' tore at that man, and he would come home mean."

Birdine tended to the children, which was a full-time job. "Sometimes you think they're all the same, little kids just eatin' and playin' and cryin', but a mother can tell them apart. They're different, all my children were different. Gerald always wanted to be a policeman. . . . George was the artist. I remember George with the drawin's most. George [would] sit in the corner and draw. I'd tell big George when little George was just two or three that that boy was goin' to be an artist, but he'd just shake his head and say, 'You stop that talk, woman. You give that boy ideas. No nigger boy grows up an artist. He goin' have to work for a livin'.'"

George Sr. held a series of odd jobs, including a stint at a slaughterhouse in Whitesboro, New Jersey. Little George was ten years old the first time his father brought him to the abattoir, where hogs are dismembered. At first little George merely swept floors and occasionally arranged frozen pig carcasses in the walk-in freezer, but eventually big George felt it was time for his son to learn the finer points of vivisection.

Whitmore led his son toward one pig, which was still alive. He stood behind his son, wrapped his arms around George's slender torso, and together they raised the meat cleaver high in the air. Little George was sweating; this was the same pig he had been playing with earlier in the day, riding it like a horse and feeding it cornmeal.

"I can't do it," he said, wriggling out of his father's grasp.

The old man hacked at the pig with the cleaver. The pig squealed; blood ran like water from an overflowing bathtub. George threw up, vomit dripping down his chin onto his apron.

"Go on home and don't come back here," said his father. "What's wrong with you, ain't you ever gonna be a man?"

THINGS CHANGED FOR the Whitmores once they moved to Wildwood, a shore town that became a chilly ghost town in the winter and then swelled with revelers—mostly Caucasian—in the summer. There was work to be found in Wildwood from late May to early September, when the bars, nightclubs, and show palaces turned the area into a blue-collar Jersey Riviera.

Racial segregation was a fact of life, rigidly enforced. On Labor Day weekend in 1959—not long after the Whitmores first moved to the area—Mr. Entertainer himself, Sammy Davis Jr., interrupted his act at the Bolero nightclub in Wildwood to tell a thousand visiting firemen that he was leaving town that night, though he'd been contracted to perform through the weekend. Davis explained that he would not work in a town where a Negro performer could not rent a motel room. After he finished the show, the club's owner—suitably embarrassed—was able to find a motel room where Davis could stay. Unfortunately, the other members of his group would have to be lodged in private homes. Davis played out his weekend gig, but his name never again graced the marquee at the Bolero or any other club in Wildwood.

There were plenty of blacks in Wildwood who had moved there to find work during the summer boom season. In keeping with the tenor of the times, most knew the unwritten rules of the segregationist North—which seemed like a refuge compared with the humiliation and terror of places like Alabama, Mississippi, and South Carolina. Few were more steadfast in adhering to racial norms than George Whitmore Sr. "I was a man who had one rule: mix with your own kind. That's what I tried to tell my wife and my kids. Mind your own business and white folks'll mind theirs. Just stay in your own back yard."

By the 1960s, however, protests in the South were stimulating a new consciousness of racial injustice around the country—and the old lines began to blur.

In the spring of 1961, George Jr. was at a school dance when word spread throughout the gym that a Negro boy had insulted a white girl. Afterward, in the parking lot, a modest rumble ensued. Bicycle chains and baseball bats were brandished, racial insults shouted back and forth. The police arrived quickly, and fifteen or twenty boys were rounded up and taken to Wildwood's new fluorescent-lighted police station. Charges were filed against a few of the boys, but all George got was a stern scolding from Lieutenant Parker Johnson.

Lieutenant Johnson was a rarity in Wildwood—and not only because he was one of the few Negroes on the police force. Johnson's family were black pioneers in the area. They had first settled in Wildwood back near the turn of the century, when the town was nothing but a small fishing village. For a long time the Johnsons owned a motel for Negroes, the Glen Oak. Parker Johnson went to Wildwood High School and then to an all-Negro university near Philadelphia, where he majored in psychology and penology. After graduation, Johnson returned to Wildwood and joined the police force. By the early 1960s, he was well known to Negro families in the area. At the age of forty-nine, he had become something of a role model to black kids like George Whitmore. Sometimes he would stop by school playgrounds and shoot baskets with the kids. Johnson got to know many of the area's Negro youths on a first-name basis—the good kids and the bad. Of Whitmore he would later recall: "Young George was a humble type of individual—meek, never went around with anybody, kept to himself. He was never in any trouble."

Lieutenant Johnson knew the Whitmore family; their wood shack near the auto cemetery was a far cry from his pleasant two-family house with yard and garage, but the lieutenant wasn't the kind of person to look down on anyone. At the station house that night, he pulled George Whitmore aside. "Now, George, you know better than to be hanging out with those troublemakers. I never want to see you in this station house again. I'm gonna let you go, but you remember what I told you."

George nodded. "Yes sir, Mister Parker. Thank you, sir."

He didn't think much about it at the time, but years later, an older and wiser George Whitmore would reflect on the role Lieutenant Parker Johnson played in his life: "I got to thinking all cops were like Mister Parker. They wanted to help you. If you told them the truth and helped them out, they'd treat you right."

The good lieutenant had inspired in George a willingness—a desire, even—to trust the police without question. Whitmore had no way of knowing it at the time, but it was this inclination—what some of his fellow black citizens might describe as naïveté—that would lead him down a road of unfathomable tribulation.

two

BUSINESS AS USUAL

AT THE TIME of the Career Girls Murders, Bill Phillips was a detective assigned to the Seventeenth Detective Squad, headquartered on the second floor of the Seventeenth Precinct station house on East Fifty-first Street. The Seventeen was south of the Twenty-third Precinct, where the Wylie-Hoffert killings had taken place. Like dozens of cops working the East Side, Phillips was momentarily roped into the investigation, assigned to canvass the neighborhood. The detective made the rounds, asking store owners, residents, and doormen in the area whether they'd seen anything unusual around the time of the double homicide. Everyone in the area knew about the murders. "Horrifying," said a deli owner on Madison Avenue. "I'm so disturbed I can't sleep at night," said the doorman of a building nearby on Fifth Avenue. Everyone expressed shock, some expressed fear, but few had seen anything useful on the day of the slaughter.

Phillips was inclined to believe the tabloids' conclusion about the crime—that one of the girls, Janice Wylie, was a cock teaser, and that some man she brought home from a bar or nightclub had raped and killed her. When her roommate walked in on things, this scenario went, the perpetrator killed her, too; then, in some kind of postcoital rage, he decided to butcher the bodies. Phillips heard the local police gossip surrounding the case, but he didn't know much more than what he read in the papers or saw on TV at night. It was a major event for the New York

Police Department, but not for Bill Phillips, who wasn't one of the lead investigators on the case. He had other priorities.

Phillips, age thirty-three, was a seven-year veteran of the department. He spent most of his day roaming the precinct looking for ways to score—that is, to extort, extract via bribe, or flat out steal money from local residents, guilty or innocent, living or dead.

Scoring was an art Phillips had learned early in his career, while still a patrolman in uniform. One of his first partners was a ten-year veteran named Kenny Keller. It was Keller who taught him how to be a cop. Years later, in a memoir entitled *On the Pad*, Phillips recalled:

> Responded to a DOA with Kenny one day. It was a fairly
> decent apartment. But the individual had been dead for several
> days and there was a tremendous odor of human body which,
> once you smell it, you can never forget. It's an excruciating
> smell; it makes you gag and it makes your eyes tear. But Keller
> was a very tough guy in his own way, not squeamish at all,
> and he proceeds to roll the guy around like he was a log. The
> more you roll him around, the worse the smell gets. All the
> secretions of fluid start coming out of the body. Sure enough,
> he finds about four hundred dollars [on the body], but the
> money is all wet and smells like the DOA. So he just takes it to
> the bathroom and washes it off, dries it on a towel and says to
> me, Willie, once it dries off the smell'll be gone and nobody'll
> know the difference.

By the time of the Wylie-Hoffert murders, Detective Phillips had developed far more sophisticated scams for stealing money off the population he was sworn to serve and protect. One reason was that he had a head start: Phillips was inculcated into the ways of the department by his father, William R. Phillips Sr., who had retired from the force with a full pension in 1959. Bill Sr. was Irish American, part of a fraternal order within the department that filled out its ranks and shaped its destiny. For more than a hundred years the Irish had used the police department as their personal patronage system, to the point where the upper ranks of the NYPD read like a refrain from one of those old Bing Crosby songs, like "McNamara's Band" or "Dear Old Donegal":

There came Branigan, Flanigan, Milligan, Gilligan
Duffy, McGuffy, Malacky, Mahone . . .

As a teenager, Billy Jr. sat and listened to his father's friends—all of them cops—brag about the legendary scores they had made. His father had been assigned for ten years to the Policy Squad, which was in charge of policing the city's thriving numbers racket; in places like Harlem, even the poor put down a nickel or a dime on the daily number. The Policy Squad was a license to steal, and it was worth $1,000 a month to Bill Phillips Sr.—at a time when a policeman's take-home pay was fifty dollars a week.

From the time Bill Phillips first passed the civil service exam and entered the police academy, the fact that his father had been "on the job" put him in a proud though not necessarily exclusive club. There were many young cadets at the academy with relatives on the job—fathers, uncles, and brothers. The talk among them often had to do with ways to profit above and beyond the lowly police salary. Phillips remembered: "There was a great awareness of this money being made in the street and a lot of the fellows made no bones about it. They just couldn't wait to get out there and start making money."

Once he was part of the system, Phillips's education was gradual and methodical. His first opportunity for an arrest came before he was even out of the academy. One night, he was on the town with another guy from the academy. They were both in their police "grays," the uniform worn by recruits not yet sworn in as full-fledged cops. Phillips and his friend had picked up a couple girls in a bar. The friend took his girl up to a hotel room, while Phillips was "stuck down in the car playing a little grab ass." From the car, Phillips saw a suspicious-looking black guy across the street approach a parked car and jimmy open the window with a screwdriver. The guy broke into the car and started gathering up items from inside.

The would-be flatfoot sprang into action:

I jumped out, try to grab the guy. He squirms away and starts running down the street. I chase him up the fucking block. Stop or I'll shoot! Stop or I'll shoot! I was so fucking scared I couldn't have pulled the trigger no matter what. Stop, or I'll shoot! He drops the screwdriver, all the clothes, and he stops.

I collar the fucking guy and I drag him back up to the parked car. I tell the broad, get lost, go to your hotel room. I figure I'm now the hero cop of the whole city.

Police squad cars pulled up from three different directions. A sergeant approached and asked Phillips, "Hey kid, what've you got?"

I told him I caught this guy robbing a car. But I didn't have nothing, no fucking evidence. All I had was this nigger running down the street with a bunch of clothes. So they go out, find the screwdriver, take the guy to the 14th Precinct station house. . . . At that time they used interrogation by police psychology—a punch in the mouth, a kick in the ass, a tap in the balls. I'm a fucking dumb kid, what the hell do I know? The detective is beating hell out of this guy. Confess, you cocksucker. Confess? Confess what? I got the guy dead to rights.

Phillips was sure this would be his first official arrest, but it was not to be. After sitting around the precinct for a couple hours, he was told by a detective, "You can go, kid. It's been taken care of."

Phillips was surprised, but he asked no questions. He figured that some money, or merchandise, must have changed hands and made the matter go away. He vowed that next time, no matter what, he wouldn't be on the outside looking in.

Phillips said years later that he didn't come onto the police force looking for ways to make cash on the side. In fact, the first time he was offered money, he tried to turn it down. One night, when he was a rookie cop in the Nineteenth Precinct on the Upper East Side, he was out patrolling in a radio car with Frankie Olds, a veteran cop in the One-Nine. "Listen, we got a few dollars to pick up," Officer Olds told him. "Do you mind?"

"Well," replied Phillips, "no, I don't mind."

Olds pulled in front of a dance club on Eighty-fifth Street and Lexington Avenue. "I'll only be a minute," he said. The veteran cop returned a few minutes later with two five-dollar bills, one of which he handed to Phillips.

"No," said the rookie, "that's okay. You can keep it."

Olds insisted. "Take it. It's yours."

"That was the first, and I still remember how I felt when I took it," recalled Phillips. "I felt, goddamn, do I have to get involved in this? I don't really want to, but if I don't take the money this guy will think I'm some kind of creep. I won't be able to hang out with the group I hang out with now."

Phillips was startled by the offer from Officer Olds, but he'd known the moment was coming.

When you first get to a precinct, you're like a wallflower. Nobody even says hello to you. Then, slowly, you begin to build up this trust and they tell you little things in the station house. Like the captain's man is making a lot of money, or the sergeant is robbing from that guy. . . . So right away you got to make up your mind. Are you going to go in for it and be one of the guys, or are you going to stay out of it and have everybody look at you like you're some kind of queer?

For Phillips, the choice was clear. "I took the five dollars. I really didn't know what else to do." Later, after he'd grown accustomed to taking money in much greater denominations on a regular basis, the process became less mysterious. "You know," said Phillips, "taking money is like getting laid. You remember the first time with a broad; after that it's a blur."

Even after Phillips joined the club, he had much to learn about how the system worked. The next stage of his education came when he arrested a kid on East Eighty-fifth Street for creating a disturbance. Patrolman Phillips, who had come upon a group of teenagers knocking over garbage cans and making noise, told the teenagers to straighten up the garbage cans and be on their way. The young punks obeyed, but half an hour later they were back at it. As Phillips put it, "One of the kids, a big kid, Irish, had to be a football player, starts to give me a little lip so I whack him right in the puss in front of all his friends. . . . He was completely enraged. He puts his hands up to fight. I grab him by the neck and I say, you're under arrest."

Back at the precinct, Phillips got more guff—not from the kid but from other cops. It was considered a bad arrest. White kid, Irish, got a little drunk, so what? Phillips overheard the desk lieutenant say, "With all the shit out there, why does he have to lock up this kid?" The implication was: we lock up spooks, spics, chinks, and white trash. We don't lock up Irish kids for no good reason.

Phillips felt foolish; it was a rookie mistake. But once you booked somebody you couldn't take it back. The kid stood charged with littering and simple assault. Not to fret: in the NYPD of the day, there was always a way out.

Weeks later, with a trial date for the case now on the docket, a former cop named Pete Meagher contacted a cop named Doc Slaughter, who worked with Phillips in the One-Nine. One day, Doc said to Phillips, "Pete Meagher wants to see you about that kid you locked up. They want to know what they can do. Pete is a one-hundred-percent guy. An ex-cop."

Phillips, the rookie, was confused. He knew Doc Slaughter was pointing him in a certain direction, but he was too green to figure it out.

"Tell you what," said Doc. "I'll make an appointment. You'll talk to Pete and we'll see what we can do."

Phillips and Slaughter met Pete Meagher in a bar on the West Side, in Hell's Kitchen. Slaughter made the introductions. In a thick brogue, Pete said to Phillips, "That's my nephew you locked up. The lad's going to college next fall, and he can't take a conviction. Now, what can we do about it?"

What did Meagher want to do? He wanted to give Phillips two hundred dollars to guarantee that the case came to a favorable conclusion.

Two hundred dollars was a sizable sum to Phillips. His take-home pay was $130 every two weeks. Besides, he'd begun to feel guilty about the arrest: with all the shit out there, why *did* he have to lock up this kid?

Phillips took the money, and everyone was happy. But now the rookie cop had to deliver.

At trial, Phillips took the stand and described the incident.

"Is this the man who did it?" asked the prosecutor, pointing to the Irish kid.

"I can't be sure," answered Phillips. It was a direct lie—a perjury.

The prosecutor was dumbfounded. "What do you mean you can't be sure?"

"Well, it was dark and there were some other people with him."

"So why did you lock him up?"

"It looked like him, but I'm not sure."

"You mean you're not sure now?"

"Well, yes, I can't be positive."

The kid was set free. The prosecutor looked at Phillips like he was the biggest idiot he'd ever seen. *How can you lock up a guy, you don't even know what he looks like?* Phillips felt stupid, and vowed that he would learn from the experience. "After a while you learn to write up the affidavit in such a loose way that you can't get nailed like that," he remembered. "You write it up so that if you can't score, boom, you nail the guy, but if you score, you don't look like a boob on the stand."

In later years, the type of behavior Phillips was engaged in would be referred to as corruption, but at the time few people—inside or outside of the NYPD—used that word. The department had a way of doing things, the way things had been done for generations, and it was rarely challenged by the press, city government, or the citizenry. It was business as usual.

There were some who didn't go along with the program. One of them was a young cop named David Durk, who joined the NYPD in 1963, just months before the Wylie-Hoffert murders. Unlike Bill Phillips, Durk was not Irish, nor was he Italian, German, or Polish—the other ethnicities that composed the bulk of the department. He was Jewish, and a college graduate to boot. Durk was a strange bird by New York police standards, and from the start he was viewed with suspicion.

Durk encountered the same kind of corruption Bill Phillips did, but unlike Phillips he refused to take money himself. This sealed his fate: other cops tagged him as an outsider, a "nut," a "rat," a "fag," and a "psycho."

Whether a cop took money or not, it didn't seem to matter. The system was the system. Graft made the world go round. Dirty money not only determined who got rich in the department, it also played a role in promotions, choice assignments, who got punished, who was seen as a threat, and who was viewed with esteem. By the early 1960s the NYPD's system of graft was deeply entrenched within the entire police bureaucracy. And it had begun to take the department's work ethic down with it, giving rise to a culture that tolerated brutality, racism, sloppiness, laziness, and police malfeasance.

It was this mentality, in large part, that led detectives down the wrong road as they scrambled to close their most sensational double homicide case in a generation.

THE CAREER GIRLS Murders lit up the city like a hit Broadway show. The case had innocent female victims, shocking brutality, and the makings of a classic whodunit. The background players were already cultural figures: Max Wylie, father of the deceased, was an advertising executive with Lennon & Newell, and the author of four novels, six nonfiction books, and three plays. His brother, Philip Wylie, was even more famous, the author of twenty-five novels, and an established figure in Manhattan literary and publishing circles. The race of the victims, the savagery of the killings, and the social standing of the Wylie family all conspired to make the story a keeper: "a good murder at a good address," as police beat reporters and cops often described their most noteworthy murder cases.

The killings were made more poignant when it emerged that Janice Wylie had intended to take part in the March on Washington on the day of her death. Worried about the crowds and the potential for violence between the police and marchers, Max Wylie had urged her not to go; the night before the march, he was relieved when she told him she'd changed her mind and decided to stay in New York.

From the beginning, the top NYPD brass announced that the investigation was being given the highest priority. One hundred and fifty detectives were searching for the killer or killers. The investigators began with a principle that is applied to nearly all homicide cases: 90 percent of the time, the victim knows the killer. The life of Emily Hoffert led detectives nowhere; she was a good girl, originally from Minnesota, a schoolteacher, clean as a whistle. Janice Wylie was also a good girl, talented and vivacious. But she was a modern woman—an aspiring actress, and one with skeletons in her closet.

When detectives discovered an address book among Janice Wylie's belongings, the names and numbers within it dictated the initial thrust of the investigation. Anyone who'd ever worked with or dated or known Janice Wylie became a "person of interest." Old boyfriends, secret lovers, even crank callers to Wylie's place of business were hunted down and interviewed. Wylie's employer, *Newsweek*, sweetened the pot by offering $10,000 to anyone who could supply information leading to an arrest. The net was thrown far and wide, with a squad of Manhattan detectives—augmented by other detectives from around the city—questioning more than five hundred persons in the first month of the investigation.

After four weeks: *nada*. Bupkis. Less than zero.

In the *New York Times,* a high police official tried to explain the lack of progress. "There is a complete lack of physical evidence, no description of the murderer, not one substantial clue, not one tangible motive." As one *Times* reporter on the case noted, the NYPD was flailing. "The police, under intense pressure to solve the crime and remove from the streets a killer whose act has frightened thousands of lonely women, have disrupted the offices of *Newsweek* by repeated interrogations of the magazine's personnel. Thirty-eight persons who attended a farewell party for a departing magazine executive on the eve of the double murder have been questioned. Persons as far away as 3,000 miles have been asked to explain their movements on Wednesday, August 28, the day of the killings. Intellectuals, delivery boys, taxicab drivers, disturbed persons with police records of sex crimes have been interrogated."

When it became apparent that their excavation of Janice Wylie's personal life was leading nowhere, detectives were forced to go in another direction. The jewelry, money, and other valuables left in the apartment had convinced investigators that the killer wasn't a burglar. They also discounted the idea that it was a random crime of opportunity; the savagery of the murders seemed to suggest something more personal. Could it have been an addict? An intriguing possibility, but police knew from experience that most junkies were single-minded in their pursuit of dope, or the means to buy it. Why would a desperate junkie take time out to rape a woman, eviscerate two people, and leave behind money and jewelry?

Even so, detectives were compelled to consider these and many other possibilities. They went back over the murder scene looking for telltale signs of entry. The apartment door had been locked from the inside, with no signs of forced entry. Neither the building's doorman nor anyone else in the building had seen anyone suspicious. The apartment's kitchen window had been unlocked and partially open, but access to the window from outside seemed nearly impossible. The window was thirty feet aboveground, a distance so remote that police photographers hadn't even bothered to snap photos of the window as a possible point of entry.

Meanwhile, a mood of fear was slowly overtaking the city's central nervous system. Janice Wylie's grieving father sought to stifle the horror and pain of his loss by doing what writers do: he penned a thirty-five-thousand-word manuscript he called "Career Girl, Watch Your Step." The sense of foreboding was shared by many. In the big cities of the North—of which New York was the crown jewel—fear could be a collective emotion. Especially in recent years, it seemed as though something ominous was happening. Much of this trepidation—felt by rich and poor, black and white—was sparked by the new prevalence of narcotics.

The junkie as an urban leitmotif was not exactly new. In New York, dope fiends and pushers had emerged on the urban landscape in the late 1940s, after the Second World War—fueled in part by an influx of veterans who'd returned nursing an addiction. At first, the scourge had seemed manageable: an early generation of heroin users were often people with jobs who found ways to function, at least until the addiction kicked in. Heroin wasn't yet that easy to find or purchase. To policemen around the city, junkies were becoming a nuisance, but their criminal activity rarely went beyond burglary or purse snatching.

In the 1950s, however, public and official attitudes toward narcotics users began to change dramatically. One reason was the increase in predatory violence associated with junkies. Another reason was race.

The massive migration of blacks from the South, which had begun as a trickle in the mid-1940s, swelled to a steady stream in the 1950s. And their arrival in New York happened to coincide with the most massive influx of heroin the city had ever seen.

The reasons for the sudden and immense availability of the drug in places like Harlem has never been fully explained. Certainly, the forces of organized crime—in this case the Syndicate, or *Cosa Nostra*—recognized the benefits in having America's urban black population hooked on dope. The sale of heroin in the black community became a kind of ghetto Gold Rush. In the 1940s and 1950s, the suppliers were almost exclusively Sicilian, Italian American, and Corsican mobsters who relied on the American Mafia for distribution. Prominent Mafiosi like Vito Genovese, Joe Bonanno, and many others created huge financial empires off the backs of street-level dope fiends. Statistics revealed that half the heroin addicts in the United States lived in New York City. The free-floating misery of this increasingly drug-dependent culture, combined with poverty and the sense of racial displacement felt by many blacks, helped lay the foundation for a crime wave that would last thirty years.

In his 1965 memoir, *Manchild in the Promised Land*, Claude Brown chronicled the effects of the heroin tsunami that first hit Harlem in the early 1950s. A community known during the Harlem Renaissance for its proud displays of sartorial splendor and artistic achievement had been shattered by dope. As Brown describes:

> Around 1955, everybody wanted a slick bitch; nobody wanted to kick the habit much. They were strung out, and they were really going down. They were ragged and beat up. Cats who had never come out of the house without a pair of shoes on that didn't cost at least thirty-five dollars, who had never had a wrinkle anyplace on them, who had always worn the best suits from Brooks Brothers or Witty Brothers—these cats were going around greasy and dirty. They were people who had too much pride to put a dirty handkerchief in their pockets at one time. Now they just seemed to be completely unaware of how they looked. They would just be walking around dirty, greasy, looking for things to steal.

Manchild in the Promised Land was a cry for help. With its publication, Claude Brown sought to bring a level of compassion and understanding to the subject. Yet few of the city's white ethnic residents were interested in that. Many of them had already concluded that illiterate, dirt-poor blacks from the South, and Spanish-speaking blacks from the Caribbean, were destroying the fabric of life in their neighborhoods. When heroin was added to the mix, it created the impression that poverty, drug abuse, and negritude were all part of the same psychosis. Spurred by genuine concern and alarmism in equal measure, many white families packed up their belongings and began their own Great Migration out of the city.

Those who stayed behind picked up their tabloid newspaper every morning with mounting dread. The subject of race became a boogeyman lurking in the shadows. The city's perceptions of urban crime were infected with a shared racial anxiety that ran like a hot wire through every major crime story in the city—including the Wylie-Hoffert murders.

The city was a fickle suitor, however. The Career Girls Murders story was like a good-looking whore: it was flashy, with sizzle and pathos, but there was always the prospect of something hotter just around the corner. Which is exactly what happened when the Wylie-Hoffert investigation—and most other aspects of daily life in New York and else-where—were shoved into the background by the events of November 22, 1963.

As a presidential motorcade wound its way through downtown Dallas that day, a bullet obliterated the skull of President John F. Kennedy; another pierced his esophagus. The president was pronounced dead at the hospital. Then, before anyone had fully processed the shock, the alleged assailant, Lee Harvey Oswald, was himself gunned down in the basement of the Dallas police department—live on television. The reverberations of these events—the news reports, the swearing-in of a new president, the unbearably poignant funeral—riveted nearly every-one, especially the media.

It would be weeks before the country emerged from its grief and began to ask: *Why?* For what reason had Kennedy been shot? The expla-nation—that the assassination was the work of a crazed lone gunman—was all well and good; for a time, sorrow outweighed the need to know. But by the early months of 1964, after the burial of JFK and the pass-ing of the torch to Lyndon Baines Johnson, clouds of suspicion began to gather. Oswald turned out to be a murky figure, with ties to many powerful forces that all had reasons to want JFK dead. Shortly before his demise, Oswald himself had insisted he was a "patsy" taking the heat for others. In time, theories about the assassination would metastasize to include conspiracy plots involving the Mob and the CIA.

Among the black community in New York and elsewhere, however, a slightly different point of view began to emerge. Given all that was hap-pening in the country, to them, this story also seemed to be about race.

The previous summer, President Kennedy had taken the dramatic step of hitching his wagon to Martin Luther King and the civil rights movement, sending the U.S. Army into Mississippi to enforce civil rights laws. To southern bigots and their supporters around the country, it was a shocking turn of events—tantamount to a declaration of war. Then, in June, the president went on national TV and framed the civil rights debate in a way no U.S. president ever had before.

"We preach freedom around the world, and we mean it," said Kennedy. "We cherish our freedom here at home. But are we to say to the world, and much more importantly, to each other that this is the land of the free except for the Negroes; that we have no second-class citizens except Negroes; that we have no class or caste system, no ghettos, no master race except with respect to Negroes? Now the time has come for this nation to fulfill its promise. The events in Birmingham and elsewhere have so increased the cries for equality that no city or state or legislative body can prudently choose to ignore them."

The day after Kennedy's speech, NAACP field marshal Medgar Evers was murdered in Mississippi. Later in the summer, President Kennedy submitted his civil rights bill to Congress. A few weeks later, in what would go down in history as perhaps the most depraved act of the era, a bomb was set off at a Baptist church in Birmingham, killing four black girls between the ages of eleven and fourteen.

Many of those following these events viewed them as part of an orchestrated reactionary campaign on the part of white supremacists, including the Ku Klux Klan and police authorities. Whenever the civil rights movement achieved a notable success, there was a shooting or a bombing in response. Whenever the president issued a statement or gave a speech in favor of equality for the Negro, terror and death followed in its wake. To many Negroes, JFK's assassination seemed to be a part of this cycle, a kind of murderous blowback for his advocacy of civil rights.

By the spring of 1964, the shock of the Kennedy and Oswald killings had been absorbed into the body politic. It wasn't that people were over it, but life went on. The city was a machine with many moving parts, a beast that needed to be fed. People returned to their lives—though perhaps with less confidence that their democracy was capable of reconciling its many contradictions.

FOR THE NYPD, the Wylie-Hoffert murder investigation had never really gone away. With media attention and public scrutiny diverted elsewhere, the detective squad in charge of the case continued to interview people and follow up on leads. The case ran into one cul-de-sac after another. Often when this happens, after too many hours of fruitless phone calls, tiring legwork, and second-guessing evidence, detectives will put an investigation on hold and come back later with a fresh eye. But this case was too prominent to shelve.

On March 11, roughly seven months after the killings, the *Herald Tribune* ran a front-page story under the headline "Our City's Number One Unsolved Murder: Who Killed the Career Girls?" After so much time, the fact that there was no hard evidence or promising suspects was a source of consternation. The press, some city officials, and the public were getting antsy. The killer—or killers—were still out there, capable of killing again.

Around this same time, in nearby Wildwood, New Jersey, George Whitmore Jr. decided he'd had enough of life with Pops. The walls of the family's three-room house, with the auto junkyard just outside, were closing in on him. "I know I should take into consideration my father had a hard life," George recalled. "Things didn't come easy, and he worked most his life. But I hated my house. I hated it when I woke in the mornin' and my father couldn't get out of bed 'cause he was drunk. And I hated the way he treated my mother—like she was workin' for him or somethin'. I know I should have had some obligations for him, but he didn't have none for me."

For a change of scene, Whitmore had often spent time in Brooklyn, where he had relatives. He would stay there for weeks or even months at a time, especially when no work could be found in Wildwood. The winter before, George had worked for three months at a metal factory on Long Island while living with his aunt and uncle in Brownsville, in central Brooklyn. George's brothers, Gerald and Shelley, were both living near Brownsville. It was a mere bus and subway ride away.

Whitmore told his mother he wanted to head out for the big city. Maybe he could find some work there.

"You sure that's what you wanna do?" she asked.

"Well, nothin' much for me to do round here."

"All right, then. Go on. But be sure now to stay with our folks, and take care of yourself, and don't stay out late, y'hear?"

A few days later, George was in a New Jersey bus station playing pinball. His mother had come along to see him off. When his bus was announced, George and his mom embraced. She thought he'd come back soon, as he always had before. George felt in his heart that he was done with Wildwood. He boarded the bus and was off.

Leaving the New Jersey Turnpike and heading toward the Lincoln Tunnel, the spiraling off-ramp offered George a panoramic view of midtown Manhattan across the Hudson River. The towering skyscrapers, dominated by the triumphant spire of the Empire State Building, were a breathtaking sight, a reminder that there was no man-made metropolis like the city of New York. George would cross under the Hudson and emerge in the Port Authority bus terminal; from there he would transfer to a subway that would take him under the East River and through Brooklyn along elevated tracks to his stop at Rockaway Avenue. There, Whitmore would descend from the station to find his destiny in a ghetto neighborhood called Brownsville.

three

THE BOWELS OF BROOKLYN

GEORGE WHITMORE DID not yet realize that he would be spending some of his nights in Brownsville as a homeless person, but he knew it wouldn't be easy. Having grown up scavenging metal from the scrap yard next door, Whitmore understood that survival was often a zero-sum game. Brownsville was a different kind of challenge: a desolate urban ghetto full of abandoned buildings, deserted, rubble-filled lots, and row after row of dilapidated brick tenements and rickety wooden homes. In nearby Bedford-Stuyvesant, another Negro ghetto, the streets were lined with glorious brownstones from a more prosperous era, now fallen into disrepair; in Brownsville there was nothing. The neighborhood's physical squalor was matched by its spiritual desperation. As one local clergyman put it: "By every number we have to measure the suffering of a community—narcotics addiction, welfare dependency, sickness and malnutrition—Brownsville is a leader. If there is a hell, the people of [this neighborhood] will take it in stride."

At first, George was able to stay with Mr. and Mrs. Blondell Dantzler, his aunt and uncle, in their cramped apartment on Hopkinson Avenue. But the Dantzlers often had other guests, and on those nights George had to look elsewhere. Sometimes he was able to sleep on a sofa at one of his brothers' apartments, though they too often relied on the kindness of family and friends for a place to stay. Occasionally, George was able to sleep at the apartment of Beverly Payne, his sometime girlfriend.

A seventeen-year-old high school student, Beverly lived on Hopkinson Avenue with her mother in a three-room railroad flat.

On the night of April 23, 1964, Whitmore had been hoping to stay at Beverly's, but her mother wasn't having it. The mother did not approve of her daughter's relationship with an unemployed grade-school dropout from New Jersey who sometimes enticed Beverly to skip school for the day and hang out with him. After George spent a few nights on a sofa in the front room, she laid down the law: no more overnight stays for him.

George spent most of that day with Beverly, but by nightfall he'd gone looking for a place to stay. Reluctant to trouble his aunt and uncle, he headed for an apartment building at 191 Amboy Street where his brother Gerald was staying with a cousin. George himself had stayed there before, but he didn't have a key, and his cousins didn't have a phone, so when George arrived at the apartment he had no way of knowing whether anyone would be home. This time no one was home, so George did what he had done before under the circumstances: he walked across the street to an almost identical tenement at 178 Amboy, where the front door lock was usually broken. Entering the building, he walked to the rear of a musty ground-floor hallway, wrapped his coat around himself, and burrowed into a small space underneath a stairwell. This would be his home for the night.

He awoke around 7:00 A.M., stiff and groggy from a night of little sleep. He stumbled out into the daylight, all nineteen years of him, gangly, pimple-faced, a veil of grime on his clothes and face. It took him a while to remember that he'd promised to meet his brother Gerald in front of a Laundromat on Sutter Avenue that morning. He quickly shuffled on over to Sutter, one block away, where he immediately spotted the familiar face of a cop by the name of Isola.

Early the previous morning, George had been standing at the same spot in front of the same Laundromat when he was approached by the same cop, Patrolman Frank Isola. The cop asked him why he was there. George willingly gave his name and told the officer he was waiting for his brother to take him to a day job at a salt-packing plant. He watched the cop jot down the information in a notepad. George didn't mind; he was eager to help.

"I know why you're asking me these questions," said George.

"Oh?" said the cop. "Why?"

George explained that the night before he'd been walking home from a pool hall when he heard shots and saw a guy running along Bristol Street with a cop in pursuit. "What was the shooting all about?" asked George.

Officer Isola explained that a woman coming home from work had been assaulted in the street.

"How low can some people get?" said George.

The cop asked George a few questions about what he'd seen. George explained that the guy being chased had disappeared into a building on Amboy Street. George even volunteered to show Officer Isola the building, which he did. Isola didn't bother to write down the building's address, but he did find it noteworthy that George had witnessed the assailant running away. From a street call box the patrolman called his sergeant, who minutes later pulled up in a squad car. Isola gave the sergeant a report. Without even getting out of the car, the sergeant stuck his head out of the window and said to Whitmore, "Between you and me, it's against the law not to tell us where a guy went to when we're looking for him."

George was startled; that's exactly what he had done. "I did tell you," he said.

The sergeant shrugged and then said to Isola, "You got this kid's name and place of employment?" Isola nodded; the sergeant drove off. Not long after that George's brother showed up and they headed off for a day of employment at the Schoenberg Salt Company.

Now, here it was the following morning and Officer Isola was back. This time he was accompanied by another guy. The guy was built like a football player, with a barrel chest and biceps that stretched the fabric of his suit jacket. They both approached Whitmore. "Mornin', Officer," said George.

The big guy spoke first: "Why did you lie to us?"

George stuttered.

Isola explained that the man with him was Detective Richard Aidala. "Your name is George Whitman, correct?"

"No," said George. "Not Whitman. Whitmore. George Whitmore Junior."

The cops looked at each other, then at George. They told him that yesterday they had gone to his place of business, the Schoenberg Salt Company. The manager told them there was no George Whitman working there. "Were you there yesterday?"

George explained that he'd gone with his brother to the factory, but when he got there he realized he'd neglected to bring along his social security number, and without that number the company was unable to employ him for the day, so they'd sent George packing.

Whitmore had answers for Isola and Aidala's questions, but the two policemen didn't seem satisfied. Aidala asked, "Would you be willing to come with us to the station house and answer a few questions?"

"Why, sure," said George. He wasn't the least bit hesitant; indeed, Whitmore had seen enough TV cop shows that he was actually excited by the prospect of helping with the investigation.

The Seventy-third Precinct station house was located near the intersection of East New York Avenue and Rockaway Avenue. It had the look of a Second World War bunker, an imposing redbrick and slate building constructed at the turn of the century in a style known as French Fortress. Like most public buildings in this part of Brooklyn, it had seen better days; there was chicken wire over the windows, a crumbling facade, and weeds sprouting from cracks in the front steps and surrounding sidewalk.

Whitmore was brought into the station house by Isola and Aidala. It was his first experience inside a New York police station. The harsh overhead fluorescent lighting seemed designed to make a person sweat. There was a sickly yellowish hue to the lighting: it had been years since the light fixtures had been cleaned or the walls painted, decades since the floor tiles had been replaced. The building's few windows allowed little natural light to intrude on the institutional surroundings. George had the same feeling many civilians did when they entered this and other precincts in black Brooklyn: that it was the kind of place a person could enter and never be heard from again.

Right away George got the sense that, despite what he'd been told, he hadn't been brought to the station house for "routine questioning." The cops inside looked at him like he was a criminal. Whitmore was taken upstairs and placed in "the cage," a makeshift holding cell in the detective squad room. The two cops disappeared.

Damn, thought George, *why they treatin' me like this? What'd I do?*

The two cops returned. Detective Aidala took George into another room and told him to stand. Unbeknownst to Whitmore, in an adjacent squad commander's office, Patrolman Isola and a woman named Elba Borrero were awaiting his arrival. It was Elba Borrero, a twenty-five-year-old Puerto Rican woman, who had been assaulted on Bristol Street two nights before.

Isola instructed Borrero to look through a peephole in the wall at a person she'd been told was a suspect. Borrero was a small woman, barely five feet tall; she couldn't reach the peephole until the cops stacked some phone books for her to stand on. She peeked through the hole and said, "That's the man." Then she thought about it for a moment and said, "I want to be sure. Can I hear his voice?"

Whitmore was instructed to say, "Lady, I'm going to rape you; lady, I'm going to kill you."

When George said the words, Borrero began to tremble. It took the cops twenty minutes to calm her down. "He's the one," she said.

George was brought into the squad commander's office to face Elba Borrero. He'd heard her through the door claiming he was the person who assaulted her. "Ma'am," he said, "you makin' a mistake. I never seen you before in my life."

The woman recoiled in horror; she was immediately led out of the room.

Whitmore stood dumbstruck. The odd confluence of circumstances that had brought him to this moment had fallen like dominoes: if Whitmore hadn't chatted amiably with Officer Isola the previous morning, volunteering information about what he'd seen on Sutter Avenue, he probably wouldn't be standing in the precinct house at this moment. If the officer had copied down his name correctly as Whitmore, not Whitman, Isola and Aidala wouldn't have concluded that George was a liar and therefore worthy of suspicion. If George hadn't been a meek and pliable person—a blank slate—he might not have intrigued Isola and Aidala as the ideal suspect, a wayward Negro boy you could pin crimes on and no one would ever know or care.

There is an expression cops use when they have a suspect who fits the profile of a perpetrator they're looking for: "I like him for that assault," they'll say. "I like him for this murder." Officers Isola and Aidala liked George Whitmore. They liked him a lot. In fact, they thought he fit nicely into another case that was being investigated in the Seventy-third Precinct—the murder of a woman in a Brownsville alley two weeks earlier.

The cops immediately called the lead investigator on that case and summoned him to the precinct. In the meantime, George needed to be softened up. The three of them—Isola, Aidala, and Whitmore—were in the squad commander's office with the door closed. As Whitmore recalled:

> The detective kept on saying that I was suppose' to have raped this lady, and then he started punchin' on me . . . and I kept telling him that "I don't know anything about this," and at the same time the officer came in and he was rollin' up his sleeves . . .and he came over and started punchin' on me, too. He had a big ring on his finger, and that ring kept hitting me in the chest, in the same spot, over and over. Then they stood me in front of a chair, and every time I said, "I never seen this lady before," I got knocked into the chair until I thought the chair was gonna break underneath me. I told them, "If I told you that I did do what you said I did, I'd be lyin'." They called me a liar and kept beatin' on me. So I just broke down and said, yes.

After thirty minutes, Detective Joseph Di Prima, the man from the homicide squad, arrived in the squad room.

Di Prima knew what to do: it was called "the Mutt and Jeff routine," or "good cop bad cop," part of a detective's official training as laid out in *Fundamentals of Police Investigation*, a manual by Charles E. O'Hara, a former NYPD detective. O'Hara described the tactic: "One interrogator, Mutt, is relentless and menacing, but the other, Jeff, is a kindhearted man. . . . He disapproves of Mutt and his tactics and will arrange to get him off the case if the suspect will cooperate."

Di Prima stepped into the role of Jeff. "Are you hungry, George?" he asked. "Can we get you something to eat?"

Whitmore nodded; he hadn't put anything in his stomach in a long time.

The detective sent Patrolman Isola out for Italian rolls and containers of coffee for the four of them. While they waited, Di Prima made small talk with George, taking care to stay away from criminal matters. He asked George about his upbringing in Wildwood and about his life in Brownsville. He asked George about his father and his mother and about whether he'd been able to find much work in Brooklyn. Whitmore was relieved to talk about something besides the crime of which he'd suddenly been accused.

The bread and coffee arrived. When George had finished his, Di Prima got down to business. The detective was there to ask George about a different crime—a murder—but he started with the Borrero incident, with the idea of working inexorably toward the other case. According to Di Prima:

I asked him whether or not he was the person who attacked Mrs. Borrero. I asked him if what she said was true. He said, in the beginning, he said, he did not attack Mrs. Borrero, he didn't know anything about it. I said inasmuch as Mrs. Borrero had identified him as her assailant there was no other thing for the police to do but to arrest him. If he wanted to tell me anything about it, it was his privilege, he didn't have to speak to me if he didn't want to. He thought it over a little while and then asked me, if a fellow was convicted for this type of crime, how much time would he do. I said I honestly didn't know, the punishment for the crime would be limited to the courts and the judge. He then turned around and says, "Well," he says, "I'll tell you the truth. I want to tell you that I'm the one that Mrs. Borrero identified as—I'm the person that she identified as assaulting her." I again reminded him that he didn't have to speak to me about this if he didn't want to, but if he wanted to tell me the truth, I would listen to him and I would relay that same truth to the court. He continued talking to me. . . . He told me later on, during the conversation, when I reminded him that there was nobody there that would hurt him, and I kept talking to him in a nice level. I asked him was he afraid of me, he said, "No, you're speaking to me better than anyone else has spoken to me in my life," he said. "My father never spoke to me like that. . . . "

With George now on his side, Di Prima moved on to the murder case. It involved a forty-two-year-old Negro woman named Minnie Edmonds who had been sexually assaulted and brutally stabbed to death in an alley near Chester Street. As the detective would later tell it:

When we were through with the Borrero case, I said to George Whitmore, "You mentioned Chester Street in your conversation with me, have you anything in your mind about Chester Street?" At first he said, "Well, the boys fight on Chester Street, you know there is a lot of jitterbugging going on." I said, "This is nothing new to the police. We know about the jitterbugging. What is on your mind or have you anything on your mind on Chester Street other than the jitterbugging." He said, "You mean about the woman that was hurt on Chester Street?" He said, "I hurt the woman who was hurt on Chester Street." I said, "Do you care to talk to me about it?" He said he would. . . .

Whitmore, of course, had a different version of his conversation with Detective Di Prima. George would contend that he knew nothing of these crimes other than the information given to him by the policemen. He did admit that, after the physical abuse he'd taken from Isola and Aidala, he'd begun to fear for his well-being. From that point on his goal—if he had a goal—was to tell the cops whatever they wanted to hear so he could get the hell out of there as soon as possible.

Occasionally Isola and Aidala came into the squad commander's office to listen in on Detective Di Prima's interrogation. Everything was going well. Di Prima fed Whitmore the details: *You approached the woman from behind, you put a knife to her throat and said, "I want to touch your pussy, I want to rape you. Be quiet or I'll fucking kill you, bitch." You tore her panties off and tried to rape her, but she began screaming. So you cut her with the knife.*

Di Prima was careful not to say that George had murdered the woman: that was part of the strategy, to get Whitmore to admit to the facts before he had any idea that he was admitting to murder.

George went along with everything. He was so pliable that the policemen could hardly believe their good fortune. He was a blank slate, an empty vessel to be filled with all the crimes they could make stick.

There was one problem: Whitmore was saying "yes" and "okay" to virtually every detail of the Edmonds murder fed to him by Di Prima— but what about the weapon, the knife he'd used in the attack?

George wanted to help; he wanted to satisfy the cops so that maybe they'd let him go. But he didn't know what to say about the knife.

At this point, Patrolman Isola entered the room and listened to Di Prima questioning George about the knife. Isola left the room, went to his locker, and returned with a knife. It was metallic, with a black handle and the image of a greyhound on both sides of the handle. "Was it anything like this?" Isola asked Whitmore.

George nodded.

The cops were excited. George had identified *a* knife, but not *the* knife. They wanted to know what he did with it. As George remembered it:

> They kept on insistin' that I had a knife, which I kept telling them that I had no such knife, and they made a statement that this knife would be the only thing that would help me, and they need it, they wanted to find it. So I told them that I had lost a knife, and I didn't know where it is, and they just insisted, so I told them that I hid it. . . .

"Where?" asked Detective Di Prima. "Show us."

George began to sweat. His first thought was that he didn't want his family or relatives to know where he was and what was happening; he was embarrassed. He could think of only one place to direct the cops where he wouldn't run into anyone he knew: his "home" under that stairwell in the tenement building on Amboy Street.

Together with Detectives Di Prima and Aidala and another officer acting as driver, Whitmore was loaded into the back of a squad car. They drove through the streets of Brownsville to the building at 178 Amboy Street. There, George led the detectives inside and showed them the spot under the stairs where he'd slept the night before. Detective Aidala got down on his hands and knees and swept his hands around in the dark space. He found some debris, but nothing else. "You look," the detective said to George.

George knelt and groped around for the knife he knew wasn't there. He could tell that the detectives weren't happy. "Maybe I made a mistake about leaving the knife under the stairs," said Whitmore. "Maybe it's over at my girlfriend's place." George regretted the words as soon as they left his mouth.

That got the detectives excited again. "Good," said Aidala. "Take us over there."

They headed to the apartment. Beverly Payne, Whitmore's sometime girlfriend, was startled to open her door and find George standing there, flanked by two white men in suits who could only be officers of the law.

Aidala and Di Prima searched Beverly Payne's apartment thoroughly. They didn't find a knife, but they did seize some clothing that belonged to George. The detectives told Beverly to get her coat; she was coming with them.

They all returned to the Seventy-third Precinct. Once they entered the station house, George never saw Beverly again. She was ushered off to a different part of the building, and George was secluded once again in the squad commander's office. Whitmore remembered: "They stated to me that if Beverly didn't—if we didn't come up with the knife, if she had it, they were goin' to send her to a girls home."

After a while, the detectives stopped talking about the knife and came up with another idea. "Let's go see the murder scene," they said.

Whitmore was put in the car once again and driven to Chester Street. The officers pointed out to George where everything happened: *That's where you grabbed Minnie Edmonds. That's where you threw her down and ripped off her panties. That's where you cut her with a knife.*

It was early afternoon by the time the detectives and Whitmore returned to the station house. Hungry and sleep-deprived, his head pounding after more than seven hours of physical and psychological manipulation, George felt as though he were tumbling in midair with nothing to break his fall.

The detectives ordered sandwiches. George was given ham and cheese. When he finished the sandwich, the detectives questioned and cajoled him for another hour or so. Whitmore told the cops whatever they wanted to hear.

By late afternoon, Di Prima and Aidala seemed satisfied. Aidala called for an assistant district attorney and a stenographer to take Whitmore's formal confession.

It took the Homicide Bureau's assistant D.A. at least an hour to get there. As Whitmore waited in the commander's office, detectives came and went. Even during his interrogation, other cops had been sticking their heads into the office to see the "perp" who'd "confessed" to two violent felonies in the precinct. One detective seemed to observe the proceedings with more intensity than the others.

Edward J. Bulger was a veteran who had seen it all. In his mid-fifties, with receding hair slicked back, and a steely glare that criminal suspects found discomforting, Bulger was a detective's detective. A legend in the Brooklyn North homicide squad, Bulger was old school, the kind of guy who always got his man—by any means necessary. He was about to insert himself into the case against George Whitmore in a way that would have a profound impact on the young Negro's life—not to mention the very nature of criminal justice in America.

WITHIN THE RANKS of the NYPD's detective bureau, there was no talent more prized than the ability to make a person confess to a crime. Some cops were good at the politics of the job, others had a nose for collecting and gathering information; these were skills that were appreciated and sometimes led to promotions. But among the rank and file, nothing was more central to the success of a detective's career than the magic touch to make a suspect say "I did it" and sign on the dotted line.

The most common method for extracting a confession was known as the "Third Degree"—a term that would become so ubiquitous in police dramas that it became a cliché. But to the NYPD it was a very specific and effective tactic, a vital means to an end. As far back as 1901, a police reporter for the *New York Times* traced the origins of the term, which he defined as a procedure that "consists largely in creating an atmosphere around an alleged criminal from which very few can emerge without having committed themselves in some way or another if they are guilty." That last phrase—*if they are guilty*—was generous: ideally, the Third Degree was applied only to suspects the police believed were guilty, but often it was used to extract information, or exact punishment, from suspects or witnesses who weren't giving the cops what they wanted.

At its most extreme, the Third Degree involved police coercion, violence, or flat-out torture. It was also known as "backroom justice" or "police psychology." Cops who were good at it knew how to beat or slap around a suspect without leaving so much as a bruise (beating suspects with a thick phone book or an open hand, for instance). Especially brutal cops were known as "mechanics" for their ability to "tune up" a suspect. Robert Daley, who would serve as the NYPD's deputy commissioner of public information for two years, recalled that "the New York police department was, in a sense, renowned for its brutality. Police brutality was considered part of the game. Not always. But let a suspect give a cop a hard time and the cop would hit him. . . . Cops would tell me about this slap-jack that certain cops had, where you could turn a man's brain to jelly without leaving a mark. Cops used to carry newspapers in the car so suspects wouldn't bleed all over the seat."

In some precincts, so vaunted was the NYPD's reputation for brutality that it wasn't even necessary to use actual violence—the mere suggestion was enough.

In his twenty-seven-year career with the force, Edward Bulger had become known as a man who knew how to extract confessions. In 1960, he broke a big case involving the shocking death of Margaret O'Meara, a seventy-seven-year-old grandmother who was raped and murdered on Thanksgiving Day 1959. The man who took the fall was David Coleman, a black man who would be tried, convicted, and sentenced to die in the electric chair at Sing Sing prison. Years later, while seeking a stay of execution, Coleman told a judge how, in January 1960, he'd been arrested for the theft of two typewriters. Detective Eddie Bulger and another detective took Coleman to a Brooklyn squad room, handcuffed him to a chair, and beat him over the head until "I thought the top of my head would come off." After fifteen hours of questioning, interrupted by five visits to various burglary scenes around the borough, Coleman gave the detectives the confession they were looking for—even though, it would later be proven, he had nothing to do with the rape and murder.

Bulger's skills were so well known that, just seven months earlier, he'd been plucked from his assignment in Brooklyn North homicide to work the most famous case in the city, the Wylie-Hoffert murder.

The rivalry between Brooklyn and Manhattan detectives at the time could be fierce. The boys from the more glamorous borough, weaned on high-profile cases that came under intense press scrutiny, considered the Brooklyn detectives rubes who sometimes used crude and sloppy tactics simply because they could get away with it.

Detective Bulger was a hotshot on his home turf, but in Manhattan he wasted no time alienating the detectives who'd been running the Wylie-Hoffert investigation for months. One day, he visited the murder scene and discovered in the bathroom a blue plastic wrapper from a package of razor blades—a wrapper not mentioned in any of the police reports. Bulger brought it to the attention of the squad commander, who scolded his detectives for the oversight. Some Manhattan detectives suspected that Bulger planted the wrapper himself. Later, unbeknownst to Bulger, it was determined that—weeks after the murders—a police officer baby-sitting the crime scene had shaved in the bathroom of the Wylie-Hoffert apartment, absentmindedly leaving behind the wrapper.

Another matter that annoyed the Manhattan investigators was Bulger's interrogation technique. Everyone knew how the Third Degree worked, but Bulger could be heavy-handed. One person of interest who was pulled in to be questioned about the Career Girls Murders was a local Negro window washer. Bulger, another detective, and a sergeant hovered over the young man, who had an airtight work-related alibi for the day of the murders. Bulger stuck a finger in the guy's face and slammed a desktop. "You're the guy who did this. You saw the door open and walked in . . . then you saw Janice Wylie nude and you had to have her."

The sergeant was forced to get between Bulger and the window washer, a guy with no criminal record. Bulger waved his hand to dismiss the man. "All right, get out of here. But I'm not through with you yet." A week later, Bulger was taken off the case and sent back to Brooklyn.

On the day Whitmore was being interrogated, Bulger had arrived at the Seven-Three station house late in the afternoon, just as Detective Di Prima was starting to tighten the screws on the young man for the Minnie Edmonds murder. After looking in on the interrogation, Bulger started rifling through George Whitmore's belongings, which were spread out on a desktop in the outer office. There wasn't much: some loose change, a paperback book, and Whitmore's wallet. Bulger flipped through the wallet and came across a photo, a black-and-white snapshot of a girl—white, with blond hair—leaning against the hood of a car in what looked like a park or a rural area with grass and trees. Bulger stared at the photo, then held it up to a couple of nearby detectives. "Hey, this looks like one of those Wylie-Hoffert girls."

The room got quiet. Bulger may have been a reject in Manhattan, but out here in Brooklyn he was still a Big Cheese. He was considered the local detective with the most knowledge about the Career Girls Murders, having pored over files, visited the murder scene, and interrogated "persons of interest" himself.

Bulger ducked back into the squad commander's office and whispered into Detective Di Prima's ear. He showed him the photo from Whitmore's wallet. And with that George Whitmore was pushed further down the rabbit hole into a world of confusion and dread.

They took him into another room, a small eight-by-twelve-foot interrogation room with a window so grimy you couldn't see through it, where Bulger told him they would have "more privacy." Careful not to mention anything about rape or murder, Bulger started interrogating Whitmore about the photo.

The questions embarrassed George. He'd found the photo months earlier while scavenging at the town dump in Wildwood. He'd liked the look of the pretty, blond-haired white girl in the photo, and put it in his wallet. Later, he wrote on the back of it: "To George from Louise." It was a ruse he hoped to use to impress friends and family: *See,* he could say, *this is my white girlfriend.*

Flustered, George tried lying to the detectives, telling them Louise was a girl he knew who'd given him the photo. They didn't believe him. Reluctantly, George told them the truth: he'd found the photo in the garbage and written the inscription on the back himself. The detectives didn't believe that, either. Di Prima asked, "Couldn't you have gotten this picture off Eighty-eighth Street? . . . Didn't you go into Eighty-eighth Street and go into an apartment and take this picture?"

At first Whitmore was resistant, but—just as he'd been doing all day long—he eventually relented and told the cops what they wanted to hear.

Linking George to the horrible events of August 28, 1963, was a slow and torturous process. Whitmore had never been to the Upper East Side of Manhattan; he'd never stepped farther into Manhattan than the Port Authority bus station, where he caught the subway to Brooklyn. If the detectives wanted to create a plausible scenario in which Whitmore somehow made his way to the Wylie-Hoffert residence, entered the apartment, raped Janice Wylie, then brutally murdered her and her roommate, they had a tough job ahead of them.

Recalled Whitmore:

> They asked me what building was I supposed to go in on 88th Street. I told them I don't know. And they said I had went into the building and went upstairs, and I told them that I didn't went into the building. They said, "Sure you went into the building and you went upstairs." And I said, "Yeah, I went to the roof." And he says, "No," he says, "didn't you see a door crack when you were going up?" And he says, "When you walked—when you pushed the door open, what was the first thing you saw?" And I didn't say anything. I waited and I said,

"The table," and he says, "Didn't you see soda bottles?" I said, "I don't know. I don't know." I was confused.

The soda bottles were an important detail. Both Wylie and Hoffert had been hit over the head with a Coke bottle before they were murdered. The killer would have to know about that.

The interrogation continued. By now, Whitmore was a willing confessor, but it would still take hours to get all the details straight.

They didn't beat me. They didn't yell at me. They didn't threaten me. They wasn't even angry. They asked me didn't I grab the little girl like I grabbed Missus Edmonds, and I tried to remember what they told me about Missus Edmonds and I told 'em, "Yes, that's how I did it." I did more. I showed 'em. I remembered and I showed 'em. They said didn't the little girl scream the way Minnie Edmonds and Missus Borrero screamed? I remembered about that from before and I told 'em that's how she screamed. They said, "If you was a burglar and you was in a home and somebody saw you, wouldn't you knock 'em out and tie 'em up?" And I said I guess a burglar would. They said if'n a burglar got scared, mightn't he cut the girls? And I said he might. I just didn't care. I was tired and I didn't care.

There were interruptions: because of a shift change, George had to be taken downstairs and booked for the Borrero and Edmonds crimes, then taken back upstairs. Somewhere along the line there was a food break, more sandwiches and soda. Then back to questioning.

"George," he says, "do you suck pussy?"
"I'm not that kind of boy," I says.
"I believe you," he says, "but everybody sucks pussy."
"I don't," I says.
"George," he says, "did you put cream in her pussy when she was on the floor?"
"You mean," I says, "when she was knocked out?"
"Yeah," he says, "when she was knocked out."
"No," I says, "I couldn't done somethin' like that. You gotta be terrible sick to do somethin' like that."

The other detective, he gets up and he yells at me—
"Listen, George, if you don't give me a straight answer in five minutes I'm gonna kick you in the balls."

After that, I told them what they wanted.

Once George figured out that the girls had been sexually assaulted and badly cut up, the thought crossed his mind that the detectives were leading him into a murder confession. "Hey," he said, "ain't those girls gonna be mad with me?" He intended it as a trick question to find out if the girls had been killed.

"Well," said Detective Bulger, "wait right here and I'll find out." Bulger left the room, then returned and told Whitmore, "I just spoke to the girls on the phone. Everything's okay. They're not mad."

By now, word had begun to spread throughout the precinct and borough command that detectives out here in the bowels of Brooklyn had stumbled across the most notorious killer in the city, and he was spilling his guts.

The first to arrive was Lieutenant Damien Salvia, the commander of the Seventy-third Detective Squad. It was Salvia's day off, but when he heard that a few of his men were about to crack the city's biggest murder case, he rushed in. He was followed by Assistant Chief Inspector Richard F. Carey, the commander of Brooklyn North Detectives. Together, the detectives and their commanders decided to wait before calling in the top brass from Manhattan. The Manhattan detectives would know the case inside out. There was still work to be done before they were ready to share George Whitmore.

Bulger and Di Prima had come up with a plausible scenario to explain how Whitmore got to the building at 57 East Eighty-eighth Street. They had even gotten George to describe how he perpetrated the act. But they needed to establish without a doubt that George had been in that apartment, that he knew the layout of the crime scene. Detective Bulger gave Whitmore a pad of paper and told him they were going to sketch a drawing of the Wylie-Hoffert apartment.

George liked to draw; it was a skill he'd once hoped would be his calling in life. But it was approaching midnight, and he was exhausted.

"Here," said Bulger, "I'll help you."

The veteran detective stood behind Whitmore. He put a pencil in his hand, then gripped George's hand with his own. Together, like a puppeteer and his marionette, they began to draw the apartment layout, room by room.

Whitmore might have done better if he had glasses on. With his poor eyesight, he could hardly make out what was being put down on paper.

I was very tired, almost falling asleep. I was in a drowsy fog. The light in the room was sweating. I was sweating. The detective put a pencil in my hand and helped me sketch. He was explainin' to me where the bathroom and the bedroom was. . . . They said, "You stay awake; you're not goin' to sleep. As soon as we're done, we'll let you get some sleep."

When George was finished, Bulger had him initial the drawing.

Now they had something; it was all coming together. Word went out over the police radio: *Subject in Manhattan double homicide being interrogated at Seven-Three precinct. Repeat, subject in Wylie-Hoffert homicide at Seven-Three.*

The Manhattan command structure arrived all at once: Assistant Chief Inspector Coyle, Detective Lynch from the Two-Three Detective Squad, Andrew Dunleavy from Manhattan North Homicide, Lieutenant Regan from the chief's office, and the man himself, Chief of Detectives McKearney.

Over the next two or three hours—well past midnight and into the early-morning hours—Whitmore was subjected to a numbing litany of accusations, harangues, and questions with predetermined answers. He was introduced to inspectors, chiefs, lieutenants, and homicide detectives. At times, as many as seven or eight men were crowded into the small interrogation room, a sea of white faces descending upon George like a blistering snowstorm. As Whitmore would later point out, "I was the only Negro guy in there. The rest of 'em were white, and at the time, they wasn't too friendly."

By 2:00 A.M. Whitmore's story was seemingly complete; the highly detailed diagram of the murder scene had been notarized by George. It had taken more than ten hours to lay out all the details of the Wylie-Hoffert murders and get the perp to regurgitate it all back to the investigators. Now came the hardest part: Whitmore would have to give his statement to an assistant district attorney and have it recorded by a stenographer.

Assistant district attorneys arrived from both the Brooklyn and Manhattan D.A.'s offices. Whitmore would have to give three separate statements for the three separate crimes. These statements would become the official version in the state's case against the accused, to be used by prosecutors, defense attorneys, judges, and jury members. They had to be perfect.

The Borrero and Edmonds confessions went off without a hitch. Seated in the squad commander's office, with the assistant D.A. and a stenographer on one side of him and detectives on the other, Whitmore gave his name, address, and date of birth, and was then led through the details of the crimes. Recalled Whitmore:

> People say you must have a wonderful memory to remember all that, but it weren't so hard. Most of the questions I could tell where they were goin' cause I had good schoolin' on that. Whenever I got into trouble and forgot my answer, I'd look sideways at my detectives and they'd hint me with shakin' their head or scratchin' their nose or somethin' like that. I think even one time they whispered an answer to me.

Getting the Borrero and Edmonds confession down on paper took about an hour. The Wylie-Hoffert confession was more problematic. To make the case as airtight as possible, Bulger had filled Whitmore's head with minute details about the case. It could be confusing, but the detectives had worked out a system with George so he could keep some of the details straight.

> My detectives told me if anybody ask you, the first girl you seen is the baby girl and the second one who comes in later is the mother. That's the way I can keep the girls straight in my memory. So I make believe to myself the left hand is the baby girl and the right one is the mother and when he ask me 'bout the first girl I make a fist with my left hand when he ask me 'bout the second girl I make a fist with my right for the mother. A game, kind of. That's my whole story. That's the whole story of a Negro boy who never hurt nobody, in the police precinct on Friday that April.

The assistant D.A. from Manhattan was Peter Koste. He should have been suspicious when the detectives warned him ahead of time that Whitmore probably believed that Janice Wylie and Emily Hoffert were still alive. That was the first of many details that went against normal protocol. It was within Koste's job description to question the detectives about their methods of interrogation, but Koste found himself in a Brooklyn precinct surrounded by two dozen detectives and high-ranking police officials, all of whom could hardly contain their excitement at the prospect of breaking the case. As far as these men were concerned, taking down Whitmore's confession was a formality. Koste was expected to do his part.

It was a nerve-racking process. George had been prepared well, but occasionally there were details that he and the detectives hadn't gone over. For instance, at one point Assistant D.A. Koste asked Whitmore about the building at 57 East Eighty-eighth Street.

Q: What kind of building?
A: About a four-story house.

Q: Four-story house, you think it was?
A: Yes.

Q: What did you do when you spotted this four-story house?
   You think it was four stories?
A: Four or five stories.

Apparently, the number of stories in the building had never come up. At this point, as the finished transcript noted, "Detective Bulger leaves room." Twenty questions later, Bulger returned and the questioning veered back to the height of the building.

Q: You mentioned that this building was about four or five
   stories, could it have been eight or ten stories?
A: I don't know if it's that high or not.

Q: Could it have been eight stories?
A: Yes.

Q: But it could have been more than four or five stories?
A: Yes.

The questioning continued in a similar manner. Whenever there was confusion about an important detail, the detectives ducked out of the room, figured out the answer among themselves, then returned. The line of inquiry would return to important details to make sure they were clarified in the transcript. The investigators were determined to cover everything. George had even been supplied with a story about how, after committing the murders, he had retrieved a package of razor blades from the bathroom. He opened the package and took out a blade, used it to slice a bedsheet into strips, and then used the strips of cloth to tie up the bodies.

The detectives and the assistant D.A. worked as a team. The inspectors and chiefs were there to make sure everyone dotted their *i*'s and crossed their *t*'s.

At 4:12 A.M., Koste said, "All right. Thank you, George. No further questions." The longest murder confession in the history of New York State was complete. Koste had asked 594 questions. The transcript was sixty-one pages long. Whitmore was asked to sign it, and he did.

A quiver of excitement rippled through the police command, all the way from the Seventy-third Precinct to the office of the commissioner. Before Whitmore had even finished giving his statement, someone had leaked to the press that a suspect in the Career Girls Murders was confessing to the crime. Reporters started arriving at the precinct around 4:00 A.M.; they were held at bay near the station house front desk by uniformed cops and told that Chief McKearney would be down soon to issue a statement.

Upstairs, Whitmore was placed in the cage and left there by himself. He had passed beyond fatigue into what resembled an out-of-body experience. Alone, away from the detectives for the first time in many hours, he began to feel something like anger. For nearly twenty-four hours he had been in police custody. Not once had detectives told him that he could make a phone call or have an attorney present. Not once had they asked him if he had an alibi for the dates and times of the crimes in question. They weren't interested in alibis. They had promised George that, after he satisfied their needs and demands, it would "all be over" and he could go. Well, obviously that was a lie. For the first time, George realized that he'd gotten himself into something he might not be getting out of for a long time.

After a while, a big group of white men in suits came and took George from the cell. Along with Bulger and Aidala and Di Prima, there was Detective Martin Zinkand, who'd arrived at the precinct as a representative of the Manhattan homicide squad. Department protocol called for the glory to be spread evenly among the various detective units involved.

With policemen holding George Whitmore by one arm and Di Prima by the other, they led the accused toward a staircase leading down to the front desk.

It was approximately 5:30 A.M. At this hour, the station house in Brownsville was usually as quiet as a cemetery. But today was not an ordinary day.

That morning, Fred C. Shapiro, a reporter for the *New York Herald Tribune* who lived in Brooklyn, was awoken by a phone call from an assistant city editor. "Get over to the East New York Avenue precinct," he was told. "They've got the Wylie killer."

Shapiro, a veteran reporter, was accustomed to early-morning calls, but this one seemed especially urgent. "Do we know the identity of the suspect?" he asked.

"You never heard of him," he was told. "It's a jig named Whitmore."

At the station house, Shapiro crammed into the front desk area with dozens of other print reporters, crime beat photographers, and TV news crews setting up lights. A buzz of excitement permeated the room, punctuated by the incessant ringing of the station house phones. Off-duty detectives were coming by to see what was going on. The reporters' cigarettes created a layer of smoke in the air.

Around 6:30 A.M. there was a rustle of expectation. Chief McKearney appeared and read an official statement from a yellow notepad: "Suspect's name is George Whitmore Jr., age nineteen . . . admitted killing one Minnie Edmonds . . . attempted to commit felonious rape on one Elba Borrero . . . was apprehended by Patrolman Frank Isola, who had engaged the suspect in a chase . . . did admit these crimes."

The reporters shouted questions: *What about Wylie-Hoffert? Yeah, the Career Girls Murders—did he do it?*

The chief continued: "Whitmore is a drifter. . . . He wandered to the apartment on 88th Street. . . . He found the door cracked . . . stabbed the girls repeatedly after binding them with a sheet. . . . Then he calmly washed his hands and left as he came." McKearney added that a wallet-sized photo of Janice Wylie had been found on Whitmore. At first, said the chief, the perpetrator claimed he'd found the picture on a dump in his hometown of Wildwood, but under questioning he admitted taking it from the apartment on the day he killed the girls.

The reporters jockeyed for position, tripping over one another to ask their questions.

The chief was tired and running low on patience. "Look fellas, we wouldn't have booked him if we weren't sure. He gave us facts only the killer could give. . . . We got the right guy—no question about it."

From the top of the stairs, Whitmore heard shouting and the sound of cameras flashing. Zinkand and Aidala were still holding him, with a phalanx of detectives behind them. When he spotted the mob of reporters below them, George hesitated. One of the detectives said reassuringly, "It's okay, George. Let's go."

They descended the stairs. Bright lights from TV cameras illuminated the dingy precinct. Phosphorescent bulbs flashed. Questions were shouted all at once: *George, why did you do it? Did they beat you? What do you have to say, George? George, was it fun?*

Fred Shapiro pushed to the front of the crowd. Years later, in a book on the Whitmore case, he would write: "The detectives made no effort to clear a path for Whitmore. . . . rather, it seemed that he cleared a path for them through massed reporters and photographers who pressed close to, but did not touch him."

Within a few moments, the prisoner was led out of the station house to a squad car that would take him to arraignment court in downtown Brooklyn.

The police station quickly emptied out, with reporters dashing off to file their stories in time for the next edition. There was nothing left to say. The NYPD had their man.

AT ARRAIGNMENT COURT in downtown Brooklyn, Whitmore felt so weak he thought his legs might give out. The room was packed with reporters, cops, lawyers, and the judge seated on high looking down on the accused. George saw some of his family in the spectators gallery—his aunt, his girlfriend Beverly, his brother Gerald—and felt a wave of humiliation.

"Do you have a lawyer?" barked Judge James J. Comerford. Though the judge had been living in New York most of his life, he had the accent of a man who'd never left the green fields of his birthplace in County Clare, Ireland.

Whitmore stood handcuffed, with Detective Aidala on one side and Detective Zinkand on the other. To the judge's question he answered, "No."

"Do you intend to get a lawyer?"

"Yes."

"I can't hear you," said the judge.

"Yes," said Whitmore.

"When will you have a lawyer of your own choice?"

Detective Aidala spoke up. "He can't afford a lawyer, Judge."

"Let him speak for himself. Is there any lawyer in court here now?"

The judge scanned the area where lawyers from the public defender's office gathered. "You," he said, pointing at Jerome J. Leftow. "Do you want to assist the court by speaking with the defendant?"

Leftow stepped forward.

This scene, intended to appear spontaneous, was anything but. In fact, early that morning, when the judge first heard that the perpetrator of the notorious Wylie-Hoffert murders was being brought to his courtroom, he summoned Jerome Leftow to his chambers. Leftow was thirty years old and relatively inexperienced as a criminal defense attorney, but he was a member of the Madison Club, a well-placed political club in Brooklyn. Years later, Leftow remembered how his political connections paid off by netting him the most famous case of his career. "In his chambers Judge Comerford said to me, 'Young man, I'm going to help you out and get your name in the newspapers. I'm going to assign you a case that's gotten national attention. The reporters are out there, and the photographers are out there.' And then he tells me what the case is about. I say, 'What about those other more experienced lawyers out there? They're gonna want to be involved.' He says, 'Don't worry about it—you're getting it.'"

And the scene in the courtroom that morning? "The judge was putting on a show," Leftow remembered. "It had already been decided."

Jerome Leftow, whose inexperience as an attorney was matched by his inexpensive suit, purchased wholesale at an outlet in downtown Brooklyn, walked over and stood next to Whitmore.

A court clerk read the docket number and charges, and then asked Detective Aidala to verify the facts of the Borrero assault and the Edmonds murder.

This was the first time that George Whitmore realized Minnie Edmonds had been killed and he had confessed to the murder.

The court clerk then asked Detective Zinkand to swear that he had arrested the defendant "on a charge of homicide with a knife which he believes he committed on August 28, 1963 at 57 East 88th Street, apartment 3C, County of New York, between the hours of 9:30 and 2 P.M. in that the defendant herein did stab and cut with a knife about the throat, neck and body of two females, Janice Wylie and Emily Hoffert, as a result of which injuries were inflicted that resulted in death of the aforesaid."

George wasn't sure, but he figured all of that must mean those two girls were dead. It was another murder he'd confessed to without knowing it.

Judge Comerford offered Leftow ten minutes to speak with his client. The lawyer pulled Whitmore aside. The kid was shaking and appeared confused. He looked at Leftow with suspicion: *Is this another white guy in a suit, working for the police and the D.A. to help make me look guilty?*

Leftow handed George a copy of the formal complaint against him. "Do you want to read this, George?"

Whitmore's eyes glazed over the complaint. Leftow saw at once that his defendant wouldn't be able to absorb the document. He was far too tired and unfocused.

"Do you understand the charges against you, George?" asked Leftow.

Whitmore nodded.

"Is it true?"

"No. Definitely not true."

Leftow took a deep breath. This was going to be more complicated than he'd expected. "George," he asked, "why did you make these statements to the police if they are not true?"

Whitmore's eyes filled. "They made me. They made me say those things." He gave a rambling minute-long explanation of how he came to sign the confession.

Leftow looked at the kid, unsure what to make of him. Lots of criminals claimed they were innocent. This kid looked and sounded sincere, but Leftow would need to spend some time with him before he could make an assessment. "George," said Leftow, "I'm going to tell the judge what you just told me."

The lawyer and Whitmore walked back over in front of the bench. Leftow cleared his throat and said, "Judge, I'm the first person the defendant has had the opportunity to discuss this matter with, besides the police officials. And at this point the defendant informs me that he made certain statements yesterday pertaining to these particular crimes he is charged with. He now states to me that the statements and confession pertaining to all three crimes he is alleged to have committed were made under duress and threats, and now he recants all confessions and statements made, Your Honor."

The prosecutor, Assistant D.A. Robert Walsh, jumped up as if on cue. "If Your Honor please, I think the officers ought to be commended for fine police work in this matter. . . . I know that this man has been wanted for quite some time for this murder in Manhattan. And I think a lot of people feel easier that he has been apprehended."

Comerford nodded. The judge was a product of the city's Democratic Party machine, a proud member of the Ancient Order of Hibernians and one of the chief organizers of the annual St. Patrick's Day parade. The police were his people.

Said Comerford, "The court wishes to point out at this time that nobody is saying the defendant is guilty, nobody is saying the defendant is not guilty. That will be a matter of due process of the law when the time comes. But the citizens of this town are very much pleased with the police department of New York City. . . . I have found out that the police department do a fine, effective police job, do it efficiently and do it properly. And the court commends the police department of the City of New York, the individual officers concerned, and . . . our citizens have much more confidence in law enforcement than they may have had a couple days ago in relation to these two major crimes."

The judge recommended that the defendant be remanded to a psychiatric facility to determine his state of mind. He banged his gavel and called the next case. Whitmore was taken away.

four

"GET THOSE NIGGERS"

A NEGRO BOY claiming he'd been coerced into confessing to a crime he didn't commit—it was a symbol of the city's zeitgeist at that moment. To those citizens who raged that the Great City of New York was being destroyed by niggers and spics, it was no big deal. To make an omelet, you needed to break a few eggs. To the city's rapidly growing black population, framing young Negro men in this way was an injustice as deep and resonant as a lash delivered during the bullwhip days. News of the arrest, and of Whitmore's claim of coercion, was one more drop of blood in the rivers of Babylon, its ripples radiating outward from places like Harlem and Brownsville to other interested quarters across the country.

In a prison in upstate New York, one young black inmate received the news. His name was Dhoruba Bin Wahad.

A few days after the arrest of George Whitmore, Bin Wahad sat at a table in the prison library looking for something to read. Great Meadow Correctional Facility—better known as Comstock, after the town where it is located—didn't have the best library, but Dhoruba was usually able to find something to interest him. There were always the newspapers, mostly New York City editions that were his only access to news from back home. The only problem was, the papers were often censored by the Department of Corrections. It was not uncommon to pick up a copy of the *Times* or *Daily News* or *Herald Tribune* and find that an entire article had been clipped out of the paper, leaving a gaping hole in the page. Since neither Dhoruba nor any other inmate was privy to the censorship process, it was hard to know what kinds of things were being cut out. Dhoruba figured that the excised articles were political in nature, probably relating to the civil rights movement down South, with their photos of police attack dogs, fire hoses, and billy clubs being used on marchers—images deemed too incendiary for a predominantly Negro prison population.

On this particular day, all the New York papers led with the same story: The police in Brooklyn had extracted a confession from a young black kid for a notorious double murder. Dhoruba looked over a copy of the *Daily News*, headlined "Confession: Stumbled into Killing Two," and read: "The Wylie-Hoffert murders were declared solved yesterday with the police-reported confession of a pimple-faced jobless laborer . . ." He picked up the *Journal American*, which devoted three full pages to the confession. One of its articles was headlined "The Wylie Killer: Boy Jekyll-Hyde," and described George Whitmore Jr. as a "Negro drifter" who was equal parts milquetoast and psychopath. The main article in the *Journal American* was headlined "How Police Broke the Wylie Case: Step by Step Account." "Police were astonished at the way the accused described the murder apartment," it read. "They marveled at his memory and quick recall." The article heaped special praise on Detective Edward Bulger, who was described as "an astute practical psychologist, as well as a crackerjack detective."

Both newspapers made special note of a devastating piece of evidence: the photo of one of the victims, which the killer had stolen from the apartment after he did the deed.

It wasn't until Dhoruba picked up the *Times* that he found, in the third paragraph of a front-page article, the following information: "But at his arraignment in Brooklyn Criminal Court, Whitmore, through his court-appointed lawyer, Jerome Leftow, recanted the confessions. Mr. Leftow said they had been obtained under duress."

Reading these accounts, Dhoruba felt in his gut that this kid Whitmore was being framed. The story sounded typical of criminal justice in America as he knew it to be, in his experience as a young black man born and raised in the ghetto.

It wasn't that Bin Wahad had been framed himself. He was guilty of the charge for which he was doing time—felonious assault with a deadly weapon. Dhoruba felt that the assault had been an act of self-defense, but he'd accepted a plea in exchange for a five-year sentence. Long before he violated any laws and wound up in prison, however, he'd come to see the police as the enemy. His attitude toward the men in blue was rooted in his upbringing on the streets of the Bronx in the 1950s.

To Dhoruba, blacks and cops in the Bronx were like cowboys and Indians. The cops were the cowboys; they had better firepower and superior fortifications. The Negroes were the Indians; they knew the terrain and how to live off the land. They shared the same territory, mostly as hostile tribes. When one of the natives became unruly and engaged in a confrontation with a cop on the beat, the cavalry was called in; the police had strength in numbers. But the natives had guile and fortitude and carried with them the spirit of a proud and unconquerable people.

As a teenager, Dhoruba sought to create his own version of strength in numbers: he joined a youth gang. The gang he chose was the Sportsmen Disciples, a division of the Disciples, a citywide gang. The Disciples had many rivals, including the Fordham Baldies, the Scorpions, the Renegades, and various divisions of the Seven Crowns—the Valiant Crowns, the Bohemian Crowns, the Collegian Crowns, and so on. In the Morrisania section of the Bronx, where Dhoruba lived, teen gang culture was a living, breathing organism. A kid joined a gang to embrace the vitality of life. Years later, Bin Wahad recalled:

> Back then, before heroin came to dominate illegitimate capitalist activity in the ghetto, gangs served a different kind of purpose—especially for black males. They were an organization that taught young men codes of manhood; i.e., your word is your bond, loyalty—if someone lied to you, you confront them. That might seem like macho posturing in this day and age, but the gang did serve that purpose. They weren't criminal enterprises to make money. We wasn't hustling for money. You only started hustling for money when you graduated out of the gang and became a thug.

Whether they were dealing dope or merely seeking solidarity, however, the police considered gangs a threat, plain and simple.

In June 1955, the NYPD initiated a special enforcement program called Operation 42, named after the Four-Two Precinct in Morrisania. Operation 42 was aimed specifically at the southeast Bronx, a squalid, overcrowded area of slums and small shops. Special patrol units were sent into the community. Commissioner Stephen P. Kennedy gave the troops their marching orders: "You shall meet violence with sufficient force, legally applied, to bring violators to justice swiftly. Mob rule and mob violence is an evil thing. We cannot compromise with evil. You must enforce the law." Youth officers were assigned to every precinct in the area. It was their job to identify the different gangs and monitor their behavior, especially in and around the public schools. Remembered Dhoruba:

> The cops who used to patrol the areas around the schools, they were really dirty. They were sadistic. And if they would catch you with your gang colors on, it was an obligatory ass whupping. It was routine. They didn't even give you a JD [juvenile delinquent] card and call your parents. They just whupped your ass. . . . They would slap you around in a squad car, but when they took you back to the precinct is where the fun and games began. . . . When you're a kid and they're slapping you upside the head, they usually got your hands cuffed. In our neighborhood, the police were bullies.

By the late 1950s, the gang problem had escalated in the city's Negro communities to the point where Commissioner Kennedy began talking about riots and racial Armageddon: "A race riot could cause more destruction of community relations than an atom bomb, and the lingering effects of such a riot would be worse for the community than that of the fallout of an atom bomb."

There were, of course, gangs of every ethnicity: Irish, Italian, Puerto Rican, Chinese, and Negro. Composed primarily of teenagers, gangs engaged in what was called "jitterbugging," later known as gang banging, or armed warfare between gangs. The dominant weapon of choice was the switchblade, but some enterprising gang brothers were known to make "zip guns," converted cap pistols rigged with a lead pipe and rubber band so that they could fire .32-caliber bullets. More than anything, the gangs were an intimidating presence in a community: they knocked over garbage cans, endangered innocent bystanders with their jitterbugging, and sometimes mugged and assaulted people.

Youth officers from the NYPD were liable to give an ass-whupping to any gang kid they caught—black, white, or Latino—but Negro gangs presented a special problem. Blacks weren't supposed to leave the ghetto, especially at night. Those who did learned quickly that New York City was a white man's world.

> I lived not far from Yankee Stadium. The stadium was
> in a Jewish neighborhood on the other side of the Grand
> Concourse [the main residential thoroughfare in the Bronx].
> Everybody there was white. I would go over there to play ball
> at Macombs Park, across the street from Yankee Stadium. If
> [you] stayed late at the park and got caught there at night, you
> were in big trouble with the police. They would throw us in
> their car and drive over to the Italian neighborhood, home of
> the Fordham Baldies. The police would dump us out in the
> middle of hostile territory—at night. You'd have to run home,
> if you were lucky enough to make it without getting attacked.

The relationship between Negro youths and the cops was circumscribed by a simple fact: the police considered it their job to keep the colored people in their place.

For Dhoruba, growing up in one of the country's most densely populated ghettos, learning the laws of the jungle was a gradual process. He was born June 30, 1944, and raised in a tenement at 166th Street and Boston Road. His name at birth was Richard Earl Moore; he was the son of Collins and Audrey Moore (née Cyrus). Collins Moore was from a southern family that had migrated from Georgia and settled in Harlem during the 1920s. Dhoruba's mother's family was from the island of Antigua in the Caribbean. It was a classic Harlem romance: a southern Negro and a child of Caribbean immigrants meeting on the streets of Harlem and falling in love while the rest of the world fretted about the war in Europe.

Dhoruba grew up mostly without a father. Collins Moore joined the army shortly after he was born; before too long, he and Audrey Moore separated. As a young boy, Dhoruba never knew much about his father, beyond the fact that his aunts and uncles on his mother's side called him a ne'er-do-well and a lowlife.

Dhoruba's mother was a young woman, barely out of her teens, who worked full-time and tried to have some semblance of a social life. By the time her only son was four or five, he was living mostly with his aunt and his grandparents, all of whom lived in the same general neighborhood.

In 1956 and 1957, the New York Housing Authority constructed two massive housing projects in the area known as Morrisania. The Morris Houses and McKinley projects changed the tenor of the neighborhood. Poor blacks from the South and Puerto Ricans flooded into the projects, and before too long what had once been a small village where everyone knew one another became a kind of armed camp. Muggers and predators were able to prey on merchants and residents and then disappear into the impenetrable maze of the projects. It was a tough environment for an adolescent.

Like many young men coming of age in the Bronx, Dhoruba found refuge in a street gang. It gave him a feeling of belonging, taught him the rituals of manhood, and shaped his feelings toward the police in ways that would determine his life for years to come.

Jitterbugging was a gas, but by the time of Dhoruba's seventeenth birthday he was ready for something more. One of his mother's brothers had been a hero in the Second World War, and she convinced Dhoruba that he should follow in his footsteps and join the army. Dhoruba was only seventeen, so his mother had to sign the enlistment papers. In November 1960, he was shipped off to basic training at Fort Dix, New Jersey, and then on to Killeen, Texas, for advanced infantry training (AIT).

Dhoruba liked the physical and weapons-related aspects of basic training, but he had a problem with authority. "I never liked the attitude of the drill instructors talkin' trash about your mama, spittin' in your face," he recalled. "Where I came from, you talk about somebody's mama and be spittin' in their face, there's gonna be repercussions. I took it for a while, but then I started to stray."

Two incidents got Dhoruba into trouble with army command. One was a time when he stole a cache of M-1 bayonets from a munitions supply barracks and took them back to the Bronx for his gang cronies. The haul made him a local hero among the Disciples, but when the military police found out about it, he was disciplined.

Dhoruba's second, more serious infraction occurred when he returned to Texas. He and two other soldiers, Jingles and Ralph, devised a scam for selling starched fatigues, which were highly prized by the rank and file. Dhoruba and his partners would steal the fatigues from another battalion's clothesline and mix them with their own battalion's laundry.

Rare camel fatigues, professionally cleaned, pressed, and creased—they sold like hotcakes.

Jingles, Ralph, and Dhoruba got busted and were given extra duty. Instead of complying, Dhoruba went AWOL, sneaking into town to get drunk. He was apprehended and thrown in the stockade. It was his first time behind bars. Two weeks later—after six months in the army—he was given an undesirable discharge and sent packing. "I look back now and I realize that rebellious attitude I had in the military served me well. If I hadn't been that recalcitrant, I would have eventually been sent to Vietnam. If I had pursued things like I thought I would when I enlisted, by '65 I probably would have been a sergeant in charge of a squad with my black ass in the Mekong Delta. The life expectancy of a sergeant wasn't too good. I would have been dead."

Dhoruba returned to the old neighborhood and resumed his life as a member of the Disciples. His military weapons training put him in good standing with the gang. He was still only eighteen, with a restless energy that earned him the nickname Torch. He was a ball of spontaneous combustion, ready to go up in flames at the slightest provocation.

In retrospect, the incident that landed Dhoruba in prison seems almost inevitable, given the level of gang tension in the early '60s. The Disciples were at war with many gangs, especially the Fordham Baldies. Dhoruba rarely went anywhere without a .32-caliber pistol.

One spring night in May 1962, he ventured into rival territory in the northern Bronx with a homeboy who was going to see his girlfriend. Dhoruba and his friend were walking through a housing project in the Soundview neighborhood when they were set upon by a group of jitter-buggers who had a beef with Dhoruba's friend. Dhoruba pulled out his pistol and opened fire, with everyone scattering for cover in the court-yard of the projects. No one was hit, and Dhoruba ditched his gun and went home. At 2:00 A.M. the police came knocking at his door. They had witnesses to the shooting, and somehow they had recovered his pistol. Dhoruba was arrested and charged with felonious assault with a deadly weapon.

Dhoruba already had one strike on his record, an attempted burglary conviction from earlier that year. After consulting with a court-appointed lawyer, he pled guilty to the felony assault charge and was given a sentence of five years.

On the eve of his nineteenth birthday, Dhoruba became an inmate of the New York State correctional system—first at Elmira, a facility for youth offenders, and later at Cocksackie, a prison full of gangbangers. By the time he was transferred to Comstock in 1964, Dhoruba had begun to see prison life as a microcosm of life on the outside. The inmates were mostly black and Latino, the guards and prison authorities exclusively white. Institutional racism was deeply entrenched:

> The racism that existed in the prison system was an advanced stage of what existed in the street; it was overt. The guards and commissary employees were mostly inbred country boys from upstate, and they were racist to the core. They had no problem calling you nigger, but they would only do that when they were all massed together in a goon squad. "Nigger, get in that cell!" They only said that when there was a whole group of them whipping on you. One on one, they wouldn't dare use that word. Because if they said nigger to a brother who was a Nation of Islam militant, they got knocked the fuck out. A brother would submit to the group ass-whupping he knew was coming later just to land one good blow.

Dhoruba clashed with guards, often landing in what was called the Box. "The first time I got sent to the Box was because a guard told me to do something, and I said no." The Box varied from facility to facility, but the concept was the same: maximum separation.

Inmates sent to the Box first spent seven days in a screening cell. On a ground floor tier known as the Flats, screening cells were stripped-down cells with only a toilet and a bed frame without a mattress. A worn, soiled mattress was delivered to the cell each night at 9:30 P.M. and picked up at 6:00 A.M. Beyond the bars of the cell, the catwalk was fenced in by a wire-mesh screen.

After a week in the screening cell, a phalanx of guards arrived in the middle of the night. In Dhoruba's case, three white guards pulled him out of bed at 2:00 A.M. for transport to the Box, which was separated from general population. Dhoruba was shackled and dragged to a freight elevator—a place where beatings routinely occurred, beyond the sight of eyewitnesses. Dhoruba was clubbed, kicked, and punched, as was routine. Inmates usually arrived at the Box with cuts, abrasions, even broken bones, their files annotated to read "inmate injured while resisting transport." Their heads were shaved bald. The Box housed everything from killers and reprobates to political prisoners; it was a true Brotherhood of the Damned, a prison within a prison.

It was during his time in the Box that Dhoruba first came into contact with a breed of militant Negro he'd never known before. On the streets of the Bronx, Dhoruba had been a mindless gangbanger with no real consciousness or sense of history. In prison, he began to see things in a new way.

A Muslim inmate by the name of Mjuba took young Dhoruba under his wing and began giving him books and pamphlets to read. Among the first of these materials were two pamphlet-sized books from the 1920s called *Four Negro Presidents* and *Sex and Race* by J. A. Rogers, a Jamaican-born historian and ethnographer who wrote from an African American perspective. For blacks whose only education had been in the U.S. public school system, Rogers's writings were mind-blowing, both for the historical information they contained and for their point of view, which did not exist in the mainstream culture. Rogers's writings were so prized in prisons that inmates painstakingly copied his pamphlets by hand so that more inmates could have access to them.

Rogers wasn't the only writer Dhoruba discovered in prison. For the first time, he read the slave narratives of Frederick Douglass, Nat Turner, and Harriet Tubman. Most significantly, it was during his time in prison that Dhoruba came under the influence of Malcolm X.

Before his incarceration, Dhoruba had heard of the fiery activist who was shaking up Harlem and the rest of New York with his pointed condemnations of white supremacy and racial trickery. But Dhoruba had been an adolescent, mostly without racial consciousness, a particle of matter bouncing randomly through space without focus or direction. The activities and exhortations of Martin Luther King, Malcolm X, and others were a distant echo to Torch, the gangbanger primed to shoot first and ask questions later. Now that he was behind bars, however, Dhoruba began to reckon with a world he had not known existed—a world of theory, logic, and righteousness that, when combined with action, had the power to ignite a revolution.

"We declare our right on this earth," said Malcolm X, "to be a human being, to be respected as a human being, to be given the rights of a human being in this society, on this earth, in this day, which we intend to bring into existence by any means necessary."

Dhoruba fell under the spell of Minister Malcolm's words, many of them contained in speeches reprinted verbatim in the newspaper *Muhammad Speaks*, smuggled by inmates into the prison. Though they were merely words printed on a page, without the power of his piercing verbal presentation, Malcolm's message stoked embers within Dhoruba's soul. Through Mjuba and other Muslim inmates locked away inside the Box, the kid from the Bronx began a process of historical reclamation and indoctrination—one that mirrored the rising tide of an entire generation.

As he sat in the prison library reading newspaper accounts of this kid named Whitmore—a young black male like himself, born in the same month of the same year, trying to exist as a human being in the white man's world—Dhoruba felt a connection. He absorbed such stories, of young black men caught in the grip of what he increasingly recognized as a racist criminal justice system, and filed them away in his mind, where they would inform and inspire his growing political consciousness.

FROM WITHIN HIS tiny room at Bellevue Psychiatric Hospital in Manhattan, George Whitmore felt his world crumbling around him. He'd been charged with two major felonies in Brooklyn and a double murder in Manhattan. He was notorious. During his brief stay at the Brooklyn House of Detention after his arrest, he'd been ridiculed by inmates: *Hey George, how was that white pussy? Damn, Whitmore, how you let those detectives play you like that?* But all the trash talk was background noise; his real concern was the words he read in newspaper accounts of his arrest: "facing two life sentences"; "if convicted, likely to receive the death penalty."

Death. It was a strange prospect for a relatively healthy nineteen-year-old boy to consider. George pondered the options: lethal injection, gas, the electric chair.

By the time he was transferred to Bellevue, George was overcome by depression. To preserve his sanity, he began scratching out thoughts in a daily diary:

I have never been in trouble in my life. And don't intend to
get in any. This just goes to show you! You don't have to get in
trouble to go to jail. . . .

I went out to see a doctor to take a test. Then I came back down and began to think. I said to myself, George you don't realize how much trouble you'er in. Even though you don't do it. And what if they say you are guilty. You know that you will be doing time for someone else who ain't worth it. The only thing that comes to my mind is when I get out. And why did this happen to me? . . .

Yesterday I was called out to talk to a doctor who seem nice. While talking to him I kept thingen is he going to help me or is he a DA's man. I have learn that you can take one thing and see it dun the other way around.

George's attorney, Jerome Leftow, visited him a number of times, first at the House of Detention and later at Bellevue. By most standards, Leftow was in over his head with the Whitmore case. Though he'd been a criminal defense attorney for seven years, he'd never tried a homicide case. Though he was anxious about taking on such a high-profile case, he was heartened by the fact that Whitmore's mother, whom he met at his office after George was incarcerated, liked him and wanted him to stay on the case.

Leftow was idealistic, and he was sympathetic with Whitmore's predicament. As he got to know George, he could see how easily he might have buckled under police questioning. "I asked Whitmore, 'Were you beaten?'" he recalled years later. "He said, 'I was pushed around.' That was the most difficult thing to understand. At first I didn't understand what George was trying to tell me. I was still thinking about police brutality in the usual sense where the prisoner is tied to a radiator and beaten up. It took me a while to realize that George was the kind of kid that, if a detective used a harsh voice, it was the same as being struck."

A psychiatrist who evaluated Whitmore's handwriting, in his Bellevue diary, agreed with Leftow's assessment. Wrote the doctor: "He is without guile, somewhat repressed emotionally, and therefore likely to be infantile in some areas. Essentially optimistic, he tries most of the time to look on the bright side of life, often having fantasies of being accepted in a world which is foreign to him wherein he dreams of himself as being admired, wanted, loved."

Whitmore was supposed to have been transferred from Bellevue after two months of evaluation, but when late June rolled around he was still buried deep within the hospital bureaucracy.

While visiting George, Leftow was stunned when a female doctor mentioned offhand that Whitmore was receiving injections of sodium amytal, commonly known as a "truth serum." Leftow was furious. "It broke every rule against self-incrimination. No written approval was ever gotten. I was never asked. His parents were never asked. This was a terribly wrong thing. I had a discussion with the doctor. He told me they had given him truth serum. The results were inconclusive. The doctor said they were studying people accused of sex crimes and they thought George would be a perfect person to test. I'm sure the district attorney's office knew. I am absolutely sure about that. But of course they never told me. It was just an accident that I found out."

Leftow tried to make an issue of these extralegal injections as a violation of Whitmore's rights, but his efforts were quickly squelched by a judge—one of many objections that would be shot down by prosecutors and judges as they tried to expedite prosecution of the Career Girls Murders case.

Far beyond the boundaries of Bellevue Hospital—where Whitmore would spend his twentieth birthday in a drug-induced haze—the struggle continued. In Washington, D.C., dignitaries gathered to inaugurate a historic occasion. On the morning of July 2, President Lyndon Johnson was joined by Martin Luther King Jr. and other civil rights leaders at the White House as he signed into law the Civil Rights Act of 1964. This legislation was seen as a direct consequence of the March on Washington—and as a tribute to the late President Kennedy, who had put the bill before Congress just weeks before his assassination.

To King and others who had been marching, protesting, getting arrested, hosed down, and beaten as advocates for civil rights, it was a momentous occasion. But out on the streets of America's big cities, it was dismissed by many as pie in the sky.

In New York City, frustration over the glacial pace of progress over civil rights was matched by mounting anger over images of black people being clubbed and attacked by police dogs and murdered by white supremacists in the South, often with official support. This seething resentment was made worse by the daily reality of poverty and hopelessness in places closer to home, such as Harlem, the Bronx, and Brooklyn.

Writer James Baldwin, Harlem born and raised, sounded alarm bells with his 1963 book *The Fire Next Time:*

> This past, the Negro's past, of rope, fire, torture, castration, infanticide, rape; death and humiliation; fear day and night, fear as deep as the marrow of the bone; doubt that he was worthy of life, since everyone around him denied it; sorrow for his women, for his kinfolk, for his children, who needed his protection, and whom he could not protect; rage, hatred, and murder, hatred for white men so deep it often turned against him and his own, and made all love, all trust, all joy impossible. . . . This is the message that has spread through streets and tenements and prisons, through the narcotics wards, and past the filth and sadism of mental hospitals to a people from whom everything has been taken away, including, most crucially, their sense of their own worth. People cannot live without this sense; they will do anything whatever to regain it. This is why the most dangerous creation of any society is that man who has nothing to lose.

For those who'd been paying attention, the city seemed a powder keg ready to blow. And that's exactly what happened, over a tumultuous six nights in July 1964.

The Harlem riots of 1964 weren't triggered exclusively by outrage over George Whitmore's coerced confession, but his story undoubtedly played a role. The arrest of a suspect in the case brought sighs of relief among white folks and the mainstream press, but the Negro community saw things differently. In the *Amsterdam News*, the city's preeminent black newspaper, the headline read: "Negro Youth Claims False Confession." The article focused not on the NYPD's success in finding the killer, but on the doubts that had been raised about his confession. The clear implication of the *Amsterdam News*'s coverage was that Whitmore was being framed. It was one more grievance to be added to James Baldwin's searing catalog of atrocities past and present.

The incident that actually set off the riots was an altercation between a cop and a black teenager. At 9:20 A.M. on Thursday, July 16, fifteen-year-old James Powell was sitting with fellow students on a stoop near a high school building on East Seventy-sixth Street. The neighborhood was predominantly Irish and German. The students, all of them black, were waiting for their summer school class to begin in ten minutes. Next door, a white resident was watering flowers in front of his house. After an unfriendly exchange of words between the resident and the black "interlopers," the resident turned his hose on the students and said, "Dirty niggers, I'll wash you clean."

Some of the students jumped out of the way, but the white man kept spraying them. In return, the kids threw a can of soda and a bottle in his direction. Then James Powell went after the man, who dropped the hose and ran away toward a nearby apartment building.

At that moment, an off-duty cop named Thomas Gilligan was leaving a television repair shop across the street. When he saw the black kid chasing the white man, he ran over to help. Gilligan was dressed in street clothes, with no indication that he was a police officer. He pulled out his gun.

When Powell saw the man he was after duck into an apartment building, he gave up the chase. When he turned around, Gilligan was standing there. The off-duty officer fired three shots. Powell went down.

A fellow student ran over and knelt beside his friend. "Jimmy, what's the matter?" he said. Powell didn't answer; blood gurgled from his mouth. The student turned to the man and said, "Why did you shoot him?"

Gilligan answered, "This is why." He took a police badge from his pocket and pinned it to his shirt. Then, according to the student, he said, "This black bastard is my prisoner. Somebody call an ambulance."

There would be many conflicting eyewitness accounts of the shooting. Gilligan claimed he told Powell twice that he was a police officer, and that each time he did, the young man lunged at him with a knife. The second time, he opened fire.

The students disputed the claim that Powell had a knife, though some conceded that he may have lunged at Gilligan. A knife was found at the scene, but its blade was closed.

Within a few hours of the shooting, James Powell was declared dead at the hospital.

Even before the news of Powell's death, trouble was in the air. A sprawling group of community activists gathered at the sight of the shooting; that night, the local TV newscasts were filled with angry protesters sounding off about police brutality. The police department kept Lieutenant Thomas Gilligan under wraps and said nothing.

The next day, Friday, the protests were more organized and even angrier. The Congress for Racial Equality (CORE) led a group of protesters—mostly blacks and Latinos, with some whites—who gathered first at the location where Powell was killed and then marched toward the Nineteenth Precinct station house on East Sixty-seventh Street. The police would not let the sprawling crowd of protesters block traffic in front of the precinct, though they were allowed to picket on a nearby avenue. The mood was angry, and once again the cameras and reporters were there to record every moment. When the crowd dispersed later in the afternoon, protesters and passersby traded insults—mostly white drivers shouting racial epithets as they passed and then quickly pulling away.

There was no official statement from the police, and little outreach between police and the community. The negative energy was building, with little or no attempt to understand what happened or anticipate what lay ahead.

Saturday was hot and humid, a typical summer day in the city. Another protest took shape, this time in Harlem. By early evening the crowd had grown to around five hundred people. Speakers and rabble-rousers roamed over 125th Street, shouting over bullhorns. Someone proclaimed, "We got a civil rights bill and along with the bill we got a dead black boy. This shooting of James Powell was murder!" Another voice said, "It's time we let the Man know that if he does something to us we're going to do something back. You kick me once and I'm going to kick you twice!"

Among the protesters was William Epton, a well-known self-proclaimed black communist and leader of a group called the Progressive Labor Party. From a soapbox on Seventh Avenue, Epton called for armed insurrection.

Someone with a bullhorn yelled, "Let's march to the station!" The growing throng began moving toward the Twenty-eighth Precinct station house on West 123rd Street between Seventh and Eighth avenues. Garbage cans were knocked over, glass broken, bottles thrown. Police commanders at the scene called in for reinforcements.

Among the officers in Harlem that day was Robert Leuci, a member of the department's highly touted Tactical Patrol Force (TPF). Just twenty-four years old, Leuci had been on the job for only three years. He was called into work that day to deal with crowd control. Leuci and his partner, Ronnie Heffernan, were sent up to the rooftops. In Harlem and other black neighborhoods, where cops were mostly considered an unwelcome presence, rooftops were a source of danger. Youths gathered atop tenement roofs to serenade the police with a symphony of bricks, bottles, rocks, and other missiles.

Around 10:00 P.M., Leuci heard a loud sound—*pop pop pop pop*—in rapid succession. He said to his partner, "Hey, you hear that? Somebody's setting off firecrackers." Heffernan listened, then shook his head. They both realized at the same time: *That ain't firecrackers. It's gunfire.*

They headed down to the street and walked into the middle of a full-blown riot. Years later, Leuci remembered the scene:

> The noise was incredible, an ocean of sound that came
> in waves—people screaming, sirens wailing, the sound of
> breaking glass, shots fired. Traffic had been diverted from
> 125th Street and was backed up on the side streets, with horns
> honking and white people in their cars looking terrified. On
> 125th Street was a battleground, with police and looters in
> hand-to-hand combat. Some cops were firing warning shots
> into the air, which caused people to scatter, regroup, and then
> come back with even more force. I bumped into another TPF
> cop, Dave Christian, who was driving a sergeant when two of
> his tires were blown out. I told Dave I could swear I saw tracer
> rounds ricocheting off a building on the avenue. Dave's eyes
> got real wide, and he smiled.

Leuci was shocked by the sheer chaos of what was unfolding all around him, but as a TPF cop who interacted with the locals in an intimate and sometimes combative way, he had sensed a reckoning like this might be coming.

TPF had been instituted in 1959, another special unit created by Commissioner Stephen Kennedy. It was designed as a kind of special forces squad—a crew of big, tough cops who climbed fire escapes, traversed rooftops, and busted down doors. Their nickname was Kennedy's Commandos.

One of TPF's assignments was to deal with youth gangs and serious criminals. In doing so, however, they often stormed through buildings and busted into the apartments of average citizens. In black and Hispanic communities, they were despised.

Some TPF cops were more brutal than others. Leuci had to pull strings to get into the unit because, at five foot nine, he did not meet the unit's height requirement. "I guess I had something to prove," said Leuci. "I was as gung ho as anybody. I was a racist cop like everybody else, but I didn't want to be."

Leuci's conscience sometimes got the better of him; his Italian American father was an armchair socialist who read the *Daily Worker* and warned his son that the oppression of Negroes in the United States would one day come home to roost. When his son became a cop, Leuci Sr. wasn't exactly thrilled.

Leuci thought his father was nuts. Like other Italian cops, he sometimes used pejoratives like *tuttsoon* or *yom* to describe black people. (Irish cops tended to favor the fully Americanized epithets—nigger, spade, and jig.) Still, he had to admit that the level of poverty in Harlem, the South Bronx, and parts of Brooklyn could be downright shocking. "There were no social services in these neighborhoods," he remembered. "Nobody picked up the garbage. In East Harlem people would throw their garbage out the back window and it piled up almost to the first-floor windows. And there were rats everywhere. More than once I saw young children who had toes gnawed to stubs because their apartments were infested with rats. In the winter people froze to death because they had no heat, and of course there was no such thing as air-conditioning at the time in those neighborhoods."

Poverty created a sense of alienation; the brutishness of police units like TPF created anger. "They hated us. And you respond to that hatred with a hatred of your own."

According to Leuci, police brutality was not uncommon. Some cops sought out tactical patrol because they were the kind of people who liked to bust heads. At the time, Leuci didn't question what he saw. Like any TPF cop, he was expected to show he had the right stuff. "I walked in on a lot of beatings. And when you walked in on a beating, you were expected to add a kick or a punch of your own to show you were with the program. Some cops were more brutal than others. Some of this was because there was brutality all around us—it absorbed us, inhabited us, and made us feel a kinship that no outsider could ever understand."

By the summer of '64, Leuci had begun to sense that something was changing. One reason was the emergence of Malcolm X and the Nation of Islam on the scene. The Nation of Islam militants, with their suits and bow ties, were sometimes open in their scorn for the men in blue. Leuci remembered one occasion when he was walking in uniform along 125th Street and came upon two Nation of Islam people. They gave him a nasty look, and one of them started singing a song that was riding the Top 40 at the time: Ruby and the Romantics' "Our Day Will Come."

"What's your problem?" asked Leuci.

"You're our problem," responded the Muslims.

The riot galvanized this kind of antipolice sentiment. For those caught in the middle of the violence, there would be many unforgettable images—cops and blacks fighting in doorways and on the sidewalks; looters being chased and clubbed; shadowy figures on rooftops throwing bricks from above. By the second day of rioting, police were no longer firing guns into the air; they were firing at people, using what cops referred to as a "gypsy gun," nonpolice issue, unregistered, and untraceable.

Bob Leuci described one shooting in his memoir, *All the Centurions* (2004):

> A young man, barefoot, muscular, stripped to the waist, was jumping up and down on the roof of a car, his face gleaming, his eyes wide with unspeakable rage. Theatrical and dramatic, he held a bottle in each hand and was throwing karate kicks at the cops who were trying to grab him. He stretched his neck and thrust his jaw forward as he screamed out, "White motherfuckers". . .
>
> He threw a circular kick and I reached up to snatch his ankle and missed. I swung at him with my stick, went for his leg, missed again, and he swiftly kicked me in the shoulder. He was dancing, spinning around, throwing kicks like a ninja warrior in a Kung Fu movie. I scrambled up onto the hood of the car, thinking that maybe I saw a motorcycle cop ride up. I couldn't figure out what he was up to, shouting for me to get out of the way.
>
> Then the guy on the roof of the car changed everything. He threw a bottle at the motorcycle cop. The cop drew his pistol, fired a shot, and blew the guy off the roof of that car.
>
> Everyone froze.
>
> Then everyone ran.

For three days and nights, Harlem burned. Then the chaos spread to Brooklyn.

In Bedford-Stuyvesant and Brownsville—the area where George Whitmore spent his lost night inside the Seventy-third Precinct station house—Molotov cocktails were launched from rooftops. The streets rang with the sounds of running feet, smashed shop windows, screams, the clicking of hooves from cops on horseback, the dull thud of nightsticks hitting bare skull. People stumbled through the street with blood running down their faces, shirts torn, a crazed glint in their eyes. Leuci and his TPF unit were moved from Harlem to Brooklyn, dispatched to catch looters. Residents were backing trucks up to storefronts, tying rope to security gates, and driving away, wrenching the gates off their hinges. Bricks shattered windows and looters flooded in and out with TVs, clothes, food. "Get those niggers!" commanded a sergeant. A wave of cops descended.

Police violence in Brooklyn was even more unfettered, with little control or oversight to stop it. Riot cops in helmets clubbed blacks indiscriminately: "Go on, you bastards, run." "Yipee-yi-yo-ki-yay, get along little doggies." A cop proclaimed: "I'm tired of you damn niggers." A Negro boy of about ten or eleven, holding his mother's hand, looked at the cop and said, "You think you're having trouble tonight, just wait till tomorrow."

After the first night of rioting in Brooklyn, Mayor Robert Wagner took to the airwaves. "Without law and order," he announced on TV, "Negro and civil rights progress would be set back half a century. Law and order are the Negro's best friend, make no mistake about that. The opposite of law and order is mob rule, and that is the way of the Ku Klux Klan, the night riders and lynch mobs."

Wagner's implication was obvious. But the era when public officials could keep the Negroes in line by evoking Klan retribution had apparently passed, and the mayor's admonitions were ignored. That night saw more rioting, more shooting, more looting and fires, more bloodshed and death.

After the third night of chaos in Brooklyn, the sky opened—first a sprinkle, then a heavy downpour. The rains saved the city from descending further into chaos. Six straight days and nights of lawlessness and terror finally came to an end.

The postmortems ranged far and wide, some citing Negro disrespect for law and order, others citing the savage police response. "Sure, we make mistakes," Commissioner Michael Murphy conceded. "You do in a war."

The official tally was one civilian dead, 118 police and civilians injured, and 465 men and women arrested. Those who were there, though, believed the real numbers were higher. "I know there was more than one dead," Bob Leuci said. "I saw more than that killed with my own eyes.

"There was a rumor among cops that, for weeks afterwards, they were still pulling dead bodies out of the lake in Central Park."

The uprising was unprecedented in recent memory. The press and the public didn't really know how to respond. Some viewed the insurrection with relief; at least now the Negroes had released their anger, had blown off some steam. It had been horrifying, but the worst was over.

That was wishful thinking. The war between the Negroes and the police had only just begun.

five

GETTING FLOPPED

JEROME LEFTOW HAD his hands full. His client, George Whitmore, had been charged with a series of heinous crimes. He had spent six months buried away inside a psychiatric hospital, the subject of secret experimentations with truth serum for which no one would ever be held accountable. As he slowly realized the full dimensions of his predicament, Whitmore was understandably depressed. He told Leftow he was suffering from severe headaches. One Sunday, he had asked a Bellevue doctor for some aspirin. "What do you mean bothering me on a Sunday?" the doctor barked. "You know I don't work on Sunday. Come back tomorrow. Who do you think you are, a private patient? Don't you understand? You're a murderer."

At a certain point, Leftow needed to separate himself from Whitmore and deal with the case at hand. As the charges against George played out, there were some bright spots. For one thing, it had been revealed that one of the key elements of the case against Whitmore—the photo from his wallet, the one he'd supposedly stolen from the Wylie-Hoffert apartment—was a fraud.

In fact, even before detectives at the Seventy-third Precinct had finished grilling Whitmore on the night of his alleged confession, they knew the photo wasn't what they later claimed it to be. Two detectives had been dispatched to show the photo to Patricia Tolles, the surviving roommate. As soon as Tolles and her brother Terry looked at the snapshot, they knew it was a red herring. "No," Patricia Tolles told the detectives. "That's not Janice Wylie." No way, said Terry Tolles, who had danced with Janice at the Stork Club. "The detectives made us promise not to talk to anyone about the photo," Terry would say later.

That same night, detectives also showed the photo to Max Wylie, Janice's father. "That's not a photo of my daughter," he said. "I have no idea who that is."

The police, then, knew from the start that the photo had nothing to do with the killings. And yet they let Chief Lawrence McKearney tout the photo as a key piece of evidence—one that nearly every major news account noted in their coverage of Whitmore's arrest.

Establishing that the woman in the photo wasn't Janice Wylie was one thing, but before the defense could clear Whitmore's name they'd also have to show that the photo hadn't come from the apartment at East Eighty-eighth Street, as George had said in his forced confession. This took weeks of diligent investigation by a newspaper reporter and an investigator in the Manhattan D.A.'s office. By establishing the location of the photo and the make of the car in the picture, they were able to track down the actual woman in the photo. The woman remembered her friend taking the photo while they picnicked near a horse stable in New Jersey. The woman later dropped the photo into a public garbage bin, which is how it likely wound up in the dump where Whitmore said he had found it—until Detective Bulger browbeat him into agreeing that he'd snatched it from a drawer at the Wylie-Hoffert apartment.

Then there was Whitmore's alibi. The detectives hadn't even bothered to check Whitmore's initial story, that he had been working on the day of the Wylie-Hoffert murders. After he was charged, however, investigators and reporters headed out to Wildwood and found three separate witnesses who signed affidavits confirming that they had seen George at the time of the murders—a moment everyone remembered because of the televised March on Washington. A dishwasher who worked at the catering hall inside the Ivy Hotel remembered seeing George all alone in front of the TV, mesmerized by the sight of King standing before the Lincoln Memorial.

THE DISCREDITED PHOTO evidence and eyewitness affidavits were steps in the right direction. As Jerome Leftow pressed on with Whitmore's case, however, the keys to the case still felt elusive to him. In part, this was because the Wylie-Hoffert murder case, though it had been "solved" by detectives in Brooklyn, would be prosecuted in Manhattan. Unbeknownst to Leftow, investigators in Manhattan had their doubts about Whitmore's confession almost from the beginning.

Melvin Glass was a young prosecutor in the Manhattan D.A.'s office who had been given a copy of Whitmore's astounding sixty-one-page confession and told to go over it with a fine-tooth comb. Glass knew every detail of the case, but even he was startled by the level of detail Whitmore had supposedly provided. It was as if it had come directly from a detective's notebook. One detail, in particular, almost made him lose his lunch.

Among the facts Whitmore was supposed to have volunteered was that, after knocking the girls unconscious with a Coke bottle, he decided to tie them up. According to his statement, he went to the bathroom and found an unopened packet of razor blades. He opened the packet, removed a blade, and then used the blade to slice a bedsheet, which he used to bind Wylie and Hoffert together. The packaging from the razor blades, according to Whitmore, was blue.

Glass read the passage two or three times in disbelief. The young ADA knew the story of Detective Edward Bulger's brief stint on the Wylie-Hoffert case the previous winter—of how Bulger had found the razor-blade wrapper in the bathroom and complained that it had been overlooked in previous reports, until it emerged that the wrapper had been left behind carelessly by a cop long after the murders. Glass had heard about Bulger's complaint, which had caused tension between the detective and his Manhattan counterparts. He'd also heard the real story behind the wrapper.

But that put Mel Glass one up on Detective Edward Bulger, who had never been told that the wrapper was unrelated to the murders.

Now, in the transcript of the so-called confession he'd given months after the murders, here was George Whitmore claiming to have left behind this wrapper from the razor packet—a wrapper actually dropped by a cop weeks *after* the murders. As he read Whitmore's statement, Glass saw only one explanation: Detective Bulger had spoon-fed Whitmore the detail.

Mel Glass decided to call Bulger in for a talk.

They met in the Manhattan D.A.'s office at 100 Centre Street in downtown Manhattan. Bulger was in a chipper mood. Along with Detectives Di Prima and Aidala and Patrolman Isola, he had recently received a special Public Protector Award by the *Journal American*. Bulger was basking in the glory of having trumped the Manhattan detectives by solving their biggest murder case in a generation. Now, unaware that Glass was having doubts about Whitmore's confession, he spoke openly with the ADA. At one point, he even confided that he had a foolproof method for determining when a Negro suspect was lying.

"Oh," asked Glass, "how could you tell he was lying?"

"Because his stomach was moving in and out," Bulger replied. "Never fails. Whenever a Negro boy lies, his stomach goes in and out. That's how I can always tell."

Glass said nothing in reply, and Bulger left the office. The ADA was beginning to suspect the worst: that the entire Whitmore confession was an elaborate concoction.

"It doesn't take much imagination to figure out how Whitmore got the facts," he told his boss, Manhattan D.A. Frank Hogan, the following day. "He got them from Bulger. . . . Whitmore was brainwashed. That confession came from the police."

Hogan asked Glass to itemize in a memo every discrepancy he found in the confession. When Glass showed his memo to Hogan, the D.A. picked up the phone and called the Brooklyn D.A., Aaron Koota. "Uh, Aaron," said Hogan, "we've found certain infirmities in the Whitmore statement."

The Manhattan and Brooklyn D.A.s were like two tribal chieftains operating in the same theater of battle, but the Brooklyn D.A. was clearly the junior partner. Hogan was asking Koota to acknowledge defeat, or at least a mistake of staggering proportions. The Brooklyn D.A. had a choice: he could accept that his office had presided over a grave injustice and botched the biggest murder case of the decade, or he could proceed full steam ahead. Koota decided to press forward. Publicly, the Whitmore case proceeded as if nothing were amiss. Before long, the Brooklyn D.A.'s office announced with great fanfare that their two cases, the Elba Borrero attempted rape and the Minnie Edmonds murder, were strong and ready to go. The Borrero prosecution was scheduled to begin on November 12, 1964.

Though Jerome Leftow wasn't privy to the backroom machinations of the two most powerful prosecutors in the city, he wasn't surprised that they would start with the Borrero case. Since Whitmore had no criminal record at all—much less a history of the kinds of violent crimes he was now charged with—the prosecution would have to dirty him up. The Borrero case was presumably their strongest, since they had an alleged eyewitness identification of Whitmore. Prosecuting George on this case would establish him as a proven sexual predator, which would only help with the later cases.

As Leftow looked at both the Borrero and Edmonds cases, it occurred to him that Whitmore may actually have been *lucky* that the cops were trying to pin the Wylie-Hoffert murders on him. "If George were only being charged with crimes against Borrero and Edmonds—a Puerto Rican woman and a black woman in Brooklyn—no one would have ever noticed," Leftow noted years later. "There would have been nothing exceptional about these cases. You have to remember, we had segregation in New York back then. The system was almost completely white—white defense lawyers, white prosecutors, white judges, white cops. And no one cared. Because it broke down that most violent crimes were being perpetrated by minorities against minorities. Most of the time, when I represented a black defendant, the victim was black. The only reason people paid any attention to the charges against Whitmore was Wylie-Hoffert, two white women allegedly killed by a black male."

As the trial date approached, Leftow was stunned by a rumor he heard from a newspaper reporter: "Hey, have you heard? Manhattan detectives have another suspect in the Career Girls Murders."

"You're kidding," said Leftow.

"No," said the reporter. "They must know Whitmore didn't do it. They're on to somebody else."

To Leftow, the implication was staggering: if the cops had another suspect for the Wylie-Hoffert murders, they must know that Whitmore's confession on those murders was bogus. And if that confession was bogus, his confessions on the other crimes were equally suspect.

Leftow rushed from his office on Court Street in Brooklyn over to the Manhattan D.A.'s office. He was given a meeting with two men: Peter J. Koste, the same ADA who had arrived at the Seventy-third Precinct in Brooklyn to serve as stenographer for Whitmore's confession, and Koste's boss, Alexander Herman, head of the Homicide Bureau. Leftow asked the two men flat out: "Is someone else under investigation for the Wylie-Hoffert murders?"

Koste and Herman were fully aware that there was another suspect. Since September police had been investigating a young junkie who had been implicated in the murders. The lead had fallen into their lap when a friend of the junkie was collared on an unrelated murder rap: in exchange for a plea, he told detectives, "You got the wrong guy on the Wylie-Hoffert murders. I know who did it. I can deliver the real killer for you." A special detective squad had begun tailing the young junkie and even placed a recording device in the apartment of his friend. The results looked promising. There was good reason to hope that an arrest and indictment were imminent.

But Koste and Herman had a dilemma. If they told Leftow about this highly confidential investigation, it would be revealed in court and likely also in the press. If the existence of another suspect was revealed, the suspect himself would likely get wind of the investigation and clam up. Things were at a delicate stage; if the Manhattan D.A.'s office lost their suspect, they would blow the opportunity to nail down an indictment in the most sensational murder case in a generation.

The ADAs had a choice: they could tell Leftow the truth, or, in the interest of protecting their investigation, they could lie, denying it even existed. At first they stalled, hemming and hawing with Leftow until the attorney pleaded, "Look, I go to trial in Brooklyn in a matter of days. You can't let Whitmore go to trial with the full weight of these Manhattan murders hanging over his head if you have another suspect. If the confession is wrong in relation to Wylie-Hoffert, then it could be wrong in my case. You have to tell me."

Finally, the two men from the D.A.'s office said, "We know of nothing that can help you with your case."

That was that: Leftow knew he wasn't getting anything more from these two men. In his gut, he knew they were lying: the Manhattan D.A.'s office was making a calculated decision to protect their investigation. Reclaiming what they believed was rightfully theirs—the Wylie-Hoffert murder case—meant more to them than full disclosure; it meant more to them than justice. Leftow's client, the illiterate Negro kid from Brooklyn, was left twisting in the wind.

DETECTIVE BILL PHILLIPS of the NYPD didn't like black people much. And he didn't try to hide it. As he said in his memoir, "I guess you could say I was raised prejudiced. I'm prejudiced against black people."

The die had been cast in childhood. Phillips was born on the East Side of Manhattan, but by the time he'd turned six, his family had moved to an apartment at West 161st Street and St. Nicholas Avenue. He came from a police family: one of his earliest memories was of a police funeral for his mother's brother, who had fallen down an airshaft while investigating a robbery.

> I was about three or four years old. That's one of the first
> things that really sticks in my mind, hanging out the window
> and watching everything. There must have been a hundred
> and fifty policemen there with a big band. They had the
> funeral from my grandmother's house because he lived there
> in a downstairs apartment. He was on what they called the
> Midtown Squad and the guys on it were chosen because of
> their appearance. He was a big, tall, good-looking guy. He was
> thirty-three years old when he got killed. It was a big thing in
> the neighborhood.

One of the things Bill Phillips noticed was that being a policeman was like being a member of a private club. Irish American cops came from white neighborhoods; many attended Catholic schools or were at least products of a Catholic environment (Phillips graduated from LaSalle Academy, a Catholic high school in lower Manhattan). Cops stuck together. And one of the common themes at police gatherings was to complain about "the niggers," how they were destroying everything.

The word *nigger*, or some variation thereof, was common among New York cops, as it likely was among white construction workers, firefighters, sanitation workers, even journalists. The criminal justice system—cops, prosecutors, judges, bail bondsmen, and so on—was overwhelmingly white, and the expression of racial bigotry went almost completely unchecked. With cops, however, antiblack attitudes seemed to hold a special distinction.

Another term that came up among cops in the 1950s and 1960s was *mau mau*. The term came from the Mau Mau Rebellion, a tribal uprising in which blacks took on British colonial rule in Kenya through a campaign of violence. The Mau Mau Rebellion was reported on in many newspapers and on the TV news, but it was written about with particular zeal in the pages of *National Review*, a New York–based, conservative magazine begun by William F. Buckley Jr. in 1955. The magazine, and Buckley himself, had become important cultural touchstones for many members of the NYPD, who considered the national media hopelessly liberal. In Buckley's publication, the Mau Mau were described as "unspeakably bestial" and their rebellion presented as a kind of cautionary tale—the black masses rising up against the white power structure. The uprising was crushed by colonial forces in 1960, but the term "mau mau" lived on as a derogatory name for blacks who were perceived to advocate violent resistance.

The Mau Mau were invoked to far different effect by Malcolm X in a speech he gave at a church in Harlem in December 1964. Speaking to representatives of the Mississippi Freedom Democratic Party, a gathering that was about one-third white, he referred to the Mau Mau as "the greatest African patriots and freedom fighters that the continent ever knew." Malcolm suggested that blacks in the United States could learn a lot about the struggle for freedom by studying the violent liberationists in Kenya. "In fact," he said, "that's what we need in Mississippi. We need a Mau Mau in Mississippi. In Alabama we need a Mau Mau. In Georgia we need a Mau Mau. Right here in Harlem, in New York City, we need a Mau Mau."

Some in the mainstream press interpreted Malcolm's speech as a provocation. By taking the terminology of the enemy and standing it on its head, he was engaging in a rhetorical counterattack that guaranteed his place in the eyes of some cops—and others on the right—as King Mau Mau.

As much as violence, the representatives of law and order in New York felt threatened by the prospect of political organization among militant Negroes. In the early 1960s, white residents looked to the police to protect them from underclass encroachment—to stop the tide of history, as it were. As poor blacks and Puerto Ricans flooded into neighborhoods that had once been Jewish, Italian, or Irish, white policemen were expected to man the barricades. It was as if they were answering a silent plea from the white working-class population who lacked the means to flee: *Please protect us. Help us hold the block. Keep the blacks away from our children and grandmothers. You are all we have.*

Some cops took this role to heart. The protector role was near and dear to many cops: even as Saint Michael protected the policemen, the policeman would protect the citizens. In the 1950s and early 1960s, this role involved white cops protecting white citizens from marauding Negroes, and some cops took to the role with fury and zeal.

In *My Father's Gun*, Brian McDonald writes that virtually every cop he knew, including his father and his brother, routinely used the word *nigger*. To Bob Leuci, who joined the force in 1961 and served with TPF units in Harlem, the South Bronx, and Brooklyn, using the word was a way of showing that you were a comfortable member of the club. If you didn't, the implication was that there was something wrong with you, that you might be sympathetic to the niggers who were running roughshod over once-respectable, working-class white neighborhoods.

Bill Phillips was certainly aware of these attitudes even before he joined the NYPD. His father, assigned to Harlem for much of his police career, was complaining about the niggers before it was fashionable. Phillips inherited his father's views, and gibed casually with other cops about the blacks, but he wasn't assigned to a black neighborhood, nor a unit like TPF that directly butted heads with blacks, so his feelings remained like a low-grade fever, active but not yet fully airborne.

For Phillips, police work was less about Saint Michael than about making money. In this, too, he was a product of the system. Like racial attitudes, a taste for graft and profiteering was passed along from experienced cops to rookies. Phillips was like a sponge; he listened, watched, and learned from the best. Early on, while assigned to the One-Nine Precinct, he studied the technique of Lieutenant William "Wild Bill" Madden, whom he came to know and appreciate as a "master extortionist." Few on the force knew how to set up a contract with the audacity and skill of Madden.

Once, when Phillips and his partner, Kenny Keller, were having trouble squeezing an illegal payoff out of a citizen they pulled over for drunk driving, they took the guy back to the station house, where Madden was in charge. As Phillips later described it, "In a half hour, Madden, who is a complete professional, is on the phone with the guy's brother." Madden coerced the drunk driver's brother to fork over five hundred dollars; no charges were filed. Madden received the money and passed along one hundred each to Phillips and Keller.

Phillips learned from Madden. He learned that suspects are much more manageable after they've been sitting in a cell for a few hours with nothing to read, no one to talk to. They're a lot easier to deal with after they've been reminded how expensive a lawyer is, how much bail bonds cost, how awkward it can be to miss several days of work—especially when there's such a simple alternative:

> [Madden] had all kinds of tricks up his sleeve. He got one guy
> on some nonsense, I don't even remember what, and he tells
> him it's going to cost him one thousand dollars. The guys says,
> All I got is two hundred. Madden takes him right to the bank,
> the guy takes out a eight-hundred-dollar loan. Madden takes
> the money and now the guy is paying off the score to the bank
> every month. . . . Get enough guys like that, you can open your
> own bank.

By the time Phillips was promoted to the detective bureau in 1960, he had developed his own reputation for excellence in the world of scoring. As a detective, he wore a nice suit and tie and circulated around Manhattan mostly unmonitored by supervisors. By late 1964, from upscale gambling operations, after-hours clubs, midtown construction sites, and various other ongoing scores, Phillips was taking in $1,500 to $2,000 a week—under the table—to augment his detective's pretax paycheck of $200 a week. And he'd learned about spreading the wealth, making sure that precinct commanders, inspectors, and lieutenants all got a piece of the action. That's the way it was supposed to be done: if you made money within a certain division, the division had to be paid. Phillips wasn't out to buck the system; he was out to use it to his advantage.

His efforts were appreciated. Detective Phillips was known as an expert "conditions man," a hustler who could examine the conditions in a precinct—construction projects, traffic issues, after-hours businesses, gambling parlors, whorehouses—and find a way to squeeze a few dollars out of the people responsible. Phillips showed talent and initiative for that kind of work, and soon commanders and partners were requesting him. He was establishing himself as a master extortionist just like Kenny Keller, Wild Bill Madden, and all the others he had learned from over the years.

Being a moneymaker gave a cop high standing among fellow officers. Phillips's stature gave him a certain swagger, which in turn enhanced his position on the street. A conditions man was someone you could see coming; the seas parted before him when he entered a room. This was the kind of cop that later became known as a Prince of the City.

Inevitably, such cops developed attitudes that spilled over from the professional into the personal. Bill Phillips had been a married man for nearly ten years. He and his wife, Camille, lived in a modest split-level home in Elmhurst, Queens, far from the hubbub of Manhattan. Camille had her own friends, and as long as Bill fulfilled his role as provider and stayed out of trouble, she was content to let him do his own thing. She was a classic police wife, accepting her husband's long hours away from home, his absences on holidays, his unwillingness to talk about even the most public aspects of his job. She wouldn't tolerate him having affairs, but she knew he was on his own, free to run his personal life as he saw fit, and she rarely asked questions.

Phillips had many women on the side—cocktail waitresses, coat check girls, stewardesses, and other "broads" who were dazzled by a detective's gold shield and the smooth patter of a professional deceiver. Some of these women were one-night stands; others were more regular, like Olivia, a model he met at Le Club on the East Side, or Dolly, a hat check girl at Ginza, a midtown disco. With his slick black hair, sideburns, and swagger, Phillips was a bona fide player—one who always had cash to throw around.

At the One-Seven detective squad, Phillips' partner was Tony Delafranco, an Italian American variant of his Irish American lothario routine. Together, they spent much of their day trying to find women they could compromise into meeting them for drinks at a midtown bar, where they would turn on the charm and impress them with their power and connections. Phillips was usually a few steps ahead of Delafranco in his willingness to push the envelope.

One night, without much preparation, Phillips told his partner that he'd worked out a scheme for them to spend a luxurious night with a couple of girls. At the internationally famous Waldorf-Astoria Hotel on Park Avenue in midtown Manhattan, Delafranco stood by, aghast, as Phillips explained to the night manager that they were two detectives working undercover on an important case. Phillips showed the manager their detective shields, then explained: "We're working on a big swindle case, very heavy case, millions of dollars involved, and we have to make a big impression on this criminal. We're going to meet him at four o'clock in the morning. We told the guy we're staying at the Waldorf and we're going to need a suite of rooms."

Suitably impressed, the manager called a bell captain over and told him, "Fix these gentlemen up with a suite. Whatever they need."

"Are you out of your fucking mind?" Delafranco whispered to Phillips. "If the boss finds out about this, he'll bury us."

"Don't worry about nothing," said Phillips. "Just sign in."

Years later, Phillips remembered the details with glee: "A hundred-and-fifty-dollar suite. Up we go. Two bedrooms, a living room, fireplace, beautiful joint. We go out, get some booze, all kinds of stuff, big platter of chicken, potato salad. Even paid for some of it. We go back up, and when [the girls] get there we're sitting in our underwear. Say, what the hell is going on here? Party time, girls."

A few weeks after the bacchanalia at the Waldorf, Phillips got a call one night from Delafranco asking if he could help him out by driving one of his mistresses home after work. Sure, said Phillips, no problem. He picked up his partner's girlfriend, took her to a bar, and got her drunk. Then he took her to a hotel, where they had sex, after which he left her passed out in the bed.

It's about eight o'clock in the morning. I get on the phone
and I call Delafranco. Hey Tony, it's Bill. I just fucked your
girlfriend. He says, You dirty son of a bitch, what'd you do that
for? I say, I don't know; I just wanted to see if I could.

Being a cop in Fun City had its privileges. Bill Phillips was floating in the deep end of the pool, free from the concerns of lesser men.

PHILLIPS WAS A bent cop, but being a bent cop wasn't what got him into trouble. What got him into trouble was stepping on the toes of another cop.

For years, Phillips had been one of many cops on the take. All around him the department was on the pad, receiving payoffs from arch and petty criminals alike. Taking money wasn't only tolerated by cops, it was expected. What wasn't tolerated were minor infractions of police protocol.

One night, Phillips and Delafranco were in a bar owned by a friend, a retired detective named Pete. In the bar, Phillips noticed two undercover cops from the police commissioner's Fag Squad, a special unit assigned to entrap and arrest homosexuals. On his way out of the bar,

Phillips figured he would warn his friend, the owner and former cop, that there were undercover detectives working his bar. "Hey, Pete," he said, "be careful, the PC's here."

"Where?"

Phillips nodded toward the two undercover detectives. Pete said thanks, and that was that—until the two detectives found out they'd been fingered by Phillips. They reported the infraction to their supervisor.

Phillips was in trouble. He and Delafranco were both called before a disciplinary board. As was customary, they sent a bottle of booze to the chief inspector investigating their case. Phillips even called in his father, Bill Phillips Sr., who still had contacts in the department. Phillips wasn't all that worried; it seemed like a minor infraction, especially for someone who was engaged in daily violations of police ethics on a grand scale. Still, he made sure he used his contacts, asked people to talk to people to talk to other people to ensure there would be no serious repercussions.

At a hearing, the chief asked Phillips and Delafranco, "What were you doing in the bar?"

"Making an inspection," answered Phillips.

"Did you make out the UF88 form?"

"Sure." To Phillips and Delafranco, it seemed like routine questioning. They explained to the chief that they never gave up anybody—that their friend the bar owner already knew that the two undercover investigators were with the Fag Squad. The hearing lasted ten minutes. Phillips left the room certain that everything was A-okay.

Three weeks later, he and Delafranco heard the verdict: they were being "flopped" out of the detective bureau and demoted to patrolmen.

Phillips was stunned. He went to the head of the Detectives Endowment Association, a kind of union for detectives, and pleaded his case. The president of the DEA said, "What have you ever done for me?" To Phillips, this was interesting; he'd spread money around to lots of people in the department, but you couldn't take care of everybody. No matter how many people got a slice, there was always somebody who didn't. Phillips had assumed that his years of payoffs were enough to protect him. Now he realized that, for every friend in the department, there was always someone else outside the loop, looking to even the score.

There was nothing Phillips could do: just like that he was back in uniform, patrolling the streets like a punk kid just out of the academy.

I was completely demoralized. Oh Jesus. . . . I was walking around in a fog. I had ten years invested in the job, am I going to throw them away? Halfway to a pension. In five years I'm vested. Fuck it, I'll do nothing and coast for a while and see what happens. . . .

Phillips was essentially an optimist, always on the lookout for a silver lining. And there it was: he was assigned to the Twenty-fifth Precinct in Harlem, nirvana for a cop on the take.

Phillips knew, from his father and from NYPD lore, that there was nowhere in the city where dirty money flowed quite like Harlem. All kinds of illegal activities were going on there, and the police were in on all of it: numbers, gambling, after-hours clubs, burglary rings, fences, loan sharks, prostitution, and narcotics. Phillips steered clear of prostitution and drugs; he was old-fashioned that way. The skells in the prostitution business were untrustworthy. And narcotics, well, that was a brave new world. Narcotics was O.C., organized crime. Dabble in narcotics and sooner or later you were going to wind up with dead cops. Phillips didn't want that on his conscience. And in Harlem you didn't need prostitution and dope to get rich; there was plenty of money to be made elsewhere.

Phillips wasn't thrilled about the idea of spending all that time in Harlem. He didn't like black people; he was a self-proclaimed bigot. But a man had to weigh his prejudices against his opportunities. And for a hustler like Phillips, Harlem was a land of opportunity, a New Frontier.

Maybe he could salvage this, Phillips thought. Maybe Harlem would be his salvation.

It was a forty-minute drive from Phillips's Elmhurst home to the Twenty-fifth Precinct station house on East 119th Street near Park Avenue. In East Harlem, Phillips drove past dilapidated tenements, debris, and human refuse, a reminder that he was no longer cruising the streets of midtown.

The first thing to do in a new precinct is drop a few bucks on the roll call men. That's so you don't get a bad post. In Harlem it's especially easy to get a bad post. . . . You could get a post like 132nd Street and Madison with fifty thousand junkies all over your back all goddamn night. You can have a three block post on Madison Avenue, from 129th to 132nd, and it's goddamn bedlam, all these ball-breaking people bothering you all night, fighting each other, stabbing each other, shooting. You can lock up a lot of them, but what good is it? Like 111th Street, all junkies and winos, a hundred people milling around in the streets, complete shitheads, scum of the earth. We call them skells.

Landing in a new precinct is always an adjustment. Phillips dropped fifteen dollars each on everyone he was supposed to, but he was still getting bad assignments. This made him angry.

I got fucked all over the precinct, all the shitty posts, all the lousy assignments. So I went back to [the people in charge], one at a time, and I says, Hey, listen pal, I'm paying you, I gave you the money; what are you fucking me around for? . . . I'm a nice guy, but I don't want to be fucked around anymore. Don't take my money and try to screw me.

Eventually, Phillips got transferred from a foot patrol to a sector car, which was a big step up. The catch was that he was given a black partner, Egbert Brown, a young cop with only two years on the job. "Most white policemen didn't want to work with blacks," remembered Phillips. But he saw the advantage in having a black partner in Harlem—and having a young partner meant Phillips called the shots.

Bert Brown was medium height, mocha-skinned, and he was a good talker. He also had contacts in the neighborhood. Within weeks, Phillips and Brown had established a network of patrolmen working for them as bagmen, picking up two and three dollars a day from street peddlers, two and three dollars from bodega owners, and even more from traffic violators. Phillips and his partner were taking in three and four hundred a month.

Through it all, Phillips regaled Brown with stories of his big scores while in the Detective Bureau. "I got a lot of friends in the bureau," he told Brown. "Stick with me, kid, and you'll be in plainclothes in a year."

"Hey," asked Brown, "you think you could make some friendly phone calls for me? Smooth the waters?"

Phillips said he would, but he never did.

If I have a hook I'd rather save it for somebody else that I really knew well. I mean it would look kind of ridiculous if all my friends are white and I call up I got a black guy I want to put in the bureau. What the fuck, are you nuts? They'd laugh at me. Like I was some kind of jerk. Let the black guy make his own connections with the black people. You don't have to do it for him.

The last straw for Phillips was when he heard that the ungrateful bastard was actually skimming on the side. Phillips found out about it while he was preparing to leave for two weeks' vacation. For a cop on the take, vacations can be a perilous time. Without the cop around to make regular pickups, poachers can move in and mess up a good thing. Phillips told Brown to handle the pickups from gamblers and policy men in his absence. When he returned, he asked his partner how it went.

"Good," Brown said. "I picked up some, but not all."

Phillips was suspicious. He went to one of his regular spots, a weekly dice, craps, and card location in East Harlem run by a wiseguy called Louis Fats.

"Hey, Louis," he said. "How you been? I come to pick up the thing for last month. I was on vacation."

"The nigger got it," said Louis.

"He got it?"

"Yeah."

Phillips couldn't believe it: he was being ripped off by a raw-assed rookie, and a nigger to boot. Phillips started setting up his own pads, cutting Brown out of the picture. "I make an extra seventy, eighty dollars a month. Every time I picked up the money I'd go, ha-ha, you fuck, and put it in my pocket."

Egbert Brown did eventually get transferred to plainclothes. Phillips was glad to see him go.

Phillips went to the roll call man and slipped him fifteen dollars. "No more nigger partners," he said. "I'd rather walk the street. You put me in with another black guy, put me out of the car. I will never again work with another one of those black bastards. They can't be trusted."

six

ON THE BUTTON

GEORGE WHITMORE WAS feeling apprehensive. In preparation for his trial, he'd been transferred temporarily to the psych ward at Kings County Hospital. Located on Atlantic Avenue in the heart of Brooklyn, Kings County housed some true crazies—killers, child molesters, dope fiends, and droolers. In his small corner of the ward, Whitmore had plenty of time to stare at the ceiling and ponder his fate. Years later, he remembered:

> I knew I hadn't done nothin' wrong, I was innocent of all charges, but I felt bad. My family had been dragged into my predicament. Everywhere they went they was related to the monster George Whitmore Jr. people seen in the papers and on the TV news. Every time my mama come to see me she cried something terrible. I held her hand and try to make her feel better, but I didn't feel so good my own self. My only hope was that once we got to the court everythin' would come out straight, a judge would see the truth and understand and it would all be over.

Whitmore's attorney was on the case. Working out of his Court Street office in downtown Brooklyn, Jerome Leftow set his sights on the Elba Borrero case. His client was charged with one count of attempted rape and one count of assault. Another public defender might have focused on the issue of racial injustice, tried to make something of Whitmore's situation in the press, but Leftow was no crusader. He was a clubhouse lawyer, and he was determined to fight the charges on their merits, with little speculation, pretrial shenanigans, or racial posturing in the press.

Without the sensational Wylie-Hoffert charges attached, the press wasn't too interested anyway. Whitmore was a black man being tried for assaulting a Puerto Rican woman—a crime among minorities on a Brooklyn street, the kind that rarely made the papers or the TV news. The system was filled with cases like this, and they usually went the same way: in the interest of expediency, a plea bargain would be arranged by the prosecutor, judge, and public defender, and the defendant would be implored to take the deal. Whitmore was offered a deal on the Borrero case, assured he'd receive minimal jail time if he pleaded guilty. To which George said, "Why would I plead guilty to somethin' I didn't do?"

Leftow was overwhelmed by the sheer volume of charges hanging over Whitmore's head—Borrero, Edmonds, Wylie-Hoffert—but he had good feelings about the Borrero charges. As far as he could tell, the D.A.'s case had many holes.

For one thing, Leftow had his doubts about whether an attempted rape had even occurred in Brownsville on the night in question. When the incident involving Elba Borrero had first been reported over the NYPD communication system, it was called a purse snatching, plain and simple. In Patrolman Isola's notebook entry, there was no mention of attempted rape or murder. The sexual dimensions of the case seemed to have been grafted on at a later date. Leftow suspected that the detectives invented the idea of an attempted rape after they decided to link Whitmore to the Wylie-Hoffert case, because it would help them establish a pattern. According to the official police accounts, in all three of Whitmore's cases he was alleged to have said, "I want to rape you, I want to kill you." Rape and murder, murder and rape: For the prosecutors it was essential to suggest that these attacks were all part of a consistent pattern of criminal behavior.

Then there was Elba Borrero's identification of the suspect. Borrero had first described her attacker as a black male, twenty to twenty-five years old, five foot seven and one hundred sixty-five pounds, wearing a hat and a long leather coat. George Whitmore, on the other hand, was a young-looking nineteen, five foot five, and one hundred forty at most. The police had confiscated a leather coat of Whitmore's at his girlfriend's house, but George said he wasn't even wearing the coat on the night in question. His brother Shelley had been wearing the coat.

Finally, there was the manner by which Borrero had identified George as the assailant: through a peephole, with no other suspects around. Even then, she had been uncertain at first. Normally, police were required to set up a lineup, or at least show the victim a set of photos and ask the person to identify one suspect among many faces.

These and additional evidentiary matters encouraged Leftow to believe he could establish that great life preserver for all public defenders: reasonable doubt. He wasn't exactly brimming with confidence as the trial approached, but he wasn't despairing either. He put his chances at fifty-fifty.

Early on the morning of November 9, 1964, Whitmore was transported from Kings County psych ward to the courthouse in downtown Brooklyn. It was his first public appearance in the nearly seven months since he had been arrested. The institutional routine of three meals a day, and a bed to sleep in, had been good for him: he had filled out a bit, and his acne, a consequence of poor nutrition, had cleared up. His hair had been trimmed, and he'd been given a bulky yellow sweater to wear. Yet none of this altered what was apparent when Whitmore opened his mouth—that he was clearly a child of the streets, with little education or sophistication.

Two days later, they had a jury: twelve white men from middle-class backgrounds. Leftow could have objected to the racial imbalance of the jury, but that wasn't his style. He was inured to the irrefutable nature of white courts, white juries, white justice.

On the first day of testimony, Elba Borrero was called to the stand. She was short and heavyset and wore a green print dress. She was only twenty-five, but with her horn-rimmed glasses and orthopedic shoes she looked ten years older. The prosecutor, Sidney A. Lichtman, led her through a series of questions to establish her story. On the night of the attempted rape, Borrero said, she was coming home from her job as a nurses' assistant at a nearby hospital. Dressed in her white uniform, carrying a purse with a shoulder strap, she descended the stairs of the IRT station and turned onto Bristol Street. It was nearly one in the morning, rainy and dark. This seven-minute walk from the subway to her apartment was Borrero's least favorite time, and that night her worst fears were realized: a man followed her from the subway station, the sound of his footsteps causing her to pick up the pace and hurry along.

Sid Lichtman was a seasoned veteran. In his early fifties, gray-haired and workmanlike, he posed each question as if it were one small piece of a larger puzzle. He also knew how to elicit sympathy from a jury, pausing so that Elba Borrero could lift her spectacles and dab her eyes as she cried on the stand. Pointing to a diagram of the location where the attack took place, Lichtman asked Borrero, "Did there come a time when you were assaulted on Bristol Street?"

"When he got to about here," said Borrero, pointing to a spot on the diagram, "he pushed me against the wall. He was standing in front of me, and he said, 'Let me touch your pussy.' And then he put his hand under my coat and under my uniform and under the slip and touched my pubic area."

"By your pubic area, you mean what?"

"The vagina."

"What was the exact language?"

" 'I want to have intercourse with you. I want to have sexual relations.' Then he said, 'I'm going to rape you. . . . I'm going to kill you first and then rape you.' I grabbed ahold of his hands then, and his coat, and I started screaming. . . . I saw a flashlight come in. . . . Then he started to run." Officer Isola had arrived on the scene. The assailant ran, the cop fired shots, and Elba Borrero breathed a sigh of relief.

The witness was asked to identify a button she claimed to have torn off the assailant's coat during the tussle. "Yes," she said, "that's the button from the coat."

Lichtman paused for dramatic effect, then asked, "Now, Mrs. Borrero, do you see the man who followed you and the man who attacked you that night? Do you see him in the courtroom this morning?"

"Yes," she answered. "That's him right there." She pointed at George Whitmore.

Under cross-examination by Leftow, Borrero maintained that she got a good look at her attacker, even though her descriptions of the assailant changed from the initial police report to the version she gave in court. Leftow asked Borrero how it was that she arrived at the Seventy-third Precinct two days after the assault.

"Patrolman Isola told me they had a man there they wanted me to look at and identify and see if he had been the man who attacked me."

"So when you looked through the peephole you knew the purpose was to see if you could identify the man on the opposite side of the room?"

"Yes."

"And when you looked at the man, you said, 'I'm not sure.' Is that correct?"

Prosecutor Lichtman stood to object, but Justice David Malbin raised his hand and said, "Wait a minute. Let her answer. Did you say you weren't sure?"

Borrero turned to Judge Malbin. "No, not exactly. I told Patrolman Isola, 'This is the man.' And then I asked him to wait a minute. . . . I asked to have him speak."

"Because you weren't sure," interjected Leftow.

"No," she answered. "Because I wanted to be sure beyond any shadow of a doubt."

Leftow did not force the issue. He could see that Borrero had been well coached. The more he challenged her, the more adamant she became. Leftow had serious doubts about her identification, but he also knew that, to the jury, this woman was the victim of a frightening attack. If he came off as too aggressive in trying to discredit her, it could backfire, and her testimony would do even more damage than it already had.

Even so, he couldn't let Borrero leave the stand without bringing up the fact that, in the weeks before the trial, she had consulted with an attorney about collecting the ten-thousand-dollar reward offered by *Newsweek* in the Wylie-Hoffert case. The accusation was particularly damning because Borrero had claimed that she'd never even heard of the Wylie-Hoffert murders.

Asked Leftow, "Do you have any other interest but of a witness in this particular case?"

"No," said Borrero.

Leftow then asked her about the ten thousand dollars.

"Do I have to answer that?" Borrero asked Judge Malbin.

"Just answer the question," he said.

Borrero admitted that she had inquired about the reward.

"No further questions," said Leftow.

Late in the afternoon, the jury was removed from the courtroom. An important moment in the trial had arrived: Justice Malbin was required to determine—outside the purview of the jury—whether or not Whitmore's confession had been extracted "under duress." If the judge determined that the confession had been coerced, it would be thrown out, and the proceedings would continue without any mention of Whitmore's signed statement. The judge's ruling was crucial since it would establish a legal precedent that could affect all of Whitmore's future cases and trials.

Patrolman Isola, Detective Aidala, and Detective Di Prima all took the stand. They were questioned by the judge about the circumstances surrounding the Whitmore confession. Then George Whitmore himself was called to testify.

To Whitmore, his arrival on the witness stand represented yet another immersion into a strange and intimidating universe: his journey from a street corner in Brownsville had led him through a police precinct, an arraignment court, two psychiatric hospitals, county jail, and now the halls of justice. The courts, in particular, were a world populated by white faces, educated people who spoke a language of legal jargon George could barely understand. Whitmore was nervous as he took the stand, but he was determined to describe the injustice that had been done to him. Once the judge heard the circumstances of his arrest and interrogation, he was certain, this charade would be over.

Whitmore's first experience as a witness did not go well. His nervousness read as defensiveness, especially when he was cross-examined by Sidney Lichtman. Said George, "[The policemen] called me a liar. Every time I told them I didn't do it, well, they hit me."

Judge Malbin asked, "Who hit you?"

Whitmore pointed at Isola and Aidala, who were seated in the front row. "They struck me in the stomach, the chest, and the back."

"On the face?" asked Lichtman.

"No. . . . They stood me in front of a chair . . . every time I said I didn't know what happened, I got knocked into the chair. Then they stood me up aside this wall and I continuously got beat until I could take it no more. So I just broke down and shook my head."

Lichtman paused, sensing that the fate of his prosecution depended on the next series of questions. "What did he [Aidala] hit you with?" he asked.

George answered, "His fist . . . in my stomach."

"How many times?"

Whitmore took a few seconds to think about it.

"How many times?" the prosecutor repeated.

"I haven't counted them."

"More than ten times?"

"Yes. It was several times."

"Ten times?"

"I don't know. I'm not sure how many times it was."

"Were they hard blows?"

"Well, I had pains in my stomach."

"Did you vomit?"

"No."

"Patrolman Isola would punch you in the stomach and Detective Aidala would punch you in the back?" Lichtman swung a few roundhouse punches to illustrate his point.

"It wasn't like that. It was fast."

"Altogether, how many times . . . about fifty punches from Detective Aidala?"

"Yes . . . and they weren't light."

"How many punches did you get from Patrolman Isola?"

"I don't know . . . I was being hit at the same time. How am I supposed to count?"

"Between ten and twenty?"

"Yes."

Seated at the defense table, Leftow winced. Whatever you do, he had told George, don't guess. Don't get suckered by the prosecutor. George had played right into Lichtman's hands. If he'd been beaten seventy times, he would have had to be carried out of the precinct on a gurney. Yet he'd already testified that, after this beating, he had sat down and eaten, drank coffee, and smoked a cigarette with these same policemen. Photographs of his body taken the next day by the Brooklyn D.A.'s office revealed no noticeable marks or bruises.

Leftow wished he had stood up to object, but it was too late now. In his embarrassment and confusion, Whitmore had likely hung himself.

Once George left the stand, it took Malbin only a few minutes to deliver his ruling: "The court finds that the evidence has established beyond a reasonable doubt that the confession was voluntary. . . . I shall permit the district attorney to offer this confession during the presence of the jury."

Whitmore spent the rest of the day in glum silence, until the judge adjourned the proceedings until the following Monday.

That weekend, in his cell at the Brooklyn House of Detention, George felt he had "never been so sad before." In a letter to a fellow inmate he'd met at Bellevue, he wrote:

> I don't think I will be a free man soon. The way things went in court, look like I was already convicted. Everyone seem to be together but me. I am innocent, but no one seems to believe me but you and my family and friends. Ever since I was put in jail I was praying. . . . I ask God to let the people see that I am not the one. But I guess my prayers wasn't answered yet. I am still praying and always will. Some day things will turn out alright. I just don't know what to do anymore. . . . Please be frank and let me know. Do you think I'll be OK? If and when you see my mother please tell her I would like to see her here. . . . Forgive me for not saying much. I've been put in the papers so bad that I don't feel like a human being any more. . . .
>
> Sincerely Yours
> George Whitmore Jr.

THE BORRERO TRIAL lasted six days. It went largely as Whitmore had expected—like a well-rehearsed stage drama, or a party to which George had not been invited. The policemen all came off as solid professionals. The defense witnesses—George and his former girlfriend Beverly Payne, who had a new boyfriend and was visibly pregnant on the stand—were inarticulate, lacking in polish or formal education. George made many of the same mistakes in front of the jury that he had when questioned in private session; he was baited by the prosecutor into repeating his allegation of receiving more than fifty punches and then sitting down for sandwiches and coffee with his assailants.

To the jury, Whitmore and Beverly Payne might as well have been aliens from another planet. Leftow seemed to acknowledge as much when he said in his closing statement, "I doubt very much if George Whitmore's friends and family would be the kind of people that you or I might come into contact with in our everyday social life." He tried to reframe George's bumbling performance as the ingenuousness of an innocent man: "[Whitmore] certainly was no match for an experienced cross-examining district attorney. . . . In his confusion and in his uncertainty we find George Whitmore's greatest strength, because when he took the witness stand, that was George Whitmore testifying; George Whitmore was telling you as best he could what had happened to him. If George Whitmore testified in any other way, you would have a right to question whether he was telling the truth."

Assistant D.A. Lichtman followed Leftow's summation with a tart condemnation of the defense. He called Whitmore's account of his night in the Seventy-third Precinct a "cock-and-bull story," adding that "George Whitmore and George Whitmore alone is on trial in this case. The police department is not on trial. . . . And let no one kid you about that fact."

After running through the key points of evidence, Lichtman ended on a curious note. The entire case, he claimed, came down to one specific piece of evidence: the button. In one hand he held the coat he claimed Whitmore was wearing on the night of the attack; in the other he held the button Borrero said she'd ripped from the coat. "Take this coat into the jury room with you . . . and put this coat alongside of the threads which are missing from the upper part, underneath the collar. . . . Is it a coincidence or is it solidly guilty circumstances that the button and the coat match? Gentlemen, mister foreman, haven't we nailed George Whitmore right on the button, in the truest sense of the word, in the truest sense of the word."

After deliberating for six hours, the jury returned a verdict of guilty on both counts.

The courtroom was eerily somber; the only sound was that of Whitmore's mother and his teenage cousin, Geraldine Dantzler, weeping openly. His brother Gerald hung his head. "I was shocked," he remembered. "We was all shocked. We knew George. We knew he wasn't capable of those things they accused him of."

George stared blankly at the judge. A few minutes later, after he was taken to a holding room, he broke into tears. A bailiff, touched by Whitmore's anguish, offered him a piece of pie from his own dinner. George ate the pie, and after a few minutes he stopped crying.

Outside the courthouse, prosecutor Sidney Lichtman stood on the front steps surrounded by reporters. "This helps to dispose of the police brutality charge," he said. "I have never had a case where the facts indicated a defendant's guilt as much as this one."

As the jurors came out of the courthouse, a few walked over to congratulate Lichtman on a job well done. One of the jurors asked the ADA why he hadn't sent the button to an FBI lab for examination, to establish irrefutably that it came from the coat.

"We did," said Lichtman. "But the tests couldn't prove anything."

The juror looked surprised. "He was really guilty, wasn't he?"

"Absolutely," said the prosecutor. "No doubt about it."

One of the newspapermen around Sid Lichtman was Selwyn Raab, a reporter for the *World Telegram & Sun*. Raab, one of a small group of crime beat reporters, had been following the Whitmore drama ever since he first heard of the defendant being buried away at Bellevue for six months—an unprecedented length of time. Raab had traveled out to New Jersey to help establish the true origins of the photo in Whitmore's wallet; he had also helped uncover the story of William Coleman, the black man whom Eddie Bulger had coerced into confession just as Whitmore had been coerced.

Raab was a terrier, short and wiry, a thirty-year-old New York City kid who'd graduated from City College and gone on to a newspaper career in Newark and Bridgeport, Connecticut, before taking a job with the *World Telegram*. He knew as much as anyone about the Wylie-Hoffert murders and the circumstances surrounding Whitmore's arrest, his contested confession, and now his conviction as a sex criminal. Raab had questions about the way the Borrero case had been prosecuted, and when he heard the prosecutor mention a lab report about the button—a report that had never been mentioned in court, much less entered into evidence—his suspicions were piqued.

Raab started asking around about the mysterious lab report. He also tracked down a number of jurors. What he discovered was startling.

The Career Girls Murders had never been mentioned during the Borrero trial; the subject had been declared strictly off-limits by the judge, who made a show of proclaiming that the notorious double homicide could not be used against Whitmore in the Borrero prosecution. What Raab uncovered, however, was that the jurors not only knew that Whitmore had been charged with the Wylie-Hoffert murders, they frequently talked about it among themselves.

After voting to find George guilty of the Borrero assault, one juror told his peers, "This is nothing compared to what he's going to get in Manhattan. We're doing him a favor." Another juror had run into defense attorney Jerome Leftow on the subway after the verdict and confessed during a friendly conversation that he had doubts about much of the evidence. "If you had so many doubts, why did you vote guilty?" Leftow asked. "Are you kidding?" the man replied. "My wife told me that if I didn't convict the guy who committed those murders in Manhattan, she'd never talk to me again."

Even more disturbing, Raab found that the all-white jury's deliberations had been riddled with open expressions of bigotry. Talking about blacks and Puerto Ricans, one juror said, "You know how these fellows are; they like their sex and they must get it someplace, so they screw like jackrabbits." Another started each day of the trial by airing his anger about how his Flatbush neighborhood was being overrun by coloreds.

What Raab uncovered about the jury's attitudes called Whitmore's guilty verdict into question. Then came the real bombshell: through a friend of a friend of a friend, Raab got a copy of the FBI lab report on the button, which Lichtman and his boss, Aaron Koota, had received two days before the trial began. In part, it read: *The Q1 button [the button Borrero tore from her attacker's coat] and the buttons remaining on the coat are different in size, design and construction. Sewing thread attached to the button is different from the sewing thread remaining on the coat in color, diameter and twist.*

This was no inconclusive report. It was clear: no match.

Throughout the trial, this report never left D.A. Aaron Koota's office, though the laws on "discovery material" clearly require the prosecution to turn over all relevant evidence to the defense. Even as the report was buried in the prosecution's files, Lichtman stood up in court and declared that they had nailed George Whitmore "right on the button."

Raab published an article in the *World Telegram* that mentioned some of what he knew, but not much. The *World Telegram* was a broadsheet, not a tabloid, and it considered itself a competitor to the *Times*; its editors weren't inclined to devote as much space to street crime stories as some of the other dailies. Raab could tell his editors weren't that interested in the Whitmore story, and the same seemed to be true of the city's other papers as well. No one seemed to care much about an anonymous Negro boy who might have been framed by the system.

Out of frustration, Raab poured all he knew about the Whitmore case into a long feature article—everything from the circumstances of George's arrest and his time at Bellevue through the recent trial, including all the improprieties and incongruities the reporter had uncovered. Raab submitted his article to an editor at *Harper's*, a magazine with a national circulation. "This is a great piece of journalism," his editor said. The magazine wanted to rush it into print.

After a week, however, the editor called him back. "We can't run your piece."

Raab was stunned. "Why?" he asked.

"Because Frank Hogan doesn't want us to."

Frank S. Hogan was a legend, a potentate who had held the post of New York County district attorney since 1933. And in the early 1960s, newspapers, magazines, and television networks rarely questioned the motives of district attorneys and police authorities. Raab's editor at *Harper's* had submitted his story to the district attorney's office for approval, but the response was negative: D.A. Hogan felt the article contained information that would be a hindrance to the fair adjudication of certain legal matters in New York County.

The editors at *Harper's* acquiesced. The article was killed.

Raab hoped to place the article somewhere else. In the meantime, he called Birdine Whitmore, George's mother. "Mrs. Whitmore, I'm a newspaper reporter. I've been following your son's case since he was arrested. I think he's innocent. We have information that calls his conviction into question and will likely affect his future cases. But I think your son needs a more experienced attorney to take over his case."

Birdine Whitmore had attended George's trial on a daily basis. She liked Jerome Leftow, but she had many questions about how the case was handled. Aware that her son's legal travails were far from over, she agreed that he needed fresh lawyers and a new direction.

Arthur H. Miller and Edwin Kaplan were young—both in their early thirties—partners in a modest law firm operating out of a store-front office in Brownsville, just blocks from where George was first questioned on the street by Patrolman Isola. When approached by Whitmore's mother, Miller and Kaplan hesitated at first. They'd read about the case, and they sympathized with Birdine Whitmore, but they had no mind to join what appeared to be a lost cause. It took a meeting with Selwyn Raab, and other journalists and legal experts who'd been tracking the case, to persuade them to come on board.

Miller and Kaplan were accomplished attorneys, but their actual courtroom experience was limited; they needed an experienced trial lawyer to spearhead their efforts in court. The man they contacted was Stanley J. Reiben.

Reiben shared many of Miller's and Kaplan's original reservations; he also recognized that Whitmore's legal predicament would likely involve copious man-hours in court for little or no money in return. At fifty-one, Reiben was in the upper tier of criminal defense attorneys in New York, with fees to match. He wasn't usually tempted to take pro bono cases. But after meeting with George Whitmore at the Brooklyn House of Detention, Reiben became convinced that he was innocent and that a grave injustice was being perpetrated by the forces of the criminal justice system.

In December 1964, Miller, Kaplan, and Reiben went to work. One of their first moves was to call for a hearing to investigate the issue of racial bias among the Borrero jury. This involved taking affidavits from twelve jurors and two alternates. At the same time, Stanley Reiben undertook a media offensive. Ever since Whitmore's arrest, the Brooklyn D.A.'s office had been leaking information to selected reporters, details that encouraged them to portray George Whitmore as a Negro predator in their stories. Reiben felt it was time to push back. In a series of newspaper and TV interviews, he enumerated some of what was known so far: that the photo in Whitmore's wallet was not of Janice Wylie, that George wasn't even in New York City on the day of the Wylie-Hoffert murders, that his arrest and identification by Elba Borrero was unconstitutional, and so on.

Reiben had a lot to talk about. Based on what he already knew, there were many legal avenues to explore. But in late January 1965, just two months after Whitmore's conviction in the Borrero case, all legal matters relating to his client were put on hold—after Manhattan police announced that they'd arrested a new suspect in the notorious Career Girls Murders case.

AFTER MONTHS OF running a confidential investigation out of the Twenty-third Precinct, a five-man detective squad led by Lieutenant Thomas Cavanaugh announced that they had their man. Richard "Ricky" Robles, a twenty-one-year-old junkie with a long history of burglary arrests, was charged with the crime.

After a laborious, uncertain process, the detectives had finally managed to get Robles on tape talking about the murders. Nathan and Marjorie Delaney, two junkie friends of Robles, had allowed their apartment to be wired with hidden microphones. Nathan Delaney, an African American ex-con in his early thirties, had started cooperating with detectives after he was arrested for the murder of a heroin peddler on a street in East Harlem. Delaney and his common-law wife, Marge, knew that Robles had committed the murders: he had come by their apartment that night, his clothes bloodied, talking almost incoherently about how he'd hacked two girls to death while burglarizing their apartment. Later, he'd told Nathan Delaney that he tried to rape one of the victims before killing her.

Now, to save himself from the electric chair, Delaney agreed that he and Marge would supply Robles with dope and lure him to their apartment on East Eighty-fourth Street, where they would get Robles talking about how the killings happened and revealing the kinds of details that would confirm his guilt.

Robles was cagey. He needed his daily fix, so he arrived at the Delaneys' apartment like clockwork, but he was careful about saying anything outright about the killings. Robles was a lean, baby-faced young man who downplayed his Spanish blood, pronouncing his name "Robe-els" rather than "Ro-bleys." He had been a bright student until he got hooked on junk at fourteen and dropped out of school. He'd been in and out of youth detention ever since. The cops knew Robles; he had once confessed to more than one hundred burglaries on the East Side of Manhattan and in the Bronx. Robles had even been brought into the Twenty-third Precinct station house for questioning after the Wylie-Hoffert murders, as detectives canvassed all known junkies and burglars in the area. But he had a plausible-seeming alibi for August 28, 1963, and the detectives let him go.

It proved hard to get Robles talking about the murders in any specific way at the Delaneys' apartment, almost as if he knew he was being bugged. But he needed his dope, so he kept coming to see Nathan Delaney, who was not only his supplier but something of a criminal mentor. Finally, at a kitchen table after shooting up, Robles started talking. From a listening post in the next apartment, a team of detectives listened.

By January 26, 1965, the investigators felt it was time to move. The conversations they'd recorded weren't devastating, but they were enough to pull him in and use against him. At 12:30 P.M., Robles was arrested on the street outside the Delaneys' building by Lieutenant Cavanaugh, Detective Martin Zinkand, and another detective. First they took him to the Delaney apartment and showed him the hidden microphones. "This is D-Day," said Cavanaugh.

"I want my lawyer," said Robles.

Cavanaugh was an eighteen-year veteran. He knew Robles would clam up as soon as he met with his lawyer, and he was determined to "break" the suspect before they got to the precinct. "Ricky," he said, "the only way to save yourself now is to confess. No one is going to listen to your lawyer. They'll listen to us."

Robles sat at the kitchen table, the same spot where he'd gotten high with the Delaneys many times, and began to squirm. His arms and face itched, his nose began to run—all telltale signs of withdrawal.

"We have you cold, Ricky. Think about your mother. She hasn't long to live. How is it going to look if we say that you showed no remorse? That you are just a cold-blooded killer?"

Robles's stomach ached; his head was pounding. He needed something—"a little taste"—to tide him over, he said.

There was nothing they could do, said the lieutenant—*unless*. If he confessed now, they'd rush him to a doctor or a clinic. Robles started to vomit, mostly dry heaves.

In the listening post, investigators from the D.A.'s office took in the conversation over headphones. They heard Robles vomiting and kept listening.

"Make your peace, Ricky. Make your peace with God and man. . . . If you don't confess and show remorse, it will destroy your mother."

Robles started whimpering. "Please. Please call my lawyer. Here's his card with a telephone number on it."

The detectives ignored the card. "We don't want to see you go to the chair, Rick. Confess."

Now Robles began to cry. For all the tears and dry heaves and whimpering, though, he didn't say much, just two things: he wanted his lawyer, and he needed a fix.

They went on like this the entire afternoon. At one point, the detectives brought Nathan and Marge Delaney into the room to help convince Robles to confess. Robles started sweating and twitching, as though he were crawling out of his skin, but the detectives were insistent: "Come on, Ricky, this is your only chance. You wanna destroy your mother?"

"I wish I could die." Three things now: lawyer, fix, die.

"I'm a Catholic, just like you are," said Cavanaugh. "After you have confessed and made your peace with God, then we'll let you see a priest."

Again Robles pleaded for a fix.

"Confess. Confess and you will have your taste."

"Please. Oh please, please, please. I just want to die."

As desperate as he was, Robles wouldn't crack. At 6:11 P.M., the tapes stopped. The detectives took him down to the Twenty-third Precinct station house and placed him in a second-floor interrogation room. His lawyer, Jack Hoffinger, had arrived at the precinct, but he was kept at bay. Another detective—Sean Downes, who knew Robles from his previous burglary arrests and had once even visited him in youth detention—brought coffee and sandwiches into the room. Robles tried to eat, but he spit the sandwich into a wastebasket. "It's making me sick," he told Downes. Sugar, that's what he needed. He loaded up the coffee with four or five packets of sugar and slurped it down.

Weary and sick, seated across from a familiar face, Robles finally unburdened himself. "I went to commit a lousy burglary and wound up killing two girls," he said.

He told the detective he'd been able to scale the wall outside the Wylie-Hoffert apartment because he was a skilled cat burglar. He climbed in the kitchen window, planning to steal whatever money and valuables he could find and sell them to buy dope. When he got inside, though, he came across Janice Wylie, who'd just come out of the shower, half-naked.

"Then what?" asked Downes.

"Well, she pulled the sheet around her. She said, 'Please don't hurt me. Take anything you want.'"

"Okay."

"Then I decided to hump her."

"Okay."

"She had a rag on. She had on a Tampax. She pulled it out of her pussy, or I did. I'm not sure. She said, 'Please don't hurt me.'"

"What did you do then, Ricky?"

"I walked her into another room. I got some Noxzema from the medicine cabinet and I put it on her ass and tried to fuck her in the ass. She complained that it hurt."

"So what did you do?"

"I made her put it in her mouth."

Then the girl's roommate came home and walked into the middle of things. Unlike Janice Wylie, who'd been terrified and compliant, Emily Hoffert talked back. Realizing he'd have to tie the two girls up, he grabbed Hoffert and held her at knifepoint while he tore strips from a sheet that he used to bind the girls together. That's when Emily Hoffert said to Robles, "Leave my glasses on. I want to get a good look at you so I'll be able to give a description to the police."

At that, Ricky snapped. He clubbed both girls over the head with a Coke bottle. Then, in a violent frenzy, he hacked them both to death— so forcefully that the knife handle broke off in his hand. "I think I hit a rib," Ricky told Downes.

That was it: the cops had what they needed. Now that Robles had confessed, he was allowed to meet with his attorney.

Late that night, at the Twenty-third Precinct station house, Ricky Robles was led downstairs by two detectives into a swarm of reporters and bright camera lights, just as George Whitmore had been at the Seven-Three in Brownsville more than a year before. *Hey, Ricky, look over here! Ricky, Ricky, one time, this way, Ricky! Hey, Ricky, you don't have to smile—over here!*

Ricky Robles, the police announced, had confessed to the Career Girls Murders. The NYPD now had two conflicting confessions to the most notorious crime of the decade.

TO STANLEY REIBEN and the legal team now working on behalf of George Whitmore, the arrest of Ricky Robles changed everything. The lawyers immediately called for a meeting with Aaron Koota, the Brooklyn D.A., and demanded that the murder charges against Whitmore in the Minnie Edmonds case be dropped at once. When Koota declined, Reiben decided it was time to call in the NAACP and identify the Whitmore case, once and for all, as a civil rights matter.

At a press conference at the NAACP's national office in Manhattan, Reiben looked on as Ray H. Williams, chairman of the Brooklyn branch's legal redress committee, announced he was drafting telegrams to U.S. attorney general Nicholas Katzenbach, New York governor Nelson Rockefeller, Mayor Wagner, and several other state and city officials calling for an independent investigation into the circumstances surrounding Whitmore's "confession." The NAACP's demands were reiterated in the pages of *The Crisis*, the organization's in-house magazine, which noted, "In coming to the aid of George Whitmore Jr. . . . the Brooklyn branch of the NAACP continues a practice and policy of the Association as old as the organization itself."

Rockefeller was one potential ally. His family had contributed money to civil rights causes in the South, and as governor he had the power to appoint an investigative body. But Nelson Rockefeller was a politician on the move; he had competed vigorously for the Republican presidential nomination the previous year and would likely run again in 1968. The governor responded quickly, via telegram, that Whitmore's fate was the responsibility of "local authorities" and he would not get involved.

Even without the governor on board, the Robles arrest put the Wylie-Hoffert murders back on the front page. The apparent framing of George Whitmore also got some ink, but mostly in the back pages, a sideshow to the main event.

Whitmore's defense team, now augmented by representatives from one of the nation's most prestigious civil rights organizations, was reinvigorated. The case against George was revealed as a race case after all, the framing of a young Negro because he was a Negro. Whitmore's predicament was elevated from a matter of court dockets and press speculation into the primary narrative of the era: not just a story about some poor kid forced to take the rap, but a story about the rising of the Negroes, their struggle for justice and civil rights.

One afternoon in late January, with the Wylie-Hoffert revelations appearing daily in the news, George met with his lawyers. Since his conviction at the Borrero trial Whitmore had been transferred from county jail to Sing Sing, up the Hudson River in Ossining, New York. Sing Sing was where they housed Old Sparky, the electric chair, and the symbolism wasn't lost on Whitmore. George asked prison guards and fellow inmates: "Tell me, 'cause I got to know. What's worse—the chair, gas, or lethal injection?" You don't want the chair, he was told. And gas, well, apparently that caused the vital organs to expand, which was painful. "I decided to go with the lethal injection," remembered George. "Figured, if and when the time came, that would be the easiest to take."

At the visiting room at Sing Sing, Whitmore met with his defense team—Reiben, Miller, and Kaplan, along with Ray Williams from the NAACP. He already knew from the papers that Robles had confessed to the Wylie-Hoffert murders. But there was another wrinkle: now Robles, too, had recanted his confession, claiming he'd been coerced.

The lawyers came bearing gifts. The NAACP had set up a legal defense fund for Whitmore, and one of their first purchases was a small but important one: a pair of glasses for their client. Few of Whitmore's lawyers knew he had poor eyesight; George never talked about it. After noticing that Whitmore was having trouble reading a legal document, though, they arranged for an eye examination, which confirmed that he was near clinically blind.

In the visiting room, George received the glasses. He removed them from their case and put them on. He looked at the ceiling, the floor, various people in the prison visiting room. The corners of Whitmore's mouth crinkled into a smile and his eyes lit up: for the first time in a long time, he could see what was going on around him.

seven

HARLEM NOCTURNE

IN LATE JANUARY 1965, Malcolm X was interviewed in a CBS television studio by correspondent Mike Wallace. It was a turbulent time in the fiery Negro leader's life. Throughout the early 1960s, Malcolm had emerged as a singular force in the budding black liberation movement, which ran alongside and sometimes served as a counterpoint to the more mainstream civil rights movement. Malcolm X presented himself as a militant alternative to the nonviolent approach of Martin Luther King Jr. and his Southern Christian Leadership Conference. Malcolm ridiculed nonviolence as a tactic, saying, "It is criminal to teach a man not to defend himself when he is the constant victim of brutal attacks. . . . It doesn't mean that I advocate violence, but at the same time I am not against using violence in self-defense. I don't call it violence when it's self-defense. I call it intelligence."

More recently, Malcolm had become caught up in a nasty public feud with his former mentor in the Nation of Islam, the Honorable Elijah Muhammad. The previous year, Malcolm X learned that Elijah Muhammad had fathered numerous children out of wedlock with young female secretaries in the Nation of Islam. This was a flagrant violation of the tenets of the Muslim faith. The revelation caused a rift that culminated with Malcolm X leaving the Nation of Islam, traveling to Mecca, and finally forming his own organization, which he called the Organization of Afro-American Unity (OAAU). The split was vituperative and violent. Throughout 1964 and into 1965 there had been threats against Malcolm's life. He was detested by the police and the establishment media, who saw him as an agitator; now he was resented by the Nation of Islam, who saw him as a traitor. In *Life* magazine, he was photographed holding a rifle and peeking out of the window of his house in Forest Hills, Queens, on the lookout for would-be assassins.

In his CBS interview, Malcolm seemed distracted—no surprise given the threats and turmoil swirling around him. But then Wallace asked him a question that brought his attention into focus. "Do you think the case of George Whitmore, the young Negro who may have been forced into signing a false murder confession, is an example of racial injustice?" asked the moderator.

"Yes," said Malcolm. "For far too long black people in this country have been dealing with racist police. What happened to George Whitmore could have happened to me or any other so-called Negro in America."

Malcolm X had spoken. In that moment, the case of George Whitmore was elevated from a local story into the annals of civil rights history.

Four weeks later, on the evening of February 21, Malcolm X stood at a podium inside the Audubon Ballroom on West 165th Street, in upper Manhattan. He had just begun to give a speech to a crowd of four hundred onlookers when a disturbance broke out in the audience. "Nigger, get your hand outta my pocket!" someone shouted. Amid the confusion, a man approached the stage, pulled out a sawed-off shotgun, and blasted Malcolm X in the chest, sending his body flying backward. Two more men approached with handguns and unloaded on the prone Malcolm, hitting him sixteen times.

Pandemonium followed. Spectators jumped on three of the assailants, some shouting "Kill them!" Cops and medical personnel arrived on the scene. Malcolm X was bleeding profusely, his jaw locked in an odd rictus grin. His limp frame was loaded onto a stretcher and whisked outside, with uniformed cops pushing through shocked and agitated onlookers toward an ambulance. The civil rights leader was dead before he reached the hospital.

News of the assassination reverberated nationwide, but nowhere was it felt more deeply than in the country's prison system. It was in prison that the slain "prophet" had made his transition from Malcolm Little to Malcolm X. To Malcolm, prison had been a reality but also a meta-

phor, a microcosm of the black experience in America, and his teachings
and example held a special resonance with black inmates. The Nation of
Islam was well organized within the system, and the split between the
Nation and Malcolm on the outside also occurred within prison walls.
When news of the assassination broke, Bureau of Prison authorities
feared it might touch off a riot.

Dhoruba Bin Wahad was at Comstock when he heard the news. He
was stunned. Dhoruba had been reading the speeches and teachings of
Malcolm X, and he'd been thinking of becoming a warrior in Malcolm's
army after he got out of prison—though Dhoruba's admiration didn't
extend to the Nation of Islam. "I never had any interest in joining the
Nation," he recalled, "even though they were the preeminent black organization in prison. I didn't feel anybody in the Nation was a free thinker.
A person should be able to explore and question and validate his core philosophy, but that wasn't happening in the Nation. It was too dogmatic.
But Malcolm was different. He wasn't a myrmidon; he wasn't just a bow
tie, a talking head. He was funny; he was witty; he was analytical."

In the days after the assassination, a fight broke out in the cafeteria
at Comstock between followers of the Nation and followers of Malcolm.
After an inmate was shanked, the prison was put on lockdown; other
New York State facilities followed suit.

At the time, Dhoruba and most other black inmates believed that
Malcolm had likely been killed by some combination of his enemies in
the Nation, acting in consort with the NYPD and/or the FBI.

Prison offers few opportunities for inmates to pursue an idea, to
take a belief or emotion and put it into action. For a young man like
Dhoruba—full of restless energy, looking to define himself—the mind
becomes the receptacle for all rebellious impulses. It occurred to Dhoruba
that the best way to honor the legacy of Malcolm X was to think like
Malcolm X, to take his message and apply it to his daily reality. And
so began the next phase of Dhoruba's education. Under the auspices of
Mjuba and other Muslim prisoners in the Box, he converted to Islam. He
began classes in Swahili. And he changed his name from Richard Earl
Moore, his birth name, to Dhoruba al-Mujahid Bin Wahad. In Swahili,
dhoruba means "he who is born in the storm."

During his stints in general population, Dhoruba spent much of his
time in the library. The library was a window into an alternate reality.
Dhoruba read *The History of the Decline and Fall of the Roman Empire* by

Edward Gibbon; the historical novel *Exodus* by Leon Uris; novels on Attila the Hun and Genghis Khan; and Karl Marx's *Das Kapital*. Much of Dhoruba's reading was political in nature. Prison became a think tank for Dhoruba, as it did for a generation of like-minded Negro inmates.

Being in general population could be numbingly dull. The daily routine might involve sweeping the gym floor, peeling potatoes in the kitchen, washing dishes, making license plates in metal shop. Inmates not assigned a job were put on "idle time," which meant being in a cell twenty-three hours a day, with one hour of release in the morning for "yard time."

Dhoruba was not a "model inmate." He talked back to guards and fought with other inmates when he felt it was necessary. Much as he had rebelled against institutional authority in the military, he clashed with prison authorities and refused to play the "good Negro."

> I definitely had a bad attitude. I was a litigator. I would litigate any way I could. I wouldn't let them get away with anything. If they locked me up for talking in line, I'd go through all the institutional procedures, administrative, segregation procedures. I would drag shit out for a month, for something I would have did seventy-two hours keep-lock time. I would contest it. Of course, I always lost. No, come to think of it, that's not true; I won a couple, to the amazement of everybody. But by then winning was usually a Pyrrhic victory, because while you're fighting this disciplinary charge, you're on lockdown. So when we finished after fighting for a month, they already got their pound of flesh out of your ass.

Around the time of Malcolm X's assassination, Dhoruba was called before the New York State Parole Board. Parole hearings were a big moment for any inmate. If all went well, the board could cut time off a sentence or even release a prisoner outright. Some inmates dreamed about the moment of their parole review, practicing responses they'd crafted to convince the Man that they truly were repentant and rehabilitated, even if they were not.

Dhoruba had mixed feelings about his parole board appearance. Yes, he would have liked to have had his sentence reduced, but the process of submission involved was contrary to Dhoruba's nature.

Still, he went through the motions. Donning a clean white shirt supplied by the Department of Corrections, he was taken to the prison's administrative building, where he sat down in front of a panel of parole officers, five white men dressed in the bureaucratic uniform of the day: gray suit, white shirt, thin black tie.

"Mister Richard Moore," said one of the men, "you come before us with a mixed disciplinary record. Are we to believe that you are remorseful for your behavior and ready to handle the pressures of civilian life?"

"First of all," said Dhoruba, "I don't go by Richard Moore no more. That's a slave name. You can call me Dhoruba al-Mujahid Bin Wahad."

The five parole officers looked at one another. "In any event," the lead suit continued, "you had an incident at the Elmira youth facility, a physical confrontation with another inmate. Would you like to tell us about that?"

Dhoruba recounted a fight he had in the Elmira cafeteria, just months after his arrival there. "It was a matter of self-defense," he explained.

"Well, this inmate was badly hurt and had to be taken to the prison hospital. Do you have any regrets about what happened?"

Many years later, Dhoruba remembered, "I believe I told them I was sorry, that I was remorseful, something like that. But it must not have had the ring of truth to it, because my parole was denied. They told me it was because of my poor disciplinary record."

Dhoruba was sent back to general population, and within a few days he was back in the Box. He didn't really care that much about being denied parole; he was three years into a five-year bit, and he knew he'd rather serve out his sentence than kowtow to the Man.

THE PUBLIC EXECUTION of Malcolm X sent shock waves rippling deep within the historical memory of the black community. Weeks after the event, it was still difficult to process what had happened. At the funeral, actor and civil rights activist Ossie Davis eulogized Malcolm as "our shining black manhood." In the street there was talk of payback, but there was also confusion about who ultimately was to blame. There was much repressed and misdirected anger, further grist for the mill in a community where frustration was building to epic proportions.

One person who felt the loss acutely was Eddie Ellis, a Harlem-born activist and journalist who, like many of his generation, was inspired by the slain black leader. Born in 1941, Ellis grew interested in Malcolm X in the late 1950s, when he was still a devout follower of Elijah Muhammad. Ellis reported on Malcolm's career for *Liberator*, a black nationalist magazine based in Harlem. He heard and wrote about many of Malcolm's speeches and interviewed him for the magazine. When Malcolm split from the Nation of Islam, Ellis also split. Like many in the community, he felt anger toward the faction led by Elijah Muhammad who most believed were responsible for the assassination.

A week after Malcolm's death, the building at Lenox Avenue and 116th Street that housed Mosque Number Seven was burned to the ground, after someone threw a firebomb through a fourth-floor window. It took seventy-five firefighters to quell the blaze and keep it from spreading. The burning of the mosque was considered an act of arson—and also an act of revenge.

"There was a lot of anger and frustration," remembered Eddie Ellis, who was among the onlookers who watched the mosque burn down. "Some blamed the police for allowing Malcolm to be set up, but there was also anger towards the Nation of Islam. The burning of the mosque was a direct shot at Elijah Muhammad."

If blacks were upset at the death of Malcolm X, so were the whites, but for different reasons. Many white citizens saw the assassination as one more act of horrifying savagery in a metropolis that seemed to be on the verge of spiraling out of control. The Wylie-Hoffert murders, the public execution of a prominent leader—these were two highly public versions of a type of behavior that was becoming the norm. There was anxiety in the air, even hysteria—and some of it stemmed from yet another high-profile murder that shocked the city.

The previous March, out in Kew Gardens, Queens, a young woman named Catherine "Kitty" Genovese was coming home after finishing her shift as a barmaid. It was three o'clock in the morning, and the streets were dark and deserted. She parked her car near her apartment building. On the short walk to her building, she was accosted by a man with a knife. What followed was a ghastly ordeal that lasted thirty-five minutes. The man stabbed Genovese, left her bleeding and incapacitated at the scene, returned ten minutes later, stabbed her again, ran away, then returned and stabbed her some more. Throughout the ordeal, the young woman repeatedly cried out for help. She died on the sidewalk three doors away from the building where she lived.

In the investigation that followed, detectives found that no less than thirty-eight people had heard Kitty Genovese's cries for help. No one so much as called the police.

Within days, police arrested a Negro male named Winston Moseley, who reportedly confessed to the Genovese murder and two other recent murders. The victims in those cases—both black women—had received scant media attention.

The announcement of Moseley's confession was a relief to some, but it was tempered by the fact that detectives were already holding another man they claimed had "confessed" to one of the other murders.

The Genovese murder was ugly on many levels, but the media and the public tended to focus on the inaction of those who heard Genovese's cries for help. The circumstances surrounding the murder, and the trial three months later, received copious attention, even in the *New York Times*, which rarely devoted so much space to a crime in the "outer boroughs." This murder, and the public-apathy story line, marked the emergence of a new identity for the city as a brutal, coldhearted urban jungle where people would let you die in the gutter without lifting a finger to help.

Fear was no good for the city's self-image, but it did sell papers. In early 1965, the *Herald Tribune* launched a series entitled "City in Crisis" that would continue for months. Focusing on issues of crime and race, two young reporters, Jimmy Breslin and Dick Schaap, chronicled the early stages of a great city's descent into hell. "Women carry tear-gas pens in their pocketbooks," they wrote. "Cab drivers rest iron bars on the front seat next to them. Store owners carry billy clubs next to the cash register. And people enter parks and the subways and side streets of New York, the most important city in the world, only in fear. The fear is justified. The weapons are justified."

And another factor added fuel to the fire: it was election season in the Big Town.

The city's three-term mayor, Robert Wagner, had tearfully announced that he would not run for another term; it was largely believed that he would have lost anyway. The media's favored candidate was a handsome, reform-minded young Republican named John V. Lindsay; his opponents were Abe Beame, a clubhouse Democrat, and the writer and magazine editor William F. Buckley Jr., who was running as an independent on the Conservative Party ticket.

Campaigning in Kew Gardens at the very spot where Kitty Genovese was murdered, Lindsay declared, "Something has gone out of the heart and soul of New York City." A Lindsay for Mayor television ad showed an image of a dark and desolate Central Park, with a voiceover proclaiming that "fear has entered the bloodstream of the city." The candidate's campaign literature was straightforward:

> No problem facing New York City and no issue in this
> campaign is more important than the problem of rising crime
> and the safety of our cities. . . . Every day New York City is a
> more dangerous place to live than the day before. . . . The fear
> which wracks our citizens today is the fear to walk the street
> and ride the subways. . . . It is fear that has made thousands and
> thousands of our citizens prisoners in their own city.

The other candidates shared Lindsay's view that crime and fear were the big issues. The conservative candidate, Buckley, made no bones about what he thought was at the root of the problem. "What is happening," he said, "or is about to happen—let's face it—is race war."

In March, Buckley kicked off his candidacy in a speech before six thousand Catholic policemen at the NYPD's Holy Name Communion Breakfast following mass at St. Patrick's Cathedral. In the speech, Buckley noted that the problem in the city and country was "a society in which order and values are disintegrating," adding, to great applause, that "the problem in New York City is too much crime, not too much police brutality." He even criticized media coverage of civil rights protests in Alabama for including images of police beating protesters with clubs, leading the *Herald Tribune* to headline its coverage of the speech "6,000 N.Y. Police Applaud a Defense of Selma Cops."

In stark contrast to Buckley, Breslin and Schaap sought to put the disturbing fact of crime in context, blaming much of what was happening on events in the South. "Every time a judge and jury [in the South] gets up from the grass and goes into court and lets a white man go because he shot a colored man, every time they make a mockery of justice in sleepy Haynesville [Alabama], we pay for it here in New York, where colored people seethe in their tenements and Puerto Ricans load up on junk, or wine, and then go out and steal for money."

Newspaper accounts of shootings, muggings, and rooftop rapes were used by political candidates to underscore their positions, whether it was for better conditions for the poor or for tougher police response. Throughout the spring and into summer, the mayoral campaign served as background noise to what was happening in the streets and in the courts, an overheated chorus in an overheated time.

As if on cue, a ten-second nightly public service message debuted on TV that seemed to feed the paranoia of the times. Over the local station's insignia, a disembodied voice announced: "It's ten o'clock. Do you know where your children are?"

Anywhere, parents hoped, but in the streets of the Savage City.

LIKE MOST COPS, Bill Phillips didn't care much for John Lindsay. To him, Lindsay was an effete liberal, a WASP blue blood who seemed eager to capitulate to the minorities. Everyone agreed that crime was out of control and fear was ruining life in the big city, but that's where the agreement ended. Most rank-and-file policemen believed that what was needed was more force, unfettered police action. There was a growing feeling among cops that civil libertarians were gaining the upper hand, that the police were being hamstrung by left-leaning politics and, in some cases, outright communist propaganda. According to this line of thinking, criminals no longer respected the dictates of law and order; they no longer feared the police.

The irony was that the use of physical force administered by police had not waned much in the ten years that Phillips had been on the job. As Phillips recalled:

> It was just part of the job: knock the shit out of a guy, kick him in the ass. You learn this as you're coming up the line. You see other people do it. . . . You find that the complete psychological interrogation doesn't work all the time and a few raps in the mouth really turns some people on.

It wasn't uncommon to walk into a squad room and see a perp strung up by handcuffs, bleeding profusely—a sight described by Phillips, Robert Leuci, and others who served during this era. As Phillips put it:

I've seen a guy brought in, cop fighter, handcuffed, hung up
in the squad room on one of those mesh cages. Then the
cops beat the shit out of him. They let him hang there all
day. . . . like Jesus Christ. Guys walk in, pow, kick him in the
balls, bust his fucking head. Unmerciful.

In his time with the TPF, Leuci encountered an almost identical
scene at the Forty-eighth Precinct station house in the South Bronx.
Walking into a squad room to get an arrest form, he came across a black
man who had been beaten and was hanging from a cage, "arms outstretched like Jesus Christ. Something had been put on the guy's head
that looked like a crown of thorns."

Leuci asked a detective, "What did this guy do?"

"Threw lye on a cop," said the detective. "You wanna take a few
licks?"

"No thanks," said Leuci. "I'm busy with some other stuff."

To many cops, Lindsay's talk of reform suggested that the NYPD's
fundamental way of doing business would be irrevocably changed if he
was elected. Methods that were deemed messy but necessary—methods
no layperson or liberal could ever hope to understand—would be out-
lawed, and the city would descend deeper into mayhem.

Bill Phillips would claim he had no special fondness for violence as a
tactic. "I mean, I'm not a merciful guy. If a guy comes at me to hurt me,
then I don't give a shit about him. No holds barred. I'll beat him within
an inch of his life. But once he's under arrest and he's in the house, it's all
over." Even so, Phillips would never have intervened in a police beating,
nor would he report it to supervisors. Being a cop meant keeping your
mouth shut.

It was also true that violence wasn't much help if your primary goal
on the job was to score. You couldn't really beat a person into giving you
money. It was far more effective to create a situation where a person was
relieved or even happy to fork it over. There was "the flake," the planting of evidence—that worked well, especially with innocent civilians.
With criminals, the best way to squeeze blood from a stone was to allow
them to operate, even *help* them to operate, and then exact a hefty tax in
return. That way everyone made out and had a vested interest in keeping
matters to themselves.

In Harlem in the summer of '65, numbers and gambling joints were the name of the game. But another racket, narcotics, showed signs of entering into another Golden Era. The war in Southeast Asia had opened up the heroin market: soldiers black and white were returning with the habit, and networks of cultivation, purchase, and distribution were being established. It was a whole new ball game.

Phillips's attitudes about taking pad money from dope were old-fashioned, but he could see that the unwritten rules about drug money were in the process of going out the window. The stakes were too damn high. In 1962, the NYPD, working with federal drug agents, scored a major bust in the "French Connection" case. The team of detectives involved in that case formed the core of a new elite narcotics squad known as the Special Investigations Unit (SIU). Almost from the start, SIU was dirty, pocketing money that dwarfed anything Bill Phillips was cobbling together from his various scores. On top of that, the dope that was confiscated in the French Connection case—dope that was stored in the NYPD's property room—was discovered to have been stolen as part of an inside job. Some believed that the dope was pilfered all at once, but Phillips suspected that detectives had lifted the dope piecemeal—kilo by kilo—over the course of many years. The street profits from this dope were likely in the hundreds of millions of dollars.

For some time, people in Harlem had complained that police in the black community were profiting from the distribution and sale of narcotics. Congressman Adam Clayton Powell Jr. first made this accusation on the floor of the U.S. House of Representatives in 1960. The flamboyant congressman charged that "the dregs of the police force" were assigned to his home district of Harlem, and that they gave "plenty of protection" to narcotics sellers, collecting as much as $3,000 a month from each narcotics "drop."

Powell named names, which got him into trouble. Along with identifying local dope peddlers such as Louie the Gimp, Slim Brown (nicknamed "Stoney"), a couple of characters named Buzz and Bikie, and many others, the congressman included the name of Esther James, who he claimed was a bagwoman for Harlem police. Esther James sued Powell for libel and was awarded a settlement of $210,000; instead of paying up, Powell skipped town, hiding out in the Bahamas.

In February 1965, the congressman was back in town. After giving another inflammatory speech from the House floor on police corruption in Harlem, he reported that his life had been threatened and turned the written threats over to the FBI.

Powell's hyperbolic nature and broad accusations made it possible for white folks to discount what he was saying. The NYPD's public affairs officer, Walter Arm, even called Powell a "liar" in the pages of the *New York Times.* But many in the Negro community believed that the congressman spoke the truth: dope, numbers, and other vice operators flourished in the ghetto under the aegis of cops on the take.

Public complaints about police corruption had come up before. In 1948, the department had been rocked by a corruption scandal involving a gambling pad in Brooklyn operated by a well-connected impresario named Harry Gross. Gross's operation made payments regularly to nearly every division in the borough, their payouts implicating public officials with ties to City Hall. The investigation led to more than one hundred arrests and convictions and eventually forced the resignation of Mayor William O'Dwyer, an Irishman from the Old Country.

Still, even crooked cops shared Bill Phillips's reservations about scoring off dope—a belief that would soon crumble as soaring drug profits led to irresistible temptation.

Like many policemen in Harlem, Bill Phillips did make money from the dope trade, though in a roundabout way. Phillips's connection was a local hustler named Freddy Clark, a brawny, dark-skinned Negro who ran a real estate office and luncheonette at 119th Street and Madison Avenue. The real estate business was a cover for Clark's real business, as a significant player in the Harlem heroin trade.

Phillips first met Clark shortly after being flopped back to uniform. At the luncheonette, Clark approached Phillips with a container of coffee in a brown paper bag. "Don't throw the bag away," said Clark. At the bottom of the bag was thirty dollars—fifteen for Phillips, fifteen for his partner. Clark asked for nothing in return; it was merely his investment in the police department. There were regular and larger payments to come.

> I go over to see Freddy for Christmas. He had a briefcase full
> of money, tens, twenties, fifties; could have been sixty, seventy
> thousand in it. I walk in and say, hello Freddy, I want to wish
> you a merry Christmas. Oh Bill, I got something for you.
> Takes three fifties out of his briefcase. That's for you. And
> here's a hundred and fifty for your partner. The word was out

on him, because the guys were lining up, everybody—cops, sergeants, lieutenants. They begin to call him Santa Claus. You seen Santy Claus? You bet your ass I seen Santy Claus.

Freddy Clark's investment in the NYPD proved to be a good move, because eventually he got arrested and charged with a triple homicide.

"Did you hear?" a cop said to Phillips one day. "Santy Claus is dead."

"Whaddya mean Santy Claus is dead?"

"Freddy's locked up for homicide."

"Holy shit," said Phillips. "There goes thirty dollars a month right down the drain."

The crime in question happened in an apartment on West 114th Street, where two brothers and a woman were gunned down execution-style while a baby screamed in the next room. After an underling of Clark's was arrested in connection with the murder, he told an assistant district attorney that he and Freddy had stormed the apartment and shot the men because they owed Freddy thirty thousand dollars. The woman, wife of one of the brothers and a potential witness, was collateral damage.

Freddy Clark knew that his alleged accomplice had turned informant. Even so, in a highly unusual move, the informant was placed in a cell with Freddy, the very person he had informed on. According to Phillips, the informant was visited in the cell by a black policeman named Charley Almanac, a good buddy of Clark's. Within days, the informant reneged on his confession. He wound up taking a plea and doing time for his role in the triple homicide; Freddy Clark served no time at all.

Clark had friends in the NYPD, and his connections paid off. To the citizens of Harlem who knew Freddy Clark was a dope dealer who paid off police on a regular basis, it was disgusting, but it was also business as usual. It was precisely the kind of relationship that Adam Clayton Powell had been railing about for years.

Bill Phillips had underworld connections like Freddy Clark. He was also constantly on the lookout for cops he could bring into the fold. Like most hustlers, he seemed to know everyone. He cultivated friends in high and low places.

Sonny Grosso was already something of a star detective in the mid-1960s when he was approached by Phillips. A cop since 1954, Grosso was the youngest first-grade detective in the history of the department at the time. He was assigned to an undercover narcotics unit in the late 1950s at a time when narcotics investigations were built on improvisation and instinct, since there was no precedent for the kind of dope epidemic then sweeping over the city. Grosso made hundreds—if not thousands—of busts and could have pocketed plenty of money and dope, or both, if he'd been so inclined.

It was perhaps inevitable that Phillips would eventually reach out to Grosso, who was becoming a legend in his own time. Grosso was revered for his role—along with partner Eddie Egan—in breaking the French Connection case, at the time the largest dope bust in the city's history. Street-smart and attuned to the rhythms of East Harlem, where he'd been raised by Italian immigrant parents, Grosso was familiar with swaggering Irish leatherheads like Phillips. His own partner, Egan, was notorious for his hyperaggressive manner, which sometimes rubbed people the wrong way. Phillips was known to Grosso—and just about every other detective in Harlem—as a former detective who'd been flopped back on the street, and as a uniformed cop with an inflated sense of entitlement. "He came to me and said he had a score set up where I could make $50 a month," recalled Grosso years later. "I told him to take a hike."

To a highly decorated detective like Grosso, Phillips was a bottom-feeder, a low-level hustler. To others, he was a more complicated figure.

"Phillips was a good cop," remembered Edwin Torres, another child of El Barrio in East Harlem, who would become the city's first Puerto Rican assistant D.A. in 1959, and later a criminal defense attorney and a legendary state supreme court justice.

Torres was a defense attorney in private practice when he first encountered Phillips in the mid-1960s. "He was tough," said Torres. "He talked like a cop from another era. He wasn't afraid to mix it up on the street."

Torres remembered a time when a client of his had been arrested on a drug charge. Phillips was the arresting officer. "He came to me the day of the trial. He told me he felt bad because he had flaked [planted evidence against] my client. He came right out and told me that, which was unusual. He even suggested that if I questioned my client on the stand in a certain way, he would be found not guilty. He gave me information that made it possible for me to establish that my client was innocent, even though he was the guy who arrested him."

Eddie Torres went on to become a famous figure in the city's criminal justice system—a judge and an author of crime novels that were made into movies—but he always remembered that incident with Phillips. In time, while many of the city's top cops, politicians, journalists, and average citizens would come to see Phillips as a poster child for police corruption, Torres always figured that, somewhere deep inside, he was a dirty cop with a conscience.

Eventually, that question—whether or not Bill Phillips had a conscience—would become a matter of public debate, with results that would rock the NYPD and the city.

AT THE ANTIOCH Baptist Church in Bedford-Stuyvesant, the Brooklyn chapter of the NAACP held a fund-raising breakfast for Whitmore. The headliner was comedian and activist Dick Gregory, author of a newly published memoir entitled *Nigger*. Gregory had arrived in New York fresh from the civil rights marches and protests in the South, where he had been clubbed by police, arrested, and held overnight in jail. Gregory's presence in Brooklyn was a sign that the civil rights movement was shifting its priorities north, from the rural backwaters of the Delta to the concrete jungles of the northern industrial cities.

Flanked by Whitmore's mother; the lawyers Stanley Reiben, Arthur Miller, and Edwin Kaplan; and a phalanx of NAACP dignitaries including Brooklyn chapter president Ray Williams, Gregory addressed an audience of more than two hundred people. "After reading about the Whitmore case," he said, "I decided there are things going on in this town that they wouldn't do to a dog in Mississippi."

Ever since it was revealed that the NYPD had indicted a new perpetrator for the Wylie-Hoffert killings, the NAACP had been calling attention to the Whitmore case and a series of other recent prosecutions of young Negro men, all involving spurious "confessions" elicited by Detective Edward Bulger. Among the men were David Coleman, who was on death row, and a defendant named Charles Everett, who had been tricked into signing a confession after detectives told him that a man he'd allegedly beaten was in an adjoining squad room. If Everett confessed, said the detectives, they would intercede with the victim to work out a light sentence. Only after Everett confessed did he learn that the victim was dead. The Second Circuit Court of Appeals reversed Everett's murder conviction on the grounds that the confession had been obtained by fraud—and yet he had since been reindicted by the Brooklyn D.A.

In his Antioch Baptist speech, Gregory used wit to soften what was actually a stern challenge to his audience. He attacked what he saw as northern Negroes' "indifference" toward the civil rights struggle. "Wake up!" he commanded repeatedly. "Don't blame the white folks. Blame yourselves." Using the previous summer's Harlem and Brooklyn riots as a point of reference, he added, "If you don't know your own power, it was demonstrated last summer. . . . Last summer proved that if you want yours, you better go out and get it."

After the breakfast, the NAACP issued a statement to the press. "The police have apparently for over a number of years, in order to get at the guilty or persons that they suspect of being guilty, been allowed by society to use apparent inhumane means . . . such as implanting in the mind of the suspect facts and circumstances of the crime. This seems a crime and ought to be penally dealt with." Among other things, the NAACP demanded that the circumstances of the Whitmore "confession" be investigated by a criminal justice panel appointed by the governor, and that the charges against Whitmore be immediately dismissed.

Though the NAACP's efforts garnered some coverage in the press, Whitmore's predicament did not change. Even the indictment of another perpetrator seemed insufficient to persuade Manhattan D.A. Frank Hogan to drop the charges against Whitmore anytime soon. To George's attorney, Stanley Reiben, Hogan's indifference was unconscionable. Reiben insisted to reporters that Hogan was leaving the Wylie-Hoffert charges hanging over Whitmore's head for one reason—so that his alleged role in the Career Girls Murders would influence Whitmore's prosecution on the other criminal charges he faced.

Meanwhile, Whitmore languished in prison. From inside his cell at Sing Sing, he was barely aware of the efforts being waged on his behalf. He had stopped reading newspaper accounts of his case, tired of seeing himself referred to as a "simpleton," a "loner," a predatory Negro with an IQ of ninety-one that supposedly categorized him as borderline retarded. He was sick of speculation that he would be fried in the electric chair, or gassed to death by the state, or sentenced to eternal incarceration.

As he waited for updates on his case from the lawyers, Whitmore's main source of refuge was his talent for drawing. When he was sixteen, an instructor at Wildwood High School had arranged for him to take a correspondence course in cartoon illustration at a branch of the Walt Disney School in Philadelphia. He had passed the exam with flying colors. The Disney School sent a shipment of free art supplies—an easel, brushes, paints, and crayons—to his junkyard home in Wildwood. When the supplies arrived, though, George's father wouldn't let the delivery men unload the truck. "Forget this nonsense," he said. "How you ever gonna make a livin' from this nonsense?" He fired a gun in the air to frighten the men away, then set the dogs on them.

After the truck drove away, George cried for days. "I guess my daddy didn't want me to have the success he never did," he remembered years later. "I never could forgive him for that."

Though his dreams of becoming an artist had been dashed, George still found pleasure in the act; sometimes he even profited from his abilities. In the weeks after the assassination of Malcolm X, Whitmore made money painting portraits of the black leader—based on a photo in the *New York Post*—and selling them for $20 apiece to Muslim inmates. Later, Whitmore made money doing portraits of inmates. He used some of the proceeds to buy art supplies, mailed to him at Sing Sing by inmates' friends and family members, and sent some of the money to his mother.

George had few visitors—Sing Sing was a long way from Wildwood or Brooklyn—but he was rarely in a mood to see people anyway. Conversations always focused on his case, which only depressed him. He usually used his daily phone call to call his attorney, hoping for good news.

In early March 1965, Whitmore was loaded onto a Department of Corrections bus and transferred back to the Brooklyn House of Detention. The following day he was dressed in nice clothes, delivered to the jail by his mother, and brought to the same courtroom where he'd been tried and found guilty for the attempted rape and assault of Elba Borrero. He was there for what his lawyers called a "hearing." George wasn't sure how a hearing differed from an actual trial, but the lawyers said it was important. George was apprehensive until he heard that he wouldn't have to testify, or do much of anything but listen.

The hearing had been requested by Judge David Malbin after Whitmore's attorneys sent him a memo claiming that various improprieties, if not illegalities, had occurred during the trial. The memo included an affidavit signed by Gerald Corbin, juror number seven at the Borrero trial, which confirmed claims of racial discrimination among the jury. The charges were disturbing enough that Malbin granted a public hearing.

Over two days, Stanley Reiben presented affidavits and signed statements supporting his claims of irregularity in Whitmore's prosecution. He also revealed, for the first time in a public forum, that the prosecution had failed to reveal an FBI lab report concluding that threads from the button presented as evidence by Assistant D.A. Sidney Lichtman did not match the threads on Whitmore's coat.

A series of jurors who had voted to find Whitmore guilty were questioned by the judge. One juror was asked by Malbin, "Did I understand you to say that you did make the statement about 'this is nothing compared to what he will get in New York'?"

"I said, 'He is a lucky boy in my opinion.'"

"Why was he a lucky boy?"

"Just my opinion."

"This was after he was found guilty?"

"That's right."

"He would have been unlucky if he were acquitted?"

"I don't know. At that time there were two murder raps going after him."

"Did you know about the Wylie-Hoffert murders in New York, sir, at the time he was tried?"

"Yes. Sir."

"Did you know about the Edmonds murder charge in Brooklyn?"

"Yes, sir."

"And you knew that he had confessed to the Wylie-Hoffert murders?"

"That's right."

Malbin asked another juror when he had made the remark "This is nothing compared to what he'll be getting in New York."

"That was during the deliberations," said the juror.

Gerald Corbin was called to the stand. When, he was asked, had he heard another juror say, "You know how these people are. They have to have their sex, so they screw like jackrabbits."

"During the trial," Corbin said.

After considering the testimony, Judge Malbin delivered a statement: "Sufficient cause has been shown to raise grave doubt whether the accused received a fair and impartial trial. . . . Prejudice and racial bias, in any of its ugly forms, has no place in an American court of justice. Deprivation of the absolute right of the accused to a fair and impartial trial reduces the process of a law to a mere sham. It destroys the hope of fundamental fairness and undermines the constitutional provisions of the Fourteenth Amendment."

Malbin then moved on to the issue of the button. Assistant D.A. Lichtman was called to the stand and asked, "Mister Lichtman, did you receive this report from the FBI in writing prior to the trial of George Whitmore?"

"I did."

"Did you submit the report in evidence during the trial?"

"I did not."

"Why, Mister Lichtman?"

"My understanding of the rules of evidence indicates that a report is not evidence. . . . Secondly . . . the report contains the expert conclusion that 'It was not possible to determine whether the button had been attached to the coat.' In view of that conclusion, it was my judgment that this report was probative of nothing." In other words, the prosecutor seemed to be saying, the report was only relevant as evidence if it confirmed his theory that the button was a match. The colloquy continued:

Judge: Although the report itself might not have been the best evidence, you could have brought from Washington, from the laboratory, whoever made the analysis, couldn't you, to testify?

Lichtman: His testimony as such would have been probative of nothing.

Judge: You say in your judgment you felt it was not worthwhile to introduce either the report or the analyst himself into evidence?

Lichtman: I said I felt in view of the conclusion . . . the conclusion indicates that the expert could not say one way or the other whether the button did or did not come from the coat.

Judge: Don't you think that the reporter or the analyst, this evidence contained in the report, should have been submitted to a jury so that they could determine?

Lichtman: I do not.

Judge: You did receive an expert opinion, didn't you, sir, as to whether the threads matched?

Lichtman: Yes, I received expert opinions that said that the threads on the button did not match the threads on the coat.

The hearing received minimal press coverage. Two weeks after it was over, on March 19, Judge Malbin delivered his ruling: "The hearing revealed that prejudice and racial bias invaded the jury room. Bigotry in any of its sinister forms is reprehensible; it must be crushed, never to rise again. It has no place in an American court of justice." As for the FBI lab report, the judge noted that although he found no "deliberate and willful suppression of any material evidence . . . the nondisclosure of this evidence to the defendant was a violation of an obligation on the part of the prosecutor, and the failure to reveal information that may be usable by an accused may be a denial of that fairness that is required under the due process clause of the constitution. . . . Therefore, the court concludes that the conviction cannot stand."

The Borrero conviction was thrown out. But Whitmore's defense team had little time to celebrate. For one thing, the very next day Brooklyn D.A. Aaron Koota announced that his office would retry Whitmore for the same charge. Even more pressing, the Minnie Edmonds murder trial was scheduled to take place in exactly one week—in the same courthouse, and with the same prosecutor, Sid Lichtman.

In that case, Whitmore was facing the death penalty.

eight

FATHERS AND SONS

THE NATIONAL ASSOCIATION for the Advancement of Colored People was a proud organization. When it was founded in 1909, by W. E. B. Du Bois among others, segregation was the law of the land. In the southern states, racist Jim Crow statutes were brutally enforced by the Ku Klux Klan, a clandestine organization that counted many law enforcement officials and civic government representatives among its members. There was no Klan or Jim Crow laws in the North, but there was still segregation, most notably in areas of housing, education, and employment. Northern whites could hang with blacks at jazz clubs and the ballpark, and segregated restrooms and water fountains were technically illegal (though they did exist), but the white population had little interest in issues of racial equality and fairness in most aspects of city life. The NAACP set about trying to change social mores by addressing the institutional nature of racism throughout the United States.

The NAACP's first official gathering took place in New York, at the Henry Street Settlement House in lower Manhattan. At the meeting, attended by forty people—some of them white—the group ratified a charter that delineated its mission:

> To promote equality of rights and to eradicate caste or race prejudice among the citizens of the United States; to advance the interest of colored citizens; to secure for them impartial

suffrage; and to increase their opportunities for securing justice in the courts, education for the children, employment according to their ability and complete equality before the law.

As the organization grew in size and stature, it developed a specific focus on legal issues as they played out in the courts. The NAACP was always something of a bourgeois organization; it had wealthy donors, undeniable social stature, and the power to influence public opinion—as in 1915, when it organized a nationwide protest against D. W. Griffith's racist epic *The Birth of a Nation*. The organization's ability to provide pro bono legal assistance was a lifeline for generations of Negroes caught in the country's institutionalized racial caste system. The NAACP was especially active in decrying the lynching of blacks throughout the United States by working for legislation, lobbying in Congress, and educating the masses.

By the early 1960s, the NAACP had more than fifty branches and close to ten thousand members, but signs of fissure had begun to appear within its ranks. The organization had long excelled at issues of legal advocacy and political lobbying, but in the late 1950s it was outstripped by a more activist movement devoted to the principles of direct action. Throughout the early civil rights era, NAACP leaders at the national and local levels had criticized Martin Luther King and his Southern Christian Leadership Conference for engaging in direct conflict with the police. The rift seemed to be generational as much as tactical: as the civil rights movement heated up in the 1960s, the NAACP risked being viewed as old-fashioned and out of touch.

In New York, the organization often clashed with CORE and other civil rights groups that had a younger membership and seemed to be moving toward a more vocal and rambunctious approach. It would take a few years for the fault lines to be clearly defined, but one thing was apparent: blacks looking to get involved in the civil rights movement would have many more organizations and points of view to choose from than they had only a few years earlier.

And yet, when it came to calling public attention to an issue—or to providing free legal assistance to victims of injustice—no Negro rights group was more formidable than the NAACP.

At the local level, the NAACP had been slow to rally around the Whitmore case. In part, the organization had hesitated because of the heinous nature of the Wylie-Hoffert murders: the media attention sur-rounding the killings, along with Whitmore's portrayal as a "drifter" and "loner," had created a broad sense that he was probably guilty of something. Even if his connection to the Wylie-Hoffert murders had been cooked up by detectives—as a discerning observer might have surmised—he'd "confessed" to two other major felonies, including the murder of a black woman.

Only after Ricky Robles was indicted for the Wylie-Hoffert kill-ings did the NAACP take an active interest in George Whitmore's case. Ray Williams and Norman Johnson, an attorney with the organization's Legal Redress Committee, asked to sit in as part of Whitmore's defense "as observers to determine whether the rights of the defendant were in any way impaired because he is a Negro."

Whitmore needed all the help he could get. His upcoming trial for the murder of Minnie Edmonds was deadly serious; if convicted, he'd be headed for a date with Old Sparky.

For weeks before the trial, the NAACP lawyers and the rest of Whitmore's defense team had been trying to pressure the Manhattan D.A.'s office to drop the Wylie-Hoffert murder charge. It seemed to defy logic, not to mention the dictates of fairness, for the D.A. to leave these charges hanging over Whitmore's head after announcing pub-licly that another suspect had been indicted for the murders—especially when Whitmore had another murder trial pending. If the Borrero jury knew that Whitmore had been charged with the notorious Career Girls Murders, surely the Edmonds jury would too. How could he possibly get a fair trial?

The behavior of D.A.s Hogan and Koota and the other prosecu-tors involved in Whitmore's legal travails was telling. Although the lead prosecutors remained intransigent, a few anonymous sources within the D.A.'s office had begun to voice doubts. Despite an in-house memo from Hogan warning that anyone caught talking to the press about the Whitmore case would be fired, one assistant D.A. told a *Times* reporter, "I am positive that the police prepared the confession for Whitmore. . . . I am also sure that the police were the ones who gave Whitmore all the details of the killings that he recited to our office." Another assistant D.A. said, "Call it what you want—brain-washing, hypnosis, fright. They made him give an untrue confession. The only thing I don't believe is that Whitmore was beaten." This unnamed source added, "If this had not been a celebrated case; if this hadn't got the tremendous publicity; if this is what we so-called professionals call a run-of-the-mill murder, Whitmore might well have been slipped into the electric chair and killed for something he didn't do."

Yet none of these prosecutors would give his name or be quoted on the record, for fear of retribution—a fact that spoke volumes about the dark cloud hanging over the case. A Negro kid had been indicted on trumped-up charges, in a way that implicated not only the cops who elicited the false confession, but also the assistant district attorneys who took down his statement; D.A.s Hogan and Koota; the other government litigators currently presiding over the defendant's slow torture by prosecution; and the press, who had initially swallowed it all mostly without question. The entire system of criminal justice was implicated in the railroading of George Whitmore.

THE MINNIE EDMONDS trial was similarly problematic. Edmonds, a forty-six-year-old Negro washerwoman, was last seen alive around 2:00 A.M. on April 14, 1964, when she left a tavern near her home in Brownsville. Her body was found stabbed and beaten, her clothes torn and disheveled, in a pool of blood just after dawn that morning in a tenement yard on Chester Street, just a block from where Elba Borrero was attacked ten days later. The cause of death was multiple stab wounds in the face, chest, and heart. At the time the body was discovered, the murder of Minnie Edmonds merited not one column inch in the city's seven daily newspapers.

The case against Whitmore for the murder was weak, almost non-existent. The Brooklyn D.A.'s office contended that Whitmore had accosted Edmonds on her way home from the tavern, chasing her into an alleyway much like the one where Elba Borrero was assaulted. There Whitmore allegedly tried to rape the woman and brutally murdered her when she resisted. There were no witnesses, no circumstantial evidence linking Whitmore to the crime. All the prosecutors had was Whitmore's confession.

Realizing that the validity of Whitmore's signed statement would come under scrutiny, D.A. Koota made a public show of launching an investigation into the circumstances surrounding the confession. His four-man team of investigators consisted of Assistant D.A. Lichtman, a Negro investigator from the D.A.'s office, and the two detectives who elicited the confession in the first place, Aidala and Di Prima. When asked by a reporter why the D.A.'s office would choose as investigators two detectives with a vested interest in upholding the confession, Lichtman said, "These two fellows were the lead investigators on the case. They were familiar with the leads and the area, particularly Dick Aidala. . . . I didn't even think of taking anybody else."

Lichtman's boss, Aaron Koota, concurred, adding in a separate interview: "Suppose [we] brought in other police officers and they found evidence to attack Di Prima and Aidala. Do you think they would have told us?"

It was an astounding statement: the most powerful criminal justice official in the borough was justifying the use of the two least objective detectives he could find because they were the only ones he could trust.

The Edmonds murder trial kicked off in Brooklyn Supreme Court, in a room down the hall from where the Borrero trial had taken place six months earlier. This trial began with a monthlong hearing—known as a Huntley hearing—in which Whitmore's defense team sought once more to have the so-called confession declared inadmissible. One by one, the detectives took the stand and laid it all out, this time for Justice Dominic Rinaldi.

At the witness table, flanked by his attorneys, Whitmore listened as the policemen came forward and told lie after lie. He had heard it all before, but with each court proceeding and each telling of the tale Whitmore developed a more pronounced sense of vertigo, a deeper feeling of descending into the rabbit hole. He remained without rancor, believing that some horrible mistake was being made, that he would one day wake up and it would all be over. But each day the earth gave way beneath his feet, and he felt his life slipping away.

Midway through the hearing, on a Thursday afternoon, a sudden groaning sound came from the spectators' gallery in the courtroom. George turned from his seat at the defendant's table to see his father collapse into his mother's arms. George Whitmore Sr. was taken from the courtroom, given air from an oxygen tank, and rushed to the hospital. The trial was postponed until the following Monday.

Their difficult relationship didn't mitigate Whitmore's concern for his father, who had suffered a heart attack. George asked himself: *What curse has befallen me that I stand falsely accused, publicly tarred and feathered, and now those nearest to me are struck down by a sudden affliction, as if by the Hand of God?*

It was another lost weekend for George, who languished in his cell at the Brooklyn House of Detention waiting to hear whether his travails had contributed to his father's death.

Whitmore Sr. recovered and was out of the hospital by Monday, but he never returned to the courtroom.

The Hundley hearing ended badly. Supreme Court Justice Dominic Rinaldi declared that Whitmore had "confessed of his own accord, without coercion by the police." His confession would stand.

"Judge," protested Stanley Reiben, "my client is doomed by this decision."

In the trial that followed, Whitmore himself took the stand. This time, he was more presentable; his new horn-rimmed glasses gave him an almost scholarly appearance. After twelve months of interrogations, depositions, incarceration, trials, hearings, and an endless recital of names, dates, times, and other details, however, Whitmore was like a punch-drunk fighter. He wanted to do well, to please his lawyers, but the process had worn him down.

"Mister Whitmore, do you recognize the man standing in front of you?" Assistant D.A. Lichtman had become Whitmore's Grand Inquisitor, a voice almost as familiar as that of his own attorney.

George looked at the man standing nearby: *a detective, probably. White man. No friend of mine.* But George couldn't be sure. "No," he said.

"Did you see him in the station house?" the judge interjected.

George looked at the man again. "Not that I recollect."

"Did he ask you any questions about Wylie-Hoffert?"

"No, sir. . . . He may have come into the room, because there were people coming in and out of the room all the time."

Even Whitmore's attorneys were startled. The man standing in front of George was Detective Eddie Bulger, the very person who had so carefully tied him to the Wylie-Hoffert murders. The jury already knew that Bulger had been among the detectives who interrogated Whitmore; they knew he had been in the squad room. Detective Di Prima testified that Bulger helped Whitmore draw a diagram of the murder scene. To George, however, Bulger was just another face among the swirl of faces that had come in and out of the squad room. His inability to identify Bulger did not help his credibility as a witness.

In questioning his client on redirect, Reiben sought to salvage Whitmore's testimony by keeping it simple. "George, did you kill Mrs. Minnie Edmonds?"

"No, sir."

"Do you know anything about it?"

"No, sir."

"Have you ever killed anybody, George?"

"No, sir."

In his final summation, Prosecutor Lichtman stood before the all-male Blue Ribbon jury of eleven whites and one Negro. The concept of the Blue Ribbon jury—one chosen on the basis of superior education and community standing—was a holdover from earlier in the century. Knowing that the jury members came from backgrounds far removed from the world of George Whitmore, Lichtman zeroed in on differences between the friends and relatives who had testified on Whitmore's behalf and the "upstanding" collection of public servants who took the stand on behalf of the prosecution.

"Now, gentlemen," offered Lichtman, "you observed Detective Joseph Di Prima as he testified. . . . Can you conceive of a more sincere and a more forthright and a more genuinely direct witness than Joe Di Prima on that stand? I ask you, didn't he fairly exude character? Didn't he fairly exude, yes, even a fatherly-type sensitivity, somewhat of a compassion, almost a sense of regret as he sat there . . . telling you the truth? . . . What under the name of heaven could possibly impel father, grandfather, and husband Joseph Di Prima to lie this defendant into a Murder One conviction? The only evidence you might even consider would be the testimony of this admitted would-be rapist killer who sat on the stand. . . . I ask you to match your observations of the detective [and] of this defendant. Match your observations of George Whitmore, sitting on the stand . . . with your observations, your mental picture of Detective Di Prima."

Lichtman harped on these perceived class distinctions shamelessly. Of Beverly Payne, he said, "George Whitmore's girlfriend, who is pregnant with another man, has a baby with another man. She lied." After a young woman named Mary Goodwin, Whitmore's cousin, testified that Detective Aidala cursed her for lack of cooperation—and that another detective, a Negro detective working for the D.A.'s office, called her "a goddamned nigger"—Lichtman dismissed her, even getting her name wrong: "Oh, Betty Goodman [*sic*], what can I say about Betty Goodman? With a different child out of a different stallion almost every year. . . . You size her up."

If race could not be used openly to hang Whitmore, class prejudice could.

"You are not going to succumb to any thought . . . that this is a civil rights struggle in this courtroom," said the prosecutor. "This is a struggle for justice in the American way."

To Lichtman, it was a simple case of good versus evil, public service versus the ghetto, but he could not hide the fact that his entire case was riding on one thing: the confession.

"Confessions have been used as a weapon, a threat, as torture, and as punishment from the first day of man," said Stanley Reiben during his summation. Like most attorneys, Reiben had strengths and weaknesses. He was thought to be average on research and attention to detail but excellent at courtroom oratory. He was particularly good at casting reasonable doubt on criminal charges by framing them in an expansive and sometimes breathtaking way.

"[Confessions] have been used by the Romans against the early Christians. They have been used in the Spanish Inquisition; they have been used in the Salem witch trials; they have been used in Nazi Germany; they have been used in Russia, in Communist China; and they are still to this day the greatest weapon to get a man to turn . . . and not all of them were voluntary. That is the only thing that the people, Mister Lichtman, the prosecutor, is presenting to you, nothing else, not a shred, not a speck, not an iota of corroboration. . . . We must beware of the law being used as a weapon by those whose sworn duty it is to enforce the laws fairly and impartially, without fear or favor, rich or poor, black or white. . . . I would like to remind you that you promised me, and that's all I ask, that you would treat this defendant as you would want to be treated. Someone else said it much better, much more simply, and much more lovingly, and I am going to ask that you please do unto George Whitmore as you would have others do unto you."

The jury began their deliberations. As the foreman later explained it, "The arguments were very bitter. The jurors never knew that the Wylie-Hoffert case was discredited. We knew that somebody else had been indicted for the murders. We assumed this guy was a partner of

Whitmore. An accomplice. We thought Robles and Whitmore were in it together."

The jury deliberated for two days, but they were hopelessly deadlocked, with a vote of ten to two in favor of acquittal. The result was a hung jury, and no resolution for George Whitmore.

Three days after the trial was over, Manhattan D.A. Hogan finally dismissed the Wylie-Hoffert charges against Whitmore. The New York Civil Liberties Union issued a statement criticizing Hogan for not dismissing the indictment before the Edmonds murder trial: "It is apparent that the only plausible reason for Mister Hogan's inaction was to aid a fellow prosecutor—Brooklyn D.A. Aaron Koota—to convict Whitmore in the Edmonds case. We expect more of our public servants."

Whitmore first heard that the Career Girls charges against him were being dropped while he was washing dishes at the Brooklyn House of Detention. Given the circumstances, the news was anticlimactic. The Brooklyn D.A. had not yet announced whether or not they were going to retry George for the Edmonds murder. His ongoing nightmare was far from over.

PRISON CAN BE a state of mind. The walls close in, the day is regimented by force of arms, dreams wither and die. A convict can be crushed by the institutionalized monotony, whether the sentence is one year or twenty. And then there are the bars. As Malcolm X expressed it in his autobiography, "Any person who claims to have deep feelings for other human beings should think a long, long time before he votes to have other men kept behind bars—caged. I am not saying there shouldn't be prisons. But there shouldn't be bars. Behind bars, a man never reforms. He will never forget. He never will get completely over the memory of the bars."

Dhoruba Bin Wahad had been behind bars for four years, and in that time he had received exactly one visitor—his mother, who came to see him at Coxsackie. The Department of Corrections made it so difficult and costly for a person of limited means to navigate the prison bureaucracy and get to the facility that visits were rare to nonexistent. While Dhoruba was behind bars, his past and future disappeared; there was only the present, a world of cement walls, cold floors, Caucasian authority, and chain-link fences topped with barbed wire.

It was not part of Dhoruba's makeup to see himself as a victim. Therefore, his time in prison was sometimes contentious. He fought with guards, stood up to the authorities, and showed little contrition when called before the parole board. Though his extensive reading in prison had raised his consciousness, the gang mentality was just as present in prison as it was on the streets of the Southeast Bronx. At Comstock, Dhoruba took part in a yard-gang rumble that got him thrown in the Box for an extended period. In late 1965, the prison administration decided to transfer him to a maximum-security facility. Dhoruba was inching closer to completing his five-year bit, but he was also sinking deeper and deeper into the system.

Green Haven Correctional Facility is located near the town of Poughkeepsie, eighty miles north of New York City, not far from the New York–Connecticut border. Dhoruba was initially housed in the orientation compound, a kind of quarantine for new inmates. After a month, he was released into general population. He had been circulating among the other convicts for less than a week when a guard told him, "Hey, there's somebody in the yard who wants to see you."

It was a gray and drizzling day. When Dhoruba went out to the yard, he saw a man huddled under an awning to stay out of the rain. The man was his father.

Dhoruba had never had any real relationship with the man who had brought him into the world—though back when he was still little Richard Moore that had never seemed like a major issue. Collins Moore, known to his friends and associates as Cokey, was a bona fide street character, a neighborhood fixture Dhoruba referred to as a "slickster." Out on the street, his hair was conked, and he wore the zoot suits of his youth. He was a talented dancer, popular with the ladies. But he was also a heroin addict whose habit diminished his status in the underworld, making him more of a street hustler than a full-fledged player.

Pops Moore was only in his midforties when Dhoruba found him in the prison yard, but he seemed withered. The father looked at the son and blinked; it took him a moment to recognize his own blood. Dhoruba remembered:

The meeting was kind of routine. That's the odd part about these abnormal encounters; they can sometime seem mundane. We just started talking about simple stuff, like what did you get busted for, when are you getting out, et cetera. I believe he was in there for boosting, probably to support his habit. Eventually the conversation swung over to family matters, my grandfather, cousins, and all that.

In childhood, Dhoruba's view of his father had been colored by the constant negative comments made about him by his mother's family. "That man is no good," his aunts and grandparents would say whenever the name of Collins Moore was mentioned. As a boy, Dhoruba sometimes saw his father working the streets or coming out of a bar, a shadowy figure with a bebop strut. Young Dhoruba wanted to approach the man and ask, "Pops, why they talk so bad about you?" But he was just a kid, without the courage to approach this unfamiliar street hustler they said was his father.

Dhoruba didn't bring it up now, either. It was Cokey Moore who broached the subject with his son. "You a young man now," he told Dhoruba. "So let me explain why I wasn't around much when you was little."

Over the course of three days in the prison yard at Green Haven, Old Man Moore told Dhoruba how he met his mother in Harlem. The mother's family were hardworking immigrants, "old-school West Indians, very clannish and family oriented." Moore was from Georgia, the southern slave tradition, with its legacy of bullwhips, lynching, and familial decimation. To the mother's family, Moore was a lazy malcontent with the heart of a hustler. "They never could accept me," he told Dhoruba.

The breaking point came in 1944, right around the time Dhoruba was born, when Collins Moore decided to join the army. He was motivated in part by a desire to show his wife's family that he could be somebody. The wife's family came from a military tradition: her father had been a merchant marine and her brother—Dhoruba's uncle—had been a war hero who died in combat during a rescue mission. The uncle's death had been a touchstone event in the family history; a plaque commemorating his service and death during the Second World War was on a wall in the house. It was one of the reasons Dhoruba had joined the service.

In 1945, however, Collins Moore went AWOL. To his wife's family this was a disgrace to the memory of Dhoruba's heroic uncle, and it was one of the factors that led to his separation from Dhoruba's mother.

From that point on, they acted as if Collins Moore had never existed—except when they wanted to curse his name.

Hearing this side of the story for the first time, Dhoruba felt an unexpected emotional connection with his father. The surroundings only added to the sense of intimacy: it took a prison encounter for Dhoruba to learn his family's secrets, the undercurrents that had shaped his African American family and set him off on his own rebellious course.

"I'm glad you told me," Dhoruba said to his father. "I never knew the whole story."

"Well, now you know," said Pops.

Their time together was brief. Three days after Dhoruba first met Collins Moore in the yard at Green Haven, he got into an altercation in the mess hall. It wasn't a serious incident—there weren't even any punches thrown—but Dhoruba's disciplinary record was so bad that any small event was enough to get him hauled off to the Box. He would spend the remainder of his sentence there in isolation, with no library, limited rec time, and only one hour a day outside the unit. He was a twenty-year-old male entering into manhood, a manchild serving out his time as ward of the state. He would spend the remainder of his sentence fixating on one thing: his release date.

GEORGE WHITMORE WAS also in prison. Since his last legal proceeding he'd been housed at the Brooklyn House of Detention, with easy access to the courts. That was the cycle that defined his weekly routine: prison to court, court to prison. Like Dhoruba Bin Wahad, Whitmore found himself surrounded by mostly African American inmates and white guards, escorted from one institution to another by court officers and armed marshals, handcuffed, searched, told to "sit right there" or "stand right there" until further notice. Unlike Dhoruba, though, George had no release date to look forward to. Not even his lawyers knew for sure how his future would play out. He was told not to lose hope, which was, of course, the battle cry of the era. Martin Luther King Jr. and other civil rights leaders implored their followers to "keep hope alive." Hope had become the placebo of an entire generation.

In the public arena, Whitmore's case had become a potent symbol of injustice. In May 1965, as the New York State Senate legislators prepared to vote on whether to abolish the death penalty, one legislator declared: "This is the year of Whitmore."

Bertram L. Podell, the Brooklyn assemblyman and attorney who spearheaded the initiative to outlaw capital punishment, used the Whitmore case as Exhibit A. In introducing the bill, he told his fellow senators: "A sixty-one page, completely detailed confession was manufactured and force-fed to Whitmore. On the basis of this confession, this defendant not only could have been, but probably would have been executed. I don't have to highlight the terrible effect Whitmore's execution would have had if the falsity of his confession and the tactics used in securing it had come out *after* the switch had been pulled, instead of before."

It was a watershed in the history of capital punishment in New York. State legislators had introduced legislation to do away with the death penalty ever since it was introduced in 1948, but every year the bills had failed. With the story of George Whitmore in the ether, though, the State Senate dramatically reversed its position, voting 47–9 to eradicate capital punishment in New York. In June, the bill was signed into law by Governor Nelson Rockefeller.

In another bill, legislators challenged the state's practice of employing well-heeled Blue Ribbon juries, which tended to find against impoverished defendants. Using the Minnie Edmonds murder trial as an example, proponents of the bill argued that Blue Ribbon juries "perpetuate a systematic exclusion of women, Puerto Ricans and Negroes . . . thereby making it a near-mathematical certainty that a defendant would be tried by a lily-white, all male jury." The bill was approved later that year, and Blue Ribbon juries became a thing of the past.

The Whitmore case was like a virus that had entered the system through the usual channels but could not be easily expunged. Whitmore now had advocates who were altering the way he was perceived by the general public. The young man scorned as a "nineteen-year-old pimple-faced hoodlum" a year and a half before was now "the most celebrated wrong man in the history of the city," according to the *Herald Tribune*. For groups like the NAACP, CORE, the American Civil Liberties Union (ACLU), and others, Whitmore was a cause célèbre, routinely cited in the press as a symbol of injustice. The newspapers, some of which had helped to frame Whitmore in the eyes of the public, took up his case on the editorial pages. When the NYPD announced it was launching an

investigation into the circumstances surrounding the Whitmore confession, the *New York Times* asked, "Can the police be relied on to investigate alleged misconduct by their own department?" It was a fair and
logical question, but also a revolutionary one: at the time it was unheard
of for a newspaper to challenge the authority of the police.

BY THE FALL of 1965, the prosecution of Ricky Robles for the Career Girls
Murders returned George Whitmore to the front pages. Among other
things, the trial promised to be a referendum on police practices in New
York City. The city's bad cops had elicited a wrongful confession from
the wrong man; its good cops had stepped in to correct their work and
nail the true killer. The Wylie-Hoffert murder trial had been years in
the making; it captured national attention and riveted New Yorkers with
all the drama of a public tribunal.

The man on trial in that fall of 1965 was Ricky Robles, but the figure
at the center of the storm was George Whitmore. For the Manhattan
D.A.'s office to prove that Robles was the man who had murdered
Janice Wylie and Emily Hoffert, they would also have to show that the
Whitmore confession was erroneous. This meant that Whitmore himself would be called to the witness stand in yet another trial—this time
for the prosecution. This was a complete reversal for George: in this
case the Manhattan D.A. was his friend, the man who would show that
his Brooklyn confession, at least with regard to the Wylie-Hoffert murders, was not to be believed. The defense attorney, on the other hand,
had a vested interest in giving the impression that the Whitmore confession was accurate, that Whitmore and not his client, Ricky Robles, had
committed the killings.

In anticipation of the trial, George was moved from the Brooklyn
House of Detention to the Queens House of Detention in Kew Gardens,
a newer and more hospitable facility. Assistant D.A. John F. Keenan,
chief of the Manhattan D.A.'s Homicide Bureau, was handling the
Wylie-Hoffert murder case. Keenan was a Hogan protégé, a fellow Irish
Catholic, with the steely will and colorless personality of a devout public
servant. He met with Whitmore once before the trial—in the presence
of attorney Stanley Reiben—to discuss George's testimony. Whitmore
was startled by Keenan's solicitous manner; it was the first time any representative of the D.A.'s office had treated him like a human being.

The trial had been under way for almost a month by the time Whitmore was called to testify, on the morning of November 12, 1965. George was twenty-one years old now. He had added some weight, his complexion clear, and he wore the black-rimmed glasses that were now a permanent fixture. He seemed more confident, perhaps because he was becoming familiar with the trappings of courtroom jargon and etiquette, or perhaps because this time he himself wasn't on trial. He had nothing to lose.

Whitmore was anxious to convey exactly how he'd been tricked into signing away his life and freedom. He was feistier on the witness stand than he had been, more willing to impute nefarious motives to his police interrogators. During cross-examination, Robles's cocounsel Jack Hoffinger read large sections of Whitmore's "Q and A transcript" from the night he was arrested. "Were you asked these questions, and did you make these answers?"

"No, sir," said George. "The question was asked, but I didn't know, so they told me."

"Who told you?"

"One of the detectives—I was asked what I saw. I said I was never in the house, that I was not in the building, so he insisted that when I went into the building and pushed the door open, the first thing I was supposed to have saw was soda bottles. Everything was suggested to me in this way."

"Didn't there come a time when [Assistant D.A.] Peter Koste came into a room, brought you in and Mister Koste himself asked you questions? Didn't that happen?"

Whitmore paused; the lingering confusion and despair that had dogged him for the last two years returned, and he started to sweat. So many names, dates, events. No, he answered, Koste had only asked "my name and address."

"Didn't Mister Koste ask you these questions I have been reading from?" George was asked.

"No, sir," he replied.

It was a curious moment: it had already been established at the trial that Peter Koste was the assistant D.A. who took down Whitmore's statement. George had nothing to gain by lying about this detail. And yet he seemed so certain in his misremembrance. Later in his testimony, he denied that he had initialed the sketch drawing of the murder scene and various pages of Koste's stenographic transcript, though the pen-manship on these pages was clearly his.

Whitmore's denial of such basic facts had little bearing on the case against Robles, but it did show how thoroughly George had been worn down. It appeared that he was no longer able to reconstruct what happened to him on that long night at the precinct in Brooklyn.

The trial's big moment came when Assistant D.A. Keenan called Eddie Bulger to the stand. Bulger had conveniently retired from the police force a few weeks before the trial began—and then disappeared. The D.A.'s office had tried to track him down, but he had apparently gone into hiding. His daughter said he was on an "extended tour of the southern states." A judge threatened to call Bulger's son, a detective in the Seventy-eighth Precinct in Brooklyn, into court to reveal his father's whereabouts. Two days later, Eddie Bulger responded to his subpoena.

Bulger strutted into court, tanned and cocky. If he felt he'd been forced to retire under a cloud, you couldn't tell by looking at him. Eddie Bulger apologized to no one.

"Mister Bulger, have you ever seen me before?" asked Keenan.

"No, sir," answered the former detective.

Keenan led Bulger through an outline of his police career, including the many commendations and promotions he'd received before his retirement, with full pension, after twenty-seven years of service. Bulger may have been lulled into a false sense of security by the time Keenan asked a seemingly innocuous question: "You have shaved with a razor, right?"

"I have an electric," said Bulger.

Keenan then led the detective headlong into his "discovery" of an empty razor packet found in the bathroom of the Wylie-Hoffert apartment. "Do you know, Detective Bulger, that blades that come from dispensers have arrows on them, did you know that?"

Bulger was confused. "Arrows?"

He admitted that he'd never seen the actual blade found in the murder room—the blade used to slice sheets for tying up Wylie and Hoffert.

Keenan showed Bulger the evidence—a blade sealed in a glassine bag—and pointed out the telltale arrows. This proved that the blade came from a dispenser, not from a wrapped razor packet, as Whitmore had supposedly "confessed" to leaving behind in the bathroom.

Asked Keenan: "Did you know there was a razor blade dispenser in the bureau drawer in the room the girls were found in?"

At one time, Bulger had believed he knew everything there was to know about the Wylie-Hoffert case. "No, sir," he answered, in a subdued voice.

"Now, when you question a suspect, Detective Bulger, are you always polite to them?"

"Yes, sir."

"You ask them what happened, you don't feed them information?"

"No, sir."

"You don't tell them they did something, you ask them did they do something, is that correct?"

"Yes, sir."

"And you speak in the tone of voice you speak to us here . . . polite, calm, when you question a suspect?"

"Yes, sir."

"Do you remember questioning a certain window washer by the name of Eddie White?"

Hoffinger, the defense attorney, interjected: "I am going to object to this, Your Honor."

The judge: "Objection overruled."

Bulger answered, "I don't recall."

Keenan: "Do you remember questioning a young Negro man about twenty-four years of age, you and a Detective Branker of the Bronx Homicide Squad doing the questioning, in December, shortly after December sixteen of nineteen sixty-three?"

"Oh, we questioned a lot of people." Bulger's response was a tad too jovial; he would have known that he'd been working the Wylie-Hoffert case in that time frame.

Keenan showed Bulger a report on the incident that Bulger had made out and signed. "Does that refresh your recollection?"

"Yes."

"Do you recall questioning a Mister Eddie White?"

"Yes."

"Do you remember saying to Mister White, leaning across the desk in the presence of Sergeant Brent of the Twenty-third Squad, and hitting your hand on the desk, 'You're the guy who did this. . . . You saw the door and walked in, you saw the bottles on the floor and picked them up, and you saw Janice nude.' Do you recall saying that?"

"No, sir."

"Do you recall saying to Mister White then, 'Alright, get out of here. But I'm not through with you yet.' Do you recall saying any such thing?"

"No, sir."

"You deny that happened?"

"No, sir."

"You don't deny that happened?"

"I do deny it."

Keenan moved in for the kill. He held up the photograph of a blond girl that Bulger had taken from Whitmore's wallet. The prosecutor asked the detective about his reaction when Whitmore told him he found the photo at a garbage dump in Wildwood. Bulger acknowledged that he told Whitmore he didn't believe him.

Asked Keenan: "When you told him you didn't believe him when he said that he got it from a dump in Wildwood, were you looking at his stomach? Did you notice his stomach moving in and out?"

Bewilderment rippled through the jury box and spectators' gallery.

"I'm sorry," said Bulger. "What do you mean?"

"Whitmore was a young Negro boy. Didn't you tell Mister Koste and Mister Glass on July thirty, in this very building, that you can always tell when a Negro boy is lying by watching his stomach, because it moves in and out when he lies?"

Bulger seemed stunned. He looked beyond Keenan at Assistant D.A. Mel Glass, seated at the prosecution table. "I don't remember saying it."

"You don't remember saying it or you didn't say it? Which?"

"I'm not saying I didn't say it, but I don't remember saying it."

"You might have said it?"

"I might have."

Keenan spent the rest of the day grilling Bulger. The following morning, he moved on to Detective Joe Di Prima.

At the Minnie Edmonds murder trial, Di Prima had been put forth by prosecutors as a paragon of virtue ("didn't he fairly exude character . . . compassion . . . and, yes, even a fatherly-type sensitivity?"). Well, that was then, this was now. Keenan set Di Prima off on a rambling, equivocating series of answers by asking, "Did anyone in your presence tell Whitmore the girls were alive?"

"No, sir," said Di Prima from the witness stand.

"Did anyone in your presence tell Whitmore the girls were dead?"

"I don't recall."

"Isn't it a fact, Detective Di Prima, that you told Mister Koste that so far as Whitmore knew, the girls were still alive?"

"I said to Mister Koste—" Di Prima paused, decided on a different tack. "I'll give you a yes answer with reservations."

Keenan asked Di Prima if he remembered testifying at the Edmonds trial. Yes, Di Prima remembered. Did Di Prima remember saying, under oath, that there was no way he could have fed the address of the Wylie-Hoffert murders to Whitmore because "he didn't even know the address"? Did he say those words? asked Keenan.

"If it is on the record, I did," answered the detective.

Keenan then established that Di Prima had, in fact, visited the building numerous times to see a physician there and knew full well that it was the exact address where the Wylie-Hoffert murders took place. "So you knew the killings were in Fifty-seven East Eighty-eighth Street before you questioned Whitmore?"

"That's right."

"But you did testify, 'I didn't even know the address of the place'?"

Di Prima turned to the judge. "Your Honor, can I elaborate on that?"

"You may not," answered the justice.

"What was the truth when you testified in court?" Keenan pressed.

"I can't answer that question without elaborating," said Di Prima. "My answer of yes would be misconstrued."

Later, in his summation, Keenan said of the detective: "Mister Di Prima's word is not worth anything." This man, who at previous trials had "exuded character," was now characterized as a common perjurer.

The remainder of the trial zeroed in on Ricky Robles, the new figure to be vilified. There were more witnesses, more evidence, arguments, and counterarguments. After closing statements and the judge's instructions to the jury, deliberations began. It took five hours and fifty-five minutes for the jury to declare Robles guilty as charged.

At a press conference afterward, a *Herald Tribune* reporter asked a police spokesman what departmental action might be considered as a result of Keenan's accusations against Bulger and Di Prima. Detective Bulger, the spokesman noted, had retired thirty days ago. He was now a private citizen, beyond the reach of departmental discipline. As for Di Prima, he said, "any action would be up to the district attorney. He is alleging a crime." But no disciplinary charges were ever filed against Di Prima; he too retired a short time later, with a "spotless record" and a full pension.

WITH THE CAREER Girls Murders trial over, and Robles found guilty, George Whitmore became a forgotten man. The press and the TV news no longer had any use for him. George remained in the system, within easy reach of local courts, but out of sight, out of mind.

In the county jail, he learned how to make cheap wine. He procured grapes and sugar while on kitchen duty, mixed them with grain alcohol smuggled in by another inmate, used cheesecloth to filter the mix, then let it ferment. It was rotgut wine, but it did the trick. As he waited for word from his lawyers that "a break in the case" was just around the corner, George Whitmore self-medicated with hooch to ease the pain. The habit he started would dog him for decades to come.

nine

FEAR

IN THE MIDDLE of the Wylie-Hoffert murder trial, John Lindsay was elected as the 103rd mayor of New York City. It was a close election: Lindsay squeaked out a victory with just 43 percent of the vote, thanks in part to William F. Buckley, whose votes were mostly siphoned away from Abe Beame, the establishment Democrat. Lindsay and his supporters, however, considered the vote a mandate—a victory for the forces of reform.

Lindsay came into office with much fanfare. His face appeared on the covers of *Time* and *Newsweek*. The *New York Times*, which had endorsed and promoted him from early in the campaign, described his victory as "astounding . . . and at the same time a vindication for high principle." Some saw Lindsay as an inheritor of the Kennedy legacy. He talked tough on crime but always made it clear that dealing with the crime problem meant improving civil rights for minorities. The theory was that opening up opportunities for blacks and Puerto Ricans—establishing fair treatment in the streets and the workplace—would lessen the level of tension in the city, and lower tension meant lower crime. It was a valid theory: in retrospect, focusing on fairness and civil rights for a group of people who had traditionally been segregated and sometimes treated like dogs was a necessary step forward in the civil rights era. What Lindsay did not fully anticipate was the level of resistance he would encounter—from other Republicans and white ethnic Democrats, but most of all from rank-and-file members of the NYPD.

The war between the Lindsay administration and the police department began almost immediately after Lindsay was sworn in on January 1, 1966. It revolved around the issue of a Civilian Complaint Review Board (CCRB). Lindsay had campaigned for office on a fifteen-point crime program called Operation Safe City, and point number five of the program was the promise of a police review board to include both police officials and nonaffiliated citizens.

In New York City, the prospect of a board to review complaints against police had long been tied up with the issue of race. The first such board, an organization called the Permanent Coordination Committee on Police and Minority Groups, had met in October 1950 to consider the problem of police "misconduct in their relations with the public generally and police misconduct in their relations with Puerto Ricans and Negroes specifically." But the police department was adamantly opposed to the board and would only agree to a compromise: the creation of a CCRB staffed exclusively with NYPD members and alumni.

In the years since, community groups and civil rights organizations had been advocating for a more democratic process, noting that the extant review board backed officers and dismissed complaints so routinely that few citizens recognized it as a legitimate entity.

One of Lindsay's first steps after taking office was to appoint a Law Enforcement Task Force to examine the operations of the NYPD. Within weeks, the task force issued a report that called for many "reforms" of the department, one of them being a CCRB that was acceptable and credible to people in the community.

Lindsay had not yet chosen a new police commissioner. The current commissioner, Vincent L. Broderick, was considered a possible candidate to continue on in the job. Though he was from the same Irish Catholic stock as so many of his predecessors, Broderick was thought to be more progressive than previous commissioners. At a promotion ceremony at the Police Academy in July 1964, the commissioner had delivered an unusually strong statement on the subject of bigotry and discrimination, telling a group of forty-seven high-ranking officers, "If you believe that a police officer is somehow superior to a citizen because a citizen is a Negro or speaks Spanish—get out right now. You don't belong in a command position, and you don't belong in the police department."

Lindsay was amenable to Broderick; he called him a "good man." But one of Lindsay's requirements was that his new commissioner must agree with his position on a reconstituted CCRB. Broderick was not that man. In response to the Law Enforcement Task Force report, he wrote a haughty seven-page letter to Mayor Lindsay—which he first released to the press. "A police review process that includes non-police personnel," argued Broderick, "would lower the morale of the police department" and "dilute the nature and the quality of protection which they will render to the public."

The commissioner's position reflected that of the rank and file, the theory being that no civilian could possibly understand or pass judgment upon cops who are called on to make hair-trigger decisions in life-and-death situations. To allow citizens representing special interests—that is, minorities—to have influence over the inner workings of the department was anathema to the very nature of the institution.

Lindsay made his choice: he replaced Broderick with a new commissioner—Howard Leary, the police commissioner of Philadelphia. Leary was another Irish Catholic who had been a New York cop for more than twenty years—but he had already worked with an independent review board in Philadelphia. He was to be Lindsay's new man in the hot seat.

As a political appointee, the commissioner was a marionette; his loyalty was to the mayor who appointed him, not the rank and file. To the average cop of Irish, Italian, German, or other European stock, a far more reliable source of advocacy was the Policeman's Benevolent Association (PBA), the cops' powerful political lobbying organization.

The PBA made it abundantly clear where they stood. Said John Cassese, president of the organization: "I'm sick and tired of giving in to minority groups with their whims and their gripes and their shouting. . . . I don't think we need a review board at all." The battle lines were drawn.

Lindsay had been in office less than two months; the city's racial problems had been mounting for years. The anger bubbling below the surface was bigger than John Lindsay or any other public official. The daily indignities of police-community relations became part of a larger narrative, a catalog of grievances that had become a malignant tumor on the body politic. Even small encounters took on huge significance until it seemed as though the city, on any given night, could fracture into a million pieces.

One February evening, an incident occurred that added to the seismic uncertainty.

It was a Sunday night, around 7:30 P.M. A police captain, a sergeant, and two patrolmen walked into Joe's Place, a tavern at the corner of 125th Street and Amsterdam Avenue in Harlem. For months, local cops had been trying to shake down Joe's Place, citing it repeatedly for bogus "violations," but the owner was resisting. The night before, two cops had come in and given the owner a summons for not having soap and towels in the restroom. Earlier in the month they had arrested several men allegedly dressed in women's clothing, a violation of morals laws.

On this particular night, a smattering of customers occupied Joe's Place. According to William Hawley, the manager, he was approached by the four policemen, who were all white. "Hello. Anything wrong?" he asked the sergeant.

The policeman told Hawley they were conducting a "routine inspection."

"I told him, 'You gave me a summons for no soap and towels in the bathroom yesterday. Is it necessary that you make a routine check every night and harass my customers?'"

One of the cops went into the restroom, then returned and nodded to the sergeant; that violation had been corrected. The sergeant then told the manager, "You need to tell your customers to stop dancing." Dancing in an establishment without a cabaret license was a violation of the city's cabaret law.

"They're not dancing," said Hawley. "They're just snapping their fingers and moving their heads to the music."

Then another policeman—Hawley recognized his uniform as that of a captain—reminded the manager about the previous arrests of female impersonators on the premises. As the captain spoke, the manager noticed that a sergeant had rounded up a few female customers. One of those customers—Gertrude Williams, a thirty-year-old mother of two—was singled out by the sergeant. According to Hawley, "He took [Gertrude Williams] by the arm and led her about seven feet to the kitchen in the back. She came out of the kitchen looking straight ahead and dazed like she wanted to cry. The officer followed her smiling."

In tears, Williams told her friends that the cop had forced her to raise her dress, lower her panties, and show him her vagina to "prove she was a woman."

Gertrude Williams called her husband, who was at home nearby. Westley Williams, age fifty-five, left his two kids in the apartment and rushed over to Joe's Place. Later, Williams would tell a newspaper reporter that he went to the sergeant and demanded, "Can't you look at her face and see she's a woman?" The policeman walked away without saying a word.

"I was hurting," said Westley Williams. "I couldn't do nothing. I can't fight the law."

The policemen left soon after the husband arrived, but not before they presented the manager with a summons for allowing "dancing."

An hour after the cops left, one of the patrolmen returned to Joe's Place. "There's no sense in you people fighting this thing," he told Hawley. "The heat is on." Then he left the bar.

It took a few days for the full effect of the incident at Joe's Place to ripple through the community. Interaction between blacks and police in the city was so poisonous, the mistreatment so routine and deeply rooted, that incidents like this usually went unreported. The pain and humiliation was absorbed into the community. But the incident with Gertrude Williams involved a kind of sexual degradation that conjured up the worst of southern-style racism. During slavery and for many generations thereafter, the dynamic between police authorities and the Negro had revolved around the emasculation of black men. Black women were sexually humiliated and even raped by plantation owners, teenage white boys, so-called upstanding members of the white establishment— all with little threat of punishment by the law. Such systematic degradation was a crime against women, but it had the added effect of striking at the manhood of black men, who were humiliated by their inability to protect their women.

The web of injustice and feelings of helplessness were monolithic— part of the racial inheritance generations of southern migrants had brought north to cities like New York. The one difference now was that John Lindsay, the city's new mayor, had been elected on a promise to reform the city's widespread corruption, and to govern with greater sensitivity to civil rights. And Lindsay's vows had been seized upon by a new generation of activists.

Ten days after the incident at Joe's Place, nearly two dozen picketers gathered in front of the police precinct on West 126th Street chanting antipolice slogans and carrying signs that read: PROTECT OUR WOMEN FROM VICIOUS ANIMALS IN UNIFORM and WE DEMAND A FAIR CIVILIAN REVIEW BOARD. The protest was led by leaders of CORE.

The next day, Roy Innis, the firebrand chairman of CORE's Harlem chapter, held a news conference at the Harlem Labor Center on West 125th Street. Among those in attendance were CORE leaders from Brooklyn, Queens, and the Bronx, as well as Gertrude Williams and others. Chairman Innis informed TV and newspaper reporters that CORE intended to continue community pressure on the NYPD and Mayor Lindsay until "vicious racist acts by the police are ended in this city."

Gertrude Williams, wearing the same dress and clothing she'd worn that night, recounted what took place. She'd gone into the tavern's kitchen with the sergeant "because I was scared," she explained. "I think he was sick."

Seated alongside Williams were other victims of the police. A fifty-year-old black man with polio, wearing a leg brace and walking with a cane, told the crowd how he'd been standing on a sidewalk in Brooklyn talking to a friend when a patrolman came up and said, "Break it up." "At the same time," the man told the gathering of reporters, "he pulled at my coat collar. Because of my stiff leg, I fell backwards. While lying on the ground, the policeman hit me across the head with his nightstick" and said "get up, you black bastard." As he struggled to stand, the cop whacked the man repeatedly on the shins.

Another victim, a twenty-four-year-old black man, described an incident that took place just the night before. The man's face was still swollen, bruised, and cut after he was set upon by a group of twenty or so white youths while walking along First Avenue with a white woman. The white youths beat him until he was nearly unconscious. When the police arrived, they shoved *the victim* around and made no effort to go after the youths who had administered the beating. As the man spoke at the press conference in Harlem, blood from a still-fresh wound trickled from the corner of his mouth.

These were the walking wounded, men and women on the receiving end of police attitudes and actions that were not uncommon in the city.

Roy Innis, a stout, barrel-chested man, spoke with righteous indignation. "This type of brutality to our men and women must end and must end quickly," he declared. Referring to the pickets, protests, and press conferences, he added, "We intend to escalate this war [against the police]."

The NYPD's response to the press conference was tepid at best. The policemen involved in the incident at Joe's Place were "temporarily transferred," according to a police department spokesman, who described the move as "a measure to reduce community tension." There were no apologies, not even an acknowledgment of wrongdoing. No one was demoted, fired, or deprived of their pension. The department handled the matter as they always had—internally.

All of this added a sense of urgency to the demand for an independent police review board. Mayor Lindsay had agitated to bring the NYPD out of the Dark Ages and make it accountable to the will of the people, and the city's largest-circulation newspapers agreed—except for the *Daily News*, which opined in an editorial that "the civilian section of a [revamped CCRB] will be infested sooner or later with cop-haters, professional liberals, representatives of pressure groups and the like."

Sensing that the Lindsay administration was about to create a new CCRB by mayoral fiat, the city's largest and perhaps most powerful pressure group—the PBA, twenty thousand strong—took matters into its own hands. Before Lindsay could act, the organization preemptively circulated a petition to put the measure on a public ballot. After securing the thirty thousand signatures necessary for such a measure, the PBA referendum was added to the upcoming November ballot.

Throughout the spring, summer, and early fall of 1966, the PBA waged an aggressive and expensive campaign in support of its referendum. PBA president Cassese set the tone by charging that "communism and communists are somewhere mixed up in this fight. If we wind up with a review board, we'll have done Russia a great service—whether by design or accident." A pro-referendum TV advertisement proclaimed: "The addict, the criminal, the hoodlum—only the policeman stands between you and him." Much of the campaign exploited the city's inflamed and tangible atmosphere of fear. A newspaper ad pictured an empty city street littered with debris, smashed storefront windows, and a cash register broken open on the sidewalk—a photo of a Philadelphia street after a recent riot. The caption read: "This is the aftermath of a riot in a city that *had* a civilian review board." The rest of the ad copy exploited the city's increasing reputation for terror: "Crime and violence are the terrifying realities of our time. No street is safe. No neighborhood is immune. New York's police force, probably the finest in the world, is all that stands ready to protect you and your family from the ominous threat of constant danger in the streets."

A number of well-financed special interest groups supported the PBA's cause. The Independent Citizens Committee Against the Civilian

Review Board placed a series of "public service announcements" in newspapers and on billboards around the city. One billboard ad pictured a terrified young white woman alone in the dark standing at the entrance to a subway station. Below the photo was a warning: "The Civilian Review Board must be stopped. Her life . . . your life . . . may depend on it."

At first, Mayor Lindsay had been slow to react to the pro-referendum campaign. But that billboard got his goat. "The only thing [it] didn't show was a gang of Negroes about to attack her," he said. "It was a vulgar, obscene advertisement if I've ever seen one."

By the fall, pro-review-board forces began to respond. Roy Wilkins, executive secretary of the NAACP, denounced the pro-referendum campaign as "the slimiest kind of racism." Wilkins wrote a letter to black religious leaders in the city urging them to preach against the referendum from the pulpit. "The PBA, the Conservative Party, the John Birch Society, the American Renaissance Party and others who want to kill the Board are no friend of the Negro," noted the NAACP executive secretary. "Remember all the Negro-haters are lined up against the Board."

Lindsay tried to rein in the debate, framing the issue as one of checking police autonomy, asking whether the people "were willing to let the police department of this city become a law unto itself." To the people at large, though, the real core of the debate was a matter of black and white. Police advocates pandered shamelessly to a climate of fear; white liberals denounced the PBA as "Nazis" and "fearmongers"; and the city's beleaguered Negroes seethed with resentment and anger in its churches, jails, and streets. Each overheated accusation and counteraccusation was another log on the pyre, each crackling ember smoldering an intimation of bonfires to come.

OFFICER BILL PHILLIPS certainly had no use for an independent Civilian Complaint Review Board. He'd been on the receiving end of citizen complaints half a dozen times in his career, and each time the current CCBA had dismissed those complaints. That was the way it was supposed to be: cops looking out for cops. Phillips felt the same way as most cops: who wanted a bunch of liberals and minority groups passing judgment on the cop on the beat? It would destroy morale, undermine the department's confidence in itself.

Phillips had another reason for resisting the idea of a truly independent review board: he knew just how much of the department, from beat cops through the command structure, was on the pad. The last thing the bosses wanted was an independent board with the power to go through the department's dirty laundry. As far as Phillips was concerned, the fearmongering and race-baiting were merely an elaborate smoke screen. What the department was really worried about was having generations' worth of graft and malfeasance opened up to public scrutiny.

Phillips, of course, knew what he was talking about. His ten years on the force had been one long gravy train. In the last few months alone he'd perpetrated an array of righteous scores.

- In a bar on the East Side, he came upon a rich drunk who had thrown a glass and broken a window. The guy was embarrassed and ashamed, willing to do anything to make the potential drunk-and-disorderly charge go away. Phillips walked him home to his ritzy apartment on Sutton Place and shook the guy down for a thousand dollars.
- While working his beat in East Harlem, Phillips found a Puerto Rican man beaten up in the gutter. He found the guy who did it, took fifteen hundred dollars for not arresting him, and gave the Puerto Rican four hundred dollars to forget about the beating.
- Arriving at the aftermath of a street fight, Phillips found a man shot in the shoulder. He found the shooter and collected three thousand dollars to let him go.
- After finding a hoodlum who was wanted for busting up a restaurant, Phillips took him to the station house and handcuffed him to a chair in the squad room. He then told the hood he'd been identified through a two-way mirror and extorted three thousand dollars for not arresting him.

In all of these scores, Phillips spread the wealth around. He gave the shift sergeant a cut, or the lieutenant, or the precinct bagman who delivered it to the captain or deputy inspector or whoever it was who let it be known they expected a cut of all action that took place under their command. It was a sweet deal—a license to steal, as long as you didn't get greedy. Phillips wasn't worried about getting caught; his hustling, for all intents and purposes, was sanctioned by the department. So many people within the system were in on it that he couldn't imagine ever being singled out for punishment or prosecution.

The money rolled in. Phillips's police salary, after taxes, netted him $140 every two weeks, but he was collecting many times that under the table. He kept no record books, never had an exact sense of what he was raking in, but it hardly mattered. "Money became just paper to me," he recalled. "I pissed it away having a good time. . . . I always had five, six hundred walking-around money."

At his house in Queens, Phillips kept cash scattered around the place—in a coffee can, under the mattress, in a shoe box in the closet. Eventually he got a safe-deposit box; later still he opened a broker-age account, which showed how little he was concerned about getting caught. Mostly, his accounts remained liquid: cash came in and was spent immediately.

> I sure had a fucking ball. It was an unbelievable life. I had a tan all year round. When I wasn't on vacation I couldn't wait to get to work. I never was late. Happy as a pig in shit. It was like every day was a new birth. . . . I used to work twelve-to-eight, get off in the morning, pick up some broad, run around all day, to the beach, get home at six, jump in bed. Never got much sleep. My wife would get home, drag me out of bed, we'd have dinner. . . . I'd take off for a twelve-to-eight, and instead of working I'd be screwing around.

In the summer of 1966, Phillips indulged a fantasy he'd had for a long time: he began taking flying lessons at MacArthur Airport, far out on Long Island. His wife, Camille, wasn't pleased; she felt it was too dangerous. But Phillips wasn't worried. As with most things, he was a quick learner, and, as he told Camille, flying a plane was a lot safer than driving a car. After a mere six hours of instruction, he was told by an instructor, "You're doing great. I think you're ready to fly solo." Phillips took to the skies:

> I'm flying around and looking at all the cars and shit down there and I look at my watch, got to go back, my hour's almost up. So I come in for a landing. . . . I'm coming in about a mile

and a half from the field, full flaps on, motor throttled back and I'm coasting in and the goddamn engine quits five hundred feet off the ground and I got no engine. I almost shit. . . . I pick up the mike, call the tower, yell Mayday, Mayday, my engine quit, I'm coming in on the [Long Island] Expressway. I make a left-hand turn, power lines—go under them; holy shit, cars going both ways, I got a thirty-foot grass strip to land on. . . . My heart was pounding. I could just see the complete annihilation of me, bent out of shape into somebody's house, in flames all over the fucking place.

Phillips's engine had run out of gas, but no one had told him that all he needed to do was switch over to the plane's backup tank. He brought the plane down on the highway without a scratch. Meanwhile, a throng of onlookers—including an official from Federal Aviation—gathered at the site. There was also a newspaper photographer there snapping photos.

The next day in the *Daily News* there was a headline: "Off Duty Officer Lands Plane on the L.I.E.," which is how Phillips's wife found out about it.

She [was] really pissed off. I can't blame her. . . . She says, goddammit, why didn't you tell me what happened? I says, it was nothing. She says, nothing? You almost got killed. Ah, it's nothing to worry about. . . . She says, well, maybe it's nothing to you, but I don't want you flying planes anymore. Bullshit. I'm going up again today. Back out to the airport.

Phillips felt immortal. He loved flying high over the city, looking down at the buildings and cars, imagining the little people with their little lives packed together like fish in cans. There was poverty and crime and ugliness in this world, but up in the sky Phillips soared with the eagles.

Eventually, he and another cop, Jack Kelly, bought their own plane, a Cessna 150, for eighty-five hundred dollars. Phillips racked up the flying hours until he was as experienced as some commercial pilots. He and Kelly decided to start their own flying club. "I put a thousand dollars down and we took a loan for the rest," remembered Phillips. "Then I set up a plan for a flying club, rules and regulations and all that kind of stuff. I called it the NYPD Flying Club and I put posters in all the station houses. Never asked permission of the police commissioner. Figured fuck him, what could he do to me? I was flopped already." The flying club was an immediate success. Cops from all over the city came out to the school on Long Island to log free flying time. It became a big social scene for policemen from many different precincts, all thanks to the largesse of W. R. Phillips, president. Before long, the NYPD Flying Club purchased two more planes, a Cherokee and a Cardinal, for a total of fourteen thousand dollars. Within a few months the club was self-sustaining; sometimes Phillips and Kelly even made a little profit.

Although Officer Phillips advertised his flying club openly in station houses, police brass asked no questions. The question of how a patrolman making less than $16,000 a year managed to finance the purchase of three airplanes, start up a costly business, and extend free flying time to cops throughout the city never set off alarm bells within the Internal Affairs Division (IAD). Phillips seemed to be untouchable.

One reason he flourished—Phillips believed—was that he knew the limits of thievery. He had an instinct for what he could get away with, and he rarely crossed that line. He also learned from the errors of others.

There was, for instance, the case of Officer Walter Jefferys. A policeman in the Two-Five who teamed up with Phillips on many scores, Jefferys was a top-notch hustler. He was especially good with traffic. He could spot license plates that were expired or had no inspection sticker, grounds to pull over a driver and shake him down. As Phillips put it, "You need a little luck to make scores, and [Jefferys] was lucky in traffic."

Even before he teamed up with Phillips, Jefferys had a reputation of being a "heavy thief." Yet he always seemed to be broke—thanks to a bad gambling habit. Huge amounts of money passed through his hands at the racetrack. Whether it was the desperation of his gambling addiction, or the sheer arrogance of a crooked cop believing he was above the law, something led Walt Jefferys to take unnecessary chances.

Jefferys made his big miscalculation on a night Phillips wasn't working. He was partnered with a rookie, a lad with perhaps six months on the job. In a squad car, Jefferys and his partner chased after a Volkswagen that they were tipped off was possibly "dirty" with narcotics. They brought the VW to a halt at 110th Street and the East River Drive. There were two young men in the car, and Jefferys and his partner commanded them to stand spread-eagle while they and the car were "tossed."

Sure enough, the search turned up four bags of heroin, a couple caps of cocaine, and assorted pills. They confiscated the dope and put the two suspects, cuffed, in the back of the radio car. They slapped them around a bit and relieved them of their valuables—forty dollars in cash and a large, expensive-looking ring from one of their fingers. In addition, they worked out a deal: the following night, one of the kids would show up at a local restaurant with three hundred dollars for the cops. In return, they would not be prosecuted.

The next day, Phillips ran into Jefferys at the police pistol range on City Island in the Bronx. The shooting range was outdoors in a bucolic setting, with trees, a breeze from nearby Long Island Sound, and the smell of cordite in the air. The two veteran cops were firing off rounds when Phillips commented on the glistening new ring Jefferys was wearing. Jefferys just smiled; he didn't say where the ring came from, but he did mention that his new partner was pretty sharp, had a lot of potential.

That night, Jefferys and his rookie partner walked into the middle of a sting set up by the Internal Affairs Division. The two people Jefferys and his partner ripped off had gone straight to IAD and filed a report. Jefferys and his partner were busted. A seal was put on Jefferys's locker at the precinct house; when it was opened the next day, they found the drugs he had confiscated, along with two unregistered pistols and other "unvouchered" material. Both cops could have received prison sentences for the crimes. Instead, they were allowed to plead guilty to misdemeanors, were put on probation, and then were dismissed from the force.

Phillips viewed it as a cautionary tale. "You smack a guy around, take his money, take his junk, take his ring, leave him destitute and say, come back tomorrow and bring three hundred dollars, he's going to be absolutely enraged. . . . My motto is: take the money and run. Don't get anybody too pissed off."

Phillips liked to think of himself as a thinking man's hustler, a man who understood the back alleys of human nature. He may have been on the take, but he wasn't stupid. He walked the city streets with a bounce in his step, confident that he was above it all—too smart to get caught.

And even if he did misstep, there was always the code.

The code was the bond of absolute loyalty that cops expected from each other—the kind of loyalty that was required of a cop who needed to trust his partner, and his other fellow officers, every day. Every cop asked himself: Will my partner be there for me? Will he back me up, both figuratively and literally? Can I trust this man with my life? If you expected that kind of loyalty from the cops around you, you had to be willing to extend the same degree of trust yourself.

"The job requires total commitment, as much as any marriage." These are the words of Randy Jurgensen, who came on the job in 1957, the same year as Phillips. Jurgensen grew up in West Harlem, and by 1967 he'd spent most of his ten-year career at the Twenty-third Precinct station house, not far from where he grew up. Jurgensen knew the terrain—poverty, hopheads, a generation of Harlemites who were hooked on dope and would steal or sell themselves to get a fix. Dope, Jurgensen knew, was a consequence of poverty and hopelessness. When he received his gold detectives shield in 1963, he was assigned to narcotics, partnered with a cop named Sonny Grosso—two white guys from Harlem, one from the West Side and one from the East.

Like most detectives who roamed the precinct, Jurgensen was aware of cops who took meals and small favors from citizens. "It was common," he remembered years later. "I'm sure I did it myself. Store owners did it as a way to show their gratitude. They gave you coffee; they picked up your check at lunch. No one thought of this as corruption; it's just the way things were done."

Other cops went farther, and Jurgensen was aware of them also. "Oh yeah, I knew who Phillips was, he became known all around the Harlem precincts. He was up to his tricks; he didn't try to hide it. Everybody knew he was bad news."

Jurgensen stayed away from Phillips, but he wasn't about to rat on him. Whether you were an untainted cop like Jurgensen, whose career would be long and distinguished, or one who was working the system, like those in Phillips's orbit—it didn't really matter. You'd never blow the whistle on a cop like Phillips because you never knew if one day he'd be called to get your back or that of one of your closest friends on the job. So you did your thing, and he did his. As long as Phillips never stepped on your toes, he'd be allowed to operate, free of judgment, free of interference—even by cops like Jurgensen, who thought he was a "scumbag."

Phillips was a time-tested member of the club. He was on the right side of the Blue Wall of Silence.

FROM HIS FIVE-BY-SEVEN-FOOT cell, George Whitmore pondered his predicament: the past was ugly, the future a big black hole. After nearly three years, his case seemed to be on a fast track to nowhere, a merry-go-round of court dates, psychiatric tests, conversations with lawyers, and other dead ends. George tried not to think about it too much, which was easier now that his name and predicament were rarely mentioned in the papers. His feelings about the system and his prospects for the future were mixed, perhaps best captured in a maxim Officer Bill Phillips once shared with writer Leonard Shecter: "A poor man goes to jail. A rich man never goes to jail." It was a principle never taught in law school, but honored by criminals and cops alike; Whitmore had heard it countless times in billiard halls and bars and on street corners in his teens. All he could do was hope that this cruel piece of street logic would spare him.

George had one thing going for him: the skilled and dedicated counsel who had taken up his case. They believed firmly that Whitmore was innocent, but the laborious and costly nature of legal justice in the city was taking its toll. The Whitmore case was becoming a financial sinkhole, which led to resentments and infighting among the lawyers involved.

Arthur Miller and his partner Ed Kaplan had put in long hours; in many ways, the case had come to dominate their practice. It was they who had brought in Stanley Reiben, the experienced trial lawyer; Reiben, in turn, had brought in the NAACP to try the case in the media, to make it a civil rights case. All of the lawyers involved had a vested interest.

By the spring of 1966, Miller decided to limit the involvement of the NAACP, which he felt was attempting to hijack the case to suit its own agenda. On the other hand, Reiben became perturbed when he heard that money was being sent by sympathetic citizens to a "Whitmore defense fund" based out of Miller and Kaplan's Brooklyn office. None of that money was making its way to Reiben. Tensions rose so high that Miller and Reiben could hardly be in the same room without yelling at each other. "I thought they might kill each other," remembered Whitmore. "I couldn't get them to agree on nothin'."

In March, Whitmore was called back to court yet again—this time to be retried for the attempted rape and assault of Elba Borrero. In the courtroom of Aaron F. Goldstein, down the hall from the location of the previous Borrero trial, the Brooklyn D.A.'s office presented much the same case they had sixteen months before. Elba Borrero took the stand and described the alleged assault on Bristol Street in Brownsville with the same level of detail as before: she was coming out of the el train station in the dead of night when a man came out of the shadows, followed and then jumped her, put a hand over her mouth, held something sharp to her throat, and attempted to drag her into an alley. As she recalled the incident, Borrero cried in all the same places she had cried in the previous trial.

To the defense, it appeared as though she had been overrehearsed. On cross-examination, Reiben tried to break her down, asking if she had thought to scream when the attacker removed his hand from her mouth.

"I didn't dare. Not while he had something pointing at my neck. I didn't dare."

When Reiben sought to bring out a minor discrepancy between her testimony now and at the previous trial, Borrero became combative. "I can't remember every word I said, but I do know that I will never forget his face."

"Is your memory better now than it was on May 6 [the date of her appearance before the grand jury in 1964]?"

"No, some things I have forgotten, some things."

"And some things you have remembered," Reiben quipped sarcastically.

Borrero pointed at Whitmore and yelled, "That is the man! I saw his face very clearly." Then she broke down crying.

After the prosecutor, Benjamin Schmier, finished presenting the D.A.'s case, it was the defense counsel's turn. Reiben startled Justice Goldstein and Schmier by mounting no defense at all; he sat mute.

Earlier, Reiben had argued vociferously that the evidence discrediting Whitmore's Wylie-Hoffert confession must be allowed as evidence at trial. There was no way you could cite Whitmore's so-called confession to the Borrero assault, he argued, without dealing with all of his confessions that day, which included Wylie-Hoffert. The judge disagreed and ruled against Reiben, prohibiting any mention of the Wylie-Hoffert case. In protest, Reiben decided to put forth a wall of silence. Neither Whitmore nor anyone else took the stand in his defense. It was a controversial strategy, one that caused further disagreements among Whitmore's lawyers, but Reiben felt it was impossible to give his client a fair trial without addressing the circumstances of the Wylie-Hoffert confession. They were better off mounting no defense and seeking to overturn a conviction on appeal.

The results came quickly—a two-day trial, and a guilty verdict for Whitmore.

Whitmore's attorneys announced immediately that they would appeal the verdict on the grounds that, by being prevented from entering the fraudulent Wylie-Hoffert confession as evidence, the defendant had been denied a fair trial.

A few days later, George and his attorneys returned to court for sentencing. Judge Goldstein announced that, before sentencing Whitmore, he wanted him committed to a mental hospital for yet another psychiatric evaluation. Reiben objected: "Your Honor, to submit this defendant to another court-ordered mental evaluation is judicial torture."

Prosecutor Schmier spoke up. He already had his conviction, but he apparently wanted more. "Your Honor, both Detectives Aidala and Di Prima time and time again in preparation of this case . . . have told the district attorney—and I state this for the first time publicly—that throughout the questioning of George Whitmore, he literally begged Di Prima and Aidala to help him. As close as I can, these are Di Prima's words: 'George Whitmore said, help me, I do these things, and I don't want to do them, and if they let me out on the street I am liable to do them again. Help, please help me.'"

Said Reiben sharply, "This is a tirade of utter garbage. This comes completely out of left field. . . . After all the other actions in this case, for the first time, this garbage comes out."

Judge Goldstein overlooked the contempt in Reiben's response and declared, "I certainly think a psychiatrist should know all about the past so the court could evaluate [Whitmore]. The court is entitled to know whether this defendant can be rehabilitated." So off Whitmore went again to Kings County Hospital for a mental examination, which he passed, as he had twice before.

On May 27, two months after the trial, Whitmore was back in Justice Goldstein's courtroom. He stood before the judge hoping that his clean mental evaluation might prove to be a mitigating circumstance, but the judge showed no mercy. He gave George the maximum sentence under the law: five to ten years on the attempted rape indictment, and two and a half years on the charge of assault with attempt to rape.

The Brooklyn D.A.'s office felt vindicated. Whitmore may not have committed the Wiley-Hoffert murders, but he'd been found guilty of something. There was such a thing as justice in Brooklyn after all.

D.A. Aaron Koota had shown unusual fervor in his pursuit of the charges against Whitmore. Now, in victory, he couldn't resist the opportunity to gloat. "It is high time to give serious consideration as to whether the pendulum of justice has not swung too much in favor of the criminal," he told a *New York Times* reporter. "There is a saying, 'It is far better that a thousand guilty men go free than a single innocent man be convicted.' This is a fetish in our society. The chances of an innocent man being convicted are extremely remote."

For Whitmore, it was a new low point. He trusted Miller and Reiben, but the infighting among his lawyers depressed him, and he couldn't fathom this strategy of losing a case in hopes of having it reversed down the road. He felt increasingly doomed.

The one good thing about being down so low was that any small ray of light, any lessening of cloud cover, was a reason for hope.

On June 13, one month after Whitmore was sentenced, the Supreme Court of the United States dropped a bombshell of a judicial ruling that affected Whitmore's case.

The *Miranda* decision, as it became known, grew out of a criminal case in Arizona, in which a suspect was tricked into giving a confession to a murder. By the time the case made it to the Supreme Court, defense attorneys cited a number of other cases that, they argued, buttressed their contention that a suspect could not receive a fair trial if he hadn't first been informed of his constitutional right to legal counsel and told that anything he said in a police precinct could be used against him. One of the primary cases cited was that of George Whitmore.

In delivering the landmark decision, Chief Justice Earl Warren noted: "This atmosphere—the back room of a police precinct—carries its own badge of intimidation. . . . The current practice of incommunicado interrogation is at odds with one of our Nation's most cherished principles—that the individual may not be impelled to incriminate himself. . . . The warning of the right to remain silent must be accompanied by the explanation that anything said can and will be used against the individual in court. This warning is needed in order to make him aware not only of the privilege, but also the consequences of forgoing it. It is only through an awareness of these consequences that there can be any assurance of real understanding and intelligent exercise of the privilege.

Moreover, this warning may serve to make the individual more acutely aware that he is faced with a phase of the adversary system—that he is not in the presence of persons acting solely in his interest."

The *Miranda* decision touched off a vigorous debate within criminal justice circles, with law enforcement officials throughout the land predicting that the ruling would lead to a free-for-all for criminals. An article in the *New York Times* noted that the Whitmore case had played a "crucial role" in the court's decision, raising the specter that a Negro could find justice in the highest court in the land, but couldn't catch a break in Brooklyn.

Two days after the article appeared, D.A. Koota announced that his office would not retry Whitmore for the Minnie Edmonds murder. The charges were being thrown out.

Whitmore's attorneys were caught off guard by Koota's sudden announcement. They quickly put together legal papers to argue in court that—now that all three murder charges against Whitmore had been dismissed—the defendant should be allowed to go free on bail pending appeal of his conviction in the Borrero matter.

In appeals court, Whitmore's attorneys made their argument. The presiding judge, Hyman Barshay, ordered yet another psychiatric evaluation for Whitmore, saying he wanted to know beyond a reasonable doubt that Whitmore was no danger to society before making any decision on bail. This time he was examined by an independent psychiatrist outside the system, a psychiatric professor at the State University of New York. The doctor declared that, although "somewhat preoccupied with his experiences" with the courts, Whitmore was "well adapted, without any evidence of mental disease." The professor added that if there was anything strange about Whitmore, it was his total lack of any rancor for his ordeal.

When Whitmore was brought from the Queens House of Detention to Justice Barshay's courtroom in Brooklyn Criminal Court for the bail hearing, he was uncertain what all the excitement was about. He knew his attorneys were working on something, but he didn't know the details. A representative of the NAACP appeared before the judge and vouched for the fact that a job awaited Whitmore in his hometown of Wildwood. Parker Johnson, who was now the first Negro police captain on the Wildwood police force, submitted a letter in which he promised to keep George under "close supervision." The cost of the bail—five thousand dollars—was guaranteed by R. Peter Straus, the progressive-minded president of radio station WMCA, who had a history of supporting and donating money to civil rights causes. He put up the collateral, the NAACP paid the bail bond premium, and on July 13—two years, two months, two weeks, and five days after he walked into the Seventy-third Precinct station house in Brownsville—George Whitmore was released on his own recognizance.

Wearing a wool suit provided by his mother and carrying his possessions in a paper bag, Whitmore squinted in the afternoon sun. Newspaper and TV reporters were on the scene.

"Did you ever think this day would come?" George was asked.

"No, I didn't," he said.

"Any bitterness?"

George thought about that. "I am hurt, yes. It would be abnormal for any person to come out and say he is not hurt when he is."

Whitmore's mother and attorney Arthur Miller led him toward a car.

"Would you like to see the police officers brought to justice?" shouted yet another reporter.

"It's not my place to say," said George.

With one hundred dollars in his pocket—the last of the money raised for him by the NAACP in Brooklyn—Whitmore got into the car and was driven away. He was taken to the same junkyard shack in Wildwood where he'd been living with his father before his troubles began. Once again, this would be his home.

As the car pulled up, Whitmore's father came out of the shack and peered in the backseat.

"Hi, Pops," said George. "It's me."

His father replied, "It's you. It's you. Thank God, it's you. . . . Boy, I am so glad to see you I don't know what to say."

The exuberance of freedom lasted for a while. But then Whitmore realized he was right back where it all began: the junkyard. Each morning, he looked around at his surroundings—the same rusted husks of old cars, piles of scrap metal and garbage, junkyard dogs rummaging for food. Then there was Pops, still bellicose and drunk most of the time, telling George what he should and shouldn't do. This was the same set of circumstances that had compelled George to flee to Brooklyn in the first place. Nothing had changed. He was still George Whitmore, Negro suspect.

NOVEMBER 2, 1966, was Election Day. Finally, the citizens of New York would decide the fate of the CCRB, Mayor Lindsay's campaign proposal. It had been a long and vituperative referendum debate. In some ways, the fight over the board was a metaphor for race relations in the city: there were loud voices on all sides, and the tone set by civic and community leaders was seized upon by race hustlers and professional agitators.

In the Brooklyn neighborhood of East New York, a group of angry white teenagers calling themselves SPONGE—the "Society for the Prevention of Niggers Getting Everything"—banded together to protest the idea. Some (especially black folks) suspected that SPONGE was a kind of youth division of the PBA, partly financed by the police advocacy group. Mostly, the organization became an excuse for impoverished white youths to loiter outside the entrance to the subway and harass black people. "Go back to Africa, niggers!" they shouted at people coming home from school or work. "Two, four, six, eight, we don't want to integrate" was another chant. SPONGE had fewer than a hundred members, but they represented a certain segment of the population: aggrieved white people who felt besieged. East New York was a stark example of the city's wrenching demographic trends: as the state census showed, in the course of merely five years, the neighborhood had gone from being 80 percent white (mostly Jewish, Italian, and Irish) to 80 percent black and Puerto Rican. This massive shift created layers of resentment, and it raised the prospect of violence.

SPONGE served as a peanut gallery to a summer of hate that spread throughout the city but was especially heated in Brooklyn. There were organized protests, racial skirmishes, shootings, and ambushes on a near-nightly basis. The hostilities cut both ways. In July, when a group of white student government interns arrived in Bedford-Stuyvesant to study ghetto conditions, they were met by Sonny Carson, the head of Brooklyn CORE, who told them:

> Get the hell out of Bedford-Stuyvesant. We don't want any
> white people in the community. It is our turf; whites are evil,
> all whites. All whites are racists; all whites including everybody
> in this room have killed our grandfathers. You're all racists.
> The CIA killed Malcolm X; you are all responsible; every

white person is responsible for Malcolm X's murder and the
CIA's actions. Slavery in the South was all backed by your
grandfathers. You all backed black slavery, and you get the
hell out of the community. Whites are no good. Get out, we
don't need you, we don't want you. The community is going to
be burned down, and you're going to be burned with it if you
don't get the hell out.

Even Mayor Lindsay was not immune to the onslaught of racial
invective. When he walked the streets in a mostly Italian American section of East New York in an effort to lessen tensions, he was told, "Go
back to Africa, Lindsay, and take your niggers with you!" The Jewish
owner of a butcher shop that had been looted during one of the summer's mini-uprisings said of the mayor, "I got him in hell—and I never
cursed anyone before."

Then it happened: on the night of July 21, 1966, at the corner of
Dumont Avenue and Ashford Street, a ten-year-old Negro boy named
Eric Dean was shot dead. As usual, accounts of what happened varied; the shooting took place during a street disturbance, with cops
and agitators present. Amid the chaos and uncertainty, police arrested
Ernest Gallashaw, a seventeen-year-old Negro. The Brooklyn D.A.'s
office alleged not only that Gallashaw had shot Dean with a zip gun,
but that he'd actually been attempting to shoot a police officer. The
D.A. claimed to have three eyewitnesses. Another witness, however,
claimed he saw a white youth identified only as "Little Joe" shoot the
black kid.

Ernest Gallashaw had no criminal record; he lived with his mother
and extended family in a city housing project. Now, he was a teenager
indicted for homicide.

The three witnesses who gave their story to the grand jury were hidden away by the D.A.'s office, but journalist Sidney Zion tracked them
down and interviewed them for the *New York Times*. The witnesses, boys
eleven, twelve, and fourteen years of age, all had histories of mental
instability. To Zion, they recanted much of what they had told the grand
jury. Yet the case proceeded anyway, with denials and counterdenials
and explosive revelations in the press.

The Gallashaw case was a good example of how treacherous the city's
racial dynamic had become. An innocent young boy had been killed

during a riot. A black kid had been arrested, though some witnesses said they'd seen a white perpetrator. Dubious eyewitnesses were assembled. The witnesses told one story, then recanted, then re-recanted. It became impossible to know whom to trust, or how to get a clear picture of what had happened. The criminal justice system—the police and the D.A.'s office—was so thoroughly discredited in the eyes of minority communities that it seemed the truth could never be known.

Outside a Brooklyn courthouse during a pretrial hearing in the Gallashaw case, a group of thirty demonstrators carried picket signs and marched in a circle. "No more Whitmores," they chanted. A handbill distributed by workers from CORE cited the Whitmore case as the kind of travesty they hoped to avoid. Under the headline "One More Whitmore," the flyer read: *The eyewitnesses who saw the white racist kill Eric Dean are being harassed and intimidated by the police. Radio station WBAI played a tape-recorded interview with people in East New York who said they saw the fatal shot fired from a passing car with four white men. The D.A. said this information was irrelevant because of the nature of the speakers. They were black.*

Given the incendiary nature of the Gallashaw case, the trial was put on a fast track. On October 13, just a few weeks before the citizenry was to vote on the CCRB referendum, Ernest Gallashaw was found not guilty of murder.

There were winners and losers in the city's unfolding racial drama. Blacks were united in their belief that the Gallashaw verdict was correct. Whites didn't know what to believe.

Around that time, the *New York Times* polled white New Yorkers for their views on race. They found that 54 percent felt the civil rights movement was moving "too fast." "While denying any deep-seated prejudice against Negroes, a large number of those questioned used the same terms to express their feelings," the *Times* observed. "They spoke of Negroes receiving 'everything on a silver platter' and of 'reverse discrimination' against whites." Social commentators began to talk of a "white backlash" against the civil rights movement.

CONSIDERING ALL THE attention the CCRB ballot measure had received, voter turnout was low. On November 2, when the votes were counted, the result came down more than two to one—67 percent to 32 percent—

in favor of the PBA referendum. There would be no newly constituted civilian review board composed of citizens not aligned with the NYPD. It was a resounding victory for the PBA, the Conservative Party, and the Friendly Sons of St. Patrick.

The people had spoken—at least those who voted. The police had maintained their exclusive right to police themselves.

But at what cost?

| PART II |

I never felt that the good Lord is that down on a hustler.

—*Bill Phillips*

ten

BLACK POWER

DHORUBA BIN WAHAD never got the chance to say good-bye to his father. On May 2, 1967, he was released directly from the Box at Green Haven prison into civilian life, leaving his old man behind. Dhoruba had spent his last fourteen months in isolation. Having served the full five years of his term, Dhoruba would not be required to report to a parole officer or a bail bondsman; he would no longer be beholden to the system in any way. He was free and clear.

The Department of Corrections gave Dhoruba ten dollars' meal money and a one-way ticket to New York City. No one met him at the gate upon release. He took a bus from Poughkeepsie to the Port Authority terminal in Manhattan, then hopped a subway to the Bronx.

While he was away Dhoruba's mother had remarried. She now lived with her new husband, Louis, in a two-bedroom apartment on the seventeenth floor of the St. Mary's Housing Project, a huge new complex at 159th Street and Third Avenue in the South Bronx. When her prodigal son arrived home, she wept.

So much had changed. On that first day back, Dhoruba walked the streets of Morrisania, trying to take in the new topography. While he was away, the Third Avenue elevated subway line had been completely demolished; the area was now dominated by two massive new housing projects, St. Mary's and the Grant housing projects.

The streets were teeming with people, more Puerto Ricans than

Dhoruba remembered, and a new generation of young Negroes—teenagers and older—who seemed ready to seize the day with a kind of restless energy, all of it set to the music of James Brown, Aretha Franklin, Smokey Robinson, and other soul and R&B singers whose music would become the sound track of a rising consciousness.

That night, Dhoruba met his stepfather; the two eyed each other warily over the first home-cooked meal Dhoruba had had in five years. Later, after everyone else had gone to bed, he sat alone in his mother's apartment in the St. Mary's projects and pondered the past and the future.

> I'll never forget this shit—my mother lived on the seventeenth floor in the project. She was high up. She had this magnificent view south of the Bronx and over into Manhattan. It was a crystal clear spring evening, and I sat up in the living room with the lights out. Everybody had gone to bed. I sat up there, just looking at the city. Maybe four hours, just looking at the city, watching it grow darker and darker. Everything in my life before then was like a dream. Now, I was another person in another place and time.

He may have been a new person, but Dhoruba was back in the old neighborhood. "Hey, did you hear? Torch is back," cried his old gang-banging homies in the Sportsmen Disciples. It wasn't long before he was back running with the gang.

> It happened fast, maybe a few weeks after I got out and was back in the Bronx. The simple fact was, I needed money. I had no job, nothing coming in. And I was back with my old cronies. And these brothers weren't jitterbugging no more; they were now full-fledged gangsters. Somebody came up with the idea to stick up this after-hours club in the Bronx. Being back in the hood, running with the boys again, I was down for that.

One of those who accompanied Dhoruba on this would-be robbery was a neighborhood kid named Augustus Qualls, who would play a major role in one of Dhoruba's later entanglements in the criminal justice system.

It was the middle of the afternoon on a Sunday. The after-hours club they targeted was known for selling liquor illegally on Sunday. Dhoruba and three others entered the club and pulled out weapons. "Nobody move!" somebody shouted. One of the gang members fired a shot into the ceiling; that caught everyone's attention. Dhoruba and the others loaded up a pillowcase with cash from behind the bar, then fled out into the street.

Someone in the neighborhood must have heard the gunshot and called the cops, because a police cruiser drove up almost as soon as Dhoruba and the others hit the street. "[The cops] didn't even say halt," remembered Dhoruba. "They just started shooting at us." He and his fellow robbers fled across the street into a vacant lot; the police car drove in reverse, with one of the cops leaning out the window firing off rounds.

Dhoruba and the others disappeared into the projects. For days afterward, Dhoruba hid out at an old girlfriend's apartment. Since none of the robbers had worn disguises during the stickup, many people knew that Dhoruba was involved, and that the cops were after him. Anxious that someone might snitch to the cops, Dhoruba had to get out of the neighborhood.

On a Saturday morning, he pulled his hooded sweatshirt tight around his head and took to the streets for the first time in days. He hopped on the subway and headed for his grandfather's house in Queens. To Dhoruba, Queens was like another country; he figured the cops would never find him there.

On the subway, he pondered his predicament. He was disappointed to find himself on the run after being out of prison only a few weeks. The gangbanger Torch might have thought it was cool, but his new self did not. He'd already lost five crucial years to the penitentiary; he didn't want to go back. His prison studies had convinced him there was more out there for him than robbing after-hours joints and counting cadence with the gang. He vowed to lie low for a while and stay out of trouble.

He holed up in his grandfather's basement in the neighborhood of South Jamaica, in the outer reaches of Queens. To Dhoruba, South Jamaica was the suburbs, but in fact it was a ghetto—a Queens version of the South Bronx. As with many neighborhoods in the outer boroughs and in Harlem, South Jamaica was struggling to deal with a huge influx of poor blacks from the South. And, just as in these other neighborhoods, a true race consciousness was beginning to take shape among its black residents.

Within days of his arrival in Queens, Dhoruba came across a modest Pan-African cultural center run by the Shakur brothers, Lumumba, Mutulu, and Zayd. Dhoruba had learned about black nationalism in prison, but the Shakur brothers were intense; they were members of Revolutionary Action Movement (RAM), a group dedicated to armed insurrection and to securing land for people of African descent in the United States so that they could establish their own state.

Having only recently been let out of prison, Dhoruba was more interested in his newfound freedom—with its promises of sex, drugs, and sweet soul music—than he was in enlisting in the Republic of New Afrika. Yes, he had changed his name, learned some Swahili, and begun a process of racial self-actualization, but Dhoruba wasn't yet nearly as radicalized as the Shakur brothers. He did, however, pick up some vinyl 45 rpm recordings of Malcolm X's speeches at the Uhuru Cultural Center, along with the book *Malcolm X Speaks: Selected Speeches and Statements*, with its cover photo of Malcolm in midspeech, finger raised, virtually spitting fire.

Down in his grandfather's basement, Dhoruba listened to "The Ballot or the Bullet" and "The Black Revolution," seminal speeches he had read in prison but was hearing in Malcolm's own voice for the first time. Dhoruba was mesmerized by Malcolm's crisp articulation and his ability to think on his feet. The speeches dealt with history, but they also addressed the contemporary situation: Martin Luther King Jr., LBJ, integration, the escalating war in Vietnam, and so on. Dhoruba was especially startled by the transcript in *Malcolm X Speaks* of a symposium Malcolm had taken part in the year before his assassination. When asked about a series of articles in the *New York Times* that quoted police sources alleging there existed an antipolice youth gang called the Blood Brothers, Malcolm said he didn't know whether the group actually existed—but that if it did, they were justified. "If we're going to talk about police brutality," he said, "it's because police brutality exists. Why does it exist? Because our people in this particular society live in a police state. A black man in America lives in a police state. He doesn't live in a democracy, he lives in a police state."

Elsewhere in the book, Malcolm was quoted putting the issue of police treatment of black people in a Pan-African context. "Recently, three students from Kenya were mistaken for American Negroes and were brutally beaten by New York police. Shortly after that, two diplomats from Uganda were also beaten by the New York police, who mistook them for American Negroes. If Africans are brutally beaten while only visiting in America, imagine the physical and psychological suffering received by your brothers and sisters who have lived here for over three hundred years. . . . It is not a problem of civil rights but a problem of human rights."

It was almost too much for Dhoruba to absorb: Malcolm's words were like a synaptic laser. He was putting the issue of police repression at the center of the struggle for human rights—in New York, Africa, and around the world.

In Dhoruba's head, as in the world beyond his basement hideout in Queens, something was happening. The civil rights movement had been under way for more than a decade, and conditions in the ghetto had gotten worse. The frustration of an older generation of Negroes was now being subsumed by a new generation waiting in the wings—people like Dhoruba, not yet fully engaged, but primed and ready for action.

The assassination of Malcolm X left a void, but in Afrocentric cultural centers and among political activists—who were less motivated by integration with whites than by the free expression of black nationalist pride—the movement was gaining steam and taking on a whole new slant.

AMONG THIS NEW generation was Eddie Ellis, who had absorbed the death of Malcolm X not as a defeat but as a call to arms. Eddie had attended the memorials for Malcolm and then, like many others, had engaged in hours of discussion and debate about what was the best way to build on Malcolm's message of empowerment. Like other blacks in Harlem and elsewhere in New York, Ellis was repelled by the idea that blacks must rely exclusively on nonviolent resistance. It was Malcolm who said that you cannot expect a man to turn the other cheek when his people are being beaten, bitten by police dogs, spit on, and hosed down by racist authorities. Ellis adhered to the words of a new leader on the scene, Stokely Carmichael, who said, "Lyndon Baines Johnson is bombing the hell out of Vietnam—don't nobody talk about nonviolence. White [policemen] beat up black people every day—don't nobody talk about nonviolence."

As far as Ellis was concerned, Stokely was the man. Of all the newcomers on the scene positioning themselves to follow in Malcolm X's footsteps, Carmichael was the one to watch. For one thing, he was a New Yorker, born on the island of Trinidad but raised in the Bronx. He had been an honor student at the academically prestigious Bronx High School of Science before heading south to join what he considered the most important calling of his generation—the civil rights movement. While still in his early twenties, Carmichael had marched with Martin Luther King Jr. in Mississippi, taken part in the Freedom Rides, and was arrested for his political activism a total of twenty-seven times. Most recently, he'd been arrested while taking part in protests stemming from the shooting of James Meredith.

Meredith had first entered the public eye in 1962 when his enrollment at the University of Mississippi led to three days of rioting and the intervention of the National Guard. In 1966, Meredith had announced that he was staging a one-man March Against Fear "to demonstrate to the people that white violence was nothing that they had any longer to fear." While walking on the highway from north Mississippi to the capital city of Jackson, Meredith was shot and injured by a sniper.

For activists like Carmichael, Meredith's attempted assassination was the last straw. At an angry rally after the shooting, Carmichael proclaimed, "The only way we going to stop them white men from whippin' us is to take over. We been saying freedom for six years and we ain't got nothing. What we gonna start saying now is Black Power."

To Eddie Ellis and others in New York who had been politicized by the words and spirit of Malcolm X, Carmichael was on point. "Stokely had that intellectual brilliance and charisma that Malcolm had," said Eddie Ellis. "He was eloquent and fearless. He spoke truth to power."

Ellis was one of dozens of black and white New Yorkers who headed south to heed Carmichael's call to "get involved." As a lifelong Harlemite, Ellis had never before been in the Deep South. He slept on hardwood floors in the homes of local farmworkers, and in Alabama, in the crucible of southern racism, he became a member of the Lowndes County Freedom Organization, a political entity that grew up around the issue of voting rights in the South. "Voting rights was the issue, but really it had to do with empowerment," Ellis remembered. "Stokely talked about Black Power not as a dream but as a right."

The idea was not complicated: philosophically speaking, black people would never attain anything resembling equality until they had power—

economic power, political power, and the power of self-determination. Carmichael detailed the new thinking in a landmark speech he gave at the University of California in Berkeley in October 1966. "This country," he said, "knows what power is; it knows it very well. And it knows what Black Power is 'cause it deprived black people of it for four hundred years. . . . The question is, why do white people in this country associate Black Power with violence? And the answer is because of their own inability to deal with *blackness*. If we said Negro Power, nobody would get scared. . . . Or if we said power for colored people, everybody'd be for that. It is the word *black* that bothers people in this country, and that's their problem, not mine."

Henceforth, the word *Negro* was out and *black* was in—soon to be augmented by the term "Afro-American."

In Alabama, the Lowndes County Freedom Organization chose as its symbol the image of a black panther. As Stokely put it: "We chose for the emblem a black panther, a beautiful black animal which symbolizes the strength and dignity of black people, an animal that never strikes back until he's back so far [against] the wall he's got nothing to do but spring out. And when he springs, he does not stop."

The black panther was a powerful image, one whose appeal reached far and wide. In Oakland, California, a number of young black activists heard Stokely Carmichael's speech at Berkeley and were suitably inspired. Two young men who were members of a local chapter of RAM, Huey P. Newton and Bobby Seale, branched out and founded a group they called the Black Panther Party for Self Defense. On May 2, 1967—the same day that Dhoruba Bin Wahad was released from Green Haven prison— the Black Panther Party for Self Defense staged a public demonstration that galvanized the attention of an entire generation of young activists. Armed with rifles—which were legal to carry in the state of California— they marched on the state capital in Sacramento to declare their right to bear arms and use them if necessary when attacked by white supremacists or the police. The sight of a dozen young black men, armed and marching in formation into the halls of the state capital building, was a powerful display of street theater beamed around the world on television news programs and commented upon with great alarm by white pundits and commentators.

The activities of the Black Panther Party in California captured the imagination of black activists in New York. In early 1967, Eddie Ellis was part of a contingent that welcomed Huey Newton to the city. In an apartment in the East Village, Ellis and a group of activists that included members of the Student Nonviolent Coordinating Committee (SNCC, commonly pronounced "snick") met secretly with Newton. SNCC had been cofounded by and was closely identified with Stokely Carmichael, who was unable to attend the meeting because he was on a speaking tour in Europe and Africa. Also at this meeting was Maxwell Stanford, cofounder and leader of RAM. The SNCC and RAM members discussed with Newton the best way to go about combining their efforts and establishing a New York chapter of the Black Panther Party for Self Defense.

According to Eddie Ellis, the meeting went well. There were philosophical differences between SNCC and Huey Newton's burgeoning Black Panther Party, but those issues were mostly ignored. Newton headed back to Oakland and announced at a press conference that Stokely Carmichael was being named Honorary Prime Minister of the Black Panther Party.

For a new generation of young black militants, it was an exciting alliance. The fact that Martin Luther King Jr., the movement's apostle of nonviolence, had expressed public misgivings about the concept of Black Power seemed only to embolden the new generation. This was not your grandfather's black liberation movement. Blacks were now going to defend themselves, and the implication was that they were going to take what was legally and morally theirs—by force, if necessary. If the police tried to beat them down, they would fight back. To young activists like Eddie Ellis, it was the dawn of a new era: "We were ready to stand and fight. There was a feeling that Malcolm's agenda had been cut short when he was killed. It was now our responsibility to carry on the legacy."

This new approach, and the role the Black Panther Party would play as a symbol and motivator for much of what followed, was made apparent in an "Open Letter to the Harlem Community" signed by Ellis and others who had attended the meeting in the East Village. The letter was circulated in the street, at political gatherings, and on bulletin boards in Laundromats, diners, and elsewhere. "The Black Panther Party has arrived in Harlem," the letter stated, noting that this was not to be a political party in the traditional sense but rather "a social MOVEMENT of BLACK people addressing itself specifically to the problems faced by black people living in the midst of white America." The letter urged all residents to take part in OPERATION SHUT DOWN, an organized effort to shut down and take over local public schools. "Our children are the future, so we should be careful what they learn and who teaches them. . . . They will mature either to become instruments of the white power structure used to keep our people politically unaware and vulnerable, *or* to become proud black men and women with love and concern for their own kind."

The letter also proclaimed that "armed self defense against the police" was one of its central tenets, adding with a sense of urgency that "TIME IS RUNNING OUT!" The letter was signed, "Yours for unity, power and self-determination."

If you were young, black, and filled with righteous indignation, it was an exciting initiative, with the promise of payback for decades of abuse and injustice at the hands of the Powers That Be. If you were a New York cop who saw the new militancy as a threat to the social order, it looked more like the mau-mauing of the American Republic.

GEORGE WHITMORE HAD never heard of Stokely Carmichael or Huey P. Newton or the Black Panther Party for Self Defense. In fact, since the day when George sat in an empty catering hall at the Ivy Hotel in Wildwood watching Martin Luther King give his "I have a dream" speech, he had completely lost track of the civil rights movement. They didn't have many civil rights in prison. George was caught up in his own ongoing legal struggles; he didn't have much time to ponder the rising of his people, despite the fact that his own case was one of the sparks that seemed to ignite the budding revolution.

For the time being, Whitmore's own legal predicament was on hold. As he awaited a ruling on his lawyer's motion to appeal his attempted-rape-and-assault conviction, he tried to make a life for himself back in Wildwood. His father and mother had separated, and his brothers and sister were living in Brooklyn, so George was living alone with his father. "He still got drunk most every day," George remembered. "Sometimes, in my weak moments, I thought I'd be better off back in prison."

There was one positive note for George: somehow, in the midst of his travails, he had managed to fall in love.

Aida de Jesus was a seventeen-year-old Puerto Rican girl whom

George had first met in 1963 during one of his seasonal visits to Brooklyn, before all his troubles began. Back then she was living with her family in Brownsville, and George with his cousins, the Dantzlers. One afternoon, he came upon Aida sitting on the stoop in front of her apartment building. He told her she was pretty and made her laugh. Their friendship blossomed into a romance when Aida came to visit George at the Brooklyn House of Detention. Sometimes, Aida would stand in the street outside the jail alongside wives and girlfriends of the inmates. The only window in the facility looked down on the street. Inmates would arrange, via phone, for their sweethearts to appear on the street at a designated time. The women would arrive, preferably dressed as sexy as possible, and the incarcerated men would try to catch a glimpse of them from the window.

Now that he was out and back home in New Jersey, George tried to stay in contact with Aida, but it was difficult with her in Brownsville. For this reason—and also because it was hard to find work in Wildwood during the winter—in January 1967 George decided to go live with his mother in Brooklyn. He was returning to the lion's den—Brownsville—at a time when the borough was seething with racial tension.

George and Aida moved in together in a small room at his mother's apartment. He almost landed a job as a security guard at a factory in East New York, but the job involved carrying a gun, so the employer was required to do a background check. It was a common problem for Whitmore. Prospective employers liked George, he was well mannered and seemingly capable—but then they would run a background check and find out he was *that* George Whitmore. "Come back after you win your case," they would tell him.

George did eventually find a part-time job as a security guard at a store in Brownsville, one that didn't require carrying a gun or a background check. He worked the night shift. One night, walking home from work, he found himself on Bristol Street, the very same block where Elba Borrero had been accosted years earlier. Suddenly, from behind, he was jumped by someone who pressed something sharp—a knife or a screwdriver—against the small of his back.

"Gimme money or I fuck you up," said the person.

George couldn't see the guy behind him, but he thought he recognized it as the voice of a local Puerto Rican gang member he knew. The guy told George to take off his shoes and hold them under his armpits.

He then reached into Whitmore's pockets, took whatever cash George had on him, then said, "Stay away from the Puerto Rican girl. Go with your own kind, nigger." Then he clubbed George on the back of the head and ran away down Bristol Street.

Whitmore had heard there were hostilities between black and Puerto Rican gangs in Brooklyn. When he walked around the neighborhood with Aida, he heard the occasional derogatory remark. It wasn't surprising: after all, he had been convicted of assaulting and attempting to rape a Puerto Rican woman in this very neighborhood. Whitmore's notoriety preceded him. George had never thought about needing protection before, but he was beginning to feel like an easy target in Brooklyn.

His brother Gerald had hooked up with a Brownsville gang—the Suicide Frenchmen, the teenage wing of the Frenchmen, a Brooklyn gang that had been around since the late 1940s. It was an all-black gang, based in Brownsville, Bed-Stuy, Bushwick, and East New York, that sometimes rumbled with white and Puerto Rican gangs—especially the Dragons, the largest Latino gang in the city. George joined the Suicide Frenchmen because belonging to the group gave him a feeling of strength in numbers. There was no initiation ceremony; all that was needed was that George be introduced to the gang by a current member, in this case his brother Gerald.

Late on the night of February 27, George was hanging out with his brother and other members of the Suicide Frenchmen at a pool hall in Brownsville. When George and Gerald went next door to a grocery store that was connected to the pool hall, they ran into members of a rival Puerto Rican gang. One of them was the guy George believed had mugged him on Bristol Street a few nights earlier. When he told Gerald, his brother and the rest of the gang decided to stand up for George. Out came the knives, bike chains, and pool cues, and a full-fledged gang rumble ensued.

Years later, Whitmore remembered: "I washed my hands of the whole thing. I didn't want to have nothin' to do with it. The last thing I needed was trouble. But trouble seemed to come my way."

The familiar sound of police sirens pierced through the streets of Brooklyn. Half a dozen NYPD squad cars screeched to a halt outside the pool hall and grocery store; more than a dozen cops wielding nightsticks flooded out of the cars and into the street to break up the rumble. In the gutter lay a twenty-seven-year-old Puerto Rican male, unconscious, who had been stabbed or beaten to a bloody pulp. He was rushed to the hospital.

The cops rounded up everybody at the scene. The various gang members were asked for identification, and the cops tried to elicit statements about what had taken place.

"Tell me what did you see," one of the cops asked Whitmore.

George had learned his lesson. "I wanna talk to my lawyer," he responded.

The cop looked at Whitmore's identification, and his eyes opened wide. He called for a sergeant, who also looked at the ID. "Are you *the* George Whitmore?" the sergeant asked.

"I wanna talk to my lawyer," said George.

This *was* the infamous George Whitmore, the cops realized—a political hot potato.

The other gang members were hauled into the Seventy-third Precinct. Rather than taking George to the site of his infamous confession three years earlier, detectives took him to a neighboring precinct and called his attorney, Arthur Miller.

The police had nothing to hold George on, so he was released into the custody of his lawyer. "You should have seen the cops," Miller said afterward. "They were so polite they were calling George 'Mister Whitmore.'"

Gerald Whitmore was not so lucky. He fled the scene of the rumble but was arrested at the building where he lived on Amboy Street. After someone identified him as wielding a pool cue that may have been used on the kid found bleeding in the gutter, Gerald was cuffed, hauled into the precinct station house, and booked. One of the detectives said, "You know what you're being charged with?"

Gerald said, "Yeah. Simple assault."

"Nope," said the cop. "Murder." The Puerto Rican kid had died at the hospital.

Upon hearing that he was being charged with murder, Gerald remembered years later, "Well, that wiped the smile off my face."

Within days, medical tests showed that the pool cue was not the murder weapon. After being held in jail for a week, Gerald was released, though at his arraignment in downtown Brooklyn an assistant D.A. could not resist a parting shot. "This does not mean that Gerald Whitmore is not responsible for the death," said D.A. Aaron Koota's chief assistant, "but merely that there is insufficient evidence at this time to warrant further prosecution."

Those closest to George and Gerald felt they'd dodged a bullet. R. Peter Straus, the radio executive who had put up the collateral for George Whitmore's bail bond, was upset to learn that George was even back in Brooklyn at all, much less in the same neighborhood where his troubles began. Arthur Miller was concerned that Whitmore's bail might be revoked. George's presence in the neighborhood was stirring up tensions between black and Puerto Rican gangs. Whitmore's mother had twice reported to local cops instances of Spanish-speaking hoodlums looking for George at her tenement building.

Whitmore knew he had to get out of town, but now a new pressing matter was keeping him in Brooklyn: his girlfriend, Aida, was pregnant. The two of them decided to get married. Given Whitmore's uncertain legal situation (he could have his bail revoked or lose his appeal and be shipped back to prison at any time), a wedding date was hastily set.

On March 9, at the interdenominational Holy House of Prayer Church in Brownsville, George and Aida were married. A few newspaper reporters and photographers attended, as did two plainclothes detectives, who were assigned to guard Whitmore and his new bride. After the ceremony, attorney Miller arranged for George to make a statement to the press. Dressed in a suit and tie, wearing his now customary black-rimmed glasses, George was poised and only a bit nervous as he told the gathering of newshounds, "What happened, happened, and can't nobody change it. As for being a news figure, it don't make me proud. I assume everything will die down eventually. There may be people who will think of me as guilty, but let's just say this is something I have to live with, and not let it stop me from carrying out plans to better my condition."

The next morning—to the relief of their friends and family, and the detectives who had been assigned as reluctant guardians—George and Aida got on a bus and left Brooklyn for Wildwood, where they had no choice but to move into the junkyard shack with George's father.

Soon George found a job driving a sanitation truck, for $1.50 an hour. That and a couple hundred dollars from the George Whitmore Jr. Legal Defense Fund made it possible for George and Aida to move into their own tiny one-bedroom apartment elsewhere in Wildwood.

A month after his marriage, George received a belated wedding gift from the Appellate Division of the State of New York. The panel of five justices who heard his appeal agreed with Whitmore's attorneys that they should have been allowed to enter into evidence the totality of Whitmore's so-called confession, not just the parts relating to the Borrero assault and attempted rape. In a written statement, the appeals judge declared: "In view of the fact that the defendant's statements on all three matters were made in the course of continuous responses to police questions, the entire statement may be regarded as one paper. . . . [Prohibiting examination of the entire confession] left the defendant at a disadvantage in that he was not free to develop his claim that whatever infirmities of compulsion and lack of truth were developed in connection with the Edmonds and Wylie-Hoffert matter likewise applied to his admission as to Borrero."

For the second time, George's conviction was overturned and thrown out.

As with all of Whitmore's legal victories, however, the celebration was short-lived. Three days after the Appellate Division's decision, Aaron Koota announced that, "in the interest of justice," the Brooklyn D.A.'s office would retry Whitmore for the Borrero assault and attempted rape. A date was set for the trial to commence in four weeks.

It was a familiar story, with one unfortunate new twist: this time Whitmore would have to proceed without Reiben, his star attorney. The animosities between Reiben and Miller had grown so bad that George was forced to choose between them. It was not a choice he wanted to make; he felt both attorneys were doing the best they could, and he appreciated how much time they were devoting to the case for so little compensation. It was Miller who told George, "Look, it's Stanley or me, one or the other."

Because Miller had been with his case longer, George reluctantly let Reiben go.

The new trial attorney, brought into the case by Miller, was Samuel Neuberger, another highly regarded veteran attorney. Neuberger was the third lawyer to represent Whitmore on the Borrero charges, which meant he needed to familiarize himself with the case by interviewing George at length about his meeting with Officer Isola on the street in Brownsville, his ordeal at the Seventy-third Precinct station house, his previous trials, and his time in prison. For George—who'd spent years being probed and interrogated about these matters in police precincts, lawyers' offices, prison visiting rooms, and psych wards—it was yet another excruciating experience, part of a process that seemed as though it would never end.

IN NEW YORK, it was unusual for a person to be put on trial a third time for charges that have been previously dismissed; most district attorneys in such circumstances would calculate the costs of further prosecution and choose to cut their losses. But Aaron Koota had a vested interest: in his eyes, the NYPD, the district attorney's office, and the city's entire criminal justice process were at stake.

The handling of the Whitmore case had been a major embarrassment to Brooklyn detectives and the D.A.'s office. In an effort to steal the infamous Wylie-Hoffert case out from under the Manhattan district attorney, Brooklyn cops and prosecutors had arrested, and pinned the charges on, an innocent man—an anonymous Negro. At the time, outward charges of racism against criminal justice officials were rare, but the perception was inescapable. Koota, who claimed to have great sensitivity on matters of civil rights and had launched his career by serving as a special prosecutor in the Harry Gross police gambling scandal of the late 1940s, was now open to charges of racism and aiding and abetting police malfeasance. The only thing that would rectify this perception was to find Whitmore guilty of something—anything—by any means necessary.

On the other hand, Koota did have a legitimate issue: Elba Borrero claimed that Whitmore was the man who'd tried to rape her on that dark night in Brownsville. With each passing legal proceeding, she became only more adamant in identifying George. Koota claimed he had no choice. "The ruling has twice been reversed on technicalities," he said, "but what we still have, as we had in the very beginning, is a woman who says she was attacked, and that George Whitmore is the man who did it."

At a pretrial hearing, Justice Julius Helfand ruled that the entirety of Whitmore's confession would be inadmissible as evidence. Neither side, prosecution or defense, was allowed to make any mention of the confession in the presence of the jury. Neuberger and Miller actually believed that this was to their advantage; the entire case would now come down to one thing—Borrero's identification of George.

It was a short trial—just three days. Whitmore did not take the stand.

Borrero did, alleging for the umpteenth time that she was "absolutely certain" that her attacker was the young black man seated at the defense table. Prosecutor Benjamin Schmier, in his final summation, pointed at Whitmore and told the jury not to be fooled. "As he sits there now, he looks like he just came from his bank, with that cute suit and white shirt and pretty tie and new hair comb." The implication was that Whitmore was a predator in disguise, a sex pervert by any other name.

The jury deliberated for six hours, then returned with their verdict: guilty.

This time, along with Whitmore's mother, there was another female in the courtroom who burst into tears when the verdict was announced—Aida, George's wife.

Three weeks later, Whitmore appeared for sentencing before Judge Helfand, a hard-nosed justice who had once been commissioner of the New York State Boxing Commission. In an appeal for clemency, Neuberger told the judge, "I am restrained to say at the outset that I cannot speak in terms of remorse. The defense persists in this position because the defendant insists upon his innocence. The court knows that this defendant has been incarcerated for some two and a half years. . . . This young man suffered punishment that I would describe as cruel and inhuman, awaiting the disposition of murder charges, and three trials in this particular case." In the ten months he'd been out on bail, the lawyer noted, George had been working in Wildwood and living there with his wife and "in all aspects behaving in a manner consistent with public morals. The interests of justice would best be served by terminating this Whitmore nightmare, and to permit him to live as a human being."

The judge was not swayed. With a minimum of ceremony, he noted that the two counts for which Whitmore was convicted "are both vicious, heinous crimes. The victim was a young mother, a nurse. She had a right to go about her business unmolested. The jury, by its verdict, has said the defendant denied her this right and subjected her to a horrifying experience. The crime cannot go unpunished." Judge Helfand hit Whitmore with the maximum sentence: five to ten years for the attempted rape and two and a half to five years for the assault. He also ordered Whitmore to undergo psychiatric evaluation at a state mental facility—his fourth court-ordered evaluation in the last three years.

Outside the courtroom, on the front steps of the majestic court-house building, Aida leaned on Birdine Whitmore's shoulder. Aida was now eighteen and noticeably pregnant. She said to no one in particular, "I thought he was going to come home with me forever. I never thought he would be convicted."

Nearby, Sam Neuberger spoke to a handful of reporters. "I would say from thirty-nine years of practicing in my borough that a Negro defendant in Brooklyn has as much chance as he has in Alabama. Perhaps less. The fear and hysteria here are greater." Neuberger pledged to appeal the verdict yet again. "We won't win in the Appellate Division, we may not win in the Court of Appeals, but we will win in the federal courts," he predicted.

As the lawyer spoke, a green Department of Corrections bus carrying Whitmore and other prisoners pulled out of the courthouse driveway and stopped at a traffic light. From inside the bus, George could see Aida, his mother, and his attorney. "I thought that was it," George remembered. "I gave up. I was so sick of all the hearings and trials and bein' sentenced to the nut house—I couldn't take no more."

George looked through the mesh caging of the dingy bus window and waved good-bye to his people. He wasn't sure if they could even see him through the metal and yellowed glass.

On the sidewalk in front of the courthouse, Whitmore saw his young wife weeping on his mother's shoulder.

eleven

"HOLY SHIT!"

THE SUMMER OF '67 was hot as hell. Hippies in California christened it the Summer of Love, but not many New Yorkers thought of it that way. The previous summer's hostilities had simmered throughout the year; the city was a tinderbox waiting for one wayward spark—a shooting, a mugging, a hostile exchange between a cop and a black kid—to kindle its flames anew.

No entity was more concerned about the prospect of violence than the NYPD. Brush fires were being stoked on many fronts: Students for a Democratic Society (SDS) and other radical groups were protesting the war in Vietnam; the ultraconservative John Birch Society was trying to expand its profile in New York, which it considered a breeding ground for liberals (or "secret communist traitors," in their parlance). No threat was more alarming to the police than the black liberation movement, with its rejection of nonviolent civil disobedience in favor of the militancy of the Black Power movement.

On June 21, 1967, the NYPD made a major effort to ward off intimations of a racial revolution by arresting sixteen members of the Revolutionary Action Movement group. In dramatic predawn raids in Brooklyn, Queens, and Manhattan, police rounded up RAM members and confiscated rifles, shotguns, carbines, and more than one thousand rounds of ammunition. One of the members arrested was Maxwell Stanford, who, along with Eddie Ellis, had met with Huey Newton the previous fall in an effort to bring RAM and the Panthers together under one umbrella.

Two of the RAM members arrested were charged with conspiracy to murder the civil rights leaders Roy Wilkins, of the NAACP, and Whitney M. Young, executive director of the National Urban League—moderate civil rights organizations, and therefore, to the militants, part of the problem.

RAM was largely an underground organization, with chapters in Chicago, Philadelphia, Oakland, Baltimore, and other American cities. In New York, they operated out of Jamaica, Queens. Police claimed that their base of operations was the Jamaica Rifle and Pistol Club, where members engaged in target practice and met to discuss how best to overthrow the U.S. government. Aside from the two RAM members who were charged with conspiracy to commit murder, the other fourteen were charged with "advocating criminal anarchy" and "conspiracy to advocate criminal anarchy." Thirteen were accused also of "conspiracy to commit arson" and seven with possession of dangerous weapons.

The arrests and indictment were announced in the most alarmist way possible. Many in law enforcement felt that the black liberation movement was now synonymous with conspiracy, even communist manipulation. RAM was described by the FBI as "pro–Red China." An assistant D.A. in Queens stated that RAM's activities were "not advocacy of ideas or opinions—it was advocacy of detailed revolution." Yet these warnings were beginning to make law enforcement officials sound like the boys who cried wolf: three summers earlier they had issued a warning about an organization in Harlem they identified as the Black Brotherhood, which they claimed was dedicated to killing policemen, but in time it became clear that the allegations were exaggerated.

The cops weren't the only ones: big city mayors and municipal officials across the country were quick to portray the black liberation movement in hyperbolic terms, stoking racial fears, alleging conspiracies, and framing the conflict as an extension of the country's cold war with China, Russia, and Vietnam.

Some of this was generational: white Americans of an earlier generation had become accustomed to the good Negro. Even Martin Luther King had been circumspect in his criticisms of the American way, though that had begun to change when he took a stand against the U.S. war in Vietnam. Black Power seemed to suggest something more radical. To Americans who had lived through World War II, the kind of black nationalism first advocated by Malcolm X and now being promoted by Stokely Carmichael and others was unpatriotic. The suggestion that black Americans should have an identity separate and above their national identity as Americans was seen as a threat to the country's internal security, and with groups like RAM stockpiling weapons, law enforcement reacted with a sense of urgency. White civic, political, and business leaders—the bloc for whom Malcolm X had coined the term "white power structure"—saw it as their duty to attack the concept of Black Power. They were unable or unwilling to acknowledge the concept of black liberation as anything other than a criminal conspiracy, and in no way an outgrowth of the battle for civil rights.

The RAM members were charged under an anarchy statute that was created in 1902 and had rarely been applied in the previous forty years. Eventually, the bulk of the anarchy and conspiracy charges would be ruled unconstitutional and dismissed.

Whether it was intended or not, the overheated rhetoric, exaggerated criminal prosecutions, and the general posture of the NYPD and other police departments around the country seemed guaranteed to bring about what William F. Buckley Jr. had predicted: race war.

The Harlem and Brooklyn riots of three summers earlier turned out to be a harbinger of things to come. Race riots around the United States were becoming a startling seasonal pattern. The previous two summers had seen major ghetto uprisings in Rochester, New York; Philadelphia; the Watts section of Los Angeles; Omaha, Nebraska; and other cities. The reasons for these uprisings were complex, rooted in local issues of poverty, substandard housing, and abysmal educational systems, but they all had one thing in common: they were touched off by a confrontation between police and the community.

In mid-July, three weeks after the RAM arrests, the pattern continued—with the worst riot yet, in Newark, New Jersey.

Just twelve miles from New York City, Newark was roughly halfway between Wildwood, where George Whitmore lived, and outer Brooklyn. A city of 450,000, Newark had one of the largest populations of impoverished black people outside of the Deep South. Like many big industrial cities, it had experienced a startling shift in racial demographics, with the now-familiar patterns of white flight and municipal neglect. Although the city was more than 50 percent black, city government and the police department were overwhelmingly white.

On the afternoon of July 12, 1967, an African American taxi driver named John Smith found himself blocked by a police squad car double-parked in the street. Rather than waiting, Smith tried to drive around the police car. He was immediately flagged down by cops, pulled from his car, and beaten in front of numerous onlookers. The taxi driver was then taken to a local precinct where, according to a police spokesman, the cops "only used necessary force to subdue Smith." According to Smith at his bail hearing the next day, necessary force included the following: "There was no resistance on my part. That was a cover story by the police. They caved in my ribs, busted a hernia, and put a hole in my head. . . . After I got into the precinct, six or seven other officers along with the two who arrested me kicked and stomped me in the ribs and back. They then took me to a cell and put my head over a toilet bowl. While my head was over the toilet bowl I was struck in the back of the head with a revolver. I was also being cursed while they were beating me. An arresting officer in the cell-block said, 'This baby is mine.'"

Word of Smith's mistreatment spread like wildfire through the neighborhood. For years, blacks in Newark, like blacks in New York City, had been complaining about police brutality and mistreatment. And, in the spirit of the times, they were no longer willing to take it sitting down.

What followed was five days and nights of chaos and violence unlike anything seen in an American city since the days of the Civil War draft riots. Rampant looting led to brutal and bloody confrontation between citizens and the police. The Newark cops, like many police departments around the country, had not yet developed effective strategies for dealing with such mass urban insurrection. They knew only one way to respond: with a massive display of force. People were clubbed indiscriminately; all black people on the street were considered to be coconspirators and treated accordingly. The populace responded with Molotov cocktails, bricks, and rocks that rained down like a meteor shower on the local police precinct.

The first forty-eight hours of the riot resulted in 425 arrests, with five dead and hundreds wounded and treated at local hospitals. By the third day, the governor of New Jersey declared that "The line between the jungle and the law might as well be drawn here as anywhere in America." He called in the National Guard.

Tanks, helicopters, and three thousand National Guardsmen stormed the city. The troops were composed mostly of white suburbanites from South Jersey towns who despised the city of Newark and everything it represented. One captain told a reporter, "They put us here because we're the toughest and the best. . . . If anybody throws things down our necks, then it's shoot to kill, it's either them or us, and it ain't going to be us."

With the coming of the Guard, the situation deteriorated into complete chaos. Rumors of snipers shooting at guardsmen and police created hysteria. The *New York Daily News*, generally a pro-police newspaper, wrote: "Reporters in the riot area feared the random shots of guardsmen far more than the shots from snipers. . . . Once a frantic voice shouted [over the radio], 'Tell those Guardsmen to stop shooting at the roof. Those men they're firing at are policemen . . .' 'They were completely out of their depth,' said one reporter. 'It was like giving your kid brother a new toy. They were firing at anything and everything.'" A *New York Times* reporter quoted chatter from a radio: "Newark police, hold your fire! State police, hold your fire! . . . You're shooting at each other! National Guardsmen, you're shooting at buildings and sparks fly so we think there are snipers! Be sure of your targets!"

The riot gave lawmen an occasion to vent their racism—and, on the other side, for rioting locals to take out their years of pent-up rage toward the police. There were many horrific episodes, but none more so than the killing of nineteen-year-old Jimmy Rutledge, who was shot dead inside a tavern. According to an eyewitness who later testified to a commission investigating the riot, a group of people were hiding out in the tavern as the riot unfolded. Two New Jersey state troopers burst in shouting "Come out you dirty fucks!" Rutledge stepped out from behind a cigarette machine and was frisked by the troopers. Then, according to the witness, "The two troopers . . . looked at each other. Then one trooper who had a rifle shot Jimmy from about three feet away. . . . While Jimmy lay on the floor, the same trooper started to shoot Jimmy some more with the rifle. As he fired . . . he yelled, 'Die, you dirty bastard, die you dirty nigger, die die . . .' At this point a Newark policeman walked in and asked what happened. I saw the troopers look at each other and smile. . . . The trooper who shot Jimmy . . . took a knife out of his own pocket and put it in Jimmy's hand. . . . Shortly after, three men came in with a stretcher. One said, 'They really laid some lead on his ass.' . . . He asked the State Trooper what happened. The Trooper said, 'He came at me with a knife.'"

After five days of mayhem, the riot was finally quelled. The official casualty totals were 26 dead, 725 injured, nearly 1,500 arrests, and property damage totaling $10 million.

The Newark riot might have seemed unsurpassable in its violence—until two weeks later, when an uprising in Detroit proved even worse. Again, the inciting incident involved police activity, in this case a special police squad shutting down a "blind pig"—an after-hours club—that hadn't been making its regular payoffs to the local precinct. The Detroit riots resulted in 43 dead, 467 injured, 7,200 arrests, and 200 buildings being burned to the ground.

In New York City, the reverberations were immediate. People watched the images on the nightly news, with shell-shocked reporters on the scene struggling to make sense of the carnage.

Bill Phillips read about the Newark riot in the papers. As with most cops, the level of civil disobedience displayed was beyond his comprehension. Phillips came from a time and place where lawmen were respected—or at least feared. The fact that idiot street hoodlums were now fighting back was a source of concern, as were reports of snipers shooting at police from windows and rooftops, an urban legend that had preoccupied police ever since the Rising of the Negroes first began. Phillips knew enough about ghetto psychology to know that the effects of the Newark riots would likely send their ripple effects into the streets of New York.

On the night of July 23—the very night the Detroit riots began—Phillips was riding in a squad car with his partner when a call came over the radio of a huge disturbance brewing in East Harlem.

> My partner and me pulled up to 110th Street and Third Avenue, four hundred people around, right? All those cocksuckers all over the roofs with bricks and bottles and shit. We get out of the car. OK, you fucks, break it up. Before we got back into the car, we were devastated with bricks and bottles and every other fucking thing they could throw at us. . . . We got back in the car. I emptied my gun at the fucking roof. . . . I could have killed four, five people. Who the hell knows? I didn't give a shit at this time. I was looking out for my own ass. There's two of us on the corner now and we're deluged

with bricks and bottles. Windows in the radio car are busted.
We have three fucking flat tires now from all the broken glass
in the street. We drove on the rims. Get the fuck out of there,
right? We go back and get our forces together now. Call for
help. Radio cars come. We get another car, we're going down
the block at Lexington Ave and 112th Street and they build a
fire in the street and we can't go through. Holy shit! We start
to back up and here comes a fucking garbage can from a roof,
full of bricks. It comes right through the windshield. We're
now covered with glass from head to foot. . . . Fucking garbage
can still sticking out of the head of the car.

To Officer Phillips, the most frustrating aspect of the riot was the
response of the police brass:

Our bosses told us, do nothing, just make them move along,
don't lock anybody up, don't shoot anybody. There were about
ten of us seasoned guys. We decided the first chance we get
we're going to get a hold of [the rioters] and beat the shit out of
them. . . . I don't give a fuck now because I can be a statistic in
the morning. I'm going out and break heads and I'm going to
break everybody's fucking head I come across because I know
these people hate us up there now and they're looking to knock
me and everybody else off. . . . We chased them into the 23rd
Precinct and up on a roof. There was about twenty of them.
We beat the living shit out of everybody. I mean beat their
fucking heads, knocked their teeth out. I left them all up there
for dead. Came down, no more riot. It was all over.

The city of New York considered itself lucky. The damage from the
East Harlem riot was minimal compared to Newark and Detroit. The
Lindsay administration claimed credit for managing the disturbance,
keeping it from exploding into an urban street version of the End of Days.

Their sense of relief was misplaced. What was happening in New York
was more like a slow-motion riot—a schism buried deep within the contours of city life that would rumble and spew for much of the next decade.

DHORUBA BIN WAHAD had been out of prison for two and a half months when the riots took place. Images of Molotov cocktails, National Guard troops, and rampaging Negroes brought back memories of his jitter-bugging days—but this was on a much larger scale. In prison, he had seen black people herded, regimented, and controlled on a daily basis; now it seemed as though freedom was synonymous with rebellion and dissent. Watching footage of the riots on television, Dhoruba had the same thought as many leaders of the Black Power movement: if only the outrage and anger could be harnessed and directed in a more productive way, then the revolution could be transformed from a dream to a reality.

A few days after the riots in Detroit and East Harlem, Dhoruba was on the subway, on his way to visit his aunt in his old neighborhood of Morrisania. He noticed that the police presence throughout the city had been stepped up, with cops in riot gear at nearly every station. He got off the train at the Jackson Avenue station in the Bronx—and walked into the middle of a police dragnet.

> I came down the stairs and the police had cordoned off the entire area underneath the train station. They had created sort of a funnel, and everybody that came into the area was detained. A group of about fifteen to twenty kids were walking together by the train station when I came down. A bunch of police came out of nowhere. With their guns out, they jumped the kids. Somehow I wound up in the middle of this. I didn't know none of these kids. But they put us all up against the wall together. They cuffed us and locked us all up, said we had burglarized or burned a school or something. It was just a way for them to sweep a bunch of youths off the street and hold them in detention for twenty-four hours.

Dhoruba was held overnight in jail and released at arraignment the next day. For the next six months he would have to make repeated court appearances to deal with the false charges before they were eventually dismissed. Not everyone was so lucky: many of the youths rounded up in the dragnets accepted plea bargains. Dhoruba saw the raid as one more indication of how the system was geared to criminalize black youths—even if they were just walking down the street or riding the subway.

Since his release from Green Haven Bin Wahad had become hyper-attuned to the possibilities of life. One aspect of his spiritual and physical rebirth involved pursuing something he'd been denied in prison: female companionship. While living with his grandfather in Queens, he met a young sister with the right combination of sass and self-possession. When Iris Bull walked into Dhoruba's life on a street in South Jamaica, it was lust at first sight. She was twenty-one years old, shapely and lean, with a smooth café au lait complexion and proud "natural" hairstyle; they consummated their physical relationship in the basement of Dhoruba's grandfather's house, but it quickly blossomed into something more: a true manifestation of the Summer of Love.

Dhoruba and Iris fell hard for each other and decided to get an apartment in the East Village, Manhattan's bohemian quarter. Along with being the location for the secret meeting that launched the Black Panther Party in New York City, the East Village was ground zero for many of the cultural strains that were blossoming and commingling to form what would become known as the "psychedelic sixties." Dhoruba and Iris moved into a street-level loft at 237 East Third Street, down the block from Slugs, a popular jazz club. The rent was cheap. Iris worked at a novelty shop on St. Mark's Place selling papier-mâché flowers and black-light posters. And Dhoruba found his own source of income: pooling his resources with a couple of friends, he bought marijuana by the pound, which he stored in a vacant apartment in the building where he lived and sold by the dime bag.

In an era of black pride and black-is-beautiful, Dhoruba and Iris were a power couple. They were strikingly handsome both individually and together, with dynamic personalities and a mutual admiration that lit up a room. The semiregular parties they held at their loft on East Third Street—complete with tabs of acid and a huge bowl filled with joints on the coffee table—became a central gathering place for a diverse collective of black militants, white hippies, artists, and activists. Fueled by hallucinogens and booze, their parties sometimes lasted an entire weekend.

Dhoruba found himself torn between two powerful drives: a hunger to exercise his newfound freedom in the hedonistic frenzy of the times, versus his intellectual drive to continue pursuing his process of political enlightenment, with all the discipline and self-sacrifice that entailed. He still played his Malcolm X records and devoured the news accounts he found in the *Liberator*, the *Amsterdam News*, the *East Village Other*, and other papers he trusted. He read Stokely Carmichael's manifesto, *Black*

Power: The Politics of Liberation in America, and also *Look Out, Whitey! Black Power's Gon' Get Your Mama* by Julius Lester, two influential books published that year. He was flirting with the prospect of becoming a full-fledged member of the Black Power movement—and his feelings only intensified when he read an article in the leftist magazine *Ramparts* by a cat named Eldridge Cleaver.

Cleaver, like Dhoruba himself, was an ex-con who had recently been released from prison—in Cleaver's case California's notorious Folsom Prison. Even before he'd been released in December 1966, Cleaver was something of a celebrity: his prison writings had been published in *Ramparts*, which enjoyed a devoted readership in the Bay Area and also in New York City. Upon his release, *Ramparts* hired him as a correspondent-at-large.

Dhoruba had read some of Cleaver's writings in the magazine, but the article that really caught his attention was one he wrote about a visit by Betty Shabazz, wife of the late Malcolm X, to speak at a political function in San Francisco. The Black Panther Party in Oakland had been assigned as Sister Shabazz's security detail in the Bay Area. "I fell in love with the Black Panther Party immediately upon my first encounter with it," Cleaver wrote. Cleaver described being seated in an auditorium awaiting the arrival of Sister Shabazz: "I spun around in my seat and saw the most beautiful sight I had ever seen: four black men wearing black berets, powder blue shirts, black leather jackets, black trousers, shiny black shoes—and each with a gun! In front was Huey P. Newton with a riot pump shotgun in his right hand, barrel pointed down to the floor. Beside him was Bobby Seale, the handle of a .45 caliber automatic showing from its holster on his right hip, just below the hem of his jacket. . . . Where was my mind at? Blown!"

After this initial introduction to the Panthers, Cleaver was honored to hear that Shabazz, who'd read an article of his about the legacy of Malcolm X in *Ramparts*, wanted to meet him. She was escorted to the magazine's editorial office by the Panthers, who were confronted by a group of San Francisco police officers alarmed by reports of a group of Negroes dressed in all black carrying rifles and handguns. In *Ramparts*, Cleaver described the encounter that followed:

> At that moment, a big, beefy cop stepped forward. He undid
> the little strap holding his pistol in his holster and started

shouting at Huey, "Don't point that gun at me! Stop pointing that gun at me!" He kept making gestures as if he was going for his gun.

This was the most tense of moments. Huey stopped in his tracks and stared at the cop.

"Let's split, Huey! Let's split!" Bobby Seale was saying.

Ignoring him, Huey walked within a few feet of the cop and said, "What's the matter, you got an itchy finger?"

The cop made no reply.

"You want to draw your gun?" Huey asked him.

The other cops were calling out for this cop to cool it, to take it easy, but he didn't seem to be able to hear them. He was staring into Huey's eyes, measuring him.

"O.K.," Huey said. "You big fat racist pig, draw your gun!"

The cop made no move.

"Draw it, you cowardly dog!" Huey pumped a round into the chamber of the shotgun. "I'm waiting," he said, and stood there waiting for the cop to draw.

All the other cops moved back out of the line of fire. I moved back, too, onto the top steps of Ramparts. I was thinking, staring at Huey surrounded by all those cops and daring one of them to draw, "Goddam, that nigger is c-r-a-z-y!"

Then the cop facing Huey gave it up. He heaved a heavy sigh and lowered his head. Huey literally laughed in his face and then went off up the street at a jaunty pace, disappearing in a blaze of dazzling sunlight.

Immediately afterward, Cleaver joined the Black Panthers, becoming their minister of information.

Just as Cleaver was impressed by the antics of Huey Newton, Dhoruba was equally enthralled by Cleaver's account of the action. The Black Panthers, Huey Newton, Eldridge Cleaver—it all left Dhoruba's head spinning in amazement. He vowed to learn more about this righteous new group, which echoed so many of the sentiments roiling in his own mind.

Politics was in the air. In October, at one of Dhoruba and Iris's regular parties on East Third Street, someone pulled out a flyer promoting a huge protest march the next day in Washington, D.C. Billed as "The

Rise on the Pentagon," it promised to be unlike anything ever staged before: a march on the Pentagon in which virtually every radical protest group and some mainstream political groups promised to attend. Anyone who was against the war in Vietnam was urged to make the trek to D.C.

"Hey," said someone at the party, "why don't we all go?" There were cars, minivans, and buses leaving for the march from Tompkins Square Park, just a few blocks away.

It sounded crazy—most everyone at the party was already high on grass, acid, and booze. But they walked over to Tompkins Square, where thousands were gathered: hippies, college students, and people from church groups and political organizations. Dhoruba and a handful of his friends climbed into a Volkswagen minibus and were off.

"When we got to the Washington, D.C., area—*damn*," said Dhoruba. "There were people walking on the highway towards the march; thousands of people walking on the shoulder of the road. I'd never seen so many white kids at one time since I got out of prison."

The march on the Pentagon would turn out to be a seminal event, an occasion for speeches, singing, chanting, getting high, and cursing at and scuffling with armed troopers. Eight hours later, Dhoruba and his crew were back on the minibus heading back to New York.

Traveling with Dhoruba was a group of black college students who had hitched a ride back to the city. Remembered Dhoruba, "One of the college students was talking about how marginalized they were on campus, how they were unable to get any respect from the institutional authorities. With all the reading I'd been doing, all the political analysis I'd been exploring, I jumped right into the discussion. One of the students said to me, 'You sound just like one of those Black Panthers from the West Coast.' I said, 'Well, if there was an organization like that in New York, I would probably join them.'"

Back in the city, Dhoruba was hurtling himself down the road toward political engagement. He read all he could find on the Panthers, and eventually visited the Panther office, a modest basement in Harlem at Seventh Avenue and West 141st Street. The group that seemed to be running the office struck Dhoruba as college kids, possibly former SNCC members who were following the community-outreach model of the traditional civil rights movement—initiating a free breakfast program for children and establishing what they called "liberation schools" to educate kids in Harlem. But Dhoruba was still half a thug, a former gangbanger whose thoughts ran more toward armed self-defense than toward organizing social survival programs. He kept his eye on the Panthers, but hoped to see them follow the example of leaders like Huey Newton and Eldridge Cleaver, cats who had a prison pedigree and sense of audacity that resonated with him.

In October, Dhoruba and Iris decided to get married. They donned matching African clothing, piled into a friend's pickup truck, and drove down to the Municipal Building in lower Manhattan for the ten-minute ceremony. The couple shared a sense of possibility; they felt ready to seize their moment in history.

Much as most New Yorkers picked up one of the city's many daily papers to read the latest about the weather or their favorite sports teams, Dhoruba always scanned the news for the latest about the Black Panther Party. On the morning of October 20, just a week after his marriage, the Panthers hit the front page: the party's chairman, Huey Newton, was in the hospital—and under arrest for shooting and killing a cop.

According to newspaper accounts, Newton and another Panther member were driving in West Oakland when they were pulled over by a police officer. Realizing that he'd just pulled over the head of the Black Panther Party, the cop called for backup. Another cop arrived. Newton was told to get out of the car. He did, and a scuffle between Newton and the first cop ensued. Newton shot the cop dead, then turned and fired—and hit—the other cop. The policeman was able to return fire, hitting Newton in the lower back. Newton and his partner then fled the scene. Bleeding profusely, Newton was rushed to a hospital, where he was treated and arrested.

Papers all over the country carried an Associated Press wire service photo of Newton on a hospital gurney, bleeding and barely conscious, handcuffed to the side of the gurney with an Oakland cop standing over him. Given that the Black Panther Party leader was proclaiming his innocence, it was a loaded image that sent shock waves through the black liberation movement.

Recovering from his wounds, Newton was transferred to Alameda County jail, where he was held without bail. Almost immediately, a "Free Huey" movement was born. It would become a huge publicity boon for the Panthers throughout the United States. The Black Panther Party was now the most famous and—among policemen—the most despised black liberation organization in the country.

For Dhoruba, the Free Huey movement was like the voice of Malcolm X himself, calling out to enlist his support in the worldwide struggle for black liberation.

BY THE EARLY months of 1968, the Whitmore case had become a lonely chorus in a loud symphony of rebellion and dissent. Riots, assassinations, and the looming specter of the Black Panther Party dominated the discussion. Stories of black kids framed by a prejudiced criminal justice system had become so common that George's story didn't even seem like news anymore. Given George's past association with the Wylie-Hoffert murders, the name Whitmore was still good for a few column inches in the back pages of the metro section, but that was it. In the racial hurricane of the late 1960s, Whitmore's travails had become a drop in the bucket.

BY THE TIME an attorney named Myron Beldock became involved in the Whitmore case, the kid's chances didn't look too good. Beldock, just thirty-five, was a skilled litigator with expertise in appellate law. The appeals process was an aspect of jurisprudence that sometimes required a talent for prestidigitation: a successful appellate lawyer was expected to create something out of nothing, or at least to zero in on a specific legal detail, using it to change the entire outlook of a case.

The Whitmore appeal was going to require that kind of magic. The accused had been convicted on charges of assault and attempted rape at three separate trials. Most recently, he'd been given the maximum sentence and remanded once again to the psych ward at Kings County Hospital, and then upriver to Sing Sing. By now Arthur Miller, Whitmore's most devoted legal advocate, seemed to be burned out on the case. Miller had asked Beldock for help, though he couldn't promise much financial remuneration in return. As Beldock remembered years later, "I'm sure Arthur used the word 'injustice' and described it as a wrongful conviction. The fact that an injustice had occurred, the strong feeling that there was a wrong that needed to be made right, was something Arthur and I would have shared in common. He knew that I would be open to the case even though, purely as a legal matter, it promised to be an uphill battle."

In many ways, Beldock was a child of the system. His father had been an appellate judge in Brooklyn for close to thirty years, and along with his years of experience in the appellate division, Beldock had served as an assistant U.S. attorney in the Eastern District of New York from 1958 to 1960. Beldock knew the system's strengths and weaknesses; he understood that justice within it was based all too often on power and influence rather than fairness.

Despite its prominence a few years earlier, Beldock was only marginally aware of the Whitmore case; like most lawyers, he tended to focus only on whatever case was in front of him at the time. But he recognized that the Whitmore case had become something of a judicial sinkhole, with its layers of bias, appellate reversals, and allegations of racial injustice—a classic example of what civil rights leaders and legal scholars had begun to refer to as "institutional racism."

The charges against Whitmore had been tried before three separate judges. Most legal matters relating to the case had been reviewed ad nauseam. Beldock had to find something—anything—to use as grounds for a new appeal. He started by reading Whitmore's sixty-one-page false confession, then worked his way through the various trial transcripts. He also read a recent book about the Whitmore case: *Justice in the Back Room*, by Selwyn Raab, the *World Telegram* reporter who'd covered the saga almost from the beginning, and whose article for *Harper's* had been squelched by the dictatorial Manhattan D.A. Frank Hogan.

Beldock was astounded by what he read. In his nine years as an attorney, he rarely used the word *racism* in describing the criminal justice system. Yet the details of the Whitmore case rang true to him: as someone who'd grown up around judges and lawyers and officers of the court, he'd often heard racial epithets dropped in conversation. "There was a basic prejudice to the system," recalled Beldock. "I heard a lawyer or two refer to black people as 'animals'—that includes defense lawyers and certainly prosecutors. Generally speaking, if you were black or Hispanic and had no particular sophistication, cops were able to get you to admit to things that were not true. I tended to not look at individual cases involving black and Hispanic defendants as racial matters because, in a sense, it was *all* a racial matter. There was prejudice across the board."

After his crash course in the case, Beldock met Whitmore at Sing Sing, where the prisoner had recently been declared legally "sane" after yet another psychiatric evaluation. In a visitors' cubicle, George seemed distracted, chain-smoking through their meeting. Beldock was the sixth lawyer he had met, the latest in a parade of advocates who had come into his life with great fanfare and then—all except for Arthur Miller— disappeared in a cloud of smoke.

After talking with Whitmore, Beldock came away with the same impression as pretty much everyone who met him. "He was sweet tempered and pretty simple. An ordinary young man. He wasn't a very well educated person. He had some learning disabilities, bad eyesight and I believe he was dyslexic. Anyone who met George would know that he was the type of person who was not very able to stand up to pressure. He would have wanted out of that police precinct and would have said and done whatever his masters told him to do. If the police had told him 'it is all going to be over, all you have to do is sign a confession to the Lincoln assassination,' he would have signed it."

Beldock told Whitmore, "What has been done here is a grave injustice, George. Myself and Arthur Miller will do everything we can to get the conviction overturned."

George was impressed by Beldock; he seemed sincere and compassionate. But Whitmore was burned out himself; he was losing the ability to focus on the details of his case. His parting words to Beldock were, "Next time you visit, could you bring a carton of cigarettes?"

"Sure," said Beldock. He returned to New York City and went to work.

Before long, Beldock zeroed in on one pertinent and unresolved issue: Elba Borrero's identification of Whitmore as her assailant at the Seventy-third Precinct station house.

Amid all the issues surrounding the Whitmore case, somehow the legality of the Borrero ID had never been sufficiently challenged by George's many attorneys. Almost everything about the identification violated the police department's own policies regarding witness identifications. According to the cops, the prosecutors, and Borrero herself, she had never been shown a photo spread of potential suspects. She was told that Whitmore had been brought into the precinct on another criminal matter, possibly predisposing Borrero to believe he was a criminal. Whitmore was not placed in a lineup; rather, she had peered at Whitmore through a peephole as he recited lines ("I'm going to rape you, I'm going to kill you") fed to him by the detectives. After initially expressing uncertainty, Borrero positively identified George despite the fact that his height, weight, and physical characteristics differed from the original description she'd given at the scene—except for the fact that he was a "Negro male."

Beldock allowed himself to be optimistic; he felt there were good grounds for an appeal on the notion that Whitmore's identification by Borrero had been illegal, unconstitutional, and a violation of his civil rights. At the very least, the attorney would file appeal papers, while submitting an application for bail on the grounds that Whitmore's conviction for assault and attempted rape was "tainted and improper." They would try to get George out of prison pending his appeal.

As for Whitmore himself, he remained behind the walls at Sing Sing, indulging his talent for making homemade wine. In March 1968, he received a letter from Aida with some good news: she had given birth to a healthy baby girl. They named her Aida Jr.

George sat in his cell. *I'll be damned*, he thought. *I'm a father.*

twelve

REVOLUTION

EDDIE ELLIS AND others in the black liberation movement had been trying to establish a beachhead for the Black Panther Party in New York,
but their efforts hadn't gone according to plan. The arrests of sixteen
members of RAM on charges of "conspiracy to commit anarchy" had
effectively wiped out what was supposed to be the military wing of the
party in New York—a devastating blow to what was supposed to be a
revolutionary militant organization. Young people in the community
who were frustrated and impatient with the predictable patterns of nonviolent protests had expected the Panthers to put some weight behind
their demand for Black Power; for them, this was a major step backward.

Ellis had wanted to build an organization that had both a militant
underground section and an aboveground political wing, like the Irish
Republican Army (IRA). RAM had been central to this plan. They had
developed an underground guerrilla strategy based on liberation struggles in Algeria, Cuba, Ireland, and South Africa. Max Stanford and other
RAM leaders were to be the Panthers' legitimate link to the practice of
armed self-defense. Now that the cadre from RAM had been taken off
the street, the New York Panthers weren't much different from other
reform-oriented activist groups like CORE or the NAACP.

There was a second problem, even more deeply rooted in the shifting
landscape of the black liberation movement: Ellis had populated his Black
Panther Party with former members of SNCC and CORE—exactly the

kinds of middle-class organizations, full of college kids, churchgoers, and conventional political activists, to which the Panthers were supposed to be an alternative. The whole idea behind the party as put forth by Huey Newton, Bobby Seale, and later Eldridge Cleaver was that revolutions were inspired and waged from the bottom up—by the "lumpen proletariat." To Newton, the Panthers should be an organization of "brothers off the block." As cofounder Bobby Seale put it: "Huey wanted . . . brothers who had been out there robbing banks, brothers who had been pimping, brothers who had been peddling dope, brothers who ain't gonna take no shit, brothers who had been fighting the pigs. . . . Huey P. Newton knew that once you organize the brothers that he ran with, he fought with, he fought against, who he fought harder than they fought him . . . you get revolutionaries."

The philosophical differences between the West Coast Panthers and groups like SNCC and CORE seemed irreconcilable. SNCC and the Black Panther Party made a public announcement that they were merging their efforts and forming a coalition, but behind the scenes, their differences were already undermining the standing of the older organizations, who were increasingly viewed as out of touch.

The impossibility of a merger was made clear in the summer of 1968, when a contingent of West Coast Panther leaders arrived in New York for a series of Free Huey rallies and a press conference at the United Nations. At the offices of SNCC on Fifth Avenue in Manhattan, the Panthers met with James Forman, veteran organizer, former Freedom Rider, and an eloquent debater and speaker. Forman had for years been attempting to move SNCC in a more militant direction and was famously quoted as saying at a rally in Montgomery, "If we can't sit at the table of democracy, then let's knock the fucking legs off."

The goal of the meeting was supposed to be finding a way for the Panthers and Forman to combine their efforts. Among the attendees were Melvin Newton, Huey's brother, and David Hilliard, a boyhood friend of Newton's who'd been named chairman of the Black Panther Party while Huey was in prison. But the meeting was derailed by a dispute between Forman and the Panther camp. Accounts would differ, as usual; the *New York Times* reported that "Members of the Black Panther Party walked into James Forman's office at [SNCC] on Fifth Avenue in late July, according to federal authorities. One of them produced a pistol and put it into Mr. Forman's mouth. He squeezed the trigger three times. It went click, click, click. It was unloaded."

This story may have been apocryphal; it grew to include claims that the Panthers "tortured" Forman in the Manhattan office and forced him into a game of Russian roulette. Forman denied there was any torture or gunplay, but he did eventually disassociate himself from any Panther alliance. "I had never worked in an organization where I felt my personal security and safety were threatened by internal elements," he wrote in his memoir, "and I did not intend to start doing it then."

To those who were hoping the Panthers would offer a new, more militant posture, rumors of the incident with Forman only added to the group's take-no-prisoners reputation. As Minister of Information Eldridge Cleaver later put it, "You're either part of the solution or part of the problem." The Panthers, it seemed, were declaring the old-guard leaders to be part of the problem.

And yet a third issue, bubbling below the surface, was causing a rift among black leaders, one that none of them—not the Panther leadership, James Forman, or anyone else—fully recognized at the time.

The account of the gun incident between the Panthers and Forman that appeared in the *Times* had been supplied by the FBI—the "federal authorities" cited in the piece. Unbeknownst to the black leaders, a number of undercover federal agents and paid informants had infiltrated SNCC, and the information they gleaned about the organization's internal plans and strategies was then being leaked to selected media outlets. It was all part of a secret Justice Department program that grew out of the cold war, a policy of spying on and seeking to undermine or even destroy people and organizations that were considered "un-American" through the use of subterfuge and the spreading of disinformation.

For more than a decade, FBI director J. Edgar Hoover had been conducting a confidential investigation into the activities of civil rights leaders, under a counterintelligence program, or COINTELPRO, code-named "Racial Matters." Although the program had been in existence since the late 1950s, it had kicked into overdrive after the August 1963 March on Washington. Shortly after King's speech that day, the chief of the COINTELPRO program sent Hoover an eleven-page confidential memo. "We must mark [King] now, if we have not before, as the most dangerous Negro in the future of this Nation from the standpoint of communism, the Negro, and national security. . . . It may be unrealistic to limit [our actions against King] to legalistic proofs that would stand up in court or before Congressional Committees."

If the FBI believed that Martin Luther King Jr. was "the most dangerous Negro" in America, one whose activities justified extralegal measures, imagine how Hoover and his people must have felt about the emerging Black Panther Party.

The philosophical differences and eventual split between the Panthers and the old-guard civil rights organizations was real, but it was also the beginning of an era when federal law enforcement would step up its lines of attack and subterfuge. Some of the efforts on the part of local police and federal law enforcement would be transparent, others covert and ultimately unconstitutional. From this point on, nearly anyone who stuck his neck out on behalf of equality and advancement for black people—especially anyone who assumed a leadership role in the Black Power movement—was designated an enemy of the state, added to what was called the Black Agitator Index, a list of names of bad Negroes whose political beliefs qualified them to be spied on, monitored, and held up to special scrutiny by the state.

IN THE SPRING of 1968, Dhoruba bin Wahad took a part-time job at a small printing plant in lower Manhattan. He was still selling weed on the side, throwing occasional parties at his loft on East Third Street, and educating himself on the symbiosis between black liberation and anti-colonial struggles around the world. Among the books he devoured was *Soul on Ice*, a collection of essays on race, revolution, and criminal justice by Eldridge Cleaver. With Huey Newton locked up in prison, Cleaver was coming into his own as the most famous and visible leader of the Black Panther Party. On TV to promote his book and at rallies, Cleaver was articulate and attractive. With his neatly trimmed goatee, tinted sunglasses, and fierce street patter (*can you dig it?*), Cleaver appeared to Dhoruba and a whole generation of young black men as a kind of street prince, the epitome of Panther chic. More than a hustler, he brought a level of philosophical insight to his politics that was exciting to like-minded, would-be revolutionaries.

In *Soul on Ice*, Cleaver identified the revolution as a conflict between personal liberation and the repressive forces of "the white mother country." Just as Malcolm X had noted that the relationship between the police and people in the ghetto was at the core of the struggle, Cleaver framed the issue of police repression in an international context:

> The police do on the domestic level what the armed forces do on an international level: protect the way of life for those in power. The police patrol the city, cordon off communities, blockade neighborhoods, invade homes, search for that which is hidden. The armed forces patrol the world, invade countries and continents, cordon off nations, blockade islands and whole peoples; they will overrun villages, neighborhoods, enter homes, huts, caves, searching for that which is hidden. The policeman and the soldier will violate your person, smoke you out with various gasses. Each will shoot you, beat your head and body with sticks and clubs, with rifle butts, run you through with bayonets, shoot holes in your flesh, kill you. They each have unlimited firepower. They will use all that is necessary to bring you to your knees. They won't take no for an answer. If you resist their guns, they call for reinforcements with bigger guns. Eventually they will come in tanks, in jets, in ships. They will not rest until you surrender or are killed. The policeman and the soldier will have the last word.

Dhoruba was hooked. Not since Malcolm had someone expressed the "truth" so vibrantly, in terms immediately recognizable to "a brother from the block." Dhoruba's social consciousness, long since hot-wired in prison, had just been waiting for an incident that would push him over the edge into action. That incident occurred on April 4, 1968.

He spent most of that morning making deliveries for the printing plant. He'd just returned to the plant when a fellow worker asked, "Hey, did you hear the news?"

"What news," said Dhoruba.

"Martin Luther King was assassinated."

Dhoruba took the news like a kick to the groin. He left the building, walked across the street, and sat down in a small park. Someone nearby had a transistor radio, and as he listened he learned more about King's shooting in Memphis. Police believed the assailant was a white man named James Earl Ray, who was still at large (Ray would be captured two months later). The killer had shot King while he was standing on the balcony of the Lorraine Motel; the civil rights leader was dead before he reached the hospital. He was thirty-nine years old.

The fact that Dhoruba had mixed feelings about King's campaign of nonviolent protest only added to the shock. For many young men of Dhoruba's generation, King had become a kind of symbol of appeasement. To allow black protesters to be hosed down and beaten by cops, to be spat upon while they engaged in peaceful sit-ins at some lunch counter in Alabama or Mississippi, was anathema to Dhoruba and almost everyone else he knew growing up in the Bronx. To black men like Dhoruba, nonviolent protest meant getting beaten by your oppressors and just standing there and taking it; at the most fundamental level, it was an affront to their manhood. As the Black Power movement increasingly dominated the headlines, King was receding from the front lines of the civil rights struggle. The idea that he, not one of them, had been violently gunned down was almost beyond belief.

They killed that dude? Dhoruba thought to himself. *He wasn't even a threat. And they killed the man.*

When Dhoruba returned to work, he was met with a surprising development: the white workers at the plant all started apologizing to him. *Why do they feel the need to apologize on behalf of that cracker who pulled the trigger?* he wondered. *Did they feel complicit in the act?* The apologies only depressed him further.

That day, he quit his job at the printing plant. Within forty-eight hours of hearing about the assassination, he headed out to Brooklyn, to what he heard was the new headquarters for the Black Panther Party in New York, an Afrocentric bookstore at 780 Nostrand Avenue in Bed-Stuy. In the window was a poster, soon to be iconic, of Huey P. Newton sitting in a wicker chair, a modern-day African warrior with a spear in one hand and a rifle in the other. Dhoruba entered the store.

"Where do I sign up for the Black Panther Party?"

The young brothers and sisters in the store, Dhoruba remembered, were sporting black berets, goatees, and Afros. One brother identified himself as the officer of the day. "Well, my brother, it ain't like that," he said. "You can't just join. We have to educate you first. You have to know the party's ten-point program and platform by heart. Also, you have to attend PE classes."

"PE classes," said Dhoruba. "What's that?"

"Political education—learning history from a black perspective. All the things they don't teach us in school, you dig?"

Dhoruba nodded. "Where do I take the classes?"

"They're held twice weekly at Long Island University in Brooklyn." The Panther officer handed Dhoruba a couple of pamphlets and an application form. "Fill this out. You have to report for class every week in Brooklyn till you're accepted into the party."

Dhoruba looked at the list of Panther reading material in a pamphlet: Frederick Douglass, Du Bois, Baldwin, *Crisis of the Negro Intellectual* by Harold Cruse. "I've read some of these books already," he said.

"Yeah?" said the officer. "That puts you ahead of the game. Where did you attend college?"

"Oh, various penal institutions upstate," he replied. "That was my college."

The officer of the day reached out and shook Dhoruba's hand. "All power to the people, my brother. You've come to the right place."

GEORGE WHITMORE WAS in the second-floor rec room at Sing Sing when the news came that King had been gunned down in Memphis. Like everyone else, he was stunned. When the network news showed footage of King giving his speech before the National Mall, George choked up. He remembered sitting in the empty catering hall at the Ivy Hotel in Wildwood that day—August 28, 1963—watching the March on Washington play out on television. If it hadn't been for the magnitude of that day and King's speech, Whitmore's coworkers might not have remembered that he'd been there watching TV at just the moment when detectives claimed he was in Manhattan raping and eviscerating Janice Wylie and Emily Hoffert.

King's speech had become Whitmore's alibi. Martin Luther King Jr. had literally saved his life.

That night, the penitentiary was put on lockdown. Worried about riots or acts of revenge by black convicts against white convicts, authorities kept the inmates in their cells twenty-three hours a day for five straight days. Mealtime was doled out in shifts, to ensure only minimal interaction between prisoners. An eerie quiet descended upon Sing Sing in those days, and it lingered until the guards lifted the lockdown and allowed prisoners to circulate in general population.

As he had after Malcolm X's assassination, George made a few dollars painting portraits of King and selling them to inmates. Sometimes, as he sketched out the contours of King's face and then painted in the details, George felt like he wanted to cry.

AS WITH MOST cops, the first thing Bill Phillips wondered after the King assassination was, When would the rioting start? In New York City, the hours and days immediately after the assassination were tense. There were sporadic disturbances around the city, with some looting, broken windows, and candlelight vigils that occasionally turned unruly. The threat became much worse on the night of April 6, as news came of full-fledged rioting in more than one hundred cities. The National Guard was sent in to restore peace in Chicago, Baltimore, Washington, D.C. Before the riots were over, thirty-seven to forty-six people were killed, with thousands of injuries and property damage of more than $50 million.

In New York, Mayor Lindsay took to the streets in an attempt to quell the growing, restless anger. There would ultimately be rioting in New York, some of it destructive and costly, but nothing like what Phillips and the NYPD had experienced the previous summer, when police cars were shot at, torched, and showered with brick-filled garbage cans from tenement rooftops. Still, the toll from rioting in New York after the King assassination was one dead, seventy police and civilian injuries, and 428 arrests. Property damage was estimated at $5 million.

One week after King was buried in a nationally televised ceremony, Phillips was cruising in a squad car with his latest partner, Eddie Lawrence. Lawrence was what was known in the department as a "hair bag," a veteran cop with close to twenty years on the job, slow, cautious, with one eye on his retirement date and dreams of suburbia.

At Park Avenue and West 122nd Street, in the shadow of the elevated tracks of the New York Central railroad, a Latina in her midtwenties came fleeing out of a building and flagged down Phillips and Lawrence.

"I've been robbed, I've been robbed!"

"When did it happen?" Phillips asked the woman.

"It's happening right now. He's still up there in the apartment."

Phillips thought about that: How likely was it that a robber was waiting up there for cops to arrive? "He's not up there," said Phillips.

The woman was taken aback. "Yes he is. He's still there."

Phillips sighed and got out of the car, followed ten steps behind by his partner. He opened the front door of the building, a run-down four-story tenement at 1743 Park Avenue. In the narrow hallway, Phillips saw a man carrying shopping bags in each hand. The man was short but well-built, black, midthirties, wearing jeans and a loose cotton shirt.

"That's him," said the woman. "Look, he's still got my things in the bag. That's my radio."

Phillips stepped forward and said to the man, "Okay, you fuck, drop the loot and get against the wall."

The man's name was Calvin McCoy. He had an extensive police record, twenty-five arrests on charges ranging from disorderly conduct to possession of narcotics to burglary. He was a junkie, likely robbing the woman's apartment for items to pawn so that he could buy smack. He had the skittish mannerisms of a junkie but looked like an athlete.

McCoy's eyes darted here and there, looking around the hallway; he had nowhere to run. He put down the bags and faced the wall. When Phillips stepped forward to frisk the suspect, McCoy elbowed him square in the solar plexus and knocked him off balance. McCoy bolted down the hallway and out the front door.

Standing outside the building, Officer Lawrence looked up to see a black dude come running frantically out the front door, with Phillips close behind.

"Grab him, Eddie!" shouted Phillips.

Lawrence tried to stop the robber but was knocked flat on his ass. He did, however, slow McCoy down enough that Phillips managed to catch up and grab him. Phillips and McCoy tussled on the street. The fabric of McCoy's shirt ripped and the shirt was torn completely off. McCoy pulled out a switchblade, and Phillips froze. The robber lunged at Phillips. The cop raised his left hand to block the attack, and the blade sliced the meaty part of his palm, sending blood spurting everywhere. Phillips jerked back his hand, pulling away. McCoy bolted down Park Avenue underneath the elevated railway tracks, a shirtless black man on the run. Phillips took off after him, his hand dripping blood. He recalled:

This guy is going like a raped ape. Zip! He's running like a

deer under the el. He's got some body on him, looked like a
weight lifter. I'm chasing him and he's gaining on me every
step. I hear Eddie yell, shoot him, shoot him. Good fucking
idea, right? He's now about fifteen, twenty yards away. I whip
out my gun and fire two shots up in the air under the el. . . .
On the corner there's a traffic stanchion. I rest my hand on
it, cock the gun and fire one shot. Get him right through the
back. He doesn't fall down, but he stops running. When I get
to him he's bleeding from the nose and mouth. The bullet
severed the lung artery. I says, holy shit, this guy's going to die.
Jesus Christ almighty, I killed this fucking guy.

Police cars with sirens wailing flocked to the scene as local residents
gathered on the street. Also among the first responders were representatives of a special Urban Task Force that Mayor Lindsay's office had
established after King's assassination for exactly this purpose—to arrive
at the scene of potentially explosive incidents and try to maintain the
peace. As people milled about, uncertain what to do, a few angry comments were shouted at the cops.

Phillips was taken to the same hospital as the robber. While his hand
was being stitched up, he was informed that Calvin McCoy had died.

"What did you have to shoot the guy for?" one of the mayor's task
force members asked Phillips. "Can you account for this shooting? You
may be in a lot of trouble."

Phillips wasn't in any trouble. The investigation of the shooting,
treated as a routine inquiry by the NYPD, found that the suspect was
killed in the line of duty. Phillips was given a special commendation for
valor, but he wasn't especially proud of the shooting.

A police officer is supposed to understand that any time he
shoots at a guy he intends to kill him. But I think, most of
us think, that most of these guys that get shot don't die. As a
matter of fact, them guys are hard to kill. Shoot these people
in the fucking head and they live, I swear to Christ. So when
I'm shooting at the guy, I figured the guy isn't going to die for
chrissakes. . . . I didn't think, I'm going to kill him. I didn't aim
at his head. I just aimed at his general body. It's really hard to
hit a guy with a handgun at that distance.

Several weeks later, a man came into the Twenty-fifth Precinct station house in Harlem and said, "I want to report a murder."

He was sent up to the second floor to see a detective. He walked into the squad room and repeated his refrain, "I want to report a murder."

"Yeah?" said a detective. "Who was murdered?"

"My brother was murdered. By Patrolman William Phillips."

The detective glared at the guy and said, "Get the fuck out of here."

There was no rioting after the shooting of Calvin McCoy. His long criminal record, and the fact that his death took place while he was in the midst of committing a crime, seemed to mitigate whatever reaction the community might have felt. Everyone breathed a sigh of relief. McCoy's death raised all kinds of theoretical issues: Does a burglar caught in the act deserve to die? Was shooting a fleeing perp in the back an act of "valor," as the department would proclaim? But this was the sort of encounter that took place regularly in the ghetto, where a cop had to make a hair-trigger decision about the use of deadly force, and the residents were left to decide if the results were outrageous enough to justify burning down their neighborhood.

A few months after the shooting of Calvin McCoy—after Phillips had been presented with his medal of valor by the NYPD—the officer was at a grand jury hearing about the shooting. In the hallway of the courthouse, he happened to walk by the mother of the man he shot. Weary beyond her years, in tremendous emotional distress, the woman looked at the cop and said, "You killed my son."

The normally loquacious Phillips had no comeback.

SEVERAL WEEKS AFTER the King assassination, on May 15, 1968, Dhoruba and his wife, Iris, attended a star-studded benefit for the Black Panther Party. It was held at Fillmore East, impresario Bill Graham's famous nightclub in the East Village, where many of the major acts of the era would perform and a generation perfected the practice of tuning in, turning on, and dropping out. On this night, there would be no acid or other hallucinogens; it was an event devoted to speeches, the staging of three short theater pieces, and fund-raising. Roughly twenty-six hundred people, black and white, witnessed an evening filled with what the *New York Times* later described as "rhetoric composed of racial paranoia, political jargon, Utopian idealism, unprintable threats, gutty 'soul' talk and shrewd humor."

Among the performers was LeRoi Jones, poet and provocateur, who had barely survived the Newark riot of the previous summer. A Newark native, Jones had been beaten by police; a photo of the aftermath, with blood streaming from his skull, appeared in papers around the country, making him an instant hero and symbol of the movement. Jones also coined a phrase that had become something of a motto for black liberation: "We are a John Coltrane people living in a Lawrence Welk world."

At Fillmore East, Jones read a long, incendiary poem entitled "Home on the Range." He was followed onstage by Kathleen Cleaver, wife of Eldridge, who'd been slated to headline the event until he was waylaid by an incident that, like the incarceration of Huey Newton, had rocked the Panther universe.

Three days after King's murder, Cleaver and a handful of Panthers got into a brutal, ninety-minute gun battle with local police in Oakland, California. Seventeen-year-old Bobby Hutton, one of the Panthers' founding members, was shot dead by cops that day; three other people were wounded, and Cleaver and five other Panthers were arrested. Authorities were unable to establish whether Cleaver had fired on police, but he was held on the grounds that he had violated the terms of his parole from prison. Cleaver's bail was set at $200,000, and the Fillmore East benefit organizers resolved to donate part of the money they raised to Cleaver's bail.

For Dhoruba Bin Wahad, the event was a coming out of sorts. He was still a probationary member of the Black Panther Party, spending his free time memorizing the Panthers' platform and Ten-Point Program, which was headed "What We Want, What We Believe." He read *Wretched of the Earth* by Frantz Fanon, the bible for Panthers with an anticolonial and Pan-African bent, and watched the movie *The Battle of Algiers*, required viewing for would-be Panthers. There were additional classes on everything from Marxist economic theory to history classes on slavery, the Nat Turner slave rebellion, Reconstruction, and Jim Crow. The reading and discussion classes were rigorous; prospective members who missed a class or came unprepared were disciplined or even denied membership.

Dhoruba excelled at the PE classes, which extended the education he'd begun in prison.

Because of my studies in the joint I already had the historical overview. I was more advanced than some of the younger brothers and sisters. Having been incarcerated gave me perspective and credibility. Plus, I had been the vice president of one of the largest gangs in the city [the Sportsmen Disciples]. I knew about organizing people who maybe didn't have a college or even high school education. I knew about fostering self-pride and group morale and how to enforce internal discipline in a way that conveys the right message without alienating the rank and file. I knew about organizing activities that had the potential of bringing us into conflict with the po po. On top of all that, I had the military training; I knew about guns.

Dhoruba not only knew about weapons, he wasn't afraid to put them to use—if and when the time arrived.

Some people joined the party to feed children through the breakfast program. Some were primarily political activists looking to change the system. All that's cool. But me, I joined the party to fight the pigs. That's why I joined. Because my experience with the police was always negative. I saw the way they ran roughshod over us, abused us, framed us, all my life. And we didn't have no say. Well, what Huey and Eldridge were advocating was self-defense, the idea that we weren't going to sit back and take that shit anymore, that we had the right to defend ourselves. And now we were going to exercise that right. Of course, this terrified the police, which was just fine by us. Nothing terrifies the police more than the image of a black person with an Afro holding a gun.

By the summer of 1968, what remained of Eddie Ellis's early efforts to launch the Panthers in New York had been absorbed into a new and improved version. A chapter officially associated with the Oakland Panthers (now known as "the Central Committee" or "national leadership") was founded in Bed-Stuy. Fred Richardson, owner of the party's bookstore headquarters at 780 Nostrand Avenue, was named the local minister of information.

On a hot day in early August, Dhoruba hopped on the Interborough subway and headed out to the office on Nostrand. That morning, he had argued with Iris about his involvement with the party. Iris was not a member. Though she was just as Afrocentric as Dhoruba, she had begun to view her husband's involvement with the movement as an extension of his former life as a gangbanger. It meant dealing with guns and hanging with the same kinds of Bronx street thugs—some of whom still occasionally visited Dhoruba, especially whenever they needed a place to hide from the law. Dhoruba's disagreements with his wife over the party would eventually undermine their marriage.

Dhoruba was caught up in the historical moment. That summer, in the wake of King's murder, Panther chapters and branches were sprouting up all over the country—not just in major cities like Los Angeles, Chicago, Baltimore, and Detroit, but even in midsized cities like Seattle and Toledo and Roxbury, Massachusetts. It was a grassroots phenomenon, attracting countless young men and women attracted by the swashbuckling image of Newton, Cleaver, and the rest, and angered by the behavior of repressive local police against political activity in the black community. That summer saw violent clashes between police and nearly any group who dared to call themselves Black Panthers. Of the many lethal confrontations, the worst occurred in Cleveland, where eleven people—Panthers and police—were killed during a shoot-out.

In New York, the police were on alert. In many ways, the Panthers were the realization of everything the NYPD had feared since Malcolm X first arrived on the scene. The Panthers' distaste for the police was brazen; it was spelled out in their Ten-Point Program, expounded upon by speakers at Panther rallies, and delineated in the *Black Panther*, the party's house newspaper, published weekly. Edited by Intercommunal News Service, the *Black Panther* emerged in the summer of '68 as a powerful promotional and fund-raising tool for the Panthers around the country. The paper sold for twenty-five cents at Panther offices, at rallies, and at corner newsstands—that is, those that weren't being harassed by police, who often confiscated and destroyed whatever copies they could get their hands on.

The average policeman would have found much to hate about the *Black Panther*. Its pages were filled with "anti-American" editorial diatribes against the war in Vietnam, in terms that supported the communist enemy; its writers repeatedly attacked the criminal justice system as inherently racist; its editors lionized Panther members on trial for shooting or killing police as revolutionary heroes. Perhaps most viscerally offensive, the *Black Panther* promoted the image of the P-I-G.

The use of the word *pig* to describe police—first circulated by Huey Newton—had caught on throughout the radical left, including among white college kids, in a way that unsettled the average policeman. The very first issue of the *Black Panther* defined a pig as "an ill-natured beast who has no respect for law and order, a fool traducer who's usually found masquerading as a victim of an unprovoked attack." This definition played off longtime police attitudes toward black people and sought to upend the notion that law and order was the sole province of the men in blue. The term was further crystallized through the artwork of Emory Douglas, the Panthers' minister of culture, whose lavish drawings and cartoons of cops as pigs appeared frequently in the *Black Panther* and galvanized the opposition. LeRoi Jones (who would soon change his name to Amiri Baraka) described Emory's pig as "a nasty scrawny filthy creature with a projected sensibility that was mostly slime lover and animal slacker, if you will. The bravura touch was the flies that always circled the creature's nasty self. Whatever one thought of the Panther philosophy as a whole, I did not meet anyone among any sector of the Movement that did not dig that pig, just looking at it would crack you up in a mixture of merriment and contempt!"

The entire posture of the Panthers, and their newspaper, involved a level of irreverence, disrespect, and hatred of the criminal justice system that mystified, if not shocked, most cops. For sheer, sustained hostility toward civic authority, there was no precedent for it in the history of American law enforcement.

Emerging as two warring tribes in a theater of battle not yet clearly defined, the Panthers and the police drew lines in the sand. Hostilities were mounting on the sweltering August afternoon when Dhoruba arrived at the party headquarters on Nostrand Avenue. There was a carnival atmosphere outside the store, with people gathering in the street. A Panther spokesperson stood on a soapbox rapping through a bullhorn, explaining the party platform and Ten-Point Program, and excoriating the cops as they drove by in squad cars to monitor the scene.

Dhoruba made his way through the crowd and headed into the store to talk to Richardson, the minister of information, about distribution for the *Black Panther*. In the two months since Dhoruba joined the party, he'd already distinguished himself as a cut above the usual inductee. His political consciousness as a black nationalist was fully formed, and with it came leadership skills he'd learned on the street. Although he hadn't yet been given a title, local Panthers and visiting leaders from the Central Committee in Oakland were already pegging Dhoruba as one to watch. He'd been assigned to handle receipt of newspaper shipments from the West Coast and distribution in the East. Given that the paper had become the Panthers' most lucrative fund-raising source, it was an important task.

As Dhoruba talked with other members, a young Panther burst in. "The pigs is vamping on the brothers outside!"

The scene outside was chaotic. Dhoruba later described it in an unpublished memoir, "The Future Past: The Biostory of a Black Revolutionary in Cold War America":

> The Panther who had earlier stood on the soapbox in front of
> the office was now in a scuffle with two or three policemen
> in the middle of the street. The cops had attempted to wrest
> the bullhorn from him. People were screaming and throwing
> rocks, bottles, and whatever they could get their hands on
> at the parked police cars. Within minutes dozens of police
> arrived, the three Panthers were snatched and whisked away
> before the crowd that had gathered could react. The police
> sped away—leaving an angry mob behind. Immediately the
> remaining Panthers rallied the crowd for an impromptu march
> on the nearest police station where it was believed the Panthers
> had been taken. A crowd of several hundred strong marched
> on the station house. I went along with the Panthers and the
> crowd.

At the station house, Dhoruba was part of a four-man delegation that entered and negotiated with the precinct commander. The police had arrested one person for illegal use of a bullhorn to incite a riot and two others for assault on police officers, including one who allegedly kicked a cop in the groin. It was agreed that the arrested Panthers would be transferred immediately from the precinct to arraignment court on Schermerhorn Street in downtown Brooklyn.

A contingent of more than two hundred supporters from the neighborhood—all black—immediately made their way to the courthouse, where they staged a loud demonstration on the front steps. Inside, the courtroom was packed with both supporters and off-duty cops who'd heard about the confrontation and showed up to support their fellow officers. An assistant D.A. and lawyers for the arrested men gave conflicting accounts of what took place on Nostrand Avenue. The three Panthers were charged and given an appearance date by Judge John F. Furey. Since they had no criminal records, Judge Furey allowed the men to be released on their own recognizance without having to post bail—a move that angered the off-duty cops.

Outside, Panther supporters and cops milled about in the afternoon heat. The crowd had now doubled in size to about four hundred. Television reporters and cameras were on the scene for what appeared to be the first major showdown between cops and the infamous Black Panther Party in New York.

Dhoruba was on the outskirts of the crowd when he was bum-rushed by a TV reporter and a cameraman. "Here's one of these Panthers," said the cameraman. The reporter hurried over. "You witnessed what happened. What do you think about the charges?"

Dhoruba recalled his reaction: "A microphone was shoved in my face, and I went off: 'This was an unprovoked attack by the police. The brothers had a First Amendment right to be out on the street. This is typical fascist pig behavior. All power to the people.'"

When Dhoruba got home that night, Iris said, "So now you're a spokesman for the Black Panther Party?"

"What are you talking about?" said Dhoruba.

"You were on the six o'clock news identified as a Black Panther spokesman."

"For real?"

Dhoruba watched the report repeated at eleven that night, and there it was: in the blink of an eye, he had gone from being a neophyte member to being the new face of the Black Panther Party in New York City.

RESENTMENT OVER THE incident in Brooklyn hung heavy in the humid air that night. A group of Panthers and cops lingered outside the courthouse on Schermerhorn Street. When they finally left, one of the brothers allegedly yelled at the cops, "You'll see some Panther Power tonight!"

Around midnight, in the Brooklyn neighborhood of Crown

Heights, a call went out over the police radio: a domestic dispute at 1054 Eastern Parkway. Two patrolmen headed over to the address, but before they reached the front door a pair of shotgun blasts knocked both the cops down.

The patrolmen weren't dead, just wounded by the buckshot from the gun. A backup team of cops arrived and rushed them to the hospital.

Combing the scene of the shooting for clues, investigators came across two empty shotgun shells in a back alley—and a white button bearing the insignia of a black panther.

The war was on.

thirteen

"OFF THE PIGS!"

GEORGE WHITMORE WALKED out of prison on June 15, 1968, but his problems with the law were not over. Although he had been released on $5,000 bail (once again paid for out of the NAACP Legal Defense Fund), he still stood convicted of assault and attempted rape. The remainder of his five- to- ten-year sentence was still hanging over his head. His most recent attorney, Myron Beldock, told him that his appeal had been put in abeyance—there would be a hearing at a future date. Until then, he would remain beyond the walls of prison but not yet free.

Upon his release, Whitmore rejoined Aida and met his daughter, less than a year old, for the first time. Aida and the baby stayed in East New York with Aida's family, but George went back to New Jersey, where there was supposed to be work during the summers in Wildwood. But no one would hire a convicted sex offender out on bail.

Journalist Fred Shapiro, who first laid eyes on Whitmore at the Seventy-third Precinct station house back in April 1964—when George was paraded before the media as the Wylie-Hoffert perpetrator—met briefly with Whitmore to interview him for a book he was writing on the case. George said to Shapiro, "I can't seem to get nothin' going with my case hanging over my head. Don't seem worthwhile to go lookin' for [a permanent job] when I know they may be sending me back to jail after all." George was especially concerned about his wife and his daughter, he told the reporter. Then he hit him up for twenty dollars.

Finally, Whitmore got some good news. His longtime lawyer, Arthur Miller, called to say they'd found him a part-time job through a federal jobs program.

"That's beautiful," said George. "What's the job?"

"You ever hear of the Nation of Islam?" Miller said.

George thought about that. "You mean the Black Muslims?"

"Yes."

"Sure, I heard of them."

"Well, you can get a federally funded job working for them. It pays minimum wage, but it's better than nothing."

Damn, thought George. The Black Muslims. Elijah Muhammad. He wasn't sure how he felt about that. "Mister Miller," he said, "you sure this might not have a negative effect on my case, me workin' with an organization like that?"

"Well, George, I spoke with them about that. I warned them they could not use the fact that you would be employed there as any kind of publicity stunt in any way. They said that was not their intention. They want you to meet with the leader there—Minister Louis Farrakhan."

"Okay."

"I'll go with you. We'll meet with Farrakhan and express our concerns and see how it goes."

On a warm summer morning, Whitmore took a bus into Manhattan, where he was met by his lawyer. He and Miller took a taxi to Mosque Number Seven, located in Harlem on West 116th Street and Lenox Avenue.

The original Mosque Number Seven had been burned down after Malcolm X's assassination back in 1965. The new version opened at the same location, the refurbished building topped with a dome and a revolving star and crescent. The mosque was in the process of expanding to include not just a religious temple but also a school, a performance space, a restaurant, and numerous shops. Whitmore and Miller met with Louis Farrakhan, a Bronx-born former calypso singer, in his thirties, who was now the national spokesman for the Nation of Islam as well as minister of its largest and most influential mosque.

Over lunch at a restaurant attached to the building, Miller explained to the minister that they did not want Whitmore's employment there to be used as political agitprop by the Nation, which they felt could poison the waters and endanger his chances of getting his conviction overturned. Farrakhan assured Miller and Whitmore that he understood their concerns. "Our goal is simply to help a brother in need, nothing more," he said.

George had a positive impression of Farrakhan, who was soft-spoken and seemed sincere. After lunch, Farrakhan introduced Whitmore to a group of fifty or so Muslims at the mosque, explaining that while Whitmore was struggling to find justice in the courts, he would be working for the Nation of Islam in a part-time capacity. "Here, you are one of us, you are a brother," Farrakhan told George in front of the group.

Whatever his reaction to Farrakhan in the moment, George had lingering reservations about the Black Muslims. His impressions of the organization came mostly from prison, where the Nation was a visible presence. They were rigidly disciplined, overtly religious, and seemed to interact almost exclusively with their own kind. George was the type of person who had always mixed easily with whites, Latinos, and anyone else who treated him like a human being. To be restricted to any one group went against his nature.

Nonetheless, he needed the work. And so Whitmore began reporting on a semiregular basis to a printing plant and office in East New York—the distribution center for *Muhammad Speaks*, the official newspaper for the Nation of Islam. The location was convenient. George moved in with his wife and daughter in a backroom apartment that belonged to Aida's mother, within walking distance of the job. Although they gave him his own desk, the job was mostly that of a glorified errand runner.

There were problems from the start: Whitmore smoked cigarettes, liked the occasional drink of vodka, ate pork, and was known to curse, all of which were forbidden or frowned upon by Muslims. Members of the Nation projected a conservative personal demeanor, with the men wearing a quasi uniform of gray suit, starched white shirt, and bow tie. While working for the Muslims, George wore the same outfit, which made him feel constricted. The most serious problem was his smoking. Whitmore had smoked since he was twelve years old; he was a pack-a-day man. There were no ashtrays anywhere on the premises. Eventually, they bought George an ashtray—a huge one, the size of a skillet. Whitmore was halfway insulted by the gesture, convinced they were implying that he should go ahead and smoke himself to death. In fact, he never felt completely comfortable with the men and women of the Nation of Islam, and after working at the office for a couple of weeks, he stopped showing up for work. It was the closest Whitmore would ever come to being directly associated with any aspect of the black liberation movement.

THE MOVEMENT WAS under way, whether Whitmore was on board or not. He was still at the mercy of the system—"plodding darkly on in resignation," as DuBois had put it, "steadily, half hopelessly, [watching] the streak of blue above." He steered clear of politics as if it were a wolf in sheep's clothing, unable or unwilling to man the barricades.

Others were there to pick up the slack.

The Black Panther Party was the latest and most vocal manifestation of an evolving process. On West 122nd Street and Seventh Avenue, a new and reinvigorated version of the Panthers put down stakes, a Harlem chapter that was separate from the Brooklyn operation. The location they chose at 2026 Seventh Avenue was under the control of HARYOU-ACT, a federal program that allowed poverty administrators to lease and rent commercial space in the ghetto (giving rise to the term "poverty pimps"). Dhoruba and Lumumba Shakur—whom Dhoruba first met while living with his grandfather in South Jamaica, Queens— were among the group that decided to appropriate the storefront office "on behalf of the people."

> I think it was Lumumba who found the space. It was a storefront, the door was locked. He said to me, 'Dhoruba, we're gonna take this office.' I said, 'Whose office is it?' He said, 'Some of those bootlicking Negroes over at the HARYOU office.' I said, 'Fuck them dudes. We'll take it over and let them pay the rent.' So we went over there, took a crowbar, popped the door open, took the lock out. The place was a mess. You had all this rotten linoleum, but underneath was a beautiful wooden floor. A group of us—sisters and brothers—got in there, pulled up the linoleum, scrubbed the floors, cleaned the plate-glass windows. We had a brother who was a plumber, he got the toilet bowl working. It was all volunteer labor. We got people in the community to donate supplies. We had the office up and running in a matter of days.

WE SERVE THE PEOPLE, read the greeting above the front door of the Panthers' Harlem office. Soon the modest storefront, with its postered windows and hand-painted BLACK PANTHER PARTY sign, was a hub of activity. The Harlem chapter also started a branch in the South Bronx, and new members started signing up at a rate of three and four a day—which mirrored the national trend. By the end of the summer the Panthers would have chapters in twenty-five American cities, and tens of thousands of members.

The growth of the Panthers was so fast and sudden that the national leadership in Oakland were overwhelmed. They tried to send emissaries to all local chapters, including New York, to ensure that any group using the Black Panther name was promoting the Panther credo—the Ten-Point Program, the mission statement, executive mandates from Newton, and so on. They could distribute and sell the *Black Panther*, but ten cents out of every twenty-five from sales of the paper was supposed to go to the Central Committee on the West Coast.

Ron Penniwell was sent to live in New York and serve as a liaison with the central headquarters in California. Penniwell would oversee the development of the Harlem office, which quickly became a show-case for curiosity seekers and media outlets fascinated by the Panthers. Political education classes were sometimes held on the sidewalk outside the office, with members dressed in the Panther uniform of black beret, black leather jacket, and combat boots. Marching exercises were performed in the street, with the young Panthers calling out in cadence:

The revolution has co-ome
It's time to pick up the gu-un
Off the pigs!

Most of the Panthers' new recruits were in their teens and early twenties. Some were attracted by the Panthers' militant image, but social and political activists of all stripes were drawn to the party.

Cleo Silvers was a social worker, originally from Philadelphia, who had come to New York City as a VISTA volunteer in late 1966. She was typical of a new breed of activist who was attracted to the action-oriented approach of the Panthers. Since arriving in New York she'd been working in the Sixteenth Congressional District in the South Bronx, an area that had the dubious distinction of having the lowest income per capita, and highest rate of heroin addiction, of any district in the United States. Cleo had been assigned to work with the Catholic Church and the New York Housing Authority as an organizer and volunteer. Remembered Silvers: "We organized rent strikes, because the housing conditions were horrible. We did the clean-up campaign with the churches, cleaning up the streets. Mostly, we dealt with addicts, trying to get them into detox."

Silvers first came into contact with the Panthers when she was involved in an attempt by health-care workers at Lincoln Hospital to take over the facility.

> The policies at the hospital were so misguided and unjust for
> people living in poverty that we decided to force the issue.
> We took over the hospital and went public with a series of
> demands. The Black Panther Party was the only organization
> that came to our aid. They were very smart and helped us
> with our strategy. They brought food and water to us when we
> occupied the administrative offices. They were kind. They sat
> down with us and taught us how to be more organized; they
> gave us ideas. They were dynamic. They had a set of principles
> that they imparted to us, even though they were younger than
> many of us who took over the facility.

Silvers was so impressed with the Panthers that she headed to the Harlem office to sign up. It was there that she met Afeni Shakur. Afeni was the same age as Cleo—twenty-one—but she was already a movement veteran, having worked for Malcolm X's organization when she was barely seventeen. Silvers remembered:

> Somebody told me to go to the Panther office and tell Janet,
> the officer of the day, that I was joining the party. Afeni Shakur
> and some of the other sisters were there. Afeni said, "So you
> want to be a Panther." I said, "Yes, they sent me down here to
> join the party." And she said, "Well, you can't join the party
> because you don't know how to wrap a gelee" [an African-style
> head covering popular in the '60s and '70s and still worn by
> some black women today]. I said, "That's true. I don't know
> how to wrap a gelee." Afeni said, "Go in there and tell Janet

to give you a cloth, so you can tie a gelee around your head
and be a proper Panther sister." I got the cloth. They wrapped
my head with the gelee real fast, then took it off my head and
said, "Now you wrap it." I watched what they did, so I was able
to wrap my gelee. Afeni said, "Good. Now you're a Panther
sister." And that's how I became a member of the Black Panther
Party.

Silvers gave up her job with the hospital to work full-time with the
party.

You can't sell the *Black Panther* newspaper, be up for the
breakfast program at 4 A.M., go to the community meetings,
work with the children and tutor them after school, go to the
PE classes, cook food, take care of the rest of your colleagues,
and have a job. . . . It was just impossible. So I had to quit
my job because I wanted to be more involved because of the
community aspect of it, the closeness and the unity of the
people.

Silvers spent much of her free time reading in preparation for her
political education class at 9:00 P.M. Her teacher was Dhoruba Bin
Wahad. "To me, the PE classes were slow, because there were people in
the party who didn't know how to read. But Dhoruba was brilliant. He
devoted himself to taking some complex political concepts and theories
and breaking it down in a way that everybody could understand. He was
firm. If he asked you a question about the PE material and you didn't
know the answer, he made you run laps around the block."

Silvers also took physical defense classes, which were held next door
to the office.

I became a green dog in karate. . . . I had stars, I had pins, and
I taught the other sisters how to use them. . . . So if a horse
run up on you, and you got to get out of the way, you got to
get that motherfucker out of your way, guess what, either the
police or the horses would fall down. If you put twenty marbles
underneath a horse's foot, guess what, the motherfucker is
going to break his fucking leg—'cause we demonstrating.

Mostly, the physical training was to instill a personal sense of confidence, not for any serious expectation of combat. "I never held a gun against a police officer," said Silvers. "I never did anything aggressive. I was never remotely violent against anyone. But if anything were to come down, I was going to be ready and able to defend myself."

Female Panthers comprised between 20 and 40 percent of the membership in New York. Their daily routine involved core tasks like selling the *Black Panther*, organizing clothing drives and the free breakfast program for children, and maintaining the "Panther pads," communal apartments around Manhattan that were available to be shared by three to six party members. Male party members followed a different routine, one colored by shared paranoia and the near-daily possibility of conflict with the police.

EVER SINCE THE night when party members had been arrested in Bed-Stuy for "attempting to incite a riot," and two cops were ambushed later on Eastern Parkway, interactions between the Panthers and the NYPD had only grown more tense. At a press conference after the shooting of the cops, Joudon Ford, a precocious, baby-faced eighteen-year-old Panther captain declared: "The Black Panther Party did not order those two policemen shot. It should be clear to all that the Black Panther Party was not involved, because if we had been . . . the pigs would be dead."

The statement enraged the police. In precincts throughout Brooklyn, a group of cops circulated a petition to banish from the bench Judge John F. Furey, who had presided over the arraignment of the Panthers who were arrested for using a bullhorn on Nostrand Avenue. In the petition, the cops claimed that Furey had "permitted members of a racist group in his courtroom to smoke, permitted them to wear their hats while the court was in session and permitted them to shout threats at the members of the Police Department and at the bench in a successful effort to have two defendants before him paroled and walk out of the courtroom."

The judge denied the allegations. In the *New York Times*, the judge was quoted saying that he hadn't seen any hats on nor anyone smoking, and that the court was quiet during the arraignment. His account was backed up by a report in the *Times* the day after the arraignment, which noted that the proceedings had been "orderly."

In general, the police felt they were "not being backed up," as a spokesman for the police petition put it. "We do not have the support of the general public. We do not have the support of the courts." When the petition went nowhere, the aggrieved patrolmen took their effort a step further.

On August 8, a group of policemen announced that they had formed an independent organization called the Law Enforcement Group (LEG), "to protect the life and welfare of police officers and to seek all the assistance possible to enable them to vigorously enforce the laws of the state."

"We're sick and tired of taking it on the chin," said John Cassese, head of the PBA, in response to a question about LEG. "Now how much can we take as policemen? We're ready to lay down our life for anybody in the city of New York or any place else. We shouldn't be ambushed by these people. . . . Among some of the militant guys in the city, war has been declared against the Police Department and I think the sniper incident in Brooklyn points it up."

But the formation of LEG went unheralded by many—until a month later, when a series of NYPD-Panther encounters brought matters to a head.

In late August, three Panthers were arrested and charged with assaulting a police office on Nostrand Avenue outside the Panther headquarters. At their arraignment, there appeared what the *Times* described as "a group of about 20 off-duty policemen, their badges hanging out of the breast pockets of their sports shirts and jackets. Most left after the hearing." The cops were angered by the fact that the Panthers had been granted a hearing to have their bail reduced on the grounds that it was "discriminatory and highly unconstitutional."

William Kunstler, the attorney for the arrested Panthers, alleged that the appearance of the policemen at the hearing was intended to create "an atmosphere of fear" and to convince the judge that "he was dealing with caged animals." At a press conference in the hallway after the hearing, the loquacious Kunstler—who would go on to become a virtual house lawyer for the Panthers and therefore the bane of policemen everywhere—noted that all over the country "large numbers of policemen invariably turn up when a black militant is on trial."

Less than a week later, five more Panthers were arrested. This time, a group that included Captain Joudon Ford were held on charges of loitering and resisting arrest. They were arrested in Brownsville and held at the Seventy-third Precinct station house, the same building where the travails of George Whitmore had begun four and a half years earlier. When Gerald Lefcourt, a young attorney working in Kunstler's office, arrived at the precinct, he asked, "Where are my clients?" A group of cops laughed and nodded toward the squad room holding cell, where the Panthers sat bloodied behind bars.

On September 4, many of the Panthers who had been arrested in recent weeks had a scheduled hearing on the sixth floor of the Brooklyn Criminal Court Building on Schermerhorn Street. They were joined by a group of about twenty fellow Panthers and family members who were there to show support. As the supporters arrived at the outer hall to the courtroom, a group of roughly 150 off-duty police officers appeared out of nowhere and pushed into the courtroom amid shouts of "White power" and "Win with Wallace!" Some of the men were wearing WALLACE FOR PRESIDENT buttons, in support of the white supremacist Alabama governor's bid for higher office.

As the crowd grew unruly, the presiding judge ordered that anyone who couldn't find a seat would have to leave the courtroom, then ordered court officers to lock the courtroom door.

Lefcourt, a twenty-five-year-old whose budding law practice was fast becoming monopolized by Panther cases, had never seen anything like it. "You could tell they were off-duty officers because they had a bulge under their shirt at the waist, where their guns were holstered. They were chanting 'White tigers eat Black Panthers.' It was the most astonishing display of racism I'd ever seen. I don't think there's been anything like it before or since."

Out in the hallway, the off-duty cops gathered in a group. A number of news reporters on the scene recognized a few of the cops, some of whom appeared to be carrying police blackjacks.

When five or six Panther supporters arrived in the hallway, one of the off-duty cops shouted, "There are the Black Panthers. Let's get them!" The cops surrounded the Panthers. According to David Burnham, a *Times* reporter, "About 150 white men, many of whom were off-duty and out-of-uniform policemen, attacked [the] small number of Black Panther Party members and white sympathizers.... Although the newsmen present could not see any of the white men actually striking the Panthers and their white colleagues during the brief melee, they could see swinging hands holding blackjacks high in the air and, immediately after the clash, blood running from the heads of at least two of those

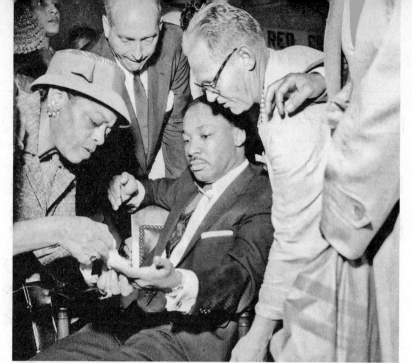

Above: Martin Luther King Jr. being tended to after he was stabbed in Harlem (note the letter opener protruding from his chest, just below his chin). *Below:* New Yorkers prepare to leave for the March on Washington, August 28, 1963. (Both © *New York Daily News*)

FINAL

DAILY ⬛ NEWS
NEW YORK'S PICTURE NEWSPAPER ®

 5¢

Vol. 45. No. 56 Cop 1963 News Syndicate Co Inc. New York 17, N.Y Thursday August 29 1963* WEATHER: Partly Cloudy, Dryer

2 CAREER GIRLS SAVAGELY SLAIN

Story on Page 2

Cop Killing Fugitive Gives Up

Story on Page 5

Janice Wylie—sought a theatrical career.

(UPI Telefoto)

Slashed in East Side Flat

The bodies of Emily Hoffert, 23, (above) daughter of a Minneapolis physician, and Janice Wylie, 21, [←] niece of author Philip Wylie, were found by Max Wylie, father of the dead girl, and a third roommate, Patricia Tolles, 21, in their E. 88th St. apartment last night. The girls had been bound hand and foot and stabbed repeatedly. —*Story on page 2*

THE FREEDOM MARCH: 6 PAGES OF PICTURES

Janice Wylie, 21, and Emily Hoffert, 23, were both brutally killed in their Manhattan apartment on the same day as the March on Washington. The murder scene was bloody, but it revealed few clues. The sensational nature of the crime put pressure on detectives to come up with a suspect. (© *New York Daily News*)

Prize catch: George Whitmore is paraded before photographers after he was coerced into signing a sixty-one-page confession, the longest in NYPD history. At far left, with cigar in hand, is Detective Edward Bulger. (© *New York Daily News*)

Whitmore is taken before a judge in arraignment court. His eyes are puffy after having spent twenty-two hours confessing to crimes he did not commit. (© *New York Daily News*)

Malcolm X inspired a generation of New Yorkers to fight for their rights "by any means necessary." (© AP Photos)

The mother of fifteen-year-old James Powell, who was shot dead by a police officer. Shortly after the funeral, a major riot broke out that raged for five days. (© Bettman/Corbis)

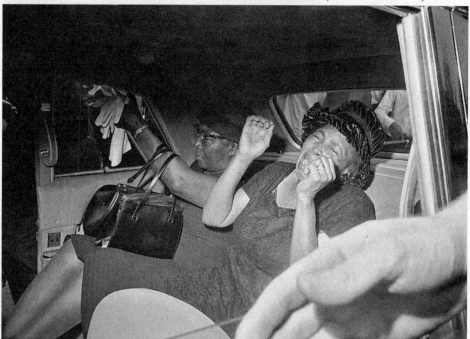

In July 1964, Harlem exploded in what would be the first major riot in a northern city during the civil rights era. *Below:* By the third night, rioting erupted in the Bedford-Stuyvesant section of Brooklyn. Residents were bloodied by what the police described as "necessary force." (Both © Bettman/Corbis)

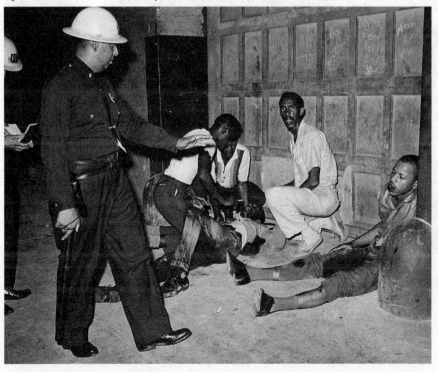

By the time the summer riots of 1964 were over, the city was changed forever. The official tally was one fatality, 722 injuries, and 423 arrests. One cop who was part of a riot squad on duty in both Harlem and Brooklyn said many years later, "I know there was more than one dead. I saw more people than that killed with my own eyes." (© Bettman/Corbis)

February 21, 1965: Malcolm X is shot multiple times inside the Audubon Ballroom while in the midst of giving a speech. Here his body is rushed to the hospital, where he will be pronounced dead. (© Bettman/Corbis)

John V. Lindsay is sworn in as mayor of New York City on January 1, 1966. (© Bettman/Corbis)

Headquarters for the Harlem branch of the Black Panther Party opened in the summer of 1968. Within months it had grown so quickly that Harlem became its own chapter, with branches in Queens and the Bronx. (© Getty Images)

Eldridge Cleaver in New York City, October 1968. Cleaver was a candidate for president on the Peace and Freedom Party ticket. (© AP Photos)

Dhoruba Bin Wahad, with microphone, speaks to Panther supporters. Standing behind Dhoruba, with her hands in her pockets, is Afeni Shakur, future mother of rap star Tupac Shakur. *Below:* a group of Panthers stands guard outside the courthouse where the Panther Twenty-one trial was being held. (Both © Getty Images)

Protestors march outside the courthouse in support of the Panther Twenty-one, while mounted police monitor the situation. (© Bettman/Corbis)

Huey P. Newton, center, holds court with the media in the Manhattan apartment of actress Jane Fonda, who was a supporter of the Black Panthers. Behind Newton, in dark sunglasses, is Chief of Staff David Hilliard. (© *New York Daily News*)

A police car occupied by officers Thomas Curry and Nicholas Binetti is riddled with machine-gun fire. The cops barely escaped with their lives. (© *New York Daily News*)

Dhoruba Bin Wahad was charged with the attempted murder of Curry and Binetti. Here he is being transferred while in custody from the 48th precinct police station to the Bronx House of Detention. (© Bettman/Corbis)

Xaviera Hollander, the East Side brothel owner who employed Bill Phillips as her Mr. Fix It within the criminal justice system. (© Getty Images)

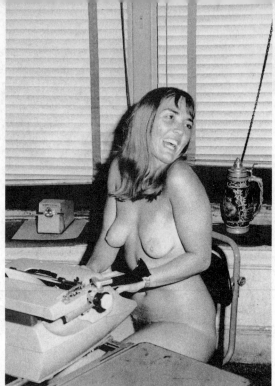

Bill Phillips, the most notorious turncoat in NYPD history, testifying at the Knapp commission hearings. (© *New York Daily News*)

The scene outside Mosque Number Seven in Harlem on the afternoon of April 14, 1972. Cops responded to a 10-13 call, "officer in distress." A shooting had taken place inside the mosque. Outside, residents rioted in the streets. Detective Randy Jurgensen was hit in the head by a rock and fell into the arms of a fellow officer. (© AP Photos)

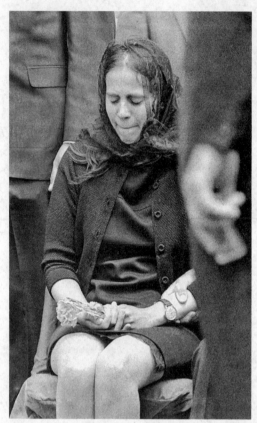

JoAnne Chesimard, a.k.a. Assata Shakur. (FBI Photo)

Diane Piagentini, widow of slain officer Joseph Piagentini. (© *New York Daily News*)

Bill Phillips, taken into custody on two counts of murder and one count of attempted murder. (© *New York Daily News*)

George Whitmore on the day of his release from prison after a nearly ten-year struggle to prove his innocence. (© *New York Daily News*)

Bill Phillips at Fishkill Correctional Facility in 2006, one year before he was granted parole and released after serving thirty-three years behind bars. (© Jason Torres)

After serving nineteen years in prison, Dhoruba Bin Wahad was released in 1990 on grounds that his right to a fair trial had been violated by cops, federal agents, and prosecutors. Dhoruba remains active as a writer, speaker, and community organizer. (© T.J. English)

It has been almost fifty years since George Whitmore was arrested and charged with the infamous Wylie–Hoffert murders. The money Whitmore received in compensation for his ordeal is long gone. The scars remain. (© T.J. English) attacked. A third member of the group said he had been kicked in the back 20 or 25 times."

As Burnham's gingerly account conveyed, the off-duty cops had overwhelmed the small group of Panthers and their supporters. Other accounts described punching and strangling in the melee. Some who were on the receiving end said they smelled alcohol on the breath of the cops. One Panther—David Brothers, a prominent leader in the Brooklyn chapter—had his briefcase stolen. The briefcase contained documents relating to activities of the Panthers.

Immediately after the brawl, the cops disappeared from the building as suddenly as they arrived.

In the hallway, a young Panther who was bleeding from a blow to the scalp said to a reporter, "Tell [those cops] something for me. If they think what happened in Cleveland was bad—it was nothing." The youth was referring to the shoot-out between cops and Panthers that resulted in eleven dead.

At least two of the off-duty cops involved in the beat-down were identified as members of the executive board of LEG, the new right-wing police group. The rest of the police gang were cops who had finished their midnight to 8:00 A.M. shift, perhaps gone for a few drinks, and then decided to go over to the courthouse and confront some Panthers.

Dhoruba Bin Wahad was supposed to be at the courthouse that morning, but he slept in and arrived late. When he got to the Brooklyn courthouse around 10:30 A.M., everyone was buzzing with shock and outrage at what happened. There were news media people everywhere. Dhoruba kicked himself for missing out on the action.

The incident at Brooklyn Criminal Court resonated far and wide. The following day, at a meeting attended by some of the Panthers who had been attacked, their attorney Lefcourt, and officials from Mayor Lindsay's Urban Task Force, Panther David Brothers removed his shirt and showed off what one observer called "a mass of ugly bruises." The mayor himself condemned the attack, announcing, "Commissioner Leary has assured me that he will take immediate and vigorous action against any individual member of the force who had violated the law or departmental regulations, including criminal prosecution if that is warranted by the facts." An official representing the NYPD even enlisted the help of the Panthers themselves, inviting them to "help us identify the assailants. We want to weed out the bad apples."

Panther captain Joudon Ford, a gangly teenager who was married to a corrections officer, stood and said, "You don't get it. It's not a few bad apples. It's the whole police force."

The NAACP's legal department called for a grand jury to investigate the incident. The *New York Times*, in an editorial entitled "Brutality, New York Style," noted that the attack occurred one week after a massive demonstration at the Democratic Party National Convention in Chicago, during which cops had brutalized protesters on national television for all the world to see. "The brutality of these off-duty policemen compares with last week's brutality of the on-duty policemen in Chicago; indeed, it is in some ways even worse. The attack in a court building makes a mockery of the rule of law and court-decreed justice. It feeds the fear of those in our society who already consider the police less their guardians than their oppressors. Mostly, it demonstrates how quickly the police-state virus can spread."

In a press release, Joudon Ford alleged that LEG (which he called "a Klan-like organization within the NYPD") was behind the courthouse attack. A LEG spokesman denied the accusation, but the perception stuck. Given the group's history of public statements against the Panthers, the attack seemed like a logical extension of their stated goals. The organization, which had applied for a state charter, was being supported by the archconservative John Birch Society, who stated in its in-house newspaper, "The battle for the control of the New York Police Department is on. Its results will be felt in every police department in every town in the United States."

LEG was not officially endorsed or supported by the upper "brass" of the NYPD, but the group did seem to represent the public view of some rank-and-file policemen. They were believed to have a membership-in-waiting of around one thousand officers.

The group's emboldened posture toward the Black Panther Party was part of a larger public relations campaign within the police establishment. There were some who wanted to show the public—and its own officers—that the NYPD could not be pushed around by a bunch of black teenagers, and that those who disrespected the police would be punished with blackjacks in the streets, the precinct houses, and even in the halls of justice. This effort was aimed as much at maintaining department morale as it was at seriously combating the rise of the Panthers. For that, a far more substantial program was under way—outside the purview of the public and even most members of the NYPD.

THE BUREAU OF Special Services (BOSS) was a clandestine branch of the police department's Intelligence Division. It had originally been set up in the halcyon days of the cold war to monitor the activities of the Communist Party in New York, which earned it the nickname "the Red Squad." By the early 1960s—especially after the Harlem and Brooklyn riots of July 1964—BOSS switched its focus from communists to what it referred to as "black hate groups." One of its early efforts had been to supply information through backdoor channels to the CBS television network, which produced a documentary called *The Hate That Hate Produced*. The documentary, produced and narrated by Mike Wallace, was an alarmist portrait of Malcolm X and the Nation of Islam.

BOSS covertly gathered information on anyone who advocated for civil rights on behalf of black people. Its most ambitious effort involved planting undercover agents within black activist organizations. They infiltrated the Nation of Islam and Malcolm X's Organization of African American Unity almost from their beginnings in New York. The organizations SNCC and CORE were rife with police informants, and undercover detectives infiltrating RAM played a major role in that group's demise.

BOSS also infiltrated the Black Panther Party. The Panther organization was growing fast, making it difficult to conduct thorough background checks on all prospective members. The leadership tried to instill quality control by enforcing a rigid initiation process. But the undercover cops were good enough at this kind of work to penetrate whatever security the Panthers could muster—and ultimately this fact created an atmosphere of paranoia within the group that was easily manipulated by law enforcement.

BOSS was able to place six different undercover agents in the New York Panthers, as well as dozens more paid informants through what they called the Ghetto Informant Program. Among the policemen posing as Panthers were:

Carlos Ashwood: Born in Panama, a former member of the U.S. Air Force, Ashwood was recruited by the NYPD for the express purpose of penetrating the Black Panther Party. He joined the police department in early 1968 and became a Black Panther a short time later.

Ralph White: After joining the NYPD in early 1968, White was recruited by BOSS. He became a Panther in June after first infiltrating an activist organization in the Bronx known as the Elsmere Tenants Association. White drank and smoked pot with the Panthers, slept with many Panther sisters, and became known as someone who liked to "talk big" by advocating the bombings of public facilities and assassination of police officers.

Eugene Roberts: Although he would eventually go down in history as one of the most notorious undercover agents BOSS ever produced, few people—including other cops and district attorneys—knew that Roberts was a member of the NYPD. He had joined the force in 1964 and quickly penetrated three different black organizations, including that of Malcolm X. In fact, Roberts was Malcolm's bodyguard on the night he was murdered; he had tried to administer mouth-to-mouth resuscitation to Malcolm as he lay dying on the floor of the Audubon Ballroom. After the assassination, Roberts maintained his cover; his presence at Malcolm's side on that fateful evening made him something of a legend in black activist circles. He joined the Black Panther Party in the summer of 1968.

BOSS's efforts to gather intelligence on the Panthers were ongoing in the summer and early fall of 1968. Few inside or outside the NYPD knew the details. The goal of the operation was not just to monitor but ultimately to bring about the demise of the black liberation movement.

These efforts were given a huge boost on September 8, when FBI director J. Edgar Hoover declared, in a front-page article in the *New York Times*, that the Black Panther Party was "the greatest [single] threat to the internal security of the country." Hoover was finally confirming in public what had been a priority of the bureau's COINTELPRO program for years. A few weeks later, the chief of the COINTELPRO program circulated a confidential memo to local FBI offices urging that the counterintelligence program against the Panthers be accelerated:

The information we are receiving from our sources concerning activities of the BPP clearly indicates that more violence can be expected from this organization in the immediate future. . . . The attached letter will instruct field to submit positive suggestions as to actions to be taken to thwart and disrupt the BPP. . . . These suggestions are to create factionalism between not only the national leaders but also local leaders, steps to neutralize all organizational efforts of the BPP as well as create suspicion amongst the leaders as to each other's sources of finances, suspicion concerning their respective spouses and suspicion as to who may be cooperating with law enforcement. In addition, suspicion should be developed as to who may be attempting to gain control of the organization for their own private betterment. . . . We are also soliciting recommendations as to the best method of creating opposition to the BPP on the part of the majority of the residents of the ghetto areas.

DHORUBA KNEW THAT the community was riddled with snitches. As he said years later, "If you accept the definition of a Negro as someone who has acquiesced and accepted the power of the status quo and was therefore a potential informant and collaborator with the status quo, then the majority of the population were Negroes." Surrounded by Negroes, the Panthers formed a security section, of which Dhoruba would become a key player. The security section was designed to insulate the leadership from the community organizations, which were vulnerable to penetration by informants. It was the job of the security section to stockpile weapons, to carry out "self-defense operations" against the police, and act as security at rallies and when members of the national leadership came into town. With his gang and prison background, Dhoruba was a natural to take charge of the security section. His official title was field secretary.

In September 1968, he and Iris moved to Harlem. It was a manifestation of his journey back to his roots, back to Africa, in the sense that Harlem was a symbol of Africa in America. Dhoruba and Iris took an apartment on West 137th Street, across from Harlem Hospital. Dhoruba gave up his weed-peddling party life among the hippies in the East Village to become, as he saw it, a warrior in the fight for liberation and justice.

The fall of '68 was full of promise but also dread. Barry McGuire's "Eve of Destruction," released in 1966, was still riding the charts almost two years later; with its vision of coming apocalypse, it was a song that spoke across racial lines. The diverse strains of dissent at play in the country were beginning to cohere.

And that fall Eldridge Cleaver finally made his New York City debut, after which the Black Panther Party in New York would never be quite the same.

After the shoot-out in Oakland the previous May, Cleaver had been incarcerated for a month and then paroled, pending criminal charges. In the meantime, he announced that he was a candidate for president of the United States on the Peace and Freedom Party ticket. Having the Black Panther Party's minister of information running for president was a stimulating national sideshow, especially among the country's burgeoning radical left. In New York State, Cleaver's age—thirty-three, two years shy of the age of eligibility—got him banned from the ballot. It didn't matter. As Cleaver said, he didn't "dream at night about living in the White House." He was running not to win, but to use the national platform his candidacy provided.

In New York, Dhoruba Bin Wahad was put in charge of Cleaver's security detail. He was finally coming face-to-face with the man whose writings in *Ramparts* had attracted him to the Black Panther Party in the first place. "Certain people," remembered Dhoruba, "had an aura about them. Eldridge was like that. *Soul on Ice* was on the best-seller list. His reputation was large, and he carried himself like a star. He was probably the most potent recruiting tool the party had at the time; he had credibility with the lumpen and the ex-cons, and he was attractive to white radicals, the New Left—even the media thought Eldridge was cool."

In an October 11 press conference at the Algonquin Hotel in midtown Manhattan to kick off a four-day speaking tour, Cleaver announced that "the purpose of my campaign is to organize people, to break some ground for a revolutionary movement, to lay the base for a revolutionary movement that will unite black radicals and white radicals." Dressed in the unofficial Panther uniform of black leather jacket and blue turtleneck sweater, he parried with the New York press like a skilled middleweight contender. When asked if his New York–based running mate, Judith Mage, had received funds from a city antipoverty program, he said, "I hope she can take all of it, take every penny she can get not only from the poverty program, but I wish that we could rip off Fort Knox. And all these hocus-pocus questions about where our money comes from—I hope that Mao Tse-tung sends me a boxcar full of money today 'cause I need it. Ho Chi Minh, send me some money. Fidel Castro, send me some money. Your momma, tell your momma send me some money 'cause we need it." He added that if Mage was getting antipoverty funds she "would be functioning in the spirit of Robin Hood."

With Dhoruba and his four-man security crew at his side, Cleaver also spoke at New York University's Washington Square campus before an audience of two thousand students. He spoke to a smaller group of Panther cadre at the auditorium of P.S. 201, many of whom were electrified. "He was spitting fire," said one Panther. His speeches were profane, sometimes angry, and often witty; people came away feeling they had witnessed an authentic cultural phenomenon.

Eldridge Cleaver giving speeches was one thing, but the Panthers were also a reality that played out in the streets on a daily basis. Both the New York police and members of the party used the word *war* to describe what was happening. As with most wars, it would sweep up many bystanders—people who weren't necessarily combatants but who were close enough to the action to become casualties.

One of these was Joseph "Jazz" Hayden. Born and raised in Harlem, Hayden became entangled in the era of the Panthers, though he was not a member of the Black Panther Party. He was known to the police as a local criminal—and he was a black male, which itself made him a suspicious character in the eyes of the law.

The incident that proved his undoing occurred in late September. Earlier that month, in California, Huey P. Newton was found guilty of voluntary manslaughter in the shooting death of the Oakland police officer the previous year. The conviction sent shock waves through the national Panther network. On September 27, Defense Minister Newton was sentenced to a term of two to fifteen years in prison. In New York, some among the armed wing of the Panthers felt it was necessary to retaliate by seeking payback against the system. It was part of a new strategy among some of the more militant element of the party—though never officially sanctioned by its hierarchy—to strike back after perceived acts of injustice on the part of "the power structure." In this case, the decision was made to respond to the sentencing of Newton in California by shooting some "pigs" in Harlem.

On the night of September 28, two uniformed police officers were sitting in a squad car at a taxi stand at 114th Street and Lenox Avenue. A black male wearing what was later described as an orange-lined black cape approached with a .30-caliber rifle and opened fire from fifteen feet away. Both officers were hit; one of them was able to return fire, emptying his revolver at the rifleman and a getaway driver. The attackers sped away in a black Cadillac. The cops believed they might have hit the fleeing gunman. The assailants were described by a police spokesperson as Negroes with mustaches, both of them tall and thin, with the driver dressed in "African garb."

The officers were wounded but in fair condition. A citywide alarm went out for the assailants. According to police, it was the fourth such attack on officers in the previous two months.

Jazz Hayden had nothing to do with the shooting. In fact, he had deliberately steered clear of the Panthers. He was a small-time hustler looking to score off the underground economy—the numbers racket, marijuana trade, dice, craps, and card games. He admired what the Panthers were doing, but it wasn't for him. "For one thing," he recalled years later, "what the Panthers was doing wasn't gonna help me pay no bills."

Hayden had been working the streets in Harlem since childhood. His father was a merchant marine who separated from his mother, leaving Jazz to fend for himself. As a kid, he'd collected pennies by selling peanuts and scrounging for empty bottles outside the Polo Grounds, where the New York Giants played ball. He ran errands for a local barbershop, dusted off coats, and shined shoes for loose change.

By the time he was a teenager, he was a different kind of hustler. Hayden described a typical day:

> You come outside in the morning and your pockets are empty.
> You cash in some bottles, get you a couple dollars. Then you
> try to get into a nickel-and-dime crap game and work your way
> up to a big crap game. Then you get a set of craps and a milk
> crate and you start your own crap game. If you made a profit
> from that, you take that profit and you put it into a couple
> bags of smoke, roll up some joints, sell them. So you start out
> with nothing at the beginning of the day and end up with
> something at the end of the day. And you start out the next day
> hustling and keep going until you build up some collateral.

The corner crap game was the lifeblood of Harlem's underground economy:

> You could start a nickel-and-dime crap game in the park.
> Then you had crap games where there was a hundred
> thousand dollars. Guys would be pulling up in cars and
> coming out with shopping bags in the trunk full of cash. Right
> there in the street; right under a lamppost. Guys dropping
> two or three or five thousand dollars. If the cops came, they
> would close it down for a minute. Cops would pull over to the
> curb, and whoever was cuttin' the game would go up and pay
> off the cops, and—boom—they was gone. And the game was
> back on. And so you had all the numbers players, all the short
> con players, anybody who had a bank was in that crap game.
> This is what I saw when I grew up and this is what I became a
> part of.

Jazz advanced thanks in part to his uncle, who was an established numbers man.

> My uncle used to take me around to all the bars in Harlem.
> He used to run a numbers business. He'd sit me on a barstool
> while he went in the back to talk to all the guys who were
> the moneymakers and the shot callers. They would be in the
> dark in the back. I might be standing there watching the door,
> everybody that came in. These were places of business. People
> met who they wanted to meet, had their conversations or
> whatever. My uncle introduced me as his nephew. I didn't know
> it at the time, but I was probably being socialized to be one of
> those guys in the back of the bar. And so I started out as a kid
> with my uncle taking me to spots, and then I looked up one day
> and I was the guy in the back of the bar.

In the late 1950s, Hayden got busted with eleven bags of heroin in his pocket. The bags sold for two dollars each. He was both a seller and a part-time user, but this was his first offense. There was no such thing as narcotics rehab back then; he was sentenced to Comstock prison for three years. He was sixteen years old. "The first night they locked me in a cell, I was rehabilitated. I'd never been away from home, never been in this kind of situation, this cement and steel. I cried."

It was in prison that Hayden learned for the first time that he was a black man living in a white man's world.

> Growing up in Harlem, I didn't know nothin' about racism
> 'cause it was all black people. In my community I could walk
> from 155th Street to 125th Street every Sunday to go to the
> movies, and every block I pass they waving, and everybody
> dressed up going to church. And now here I am caught up
> in this black/white dichotomy. The guards were all white,
> country boys; they had tobacco juice dripping down their
> shirts. Clubs big as baseball bats. They ran everything. All
> the good jobs in prison went to the white guys. They had
> all the positions of power. Whites had their handball courts
> and the others had theirs. If your ball went on to one of their
> courts and you went to get it, you'd get a beating. It was crazy.
> I came out of there after three years, and I was politicized. I
> was bitter, angry, and dangerous. It literally turned me into an
> animal.

As an ex-con back in the hood, Hayden could not find gainful employment. "I had no skills; I had nothing." One thing he did have was an instinct for the streets. Narcotics had supplanted gambling as the vice of choice, so he sold weed and heroin to get by.

By 1968, Hayden was well aware of the Panther phenomenon.

> I observed them in the neighborhood and I'm saying, "Yeah."
> Bunch of kids out there with black jackets and tams on,
> starting these lunch programs and the rest of this stuff. And
> then they started stepping up their program and taking on
> the police, that's when they became targets. But then—what's
> the saying?—"It ain't no fun when the rabbit got the gun."
> Suddenly the hunted turned the tables. It was a whole new ball
> game. Of course I felt pride in that. But at the same time—
> survival. The economic circumstances are critical. I stayed
> away from the Panthers because I had business to take care of.

Jazz Hayden wasn't aware of Huey Newton's sentencing, or the ambush of two cops in Harlem, when he went strolling along Lenox Avenue with a friend on a crisp evening in October. He was carrying a bag of groceries. As they approached the intersection near Hayden's apartment building, they noticed a lot of police gathered at the corner. "It was not unusual to see police activity on the street, but as we got closer, we noticed a van with police pouring out. It looked like they was raiding a building or something. My friend said, 'Oh shit, they must be after somebody out here.'" As Jazz and his friend got closer, they noticed local residents ducking into doorways, as if they were getting out of the line of fire. When the cops saw Jazz and his friend, they swung into action. A handful of police popped up from behind, and a cop yelled, "Hold it!" That's when Jazz and his friend realized they were the ones the cops were after.

> My friend who was with me, he didn't hesitate. He ran. He disappeared into a tenement building. And as he was going through the doorway, all I could hear was POW POW POW-POW-POW! I mean, the police tore that doorway up with gunfire. And I'm standing there with these groceries in my hands. I look around and see that the cops pretty much have me surrounded. My friend who went through the doorway, he's gone. And I'm standing there looking. The cops yell, "Freeze!" I did have a gun on me. Part of me said freeze, too, but another part of me said, "Man, fuck this." I just threw the groceries with the milk and everything up in the air, and broke straight for the police. I saw an opening and was turning back towards Lenox Avenue. A few of the cops drop to one knee and start firing—POW POW POW POW! I'm running, I'm high stepping, and I don't know, the bullets must have been going between my legs or something. I got past them. But one of the detectives was running after me. He almost had me, but he tripped and fell at the corner as I hit Lenox Avenue. I ran straight towards the mosque on 116th Street; there's a subway entrance there. I figure with all the people around, I'm safe, the detectives can't shoot with all those people coming out of the subway. It's too dangerous. But they didn't stop, they kept firing. They wanted me dead or alive.

Hayden was able to escape down an alley and up to a rooftop. From the roof, he looked down on the dozens of police scouring the neighborhood. "I stayed on the roof and wound up sleeping there that night. I woke up in the morning, looked out, and the coast was clear. I got out of there."

The next day Hayden tracked down his friend to trade notes on what happened. "We didn't have any idea what the cops wanted. Were they after both of us? Were they after me? Him? We didn't know."

That afternoon, he and the friend were walking on Park Avenue when a car full of detectives pulled up, guns drawn. "Once again, my friend, he broke. He ran one way, I ran another. Only this time, the cops followed me. The shooting commenced. I used the same tactics to get away, running into crowds. I ended up shaking them, but now I realized that I was the target. They had let my friend go and come after me. I was the one they wanted."

Hayden went into hiding. He called a black detective he knew in the local precinct and asked, "What the hell is going on?" The detective said, "Listen. The only thing that's keeping you alive is me. All them white cops, if it was up to them, you'd be dead. What you need to do is come into the station so we can talk."

Jazz smelled a rat. "I had no intention of goin' in. He wouldn't tell me what it was. I had no clue. I didn't know why they was shooting at me. Come in and talk about what?

"They hunted me throughout Harlem, and they hunted me in the Bronx. Every time I'd be somewhere, I'd leave just before they got there. Somebody was giving them information."

Hayden didn't read the newspapers much. If he had, he might have seen an article in the *New York Times* dated October 26, with the headline: "Suspect, 26, Seized in Harlem Shooting of Two Patrolmen." The article explained that a man named Stanley Stewart had initially been arrested for the shooting of a fellow drug dealer but was also being charged with the shooting of the cops. Stewart was a sometime hustling partner of Jazz Hayden. Stewart insisted he hadn't done the shooting. Fine, said the detectives, you tell us who did and we'll let you slide. Stewart fingered his partner, Jazz Hayden.

At the time, Hayden knew none of this. He was a man on the run, and he had no idea why. "They put out a ten-thousand-dollar reward on me. So all the numbers places, after-hours joints, they closed down everything. They said nobody is going to be able to hustle till we find this guy."

It all came to an end after a month, in the Bronx. Hayden recalled:

I was hiding out with my girl. We was coming out of the apartment one day, and I seen all these flashing lights outside. The police were coming to the door. I left my girl and ran up to the roof. I looked out over the roof. Man, the streets were flooded, there must have been a whole precinct out there. They had just missed me in the apartment. So, once again, I'm on the roof. I got nowhere to go. There was nothing I could do. I couldn't go down the stairs. I couldn't jump. I was stuck. But they didn't come up. Once again, I slept on the roof till the morning, when I noticed snow was coming down.

Hayden hid out a few days more, but they finally tracked him down at his girlfriend's place, lying on a sofa with his gun out on a pillow for ready use. "I was half asleep. My girl was coming up the stairs. She was saying, 'Jazz, Jazz!' Then I saw the detectives behind her. She comes through the door, and they're right behind her. They got the shotguns out. One of them said, 'Watch it! He's got a gun!'"

"I don't know how I survived that. That was a license to kill for them. They rushed over to the sofa. They grabbed the gun. They grabbed me. The first thing they do is start examining me." Jazz thought they were probably looking for bullet wounds—they'd shot at him so many times while he was running away that he must have been nicked somewhere.

Only after he was taken into custody did Hayden learn why the police had been hunting him. He told his public defender, "This is insane. I had nothin' to do with that shooting. It was a Panther shooting. I ain't no Panther." The lawyer reassured him that the case against him was weak: eyewitness descriptions of the shooter said he was six feet four; Hayden was a little guy, five feet five and a half. The lawyer told Jazz that even the cops probably didn't think he was the shooter, but he was still charged with attempted murder and held without bail.

A week later, his lawyer came to Jazz with a new development. "The arresting detectives want money or they're going to charge you with another crime. They say you fired on cops when you were being pursued. That's a second count of attempted murder."

"Let me get this straight," said Hayden. "They want me to pay them to not frame me when they're already framing me on the other charge." Years later, Hayden remembered, "My attitude was, 'Kiss my ass. I'm gonna pay you not to frame me when you're already framing me?' Sure enough, they charged me with another count of attempted murder, said that while I was fleeing arrest I turned and fired on the officers."

Hayden was indicted on two counts of attempted murder. By the time his case went to trial, the prosecutors had dropped the original charge against him—but he still went on trial for allegedly shooting at cops while fleeing arrest for the crime they now acknowledged he didn't commit. He was found guilty and sentenced to eight and a half to twenty-five years. "They shipped me off to prison," said Hayden. "Ultimately, the conviction was reversed. But during the year and a half I spent in the system, I spent my time at Attica. And during that time, my politicization was completed."

Jazz Hayden would remain a hustler, but he never was a Black Panther. In a time of war between the NYPD and the black liberation movement, he was collateral damage.

The theater of battle was expanding. No one was safe.

fourteen

WHITMORE'S LAST STAND

LIKE MOST COPS, Bill Phillips followed the war between the NYPD and the black radicals with great interest. The Panthers were an item nearly every day in the newspapers, especially the *Daily News*, which made a special effort to reflect the police point of view. There were regular reports of new shootings attributed to the Panthers and speculation on where the next ambush might come from. Some cops were disturbed by what the ongoing street war might mean for the city at large; others followed every confrontation between the Panthers and the police as if it were a sporting event.

Phillips was not a foot soldier in the Panther-police war—at least not directly. The battle was being waged mostly by commanding officers in the city's various black precincts, by beat cops, riot squads, and the undercover cops working for BOSS. Like many cops, Phillips saw the militancy of the Negro fringe as a direct threat against him and every other policeman in the city. When Phillips read statements of solidarity with the Viet Cong in the *Black Panther*, his blood boiled. When the Panthers railed against the "pig power structure" and declared that "the only good pig is a dead pig," it was hard for Phillips, or any cop for that matter, not to take it personally.

For Phillips, the hustle was still the foremost element of his daily routine.

By now, Phillips was a true veteran; he'd been in the Two-Five

Precinct in Harlem for close to four years, and now he was schooling younger cops on the secrets of scoring, just as he'd been schooled himself. One of the novices he helped educate was a kid named Jerry Lee who seemed ready and willing to learn from a master.

One of the first scores Phillips set up with Lee was a shakedown at a policy operation inside a men's club on 117th Street and Second Avenue, in East Harlem. Phillips and his rookie partner spent weeks trying to track down the owner of the club; eventually, they found the guy hiding out in the men's room of the club.

> So I says, OK you son of a bitch, now I got you. He says, I'll give you fifty dollars. I say, fifty dollars? Listen, my reputation in the neighborhood would be ruined. I don't walk around wearing a four-hundred-dollar watch so you can give me fifty bucks. . . . We drag him outside, get him up to the radio car and he says, all right, what do you want? I says, I want five hundred dollars. He says, oh my God, I ain't got five hundred. OK, get in the car. He's haggling and screaming and I'm saying, forget it, you're under arrest and here comes this friend of his, also a policy guy I scored not long ago. He taps me on the shoulder and says, look, let's talk. I go in a hallway with him and I says, listen, he's got two minutes to make up his mind; I get five hundred or he goes in the can.

Two minutes: that was the amount of time a hustler received to make a life-altering decision on the street. In this case, the policy guy coughed up the money. Two fifty up front, the rest the following day.

> We make a meet for the next day. I get the money and I divide it up with Jerry. Boy, he says, you're fantastic. And that ain't all. I put the policy guy on the pad for fifteen bucks a month and later on I sell him to another cop for a hundred bucks. The guy goes in, gets five hundred and gives us a hundred. Beautiful, Jerry says. Beautiful.

Phillips was so popular in the Two-Five that other rookie cops paid five dollars to ride with him on Jerry's off days to learn how things were done.

Phillips spent his working days in Harlem, but he didn't socialize much there. Usually, he hung out in his old stomping grounds in the One-Seven in midtown Manhattan. His favorite spot was P.J. Clarke's Saloon on Third Avenue at East Fifty-fifth Street.

Clarke's was a famous Manhattan watering hole frequented by celebrities: middleweight contender Rocky Graziano, whom Phillips knew personally; actors like Ben Gazzara; and sportswriters like the legendary Jimmy Cannon, among others. Being a regular at Clarke's was like being a member of an exclusive club whose membership filled out the Hollywood gossip columns and social register—not so much among the blue bloods (who favored the Stork Club), or the wiseguys (who filled the Copacabana), but the boxers, tough guy actors, newspapermen, cops, and the women who loved them—or at least depended on them for the rent.

Clarke's had the look of a Prohibition-era speakeasy, with lush mahogany wainscoting, tiled floors, and a tin ceiling. Phillips had his own regular spot at the bar. He was always dressed impeccably in suit and tie, expensive watch, Gucci shoes, with his police-issue .38 bulging only slightly underneath his coat. He usually nursed a glass of Johnnie Walker Black with water. The phone booth at Clarke's, which hadn't changed since the 1920s, was a veritable office and base of operations for Phillips, whose daily routine was similar to that of a bookie. He was constantly on the phone, making plans, setting up deals, checking in with the wife or his latest mistress.

Outside on the street, somewhere nearby, was Phillips's pride and joy, a fire engine red Triumph 250 sports car. He parked the car wherever he wanted: in front of a fire hydrant, in a loading zone, it didn't matter—with his policeman's ID on the dash, his car was immune to parking tickets.

One night at Clarke's, Phillips got the idea to stop by the office of a "friend"— Phillips's word for someone who had once buckled under to a shakedown. The guy's name was Jimmy Smith.

Normally, police officers weren't supposed to perpetrate scores in precincts other than their own. But Phillips wasn't worried about that. He was still known in the Seventeenth Precinct from his time in the Detective Bureau there. Plus, Jimmy Smith belonged to him.

Back in 1965, Phillips and Tony Delafranco, his partner at the time, had put the squeeze on Smith, who was running both a brothel and a bookmaking operation out of an apartment nearby on East Fifty-fifth Street. He and Delafranco had entered Smith's place of business and demanded five thousand dollars not to close it down. Smith, who wore glasses and spoke with a vaguely southern accent, talked the two detectives down to three thousand, but he didn't have the cash on him. So Smith and Delafranco headed out to find a loan shark, while Phillips sat in the apartment with two prostitutes, sipping on scotch and water, waiting for the others to return. The women told him how grateful they were that he was taking Smith's money instead of arresting everybody and shutting the place down. It was a long wait, maybe two and a half hours, before Smith and Delafranco returned—and when they did Smith had only half the money, with a promise to pay the rest the following week. Phillips stopped by a few times in the following days, but Smith always begged off with some slick excuse.

Now, three years later, Phillips heard from somebody at P.J. Clarke's that Smith was operating out of an apartment on East Fifty-seventh Street. Phillips headed over on foot and knocked on the door. "He didn't look too happy to see me," noted Phillips.

Smith knew why Phillips was there. He complained about how bad business was, pleaded poverty—and then told Phillips about a good gambling scam he had going. He had a bookie in Las Vegas who was an expert at "past-posting," a technique that allowed bettors to take advantage of the East Coast–West Coast time difference and register a bet on college football games seconds after the game ended. "I was skeptical," remembered Phillips, "but I went along with it. I put down fifty to a hundred a game and, over the next few weeks, won every bet."

Eventually, Phillips lost contact with Jimmy Smith. He was one of literally hundreds of fellow hustlers with whom Phillips would form a fly-by-night partnership over the years—only, in this case, the relationship with Smith would lay like a dormant cancer cell, seemingly benign, until it surfaced to eat the flesh off a cop who had always believed he was immune to getting caught.

FOR THE MOST part, Phillips kept his police life completely separate from his home life. Not only did he never talk with his wife about his hustling pursuits, he rarely told her anything about the job at all. When Camille read in the *Daily News* about his shooting the burglar in Harlem, she said, "I never knew you were back in uniform." It had been three years since Phillips was flopped out of the Detective Bureau.

This wasn't unusual among police marriages. In Phillips's case, he was bringing home the bacon—bringing home piles of cash, in fact, above and beyond his police salary. Camille didn't ask questions, and Phillips never offered details. It was all part of the schizophrenic reality of life as a New York cop.

Occasionally, events had a way of intruding on Phillips's neat little arrangement. In early 1969, for instance, his father seemed to be nearing the end of the road, and it would have profound consequences not only for Phillips but for the entire city.

Bill Jr.'s relationship with his father was complex. When Phillips was a preteen, his father had physically abused him, boxing him around in the kitchen, punching him in the face till he drew blood. It was all just to toughen the kid up, he said. Bill Jr.'s resentment toward his old man was one reason he had initially resisted joining the NYPD. He spent a few years in the air force in Arizona, where he met his wife, before returning to New York and finally joining the force after struggling to find other stable work. Only after becoming a cop did he begin the process of reconciliation with his father, an effort that continued for the next decade.

The old man liked to drink. In the early 1960s, when Phillips was still in the Detective Bureau, his father nearly drank himself to death. Once a big man who weighed close to two hundred pounds, he dropped down to ninety-eight. Remembered the son, "He got to be a pain in the ass with his drinking. . . . He went from being a big strapping guy down to a little skeleton. . . . I said, listen, if you want to keep on drinking we're going to put you in a box and carry you out of here. So he got the shit scared out of him and he stopped. . . . Drank [only] ginger ale, even at parties. I really admired him."   Phillips Sr. stayed clean for eight years, then began to feel ill again. X-rays showed a spot on his lung. He smoked two packs a day, so his chances weren't good. His son was with him when they brought him in for exploratory surgery.

"I don't want the surgery," said the father at the eleventh hour.

Said Phillips, "Go in and get the fucking thing over with, will you? They got to check it out and see what the hell it is and then you're finished."

After the operation, Phillips was shocked by his father's condition.

His father had a cancerous lung removed and was in desperate shape. He needed round-the-clock attention, which was costly. One afternoon, Phillips showed up unexpectedly at the hospital and was angered at what he discovered:

> We're paying thirty dollars a shift, a hundred and something
> dollars a day and he's fucking all by himself. He's got tubes
> in him, whacked out, alone. I raise fucking holy hell. Where's
> that administrator? I says, you son of a bitch, where's the nurse
> who's supposed to take care of him? He's getting treated like a
> dog up there. If you don't take care of him, I'm going to break
> balls like you never saw.

The hospital administrators promised Phillips it would never happen again.

On the job, Phillips kept working his scores, hustling like never before; pushing the envelope at work seemed to take his mind off the fact that his father was dying. Sometimes, between scams, he'd come by the hospital while still in uniform. Phillips was there as often as three or four times a day, the dutiful son. One night when he arrived, his father had been whisked into intensive care.

> This is the worst sight I've ever seen. He's propped up in bed,
> all kinds of bandages, tubes and shit all over him. He's got all
> kinds of beep-beep-beep things going all over the fucking
> room . . . and he's gasping for air. He's dead. Absolutely dead.
> They're just keeping him alive. There's no way he can survive.
> I looked at him, holy shit, I almost died. . . . [The next night] I
> got to the hospital about ten-thirty . . . and I stayed until about
> four in the morning. I went home and he died shortly after I
> left. He was sixty-four years old.

Phillips's attitude about life and work changed after that. It would be tempting to say that he lost his moral bearings—except that, with Phillips, morality had always been relative. But he seemed to stop caring as much about the job after his father died. Having the old man around had instilled in him a strong sense of fealty, not to the people of New York but to the job, to the tribe. Bill Phillips was a cop's cop; he took care of his partners and would never have dreamed of violating the department's unwritten code of silence.

Yet that sense of commitment to the force seemed to erode with the passing of the old man—an irascible Irishman, a keeper of the code, a New York policeman to the bone. Now the very embodiment of the Blue Wall of Silence was dead, and his son couldn't shake the feeling that the code had died with him.

ONE DAY, GEORGE Whitmore came home and found a baby in the crib that wasn't his. A few months earlier Aida had told him she was pregnant again, but now they had the baby and it didn't even look like George. Someone else was the daddy. George and Aida started arguing, and George started asking around, and eventually he found out she had a boyfriend on the side. That made him feel like running away. He moved out of their apartment and returned alone to Wildwood, where his brother and some cousins lived.

One person George didn't have around anymore was his father, who passed away in early 1969. A couple weeks after that, the house at the auto junkyard where George grew up caught fire and burned to the ground. By the time George returned to Wildwood, all that remained was the charred frame of the place where he and his pops used to live. It was a bittersweet memory—his father drunk and violent with his mother, George fishing out his back window with a homemade fishing pole, hoping to catch something from the inlet that sometimes lapped up against the house. It was all gone now.

One day George was drinking with a friend named Nate at a bar in Wildwood. After they downed a few pitchers of beer, Nate said, "Hey, we should go to Mexico. I hear the sun always shines there and they got pretty girls."

"Damn," said George. "You right. Let's go."

"I mean it," said Nate. "We could hitchhike and be there in a few days. What's stopping us?"

"Okay. Let's go now."

"Yeah, let's go."

What followed could be described as George and Nate's Excellent Adventure. Years later, Whitmore recalled it only in bits and pieces, like a movie with the reels shown out of sequence. "I was drunk when we started hitchhiking. When I woke up, we were in Ohio." They were carrying one suitcase with both their clothes and one hundred dollars cash each. Tijuana was the only Mexican town either of them had heard of, so that's where they headed. The western sun beckoned, but it was damn cold in the East and Midwest. George and Nate stuck out their thumbs; drivers picked them up, drove in the direction they were headed, then dropped the boys off. At one point they hopped a freight train. George had never before seen the wide open spaces of the central plains, land as far as the eye could see with no buildings in sight. He felt as though he were traveling on another planet.

Somewhere in Wyoming, George and Nate discovered an abandoned car and slept in it, until they were awakened by a police sheriff wearing a cowboy hat shining a flashlight in their faces. "You boys have identification?" asked the sheriff.

George and Nate showed their IDs and explained that they were on their way to Tijuana. They were a little worried—as far as they could tell, there wasn't a single black person in all of Wyoming—but the sheriff was friendly. "I'm gonna do you fellas a favor," he told them. "I'm gonna hold you overnight in the county jail, which means you'll have a warm place to sleep and a good breakfast, courtesy of the state of Wyoming."

The sheriff was true to his word: the jail was warmer and more comfortable than the abandoned car. The next day, after a meal of eggs, grits, and coffee, Whitmore and his pal were back out on the road.

It took them six days to travel all the way to Tijuana. Years later, all Whitmore could remember about the place was an "old, raggedy-ass pool hall" where he and Nate hung out. There they met two Mexican girls who agreed to travel with them up the West Coast. They took a Greyhound bus to Portland, Oregon, and by the time they got there they were flat broke. The two Mexican girls turned out to be "a couple of bull dykes. Lesbians." George and Nate cut them loose. They discovered a bar in Portland where a farmer came in at 8:00 A.M. and offered day work chopping beans to anyone who'd come. It paid enough to buy a bowl of soup and a slice of bread. They lived at a boardinghouse until they ran out of money, then crashed at a local movie theater, hiding in the balcony and sleeping there overnight. Sometimes, they raided the hot dog machine and ate cold dogs with mustard for breakfast.

Eventually, the boys got jobs in Portland with the Salvation Army. They drove around town in a company truck, carrying clipboards and picking up clothing donations. There weren't many more black people in Portland than in Wyoming, but George found the white folks more hospitable than back east. Even so, he never once thought about skipping bail. He could have stayed out west as an anonymous Negro and never returned to New York, where his freedom hung in the balance. But the thought never crossed his mind. "If I jumped bail, my whole life I would've been a convicted rapist, a criminal. I already spent too much time trying to clear my name to give up now. I always knew I would have to go back."

Late one night, George found a pay phone and called his lawyer in New York. He'd been told to check in, but it had been more than six weeks since he'd last spoken with Myron Beldock. George was unaware that there was a three-hour time difference between the two coasts. When Beldock answered the phone, he sounded half asleep.

"George, where are you?"

"I'm in Portland," said George.

"Portland, Maine?" asked the lawyer.

"No, Portland, Oregon."

"George, you need to get back here soon as you can. We have a hearing scheduled in three days."

"Damn. Okay, Mister Beldock. Don't you worry. I'll be there."

George caught the first bus out of Portland and headed due east. He made it as far as eastern Pennsylvania, where he was picked up by his cousins and driven the rest of the way back to the New York area.

On March 27, 1969, George Whitmore appeared in Brooklyn Supreme Court, wearing his now-familiar suit and tie—the only ones he owned. He was accompanied by his attorneys, Beldock and Arthur Miller. Acting Supreme Court justice Julius Helfand—the same judge who presided over Whitmore's last conviction—opened the hearing. George looked around the courtroom, suddenly wondering if his entire eight-week journey across the country and into Mexico had happened at all.

Reality hit home with a familiar force when Elba Borrero took the stand. The purpose of this hearing was to determine whether or not Whitmore deserved a new trial based on the grounds that Borrero's identification was a violation of police procedure and therefore unconstitutional. All other legal issues had fallen by the wayside. The credibility of Borrero's ID had become Whitmore's last stand.

For the past year, Elba Borrero had been living in Puerto Rico, her country of birth. She had moved away from Brooklyn in part to gain distance from the never-ending hassle of her case. She would have preferred to forget all about that night five years before. With each court appearance Borrero seemed to have put on more weight, until she was now portly. She was feisty, complaining on the stand about having had to testify to the same events six times, and she wasn't pleased to have had to leave her tropical homeland to return to a drab Brooklyn courtroom and do the same thing all over again.

This time, however, there was one difference: Myron Beldock was getting his first chance to question Borrero on the witness stand. After looking through all the evidence, Beldock had come up with something astounding that had never even been mentioned in the previous trials. In his very first interview with Borrero, Detective Richard Aidala had scribbled down in his police notebook the following words:

> Sister-in-law saw he grab me from her window (Celeste Viruet).

This quote was accompanied by the familiar description of the assailant: *male negro, tan or beige coat, long coat, cloth, no hat, five foot seven or eight, twenty-six or twenty-seven.*

As he examined the notebook entry, however, Beldock stopped on that parenthesis: (*Celeste Viruet*). The physical description that followed—had it come from Borrero or her sister-in-law, Celeste Viruet? If it came from Viruet, he believed it represented an independent description that was favorable to the defense, since the description did not fit George in any way beyond the fact that he was a "male Negro." If it was Borrero's description, it showed that her initial account—usually considered the most credible—contradicted her later identification of Whitmore as the assailant. Either way, it gave Beldock cause to launch a spirited impeachment of Borrero's previous testimony.

"You got a good look at the assailant that night?" Beldock asked the witness.

"Yes," answered Borrero.

"And you're absolutely certain that it was this man, the man you identified, George Whitmore."

"I am certain."

Beldock was not surprised. "Lawyers who do eyewitness identification cases," he remembered years later, "expect people to say, 'I'll never forget that face. I am certain that is the one.' Then the witness gets emotional and backs it up—and, indeed, not to be lying necessarily, but because they believe it, they have come to believe it's true even when they are completely wrong. People are trained somewhat to do this by their handlers—the assistant district attorneys and the cops tell them, 'This is what you should say. Say it this way, say it that way.' So, of course, [Borrero] said, 'I'll never forget that face.'"

Beldock kept bringing up inconsistencies in Borrero's testimony, one by one. But finally the witness broke into tears and shouted, "All I know is, George Whitmore attacked me that night! Stop bothering me. I know it, he knows it, God knows it."

When Beldock objected to this, Borrero jumped up from the witness chair and said, "You weren't raped that night, sir." Then, turning to Justice Helfand, she continued, "Judge, do you know what it is to go through this for five years?"

To which Beldock interjected, "Do you know what it is to spend three years in jail?"

Beldock thought he'd done a reasonable job of poking holes in Borrero's testimony, but the judge disagreed. Two weeks after the hearing, he reaffirmed Elba Borrero's identification of Whitmore, noting that her testimony "had the unmistakable ring of truth. It was direct; it was positive; it was clear and convincing."

"George," Beldock told Whitmore, "we will keep fighting. We will seek a favorable ruling in the Appellate Division, and if we don't get that we'll appeal to the state supreme court and, if we have to, all the way to the U.S. Supreme Court." Until then, Whitmore would remain free on bail.

If anyone needed a reminder of the disparity between the daily reality of Whitmore's legal travails and the larger framework under which he was being prosecuted, it came a few weeks after Judge Helfand's decision. The *New York Times* revealed for the first time that, in early 1965, Governor Nelson Rockefeller had ordered an investigation of the circumstances surrounding the Whitmore "confession." A separate in-house NYPD report had sought to clear policemen Isola, Aidala, Di Prima, and Bulger of any wrongdoing, but the governor's report spelled out at least nineteen separate discrepancies between the facts of the

Wylie-Hoffert murders and what Whitmore supposedly told the detectives. The report made clear what some in the black community had alleged: Whitmore had been willfully framed by detectives. The frame-up was accepted and furthered by prosecutors in Brooklyn.

After Governor Rockefeller's ninety-two-page report was completed in June 1965 and delivered to the State House, the frame-up became a cover-up. Not one person within government or civil service—not Rockefeller, Mayor Wagner, the district attorney, or anyone connected with the NYPD—was willing to release the findings of the report to the public, though many knew of its existence. The Rockefeller report was buried for four years before it was finally leaked to the *Times* "by a source outside the Police Department."

An innocent black youth had been framed on charges of murder—a frame job that was sanctioned, facilitated, and covered up by police authorities, judges, prosecutors, and other high government officials. But not a single public official accepted responsibility or was punished or even reprimanded. A few of them even received promotions.

Meanwhile, George Whitmore remained entangled in the system, and life in the city continued.

FOR THE BLACK Panther Party in New York, the year 1969 would be a point of no return. This was due in part to the election of Richard M. Nixon, who was sworn in as the thirty-sixth president of the United States on January 9. Nixon had been voted into office on a hard-line law-and-order ticket. Like most public officials, he lumped the Panthers together with the antiwar movement, the counterculture, women's liberation, and anything else that represented a threat to the established order.

It was no accident that, two weeks after Nixon was elected, the Panthers' leading national spokesperson, Eldridge Cleaver, had his parole revoked, and a federal warrant was issued for his arrest. Rather than return to prison, Cleaver jumped his $50,000 bail and fled into exile, first to Cuba and eventually to Algiers. From Algiers, Cleaver announced that he was establishing an international chapter of the Black Panther Party. In the coming months he would meet with leaders of the Palestine Liberation Organization (PLO), the African National Congress (ANC), and other liberation movements from around the globe.

Stateside, with Cleaver in exile and Newton in prison, the Black Panther Party was without clear national leadership. Individual regional chapters began to undertake initiatives of their own. In New York, there was much unfinished business between the Panthers and the police stemming from the beat-down at the Brooklyn courthouse the previous summer. A series of tit-for-tat incidents occurred throughout the winter, including a November 1968 dynamite explosion at the Twenty-fifth Precinct station house that shattered two windows. Bomb squad detectives traced explosive material to an apartment in Brooklyn rented by a woman whom a spokesperson for the NYPD described as "a lieutenant in the Black Panther Party." The woman and a Panther spokesperson denied that she had anything to do with the party.

The bombing incident, and the police response to it, were part of an emerging pattern. When an act of aggression was perpetrated against a police officer, or a bombing occurred at a station house—or bombing material was found planted at a station house—an NYPD source was quoted in the press linking the incident to the Black Panther Party. In some cases, there was actual evidence to suggest such a link; in other cases there was not. Either way, the police were using the media to reinforce the idea that the Panthers were purely a militant underground group dedicated to killing cops, not in any way a community-based social service organization. In the war between police and the Panthers, this propaganda campaign would become a self-fulfilling prophecy for both sides.

On the night of January 17, an incident occurred that brought matters into focus. In upper Manhattan, alongside a stretch of the Harlem River Drive, two motorcycle patrolmen had pulled over to do some paperwork after issuing a speeding ticket to a motorist. They noticed a red Dodge Dart parked in a dark, grassy area near the Harlem River. The two cops—one white, one black—thought the car was disabled. As they dismounted from their motorcycles and approached the car, they noticed two men, one standing at the rear of the car with the trunk open, one standing alongside the car, and a female seated behind the wheel. All three were African American.

"What's the trouble?" one of the cops asked.

The man standing by the trunk was Kuwasi Balagoon. The other man was Sekou Odinga. Behind the wheel was nineteen-year-old Joan Bird. All three were members of the Harlem chapter of the Black Panther Party.

They all glanced at one another. "No big deal, Officer," Balagoon told the cop. "Just engine trouble." Then he and Odinga pulled out guns and started firing at the cops. The cops returned fire, hitting the Dodge Dart and shattering the windshield. One of the cops was hit in the hip, but the bullet was stopped by a thick pouch on his belt. The cop retreated back to his bike and called for backup.

The two shooters ran off, disappearing into a wooded area.

Screaming sirens and flashing cherry-tops converged on the scene, nearly a dozen police cars in all. A swarm of officers spilled out and slowly approached the vehicle, guns drawn. Inside, scrunched down on the floor, was Joan Bird. "Don't shoot. I'm not armed," she said.

The cop who'd been hit in the pouch grabbed Bird by the feet and pulled her from the car. The cops cuffed Bird, then searched the car. In the trunk they found a .308-caliber Winchester rifle.

Later that night, Mrs. Charles Bird, Joan Bird's mother, was called to the Thirty-fourth Precinct station house. When Mrs. Bird, a Jamaican national, arrived, detectives recounted a version of what had taken place. As they were talking, she could hear her daughter screaming somewhere in the station house. When she was eventually led to a back room to see her daughter, she was shocked. Joan Bird had a black eye, her lip was swollen, her face bruised.

"Dear God in Heaven, who did you like this?" asked Mrs. Bird.

The daughter, crying and trembling, nodded toward the arresting officer, the one who'd been hit by a bullet and then pulled her from the car.

Bird was sent downtown to central booking, processed on charges of attempted homicide and assault, and released the following night.

The incident was the latest ball of confusion: a photo of Joan Bird's face with black eye, bloodied lip, and multiple bruises was printed in the *Black Panther*. The Panthers claimed Bird had been tortured; the police countered with a statement claiming that Bird had told them she'd injured herself during the shoot-out, banging her head on the steering wheel as she ducked to the floor when the shooting began.

By now, BOSS had penetrated most local Panther branches. Through their network of informants, they were told that Bird, a former VISTA volunteer, had volunteered to drive that night to prove herself and earn her stripes as a Panther. They had parked the Dodge Dart by the side of the road to set up a sniper post. The Panthers had supposedly rigged a bomb to go off later at the Forty-fourth Precinct station house, across the Harlem River in the Bronx; the idea was that, after the bombing, Balagoon and Odinga would open fire on the cops from across the river as they came flooding out of the station house.

Stories like this, which were passed along from Panther informants to police supervisors and then spread through the rank and file like wild-fire, fueled a kind of police hysteria about the Panthers. Never mind that no bomb was ever found planted at the Bronx precinct. Never mind that, from the location of the supposed "sniper post," there was no clear shot at the door of the station house or anywhere else where cops might come running out of the building. The story defied logic, but that didn't seem to matter. It fed into an anger and fear among the NYPD about what the Black Panthers represented: a Communist-inspired black vigilante group looking to exact revenge on local symbols of law and order by blowing up station houses and sniping at policemen from riverbanks and rooftops.

As one of the leaders of the Panthers' Harlem chapter, Dhoruba immediately recognized the value of the Joan Bird incident as a pro-paganda tool. He had copies made of the photo of Bird's bruised and battered face and had them posted all over the city. Frustrated by the California-based *Black Panther*'s inattention to events in New York, Dhoruba created his own grassroots pamphlet called *It's Time: Cadre News*. Written and mimeographed at the Harlem office, it was distrib-uted through the Harlem-Bronx ministry of information. In the very first issue (vol. 1, no. 1, January 1969), under the heading "OUR JOB," Dhoruba wrote, "It is the duty of those that profess to be revolutionaries to grasp revolutionary principles and apply them in the form of revolu-tionary action. The duty to the people's struggle impels us now to raise the conscious level of Black people within the confines of Gomorrah, this whore of the west. We must educate the people through propa-ganda. With this goal of political education, the people can best deal with this Pig Power structure. The method of education that the Black Community responds to best is—*action*."

By now, Dhoruba had become one of the Black Panther Party's most vocal and visible leaders in New York. He gave speeches throughout the city, at colleges, political rallies, fund-raisers, and symposiums. He had adopted the Panther look—black leather jacket, turtleneck, and neatly trimmed goatee—and adopted the Panther rhetorical style, a torrent of in-your-face language, liberally peppered with quotes from Marcus

Garvey, Karl Marx, Malcolm X, Che Guevara, and other revolutionary thinkers. As field secretary, Dhoruba traveled to Baltimore; Washington, D.C.; and New Jersey to oversee the setting up of chapters and settle disputes. For the first time his life had focus and purpose.

Dhoruba's high profile inevitably brought him to the attention of NYPD undercover officers and FBI field agents, who were tripping over one another in their efforts to monitor the Panthers' daily activities. An FBI COINTELPRO report from January 1969 noted:

> On January two nineteen sixty nine [a confidential informant] advised that at a meeting of the Black Panther Party political education class in Harlem, New York, it was stated that all Panthers are to obtain "a piece" (meaning a gun) by the middle of January. . . . Some Panthers are to leave for Texas (no place specified) in order to secure several pieces, one of those believed traveling to Texas is Diruba (ph) . . . Subject, also known as Richard Moore, was heard making inquiries as to where he could obtain grenades and other explosives. He is quoted as having expressed a desire to kill a law enforcement officer. In a speech, he called for revolution by the black race . . . he was observed carrying two pistols. IN VIEW OF SUBJECT'S EXPRESSED DESIRE TO KILL A LAW ENFORCEMENT OFFICER, AND HIS POSSESSION OF FIREARMS HE SHOULD BE CONSIDERED ARMED AND DANGEROUS.

In later years, Dhoruba and other Panthers would contend that much of the overheated and incendiary rhetoric at political education meetings was deliberate; they knew it would go directly into the files of law enforcement. In a propaganda war, the idea was to keep the other side in a state of paranoia. If the cops believed that the Panthers were out to kill them, they could be kept off balance. But it was a dangerous game for both sides. Confidential police and FBI reports from early 1969 show that law enforcement not only felt threatened by the Panthers but also felt the movement was predicated on murder and revenge. Every black nationalist rally, black cultural gathering, or statement of black liberation by the Panthers was recorded and seen as part of a conspiracy to kill police officers.

Ralph White was one Panther whom Dhoruba stayed away from. Dhoruba suspected that White was an informant from the day they first met. At PE meetings, White was usually the most vocal and militant in his calls for violent action against the police. Throughout early 1969, White had begun stockpiling material to make explosives, laying out plans for what he called "a day of terror" in New York City. Years later, Dhoruba remembered, "He was full of shit. I mean, the party had many people who talked a good game. They were usually the least likely to follow through. Ralph White was often high or drunk, talking 'bout blowing up buildings or monuments. He was a classic agent provocateur. I suspected he was either a spy or a bullshit artist."

One member Dhoruba *didn't* suspect was Gene Roberts. Having knelt alongside Malcolm X seconds after he was riddled with bullets at the Audubon Ballroom, Roberts had a pedigree that seemed beyond reproach. He was older than Dhoruba and the others, a veteran of the movement who no one suspected had been working undercover for almost four years.

Early in 1969, Roberts was assigned to the Panthers' security section, where he would work directly with Dhoruba. From January through late March, Roberts, Dhoruba, and a few other Panthers made a series of weapons procurement or TE (technical equipment) runs to various locales around the country. These were among the most perilous activities a Panther could undertake—driving under cover of darkness to Texas, Louisiana, or Virginia, buying handguns, rifles, and machine guns from local dealers, loading them in the trunk, and driving back to New York. In his unpublished memoir, Dhoruba described these missions as an almost spiritual undertaking, a metaphorical visit to what he called "The Church of Saint Nat Turner What's Happening Now."

> We traveled like shadows trapped behind enemy lines intent on making it to the nearest border and sanctuary before the light of false dawn. That was the script; the way we flowed. There was a distinct difference between "revolutionary theater" and theaters of revolutionary operations. We fully identified with the perception that ever since Plymouth Rock, Africans in America were behind enemy lines.

In the early-morning hours of April 1, 1969, Dhoruba was in the backseat of a car returning from a gun-running mission in the Baltimore area. Also in the car were Roberts and fellow Panthers Kwando Kinshasa (aka William King) and Cetewayo (aka Michael Tabor), who was driving. Dhoruba dozed off, and when he awoke, Gene Roberts was behind the wheel. The first thing Dhoruba saw was the Pentagon Building straight ahead. Apparently, Roberts had made a wrong turn off the expressway and got "trapped in a traffic loop to possible oblivion."

> The vast parking lot around the Pentagon loomed ahead deserted and lit by powerful security lights, and there we were: four Harlem Panthers in a car loaded with weapons, albeit purchased legally, who had lost their way and wandered into the parking facilities of the most powerful military establishment on the planet. A tense moment to say the least. After getting back on track and pointed in the right direction, the discomfort I felt over the incident and our new driver never fully subsided.

For the first time, the thought entered Dhoruba's mind that Gene Roberts was an undercover agent or a spy. He let it pass, figuring it was a product of the mix of suspicion and paranoia that was endemic to life as a Black Panther.

Dhoruba got home at dawn and slept most of the next day. He and Iris had recently moved from their apartment near Harlem Hospital to a larger apartment on West 142nd Street near St. Nicholas Avenue. That night, there was tension between Dhoruba and Iris. Dhoruba's deepening involvement with the Panthers was taking him away from home for longer and longer stretches, and the relationship was suffering. It didn't help that Dhoruba had been sleeping around with Panther women, and Iris herself had begun to stray. They were still living under the same roof, but the marriage had drifted down the priority list in both their lives.

In the early-morning hours of April 2, Dhoruba and Iris were sound asleep in bed. Suddenly, there was a loud banging on the front door. From the other side of the door, someone shouted, "Welfare agency! Is Iris Moore home?"

Welfare agency at 4:30 in the morning? Dhoruba thought. *I don't think so.* He got out of bed and approached the door in his underwear.

At first I didn't answer, realizing that to do so might invite a fusillade of gunfire through the front door. But the pounding grew louder, more insistent. Between the pounding on my front door, and the adrenaline rush of anticipation, anxiety, fear, and impending combat, I got quickly dressed. Standing to the side of the door, I boomed back, "Who is it?"

There was a pregnant silence, then a Black voice responded, "Police. Open the door."

I knew the disembodied voice was that of a Black man. I eased around to the peephole and sure 'nuff, hovering over the peephole was a sweaty black face. . . .

"How I know you're police? And what you want anyway?" I shouted back.

"Police! Open the door or we'll break it down. . . . Police, open the . . ."

As I unlocked the door, I couldn't help but think that if I lived through the next few minutes, my life would never be the same.

A phalanx of more than twenty cops in commando gear burst through the door. Dhoruba was pushed up against a wall and cuffed. Iris, disheveled, in her underwear, was told to sit on the sofa and not to move. The cops proceeded to ransack the apartment. They found an unloaded pistol in a dresser drawer, which made them search even harder. To Dhoruba, they seemed disappointed to find only that one gun on the premises.

I was pushed, shoved and half dragged down four flights of stairs and thrown into the back of an unmarked police cruiser. The street outside was teeming with uniformed cops. . . . Sirens blaring, I was sped downtown squeezed between two Old Spice smelling detectives in the back seat of an unmarked police car. The ride downtown was pregnant with tension and the silence broken only by the sporadic crackle of police chatter over the car radio.

From the radio chatter, Dhoruba got the sense that something heavy was going down. He was right. That night, similar raids and arrests were taking place all around Harlem, Brooklyn, Queens, and the East Village, executed by a team of more than one hundred well-armed Emergency Service officers. Doors were busted down, Black Panthers chased down hallways, rousted from bed, cuffed, and thrown in the back of paddy wagons and cruisers. When it was all over, twenty-one people had been arrested; one further suspect—Sekou Odinga—escaped capture down a tenement drainpipe and disappeared into the early dawn. (He would resurface weeks later in Algiers alongside Eldridge Cleaver.)

At central booking in downtown Manhattan, Dhoruba was held in an isolation cell. It wasn't until he was brought into arraignment court the next day that he was hit with the full magnitude of what was taking place. The arrested Panthers, male and female, were marched into a courtroom packed with reporters, cops, and officials from the Manhattan D.A.'s office. Dhoruba and the other Panthers were being charged with more than two hundred counts of conspiracy. In one fell swoop, the Forces of the Law had tried to take out the entire upper echelon of the Black Panther Party in New York City.

[fifteen]

THE ROT WITHIN

IN JUNE 1970, George Whitmore finally succumbed to the pressures of a criminal justice system that seemed determined to define him as a lawbreaker. It happened in New Jersey, where Whitmore had moved after separating from Aida. He was out drinking with Nate, his friend from the cross-country hitchhiking adventure. At some point that evening, Nate said, "Hey, I know a guy who stole something from me, and I'm gonna go get it. Will you help me out?"

George had no idea what Nate was talking about, but he felt indebted to his traveling partner, so he agreed.

At the time, George was working three days a week driving a truck for the Colson Lumber Company. Sometimes, like tonight, he got to keep the truck during off hours. He and Nate climbed into the truck and drove to the nearby township of Rio Grande, not far from Wildwood. George began to suspect something was wrong when Nate insisted they stop at a place called Krown's Record Store, and Nate got out of the truck with a crowbar.

"Wait a minute," said George.

"I know what the hell I'm doing," replied Nate.

Too drunk to argue, George stood by as Nate started jimmying the door of Krown's Record Store.

Neither of them even noticed the police car as it turned off its headlights and pulled up slowly behind George's truck. Patrolman Ronald

Brown got out of the car, his gun drawn, and approached the two men.

"Stop right there," he said. "You're both under arrest."

George was so inebriated he hardly remembered what happened. He woke up the next morning in the county jail and was told he'd been charged with attempted breaking and entering and possession of burglary equipment (the crowbar).

It was all pro forma: a county defense lawyer informed George that if he pleaded guilty to attempted breaking and entering, the other charge would be dropped. He would be fined $150, placed on two years' probation, and allowed to walk.

It was a good deal; George took it. The only problem was that Colson Lumber wasn't happy to hear he'd used the company truck in an attempted burglary. He was fired from his job.

George was broke. His remaining NAACP Legal Defense Fund money had long since dried up. He was able to get by for a time on public assistance, but by October he was without money to pay his bills or help Aida out with the kids. At the end of his rope, George did something he'd never done before: he willingly set out to commit a crime.

Again, it was late and he was drunk. Using the same crowbar he and Nate had used, George broke into Allen's Delicatessen, a corner store on Route 9 in the town of Cape May Court House. It was 3:00 A.M. Police caught him coming out of the store with $132.32 in stolen cash in his pocket.

George was charged with "B and E," larceny, and possession of burglary tools.

From his cell at the county jail, the biggest emotion George felt was shame. He wondered if he had messed up his case in New York by getting arrested. He wondered if his lawyers Miller and Beldock would now abandon him.

To defend him, Whitmore used a local attorney. A few weeks after his arrest, as they talked in the county jail's visiting room, the attorney suggested that they might be able to plea-bargain. By now, George had lost his glasses; he could hardly see.

"Listen, son," the lawyer said, "you're gonna have to do some time."

"How much?" said George.

"Well, I'll get them to drop the possession charge. You cop to the B and E."

George sank back into his chair. Before he could take the deal, he needed to talk with his New York attorneys. He was afraid that if he were convicted of a crime, even a relatively minor first-time offense, Beldock and Miller would give up on him.

Beldock was reassuring. Pleading guilty to a burglary charge, he said, should have little or no adverse effect on any ruling in the Borrero attempted rape conviction. "Take the plea," he told George over the phone. "Do the time. We'll deal with legal matters here in New York when you are released. And George?"

"What, Mister Beldock."

"Stay out of trouble."

"Yes, Mister Beldock."

Whitmore pleaded guilty and was sentenced to nine months.

He did his time at the Cape May Court House county jail, just down the street from the deli he'd tried to rob. For the next nine months, he didn't have to worry about rent or any other bills. He was George Whitmore, forgotten man.

George wasn't able to make rotgut hooch while doing county time; they didn't have the facilities. That was one thing he noticed: in prison, the days passed more slowly when you couldn't get drunk.

THE VENERABLE DISTRICT attorney stood at a microphone before flashing lights and television cameras—a rarity for the white-haired eminence of 100 Centre Street. By assuming the task of delivering news of a criminal indictment directly to reporters, Frank Hogan was signaling its importance in the larger scheme of criminal justice in the Big Town. The personification of Irish Catholic rectitude, Hogan stood stiff and motionless—*underplaying*, Stanislavsky would have called it, seizing command through a Zen-like force of will rather than histrionics.

In a simple monotone, Hogan let his plain words drive home the message: "The grand jury has returned an indictment containing twelve [major] counts, all felonies, charging members of the Black Panther Party with conspiracy to bomb New York City department stores, Macy's, Alexander's, Korvette's, Bloomingdale's, Abercrombie & Fitch, during the Easter shopping season. These bombings were to be coordinated with similar bombing attacks on the Forty-second Police Precinct station at Third Avenue at One hundred and sixtieth Street in the Bronx and six locations along the New Haven Railroad right of way. . . . And the target date was April third, tomorrow."

The Black Panther Party had also planned to bomb the Bronx Botanical Gardens and the city subway system, Hogan added. In total, the indictment included 156 separate criminal counts.

If headlines could scream, the following day's papers would have contracted laryngitis. "Smash Plot to Bomb Stores," read the *Daily News*, with a subhead: "Indict 21 Panthers in Store Bomb Plot." The *New York Times* declared, "Bomb Plot Is Laid to 21 Panthers; Black Extremists Accused of Planning Explosions at Macy's and Elsewhere." The *Post* updated the arrest tally in their afternoon edition: "Nab One More in Panther Bomb Plot."

Filled with quotes from "sources close to the investigation," the articles explained that the police had conducted more than a dozen raids around the city, confiscating "African clubs, spears, cane swords and a long-barreled gun that shoots fire, like a flame thrower," along with guns, knives, and other weapons. To many, the haul seemed to confirm Buckley's prediction that the Mau Mau were on the rise in America. But the exotic assortment of spears and clubs could hardly have sufficed to pull off the kind of plot described in the indictment. A spokesman for the prosecutor tried to explain the discrepancy, telling the *Times*, "We believe they have other material packed away. We have not recovered everything." A police spokesman reported that detectives had contacted the department stores named in the indictment and that "precautions had been taken." The stores themselves were taking "special security measures." The *Daily News* noted that "additional police [were] being assigned to the area around St. Patrick's Cathedral, focal point of [the] Easter Parade."

In all of the newspapers accounts, the Panthers were characterized almost exclusively by police and prosecutorial sources. The *Daily News* described the party in New York as consisting of one hundred "hard-core" members and three thousand "fringe" members, a portrait that was "pieced together from information supplied by police who infil-trated the outfit, foiling the alleged plot only a day before its scheduled execution, and from others close to the three-year investigation." Party members strictly followed "the hard-line Mao philosophy, using the so-called Red Book of the Chinese Communist boss as their text." "The gang" was "run on military lines," and party members, according to the police, "have infiltrated the school system, with some Panthers working as teachers."

The Panthers were also linked to Cuba. "High police sources" claimed that the New York Panthers were being financed through Cuban officials at the United Nations, though there was nothing in the indictment to back this up and the charges were never substantiated.

And, as if all this weren't enough, there was this: "The Federal Bureau of Investigation is quietly probing the possibility that Panthers represent a 'national conspiracy against the white power structure'— a possibility supported by the fact that individual Panthers range the nation on Party business."

The investigation and arrests were presented as a rousing victory for the NYPD. A lead editorial in the *Daily News* noted that the indictments were the results of "superior police work." It seemed to promise an end to the NYPD-Panthers conflict that had raged for more than a year. The indictment in Manhattan of what would come to be known as "the Panther Twenty-one" showed not only that the Black Panthers were hostile toward cops, but that they were determined to kill innocent people—black and white—on a prominent Christian holiday. They were communists, terrorists, and "black extremists" all rolled into one.

They were also a terrific diversion.

There's no doubt that most police officers genuinely felt the Panthers were a threat to their lives; lethal shoot-outs between police and Panthers had been occurring around the country for some time. But in New York City, the war with the Panthers served an additional purpose: it gave the NYPD a convenient way to frame their ongoing battle in heroic terms— good versus evil, law and order versus anti-Americanism and disrespect for the law. This took the focus off a growing problem within the department: a degree of moral rot among its members that, if exposed, would make the Harry Gross corruption scandal of the late 1940s look like a minor infraction.

Deep within the bureaucracy—in the Lindsay administration and, by extension, among sources "in the know" within the police department—there were disturbing signs on the horizon.

Nearly two years earlier, in 1967, a Lindsay administration official named Jay Kriegel had been approached with explosive information about the systematic corruption in the NYPD. Through an intermediary, two plainclothes cops—one a patrolman, the other a sergeant—

described to Kriegel exactly how the pervasive system of illegal payoffs within the department worked. Money from illegal narcotics, gambling, extortion, and other criminal rackets—some of it skimmed from criminal operations outside the department, some of it generated by dirty cops within—had become the norm in virtually every division in the city. And not only did the higher-ups in the department know about it, they were benefiting from it, collecting payoffs via bagmen and other designated emissaries.

The mayor's man was stunned by what he heard. Both the cops had impeccable records as policemen, and they made it known that they were willing to go public with their allegations, at great risk to their careers and even their lives. One of them was Sergeant David Durk. The other, the patrolman, was Frank Serpico.

For months, Kriegel stonewalled the two cops. Finally, in early 1969, he approached Lindsay with the information. Facing a vituperative reelection campaign in November, Lindsay was reluctant to stir up the wrath of the PBA and the police department. Durk, and especially Serpico, eventually became so frustrated and disillusioned that they nearly gave up hope.

In November, Lindsay was reelected with 43 percent of the vote.

How long could the dam hold? When it came to corruption, the police bureaucracy was filled with people who had a vested interest in obscuring the truth. By now *New York Times* reporter David Burnham was quietly investigating the claims made by Serpico and Durk, and the questions being asked reverberated throughout the NYPD's command structure. The department's manner of doing business—payoffs, graft, the pad—had been going on for so long that many cops took it for granted; the idea that it might be exposed was terrifying. Many cops would go to jail, their lives ruined.

So the NYPD's decision to take down the Black Panther Party in New York had its self-serving purpose: it engendered sympathy toward the police on the part of white ethnics (the *Daily News* was their newspaper), and it provided a major smoke screen. The cops and prosecutors who arrested and indicted Dhoruba Bin Wahad and the other black radicals on charges of conspiracy and attempted murder could have done so without ever mentioning the Black Panther Party. It was not illegal to be a member of the party. But the indictment was full of references to the Black Panthers—because the cops and the D.A.'s office saw this case as their opportunity to put the party itself on trial. Many whites in the city considered it downright un-American to question the ethics or motives of the police when they were engaged in a struggle to the death with communist infiltrators, radicals, and black reverse-racists.

For a time, the tactic seemed to work. Throughout 1969 and into the new year, revelations stemming from the Panther Twenty-one arrests and indictment dominated the press. By now, the conflict between the Panthers and the police had become a nationwide war: from 1967 into 1970, ten Panthers in cities as diverse as Oakland, Los Angeles, Chicago, and Seattle were shot and killed by police, in what Charles Garry, a lawyer for the Panthers, called "a pattern of genocide." In six of those ten killings, an officer or officers were seriously wounded and had reason to believe their own lives were in jeopardy. As the Panther-police war dominated the headlines, the deeper question of police corruption—including systemic racism, brutality, and economic extortion in ghetto communities—remained buried beneath the surface.

By the spring of 1970, that finally began to change. On April 25, the *New York Times* began publishing a series of articles by David Burnham describing the culture of graft and payoffs within the NYPD command structure. Serpico and Durk were named as sources in the articles. The cat was out of the bag.

Though Mayor Lindsay had known about the Serpico-Durk allegations for nearly two years, he reacted as if he were hearing them for the first time. Now safely ensconced in his second term, the mayor announced with fanfare that he was establishing, via executive order, an independent commission to look into the extent and nature of police corruption in the city. To oversee the commission, he selected Whitman Knapp, a respected Wall Street lawyer. The commission was given a small staff, a modest budget, and a vague mandate. The *Times* covered the announcement on page one, but many other newspapers—including the *Daily News* and the *New York Post*—relegated the Knapp Commission story to a few column inches in their back pages, near the obituary section.

In the upper echelons of the NYPD, sabers were rattled. A few months after the commission was created, Police Commissioner Leary resigned; he was replaced by Patrick V. Murphy, another homegrown Irishman, though one with a solid reputation as a reformer. Murphy was soft-spoken, deliberate, more like an academic than a field general. At his first press conference as commissioner, Murphy announced he was enacting sweeping new policies to root out corruption and punish any-one caught or believed to be violating the high standards of the NYPD.

Among the officers who should have been concerned was Bill Phillips. Any number of citizens and policemen could have identified Phillips as a bent cop. Rarely had he tried to hide his activities; he took money under the table and spread it around fearlessly. He threatened citizens with summonses, arrest, sometimes even physical violence, all in the name of good old-fashioned extortion. His partners and supervisors knew about it; his payoffs went all the way up the chain of command.

Phillips wasn't the least bit worried. Sure, he'd heard there was some half-assed commission appointed by that dick-wad mayor who hated cops—but Phillips knew the cops hated Lindsay just as badly. He was sure no self-respecting cop would talk to any commission. That was one of the reasons Phillips had always been so diligent about spreading the wealth within the department—he felt it inoculated him. The more cops who were on the pad, the less likely it was that anyone would ever flip. It was almost inconceivable to Phillips that the department's way of doing business would ever change. Like most cops, he believed the Blue Wall of Silence was impregnable. The mayor and his investigators were so far removed from the daily realities of life in the precincts and on the street, they might as well have been operating from Uranus.

PRETRIAL HEARINGS IN the case against the Panther Twenty-one dragged on for months. The defendants were being held on bail of $100,000 each, an astounding sum, and were confined at separate correctional facilities, making it difficult for them to coordinate their legal defense. Each morning, Dhoruba and the other defendants (whittled down from twenty-one to thirteen after various trial separations) were retrieved from holding pens in Queens, Brooklyn, and Manhattan and trans-ported to the Criminal Court building at 100 Centre Street in lower Manhattan. Along with Dhoruba, on trial were Lumumba Shakur, Afeni Shakur, Michael "Cetewayo" Tabor, William "Kinshasa" King, Curtis Powell, Robert Collier, Ali Bey Hassan, Alex McKeiver, Clark Squires, Baba Odinga, Lee Roper, and Joan Bird.

In a courtroom on the sixth floor, the proceedings were boisterous and sometimes chaotic. Taking a page from the New Left playbook of the 1960s, the defendants turned the trial into a burlesque of justice. They openly defied, insulted, and berated Justice John M. Murtagh, a rigid, old-school judge who was the embodiment of much of what the Panthers were fighting against. The son of a fire battalion chief, an Irish Catholic who was closely aligned with the NYPD, Murtagh had served as commissioner of investigation during the Harry Gross gambling scandal. He'd actually been arrested and charged with "willful and unlawful . . . neglect of duty" for failure to report evidence of police corruption during that episode, but the charge was later dismissed on a technicality and had no adverse effect on his career.

Early on, Judge Murtagh declared, "This is not a political trial; it is a criminal matter." And yet much of the prosecution's evidence revolved around political literature: they would enter as evidence copies of Mao's Little Red Book, the *Black Panther*, and books on guerrilla warfare seized in the defendants' apartments, along with the movie *The Battle of Algiers* and even posters of Malcolm X and of John Carlos and Tommy Smith giving the Black Power salute at the Olympic Games in Mexico City. They used these items to support their case that the defendants were bent on committing acts of terrorism and advocating the overthrow of the government.

The defense of the Panther Twenty-one was handled by a collective of like-minded lawyers, many of them protégés of the radical defense attorney William Kunstler. They proved to be skilled legal advocates, but it was clear early on that many of the Panthers would not hesitate to speak for themselves. The most vocal was Dhoruba, who announced to the court, "We are going to tell people we're not going down like all those other niggers." Years later, Dhoruba remembered, "I was referring to George Whitmore and all the others who had been mistreated and framed by a corrupt criminal justice system ever since black people were brought to this country."

"Now, if this court does not give us justice," Dhoruba told the judge, "we're going to tear this raggedy, filthy, injustice pigpen inside out every single day. . . . All we ask for is justice. That's all we ask for. Four hundred and fifty motherfuckin' years, we ask for justice. And you get this punk [the prosecutor] calls us terrorists and you get the Gestapo in our community murdering us; because of punks like that we got guns."

Murtagh responded by citing Dhoruba for contempt. At one point he suspended the proceedings entirely until Dhoruba and the other defendants agreed to promise—in writing or via recorded statement—not to disrupt the trial or use profane language in the courtroom. The defendants responded by composing a long, detailed political treatise on racial repression in the United States, from Plymouth Rock through Frederick Douglass, from the horrors of the KKK and Jim Crow through police violence in the modern era. The "Panther Twenty-one Manifesto" was recorded in its entirety by Cetewayo, who had a booming theatrical voice in the manner of Paul Robeson. Then they announced that they had prepared what they called an "apology" and requested that it be played in open court.

As the defendants languished in lockup, the voice of Cetewayo intoned the Panthers' Trojan horse diatribe before an audience of spectators and the press. As he listened to the defendants rail against "four hundred years of oppression," Murtagh grew apoplectic, suspending the proceedings again. The trial would drag on in this way for months to come—twenty-four months in all, making it the longest criminal proceeding to date in New York State history.

Handling the prosecution was Joseph A. Phillips (no relation to Bill Phillips), a veteran assistant district attorney. Like Murtagh, Phillips was a classic product of the system. He presided over a bureau within the Manhattan D.A.'s office responsible for prosecuting corrupt cops, but not a single major police corruption case had been mounted during his tenure. Phillips's fealty to the bureaucracy led one defense attorney to note that "the Panthers are on trial for conspiracy before a white Irish Catholic judge selected by a white Irish Catholic assistant D.A. to hear the testimony of white police officers from a police department historically controlled and disproportionately populated by white Irish Catholics."

When the city's law enforcement authorities made their calculated decision to eradicate the Panthers, one thing they failed to anticipate was that their prosecution of a smattering of loosely connected defendants would become a lightning rod for the entire era. Like the trial of the Chicago Eight, which was unfolding in the Windy City at the same time, the Panther Twenty-one trial became a proscenium on which a particular brand of radical theater was staged.

On the sidewalk in front of the courthouse, hundreds of Black Panthers, Panther supporters, and sympathizers gathered daily on Centre Street. The Panthers marched and called out in cadence as protesters carried hand-painted protest signs and chanted. Hundreds of uniformed officers, on foot and on horseback, were called in to surround the protesters, who gathered on the sidewalk and spilled out into the street. The rallies became a gathering point for much of the dissent and civil disobedience building throughout the city and country. Up until then, the civil rights movement, with its roots in the Deep South and its moral compass located in the ghetto, had vied for national attention alongside the antiwar movement and the rising of the counterculture. The trial of the Panther Twenty-one proved a magnet for the various protest movements, with many of the "stars" of the counterculture making an appearance on the sidewalk outside Manhattan Criminal Court. One of the most visible was Abbie Hoffman, who used part of a publisher's advance and movie option for a book called *Revolution for the Hell of It* to post bond on behalf of Dhoruba Bin Wahad.

For Dhoruba, the trial was a showcase for his most rebellious tendencies; it also came perilously close to sounding the death knell for an organization that had come to inhabit the center of his universe. Dhoruba's identity was wrapped up in being a Panther. As the party grew in stature and notoriety around the city, Dhoruba became more invested in its salvation. His personal biography, as a former gangbanger turned Panther field secretary, was central to the narrative of the Panthers in New York, who had risen organically from various Afrocentric community organizations around the city and provided fuel for a national trend. The Black Power movement was coming into its own, and Dhoruba was one of its rising stars.

Being a recognized leader in the movement had its complications. In Dhoruba's case, he was called to answer for the infiltration of the Panthers by undercover police officers and paid informants, which composed the backbone of the government's case against the Panther Twenty-one.

While the case was still tied up in seemingly endless pretrial machinations, Dhoruba was met in a jailhouse visiting room by David Hilliard, chief of staff and acting boss of the Panthers while Huey P. Newton was still in prison. Hilliard had flown out from national headquarters in Oakland, where party leadership was in a rage over the New York indictments. Huey Newton, Hilliard, and others were afraid that the New York Panthers might take the entire national organization down with them.

"We're gonna close down the New York chapter," Hilliard told Dhoruba.

Dhoruba was shocked. "You can't do that."

"Why not?" said Hilliard.

"Why not!? Because this is New York, that's why not. Harlem is here, brother. This is the center of black culture in the United States. You can't close the Black Panther Party in Harlem. This is where Marcus Garvey spoke on street corners. This is where Malcolm X launched his career."

Dhoruba was dumbfounded. Hilliard had risen to his position within the party largely because he was a boyhood friend of Huey Newton, but Dhoruba knew he wasn't respected among the party's rank and file. During the shoot-out between Panthers and Oakland police in June 1968, in which Bobby Hutton was killed and Eldridge Cleaver was shot in the leg, Hilliard had hid in an empty bathtub in a Panther safe house. As far as Dhoruba was concerned, David Hilliard was a punk.

Dhoruba also saw Hilliard as a conciliator, like many of the "country boys" from Oakland. "I was and still am a black nationalist," remembered Dhoruba years later. "I was raised in the ferment of Harlem, where Garvey and Malcolm talked about forging a black identity, a unique black culture. We were not just interested in civil rights, or integration, even though that was part of it. We were talking about the right to assert our individual identity as the descendants of African slaves in America."

Hilliard was insistent. "The problem," he told Dhoruba, "is that the Party here in New York is infiltrated with agents and jackanapes. Nobody can be trusted." He cited the case of Alex Rackley, a New York Panther who'd been tortured and summarily executed with two bullets to the back of the head in a swamp in rural Connecticut the month before. Local Panthers had killed Rackley on the suspicion that he was an informant. One of the people involved in the murder, George Sams, was himself an informant. A former mental patient who'd been recruited by the FBI to serve as a snitch, Sams had insinuated himself into various East Coast chapters of the party. Sams claimed that the Rackley murder had been authorized by national chairman Bobby Seale, who was now under arrest in New Haven for his role in the murder.

"Okay," said Dhoruba. "We got informants. That's a legitimate security issue. But you can't say nobody can be trusted. There are dozens—*hundreds*—of young brothers and sisters out there picking up the slack. How you gonna let these white crackers run the Panthers out of New York? Besides, this trial here is gonna be a fund-raising bonanza for the Party."

The mention of fund-raising stopped Hilliard's complaining and started him listening. A support group of radical lawyers, celebrities, and others had formed the Committee to Defend the Panther Twenty-one, soliciting funds from an office they opened on Union Square in Manhattan. Donations were pouring in.

"Well," said Hilliard, "maybe you're right. I'm gonna discuss this further with the chairman. But in the meantime we have to take some measure to show that discipline will be enforced. As of today, the entire New York chapter is under suspension, except for the brothers and sisters in jail. I'm headed up to New Haven to meet with the chairman. We gonna get to the bottom of this." Dhoruba returned to his cell feeling he'd averted a disaster.

Later, in sessions with their lawyers—when the defendants were able to meet with one another in a holding pen adjacent to Manhattan criminal court—Dhoruba discussed the situation with Lumumba Shakur, Cetewayo, and others. Some of the New York Panthers were livid when they heard that the national leadership had been ready to sell them down the river. Lumumba suggested that they break away from the Black Panther Party and form a splinter group.

Dhoruba argued for patience. "Look," he said, "if we could just get through to Minister Huey P. Newton, and explain our vision for a national party based in New York City, I know he would agree. The problem is Hilliard. He controls access to Huey while he's in the joint. If we could just get to Huey, he'd realize that now is not the time to bail out on the party in New York. On the contrary, this trial could be the basis for a whole new initiative—national, even international."

The others were impressed. Dhoruba was taking leadership; he was stepping into the breach.

In a matter of months, Dhoruba Bin Wahad would get his wish, meeting face-to-face with Huey P. Newton. But the man Dhoruba met wasn't the same man who had spawned the Black Panther Party for Self Defense a few years earlier, before he went off to prison for the killing of an Oakland police officer. And the BPP that Newton envisioned back in 1966—small, localized, and politically parochial—had grown unmanageable while he was away. Growing pains, internal conflicts, and the persistent counterintelligence efforts of the FBI had begun to eat away at the foundation of the black liberation movement in New York City.

IN MARCH 1970, Dhoruba caught a break. After eleven months of incarceration, and just weeks before opening statements were scheduled to begin in the trial of the Panther Twenty-one, the New York State Supreme Court ruled that some of the defendants could be released on bail. The defendants selected for bail were Afeni Shakur, Joan Bird, Cetewayo, and Dhoruba. According to attorney Gerald Lefcourt, lead counsel for the Panther Twenty-one, Dhoruba was chosen "because he was brilliant; he was very articulate and could help raise money for the cause by giving speeches."

Over the next few months, Dhoruba undertook what was his most active period as a member of the BPP. He gave speeches all around New York City and traveled to Los Angeles, Dayton, Cincinnati, Baltimore, Washington, D.C., Philadelphia, Buffalo, and North Carolina to talk at political forums and rallies about the case of the Panther Twenty-one. He hosted visiting "dignitaries" who wanted to meet with leaders of the now internationally famous Black Panther Party. Dhoruba met with representatives from the African National Congress, the Irish Republican Army, the South West Africa People's Organization (SWAPO), and other self-proclaimed revolutionary groups who felt a kinship with the Black Panthers. He even escorted the French author and existentialist Jean Genet from New York to San Francisco via plane to meet with David Hilliard, Donald Cox, and other Panther leaders.

Almost every weekend, Dhoruba flew on a commercial airliner to Oakland to meet with the Central Committee, taping updates on the Panther Twenty-one trial on a portable cassette recorder for Huey Newton to listen to in prison. In return, Newton sometimes recorded thoughts and observations of his own, returning the tapes to Dhoruba through his attorney, Charles Garry. Dhoruba found the process frustrating, but with Hilliard blocking him from direct access to Newton, it was his only lifeline to the leader.

Dhoruba was also grappling with a serious philosophical conundrum. From Algeria, Eldridge Cleaver had been sending out proclamations calling for the Black Panther Party to become the "vanguard organization" in a worldwide black socialist revolution, with underground cadres in Palestine, Korea, North Vietnam, and all over Africa. Cleaver was promoting armed insurrection as the natural goal of this shared struggle. Huey Newton, on the other hand, was publishing a series of articles in the *Black Panther* advocating what he called "intercommunalism," a form of community-based political organizing. Newton ridiculed cultural separatism, calling it "pork chop nationalism," and seemed to be retrenching from any kind of armed confrontation.

These differences troubled Dhoruba, and soon they threatened to disrupt the tectonic plates undergirding the Panther universe.

In the wake of the Panther Twenty-one arrests, amid mounting fears that the East Coast Panthers were riddled with informants, the party's Central Committee decided that the entire operation needed to be monitored by Oakland. In Brooklyn, Harlem, and the Bronx, overseers arrived from California with the authority to call the shots. One of the first edicts passed by the West Coast overlords was that Black Panthers were no longer to wear dashikis, gelees, or other African-style garb. This rule was a dagger aimed at the heart of New York's black nationalist identity, and it didn't sit well with the party's foot soldiers. "Can you imagine?" said Cleo Silvers, for whom learning to wrap her hair in a gelee had been a rite of passage into the Panthers. "This showed that there were people in leadership positions in the organization who didn't know the first thing about our culture."

Like most New Yorkers, Dhoruba was not happy with the situation. He referred to Thomas Jolly, Robert Bey, and the other Central Committee envoys as "knuckleheads" and "fools." But he remained loyal to the concept of the Black Panther Party. For Dhoruba, Huey Newton was an icon; his personal sense of courage was beyond reproach. Which is why, on August 5, 1970, Dhoruba and the rest of the Panther universe was ecstatic when the word circulated that Minister Huey was free.

After more than two years in prison, Newton saw his conviction for voluntary manslaughter overturned on a technicality. Although prosecutors in California were already planning to retry Newton, he was released on bail, free to travel within the United States, giving speeches and raising money on behalf of the Black Panther Party.

With his insinuating Louisiana drawl and quick wit, Newton had charisma to spare. When he first walked out of the courthouse where he was held in a cell pending release from prison, the light-skinned Newton tore off his shirt and stood atop a parked Volkswagen with his buff prison physique, as if to proclaim "Look, Ma, top of the world!" It seemed as though a new Panther era was under way.

The enthusiasm didn't last long. Dhoruba recalled:

When Huey and them founded the party, it was a community organization in Oakland with maybe two dozen members. When Huey came out of prison he had a national organization with forty-something chapters that had spawned dynamic leaders like Eldridge and Kathleen Cleaver, Fred Hampton in Chicago, George Jackson, Geronimo Pratt, Angela Davis, and others all over the country. That freaked Huey out. He became concerned about maintaining control. To get to Huey, you had to go through David [Hilliard]. And David was intimidated by New York. All them country boys from Oakland were intimidated by New York. We used to take Huey and them up to Harlem; they were never comfortable in concentrated urban areas. Huey used to look at the buildings and say, "Wow, man, you're all stacked up on top of one another. How many people you got in this one box?" They used to adopt our style, 'cause we wore all the New York–style shit. We used to wear wide-brimmed gangster hats and soft, full-length leathers. We weren't wearing waist-length jackets like Huey and them wore. We were wearing the Heaven's Gate shit, full-length leather dusters, with wraparound shades. We were on some shit. So when they came here, Huey used to say, "Set us up with some of them hats, Dye-ruba."

The differences were more than just stylistic.

These motherfuckers had no sense of history. One of the things that corrupted the California Panthers and made Huey so corruptible was because they had no nationalist culture. They had no culture. They came from a people who had migrated there from the South only recently, less than a generation before. They had come to Oakland to work in the navy yards building the ships. That's when they built the housing projects. And the racist cops, people who became cops were crackers from Louisiana and Texarkana. This was the dynamic they knew; they were transplanted country boys. And therefore, when they came in touch with real urban ghettos in Chicago, Philly, Baltimore, they were confronted with a whole different thing. And in New York the differences were significant, because Harlem was the geopolitical center of black nationalism and Pan-Africanism. The Panthers from Oakland never really could grasp that there was this vast international black culture.

Dhoruba had hoped that Newton would bond with the New York Panthers, but it was not to be. On trips to New York, Huey did not stay with "the people" in Harlem or Brooklyn; he stayed downtown in lofts owned by wealthy radical benefactors, or in the Upper East Side apartment of actress Jane Fonda, a vocal Panther supporter who was often out of town filming a movie or participating in some antiwar activity. Newton kept his distance from the New York leadership. Though he oozed a brash confidence in public, when it came to interacting with the New York Panthers Newton seemed to have an inferiority complex.

One of the first indications that the divisions were personal in nature came with the staging of a major event—the People's Revolutionary Constitutional Convention, which would include speeches by Panther representatives at large-scale gatherings in Philadelphia and Washington, D.C. Newton had been out of prison barely a month, but he had been a constant presence in the imagination of Panthers on the East Coast, many of whom still had the iconic poster of Newton in his wicker chair on their walls. The Constitutional Convention was the first time many would see and hear the man they had worshipped for the last three years.

Before Newton took the stage at Philadelphia's Temple University, the large crowd was addressed by Cetewayo, representing the Panther Twenty-one. As he had with his basso profundo rendering of the Panther Twenty-one Manifesto, Cetewayo used his impressive vocal instrument to deliver a rousing, militant speech.

In contrast, Newton was a disappointment. His high-pitched nasal twang paled after Cetewayo's delivery, and his didactic lecture on intercommunalism was condescending and esoteric. Having come to salute their newly released revolutionary hero, the audience grew restless after discovering he was only a man. Some even booed.

After a forty-five-minute speech that seemed to go on forever,

Newton left the stage in a rage. He had been reluctant to take part in the convention in the first place, since it had been initiated by Cleaver from Algeria. Now Huey had been humiliated on the East Coast, which he was beginning to view as hostile territory. He headed back to California convinced that the New York Panthers had set him up to look like a fool.

Paranoia had always played a part in Newton's temperament. But now, as he realized the Panthers had grown beyond his control, his insecurities kicked into overdrive. He was being courted by famous intellectuals and Manhattan celebrities at parties, plied with high-priced cognac and the new social drug: cocaine. Giving Newton cocaine, noted Dhoruba, "was like pouring gasoline on a brush fire"; his ego flared in a million different directions. Newton came to believe that people were out to get him—and his fears played right into the hands of the FBI's rejuvenated COINTELPRO initiative.

Ever since Newton's release from prison, the bureau had stepped up its counterintelligence program, aiming to exploit the growing rift between the Cleaver and Newton factions of the Black Panther Party. As one confidential memo confirmed, the purpose of COINTELPRO was to "attack, ridicule and to foment mistrust and suspicion amongst the current and past membership [of the Party]." The operation forged letters purporting to be from a Panther member to various party leaders, alleging that a particular member was sleeping with another member's wife, or that a certain Panther was a police informant, or that another was stealing money from the organization. The cumulative effect of this full-scale disinformation campaign was devastating to the party, with each success noted in an FBI memorandum:

> To create friction between Black Panther Party (BPP) leader
> Eldridge Cleaver in Algiers and BPP Headquarters, a spurious
> letter concerning an internal dispute was sent Cleaver, who
> accepted it as genuine. As a result, the International Staff of the
> BPP was neutralized when Cleaver fired most of its members.
> Bureau personnel received incentive awards from the Director
> for this operation.

J. Edgar Hoover took a hands-on approach to COINTELPRO, often pushing his agents to go further in their counterintelligence efforts. In an Airtel sent by Hoover to all forty-two field divisions participating in the program, the director castigated a particular division for objecting to one proposal because it involved the spreading of untrue information. Wrote Hoover:

> Purpose of counterintelligence action is to disrupt BPP and it is immaterial whether facts exist to substantiate the charge. If facts are present, it aids in the success of the proposal but the Bureau feels that the skimming of money is such a sensitive issue that disruption can be accomplished without facts to back it up.

In another instance, an FBI division questioned a proposal to send Newton a letter, supposedly from a specific Panther member, claiming that his chief of staff, David Hilliard, was looking to have him murdered. The division expressed a concern that the letter "could place the Bureau in the position of aiding or initiating a murder by the BPP." When Hoover responded, his only concern was that the forged letter shouldn't be tied to a specific Panther member.

> Should reword this letter to convey the same thought without directly indicating that it is from a specific member of a rival group. The letter could imply that the writer would soon get in touch with Hilliard to see what he would pay to have Newton eliminated.

Hoover expressed no objection that his agents' activities could lead to murder—as long as it couldn't be traced back to the bureau.

Black Panthers eliminating other Black Panthers—that was the unspoken goal of COINTELPRO. And by late 1970, the program had begun to bear fruit. In the California desert, Fred Bennett, a Panther known to be sympathetic to the Cleaver faction, was tortured, doused with gasoline, set on fire, and shot to death. His body was then cut up and buried in the desert. It was believed that the murder had been ordered by Newton. In a confidential Airtel memo, Hoover could hardly contain his glee:

> Increasing evidence points to rising dissention within BPP causing serious morale problems and strained relationship

among Panther hierarchy. Primary cause for these internal problems appears to be the dictatorial, irrational and capricious conduct of Huey P. Newton. His extreme sensitivity to any criticism, jealousness of other leaders and belief he is some form of deity are causing severe problems within the group. . . . He has recently expelled or disciplined several dedicated Panthers including . . . the "New York 21" who were a leading cause celebre of Pantherism. . . . This dissention coupled with financial difficulties offers an exceptional opportunity to further disrupt, aggravate and possibly neutralize this organization through counterintelligence. In light of above developments this program has been intensified by selected offices and should be further expanded to increase measurably the pressure on the BPP and its leaders.

Like many prominent New York Panthers, Dhoruba was in the thick of the FBI's disinformation campaign. He was identified in COINTELPRO files as a "field secretary" and also "street leader" of the Panthers. According to one confidential memo "Diruba [*sic*] is angry over leadership decisions" made by party headquarters, and, according to a confidential informant, "has plans to take over the entire New York chapter."

Dhoruba's dissatisfaction was no secret. At a party central staff meeting held at a community center on Northern Boulevard in Corona, Queens, Dhoruba spoke up on behalf of the Panther Twenty-one. All the party's national leaders were in attendance—Newton, Hilliard, Elbert "Big Man" Howard, Bobby Rush from Chicago, and seventeen others. At the meeting, Dhoruba complained that "there has not been proper accounting of funds raised by the Defense Committee."

Dhoruba was raising a touchy subject. In recent months, COINTELPRO agents had begun leaking information to reporters that Huey Newton was living a lavish lifestyle high in a penthouse apartment in Oakland. The accusations happened to be true: funds raised by the Committee to Defend the Panther Twenty-one in New York were being diverted to the Central Committee, and Newton was using some of the funds to finance his burgeoning cocaine habit.

At the staff meeting in Queens, Newton rose to defend himself.

Instead of addressing the issue directly, he rambled for nearly two hours, talking mostly about political developments in China and Cuba, the need for oppressed people to unite in the struggle against imperialism, the need for greater sales of the party newspaper—everything *except* the Panther Twenty-one case. Clearly, Newton, Hilliard, and others from party headquarters in Oakland would not hesitate to use funds from the Panther Twenty-one Defense Committee to suit their needs, but they weren't interested in discussing a strategy to support the defendants.

Dhoruba was caught in between. Monday through Friday, he arrived in the courtroom in lower Manhattan, often exhausted from traveling on weekends, giving speeches, and organizing activities on behalf of his fellow defendants. Still, some of those who were still in jail resented the fact that Dhoruba was free. As the primary liaison between the defendants and the Panther hierarchy, he received the brunt of their complaints about the party leadership. They also had major philosophical problems with what they saw as Newton's efforts to lead the party away from its militant agenda toward the less radical realm of social and political reform.

Locked away in prison, with no end in sight to their legal travails, the frustrations of the Panther Twenty-one and their defenders had been building for months. In early January 1971, it exploded when eleven of the defendants decided to publish an open letter that criticized the leadership of Huey P. Newton and demanded the expulsion of David Hilliard as chief of staff.

The letter, published in the underground weekly the *East Village Other*, was presented as an open letter to the Weather Underground, a radical organization that had begun a bombing campaign against "symbols of U.S. oppression." Among other bombings, the Underground had set off an incendiary device in front of Judge Murtagh's home in upper Manhattan, garnering some press coverage but creating no injuries and little property damage.

In their open letter to the mostly white radical group, the Panther Twenty-one stated that as far as they were concerned the Weather Underground—not the Black Panther Party—was now the preeminent revolutionary vanguard organization in the United States.

Dhoruba consulted with the Panther Twenty-one about the letter.

I told them not to publish it. It wasn't that I didn't agree with them—I did. But I knew [the letter] would be viewed as a provocative act. Lumumba and them said, "Man, you soft, you out there letting them do what they wanna do. Maybe we should have your ass back in jail." So now my [fellow defendants] are plotting to riot in the courtroom so my bail will get revoked at the next hearing.

As Dhoruba had predicted, Huey Newton saw the letter as a threat to his leadership. In an interview on a national radio program, Newton referred to the Panther Twenty-one as "traitors and jackanapes." All eleven Panthers who had signed the letter were immediately expunged from the party by Newton, and it was declared that the party would no longer support the Panther Twenty-one. Dhoruba had not signed the letter, but he was guilty by association: though he was not purged, he was immediately suspended by executive order, along with Cetewayo, Joan Bird, and Afeni Shakur.

Relations with the Central Committee were at an all-time low and getting worse by the day. Later that month, it was announced that Newton and his entourage would be traveling east to speak at a large Panther rally in New Haven, Connecticut, in support of party chairman Bobby Seale, who was about to go on trial for his alleged involvement in the murder of Panther Alex Rackley.

Even before Newton arrived on the East Coast, rumors were swirling. Dhoruba and his people had a well-placed spy in the Newton camp: Cetewayo's wife, Connie Matthews, was Newton's secretary. Newton himself had instructed Cetewayo to marry Connie Matthews, who was a Jamaican national in danger of being deported. But Newton was also sleeping with Matthews, who was elegant and attractive. He hadn't anticipated that Connie would eventually fall in love with her own husband.

Matthews was becoming increasingly concerned about Huey's erratic behavior. He had begun to refer to himself as supreme commander and was having delusions of grandeur. High on cocaine much of the time, Huey walked around in his office and apartment brandishing a gun, and he railed frequently against the New York Panthers, especially Dhoruba, whom he referred to as "a murder mouth." Connie Matthews wanted out, but she was being held captive by Newton, who rarely let her out of his sight and had her followed by fellow Panthers when he did.

A few days before Newton arrived in New York, Connie managed to get a message out to Cetewayo, who immediately met with Dhoruba.

"You know," Cetewayo told Dhoruba, "Huey and his crew are coming out here to whack our ass. He believes that the Twenty-one, when he comes out here to show his support for Chairman Bobby, we wanna take him out, that he's being threatened, that his leadership is being threatened, and that you are behind all this."

"How you know this shit?" asked Dhoruba.

"Connie. That's why he's not letting Connie out of his sight. And he won't let me near her no more."

What Cetewayo and Dhoruba didn't know was that, at the same time, COINTELPRO agents had sent a fraudulent letter from an anonymous "Panther cadre" to Huey Newton's brother, Melvin, alleging that a hit squad led by Dhoruba was preparing to assassinate Huey when he arrived in New York. Melvin Newton showed the letter to Huey and said, "Don't go to New York. They're gonna try to kill you."

"I have to go," said Huey. "Chairman Bobby needs us."

Huey had plans of his own. When he returned from the East Coast, the threat to his leadership among the New York Panthers would be eliminated, one way or another.

Along with Cetewayo, Dhoruba's inner circle included Eddie "Jamal" Joseph, an eighteen-year-old Panther who looked up to Dhoruba like an older brother. At a Panther pad in Harlem, the three talked strategy with Afeni Shakur and Joan Bird. The group was in constant contact with their fellow Panther Twenty-one defendants. Having been purged from the party they'd given their freedom to support, Lumumba Shakur and his codefendants wanted revenge; they wanted the New York Panthers to strike first and kill Huey P. Newton.

Remembered Dhoruba:

> This was some heavy shit. A couple years earlier Huey was one of my heroes. Cetewayo used to come to the Panther Twenty-one trial wearing a T-shirt with Huey's picture on the front. But now . . . well, first of all, there was a conscious decision made by all of us on the street that no one would try to assassinate or eliminate Huey P. Newton. Because after Malcolm X, after Martin Luther King Jr.—all our leaders—for Huey to go out like that would have been tragic for us and for

what the Black Panther Party was supposed to stand for. So
Huey survived us; he was off-limits. We weren't off-limits to
him, but he was off-limits to us.

Dhoruba and his group resolved to try one last time to reason with
Huey, to get him to agree to some sort of monitoring system to pre-
vent further funds from being embezzled from the Panther Twenty-one
Defense Committee. They also wanted to address the issue of national
representation. As Dhoruba recalled, "Most folks [in New York] wanted
Huey and them to understand that we weren't talking about challenging
national leadership; we were talking about having national leadership
that was truly national, a Central Committee that was represented by
leaders from chapters around the country." If Newton refused to listen,
Dhoruba and the others decided to enlist the help of Connie Matthews,
an ally. As cosigner of the party's legal entity, Stronghold LTD,
Matthews had the authority to sign checks and distribute funds. She
also had in her possession ledgers and documents that could prove that
the Committee to Defend the Panther Twenty-one was being fleeced by
Huey P. Newton.

When Newton arrived in New Haven to speak at the rally, held on
the campus of Yale University, he was infuriated to find that his local
security team was composed of New York Panthers. His paranoia kick-
ing in, he had his people call Boston and send down a contingent of
bodyguards with no connection to the New York chapter.

After he gave his speech and retired to his hotel room, Dhoruba and
Cetewayo were allowed through security to speak with Newton. What
they witnessed was not encouraging. There were decanters of cognac
and lines of cocaine on the coffee table, and marijuana smoke wafted in
the air. Newton's entire entourage was high. Two or three young women
had been brought from the rally to entertain Newton and his bodyguards. "They were all coked out, zonked out, and they had some freaks
up there," Dhoruba remembered. The supreme commander was in no
position to have a coherent conversation, much less make important
decisions about party matters. Cetewayo and Dhoruba left the room.

The moment had arrived. Inside the room, Connie Matthews told
Huey and his crew that she was going to take a shower. While they were
preoccupied, she gathered some Panther financial ledgers, disappeared
into the bathroom, and locked the door. She turned on the shower loud

enough to be heard in the other room, then opened the bathroom window and climbed out onto a fire escape. She scurried down the metal stairs to a car where Dhoruba, Cetewayo, and Jamal Joseph were waiting.

The renegade Panthers drove north, and kept driving until they crossed the Canadian border. Cetewayo and Connie hopped a plane into exile in Algeria; they never returned to the United States. Dhoruba and Jamal went underground, first in Canada and then to various locations around the States.

On the morning of Monday, February 8, Dhoruba and Cetewayo failed to show up for court at 100 Centre Street. Judge Murtagh issued a warrant for their arrest, effective immediately. Bail was immediately revoked for Joan Bird and Afeni Shakur, who was four months pregnant at the time, and the Panther Twenty-one trial was temporarily suspended.

In the days that followed, Huey Newton issued a statement, which was mimeographed and distributed to Panther supporters outside the criminal court building and later published in the *Black Panther*. Newton proclaimed Dhoruba and Cetewayo to be "enemies of the people" for "disappearing" from the trial and giving new life to the government's "dying case." All of the renegade Panthers were purged from the party.

The mood in the Panther universe shifted from dismay to anger and, finally, paranoia. Rumors of hit men heading east and west to exact revenge swirled in the air. James Brown's hit song "The Payback" seemed to capture the mood:

Hey! Gotta gotta get back (the big payback)
Revenge! I'm mad (the big payback)
Got to get back! Need some get back!! Payback! (the big payback)
That's it!! Payback!! Revenge!! / I'm mad!!

One month after Dhoruba and the others jumped bail, the festering tensions within the party were finally expressed through the barrel of a gun.

On 125th Street, in the heart of Harlem, a Panther named Robert Webb surfaced from underground. After Newton expelled Dhoruba and the others, calling them enemies of the people, most of those closely aligned with the New York Panthers were afraid for their lives. Webb, twenty-two, was close to Dhoruba, often serving as a bodyguard for him at Panther speaking engagements around the country. As part of what COINTELPRO files routinely referred to as "the Cleaver faction" of the party, Webb had been advised to lie low until the heat blew over.

What caused Webb to surface was that he heard the *Black Panther* was being sold in Harlem. The newspaper had become a symbolic flashpoint in the split between the Newton and Cleaver factions of the party; the New York Panthers had even begun publishing a paper of their own, called *Right On!* The original Oakland paper, the *Black Panther*, had slowly disappeared from New York streets.

On the afternoon of March 8, Webb confronted a group of Panthers, loyal to Newton, who were selling the *Black Panther* on New York Panther turf. In retrospect, the operation may have been a trap to lure the New York Panthers, who were in hiding, into the light of day. Webb was ambushed, shot multiple times. He died in the gutter on 125th Street, not far from the Apollo Theater, where the masses had gathered eight years earlier and boarded buses to the nation's capital to hear Martin Luther King speak.

According to Dhoruba, "That crew who killed Webb were some boys from Boston and a Panther from the Midwest by the name of Redwine. That's the same crew who was supposed to kill me and Cetewayo. When Robert resurfaced, he became a target of opportunity. They took him out."

The war over black liberation had become a war of Panthers killing Panthers.

sixteen

PANTHER JUSTICE

THE NYPD KEPT its collective eye on the Black Panther Party. Though the New York chapter had been torn asunder by the debilitating and long-running Panther Twenty-one trial and the FBI's COINTELPRO initiative, the agents of BOSS continued filing their daily reports of the coming apocalypse. This on October 29, 1970, from the commanding officer of Special Services to the chief inspector:

> It has been reported [via confidential informant] that the BPP
> has made a policy decision to examine the drug situation in
> the inner city in order to determine which police officials
> are receiving "kick-backs" for "looking the other way"
> while the drug traffic flourishes. These officials will then
> be systematically murdered. The Black Panther Party will
> quietly take credit for the activity. The operation is ostensibly
> intended to eliminate some of the black ghetto's drug problem;
> gain the sympathy and financial backing of both blacks and
> whites; terrorize elements of the Mafia and the syndicate; and
> force the police to clean up the drug problem. It is hoped that
> a byproduct of the activity will be a substantial increase in the
> number of youths who will join the BPP. . . . The first murders
> of "bad cops" are planned for the Harlem section of New York
> City.

The BOSS memos were starting to read like something out of a blaxploitation movie—*Shaft* meets *Superfly* by way of *Black Caesar*. Never mind that the organizational structure of the Panthers in the city was in disarray. A wounded panther was dangerous and unpredictable, capable of lashing out in an irrational manner.

Of all the party initiatives that troubled the NYPD, one that received copious attention in the BOSS files was the call for community oversight and decentralization of the police—an approach known as "community policing." In a petition circulated to protesters at rallies outside the Criminal Court building during the Panther Twenty-one trial, the party called for a police control amendment to be added to the city charter:

> This amendment would give control of the police to
> community-elected neighborhood councils so that those whom
> the police should serve will be able to set police policy and
> standards of conduct. . . . The councils shall have the power to
> discipline officers for breach of department policy or violations
> of the law. (Against the people.) They may direct their police
> commissioner to make changes in department-wide policy
> by majority vote of the said department commissioner. The
> council can recall a commissioner appointed by it at any time
> it finds that he is no longer responsive to the community. The
> community can recall the council members when they are not
> responsive to it.

The notion of community control of the police seemed democratic on the face of it, but the Panthers knew full well that what they were calling for flew in the face of historical precedent in New York and virtually every other major city in the United States. In general, urban police departments had been formed by the property-owning class to protect their assets. A police officer could shoot a looter during a riot situation and know he would be exonerated because many municipalities had determined—unofficially, and in selected situations—that property was more valuable than human life. By the late 1940s and into the 1950s, with the great migration of southern blacks to the northern cities, this dynamic took on a racial cast.

Some Black Panther Party leaders—Huey Newton in particular—

had tried to make the argument that the police were mere tools of the ruling class. In New York City, after all, real estate concerns were a primary force behind racial segregation. Real estate money was invariably behind the election of politicians, and the development of property determined where city resources were focused. The fact that the city was so densely populated, with a rich neighborhood like the Upper East Side just blocks away from a poor neighborhood like East Harlem, required the police to man the barricades with due diligence; they were the first and the last line of defense.

The argument that the police were being used by larger capitalist forces may have had some merit, but it was also a Marxist analysis that fell on deaf ears. Cops weren't interested in being portrayed as "instruments of the white power structure." And for black citizens living in impoverished communities, the theoretical reasons behind police brutality were less interesting than the reality of a nightstick across the skull.

Community policing was an attempt to alter the priorities of law enforcement, to remove them from the influences and pressures of the city's larger economic structure and put it in the hands of the people. To dismiss this as utopian or Marxist was beside the point. The vanguard of the BPP was calling for revolution, not social reform.

To the cops, community policing reminded them of the mock trials that the Panthers had instituted to call attention to police actions they felt were beyond the pale. One such "tribunal" took place at the Marcy Housing Projects in Brooklyn, where a "legal proceeding" was held to determine the guilt or innocence of Patrolman Thomas Johnson, shield number 2420, who had shot and killed a local teenager on Flushing Avenue during an arrest gone bad.

As noted in a BOSS confidential memo, "The trial procedure included a judge, jury, prosecutor, and defense attorney. The members of the jury were made up of persons of the community and members of the BPP, who in addition, formed a security detail to physically search all persons wishing to gain access to the proceedings. . . . Information gained from another source reveals that Ptl. Johnson was found guilty of murder and sentenced to death by the Black Panther Party. No mention was made of any planned action to enforce this judgment."

Access to BOSS files was restricted, but information leaked out, creating a rumor mill through which legitimate threats, hypothetical possibilities, and police paranoia were disseminated into the community. When it came to the subject of community policing, most cops were worried less about mock trials than about the very real possibility that the department's deeply engrained corruption might soon be dragged into the light of day.

Bill Phillips was aware of the possibilities. By early 1971, he had moved most of his hustling activities out of the ghetto, where operations like the Special Investigations Unit (SIU) were skimming narcotics profits in places like Harlem on a scale beyond anything Phillips had ever attempted. SIU was a virtual rogue unit within the department, relatively unmonitored by the NYPD command structure or anyone else.

Sensing, perhaps, that the level of graft in the narcotics age had skyrocketed, Phillips narrowed his own reach, focusing on the tried-and-true scams he knew best. He confined himself mostly to midtown Manhattan on the East Side, home of the Seventeenth Precinct. Payoffs from bars, nightclubs, construction sites, and gambling operations were still the best moneymakers, but like any veteran hustler, Phillips was always on the lookout for new scores.

One night in early April, he was having a drink at P.J. Clarke's, where everyone still thought he was a detective, when another cop—this one an actual detective—pulled him aside and excitedly told him of a potential score. Just a few blocks away, on East Fifty-fifth Street near Madison Avenue, a high-class madam was running a prostitution operation. Having been busted a week earlier, she was now looking for a cop who could put her on the pad in exchange for protection.

The words of his father rang in Phillips's ears: prostitution, like dope, was usually more trouble than it was worth. But Pop was dead now. Money was money. Who was Bill Phillips to say no to a potential score?

Phillips and the other cop left Clarke's and walked over to the whorehouse in an apartment building at 155 East Fifty-fifth Street. It was an immaculate building with a doorman, and the madam running the place was a class act. Her name was Xaviera Hollander. She was a Dutch immigrant, blond, blue-eyed, a professional hooker and serious businesswoman at the age of thirty-five.

Phillips introduced himself. At first, Hollander doubted he really was a cop; she'd been ripped off before by fake cops. Phillips gave her his badge and department ID number. "So," he said, "I heard you've been having problems and are looking for someone who can make them go away."

Hollander told him the story of the recent bust at her place. She and her girls had been taken downtown and thrown in the Tombs like common criminals. She described to Phillips how they were leered at by predatory Negro junkie streetwalkers. Years later, in a published memoir, Hollander put it like this: "Almost from the moment we were herded into the crowded cattle pen of a prison cell . . . the jail-toughened black hookers gave us nothing but misery. 'Hey, bigshit madambitch, bet you ain't got no black cunt turnin' tricks in your high-class fuckin' house!' . . . In the hooker hierarchy, we were the aristocrats, they were the serfs, and jail, by God, was the great leveler. I stood with my girls huddled together against the cell bars, putting as much distance as possible between us and the black streetwalkers."

Phillips listened sympathetically to this European lady's tale of woe amid the black rabble of the city. "Who was the arresting officer?" he asked. Hollander gave him a name, and that was that. Then they went over to P.J. Clarke's for a drink. Hollander was impressed with Phillips, especially when he mentioned that he had his pilot's license and ran a flying school. "You seem to be able to get around pretty well," she said.

"Yeah," said Phillips. "I move pretty good."

Over the next few weeks, Phillips went to work. Through his contacts at the local precinct, he was introduced to a patrolman named O'Keefe, whose beat included East Fifty-fifth Street. Phillips told O'Keefe: "I got a good operation up there. She's making a good buck and wants to go on the pad. What's it going to cost me?"

O'Keefe thought about it; he didn't really know. Sometimes, coming up with an equitable number was not easy. The money had to be spread around. How about $500 a month? The price included all the protection that O'Keefe could provide, plus an early-warning system. If the cop heard of any raids being planned for the madam's premises, he would call and tell her Mister White was coming to town, and at what time.

"That's a fair price," said Phillips. "Let me run it by Xaviera."

At a meeting with Hollander, Phillips made his pitch. Also present in Hollander's small office on East Fifty-fifth Street was a guy named Teddy Ratnoff, who had been introduced to Phillips as Hollander's "boyfriend." The term, Phillips gathered, was being used loosely. Hollander likely had many boyfriends, some of whom she dated because they knew how to fuck, some because they paid money for the privilege, and some who offered services in return. Teddy Ratnoff was a guy who had worked in various city agencies, knew people in government, and advertised himself as a kind of Mister Fix It. Ratnoff presented himself as Hollander's "financial adviser," but to Phillips he seemed more like "a towel boy in a whore house." At the age of thirty-three, prematurely bald, paunchy, with oversized glasses and perennially sweaty, Teddy seemed harmless—which is why Phillips was unconcerned when he sat in on their business discussion.

"Good news," Phillips told the madam. "I got a cop at the One-Seven who will be your rabbi. All it's gonna cost you is two hundred for the precinct, five hundred for the division, three hundred for the borough, and a lousy one hundred for me."

Hollander winced. "That's eleven hundred a month."

"Hey," said Phillips, who was hoping to pocket six hundred a month on the deal, "you ask me, it's a bargain." To impress her, Phillips gave them names of real cops and commanders in the precinct he was supposedly paying off.

Ratnoff was perspiring, Phillips noticed . . . but then Ratnoff was a sweaty guy.

He was also wearing a wire. Teddy Ratnoff was recording the entire conversation as a part-time operative for the Knapp Commission.

IN THE NEARLY six months since its inception, the Knapp Commission had toiled mostly in obscurity. From the beginning, it struggled with mandate issues and budgetary constraints. The commission had been created by executive order, which gave it the power to hold public hearings and the right to get subpoena power. Its initial funding came from a federal Law Enforcement Assistance Administration (LEAA) grant, but that was hardly sufficient or sustainable. Even some members of the commission felt the initiative had been set up to fade out and disappear as soon as possible.

As chief counsel for the commission, Knapp selected Michael Armstrong, a square-jawed, thirty-one-year-old attorney with a boyish shock of brown hair and an impeccable reputation. From the beginning, Armstrong took the assignment seriously. If the Knapp Commission was supposed to be a paper tiger, nobody told Mike Armstrong. He immediately set up meetings with various leaders in law enforcement, the district attorney's office, and in the community, to let it be known that the Knapp Commission meant business.

In Harlem, Armstrong met with the editor of an African American newspaper. When he asked the man if he knew of any cops on the take in the black community, the editor was incredulous. "You gotta be kiddin', right?"

"Well," Armstrong persisted. "In your opinion, who are they? Which cops are on the pad in Harlem?"

The editor answered, "The dudes that are taking the money are the dudes that are breaking hands." It took a few days for the meaning of this remark to dawn on Armstrong: the NYPD's habit of physical abuse went hand in hand with its pattern of financial corruption. The department's use of excessive force instilled fear everywhere in the community; it was the nonverbal facilitator behind many police corruption rackets.

In his role as the commission's chief liaison with the criminal justice community, Armstrong also met with assistant D.A. Joseph Phillips. Along with serving as prosecutor in the still ongoing Panther Twenty-one trial, Joe Phillips helmed the bureau that dealt with police corruption cases in the NYPD's plainclothes division. He struck Armstrong as highly defensive, in deep denial on the subject.

"You guys think everybody in the department is corrupt," the ADA snarled at Armstrong.

Also present at the meeting was Richard Condon, an NYPD deputy inspector working on corruption cases in conjunction with the D.A.'s office. Condon sat quietly smoking a pipe as ADA Phillips insisted there was no widespread corruption in the NYPD. At one point, Phillips turned to Condon for backup. "Go ahead, Dick, tell him. How many bagmen would you say we've got in the whole division?" Phillips was no doubt expecting Condon to lowball Armstrong—to put his estimate somewhere in the single digits, or maybe shrug and say "none to my knowledge." Instead, Condon—a straight-arrow veteran who would years later become police commissioner—took his pipe from his mouth and said dryly, "Ninety-eight."

Armstrong tried not to laugh out loud. Phillips was apoplectic.

Beyond grappling with the commission's financial constraints—it would eventually reduce its staff from twelve to four—the agents also had a hard time focusing their investigation. They narrowed police corruption down to three main areas of operation: gambling, prostitution, and narcotics. The commission did uncover one major lead early: in 1969, Robert Leuci, the young New York cop who had found himself in the middle of the July 1964 street riots in Harlem and Bed-Stuy, had come forward to detail corruption within the SIU, which involved proceeds that dwarfed anything ever seen in the history of New York police corruption. Leuci's revelations—initially unknown to anyone outside the Knapp Commission—were so massive in scope that Armstrong concluded that they were beyond the means of the commission to investigate. Reluctantly, he turned Leuci over to the office of U.S. Attorney Nicholas Scopetta, who initiated an undercover investigation that lasted years and eventually resulted in unprecedented prosecutions of police officers.

Then there were Serpico and Durk, the cops who'd approached the mayor's office and then told their stories to the *New York Times*. The two were willing to cooperate, but Serpico and Durk were well-known clean cops who knew only about corruption that they had turned down. They were useless to the Knapp Commission as undercover operatives.

What the commission needed was a dirty cop, someone actively engaged in criminal scores that reached throughout the police command structure.

"Frankly," remembered Armstrong years later, "we had little reason to be hopeful. We were flat on our asses."

And then Teddy Ratnoff walked in the door.

A self-proclaimed eavesdropping expert, Ratnoff was known to investigators around the city and state. One day, an IRS investigator named Brian Bruh, who was working with the Knapp Commission, mentioned to Ratnoff that they were looking to nail cops on the take in the prostitution business and were looking for a way in. "Any ideas?" Bruh asked Ratnoff.

Teddy's eyes lit up. "Have I got a prostitute for you. Xaviera Hollander. High-class European. She's paying off a cop named Phillips."

The Knapp Commission didn't know who Phillips was, and they couldn't start asking around without arousing suspicions. The only way to proceed was to wire up Teddy Ratnoff and have him ingratiate himself with this cop, who Ratnoff said was tied into corruption at many levels of the NYPD.

Ratnoff devised his own equipment, a transmitter he strapped to his chest underneath his clothing. The device picked up conversations and transmitted them to a recorder, manned by eavesdropping agents, at a separate location. Ratnoff's equipment was homemade but state-of-the-art; he was something of a pioneer in the surveillance business, a man without much of a personal life who made his living spying on the lives of others. Still, corroboration was needed. When Ratnoff met Phillips at P.J. Clarke's to make Hollander's first payoff, Bruh and a handful of other agents were on-site, mixing in with the clientele as they monitored the transaction.

"I got the five hundred for you," Ratnoff said to Phillips as they stood at the bar.

"Where's the rest of it?" said Phillips, giving Ratnoff a hard look.

"You'll get the rest of it tomorrow," said Teddy. For a little guy dealing with a swaggering cop, Ratnoff was surprisingly calm. In dealing with Phillips, he said later, "I was never afraid. I was convinced that Phillips was so hungry [for money] that he would never consider I was recording him."

Later that day, meeting again at Clarke's, Phillips was met by Officer O'Keefe. "How are you, kid," said Phillips, slipping an envelope to the cop. "Five hundred. Everything taken care of?"

"Fine," said O'Keefe. "Everything's fine."

In the weeks that followed, the Knapp Commission investigators monitored the daily routine of Bill Phillips. He never suspected he was being followed; such a thing would have been inconceivable to him. If it had been an interdepartmental investigation that was closing in on him, he would have been tipped off about that. The problem for Phillips was that the Knapp Commission was not under the purview of the NYPD.

There were more deals and more payments on behalf of Madam Hollander, all of them partially facilitated by Ratnoff. By early June, Phillips felt comfortable enough with the Hollander people that he even brought a contact of his own in on one of their schemes.

Hollander had a friend who had been arrested on charges of possession of a fraudulent check, and she asked Phillips if he could make the charges go away. "Anything's possible," said Phillips. He reached out to a criminal defense lawyer he knew named Irwin Germaise. A well-connected, highly successful attorney, Germaise also happened to be crooked. When Phillips explained the situation, the lawyer said he could fix the case for $10,000 if they got it before the right judge.

Fixing a case with an under-the-table cash payment to a judge was not uncommon at the time in New York; tales of judicial scandal hit the tabloids on a semiregular basis. Ratnoff and the Knapp Commission investigators were excited by the prospect: high-priced madam, crooked cop, crooked judge. That was big city corruption in a nutshell. There was only one problem: when Ratnoff explained the scam to Hollander, she balked at the price. She could make a small portion of the payment, but she didn't have the whole ten grand.

"So we scrounged the money together ourselves," Armstrong remembered. "Some of it came from the State Crime Commission. The rest we all pitched in out of pocket. I borrowed some of it from petty cash at the law firm where I worked. That's how we came up with ten thousand."

Irwin Germaise had a bad feeling about Teddy Ratnoff. He told Phillips, "That fuck. He's a slimy character and I hate his guts. He's the worst kind of guy in the world and if it wasn't for the ten thousand, I wouldn't have anything to do with him."

Phillips chuckled. Ratnoff was a weasel, all right, but for some reason he found him endearing.

After meeting with Teddy a few times, the lawyer got spooked. At one meeting in particular, at Germaise's penthouse home, he pointed a cane at Ratnoff and told him the cane was actually a gun that fired .45-caliber bullets. "One word from me and you're dead," Germaise told Ratnoff.

A few days later, Germaise expressed his concerns to Phillips. "Bill, I think I talked too much to that guy. I did a little drinking and did a big mistake. I've been thinking about it now all weekend and I've decided the guy's wired."

"Ah, no," said Phillips. "He's not wired. He's a shithead, a schmuck. He's nothing."

"No, I think he's wired."

"He can't be wired. He's not that smart. He's like a flunky in the whorehouse, that's all."

"Well, he's coming by the office at four tomorrow. I want you here when he gets here. We'll find out if he's wired."

The next day, Ratnoff showed up at Germaise's office, wearing a wire. The office was in a high-rise building on Fifth Avenue, not far from Hollander's bordello. Brian Bruh and another Knapp investigator were in the back of a van outside, listening in.

Phillips and Germaise were waiting when a secretary ushered Ratnoff in. Phillips stood up. "Ted, come in. How you doing, kid?" He smiled and ran a hand over Ratnoff's chest. The smile disappeared. He grabbed Ratnoff by the scruff of the neck and lifted him off the ground.

"What's the matter?" said Ratnoff, choking. "What's the matter?"

"Irwin, the man is loaded," Phillips said.

Ratnoff tried to laugh it off. "With what? What am I loaded with? Money?"

Phillips reached inside Ratnoff's jacket and ripped his shirt open, exposing wire, adhesive tape, and a small electronic transmitter. The recorder picked up the following conversation:

Phillips: What is that?

Ratnoff: It's a paging system.

Phillips: Yeah, take it off.

Ratnoff: It's a paging system, Billy. . . . Pick up the phone, I'll show you. It's a paging system.

Phillips: Take it off.

Ratnoff: It's a paging system.

Germaise: What do you page?

Phillips: How come you're so shaken now?

Germaise: What do you page?

Ratnoff: I'll show you. Pick up the phone and I'll page, right?

Phillips: I'll tell you what, if this is what I think it is, you know what you are?

When they heard what was happening, Brian Bruh and the other Knapp investigator jumped from their vehicle, ran into the building, took an elevator to the eighth floor, and burst into the office. "I could see Ratnoff sitting, like, on a little stool," Bruh remembered. "His clothes were ripped off, and Phillips was standing over him. You could see Germaise had been standing over him, too. He said, 'What are you doing, sir?' or words to that effect. I said I was from the Knapp Commission, and I wanted that man [Ratnoff] out of here."

Later, in his memoir, Phillips remembered the moment when his life turned upside down:

> I thought, shit, he's wired, my life is gone, ended, obliterated by this one individual. It's finished, dead. My reaction was, if I could just take this guy, and not kill him, but beat the shit out of him. I don't know. Maybe throw him out the window.

What the Knapp investigators did next was risky. Instead of arresting Phillips immediately, they let him stew on the situation for a few days. They were certain he wouldn't flee: for such a hotshot, a man about town, his world was small. He lay on the sofa at his house in Queens for a few days and considered his options.

Three days after the incident with Ratnoff, Phillips was having a drink at P.J. Clarke's when Bruh and two other investigators appeared and asked him to "come downtown." They brought him to 51 Chambers Street, Room 1130—the headquarters of the Knapp Commission.

Phillips was introduced to Mike Armstrong. "We thought we were going to have to turn the screws," remembered Armstrong. "But he had already made up his mind."

Armstrong still felt he needed to drive home to Phillips the gravity of what would be required of him—that he would have to come clean on everything he knew. "I started giving him the standard bit, you know. 'You'd better realize that if you come across, you've got to come across all the way; we don't want to hear anything from you that isn't true because you think we'd like to hear it.' All that crap. 'Some time in the future there is going to be a cross-examination in criminal cases on this, and you're going to have to be subjected to it, and if you want a deal for yourself, you'd better be telling the truth right now.' Well, I'm in the routine and he stopped me. He said, 'Hey, Mister Armstrong, I've been sitting where you're sitting, and I've had people sitting where I'm sitting. I know what I got to do.'"

Afterward, the Knapp investigators took Phillips to dinner at the Old Homestead, a venerable steakhouse in the city's Meatpacking District. There, Phillips regaled the investigators with stories from his career—some sad, some hilarious, all of them fascinating. Bill Phillips, second-generation NYPD, crooked cop, engaging raconteur, was about to become the most infamous snitch in the history of American policing.

CORRUPT INSTITUTIONS ARE traditionally brought down from the inside. Dishonesty feeds on itself. In the NYPD, certain ways of doing business had gone unexamined for generations; the common belief was that the Blue Wall of Silence was like the code of *omerta*, a bonding agent more powerful than the sun. Shine a light in the darkest recesses of the NYPD and the glare from a policeman's badge just might blind you.

Mike Armstrong knew the score: no cop had ever been compelled to wear a wire and take down fellow cops. But he wasn't willing to defer to the power of the Blue Wall. Armstrong had another theory: "Maybe it's because nobody ever tried."

The Black Panther Party was another organization that demanded internal discipline and loyalty. Contrary to how the Panthers had been portrayed by some in law enforcement and the media, the organization was not created to kill cops. And yet there were Panthers who shot at cops and planned acts of violence against the police, who fantasized about taking their revenge against law enforcement. The gun was at the center of the Panther mystique, and violence—whether theoretical or practical—was an accepted mode of discourse.

Sometimes, in times of crisis, violence turns inward. The murder of Robert Webb on 125th Street was an act of provocation that the New York Panthers would not let stand. The Panthers, after all, were a street organization, "brothers from the block." There were ex-gang members and ex-cons mixed in with the college kids and community organizers. And the hard core of the party was ready to rumble.

At a press conference following Webb's murder, Zayd Malik Shakur, brother of Lumumba Shakur, pointed the finger at Newton and Hilliard. "We have documented evidence that these two madmen gave the orders to have Brother Robert Webb killed." Shakur added that the Central Committee in California had sent "seventy-five robots" to New York as hit men to wipe out selected opposition leaders.

Dhoruba was on that hit list, but he had gone underground. The rumor in the street—and in the files of the NYPD and the FBI—was that he was in Algeria with Eldridge Cleaver. In truth, Dhoruba and

Jamal Joseph had snuck back into the United States from Canada; they were hiding out in the Bronx, moving from Panther pad to Panther pad—and redoubling their studies of the philosophy and lifestyle of the urban underground.

Much of what they knew came from reading Carlos Marighella's *Mini-Manual of the Urban Guerrilla.* As a leader of National Liberation Action (ALN), a Brazilian guerrilla organization fighting the military dictatorship in Brazil, Marighella offered practical advice on how to live as an urban revolutionary:

> The urban guerrilla must know how to live among the people, and he must be careful not to appear strange and different from ordinary city life. He should not wear clothes that are different from those that other people wear. Elaborate and high-fashion clothing for men and women may often be a handicap if the urban guerrilla's mission takes him into working class neighborhoods or sections where such dress is uncommon. . . . If [the urban guerrilla] is known and sought by police, he must go underground, and sometimes must live hidden. Under such circumstances, the urban guerrilla cannot reveal his activity to anyone, since this information is always and only the responsibility of the revolutionary organization in which he is participating.

Dhoruba and his crew felt they were under the gun on two fronts: in the war between law enforcement and the black liberation movement, and in the war between the East and West Coast Panthers.

Revenge was the talk of the day. The New York Panthers wanted revenge for the murder of Robert Webb, but that wasn't the only issue that had gotten under their skin. Adding insult to injury, the Huey Newton faction of the party had set up shop in New York. They'd moved the *Black Panther* publication offices to an office in Corona, Queens, and soon the paper was selling four times as many issues in New York as in any other city in the United States, including the Bay Area. And yet none of the proceeds went to the New York operation. Ever since Newton had purged the New York chapter, the city had become nothing more than a source of plunder for the Central Committee—a flagrant act of financial buggery that wasn't going down easy with the brothers from the block.

On the evening of April 17—five weeks after Webb's shooting—Dhoruba, Jamal Joseph, and a handful of others met at a secret location in the Bronx. They had already decided to retaliate by burning down the *Black Panther*'s office and distribution center on Northern Boulevard in Queens. After staking out the location, they decided to strike at night. After renting a U-Haul truck and loading it with handguns, rifles, a machine gun, and cans of gasoline, Dhoruba and five others piled into the truck around 10:00 P.M. and drove across the Whitestone Bridge and into Queens.

Among the Panther faithful, the split between the Newton and Cleaver factions of the party had created a mood of foreboding. The Panther Twenty-one trial had been going on for nearly two years, and efforts to rally support for the prisoners had been scuttled by dissension within the party. The Central Committee in Oakland had abandoned and excoriated the defendants, who had been locked up without bail and driven virtually insane by an interminable legal process. Newton had forbidden any mention of the group in the pages of the party's own newspaper. They had been demonized.

As the split began to take shape, many Panthers were caught in the middle. One was a young Panther named William "B.J." Johnson, who had joined the Jamaica, Queens, branch and then transferred to Corona, Queens, to work on distributing the *Black Panther*. B.J. was a former heroin dealer from Brooklyn who became involved in the Panthers' Drug Relief Program, which involved recruiting members who were in rehab and offering them a path to getting clean by working for the party.

At the Corona branch, Johnson became close to Sam Napier, the *Panther*'s national distribution manager. Napier had come to Corona from Oakland, where he'd known Newton and Hilliard since the party's early days in the Bay Area. Napier was well liked by those who knew him, but his strong connections to the California Panthers made him a visible symbol of the Newton faction in New York—not a comfortable position as tensions mounted.

Johnson was a rank-and-file member of the party; he did not see himself as being affiliated with any faction, Newton or Cleaver. But as feelings became more heated, and Panthers started killing other Panthers, neutrality was not an option. Remembered B.J.:

After the Webb murder, for a time we stopped selling *The Black Panther* in Harlem. It seemed crazy to do that with all the bad blood. Then Huey Newton gave the order to resume circulating the paper in Harlem. Sam [Napier] did as he was told. "Circulate to educate." That was his favorite phrase. Sam was a stickler for structure and following the rules. He told us to get back out there. I didn't agree with it at all. I argued against it. We didn't need Harlem. We were meeting our quota selling the paper in Brooklyn and Queens. The Harlem people had their own paper called *Right On*. Let them have Harlem. See, I know how New Yorkers are. We are very territorial because we all grew up in gangs and each gang had their own block or their own [housing] project and if you went into somebody else's neighborhood and don't know nobody, they whip your ass. So, you know, I didn't want to go to Harlem, but them motherfuckers in California didn't understand.

On the night of April 17, Johnson and a fellow Panther named Omar were in Manhattan distributing copies of the paper. From a pay phone, Johnson called Sam Napier, who told them, "Get your ass back to the office." There had been threats against the office all week, and Napier was concerned that there were no security guards on the premises.

Johnson and Omar were driving back to the distribution center when they heard fire trucks behind them. They pulled their van over to the side of the street and let the trucks pass. As they approached the distribution center, there was smoke billowing from what they thought was a storefront next to the office. Then they got closer and saw what was happening. "Oh, shit!" B.J. cried. "It's the office. We been hit!" They pulled over and jumped out.

As Johnson knew, Napier was in the office—along with a woman who was babysitting the child of a Panther secretary. He ran into an apartment building next to the Panther office, headed down to the basement, and crossed over to the distribution center building. In a closet on the ground floor he found the woman tied up with tape over her mouth. When Johnson pulled off the tape, the woman exclaimed, "The baby! Get the baby. It's in the backyard!" He ran into the yard, and sure enough there was a baby crawling around in the dirt. He grabbed the child, handed it to the woman, and the three of them hurried out of the burning building. B.J. remembered:

On the way out, I asked the sister, "What about Sam? Where's Sam?" She said she didn't know. Some brothers with guns had came into the office. They blindfolded her the whole time. The last thing she saw they was takin' Sam to the basement. "Did they kill him?" I asked. "Is he dead?" She said she didn't know, but when they took him to the basement she heard gunshots.

When Johnson, the woman, and the baby arrived back on the street in front of the building, the situation was chaotic. There were at least four fire trucks, all of them spraying water. A dozen police cars had arrived on the scene from different directions, lights flashing and sirens blaring. At one point, Johnson broke away to call Oakland and tell them what had happened. "I need to talk to someone in charge," he said to whoever answered the phone.

"That's me," said the person. "I'm the officer of the day."

"Well," responded B.J., "I need someone higher than you. The shit done hit the fan out here. East Coast distribution is on fire. I need to talk with somebody else."

"Hold on, brother." The person handed the phone to someone who sounded like David Hilliard. Johnson explained the situation. "I told them I got the sister and I got the baby out. I said, 'The place is on fire, it's burning up.' I told them if Sam was in there he's a goner and we're gettin' ready to get out of here." That's when Hilliard told Johnson he needed to let the fire marshal know that Sam was in the basement. "He might be trapped down there," said Hilliard.

Johnson's instinct was to flee the scene before the police locked him up as a material witness, but he was a good soldier. He approached the firemen and told them to check the basement. They did—and, sure enough, Sam Napier's bullet-riddled body was found smoldering in the embers.

B.J. Johnson was arrested and held in custody for nearly a week, interrogated by Chief of Detectives Albert J. Seedman. He stalled the police as long as he could before relenting and telling them about the Panther split. Eventually the cops came across other leads and let Johnson go.

The details of the Napier murder spread like a malodorous breeze through the Panther universe; the callousness of the killing was a portent of things to come. Napier had been tied up, then shot in the back of the head and set on fire. One former Panther noted that his body "was found charred beyond recognition." The supervisory fire marshal investigating the blaze told the *Daily News* that "Mister Napier's eyes had been bound shut with tape and his body appeared to have been set afire with flammable liquid." He said the dead Panther had been shot four times.

To Dhoruba, the Napier killing was part of a chain reaction, the tragic consequence of a dirty war that made his death seem almost inevitable. In a sense, Napier had died for the sins of Huey P. Newton. Dhoruba and six New York Panthers had stormed the office, guns drawn. Napier was bound and gagged, but it was never the plan for him to be executed. That occurred when Irving "Butch" Mason, one of the group, decided to shoot Napier in the back of the head after he was taken to the basement. Dhoruba remembered:

> The hit on the Queens distribution office was an act of retaliation for Robert Webb. The location was the target, not Sam Napier. That office was the hub of Huey Newton's activities in the area. They had this little enclave of Newton sympathizers based out of the office. They continued to raise money in the area while at the same time denigrating and attacking the local chapter of the BPP. Our objective was to run the scoundrels out of New York, and that's what we did. It had the desired effect. Big Man Howard and all of them abandoned New York. They left. They wound up taking root in Boston.

After the Napier killing, Dhoruba and Jamal Joseph went deeper underground. They stockpiled weapons, stayed indoors for days on end, and relied on a sprawling cadre of supporters in the urban underground.

Followers of the Panthers knew that the Napier killing was fallout from what was routinely referred to as "the split," but if they knew who the perpetrators were, they kept their mouths shut. Most people, including law enforcement, still believed that Dhoruba was in Algeria, a ruse that was unknowingly aided and abetted by the *New York Times*.

Since Dhoruba, Jamal, and Cetewayo had been demonized by Newton for skipping bail in the Panther Twenty-one trial, Dhoruba felt the need to explain the reasoning behind his actions. He penned a letter to the *Times*, which he submitted for publication a few days after he and Cetewayo first went underground, arranging to have it postmarked by way of Algeria. The paper sat on the letter for three months before finally printing it on the editorial page on May 12, three and a half weeks after the Napier killing. Printed under the headline "A Black Panther Speaks," the article was accompanied by an explanatory note that claimed the author "wrote this from Algeria."

> First, let it be understood that the only reason that I undertook
> to explain why it was necessary for I and Cetewayo to leave the
> Fascist Farce of a Trial Presided over by the evil likes of John
> Murtagh is because it has come to my attention that there is
> confusion as to why we did it. . .

Along with denouncing the trial and prosecution as fraudulent, Dhoruba explained how fundamental differences between the New York Panthers and "the revisionist clique of west coast pimps headed by Huey P. Newton" had threatened to derail the revolution. He criticized the policies of the Central Committee, which seemed more devoted to "survival programs" than revolution, and personally called out Newton for living in a plush penthouse apartment all at the expense of "the people's struggle."

> These internal contradictions have naturally developed to the
> point where those within the party found themselves in an
> organization fastly approaching the likes of the NAACP—
> dedicated to modified slavery instead of putting an end to
> all forms of slavery. Outlaws cannot enjoy penthouses and
> imported furniture. It is this type of leadership that saw the
> slogan substituted for the action.

There were those in the movement who felt that Dhoruba had gone off the reservation and become a danger to society. But one thing he couldn't be accused of was abandoning his vision. While Huey P. Newton spent his time socializing with starlets and appearing on radio and TV,

Dhoruba was underground, living off the land, stockpiling weapons, and plotting revolution.

ON MAY 12, 1971, a verdict was finally delivered in the Panther Twenty-one conspiracy trial. After two years and two million dollars—the most expensive trial in the history of New York State—the jury deliberated a mere ninety minutes before finding the defendants not guilty on all charges. Reading the verdict aloud required the foreman to repeat the phrase "not guilty" one hundred and fifty-six times. Dhoruba and Cetewayo were found not guilty in absentia.

It was a stunning defeat for ADA Joe Phillips and Manhattan D.A. Frank Hogan. They could have tried the defendants in a series of more manageable cases, on charges of arson, weapons possession, attempted murder, and so on. Instead they had gambled on fear, decrying the maumauing of America—and they had lost.

To those in law enforcement, the battle hadn't been a complete loss. As the steady stream of memos in the COINTELPRO and NYPD intelligence files confirmed, the Black Panther Party was in disarray. One memo noted that the party's entire New York chapter had exactly $29.95 in its bank account. Panthers were killing Panthers; the Harlem chapter had been virtually wiped out by the pressures of the trial and by internal disputes. The trial may have ended in acquittal, but its goal was accomplished: the Black Panther Party in New York was beyond recovery.

As with any social conflict, the magnitude of any setback or success depends on where you sit. Within the black liberation movement, the Panther Twenty-one verdict was a cause for joy but also anger. One juror, Edwin Kennebeck, who would later write a book about the case, asked, "How did the grand juries decide to bring those heavy indictments? There is something wrong with the way those august bodies are constituted. They are mainly the fat cats of the community, who, like most of us comfortable folks, have not heeded Martin Duberman's advice to be in touch 'with the felt experience of others'—the poor, the disaffected, the angry underdogs—to have some concept of their lives, their feelings, their language." To the most militant within the movement, the fact that even a predominantly white jury saw the Panther Twenty-one prosecutions as a disgrace was like a kick to the solar plexus.

After two years of incarceration and prosecution under the most severe conditions, the defendants were set free. The Black Panther Party's New York chapter was destroyed, but the underlying causes of the movement had not changed. Authors and sociologists described the mood as one of "black rage," a feeling of disenfranchisement that led a generation of black youths to throw themselves into the whirlwind. The demands of Black Power activists remained the same, and few in government or the criminal justice system seemed capable of addressing the subject in an enlightened or honest way. All of which begged the question: *If the Black Panther Party is finished, then what comes next?*

The answer came hard and fast. On the night of May 19—six days after the Panther Twenty-one defendants were set free—Patrolmen Thomas Curry and Nicholas Binetti were guarding D.A. Hogan's apartment building at Riverside Drive and 112th Street. A police guard had been posted outside Hogan's place of residence since the firebombing at Judge Murtagh's home the year before. Curry and Binetti were sitting in their vehicle when an aqua-blue Ford Maverick drove past them traveling south in the northbound lane on Riverside Drive. They took off after the car, circling around the block and finally catching up with the car at Riverside Drive and 106th Street. When the police car pulled up alongside the Ford, the cops barely had time to glance into the car when the driver ducked and the passenger, a black male, poked a .45-caliber machine gun out the window and opened fire. Binetti, who was driving the police car, hit the gas pedal, but it was too late. Both cops were riddled with machine-gun fire. The police car lurched forward, running into a parked car. The blue Maverick sped away.

The two cops were badly hurt—Curry disfigured and brain damaged, Binetti paralyzed—but both miraculously survived.

Two days later, a package arrived at the editorial offices of the *New York Times* and another at the studio of WLIB, a black-owned radio station. Inside the package was the license plate of the car sought by police in the shooting, wrapped in pages from the *New York Post*, accompanied by a typed note that read:

Here are the license plates sort [*sic*] after by the fascist state pig police. We send them in order to exhibit the potential power of oppressed people to acquire revolutionary justice. The armed goons of the racist government will again meet the guns of oppressed Third World Peoples as long as they occupy our

community and murder our brothers and sisters in the name
of American law and order. Just as the fascist Marines and
Army occupy Vietnam in the name of democracy and murder
Vietnamese people in the name of American imperialism
are confronted with the guns of the Vietnamese Liberation
Army, the domestic armed forces of racism and oppression will
be confronted with the guns of the Black Liberation Army,
who will mete out in the tradition of Malcolm and all true
Revolutionaries real justice. We are revolutionary justice. All
Power to the people.

Few cops had ever heard of anything called the Black Liberation
Army. Those who had found the reference ominous. As some had feared,
out of the ashes of the Black Panther Party had arisen something potentially more lethal and militant.

That night, as news of the BLA note made its way through the police
grapevine, two cops responded to a domestic disturbance call at the
Colonial Park Housing Project at 159th Street and Harlem River Drive,
where the Polo Grounds sports stadium had stood until it was torn down
in 1960. Patrolmen Waverly Jones and Joseph Piagentini entered one
of the eight massive apartment complexes that composed the Colonial
Park projects, only to discover that the call had been a hoax. As the two
uniformed policemen—one black, one white—were leaving the grounds
of the project, they were ambushed from behind by two assailants later
identified as black males. Jones, African American, was shot dead with a
bullet in the back of the head. The white cop, Piagentini, was shot and
fell to the ground. One of the assailants approached, pulled the officer's gun from its holster, and blasted away at point-blank range using
Piagentini's own service revolver. The assailants then fled the scene on
foot. Piagentini, shot thirteen times, died in an ambulance on the way
to the hospital.

The next day a typed note arrived at the offices of radio station
WLIB claiming credit for the killings. The wording was similar to the
previous message, and it was signed REVOLUTIONARY JUSTICE.

There had never been anything quite like this in the history of the
NYPD: cops being executed randomly, regardless of their identity or
even skin color. It was open season on the Men in Blue.

"We're in a war," declared Edward J. Kiernan, president of the PBA, as he arrived at Harlem Hospital into the middle of television news cameras and a gaggle of reporters. The head of the PBA was traditionally a stalwart and sometimes bellicose defender of his tribe, and Kiernan was no exception. "I refuse to stand by and permit my men to be gunned down while the Lindsay administration does nothing to protect them. Accordingly, I am instructing them to secure their own shotguns and to carry them on patrol at all times."

"Do you think that will make a difference?" asked a reporter.

"I don't know," said the PBA president. "But we'll do whatever is necessary. If we have to patrol this city in tanks, that's what we'll do. This is a war. I want all my men to understand that in any situation in which they have to draw their weapons, they are to shoot to kill. This is a battle to the death, and I want everyone to know that we won't be the only ones taking casualties."

Three blocks away, in a detective squad room on the second floor of the Thirty-second Precinct station house, Mayor Lindsay and Commissioner Murphy hosted a somewhat more sedate gathering of the Fourth Estate. Describing the shootings as "an organized attempt . . . deliberate, unprovoked, and maniacal," the commissioner released to the press a copy of the note from the BLA in response to the Curry and Binetti shooting. When a reporter told Murphy that the PBA president had "ordered" his men to carry their own shotguns, the commissioner blanched. "Police officers will carry regulation firearms," he said, refusing to comment further.

Moments later, the commissioner and the mayor left the station house, a four-story brick fortress, and came face-to-face with a gathering of twenty-five to thirty off-duty cops. The men stood between the officials and their waiting limousine.

"Jonesy and Joe are dead," someone shouted. "What are you gonna do about it?"

"What are you gonna do about *us*?" another cop demanded, with a chorus of voices sounding their approval.

"I don't know about you guys," said another cop, "but the next time I go out there I got my shotgun with me."

In a soft voice, Commissioner Murphy said, "That's not the answer. Those two patrolmen were ambushed from the back. Shotguns wouldn't have done them any good."

"That's them. I gotta be able to protect me."

"That's not the answer," Murphy repeated.

Mayor Lindsay said nothing. He was out of his element, surrounded by hostile officers who viewed him as the enemy. As he and Murphy moved toward their waiting car, a young patrolman stepped forward and spoke directly to the mayor. "We're targets. Every day we go out there, we're targets. They don't fear us or respect us. Maybe if we carried shotguns, maybe if we got tough with them . . ." The cop's voice trailed off.

The mayor nodded and climbed into the limo with the police commissioner. Their car drove off, leaving behind a handful of cops muttering to themselves, feeling angry and wounded.

IN LATE MAY, George Whitmore was released from jail in New Jersey after serving nine months for attempted robbery. He moved in with cousins at a tenement apartment in Brooklyn. As with most of his periodic stints behind bars, Whitmore returned to a society that seemed to be worse off than when he went into prison—fewer jobs, more crime, more overt hostility. This time, Whitmore rejoined the civilian population at a time when New York City seemed to be in the midst of a war. News about police shootings, or attempted shootings, were in the tabloid headlines nearly every day. In the black community there was a heated debate about the morality of the shootings. Although the BLA had its defenders, most people were disturbed by the random killing of police officers, either black or white. An editorial in the *Amsterdam News* captured the mood:

> There are those who call themselves your brothers. They stand on rhetorical platitudes and shout at the top of their voices that they are fighting for the rights of their black brothers. But how black are they? Black is not only a color as it applies to us. It's a state of mind that stands for courage. And most of all, pride. A pride that would not allow a black man to cravenly shoot down another man when his back is turned, and then condone the act by calling it justice. Especially another black man who has sworn to protect and stand between his people and harm. Cast them out for they are not of you, they have become infected with a poison that could kill us all.

Whitmore skimmed the articles, read the headlines, and scratched his head. He did not support the black radicals. He was against random killing on moral grounds. Most of all, he couldn't see how shooting cops was anything but counterproductive. George came from a generation who believed that if you challenged the police, they would only use it as an excuse to bring the hammer of repression down on you even harder. George also had personal reasons for being concerned about the social agitation of the black militants: it was bad for his case. Somehow, he feared, the actions of the black revolutionaries could be exploited to deny him his freedom.

That freedom was hanging by a thread. Whitmore was out of jail, but still firmly in the clutches of the system. He and his lawyers were waiting for a final ruling from the Appellate Division of the State Supreme Court on whether Elba Borrero's identification of him as her assailant back in 1964 would stand. The judge could call for a new trial, or, better yet, dismiss Borrero's identification altogether, throwing the ball back into the court of the Brooklyn D.A. Of course, there was also a third possibility: the judge could uphold Borrero's identification and Whitmore's conviction—in which case George would immediately be taken back into custody and serve out the remainder of his five-to-ten-year term for assault and attempted rape. There was no way of knowing which way it would go.

Meanwhile, George, as usual, was broke and without a job. With each new round of legal complications, his rap sheet grew and the likelihood of his ever finding meaningful employment faded further.

In the midst of his now familiar cycle of legal limbo and poverty, George got a surprising call from Myron Beldock, asking George to come to his office. There was someone who wanted to meet him—a famous Hollywood screenwriter.

Abby Mann was a Hollywood player at the top of his game. Having won an Academy Award in 1961 for his screenplay *Judgment at Nuremberg*, which had started out as a teleplay for the prestigious CBS drama series *Playhouse 90*, he was considered a go-to writer for subjects of serious social import. Now he wanted to adapt George Whitmore's story for film. Universal Studios had purchased the rights to Selwyn Raab's book *Justice in the Back Room* and hired Mann to work it up into a script—but in the interest of authenticity, Mann wanted to meet directly with the man at the center of it all.

George took the long subway ride into Manhattan to Beldock's midtown office, where he met the screenwriter. In his midforties, with jet-black hair and a perennial suntan, Mann had the look of an authentic Hollywood character. He told George he wanted to create a movie that was "faithful to the true story of George Whitmore." It was his intention, and the producers', to use real names and real locations for the picture, which was slated as a feature film for theatrical release.

George was intrigued, but he kept waiting to hear the words "and you will be paid this amount for your participation." Mann suggested that he might be hired as a technical adviser, but no promises were made.

George had to borrow thirty-five cents from his lawyer for the subway back to East New York.

As the train emerged from the tunnel onto the elevated tracks in Brooklyn, George peered from the window at the dingy tenement buildings, liquor store signs, and church spires of the borough's skyline. He'd often been told by lawyers, journalists, and civil rights activists that his story was incredible; now a famous Hollywood screenwriter was saying the same. He had suffered a terrible injustice, they said; if people knew the details, the criminal justice system would be reformed forever. He was an important man, they said, and his case was a part of history. Hearing all those kind words made George feel good; it gave him a feeling of relevance, gave his life a sense of purpose. But then they would go back to their lives, and George would go back to his, and nothing had changed. In fact, his financial situation only seemed to get worse as time went on, and his legal situation was like an artifact from another age, mired in sludge, calcifying further with each passing day.

Your day will come, they told George. But his daily routine, his struggle for shelter, work, sustenance, and survival weighed on his shoulders like a bag full of bricks. Out on the streets and in the courts, nothing seemed to change. Some people looked at this reality and became angry—they robbed and they shot at police and engaged in acts of civil disobedience. Whitmore mostly felt despair. No matter how hard he tried, in the collective eyes of the city he remained a nigger with a rap sheet.

seventeen

NEWKILL

THE RAT-A-TAT-TAT OF machine-gun fire strafed the ceiling at the Triple-O social club. Plaster, dust, and debris rained down on the patrons, huddled together in only their underwear. The group of fifteen men and fifteen women had been ordered to strip by Dhoruba Bin Wahad. After they'd dumped their clothes in a pile in the middle of the floor, he called for everyone to "shut the fuck up!"—and unloaded a round of bullets into the ceiling for emphasis. Everyone shut the fuck up.

"Get the money," Dhoruba told Jamal, who had already grabbed cash from behind the bar and dumped it into a bag. Another accomplice, Augustus Qualls, fleeced the patrons' clothing for cash and other valuables.

"Stay cool and you won't get hurt," Dhoruba told the patrons.

The employees, and some of the patrons, knew the routine. Robberies were a common occurrence at the Triple-O, a gambling and narcotics joint located on a desolate stretch of Park Avenue at 171st Street in the South Bronx. The place was an illegal after-hours club, so the owners weren't likely to call the cops to report a robbery. The only way a club like the Triple-O could protect itself was to have plenty of security on the premises, but Dhoruba and his crew—Jamal Joseph, Qualls, and Butch Mason—negated all that by showing up with an arsenal big enough to intimidate a small army. Dhoruba brandished a .45-caliber M3A submachine gun, also known as a "grease gun." Jamal carried a double-

barreled sawed-off shotgun in one hand and a 9-millimeter Browning
automatic in the other. Qualls had a sawed-off shotgun and a .357 Smith
and Wesson Magnum. Mason had a Colt .45-caliber revolver. In the
glove compartment of their getaway car, they'd brought along a U.S.
Army hand grenade, for good measure.

In the four months since Dhoruba had gone underground, he and
a small core of supporters had been living off what Carlos Marighella,
in his urban guerrilla manual, referred to as "expropriations." Wrote
the Brazilian revolutionary: "It is impossible for the urban guerrilla
to exist and survive without fighting to expropriate." In other words:
one must steal to survive. In Marighella's case, expropriation involved
"government resources and the wealth belonging to the rich business-
men, the large land owners and the imperialists." For those in the black
urban underground in America, it meant robbing banks, bars, gambling spots, and social clubs. Black Liberation Army members referred
to this as their "narcotics eradication program": they targeted known
drug spots—especially those suspected of making regular payoffs to
the police—which allowed them to claim they were doing good for the
community while expropriating the one thing they needed most: cash
money. According to Dhoruba,

> The black underground had taken on the campaign of
> eradicating drugs with direct action. We would raid the after-
> hours places and destroy the drugs, and when it was necessary
> we would punish the drug dealers ourselves.

Dhoruba's crew had chosen the Triple-O partly because of its desolate location. One thing they hadn't anticipated was that a gypsy cab
driver would drive by as they were entering the club, guns in tow. The
cabbie alerted two cops in a squad car a few blocks away, and the cops
were driving up to the club when they thought they heard machine-gun
fire inside the building.

Butch Mason was standing guard outside the club when the green-
and-white cop car approached. It was Mason who'd lost his cool during the assault on the BPP newspaper distribution center in Queens
six weeks before, killing Sam Napier; Dhoruba had posted him outside
to keep him away from the action in the club. With his .45 tucked in
his belt, Mason saw the cop car driving up just as he heard the sound

of gunfire inside. Mason turned and ran in to see what was happening.

Dhoruba, Jamal, and Qualls were gathering up cash and valuables when Mason rushed in. "Hey, what the hell's going on in here? There's cops out there."

"How many?" asked Dhoruba.

Just one car, Mason said—but they were bound to call for backup after hearing the gunfire.

Dhoruba ran over to the window and peeked from behind a curtain at the street below. He saw four squad cars, with more arriving from all directions. There were half a dozen cops in the street with their guns drawn, motioning others to cover the rear entrance.

Damn, Dhoruba mumbled to himself. *These motherfuckers got us surrounded*. The words of Marighella rang in his ears: "The urban guerrilla is characterized by his bravery and his decisive nature. . . . [He] must be a person of great cleverness to compensate for the fact that he is not sufficiently strong in weapons, ammunition and equipment."

Turning back to the patrons, Dhoruba said, "Okay, folks, put your clothes back on. There's a bunch of pigs outside. Let's all be cool. We're gonna act like nothin's happening, you dig?"

The patrons did as they were told. By the time the cops came through the door, everyone was mostly dressed—shirttails hanging out, one shoe on and one shoe off, but presentable. Stashing their guns under a table, Dhoruba and his crew mixed in with the patrons.

"What's going on here?" asked a police sergeant.

"Nothin'," said one of the patrons.

Something was odd; the patrons were unusually somber.

"We heard shots being fired," said a patrolman.

The patrons looked around at one another.

"No, there wasn't no shooting here," one woman said.

"Yeah, some dudes tried to rip us off," a man said. "But they ran out the back. They gone."

The cops looked at one another. The patrons looked down at the floor. Then someone spoke up from the back of the group. "No, that's not true. The cats you looking for are right here. That's him, and him and him and him." He pointed at Dhoruba and the others. The people moved aside, and the cops cuffed Dhoruba and the others without a struggle. A few minutes later, they found the small arsenal of weapons under a table.

The cops didn't know who they had. Dhoruba and Jamal were carrying false identification, Qualls and Mason no ID at all.

One item that immediately caught the attention of the police was the .45-caliber submachine gun, the same type of weapon used in the shooting outside D.A. Hogan's home three weeks earlier. The machine gun was immediately rushed to the ballistics lab.

Meanwhile, the four robbery suspects were loaded into separate vehicles and taken to the Forty-eighth Precinct on Bathgate Avenue in the Bronx, where they were photographed and fingerprinted. Remembered Dhoruba:

> We were lucky to be taken alive. The only reason we weren't killed is because of the confusion surrounding our arrest at the club. The police didn't know who we were at first. If they had, I'm pretty sure we would have been dealt with at the club or, even better for them, in the street where there were no witnesses.

At the precinct, Dhoruba, Jamal, Qualls, and Mason were all held in separate interrogation rooms. Dhoruba and Jamal kept their mouths shut, but Qualls and maybe Mason—Dhoruba wasn't sure—started to talk. Before long, word was circulating throughout the precinct and law enforcement circles throughout the city: The cops were holding Dhoruba Bin Wahad, aka Richard Moore. It was almost too good to be true: one of the most wanted of the black radicals terrorizing the city had fallen into their collective lap during a bush-league robbery.

There was plenty of work to be done—evidence to be gathered, witnesses to be sought and massaged. But the police had their first big break in solving one of the most heinous crimes against American law enforcement anyone could remember.

THE FUNERALS FOR Officers Jones and Piagentini were held in late May. The grief felt by the families of the deceased and by the police department in general was without precedent. These cops had not been killed during the commission of a "crime" in the traditional sense, which would have been bad enough. They had been executed, shot down simply because they were police officers. To most white cops, the motive for these murders was beyond comprehension. For black cops, it was cause for alarm, because the BLA had announced that a cop's race didn't matter: "Every policeman, lackey or running dog of the ruling class must make his or her choice now. Either side with the people, poor and oppressed, or die for the oppressor."

The reaction was immediate. Before the funereal bagpipes of the department's Emerald Pipe Band had even sounded, virtually every division within the force was involved in the investigation. The two incidents—the Curry and Binetti shooting and the Jones and Piagentini killings—were dovetailed into one investigation. Forty-eight detectives and ten supervisors were assigned under the command of an inspector and a lieutenant. A specialized unit of forty detectives and four supervisors worked back-to-back tours, from 10:00 A.M. to 6:00 P.M., and 6:00 P.M. to 2:00 A.M. Within a matter of weeks, they had interviewed nearly five hundred witnesses, suspects, and persons of interest. According to a status report written by the inspector overseeing the investigation, "Approximately 1000 DD-5's [police department activity reports] were submitted, 450 telephone calls were checked out. In addition, approximately 450,000 prints have been scanned from the micro-film file, 85,000 prints in the latent file, 300,000 manually from the main file and all prints from daily arrests have been checked."

Eventually, the investigation of the police shootings would lead to sixty-two arrests—mostly incidental arrests of people wanted for unrelated crimes—and result in the seizure of thirty-three handguns, twelve rifles, four shotguns, one machine gun, and more than three thousand rounds of ammunition.

The manpower and hours devoted to the investigation would make it one of the most extensive in the history of the NYPD, but the fallout from the police shootings would reach well beyond local police.

On May 26, 1971, less than a week after the killings of Jones and Piagentini, J. Edgar Hoover discussed the recent outbreak of urban violence with Richard Nixon. The president, whose reelection campaign in 1972 would be determined in part by how well he had delivered on his promise of "law and order" in cities like New York, was disturbed by the spate of shootings attributed to black militants. Nixon told Hoover that he should "take the gloves off" when dealing with Black Panthers and the like. Hoover passed the president's comments on to field agents via a confidential memo, authorizing a new round of counterintelligence and investigative activity.

Together, the FBI and NYPD inaugurated OPERATION NEWKILL, which would be devoted solely to seeking out and taking down anyone even peripherally involved in the police shootings or recent activities of the Black Liberation Army. The NYPD liaison was Chief of Detectives Albert Seedman, a cigar-chomping cop from the old school who undertook his duties with swagger and confidence. Hoover promised Seedman and the NYPD access to the latest fingerprinting and ballistics technologies, as well as use of the FBI's Black Agitator database. Dozens of agents would be assigned to augment interrogations, interviews, and stakeouts. In return for this unusual level of interdepartmental cooperation, Hoover demanded only one thing: that the FBI's involvement would never be acknowledged. NEWKILL would be a confidential investigation, known only to the police commissioner, the chief of detectives, and a handful of other high-ranking members of the NYPD.

Almost from the beginning of NEWKILL's formation, Dhoruba Bin Wahad was designated as a key target. In mid-May, the FBI's latent print lab had made a startling discovery: fingerprints matching those of Dhoruba and Jamal Joseph had been found on the copy of the *New York Post* that was used to wrap the license plate delivered along with the BLA's communiqué claiming credit for the Curry and Binetti shooting. The feds and local police were surprised: their sources had insisted that Dhoruba and Jamal were in Algeria, an impression that seemed to be confirmed by Dhoruba's article in the *New York Times*, with its Algiers dateline. The copy of the *Post* with Dhoruba's fingerprints was from May 20, putting him in the United States as of that date. A confidential teletype from NEWKILL's special agent in charge (SAC) to Hoover noted the finding:

> **Due to the fact that latent impressions obtained . . . are identical to the fingerprints of richard moore aka dahruba [sic] . . . it appears moore could be directly involved or possess positive knowledge of the shooting of nycpd officers on five nineteen seventy one and also may be implicated in captioned matter. . . . intensive and vigorous investigation currently underway by nyc to locate and apprehend moore, and sufficient manpower being utilized to effect same.**

Five days after this memo was transmitted, Dhoruba, Jamal, and the others were busted at the Triple-O social club.

At the Forty-eighth Precinct station house in the Bronx, Dhoruba sat in the interrogation room, saying little beyond "I know my rights. I wanna see my lawyer." The fact that the cops hadn't killed him, or physically abused him in any way, suggested to him that he was a prize catch. When an FBI agent entered the room and introduced himself, Dhoruba sensed for the first time that the authorities might well try to pin any number of recent BLA crimes on him, including the shootings of the police officers in Manhattan.

Eventually, Dhoruba was transferred to the Bronx House of Detention and placed in solitary confinement. Later that day, he learned from an attorney that the NYPD had issued a press release confirming that the .45-caliber submachine gun seized at the Triple-O club was the same gun that had been used in the shooting of Officers Curry and Binetti.

Now they had him. Locked in his four-by-six-foot cell, Dhoruba could feel the full weight of his situation closing in. If Qualls and even Mason were talking, the cops might soon have enough to name him as an accomplice in the Sam Napier murder. Now they were trying to pin that Riverside Drive cop shooting on him; they might even try to nail him for the other cop shooting too, the one where the two cops were killed. Dhoruba was in what is commonly known on the street as a fucked-up predicament.

The lawmen were excited. NEWKILL had been in effect less than two weeks and they'd already landed a Big Fish. As with most investigations, the best results sometimes came through hard work—but sometimes, when you created the proper environment, they just fell right into your lap. Bin Wahad had screwed up and got himself caught at the Triple-O; that was luck. What came next was more like divine intervention—a lead so unanticipated that it made the agents working OPERATION NEWKILL believe they were on the side of the angels.

On the afternoon of June 12, a call came in on the investigator's hotline, a phone number that had been posted on flyers all over the city. It was the voice of a young woman with a slight Caribbean accent. She told a detective, "The four men you are holding are not the ones who shot the cops. They may know who did it. They did not do it, neither the Riverside Drive shooting nor the Harlem shooting. They were at my girlfriend's house, 757 Beck Street in the Bronx. Her name is Pauline Joseph. She's the common-law wife of Jamal Joseph. They did nothing until the social club robbery. I don't want to see the innocent accused. I will call again."

The detectives didn't wait around for the woman to call again. They immediately drove over to 757 Beck Street and discovered that the woman who had made the call was herself Pauline Joseph. A petite black woman of twenty-two, Pauline was a native of the U.S. Virgin Islands. She worked as a receptionist for a doctor and had a baby named Brenda. The baby's father was Jamal Joseph.

Pauline allowed the cops to search the premises. What they discovered was the remnants of an underground guerrilla pad, with an entire room full of medical supplies for treating wounds, revolutionary literature strewn about, bottles for making Molotov cocktails, and the like. The cops asked Pauline if she would be willing to come to the precinct to be questioned. She agreed.

What followed would continue to one degree or another over the next two and a half years. Pauline Joseph talked. Sometimes she didn't even have to be asked a question before she began giving detailed explanations and stories of what had taken place at 757 Beck Street over the last several months. The apartment, it seemed, had become the central location for a highly active cell of the Black Liberation Army. Dhoruba and Jamal had been semiregulars there since they'd first skipped bail in the Panther Twenty-one trial. Sometime around the announcement of the verdict in that trial, they moved in permanently. And there were others who came and went—a veritable who's who of BLA militants, suspects in a spate of bank robberies, shootings, criminal conspiracies, and cop killings around the city. To the detectives, this looked like the mother lode.

Gradually the questioning zeroed in on the Curry and Binetti shooting. Joseph told the investigators that she'd heard Dhoruba and others talking about how they were going to "off a pig." Dhoruba was the leader; he rarely went anywhere without his .45-caliber submachine gun, which he carried in a duffel bag and affectionately referred to as "the grease." On the night of May 19, Pauline was in the apartment when Dhoruba and two others, Frank Fields and Michael Dennis Hill, showed up at the apartment in a state of excitement. They turned on the news and watched, mesmerized, as a news bulletin described the police shooting on Riverside Drive.

"We need to clean out the car," said Dhoruba. "Pauline, give us a hand." They all went down to the blue Maverick. While the others removed the license plate from the car, Pauline felt around in the front seat for spent shell casings and noticed Dhoruba's machine gun under the seat. She heard Dhoruba say to Michael D. Hill, "You handled the grease gun real good but not good enough. The two cops lived."

Later, the men regrouped in the apartment. Jamal was upset. "You know I wanted to go," he told Dhoruba. "We gonna ice some pigs, I want to be there." Jamal suggested to the others that they go over to Harlem Hospital and finish the job. "We can't," said Dhoruba. "There are cops crawling all over the place."

The NEWKILL investigators felt their pulses quickening. Pauline Joseph was giving them the goods. She told them that Dhoruba and Patricia "Kisha" Green, an activist with the Third World Woman's Alliance who had become his "revolutionary wife," composed and typed out the BLA letter to the *New York Times* and WLIB Radio using a portable Smith Corona typewriter in the apartment. In a search of 757 Beck Street, detectives found a typewriter and later confirmed it was a perfect match for the letter.

Joseph also told them about the Sam Napier murder: on April 17, the day of the killing, she bought adhesive tape at Sherman's Drug Store for a crew that included Dhoruba, Jamal, Michael D. Hill, Butch Mason, Mark Holder, Andrew Jackson, and Frank Fields. The crew left the house with the tape, several rifles and guns, cord from a venetian blind, and Molotov cocktails that Pauline, Patricia Green, and two other revolutionary wives had prepared. Hours later, the crew returned to the house and listened to a radio news bulletin about the fire and how an unidentified body had been discovered in the basement. Joseph claimed to have heard Butch Mason say, "I shot him in the head, pow, pow, pow." When detectives went back to 757 Beck Street to follow up on the leads, they found a venetian blind cord that matched the one used to tie up Sam Napier, as well as the roll of adhesive tape and leftover Molotov cocktails.

One disappointment stemming from the questioning of Pauline Joseph concerned the Jones-Piagentini murders. On the night of the shooting, Joseph said she'd been at the apartment eating pepper steak and drinking Boone's Farm Apple Wine. Dhoruba, Jamal, Kisha Green, and a few others had just returned from dropping off the BLA letters at the offices of the *Times* and WLIB. They had the radio on, half-expecting news of the letters to come over the airwaves, when Butch Mason burst into the apartment.

"Hey, did you hear? Two brothers just offed two pigs in Harlem."

Within a few minutes, a report about the shooting came on the radio. Later, the crew gathered around to watch a more detailed report on the eleven o'clock TV news, which carried footage of the crime scene, a somber press conference with Mayor Lindsay and Commissioner Murphy, and comments from people at the Colonial Park Housing Project, where the shooting took place.

"Damn, Butch, find out who iced those two pigs," Jamal told Mason.

"I'll try," said Mason.

The detectives listened to Joseph, but they weren't sure. Just to be sure, they rounded up Dhoruba, Jamal, Mason, and Augustus Qualls— all four of the men arrested at the Triple-O—and paraded them in a lineup before witnesses of the Jones and Piagentini murder. None of the witnesses identified Dhoruba or any of the others as the shooters.

In police parlance, Pauline Joseph was a "prize informant." She was not herself a political militant, but she had sat ringside as perhaps the city's most active BLA cell plotted and carried out crimes. Still, as a potential trial witness, she was far from perfect: though much of what she told the detectives checked out, her stories had a way of changing. And her memory was open to suggestion, which was both good and bad.

An assistant D.A. was assigned to the case—John Keenan, head of the Manhattan D.A.'s Homicide Bureau, the same man who had prosecuted Ricky Robles for the Wylie-Hoffert murders back in 1965. You couldn't get much higher in the D.A.'s office than Keenan, who was rumored to be in line for the top job if and when D.A. Hogan decided to step down.

At Keenan's insistence, Pauline Joseph became a virtual ward of the state. She was set up in a room at the Commodore Hotel in midtown Manhattan and kept under armed guard twenty-four hours a day, with a female detective assigned as her full-time guardian. Detectives and FBI agents from OPERATION NEWKILL interviewed her almost daily.

Joseph was a troubled woman. She had twice done stints in a psychiatric hospital and been diagnosed as a paranoid schizophrenic. She had depended from time to time on both street prostitution and welfare for a living. Her motive for cooperating with the authorities was hard to discern: she told the investigators that her greatest dream was to be accepted into the U.S. Army, and they promised her that, if she proved helpful in her testimony, they would help make that happen.

It would be a while before investigators decided whether Joseph would hold up as a credible witness at trial, but in the meantime she offered them a treasure trove of useful information, presenting her account of events before various grand juries unfettered by cross-examination. The investigators parsed the information as it was released to the press, hoping to put maximum pressure on the accused. An unusual number of D.A.s and prosecutors were involved. Dhoruba and his crew had been arrested in the Bronx, but they were suspected of major crimes that would be prosecuted in Queens (the Napier murder) and Manhattan (the Curry and Binetti shooting).

That summer the indictments were rolled out one by one, like a series of explosions designed to shatter Dhoruba Bin Wahad's resolve. In the Bronx, D.A. Burton Roberts announced a seventy-five-count indictment against Dhoruba, Jamal, Qualls, and Mason on charges that included robbery, grand larceny, possession of a weapon as a felony, burglary, assault, and reckless endangerment. The following month, at a news conference in Queens, D.A. Thomas J. Mackell, accompanied by Chief Seedman, announced that seven men were being arraigned on charges of murder and first-degree arson in the death of Sam Napier. Dhoruba, Jamal, and Mason were among those charged; the other four were still at large.

The very next day—July 31—over in Manhattan the gray eminence himself, District Attorney Frank Hogan, made the announcement that everyone in law enforcement had been waiting for: Richard Moore, aka Dhoruba Bin Wahad, was being charged with attempted murder in the shooting of Officers Curry and Binetti outside Hogan's own home.

At his arraignment, Dhoruba refused to enter a plea to the charges against him, protesting that there weren't enough black folks on the grand jury to make it a genuine panel of his peers. Supreme Court Justice Xavier Riccobono entered a plea of not guilty on Dhoruba's behalf and ordered that he be held without bail.

FOR THE NYPD, it should have been a time of great public sympathy. Cops were under assault from what some in the press referred to as a "black army." Where the Black Panther Party had enjoyed some support in the media and among white liberals, almost no whites and not many blacks were willing to get behind the Black Liberation Army. The BLA made no pretense of promoting breakfast programs for children or the kinds of social services Huey Newton described as "survival programs." The BLA's agenda was armed revolution, the sooner the better.

If the detectives and agents of NEWKILL thought taking down Dhoruba and his crew would defuse the BLA, they were wrong. Starting in the spring and into the fall, a number of BLA-affiliated militants whom Pauline Joseph had named as regulars at the 757 Beck Street safe house were involved in head-to-head combat with the police. In April, two cops were injured in a shoot-out in Harlem with BLA members. One of the black militants was shot and killed, another was captured, and a third—Robert Vickers—was shot and wounded but escaped.

In August, a crew of five heavily armed bank robbers stormed a Bankers Trust branch in Jackson Heights, Queens. The crew included Twymon Myers, a twenty-one-year-old known for his sweet disposition, and JoAnne Chesimard, aka Assata Shakur, an attractive woman with a majestic Afro whom police had identified as "the soul of the black militants." Assata, her boyfriend, Andrew Jackson, and their crew were believed to be responsible for securing false IDs for the BLA and facilitating an "underground railroad" for members on the run, usually through Detroit or upstate New York into Canada and often on to Algeria. At the Bankers Trust in Queens, Myers, Assata, and the others made off with $7,697. Assata and her distinctive Afro were caught on a surveillance camera.

A few months later, in another part of Queens, two policemen were chasing three men and a woman in a stolen car when the fleeing suspects tossed a grenade at the police car. Amazingly, the two cops escaped serious injury, but their patrol car was demolished. Working from FBI photos, a witness identified Assata and Andrew Jackson as the car's occupants.

It was a bitter harvest of BLA shootings, bombings, and threats against the police—yet public outrage over the incidents was noticeably lacking. By the fall of 1971, the exposure of rampant criminal behavior within the NYPD itself would make it hard for many to view the ongoing war between law enforcement and black radicals as a battle of good guys versus bad guys. And the man responsible for that shift was Bill Phillips.

FOR FIVE MONTHS, from June through October 1971, Phillips circulated as an undercover operative for the Knapp Commission. To facilitate his work, he was restored to the Detective Bureau as a third-grade detective. Out of uniform and back in suit and tie, Phillips made the rounds much as he always had, except now he was wearing a recording device specially created by the man who had entrapped him—Teddy Ratnoff.

Phillips applied the same enthusiasm and initiative to his undercover work as he had to his life as a bent cop. He put major construction projects on the pad, then acted as bagman, making cash payments up the chain of command. He took payoffs from organized crime figures in East Harlem, protecting all manner of bookmaking, numbers, and narcotics operations, and made sure the local precinct received its "nut." He spread the money around—though some on the Knapp Commission worried that Phillips was pocketing some of the cash himself. Brian Bruh, one of the investigators, considered Phillips "a crook." "I didn't trust him," he recalled. "So what I made him do was, he was under instructions to call me every single night. . . . If he was not working with me during the day, he had to call me during the day. I had to know where he was all the time."

Another concern the commission had with Phillips was his use of language. As a product of the police culture, he used the word *nigger* frequently. Even while he was wired, he would refer to people as "that fucking nigger." The investigators intended from the start for Phillips's secret recordings to be used as evidence for the prosecution at trial. But they knew that such casual use of racist language might offend potential jury members, black or white. Bruh tried to get Phillips to tone it down, but their star informant resisted: "I'll try, but I can't worry about that because that's the kind of language I use. That's the way New York cops talk."

It was a testament to his skills at deception that Bill Phillips managed to stay undercover as long as he did: the very fact that this flopped detective, banished to East Harlem, had suddenly been reinstated to plainclothes status downtown was enough to raise suspicions. By September, though, rumors about Phillips had begun to spread. The final straw was a phone conversation taped by the district attorney's office in an unrelated investigation. Two detectives, known to Phillips as friends and fellow "conditions men," were having a conversation:

Detective #1: Lou, about that guy.

Detective #2: What guy? The old friend or the new guy?

Detective #1: The old friend. Think the worst. Think the worst about that guy.

Detective #2: Wow! Jesus. I'll talk to you later.

The Knapp investigators called Phillips in to play him the tape. After listening to the conversation a number of times, Bruh asked him, "Are you blown?"

"I'm blown," said Phillips.

Phillips had gotten so caught up in his undercover job that he never really thought much about how it was all supposed to turn out. He knew he was likely to be called to testify at trial, but he assumed those trials would take place mostly outside the glare of public scrutiny. There may have been some mention of his having to appear at a public tribunal to discuss his career as a crooked cop, but Phillips never worried much about that. It wasn't until he was taken off the street, housed at a secret location, and told that he'd be called to testify live on television that it finally hit home. *How the fuck did I ever agree to do a thing like this?* he asked himself.

On October 18, 1971, the day the Knapp Commission hearings were scheduled to begin, a bomb threat was called in at the building on West Forty-fourth Street. An NYPD bomb squad arrived and searched the premises of the New York City Bar Association, home of the commission. There was no bomb. But what followed was potentially more destructive to the reputation of the police than any explosive device.

For a commission that began so inauspiciously—hampered by budgetary problems and a decided lack of political will—the public hearings were a sterling production. In the cavernous, baroque auditorium, with its wall-to-wall carpeting, mahogany wainscoting, and framed portraits on the walls, the room was charged with an air of both excitement and doom. Chairman Whitman Knapp, bespectacled, patrician, sat at a large dais flanked by fellow commission members, looking like a modern Pontius Pilate. Two tables were set up in front of the dais, one for the witness and one for the grand inquisitor—lead counsel Mike Armstrong. A gaggle of microphones was set up on each table, and the room was adorned with klieg lights and cables that snaked across the floor. The room was packed with media and spectators. There had been nothing like it since the Kefauver hearings on organized crime back in 1950, or perhaps Senator Joe McCarthy's House Un-American Activities Committee hearings, which had unfolded in a similar atmosphere of hushed seriousness and high drama.

On the first day, Mike Armstrong sat before a bank of microphones to address Chairman Knapp and the commissioners. Armstrong explained that the findings of his investigation would reveal a vast system of police corruption that was spread throughout the department, but which primarily flourished in the plainclothes division. The first witness, whom Armstrong identified only as "Patrolman P," would be a police officer who had been caught setting up a pad for the protection of an East Side madam named Xaviera Hollander. Undercover video footage was shown of what were said to be illegal payoffs between cops that included Patrolman P. For the time being, Armstrong said little more. It was titillating stuff—a fitting introduction for Phillips, whose name and face would not be known to the public until he stepped before the bright lights of the Knapp Commission to became the most infamous police informant in history.

By the time the star arrived to give his testimony, he had overcome his fears and was ready to perform. As usual, when Phillips committed himself to proceed, he did so at 100 percent. It helped that he looked like a New York detective out of central casting: nice suit, stylish tie, dark hair slicked back, sideburns worn down to the bottom of the earlobe in true 1970s style. His voice had the tone and timbre of the outer boroughs, what one reporter described as a "Queens-Irish-cop brogue." He sat down at the witness table before an array of microphones lined up like a Mob hit squad; behind him sat a group of government-supplied bodyguards who would be his constant companions for the foreseeable future.

Facing Mike Armstrong, surrounded by government officials, Phillips laid it all out: "There is a pad in every plainclothes division in the city of New York."

In a manner that was eerily calm and matter-of-fact, Phillips chronicled his immersion into the department's underbelly of corruption—starting all the way back in the Police Academy. On why he became a cop, Phillips said, "I wanted to get into a career where I could advance myself by my own initiative." And so he did. "I worked in every precinct in Manhattan from the Thirty-second to the First, East and West, in one capacity or another—as a detective, uniformed patrolman, plainclothesman, youth squad and a detective in a district cruiser car," he said proudly. And in every precinct and every division he got to know the "standup cops," his term for officers on the take.

Occasionally, Commissioner Knapp interjected a question from on high:

Knapp: And speaking not about your own group but about your knowledge of the division plainclothes who have the primary responsibility in that area, what percentage of the plainclothes men assigned to the division, to the Sixth Division at that time, do you feel participated in the pad?

Phillips: Everyone, to my knowledge.

Knapp: Everyone?

Phillips: Everyone.

As much as Phillips's actual revelations about corruption, what mesmerized spectators watching in the room and on TV was the language that rolled off his tongue. The *Times* felt it necessary to print a glossary of references "unfamiliar to the general public." Terms like *bagman, pad, flake, kite, score,* and *conditions man* entered the general New York lexicon for the first time. Citizens who caught even snippets of Phillips's testimony were getting window into a hidden subculture, with its own language, codes of behavior, and elastic morality. Phillips's casual attitude in describing the department's culture of corruption shocked many, but that brutal honesty and apparent lack of remorse was the very thing that lent credibility to his words. You didn't have to like Bill Phillips, you only had to believe him.

For the better part of three days, Phillips named names and listed the exact figures that various divisions collected in exchange for allowing gambling and other illegal operations to remain in business. Among other tales, he told the story of a plainclothes officer in Queens who walked out of a precinct with a paper bag containing $80,000 in proceeds from narcotics sales that he'd stolen from the property room. Such brazen theft was allowed to occur because the detective had already made sure his superiors were also getting a taste, right up the chain of command.

Phillips also walked the commission through various tape recordings that were made during the months he spent undercover. On one tape, he discussed setting up a lucrative card game in Queens with the help of an officer named Fritello. When Phillips saw Fritello, he said, "Hey, you son of a bitch. I hear you made a big score and you're set for life?"

"Nah," said the cop. "Not that good. Only eighty thousand."

"Eighty thousand? How the fuck did you get eighty thousand dollars?"

Easy, said Fritello, describing how he'd set up the game and who within the division got paid. As he spoke, his voice flowed through a transmitter strapped to Phillips's chest, which routed it to a recorder manned by Knapp investigators in a nearby van. Now it was being reviewed, in tape and transcript form, by a rapt audience at the commission hearings.

By the time Phillips was done, the public image of the NYPD had changed forever. New Yorkers would never again assume that corruption in the department was confined to a few rotten apples. The system Phillips described was elaborate and deeply entrenched—layer after layer of street cops, detectives, precinct captains, and division commanders, all of them on the take. The dirty money worked its way through the machinery like crude oil, greasing the wheel, making the world go round.

"Thank God his dad's gone," one spectator told a *Times* reporter, watching Phillips testify. The spectator said he remembered Phillips as "a very decent lad, just like his father. I never guessed it would end this way."

Of all the people who were floored by Phillips's testimony, no group was more startled than the members of the NYPD itself. Rank-and-file cops, veteran detectives, inspectors, and deputy commissioners all saw their world being turned upside down—not necessarily because they were on the pad themselves, but because the Blue Wall of Silence was considered more impenetrable than the Berlin Wall. Phillips alone hadn't absolutely dismantled the wall, but his testimony was like an explosives-laden truck driven into the side of it, inflicting a level of damage few would have believed possible.

Sensing the crisis within the ranks, Police Commissioner Patrick Murphy did something that hadn't been done in twenty-five years: he made a shortwave radio address that went out to every precinct and squad car in the city. "There is no reason to be ashamed because one or another traitor to the uniform that you are wearing so proudly seeks to justify his own dishonesty by pretending that none of you are honest," he declared.

Murphy also held a nationally televised press conference, in which he tried to contain the damage by maligning Phillips: "A very long story is being told by a corrupt policeman. A man who admits to a pattern of corruption over a long number of years in the department. A man who was caught in the commission of a very serious crime, and who obviously now is a man on the hook—squirming, squirming—to get the best possible deal for himself. And it's understandable to me, and I hope it will be understandable to every citizen, that a man in that position, a man who admits that he's been a bagman, a man who's attempted to make deals and probably has made many, that it will serve his own selfish purposes to attempt to create the impression that the kind of behavior he is engaged in is commonplace in the department."

Kiernan, head of the PBA, took the occasion to attack not only Phillips but Mayor Lindsay, whom he blamed for the entire fiasco. Kiernan announced at a press conference that he was shocked at the "political implications" of the Knapp Commission hearings, and said he'd learned they were being held only because Lindsay planned to run for president of the United States. "He should immediately take steps to end this vicious unsubstantiated smear of the entire department," said Kiernan.

There was one problem with these arguments: the Knapp Commission's revelations wouldn't end with Bill Phillips. In the following weeks two more policemen were called to testify, and their accounts corroborated everything Phillips said. Edward Droge, a former patrolman in Bedford-Stuyvesant, explained that the system of payoffs from numbers banks and dope dealers in Bed-Stuy was the same as in Harlem. Like Phillips, Droge had gone to New York City Catholic school; he was considered a good cop, with six Excellent Duty citations and two meritorious citations. Droge said he was "surprised at first" by the prevalence of graft in the department, but that the practice of bribery "became so common it just grew on you."

Another witness was Waverly Logan, a thirty-year-old black cop who had been bounced from a unit known as Preventive Enforcement Patrol (PEP) for taking $100 from a narcotics suspect. Logan said that every division gambling unit in the city was netting $400 to $1,500 a month for each plainclothesman. In the ghetto, said Logan, narcotics informants routinely stole money for cops in return for drugs.

There were more witnesses, including a tow-truck operator whom the Knapp Commission had wired up and sent out on the streets to ensnare dirty cops. In one of his many bribery encounters with a policeman, the tow-truck driver told a cop that he was worried about exchanging money near a precinct, where the transaction might be spotted. The cop was reassuring: "The cops are nothing. You know what we should have done? We should have taken you right into the station house."

"The cops are nothing?" repeated the driver.

"Well, that's the easiest. Cops you never worry about."

After two weeks, the hearings closed with a dramatic moment: Frank Serpico, the good cop who had tried for years to alert superiors about systemic police corruption, appeared before the commission and the media to deliver a statement. After the *New York Times* had identified Serpico as a whistle-blower, he had been shot in the face during a narcotics raid gone bad, and rumors inside and outside the department suggested that he'd been set up by disgruntled cops. Now Serpico described his efforts to alert his department supervisors about the corruption he'd encountered, efforts that were rebuffed at every turn. By the time Serpico finished speaking, the reputation of the NYPD was in shambles.

The Knapp Commission hearings seemed to capture the historical moment—and ultimately it was the good cop Frank Serpico, not the charismatic rogue Bill Phillips, who came to symbolize the event. A mere two years later, Al Pacino would play Serpico in a major Hollywood film, portraying him as an idealist and "flower child" who was crushed and disillusioned to discover corruption in the NYPD. Some in the mainstream media echoed this innocence-lost story line, claiming to be "shocked, shocked" by the level of corruption in the department.

In the African American community, it was another story. When it came to policing in the Savage City, black people had lost their innocence a long time ago. Some in the community had been sounding alarm bells for quite a while: Rev. Adam Clayton Powell Jr., for instance, had spoken out in public about police payoffs in Harlem. But his accusations had only gotten him ridiculed in the press and labeled a liar in the *New York Times* by the NYPD's deputy of public information, Walter Arm. Powell was hounded by prosecutors and eventually convicted for naming names in public. Though few acknowledged as much in the press at the time, the testimony of Phillips and others in the Knapp Commission hearings was a vindication for Powell.

As illuminating as the hearings were, however, one crucial piece of the puzzle was missing. Underlying the portrait painted by Phillips, Droge, and Logan was the fact that the most rampant corruption in the force took place in the ghetto. The culture of graft was allowed to flourish in Harlem, Bed-Stuy, and other disadvantaged neighborhoods. It was true that marauding hustlers like Phillips would seek scores anywhere they might be found—midtown, uptown, all around the town—but places like Harlem were, as Phillips himself put it, "paradise" for a dirty cop, especially a white cop who felt no great identification with the community or its people. Phillips, in his memoir, expressed his feelings about the ghetto this way:

> The whole fucking Harlem stinks. Every hallway smells of piss, garbage, smelly fucking people. I hated the fucking place. I'd go on some of these family fights, and I'd walk in and I would be an absolute hostile fucking maniac. When I had a rookie with me, he'd shit at what I used to do. We'd go on a family fight—if I decided to go on the job, most of the time I didn't even bother—and here's some big fucking drunken hump, some Puerto Rican or some colored guy laying there, drunk. His wife's all bloody, the kids all fucked up, there's no food on the table because he drank up the welfare check. . . . I would go into a complete rage. OK, you cocksucker, you're leaving. Ah, you ain't throwing me out of my own house. I ain't, huh? I'd pick him up bodily. Open the door. Throw him right down the fucking stairs. . . . I must've thrown guys down the stairs like that ten, fifteen times.

The truth was, most cops hated the ghetto. And for many it was a short leap from being disgusted by the people and the conditions of that environment to fleecing it shamelessly for personal profit. Was it possible that racism contributed to the practices that Phillips, Droge, Logan, and Serpico had described? Was there a connection between the attitude that made it possible for a group of detectives to frame a young black kid like Whitmore for murder and the belief that the ghetto was a shithole to be plundered?

Such questions were beyond the purview of the Knapp Commission. And the press of the day seemed incapable of placing the subject of police corruption in a racial context. The commission hearings were historic in their detailing of the finer points of a diseased system, but the underlying attitudes that may have contributed to the system's pathology remained safely out of reach—and would continue to fester within the institution for decades to come.

Even with its limitations, the Knapp Commission hearings rocked the lives of many within the police universe—not the least of whom was Phillips's wife, Camille. As was his custom, Phillips even kept her in the dark about the fact that he'd flipped and was cooperating with the government. Until the day it happened, she had no idea he was slated to testify at the hearings; she read about it in the newspaper—in her case the *Daily News*—like everyone else. The news caused a neurological short circuit:

> I didn't know what to say. I couldn't believe it. I just sat there
> numb. I didn't even read it. I just sat there, crying, trying to
> put myself together. The next thing I remember I was home,
> sitting on the couch, crying. . . . I read the paper and put
> on the television. I would say for three days I didn't move
> from the couch. I didn't sleep. I didn't eat. I didn't answer
> the telephone. I wouldn't see anybody. It hit me like a ton of
> bricks. . . . For seventeen years I was married to a hoodlum,
> and I didn't know it.

THE KNAPP COMMISSION hearings dominated the headlines in the fall of 1971, but the war between the NYPD and the BLA hadn't gone away. For weeks, like two sides of the same coin, the two stories vied for space in the tabloids. Fallout from the hearings, and new revelations about BLA suspects plotting attacks on cops, seemed to suggest a police apparatus that was fighting for its very survival—attacked from both the outside and within. Unnamed sources told reporters repeatedly that morale among the NYPD rank and file was at an all-time low.

That same year, a college professor named Nicholas Alex was granted clearance to interview dozens of NYPD officers as part of a survey of views within the department. The study, eventually published in book form as *New York Cops Talk Back: A Study of a Beleaguered Minority* (1976), gave voice to a cross section of officers at a critical moment in the department's history; they were markedly forthcoming in their comments, in part because they had been promised anonymity.

"I don't think we will ever come back in the eyes of the public the way we were six or seven years ago," said one cop. "The damage has been done." Another cop complained that "The Knapp Commission was crying out corruption, corruption, corruption. They publicized it. Even if there was what they say there is, they shouldn't publicize it . . . because it is demoralizing to honest cops to see other cops taking graft, being arrested, et cetera. It doesn't look good." Said another cop: "[They] put it right on television just before the kiddie show. When my daughter usually watched *Sesame Street* the Knapp Commission was on TV telling everybody how corrupt we are. What do you say to a kid who hears this stuff? It's like being a saint—the more you protest the crazier you look."

There was one notable trend within the comments Alex gathered: even when they were being asked specifically about corruption, many of the cops wound up talking about race. Said one patrolman, "Blacks have more rights than they ever had and they want more. They don't want to be equal to whites, they want to be superior to whites! They want reverse position with whites, that's all they want. Blacks are a different breed of people. The way they think. They have no family life. . . . There is no one supervising them. They want to do things for kicks. And they want more and they don't want to work and it's easier to steal. They love to commit crime. They love it. They love to stick a knife into you. They have a revenge for doing this and they get money for it, too. They are ruthless people."

Some white cops expressed dismay about how black residents viewed them, but it never seemed to cross their minds that it might be because of the way blacks were treated by cops. "A call came over one night on the radio car that they wanted an ambulance. A lady's son was very sick and she would not let policemen into her house because they were white and she was black. They wanted a black policeman, plus a black ambulance attendant to come. Now this brings up two things: the public doesn't want you, and in this case, the person doesn't want you because you are white. We are helping her and yet she still rejects us."

One white officer assigned to Harlem reported that "Nobody likes you in Harlem. And I'm not the only cop who feels that way. They ragmouth you. They will say anything. They know they can get away with it. . . . Out in Brooklyn, forget it. Black kids have never respected us anyway. They call you a pig and a motherfucker. This is not something new. They see you in a car and call you a motherfucker and spit at the car. If I get out of the car it would be an incident, so I stay in the car. Sometimes I might say, 'Do you know me to call me that?' "

Most cops had resigned themselves to hostility from blacks, but the Knapp Commission hearings left them convinced that the entire system was against them. "To me it's understandable why a great many of the men have the idea that the least I do the better off I am. I don't have to worry about civilian complaints. I don't have to worry about going out and having to answer for my actions to some review board because I haven't done anything. I pick up my paycheck every two weeks. I don't give a damn what happens."

ON A FREEZING night in late January 1972—not long after the Knapp Commission hearings wrapped up—a cascade of bullets once again pierced the vital organs of two policemen. This double shooting was, if anything, even more disturbing than those that came before.

On Avenue B and East Eleventh Street in the East Village, Officers Gregory Foster and Rocco Laurie—rookies who had both served as combat marines in Vietnam—were ambushed from behind by multiple gunmen and executed in the middle of the intersection. A total of fourteen bullets were unloaded on the two officers, many while the two men lay on the ground. Patrolman Foster had his eyes shot out, his brain matter reduced to liquid on the pavement. Witnesses described one gunman—a black male—standing over Patrolman Laurie. "Shoot him in the balls," said an accomplice. The gunman shot Laurie in the groin at point-blank range; then, according to a witness, he danced in the street and fired shots in the air in celebration.

The East Village was a hub of narcotics activity, and at first there was speculation—even among some in the police department—that one or both of the cops might have gotten mixed up in the dope trade. It was a nasty issue to raise, an insult to the memory of the two cops, but a logical question at a time when police corruption was the number one topic of the day.

The day after the shootings, a letter concerning the shootings arrived at the offices of United Press International. It read in part:

> This is from the George Jackson Squad of the Black Liberation
> Army about the pigs wiped out in lower Manhattan last night.
> No longer will black people tolerate Attica and oppression and
> exploitation and rape of our black community. This is the start
> of our spring offensive. There is more to come. . . .

The letter, which was immediately forwarded to Chief Seedman at police headquarters, was signed by the "George Jackson Squad," a reference to a prominent Black Panther who'd been killed while attempting to escape from California's San Quentin prison. The reference to Attica concerned a notorious riot at the Attica prison in upstate New York three months earlier, which was still under investigation. After the riots began, Black Panther Bobby Seale had flown in to facilitate negotiations between rioting inmates and prison authorities, but his efforts were in vain: the four-day riot had ended only after a National Guard unit called in by Governor Rockefeller had massacred the rioters. Thirty-nine people were killed, including twenty-nine inmates, all of them black and Hispanic.

The Foster-Laurie killings were a chilling codicil to both the Attica riots and the Knapp Commission hearings, and they touched off a new round of hysteria in the press. Commissioner Murphy, normally circumspect in his public statements about the Black Liberation Army, went on the offensive, describing the BLA as a highly mobile group of approximately one hundred members spread throughout the United States. "Too many policemen have been killed," said Murphy. "Too many policemen have been wounded. And obviously there has been a pattern. I think the hunt for these men should be one of the highest priority problems in the country."

By now, a number of corruption cases stemming from the Knapp Commission hearings were starting to get under way, and some suggested that Murphy's daily press bulletins about the BLA were an attempt to divert public attention from the department's internal scandals. In the Eastern District of New York, Assistant U.S. Attorney Nicholas Scopetta was building a series of criminal cases against cops, using former narcotics detective Robert Leuci as the star witness, that promised to make the Knapp revelations look tame in comparison. The NYPD's public relations nightmare was far from over.

Commissioner Murphy's possible motivations in leading the charge against black militancy were not lost on Dhoruba Bin Wahad's attorney, Robert Bloom. As a veteran of the Panther Twenty-one case, where he represented Curtis Powell, Bloom was a seasoned combatant. His strategy was to always land the first blow. In February, Bloom filed an injunction in court to prohibit the police commissioner from making further public statements about the BLA. Bloom contended that Murphy was polluting the jury pool for upcoming trials, trying to win sympathy for the department at a time when their standing in the community had reached a new low. Federal court judge Charles H. Tenney disagreed; he ruled against the plaintiff and stated that Commissioner Murphy's statements about the BLA—whatever his motives—interfered with no one's right to a fair trial.

The battle lines were drawn: the police on one side, the black army on the other.

AS MUCH AS he may have wanted to, George Whitmore could not escape the times in which he lived. As a black man fighting for his freedom, he had seen the quaint days of "I have a dream" give way to a culture in which cops were lethally ambushed on city streets, peaceful civil disobedience had given way to organized radical violence, and prison riots filled TV screens with images of death and destruction. In 1971, soul singer Marvin Gaye released a hit song asking "What's Goin' On?" There were no easy answers.

On February 12, 1972, with the shock of the Foster-Laurie killings still very much in the air, Whitmore once again walked into court to hear his fate determined by a judge.

It had been almost nine years since the Career Girls Murders, eight and a half since that fateful night when Whitmore was led into the Seventy-third Precinct station house in Brownsville by two policemen. Twenty-three hours later, he had signed the longest written confession in NYPD history. Before that, however, Elba Borrero had given her much-contested identification of Whitmore as the man who tried to rape her. The questions surrounding that identification had become the tiny glimmer of hope on which Whitmore pinned his daily dreams of exoneration.

Attorneys and civil rights activists had tried everything on his behalf. Most recently, Myron Beldock had argued the case before the New York State Court of Appeals. He had come close, but Whitmore's conviction was upheld by a 4–3 vote. This led to a final Hail Mary pass, an appeal to the United States Supreme Court to hear the case. Beldock had filed his papers; the arguments had all been made. Now, at the federal courthouse in the Eastern District of New York, George Whitmore would learn whether the Supreme Court would free the "Negro drifter" from Brooklyn.

He had few supporters in the courtroom. George and Aida were estranged, heading toward divorce. His brother Gerald was upstate doing time on a burglary conviction. His longtime attorneys, Miller and Beldock, were there, as was his mother, who had stuck by her son through every trial.

It took all of thirty seconds for the court to deliver its verdict. Whitmore's appeal to the Supreme Court was denied.

Whitmore was beyond tears. It appeared as though his fight was over. He was put on a Department of Corrections bus and taken to the Brooklyn House of Detention, where he was held for a few days before being shipped upstate to Green Haven prison.

A week after he was returned to custody, Whitmore was visited by Selwyn Raab, the former newspaper reporter. Raab, who had never stopped following the case, was not surprised by the Supreme Court ruling. "All those stories in the press about the black liberation movement and the Black Liberation Army—that did not help Whitmore's chances," remembered Raab. "It created a climate that made it difficult for people like Whitmore to get a fair hearing."

At Green Haven, Raab found a young man who had given up hope. Until now, George had always found a way to stay positive, but the years of legal struggle had taken away his spirit. George showed some curiosity about the movie that was being made of Raab's book, but even that was a source of disappointment. The project was now being produced by Universal Studios as a TV movie for CBS, with Abby Mann as screenwriter and executive producer. Universal had promised to hire Whitmore as a technical consultant, but they'd reneged on the offer and never paid Whitmore a dime, even though the production was almost complete. Raab promised to look into it.

"Next time you come, can you remember to bring cigarettes?" asked George. It was his standard parting request to all visitors: cigarettes seemed to be the only thing he had left to care about. "You won't forget?"

"Sure, George," said Raab. "I won't forget."

Raab left the prison more convinced than ever that Whitmore was innocent. *There must be something to do about this*, he thought, *some way to make it right.*

eighteen

LONG TIME COMIN'

AFTER VISITING WHITMORE at Green Haven prison, Selwyn Raab put in a call to Myron Beldock. As the journalist and the lawyer hashed over the case, searching for anything that could form the basis of a new appeal, they agreed that one last thread was still dangling, one detail that had never been adequately investigated: Elba Borrero's sister-in-law, Celeste Viruet.

From the beginning of Whitmore's ordeal, none of the many patrolmen, detectives, and assistant D.A.s involved in his trials and hearings had ever mentioned Viruet's existence. It was only after Beldock joined Whitmore's team that the handwritten note about Viruet in Patrolman Isola's notebook came to the defense lawyers' attention. Beldock had discovered the entry almost by chance:

> Sister-in-law saw he grab me from her window (Celeste
> Viruet).

That one scrawled line was like a beacon: a description of the assailant that conflicted with Whitmore's appearance in every detail except for the fact that he was a black man. Was the description from Borrero or from Viruet? The question had never been answered. No one acting on Whitmore's behalf had ever spoken with Celeste Viruet. She was a phantom. Of course, it was quite possible that there was nothing to it;

if questioned, the woman might ultimately back up her sister-in-law's account of that night. But the very fact that police investigators had never conducted a follow-up interview with her—that Viruet was never produced to corroborate Borrero's version or even mentioned in court by detectives or prosecutors—led Raab and Beldock to suspect that there was a reason she'd become a phantom. Chances were, her version didn't fit the prosecutors' version of the crime.

"I'm not sure who came up with the idea first," Beldock said, "but Selwyn and I both realized that we needed to find Celeste Viruet. She was our last hope."

It wasn't going to be easy. No one from Elba Borrero's family was going to help Whitmore's lawyers find Celeste Viruet. She was a transient Puerto Rican who lived part of the year in Brooklyn and part of the year in her home country. After some preliminary inquiries in and around Brooklyn, Beldock and Raab came up empty. She didn't live there anymore; she hadn't been seen by anyone in a long time.

Finally, the two men pooled their resources and hired a private investigator—a former FBI agent with the unlikely name of Richard "Dick" Tracy. The P.I. with the famous cartoon name followed Celeste Viruet's trail to the Bronx, where she had moved after leaving Brooklyn. But Viruet didn't live in the Bronx anymore. She had moved back to Puerto Rico. An acquaintance told the P.I. the two things she knew: that Viruet lived in Isla Verde, and that she owned a store with the word *naranja* (Spanish for "orange") in the title. That's all they had to go on.

Dick Tracy turned the information over to Raab and Beldock. They were on the case.

Raab came up with a way to finance most of the trip to Puerto Rico. For the last year he had been working as a segment producer for a news-magazine show on public television called *The 51st State*. The show had debuted in February 1972 as a one-hour program, airing four nights a week. Staffed largely by former print journalists, *The 51st State* was designed as a forum for longer and more in-depth stories than those shown on network news programs. Raab persuaded the producers to supply him with a modest budget to produce a segment on the Whitmore case, revolving around the hunt for Celeste Viruet. He would travel to Puerto Rico with Maria Mena, a young reporter at Channel 13 who spoke fluent Spanish; Myron Beldock; and a two-man crew.

The capital city of San Juan was seasonally warm when they arrived.

Raab, Beldock, and the crew all stayed at the same oceanfront hotel. The morning after they arrived, Raab and Beldock met poolside to strategize. They weren't sure where to begin.

"Well," said the lawyer, "why don't we start by asking the first person we meet if they know of a shop with the word *naranja* in the name?"

Raab chuckled. He thought Beldock was joking.

"I'm serious," said Beldock. To illustrate his point, Beldock asked the busboy, who spoke passable English, if he knew of such a store.

"Yes," said the busboy. "In Isla Verde there is a store named La Naranjal, the orange grove."

Raab and Beldock looked at each other.

"Do you know this place?" Raab asked the busboy. "Have you been there yourself?"

"Si, señor. I know the place. It is owned by my wife."

"Excuse me," interrupted Beldock. "Did you say the store is owned by your wife?"

"Yes, sir, that is what I say."

Raab said, "Your wife, if I may ask, what is her name?"

"My wife's name is Celeste Viruet."

THE TWO MEN and their translator made arrangements to meet the busboy later that day. He led them from the hotel to La Naranjal, a store in the nearby resort area of Isla Verde. There they met Celeste Viruet, a simple, plainspoken women in her midtwenties.

The translator explained to Viruet why the two men had come from New York City to see her. Viruet did not seem surprised. Raab and Beldock began by asking questions about what she saw on the night of the alleged assault. Right away she mentioned that her sister-in-law Elba Borrero had told her things that no one else had known—including the fact that her assailant that night had spoken to her in Spanish as well as English. At the time of the assault, George Whitmore did not know a word of Spanish. And she volunteered other startling details to Raab and Beldock, all of it in a matter-of-fact manner. They couldn't believe what they were hearing.

Given the notoriety of the Whitmore case, and the fact that it may have involved corrupt behavior on the part of powerful municipal officials, Viruet would not agree to do an on-camera interview. She would, however, answer any questions they had, and she allowed them to audio-tape the interview. Over the next two days, Raab and Beldock asked Viruet every question they could think of, using a tape recorder and taking notes.

Viruet had witnessed the assault on Borrero. Though she hadn't gotten a good look at the face of the assailant, her description in terms of height, weight, and clothing didn't match any of the identifications supplied by the various police accounts. Other than the two people involved in the attack that night, she was the only known eyewitness to an alleged felony assault—but she had been interviewed by police only once, and never questioned again or even contacted by anyone from the district attorney's office. It was as if she didn't exist.

If nothing else, the fact that Viruet was known to investigators—but never produced at any of Whitmore's many trials or hearings—was possible grounds to reopen his case. Beyond that, the substance of her statement was that Borrero had told her a version of her story that was substantially different from what she had been contending in court all these years. If that could be proven, Whitmore's conviction for assault and attempted rape could even be dismissed.

Raab and Beldock returned to New York City with what they hoped was the raw material to blow the Borrero identification out of the water. They were energized by their improbable discovery—which had descended upon them as if by divine intervention—but they knew that any appeal for a new trial, or even a reexamination of evidence, would be a long shot at best. Whitmore's previous appeals had already been dismissed at every level of the legal system, right up to the United States Supreme Court. A judge could dismiss a new appeal on any number of grounds—that it was too late, or that Viruet's statement was not rel-evant, or for any number of other technical reasons.

Beldock filed papers in the appellate division in Brooklyn court seek-ing a reexamination of the evidence in the case, alerting the court that "important new evidence" had come to light. Meanwhile, Raab and his production team at *The 51st State* began splicing together their minidoc-umentary on the strange case of George Whitmore, which they hoped to have broadcast on public television in time to have some bearing on the judge's ruling.

They had one new development going for them: a new district attor-ney had taken over in Brooklyn. After ten years in the office, Aaron

Koota, who had taken such a hard line on the Whitmore case, had decided to step down. The persecution of Whitmore, from the time of his arrest through the Edmonds and Borrero trials, had spanned much of Koota's tenure. In Raab's eyes, the D.A. had "made a fool of himself" by staking his reputation on the conviction of Whitmore even after the circumstances of George's arrest and bogus confession were exposed. Koota had chosen to become the defender of a system from another era, a clubhouse environment in which a black teenager accused of horrific crimes, facing the death penalty, could be assigned counsel based on the fact that the judge and the defense lawyer were members of the same political club.

The new Brooklyn D.A., Eugene Gold, did not carry the same ideological baggage as Koota. His arrival as top prosecutor was the sort of sea change that criminal defense attorneys dream about. Eugene Gold had no vested interest in maintaining the status quo; it wasn't his regime that had run Whitmore, the hapless Negro, through the proverbial prosecutorial gauntlet. It looked like the Whitmore case might finally get something it badly needed—a breath of fresh air, and a reason for hope.

TO DHORUBA BIN Wahad, hope was an illusory concept. He'd been hopeful once. Back in the fall of 1968, when Eldridge Cleaver first came to town as a candidate for president, the Black Panther Party seemed like an idea whose time had come. Party chapters were sprouting up all over the country; the possibility of global revolution seemed to be within reach. Student protesters, antiwar activists, and leading lights of the counterculture had begun to coalesce around similar movements all over Europe, Africa, Latin America, and Southeast Asia. Disenfranchised people all over the world were rising up, and the concept of black liberation was a powerful and attractive component of the international groundswell. In New York, the movement revolved around the Black Panther Party, and the party revolved around leaders like Dhoruba, who was committed enough to put his life on the line.

Then, in a short period of time, that dream went up in smoke. The philosophical differences between the East and West Coast factions of the party might have been resolved if the counterintelligence efforts of BOSS and COINTELPRO hadn't exacerbated them. The infighting, in turn, had brought about a bad case of revolutionary suicide. Cops killed

Panthers, Panthers killed Panthers, Panthers killed cops—the vicious cycle seemed to take the struggle from its goals of civil rights, and then Black Power, into the realm of revenge. The big payback.

Dhoruba had been at the center of the maelstrom, and now he was suffering the consequences—charged with an assortment of crimes that could put him behind bars for multiple lifetimes.

By nature, Bin Wahad was a fighter, a South Bronx survivor who often quoted Frederick Douglass: "Without struggle, there can be no progress." He was preconditioned to see his current predicament as part of the broader struggle. Had he been charged only with the Triple-O robbery and his role in Sam Napier's murder, Dhoruba might have been depressed; after all, those were crimes he'd actually committed. By charging him with the double shooting of police officers, though, the prosecutors were making it political—giving Dhoruba, his attorney, and his supporters reason to view his plight as another chapter in the ongoing fight against racism and corruption in the criminal justice system.

Throughout 1972, the legal maneuvers came fast and furious. Under legal advice from his attorney, Robert Bloom, Bin Wahad pleaded guilty to the armed robbery and attempted grand larceny charges. In a Bronx courtroom, he was given seven years in prison, the sentence to begin immediately.

In March, Dhoruba traveled to Queens, where he and three other defendants were tried for the murder of Sam Napier. The trial was defense attorney Bloom's first opportunity to hear and cross-examine Pauline Joseph, who would become a fixture at trials involving Dhoruba and others associated with the BLA over the next few years. Joseph described how a group of revolutionaries left 757 Beck Street to burn down the *Black Panther* offices in Queens, and then returned to tell her that Butch Mason had shot Napier in the head. But her testimony was shaky, and, without an eyewitness to the actual shooting, prosecutors were unable to present a coherent account of who did what. After a six-week trial and seventeen hours of deliberation, the jury announced that it was hopelessly deadlocked. With ten jurors leaning toward acquittal and two toward a guilty verdict, the trial ended in a hung jury.

The Queens D.A. immediately reindicted Dhoruba and the others and announced they would be retried on the same charges.

Dhoruba was being held at the Manhattan House of Detention, better known as the Tombs. He eventually pled guilty to a reduced charge of attempted manslaughter in the second degree for his role in the Napier killing, receiving a four-year sentence to run concurrent with his grand larceny plea conviction. As with the Bronx charges, Dhoruba was willing to accept culpability for crimes in which he had played a role, in order to better fight the charges for which he claimed he was being framed.

In November, a smattering of protesters gathered on the sidewalk outside 100 Centre Street, where the long-running Panther Twenty-one trial had occurred two years before. This time, Dhoruba was on trial alone for the shooting of police officers Thomas Curry and Nicholas Binetti. A group calling itself the Committee to Defend Richard "Dhoruba" Moore tried to rally the troops, but the days of rambunctious support for a Black Panther in New York were over. Among the small group of supporters was Kisha Green, Dhoruba's common-law wife, who had been held in jail as a material witness for several months, even while she was pregnant with Dhoruba's child. She had recently given birth to a baby boy—a child whom Dhoruba, the father, hadn't yet met.

The press flooded the thirteenth-floor courtroom: Manhattan D.A. Frank Hogan was rumored to be nearing retirement, and he had a lot riding on this prosecution—even beyond the fact that the case involved the shooting of two cops who'd been guarding his own apartment building. Hogan had come under fire for publicly criticizing the jury in the Panther Twenty-one case for having been influenced by "the political climate," when Hogan's own critics were accusing him of the very same thing. Dhoruba's prosecution was a crucial step in the D.A.'s efforts to show that they were not toothless in the ongoing war between black radicals and the police.

Curry and Binetti both testified. Neither had much recollection of the assault, and neither was able to positively identify Bin Wahad as the shooter. But their appearance on the stand—two white police officers, one permanently paralyzed, the other partially disfigured—made an impression. One of the jurors, a twenty-five-year-old white male from the Bronx named Frank Treu, later said: "Here [were] two damaged white people. And they're police officers, whom we're supposed to trust. What gripe did they have that caused them to be shot? . . . [A]s far as any value as witnesses, there really was none. But it set the tone. And the tone it set was: somebody has to pay."

The primary witness was Pauline Joseph. Her testimony was well rehearsed—perhaps too much so. Throughout the trial, defense attorney

Bloom reminded the court repeatedly that the prosecution was required to turn over all notes from interviews of Joseph by investigators—documentation commonly known as Rosario material. ADA Terrence O'Reilly claimed that the only such document was a one-paragraph statement by Joseph that had already been admitted into evidence.

Dhoruba and his attorney believed this to be a lie, and their suspicions seemed to be supported by an article in *New York* magazine by Robert Daley, the NYPD's recently retired press information officer. In the article, Daley described how Joseph was cultivated as a witness—with a level of detail that suggested there was more to the written record than the prosecution was presenting in court. Had Daley made it all up? Or was his account based on police reports and incriminating FBI interview notes not entered into evidence? The obvious solution would have been to call Robert Daley to the witness stand, but the judge, Joseph A. Martinis, refused to authorize a subpoena, taking the D.A.'s office at its word.

On the stand, Joseph was caught in lies relating to her psychiatric history, her time as a street prostitute, and the fact that she'd been on welfare. "She [testified] for three days," said juror Treu. "And by the end of the third day, in my mind, there was enough inconsistency that it was hard to tell 'Was she telling the truth here or was she telling the truth there?'"

The prosecution's case was riddled with doubt, but they did have one key piece of evidence: the gun. Although no witness was able to give an account of who actually pulled the trigger on the night of the shooting, the prosecution tried to link the gun to Dhoruba through a jailhouse conversation that ADA O'Reilly characterized as a "confession" on Dhoruba's part. His crew member Augustus Qualls, an admitted heroin addict and recidivist criminal, while the two were sharing a cell after their arrest for the Triple-O robbery, asked Dhoruba, "Why didn't you tell me the gun you used was the one that was used in the shooting of those two pigs?"

"If I had told you that, would you have come with us?" Dhoruba allegedly replied.

During his closing statement, ADA O'Reilly handed the machine gun to a juror and asked that it be passed around among the jury. It was a powerful bookend to the prosecution's opening presentation: having begun with the spectacle of two damaged cops, their lives altered irrevocably, the prosecution was closing with the weapon that had injured them. And there, ladies and gentlemen, at the defendant's table, was the man behind it all—the man who, according to Pauline Joseph, loved that gun so much he gave it a nickname.

"That man," said O'Reilly, "Richard Moore, known to some as Dhoruba, he shot those two police officers."

Treu recalled that emotions ran high during deliberations: "One of the other jurors says, 'What's the difference if he did it or not? You want a guy like this running around on your streets? . . . My feeling now is that I want to take this guy and shake him and say, 'This is America, you idiot. We don't do it this way.'"

He wouldn't get that satisfaction. After deliberating for two and a half days, the jury of eleven men and one woman announced to the judge that they were deadlocked. Justice Martinis had no choice but to declare a hung jury.

D.A. Hogan wasted little time getting Bin Wahad back into court on the same charges, but by January 1973 that effort ended in another mistrial, after the judge became ill during jury selection.

Finally, in June, the D.A.'s office got the conviction they sought. After a four-week trial that was virtually identical to the first proceeding, a jury took just forty-five minutes to declare Dhoruba Bin Wahad guilty.

After the verdict was announced, Justice Martinis individually polled each of the jurors. From the defendant's table, Dhoruba jumped to his feet and pointed at the judge. "You did everything in your power to deny me a fair trial. I did not want those twelve men, but you forced me to accept them. Now they have convicted me of a crime I didn't commit." Then he turned to the jury and told them: "Anything that happens from now on, it is on your shoulders, not mine."

"It's on yours," said the judge.

"No, it's not. It's on theirs," countered Dhoruba.

After Dhoruba was taken away, the D.A.'s office allowed itself a moment of self-congratulation. ADA O'Reilly, who the *Times* described as "jubilant with his victory," noted at a press conference that Bin Wahad was the first black militant in New York to be convicted of attempting to kill policemen. D.A. Hogan called the verdict "a major triumph."

At his sentencing hearing a month later, Dhoruba remained angry and unrepentant. He told the judge he would leave the courtroom and stay in the nearby detention pen unless all detectives and prosecutors were removed from the courtroom. When the justice refused to comply, Dhoruba stalked out, leaving it to his attorney to explain, "Many people here in the courtroom—police officers and others—have conspired to convict Mister Moore on perjured and unlawful testimony. In their own specific way they've seen to it he could not receive a fair and impartial trial."

The judge stood firm. Holding her new baby, Kisha Green cried, "Please, Judge, as a matter of human dignity . . ."

"I order that woman removed from this court," Justice Martinis yelled.

"But, Your Honor, that is Richard Moore's wife," Bloom pleaded as guards escorted Green and child from the courtroom.

"I don't care who she is," said the justice. "I'll have order in this courtroom."

Martinis then announced that he was sentencing Dhoruba to life in prison.

A court clerk was sent to the holding pen to inform Dhoruba of his right to appeal. The clerk returned with a message from Dhoruba: "My appeal will be over the barrel of a gun."

"What?" cried the judge.

"My appeal will be over the barrel of a gun," the clerk glumly repeated.

Later, while he was biding his time at Rikers Island Correctional Facility before being moved upstate, Dhoruba was more sanguine. "They cannot break my spirit," he told his attorney. "I will fight this. I will fight until the day I die."

IN DECEMBER 1972, the Knapp Commission issued its final report. In the history of the NYPD there had never been a more thorough and embarrassing exposure of corruption within the ranks. This was not a report on wrongdoing within a certain division or a scandal in one of the city's boroughs—it was a highly detailed dissection of the entire rotten organism.

Among other things, the Knapp Commission Report on Police Corruption identified two primary classes of bent cop. One group—the "grass eaters"—were those who "accepted gratuities and solicit five, ten, twenty dollar payments from contractors, tow truck operators, gamblers, and the like but do not pursue corruption payments." Grass eating was passed from officer to officer; it was a way for officers to prove their loyalty within the brotherhood, and it was widespread and widely tolerated throughout the department.

The other group—the "meat eaters"—were police officers who "spent a good deal of time aggressively looking for situations they can exploit for financial gain." Some cops justified activities like shaking down pimps and drug dealers for money by pointing out that the victims were criminals anyway and deserved it. But meat eaters didn't always stop there; they were willing to extort money from civilians, too. They spread the illicit proceeds from scores throughout the command structure, confident that widening the net would inoculate them from possible trouble.

The designation of dirty cops as grass eaters and meat eaters would be the Knapp Commission's most lasting legacy. The rest of the report was overshadowed by a development no one had expected: the commission's own star meat eater, Bill Phillips, was accused of being a homicidal maniac—a charge that came as a shock even to those who knew Phillips's dirty side.

During the live broadcasts of the Knapp Commission hearings, a veteran detective named John Justy saw Phillips on TV and thought, *That face looks familiar.* Three years earlier, on the night of Christmas Eve 1968, a brutal double murder had taken place in an upscale whorehouse in an apartment building at 157 East Fifty-seventh Street, which was within Justy's precinct. Jimmy Smith, the brothel's proprietor, and a nineteen-year-old prostitute named Sharon Stango were executed with bullets to the head at close range. A customer named Charles Gonzales was also shot, but survived.

Detective Justy caught the case of the whorehouse murders, but the killings went unsolved. A composite sketch of the killer was made from details provided by Gonzales and a handyman who saw the killer leaving the building. After seeing Phillips on TV, Justy dug up the sketch and reopened the case. He tracked down various former employees of Smith's prostitution business and showed them photos of Bill Phillips. A number of them said they'd seen Phillips on more than one occasion at the whorehouse. One prostitute claimed that on the night before the Christmas Eve double murder, she was present at Smith's eleventh-floor apartment when Phillips told Smith, "If you don't have my one thousand dollars I'm going to come back here tomorrow night and blow your fucking head off."

The next evening, Justy concluded, Phillips returned to apartment 11-F. Smith was in the front room with Stango and her john, Gonzales, when Phillips told Smith, "You owe me a thousand dollars."

"I can pay you at the end of the week," Smith replied.

"I'm not going to wait until the end of the week," said Phillips, "I want my fucking money now." Then he pulled out a .38-caliber gun, put it to Smith's head, and pulled the trigger. Blood spurted everywhere, and down went Smith.

Stango screamed.

"Shut up, bitch," said the assailant, turning the gun on Stango and pressing the muzzle against her head. "Please, please," she cried hysterically. Then he pulled the trigger twice. Blood poured down the front of her shirt, and she fell to the floor.

The killer now turned to Gonzales, a short, pudgy man of forty. "I have four children," pleaded Gonzales.

The shooter fired on Gonzales, but the john raised his arm, deflecting the bullet so that it hit him in the abdomen. The man went down. Thinking he was dead, the shooter stepped over him and left the apartment.

Gonzales struggled to his feet, staggered out into the hallway, and fell to his knees. He looked down the hall at the shooter, who was waiting for the elevator. "Merry Christmas," the shooter said, then disappeared into the elevator. Gonzales slumped to the floor and passed out.

The slaughter on East Fifty-seventh Street hadn't made a lot of headlines at the time. In the Savage City of 1968, lurid crimes of violence had become commonplace—even those involving white victims shot in Upper East Side apartments. Now, three years later, with the perpetrator of the crime being named as the very same cop who had torn his department down in front of the Knapp Commission just months before, the story shocked even the most jaded New Yorkers.

No one was more shocked than Bill Phillips. Ever since the end of the commission hearings, Phillips had been helping prosecutors prepare cases stemming from his testimony. Then, one afternoon in March 1972, Detective John Justy and ADA John Keenan intercepted Phillips at the D.A.'s office, leading him to a private conference room to inform him that he was being investigated for the whorehouse shooting. Phillips recalled: "It was around three in the afternoon. . . . I was in such a state, mentally and physically, I couldn't do anything. I couldn't sit down, I couldn't drink anything; I couldn't eat. I went home that night in a terrible state of mental torture." Right away, Phillips's gut told him he was being framed by the NYPD as payback for his Knapp testimony. What else could it be? He knew John Justy. Years earlier he'd offered to help Justy fix a case the detective was working on. Justy was amenable, but the case never advanced, and nothing ever came of it. Phillips also knew that one of the cops he'd fingered during the Knapp hearings had been a friend of Justy's; humiliated by the public exposure, he had committed suicide soon afterward. Phillips heard that Justy was distraught and angry about his friend's death.

Even so, Phillips was dumbfounded. He himself had named Jimmy Smith to Knapp investigators as someone he had once scored. He hadn't visited Smith's place since 1968, when he'd briefly taken part in a past-posting sports betting scam. Why on earth would he willingly link himself to Smith if he was the one who'd killed him? There could be only one answer. *They want to bury me,* Phillips thought. *That way they can destroy all the Knapp-related cases, the state cases, the federal cases, all the police corruption cases. Everybody walks.*

On March 20, Phillips was indicted on two counts of murder in the first degree and one count of attempted murder.

A few weeks later, an incident occurred that seemed to symbolize the moral chaos that had consumed the city. In Harlem, a handful of cops responded to calls of a "10-13"—*officer down.* The location of the reported disturbance was at Lenox Avenue and 116th Street, an address the cops didn't immediately recognize as the Nation of Islam's Mosque Number Seven. Inside the mosque, a rumble broke out between the cops and a group of Muslims. One cop, Patrolman Phillip Cardillo, was shot and killed in the melee. Additional cops flooded to the scene, but they were surrounded by a huge throng of Harlemites that had gathered on the street and sidewalk in front of the mosque. Before long, the crowd was attacking the cops with bricks, rocks, and even gunfire raining down from rooftops nearby.

One of the cops responding was Detective Randy Jurgensen, who had been undercover in a gypsy cab, staking out the apartment of a BLA member's girlfriend, when the call came over the radio. Jurgensen drove to the scene, but the mob of pedestrians was too thick to get close, so he left the car and ran toward the mosque on foot. Behind him, angry rioters turned over his gypsy cab and set it on fire. Jurgensen was hit in the head with something heavy—a rock, a brick, maybe a baseball bat.

"I thought I was shot," he remembered. "I was coughing up blood, gasping for breath." Jurgensen collapsed, unconscious. When he came to he was in the arms of a fellow officer, being dragged away from the mob as another officer fired his gun in the air to keep the rioters at bay.

"Die, you pigs!" shouted someone in the crowd. "Kill the pigs!" shouted another.

The riot raged until enough police arrived to quell the crowd. From the stoop in front of the mosque, Minister Louis Farrakhan attempted to control and disperse the angry residents. It had been a sudden and frightening explosion of violence, with numerous injuries. The shooting of Patrolman Cardillo inside the mosque was revealed only later; no one was arrested for the crime. In fact, city and police authorities weren't even willing to say a murder had taken place, though officers on the scene claimed that Cardillo had been beaten and gunned down in cold blood by a member of the Nation of Islam inside the mosque.

The politically explosive nature of the incident seemed to enshroud it in mystery. The 10-13 call that initially drew cops to the mosque, it turned out, was a false alarm. Had police been deliberately suckered into a confrontation? Did the police have the right to storm unannounced into a religious place of worship? And who shot Officer Cardillo? Muslims claimed he'd been killed by friendly fire during the mayhem, and that cops, humiliated and disgraced, were trying to blame it on them. Outside, on the street, a throng of local residents had almost lynched a group of cops who'd been called to back up fellow officers in distress. It was an afternoon of utter mayhem.

No one representing city government—or anyone else—was able to give a clear accounting of what happened that day, but that was hardly surprising. The city could no longer be broken down into simple categories of good guys and bad guys. Black was white, white was black. The old ways had been turned inside out.

As if to further illustrate the moral ambiguity, in the summer of 1972—eight weeks after the mosque riot—Bill Phillips was brought into Manhattan criminal court to be tried on charges of murder and attempted murder.

The judge presiding was John Murtagh. It was his first major trial since the debacle of the Panther Twenty-one prosecution, after which a number of jurors had signed an affidavit calling his conduct prejudicial and unfair. Murtagh had been berated by the Panther defendants and their political allies for two years; his home had been targeted for bombing by the Weather Underground. The defendant in this new case, Bill Phillips, wasn't likely to jump up and call Murtagh a "crypto-fascist," but there were other issues.

For one thing, Phillips's attorney, the celebrated Boston attorney F. Lee Bailey, was famous for trying to influence the outcome of his trials both inside and outside the courtroom. In the weeks leading up to the trial, Bailey stoked the flames of controversy by promoting Phillips's claim that the charges were simply payback for his Knapp testimony. In pretrial hearings, Justice Murtagh made it clear to Bailey that any such allegations of a police department conspiracy, made without evidence, would be ruled out of order.

As for the prosecution, Keenan decided he would try the case himself—a rare move for a bureau chief. Fresh from supervising the successful conviction of Dhoruba Bin Wahad, Keenan was a veteran in the city's race and corruption wars; he'd even prosecuted Ricky Robles in the Wiley-Hoffert case. Keenan was upright to the point of drabness, a pillar of propriety who never pronounced curse words outright in court; in his mouth the word *fuck* became "the f-word," and *shit* became "a reference to certain human bodily functions." His very presence was a rebuke to the salty demeanor of swaggering Bill Phillips.

Once the trial commenced, the prosecution presented a startling array of eyewitnesses. Four different prostitutes who had worked for Jimmy Smith testified that they'd seen Phillips on the premises numerous times, including the night before the murder, when he threatened Smith. The handyman at the apartment building, who did not know Phillips by name but had seen him at the building "five or six times," testified that the defendant had arrived just before the murders took place, gone to the eleventh floor, and then left the building after the slaughter. Even more damaging was the testimony of Charles Gonzales, who showed the jurors his gruesome scar from the shooting; when asked to identify the assailant, he stepped down from the witness stand, walked over to Phillips, and said, "That's the man who shot me."

An eyewitness account from the survivor of a brutal criminal act was powerful testimony, but the single most effective evidence against Phillips may have been his own words. When Phillips took the stand to testify in his own defense, Keenan played him a recording made by Teddy Ratnoff not long after the two men first met. Phillips did not know Ratnoff was wired. At one point on the tape, Ratnoff asked Phillips about some commendation medals on the front of his police uniform:

Ratnoff: What's that??

Phillips: Oh yeah, I killed three fucks up there.

Ratnoff: You killed three—yeah?

Phillips: Yeah. Oh yeah. I blow 'em away like they're fucking nothing.

Phillips had killed one man in the line of duty; the prosecution contended that the other two victims he was referring to were the pimp and the prostitute. Phillips would dismiss his words as idle bravado, the inflated rhetoric of a professional hustler with a couple drinks under his belt.

Bailey was able to put forth a strong alibi defense for his client. The crime had taken place on Christmas Eve, which made it easy for Phillips to reconstruct his whereabouts that night. After attending a dinner party with his wife and relatives, Phillips had driven around to the homes of other relatives to offer Christmas greetings. At his aunt and uncle's house, they all stopped to watch news reports of the first U.S. astronauts to circle the earth. It was a memorable evening, and Bailey paraded a host of Phillips's relatives before the jury to confirm Phillips's account of his whereabouts.

The trial lasted six weeks. For four days the jury deliberated. Then they returned to the courtroom to inform Justice Murtagh that they were deadlocked, 10–2 in favor of acquittal. There would be no verdict. Hung jury.

Within days, Hogan and Keenan announced that Phillips would be retried on the same charges. Phillips didn't seem overly concerned; he was out on bail, living with the ever-faithful Camille, who had apparently reconciled herself to the fact that her husband was a hoodlum. He had even arranged to publish a memoir, *On the Pad*, written with Leonard Shecter. Phillips had always been a man of great confidence; he had little doubt he would beat the charges at the next trial.

As he waited, the revelations of the Knapp Commission were debated by journalists, politicians, and policymakers. It was a true sign of the times that the man who had made the revelations possible—the man who breached the Blue Wall as no one ever had before—was facing an indictment that, if true, made him the dirtiest cop of them all.

What was the public supposed to make of that?

AT GREEN HAVEN prison in upstate New York, Whitmore received a rare visit from the warden. For a lowly inmate, it was like an audience with the pope. Whitmore knew it meant something out of the ordinary.

"George," said Superintendent Leon Vincent. "How you feeling?"

"Okay," said Whitmore.

Vincent was known as tough but fair. "Well, son," he said to George, "I got a proposition for you."

"What's that, sir?"

"Tonight on television they're showing that movie based on your case. I was thinking of sending you to the sick ward so you can watch it in privacy. This way, nobody's gonna bother you in the TV room. What do you think?"

"I appreciate that, Warden."

For three days, George had a bed in the prison hospital ward—the only place in the prison where inmates got private TV privileges. On the night of March 8, 1973, he had the unusual experience of watching a major motion picture that purported to be based on his life.

George had mixed feelings about the project. Selwyn Raab and Myron Beldock had finally shamed and cajoled Universal Studios and CBS into making Whitmore a modest payment of three thousand dollars. But their promises to hire him as a technical consultant never panned out—and, worse yet, the movie itself had taken a sharp turn away from the docudrama they had originally pitched. What had begun as a feature film to be called *The Wiley-Hoffert Murders*, using the real names and details of George Whitmore's case, had been transformed into a fictionalized TV movie called *The Marcus-Nelson Murders*, with a screenplay "suggested by" Raab's book *Justice in the Back Room*.

Even so, it was a heady experience for Whitmore sitting alone in the sick ward at Green Haven watching a three-hour movie so clearly based on his story. The actor playing the Whitmore character—Gene

Woodbury, a young African American in his first major role—had written George a number of letters in researching the part, and much of the filming was done at locations in Brownsville and elsewhere in Brooklyn where the actual events had taken place

At times, for George the movie was almost too painful to watch. The sequence in which the Whitmore character is broken down by detectives until he signs a false confession was taken directly from Raab's book, which relied heavily on the actual transcript of George's interrogation. The scene had him in tears—consumed with shame that he hadn't stood up to the detectives.

By the end of the movie, though, George's shame was eclipsed by annoyance. Ultimately, the star of *The Marcus-Nelson Murders* was a crusading detective who senses immediately that the Whitmore character has been framed—and then becomes a tireless advocate for justice, securing a top trial lawyer for the black kid and spearheading the investigation that eventually exonerates him of the murder of two white girls.

The detective character was a composite of several detectives who worked the real Wiley-Hoffert investigation, most notably Lieutenant Thomas Cavanaugh, the cop who tracked, wiretapped, and interrogated Ricky Robles. In the movie, the detective was named Lieutenant Theo Kojak and played by the charismatic, bald-headed actor Telly Savalas. The character was such a hit that he was later spun off into his own series, entitled *Kojak*, which would become one of the most iconic TV cop shows in American TV history.

The day after the movie aired, George was returned to his regular cell. Some inmates congratulated him about the movie, but his familiar ambivalence toward the public exploitation of his case soon returned. Sure, the movie had been a success; it made other people rich and famous. But what had it done for Whitmore? The three grand he'd made from Universal had gone right to his attorneys. And there he sat, still in prison, still guilty in the eyes of the law.

George did not know that, beyond the prison walls, his case was perched on the edge of a startling reversal.

The previous December, shortly after returning from Puerto Rico, Beldock had filed papers with a state supreme court justice in Brooklyn, including the affidavit signed by Celeste Viruet. At around the same time, PBS aired Selwyn Raab's segment about the Whitmore case on

The 51st State. Both of these events caught the attention of Eugene Gold, the new Brooklyn D.A. Gold recognized that the existence of an eyewitness to Elba Borrero's assault, who had never been thoroughly questioned by investigators, was a stain on the Brooklyn D.A.'s office. And so he did something that his predecessor, Aaron Koota, would never have done: he sent two investigators from his office down to Puerto Rico to question Celeste Viruet. The trip confirmed what Raab and Beldock had already discovered: that the account of the attack Borrero had given Viruet cast major doubts on the official record.

Two days before Christmas 1972, Gold announced that the Brooklyn D.A.'s office was reopening the Whitmore case.

Beldock and Raab were ecstatic. In the interest of caution, though, they decided not to tell Whitmore. Gold's willingness to reopen the case was a good sign, but there was a chance that it would go nowhere; he might still decide that Borrero's identification of George was valid— or he might even call for the case to be tried once again, for the fourth time. Whitmore had already been through hell, subjected to an endless array of legal and emotional ups and downs; Beldock didn't want to get his hopes up until they were relatively certain that there would be a positive result.

Weeks passed. With *The 51st State* segment and *The Marcus-Nelson Murders* generating considerable press attention, there seemed to be a new groundswell of curiosity about what had happened to George Whitmore. After a decade of civil rights marches, riots, Black Power speeches, high-profile trials, Panther frame-ups and assassinations of cops, was Whitmore's case a major miscarriage of justice that had slipped through the cracks?

Late one April afternoon, Beldock got a call from an assistant D.A. in Brooklyn. A date had been set for a hearing in the courtroom of Justice Irwin Brownstein in state supreme court, he said—and D.A. Gold himself would be in attendance. This was significant: the presence of the district attorney suggested a major development.

"Would you like to give me some indication of which way this is going to go?" Beldock asked.

"No," said the ADA. Then he cleared his throat. "I think it's safe to say that it will be a ruling that you and your client will find favorable."

Beldock hung up the phone, his heart thumping in his chest. It wasn't clear whether this meant a new trial or a dismissal, but it sounded promising. One of the first people he called was Selwyn Raab. "Selwyn was pretty certain it was going to be a dismissal," he recalled. "I wasn't so certain. We decided it would be best to keep George in the dark, so to speak, for his own state of well-being. If it was a ruling in our favor, there would be plenty of time to celebrate after the fact."

ON THE MORNING of April 9, 1973, George Whitmore was in his cell when he got word that he would be picked up later that day and transferred to New York City for a court appearance the following morning. Although Beldock had mentioned that he had a court date coming up, George didn't know what to make of it.

It was a time of considerable unrest at Green Haven, with riots and other disturbances occurring on a semiregular basis. The previous September, not long after Whitmore arrived, Green Haven had seen a major riot between two rival groups of black inmates, one a Black Muslim sect faithful to Elijah Muhammad and the other described by prison authorities as a group of former Black Panthers. After a major rumble in the prison yard, seven inmates were rushed to a hospital in the nearby town of Poughkeepsie. Superintendent Vincent declared a state of emergency, and the entire inmate population was placed on lockdown. Two months later a prison guard was slashed in the neck with a knife. Once again, full-scale lockdown, with periodic cell searches for weapons.

By March 1973, the atmosphere had quieted down, until one afternoon when maggots were discovered in the food served in the mess hall. This touched off another riot. A group of prison riot police—separate from the guards employed by the Department of Corrections—were periodically raiding individual cells and beating prisoners.

With the atmosphere so fraught with violence, Whitmore spent much of his time at Green Haven in a state of terror. One day, when prison authorities made an unscheduled visit to his cell, he was certain they had come to beat him up. Even after they told him he was being transported to New York later that day, he was still skittish, half-convinced he was being set up for a beating.

Around four in the afternoon, Whitmore was retrieved from his cell. "What's this all about?" he asked the guards.

"Sorry, George," one of the guards replied. "We are under strict orders not to tell you anything."

Whitmore was startled to find that they were taking him to New York by helicopter. He'd never been in a helicopter before. Yet he still couldn't shake the fear that he was being taken somewhere for a beating. At one point, one of the guards joked, "If you wanna try to escape, George, go ahead, we won't stop you." George wondered if they were trying to trick him into fleeing so they could shoot him down like a dog.

As the chopper approached the city, George's anxiety settled into an unusual sense of comfort. The flight was so strange—like an amusement park ride, with the city's lights twinkling like diamonds and the skyline like the world's biggest Erector set. Whitmore had seen the New York skyline many times before, but always through the windows of a Greyhound bus coming from New Jersey. Seeing it from above, as he hovered in the sky—this was incredible, and it filled George with the sense that something monumental was about to take place.

They landed at Kennedy Airport. George was escorted by his bodyguards to a car and driven to a nearby motel.

"This is where we stay tonight," they told George. He was given a room that was connected to one where the guards would stay. Once again, one of them said jokingly, "Now remember, George. If you wanna run away, you go right ahead. We won't stop you." The others laughed.

George allowed himself a smile, but he still didn't know what the hell they were talking about.

The guards stayed up all night playing cards. Whitmore slept until they woke him up in the morning. He showered, combed his hair—he was now wearing it in a kind of mini-Afro style—and put on his black horn-rimmed glasses. He was given a fresh suit, white dress shirt, and black tie to wear. Standing in front of the mirror dressed in his new clothes, he felt reborn.

The guards put George in the car and drove into Brooklyn, to the state supreme court building on Court Street. George was loaded onto a freight elevator and then taken to a small room "no bigger than a bathroom." There was a small desk in the room. George was given a breakfast of cereal, some fruit, and a cup of coffee.

"Stay put until we come to get you," they said. "Do not open the door unless you hear this knock." One of guards tapped out a code, *taptap, tap-tap, tap-tap.* George nodded. The guards departed.

George sat alone in the tiny office. He tried to eat the food, but he was so filled with excitement and apprehension that he couldn't stomach the meal.

Twenty minutes later he heard the coded knock on the door. He opened the door.

"Okay, Mister Whitmore. Time to go."

George followed the guards into the elevator, up a few flights, then down a hallway and into a courtroom.

Whitmore was unprepared for what he found there: a roomful of people, reporters with notepads and pens, uniformed guards lining the room, lights so bright that for a few seconds he was blinded. Eventually, he noticed familiar faces—his attorneys Beldock and Miller, his mother, his brother Gerald, maybe some others he knew. He was led over to a table where Beldock and Miller stood smiling.

Within a few minutes of his arrival, Judge Irwin Brownstein entered the courtroom. "Mister Gold, I believe you have a statement you would like to read to the court."

A man George didn't recognize stood at the prosecutor's table to speak.

"Who's that?" George asked Beldock under his breath.

"Eugene Gold, Kings County D.A.," the attorney told his client.

Gold announced that "fresh new evidence" uncovered by his office had shown that Elba Borrero's identification of George Whitmore as her assailant was "hopelessly suspect." Borrero's relatives, Gold stated, now declared that she had told them a number of things that "either contradict or undermine the testimony she has given against Mister Whitmore." Among other things, Gold noted, his office had learned from Celeste Viruet that, before Elba Borrero identified Whitmore at the Seventy-second Precinct station house in Brownsville, she had first been shown a collection of mug shot photographs by the police—and identified one among them as her assailant. It was not George Whitmore. This fact— that Borrero had identified someone else as her assailant before she ever identified Whitmore—had never been revealed by cops, prosecutors, or Borrero herself in all the criminal proceedings Whitmore had been sub- jected to over the years.

Gold stopped short of affirming Whitmore's innocence. But the new evidence, he declared, "renders the case so weak that any possibility of conviction is negated." Gold asked the judge to vacate Whitmore's conviction, to dismiss the indictment, and to have the defendant discharged immediately.

Cheers broke out in the courtroom. Whitmore felt his knees go weak. He was afraid he might fall to the floor.

Gold had one final comment: "Your Honor, if in fact George Whitmore is guilty of these charges, surely his debt has been paid by his incarceration. If in fact he is innocent, I pray that my action today will in some measure repay society's debt to him."

The attorneys Beldock and Miller were allowed to add their own pleas for dismissal. Then the judge spoke.

"Gentlemen, I won't waste any more of your time. It is indeed disgraceful that this defendant has been subjected to nine years of prosecution and appeals. I hereby declare that he be released from custody immediately and that all charges against him be dismissed."

Again, the courtroom erupted in spontaneous applause.

Then the judge turned to George. "Mister Whitmore, I would like to say to you on behalf of the Supreme Court of the State of New York, I am sorry for what you have had to go through."

Now George felt tears coming to his eyes. In all his years struggling to break free from the chains of false prosecution, he had never dreamed that one day a judge would look him in the face and apologize for what happened. Whitmore felt a lump in his throat; he was speechless.

The people spilled out of the courtroom. George was led by his attorneys out onto the steps in front of the courthouse. It was a bright spring day. Whitmore squinted in the sunlight. A reporter shouted a question: "George, what do you have to say?"

After nearly giving up hope for so many years, Whitmore tried to summon his feelings. The rush of emotion was almost too much.

"I feel it's just beyond expressing," he said, shaking his head in wonder. "They dropped my case. I'm overwhelmed."

Years later Whitmore recalled:

I never expected to see the day when I would be cleared, so I
didn't allow myself to think about it too much. When it did
come, I was in shock. I kept thinking of all those years earlier,
when they told me I was facing two death penalty charges.
That weighed heavy on my mind for a long time. Even after
the Wylie-Hoffert charges was dropped, I couldn't stop

thinking about it. Electric chair, lethal injection, which was the most fast and least painful. Would I be ready to die when the time come? Would I cry or feel any pain? Now, well, they let me go. I got to go home. Man, I was so happy.

George was taken by his attorneys to a waiting car. Someone asked him something about getting revenge against the prosecutors. "I'm not bitter," George told a reporter. "I appreciate greatly what the D.A. did."

From the backseat, he waved shyly to the crowd. Then the car drove away.

For George, the next three days were one long parade of press conferences, interviews, and TV appearances. The news reports tried to sum up the Whitmore case in sixty-second spots—but there was more to the story than any report could contain. It had been ten years since the horrific murders of Janice Wylie and Emily Hoffert, nine and a half since Whitmore was plucked from the streets of Brooklyn and thrust into a drama that would destroy his life and call into question the basic fairness of the city's justice system. From the time of the Career Girls Murders, the city had descended into a kind of urban madness; a tidal wave of injustice and insurrection, ambushes and assassinations, led some to believe that the city could not be saved. White people continued their exodus from the city, and black people stepped forward to claim what they felt was rightfully theirs. Others—black and white—tried to cauterize the trauma with words of caution, with nonviolent protests and peaceful marches, but the historical moment seemed to hold forth its own bloody agenda.

Ten years earlier, the voice of a prophet had echoed throughout the city's concrete canyons: "We can never be satisfied as long as the Negro is the victim of unspeakable acts of police brutality." In a speech that heralded the beginning of a new era in the struggle for human dignity, King called on a nation to "live up to the meaning of its creed." The nation had been trying to do so, but the process was not pretty. The costs were nearly incalculable. The framing of a semiliterate Negro youth for one of the most heinous double murders in a generation had been one of many sparks for the racial conflagration that followed, troubling the collective conscience of those who cared about social justice.

In the year 1973 most would have agreed that the struggle was far from over. But a weary people will take their moments of triumph wherever they can be found. The story of George Whitmore symbolized the injustice that had long pervaded the system. Now, it seemed, the wheels of time were moving forward. Police corruption, prosecutorial malfeasance, civil unrest, and institutional racism still existed, but at least one grave injustice had been undone, one crooked place had been made straight.

George Whitmore was a free man.

EPILOGUE

ONE PERSON'S HARDSHIP is another's opportunity. The Savage City was like a kaleidoscope, its moods and shadings shifting with the angle of the instrument and the perspective of the participant. The cliché was that the city could make or break a person. The harder truth was that life in the big town could set an individual off on a blind path, one that could change a person in ways that were difficult to assess. You could attain high levels of accomplishment and still become lost in a world of self-righteous illusion. And, yes, on any given day you could be crushed by the wheels of progress.

To Mayor John Lindsay, the era of civic disorder and rising crime over which he presided was a sign that the American city was struggling to redefine itself. It was also in great danger of being abandoned by the federal government. In November 1971—against a backdrop of police executions, spectacular criminal prosecutions, and a level of racial conflict that had become the norm—Lindsay reasserted his mission as self-appointed guardian of the urban ideal and used it to announce that he was running for president of the United States.

There was no great clamoring for Lindsay to run. His poll ratings in New York City were low, though he was in good standing among black voters. Lindsay took this as a sign that his day had arrived. He switched his political affiliation from Republican to Democrat and traveled south to Florida to take part in the presidential primary. His pitch to voters was based largely on the argument that the country's future depended on the health of its major metropolitan areas. But Florida was a state filled with New Yorkers who had fled the city during Lindsay's years as mayor. As far as they were concerned, he was prescribing a medicine they did not want to take. Lindsay finished a distant fifth in a field of six candidates, with 7 percent of the vote. The winner of the Florida Democratic primary, with 42 percent of the vote, was George Wallace, an avowed segregationist.

After a couple more disastrous primaries in other states, Lindsay returned to the city a beaten man. He finished his term as mayor in 1973, but his political career never recovered. In the end, he was one more casualty from an era that claimed many victims.

There were still some scores yet to be settled. The war between the NYPD and the Black Liberation Army continued down a dark alley. The battlefield spread nationwide; there were BLA–law enforcement shoot-outs in St. Louis, San Francisco, Florida, and elsewhere. All of these confrontations ended with BLA members succumbing to overwhelming police fire-power. Between 1971 and 1974, the BLA killed ten police officers around the United States; dozens of militants were captured or killed.

The last to go out in a blaze of glory was Twymon Myers, who was believed by police to have been involved in the murder of Officers Foster and Laurie in Manhattan and also another shooting of a policeman in Brooklyn.

On November 14, 1973, at 152nd Street and Tinton Avenue in the Bronx, members of a joint FBI-NYPD task force surrounded Myers outside the apartment building where he had been hiding out. According to the police version, "Myers turned, pulled a 9-mm automatic pistol from under his coat and opened fire." The lawmen then returned fire, hitting Myers "multiple times." Eyewitnesses in the neighborhood offered a different account: Myers did have a weapon, they said, but the police fired first. Four officers were hit by bullets; one witness suggested that it was another case of friendly fire, as more than a dozen cops and agents unloaded their weapons in a shooting frenzy. Riddled with bullets, Myers died in the street. He was twenty-three years old.

Said Donald F. Cawley, the newly appointed police commissioner: "Tonight we've culminated a very long journey that involved the final capture of Twymon Myers, who we consider the last of the known leaders of the Black Liberation Army. We believe we have now broken the back of the BLA."

But the BLA's bloody rise and fall wasn't quite played out. There was one last saga; this one involved Assata Shakur, aka JoAnne Chesimard, occasional bank-robbing partner of Twymon Myers.

Since she'd gone underground in late 1971 Assata had been linked to a staggering array of bank robberies, attempted murders, kidnappings, and other crimes on the East Coast. Her face appeared on FBI wanted posters in New York and elsewhere around the country. In his 1973 book *Target Blue*, Robert Daley described her as "the final wanted fugitive, the soul of the gang, the mother hen who kept them together, kept them moving, kept them shooting."

Assata was captured in May 1973 after a ferocious shoot-out on the New Jersey Turnpike between state troopers and three BLA members—Assata Shakur, Zayd Shakur, and Sundiata Acoli. Zyad Shakur was killed in the shoot-out, as was one of the state troopers. The other trooper and Assata were injured. Acoli and Assata tried to escape, driving five miles along the turnpike until their car was surrounded by state troopers. Bleeding from gunshot wounds in both arms and a shoulder, Assata surrendered to troopers at the scene.

From 1973 to 1977, Shakur was indicted ten times in New York and New Jersey, resulting in seven different trials. She was charged with two bank robberies, the kidnapping of a Brooklyn heroin dealer, the attempted murder of two Queens police officers, and eight other felonies related to the turnpike shoot-out. All the charges for which she was originally hunted by the FBI were either dismissed or ended in acquittal at trial. She was, however, found guilty at trial on all eight felony counts relating to the shoot-out on the turnpike. Her role in the murder of the state trooper brought with it a mandatory life sentence.

During her incarceration, Assata had a child by one of her codefendants, James Hinton. Her imprisonment, which included long stretches of solitary confinement—and instances of physical abuse, claimed Shakur—was condemned by a panel of jurists representing the United Nations Commission on Human Rights, who stated that her treatment "was totally unbefitting any prisoner." Her cause as a political prisoner was championed by the dwindling faithful in the black liberation movement.

No doubt there were those who cheered when, on November 2, 1979, Assata was sprung from the Clinton Correctional Facility for Women in New Jersey in a daring escape engineered by, among others, former Black Panther Sekou Odinga and Mutulu Shakur. Using false IDs, the team of BLA members penetrated prison security, then seized two guards as hostages and used a prison van to escape. Assata was able to evade an intensive FBI manhunt and live underground in the United States for nearly five years. In 1984, she fled to Cuba, where she was granted political asylum and still lives in exile.

Assata Shakur was one of many whose lives were scattered to the winds by events of the 1960s and early 1970s in New York City. For the three main players in this narrative—Phillips, Bin Wahad, and Whitmore—the years that followed were no less dramatic:

BILL PHILLIPS

After the hung jury in his first trial for the double murder of a pimp and a prostitute, Phillips began his retrial in November 1974 expecting to be found not guilty. In terms of the evidence, the second trial was a replay of the first, but this time Phillips was without the services of star attorney F. Lee Bailey, with whom he parted ways after a dispute over the lawyer's fee. At trial, Phillips's new attorney, Harold Rothblatt, was unable to undermine the eyewitness testimony of the surviving victim, Charles Gonzales, who, when asked if Phillips was the man who shot him, said, "Yes sir. I'll never forget his face as long as I live." After an eight-week trial, the jury deliberated eleven hours over two days before finding Phillips guilty on two counts of homicide and one count of attempted homicide. "The 44-year-old defendant blanched and sank into his chair at the defense table after the foreman replied 'guilty' when asked for the verdict on each of the three counts in the indictment," the *New York Times* reported. Phillips was sentenced to twenty-five years to life in prison.

For the high-flying corrupt cop who became a media star during the televised Knapp Commission hearings, it was a fall of mythic proportions. Phillips did not fear many things, but he did fear prison. As he put it in his memoir, "I could never, never spend the rest of my life in fucking jail. I would kill myself first. The thought of suicide is the only escape. To be locked up like an animal in some fuckin' jail, I couldn't do it. I couldn't survive. I'd have to find some way to end it."

Given Phillips's trepidation about being an ex-cop locked up with criminals, the next thirty years of his life were a time of considerable accomplishment. He was first sent to Attica, a correctional facility seething with racial hostilities in the wake of the infamous riot that had taken place three and a half years earlier. In general population, Phillips was "terrorized" every minute of every day, as he would later put it.

Around 1978 Phillips began spending nearly all of his free time in the prison library studying the law. At first it was just a hobby, but eventually he began helping out fellow inmates with their cases. He took full advantage of educational programs that were instituted in the state prison system as a result of reforms brought about by the Attica riot. Eventually, he earned a bachelor's degree from Empire State College and a master's degree from Buffalo State University with a 4.0 grade point average. He earned a state certification in legal research and taught a course on the subject at Attica. He helped dozens of inmates with their cases, and in the late 1980s he was profiled on the CBS newsmagazine *Street Stories*. The program's producers interviewed inmates whom Phillips had helped get released from prison through his legal work. "I've been championing the cause of the underdog in here," Phillips would say on the program.

Phillips would eventually be transferred to various other state penal facilities. He used his incarceration time well, doing charity work through an upstate Quaker group, rewriting a prison substance and alcohol abuse treatment program, and receiving counseling from a Mormon prison organization. By the time of his first parole hearing in 1999, he had become known as a "model inmate" who was respectful to prison authorities and helpful to other inmates.

As the hearing approached that September, Phillips had reason to believe he might have a favorable reception. He had letters of recommendation from Whitman Knapp and Mike Armstrong, the Knapp Commission's chief counsel, who wrote that Phillips had been "resourceful, courageous, tireless, and extremely effective" in his work for the Knapp Commission. "It is fair to say that, without the undercover work and testimony of William Phillips, our committee would not have been able to hold its public hearings."

Yet the pleas on Phillips's behalf were to no avail. He was turned down for parole; the board called him "a criminal of the worst kind whose danger to public safety is to the highest degree." Of the parole board members, Phillips said only, "Most of these guys were in diapers when I was testifying. They don't know what it's about. They have no idea about my story."

From 1999 on, Phillips went before the parole board every two years, and was turned down every two years, until he was one of the oldest inmates in the state prison system. Over the years, he had three cancer surgeries, including one that claimed his left eye. He suffered a minor stroke and developed diabetes. Despite his infirmities, Phillips kept himself in shape in the prison gym and never lost hope that he would eventually see the light of day.

The problem was, Phillips was not only unwilling to express remorse for the double homicide for which he'd been convicted, he wouldn't even admit to the killings. To Phillips, the reason was clear: he didn't do it. At his first hearing in 1999, he was asked,

Parole board officer: So it is your position on these convictions that you're innocent of these crimes?

Phillips: Well, I was convicted by a jury so I'm stuck with that.

Parole board: Do you suppose the witness could be wrong about who shot him?

Phillips: I believe so.

Phillips was asked if he had any ideas about who might have done the actual murder.

Phillips: Yes, I have a theory. It was a loan shark. Every report that was put in this case was put in by the detective that it was a loan shark. This individual [Jimmy Smith] had 33 or 35 arrests. He owed everybody money. He had been beat up on several occasions for nonpayment of his loan shark bills, and my theory of the case is that, yes, it was a loan shark.

Parole board: You are saying that another person was responsible?

Phillips: My theory, yes.

After three or four parole hearings over an eight-year period, it became clear to Phillips that he would never be released unless he copped to the killings. In 2007, a new regime took over control of the state parole board. Phillips was informed by his attorney that there was a good chance he could get a favorable ruling, but he would have to say the magic words: *I did it.* This was easier said than done. The parole board

was likely to ask Phillips specific questions about the night of the shootings. He would have to come up with a scenario that matched the actual
details of the crime.

On September 19, Phillips came before the board in what would
likely be his last shot at receiving parole. When he was asked "How are
you feeling today?" he answered, "A little nervous. It's my fifth time
before the parole board." He was told, "Take a few minutes to calm
down. Take your time, sir. Take a deep breath. It's a fresh, new panel."

Phillips decided, at last, to tell the board what it wanted to hear—
that he had shot the three victims in that whorehouse in 1968. He proceeded to take the board members through a rambling description of the
crime, seeming at times incredulous at his own words:

> Going back now, I can't possibly imagine that I could do such
> a thing and act like that. It's just beyond me. . . . I never had a
> problem with people and money on the Force, and things like
> that, or threatening people. I don't know what came over me
> to do this. It's just like out of my character, you know. Okay,
> I took money as a police officer but I never was involved in
> hurting nobody to collect money or attempting to kill them or
> kill them. This is something I can never fully explain.

Phillips's account of the events of that night was nearly incompre-
hensible; when asked about details, he floundered, confusing one of the
two dead victims with the survivor. He sounded like a man determined
to convince the board he was guilty—and remorseful—for a crime he
didn't commit. Ultimately, his act was successful: on November 10,
2007, after serving thirty-three years in prison, Bill Phillips was released
on parole. He was seventy-eight years old.

Upon release, Phillips went into hiding. After living for a time in a
U.S. veterans halfway house, he was taken in by the Mormon group he'd
become associated with in prison. As of 2010, he was working with two
filmmakers who planned to produce a documentary about his life.

DHORUBA BIN WAHAD

In the late 1970s, while incarcerated at Green Haven, Dhoruba started
reading about a covert FBI counterintelligence program that had been

revealed during Senate hearings in Washington, D.C. In the wake of the Watergate scandal, the Senate had vowed to usher in a new era of transparency in government. A committee was formed to investigate the activities of U.S. intelligence agencies. The Church Committee hearings, headed by Senator Frank Church of Idaho, focused in part on the activities of the FBI under J. Edgar Hoover (who had died of natural causes on May 2, 1972). For the first time, the American public learned of the FBI's efforts to infiltrate and destabilize the black liberation movement via COINTELPRO.

Dhoruba became convinced that he might have been a target of the FBI's counterintelligence efforts; if that was true, he might have grounds to claim that his civil rights had been violated. COINTELPRO had engaged in the use of illegal wiretaps, paid informants, and the spreading of false information that, in some cases, led directly to the deaths of people in the movement. If Dhoruba had been a target of the program, it also bolstered his argument that police authorities had targeted him, because of his politics, to take the rap for the shooting of police officers Curry and Binetti.

The problem for Dhoruba was that he was locked away in prison on a life sentence. No lawyer was likely even to listen to his claims, much less devote time and effort to helping him prove his theories. Then, in 1975, he got lucky. A group of college students visited Green Haven prison. Among the group was Robert Boyle, a twenty-year-old student majoring in sociology. Boyle met Dhoruba and became convinced that, if what the imprisoned black militant was saying was true, it might open a window onto a pattern of FBI wrongdoing that had affected an entire generation of civil rights activists.

Thus began a legal saga that would last the next fifteen years. Boyle decided to become a lawyer. He attended Brooklyn Law School and was admitted to the New York State bar in 1981. At the same time, he brought Dhoruba's case to Elizabeth Fink, a civil rights attorney whose career had been inspired by William Kunstler. Together, Fink and Boyle began a long process of filing legal injunctions against the FBI and the NYPD in an effort to get their hands on any and all files relating to Dhoruba Bin Wahad.

At every turn, government lawyers stonewalled. At first, they claimed there were no secret files. Then they claimed there *had* been files, but that they were destroyed or lost. Finally, in 1989, the government not only revealed that FBI and NYPD intelligence files did exist, but they also launched a counterstrategy: they released a mountain of files, more than three hundred thousand pages in all, hoping to overwhelm Dhoruba and his attorneys.

Over the next ten months, the lawyers pored over the files—and were astounded by what they found. Not only was the name of Richard Moore aka Dhoruba all over the FBI files, they uncovered extensive documentation of the covert program known as NEWKILL—the first time that program was revealed to anyone outside of law enforcement. The implications were explosive: the files proved conclusively that the Manhattan D.A.'s office had been lying when it insisted that there were no relevant files or notes concerning Dhoruba's case. In particular, the NEWKILL files revealed that—despite the prosecution's repeated denials during Dhoruba's trial—star witness Pauline Joseph, whose testimony helped convict Dhoruba and others at numerous BLA-related trials, had been briefed and interrogated dozens of times over a period of two years, and much of what she told detectives and prosecutors contradicted what she had testified to on the witness stand.

Fink and Boyle believed they had hit the jackpot. They filed a motion to have Dhoruba's conviction overturned, citing (among other factors) the fact that the government had failed to turn over essential Rosario material at trial.

At first the motion was denied; then the denial was overturned. Finally, in March 1990, Dhoruba's case came before Justice Peter J. McQuillan. After examining the motion filed by Dhoruba's lawyers and all the relevant material from the NEWKILL files, McQuillan rendered his verdict. "I acknowledge that [my] decision is not free from doubt," said the judge. "The Rosario materials do not contain clearly exculpatory statements, nor any statements that would undermine a witness's entire testimony. But they do include statements by Pauline Joseph which depart significantly from some of her most crucial testimony, and that testimony was essential to the People's theory of the case. It follows, then, that there is a reasonable possibility of a different verdict if the defendant had been afforded the opportunity to cross-examine her with these statements. To vacate a conviction some twenty years after the jury's verdict on the basis of a possibility, however reasonable that possibility may be, is not a pleasant duty. . . . A conviction that can no longer be called a just conviction . . . must be remedied no matter how much time has passed. Accordingly, the motion to vacate the defendant's conviction is granted."

After nineteen years of imprisonment, Dhoruba walked out of court a free man.

Immediately, the former Panther and underground guerrilla became a symbol to a generation of activists who had been beaten, shot at, hunted down, and incarcerated during the years of conflict between police and the black liberation movement. Dhoruba became a popular speaker at political rallies and, occasionally, on television. After a 1992 appearance on *The Phil Donahue Show* alongside rapper Sister Souljah and Princeton University professor Cornel West, Dhoruba was derided by a *New York Times* reviewer for his "soapbox radicalism." In speeches and essays in leftist journals, Dhoruba's rhetoric remained fiery and unrepentant, though in many ways the movement he helped forge had since moved on.

The inevitable civil litigation followed. Dhoruba sued the FBI and the NYPD. In a 1995 settlement with the federal government he was awarded $400,000. Five years later, in a settlement with the City of New York, he collected a further $490,000. Some of this money went to pay legal fees, some to taxes. The rest Dhoruba used to finance a project he had dreamed about while he was in prison. In the late 1990s he moved to Ghana, Africa, and, in partnership with the local government, constructed a school for children. Dhoruba became something of a player in African politics, jetting back and forth between the continent and the United States. In 1999, he introduced Nelson Mandela at a rally in Harlem. A documentary about his life called *Passin' It On* was produced and shown on PBS. But by the early years of the new century, Dhoruba's ventures in Ghana had fizzled out. His school was forced to close after financial improprieties by his business partners, and the political party he had supported was voted out of office.

Dhoruba moved his African wife and child back to the United States, where he settled in New Jersey. For a time, he resumed his role as a speaker at political forums and rallies. But increasingly Dhoruba's politics and uncompromising point of view seemed to reflect battles from another era. He routinely attacked ostensibly progressive activists and political figures whom he considered insufficiently radical. Dhoruba was still a revolutionary, but the revolution he advocated had been put to rest long ago.

In November 2008, at the age of sixty-three, Dhoruba became a father for the fourth time. His new child caused him to reflect back on the years of his youth, when he and others of his generation had thrown themselves into the whirlwind.

I don't know if I ever thought what the endgame of joining the Panthers would be. Maybe I thought the endgame would be a victory march down Madison Avenue with black, red, and green flags. You woulda had [police commissioner] Murphy and Lindsay and all of them in the hoosegow under charges of corruption. . . . I thought that maybe we would succeed in getting the type of respect that would allow us to basically build our own lives and maybe our own future. Because almost everybody I grew up with was either in jail or dead. . . .

My major motive was to make these motherfuckers respect us. Because I came from an environment where respect from [the police] didn't come because they admired your intellect or creativity. They thought you were a whole different level of human being, if you were a human being at all. I really believed that there could be no true reconciliation unless there was pain on both sides. People only reconcile when they're tired of the pain and tired of what's happening.

I think our mission was to show that you couldn't employ violence, intimidation, and fear on black people without a consequence. That was the whole thing: a political consequence. If you do [something], there is a consequence.

Bin Wahad, the former gangbanger from the South Bronx, had over the years embraced a Pan-Africanist perspective. The more he became immersed in the struggle for civil rights in the United States, the more acutely aware he became that he and his fellow revolutionaries were merely displaced Africans living out the legacy of slavery. His forays in Africa sometimes took him to his sharpest levels of reflection.

I used to drive through Africa and see devastated villages and kids running across the roads, and you realize war doesn't bring anybody anything. It destroys shit on a really deep, profound level. And war usually comes from those who have power, the people who have other people willing to kill you, willing to brutalize you, willing to murder you. These are the people who have the upper hand. So, at what point does a man have a right to fight, to use violence, at what point? Because if there's no forces or organization or movement exacting a consequence on those who wield power over you, what can you do? I'm not saying everything is reducible to violence and that's the only way. But if people feel free to exercise power over you, there's nothing you can do about it. They're gonna exercise power over you in their own interest, and they don't really care what you have to say about it.

Dhoruba's opinions were far from flippant; they were hard-earned. You could disagree with his views and actions, but it was hard to question his bona fides. His philosophy was tempered in the streets and during twenty-four years behind bars, nineteen of those for a crime he maintains he did not commit.

By early 2010, the former Panther had put together the pieces of a new business venture that involved ibogaine, a highly touted though controversial drug used as a treatment for narcotics addiction. Ibogaine is derived from iboga, a hallucinogenic plant of West African origin. Together with partners in Ghana, Dhoruba was looking to build a narcotics rehabilitation clinic somewhere in Saudi Arabia. Often, after negotiating some detail of the plan from his cell phone driving around New York and New Jersey, he would hang up the phone and say to himself, "I gotta get back to Africa."

GEORGE WHITMORE

Life wasn't easy for Whitmore, a man whose existence was changed forever by a chance encounter with a policeman on a Brooklyn street. Upon his release in 1973, George moved back to the same area of New Jersey where he had lived most of his life. He tried to live an anonymous life, but his story as a wronged man was still fresh, and people asked him about it constantly. Remembered George, "I got tired of everybody saying, 'Hey, aren't you Whitmore?' and reciting all these things I was trying to forget. I was polite and nice about it and everything, but I said, Well, it's time for me to move. I lived in Whitesboro, Wildwood, Denisville, Woodbine. Everywhere I went, people knew my case."

Through his attorney, Whitmore filed a lawsuit against the City of New York for improper arrest and malicious prosecution. It took five years to get a ruling. In 1979, a judge dismissed Whitmore's suit, saying that parts of it had been filed too late. The judge also declared that there was "no proof of actual malice" by the Brooklyn D.A.'s office in trying Whitmore three times on the same false accusation.

In a rare display of discord, George was quoted in the *Times* saying, "They wrecked my life and they still won't admit they did anything wrong. If justice prevails, let it prevail for me." And, eventually, it did: the judge's decision was overturned on appeal, and in 1982 Whitmore received $560,000 in a settlement with the city.

As often happens with people from humble beginnings who come into a large sum of money, the influx of cash was a mixed blessing for Whitmore. Relatives, friends, acquaintances, and would-be business partners came out of the woodwork. George gave some of the money away to family members in need. He invested half of the money in a cattle business, but his partner, a former schoolmate, fleeced Whitmore of nearly $100,000. The crooked business partner went to jail, but Whitmore was unable to recoup his losses.

In Denisville, a pleasant, mostly white suburb on the other side of the tracks from Wildwood, Whitmore bought a beautiful, spacious home ("a mansion," he called it) on a tree-lined street. He got a good deal: the asking price was $100,000, but since the previous occupant had killed his wife and himself in the house, George was able to buy the house for $75,000.

George moved in with a lady friend and three kids—two of his and one of hers. He knew about the killings that had taken place in the house, but what he didn't know was that the place was haunted. "One morning I woke up and all the silverware had been pulled out of the drawers and thrown on the floor. That was only the beginning; there were ghosts in that house." George bought sheets of plywood and boarded up part of the house to keep the ghosts away.

There was another problem. One day, George came home and someone had painted the words *Nigger Get Out* on the side of his garage. Whitmore contacted the local police, but they seemed uninterested in what George called his "KKK problem." When the racial harassment continued, George decided he wasn't wanted in the lily-white suburb of Denisville. He sold the property at a loss and moved back to Wildwood.

It was the mid-1980s, and Whitmore's money was running out. He took what he had left, bought a scallop boat, and started his own fishing business. George had always loved the water, ever since his days of sticking a homemade fishing pole out his bedroom window when he was a child. With a crew of four or five men, George went out to sea and stayed there through the fishing season. "Out on the ocean seemed to be the only place where I could get peace of mind," he recalled. "Nobody knew me or bothered me. I wasn't no famous man who went through hell. I was anonymous."

One day, out on his fishing boat, George was hit in the face by a steel cable and broke his nose. He bled all over the boat, but he stayed at sea until he and the crew met their scallop quota. By the time he returned to land and went to the hospital, it was too late to reset his broken nose. Forever after, George would have a noticeably crooked nose.

Eventually, like many things in Whitmore's life, his fishing business took a bad turn. His boat was repossessed for lack of payment. By the 1990s, the money from his settlement with the City of New York was long gone. He lived off welfare and disability payments from the State of New Jersey. His drinking problem, which had begun in prison, grew worse, and when George drank he sometimes got ornery. His girlfriend took out a restraining order against him, which George routinely violated. Thus began a series of arrests for things like criminal trespassing, violating a protection order, simple assault, contempt of court, defaulting on bail, and driving while intoxicated. Between 1990 and 2005, Whitmore was arrested twenty-four times. He became a well-known figure at Middle Township Municipal Court and other courts and jailhouses in and around the Wildwood area.

Into the new century, now in his sixties, George stopped getting into trouble with the law, but his life of hardship did not let up. He had three separate heart attacks and was once declared legally dead. He broke more bones than he could count. Whitmore had developed a knack for disaster. He was like a tumbleweed blowing in the wind, freewheeling, trying to stay a few steps ahead of the next catastrophe. Nearly every day he self-medicated with vodka, beer, and cigarettes.

One day in January 2010, George was at the Western Union counter at a check-cashing store in Rio Grande, New Jersey, picking up money sent to him by a friend in Manhattan. Standing nearby, George noticed a man wearing a surgeon's mask over his face, but he didn't think too much about it: There was lots of talk on the news about the swine flu, and sometimes people wore masks. Whitmore picked up his money, $250 in cash. Then, before he had a chance to put it in his pocket, the man with the mask snatched the money out of his hand and dashed out the door.

Whitmore ran after the thief, heading out into the street, when—BAM!—he was hit by a car. The vehicle dragged him twenty feet. Whitmore was unconscious when paramedics arrived on the scene and determined that the victim needed to be transferred to a hospital in Atlantic City. The fastest way to get there was by helicopter.

When Whitmore awoke, he was high in the sky—the first time he'd been in a helicopter since the day in 1973 when he was flown to New York City for the court hearing that would eventually lead to his freedom.

Whitmore suffered numerous broken bones and a concussion in the accident, but he escaped life-threatening injury. Soon he returned to his home at a motel off Route 9 in the town of Cape May Court House, where he convalesced. Said George, "I've had three heart attacks, been declared dead, got a stent in my heart, been harassed by ghosts, the KKK, broke my nose—you name it. But I'm still here. I ain't going nowhere. I'm a survivor."

IN THE CITY of New York, the wheels of progress continue to turn. The forces that shaped the lives of Whitmore, Phillips, Dhoruba, and others seemed to linger for decades—and things got worse before they got better. In the 1980s, the explosion of crack cocaine in the ghetto would lead to levels of violence and mayhem that far surpassed the heroin years of the 1950s and 1960s. The result was a staggering rate of incarceration for black males in their teens and twenties. The number of homicides in the city doubled from its total of one thousand in 1970 to more than two thousand in 1990. The city's crime rate continued to climb until, coincidentally, New York elected its first African American mayor, David Dinkins, in 1990.

The 1990s, when former federal prosecutor Rudolph Giuliani became mayor after Dinkins, saw a continuation in the decline of violent crime, but it was also a period characterized by instances of police brutality that far outstripped anything that had happened to George Whitmore. A Haitian immigrant was tortured and sodomized in the back room of a Brooklyn station house; an African immigrant was riddled with forty-one bullets by a team of cops while he reached for his identification in front of his home in the Bronx. Protesters marched on police headquarters and City Hall. Eventually, Giuliani, like John Lindsay, headed to Florida to run for president. In the Republican Party primary of 2008, he somehow managed to do even worse than Lindsay, garnering a total of zero delegates before dropping out of the race.

Since the infamous 9/11 terror attacks of 2001 the crime rate has remained low. In 2009 there were 496 murders in New York, the lowest total since the NYPD began keeping detailed crime statistics in 1963. The Savage City is now the Safest Big City in America. But many of the fissures remain. Within the criminal justice system, assumptions based on race and class are still the norm. Out on the street, police stop and frisk African American and Latino youths at a rate nine times higher than whites. The city's jails are disproportionately filled with young black men. More cops than ever live in the suburbs, outside the city they police. When it comes to poor and minority neighborhoods in places like Brooklyn and the Bronx, they are strangers in a strange land.

Crime may be down, but the system is still based on fear. Mayors and police commissioners come and go; they tout new programs and produce statistics to show they're doing their job, but the institutional roots are largely the same. A criminal justice system that was designed to separate the races, and to enforce a racial caste system, does not change overnight. In fact, it doesn't change at all unless the general populace, and those who enforce the system, are willing to recognize the problem.

The Savage City may have drifted from memory; the names and events of a tumultuous era have been paved over and buried away. But the scars, emotions, and underlying causes are still present. They remain embedded below the surface of the city like a dormant but smoldering volcano, one that could rumble to life at any time.

Today, the city projects an image of security. But the fault lines remain. Lift up the rock and you will see.

AFTERWORD

SEVERAL MONTHS AFTER the hardcover edition of this book was published, I received an email message from Bill Phillips. *After reading your book*, it read, *I feel we have much to discuss.*

During the course of researching *The Savage City*, I had tried in vain to track Phillips down for an interview. When I began my research, he had only recently been released from prison. I contacted an attorney who had helped Phillips get parole, but the attorney told me he hadn't heard from Phillips since his release in December 2007. The attorney had made plans with Phillips to meet him on the very day of his release, but Phillips never showed at the agreed-upon time and location. The attorney never saw him again. For all intents and purposes, Bill Phillips had disappeared.

As I carried on with my work, I kept trying to track Phillips down. I wasn't as concerned with meeting and speaking directly with him as I had been with Whitmore and Bin Wahad, the other primary subjects of my research, because in a way I already had his voice: his book *On the Pad*, an unusually thorough explication of his activities and thinking during his years as both a corrupt cop and an operative for the Knapp Commission. Published in 1973, after Phillips's first murder trial and before the second, it reflected the detective's fresh memories and his willingness to be open and candid about his police career. Even if I should manage to find and interview Phillips, I knew, given the passage of time, he wasn't likely to add much to what he'd laid out in *On the Pad*.

I finished the book without any further solid leads on Phillips, and it was published in March 2011. Still, not having met Phillips face-to-face, as I had Whitmore and Bin Wahad, rankled my sense of duty as a reporter. So when he summoned me via email, I quickly responded. We arranged to meet in the small upstate New York town where he lives today.

Phillips had no real complaints about *The Savage City*. "You told it the way it was," he said when we finally met. He just wanted to give me his "two cents," as he put it—to reflect back on his years as a corrupt cop, to shed further light on why and how he'd become an informant for the Knapp Commission. "I knew that one day I was going to get caught," he told me. "And I didn't care. I had become disgusted with myself. My morals went right down the sewer. I wasn't happy with the way I turned out to be, having to live a hidden life. My family didn't know; my wife didn't know. Hiding money all the time. And, of course, you get a little leery. Your phone rings at three or four in the morning, that kind of shit. You know it ain't gonna last forever. Something's gonna go haywire."

Even at eighty-one, Phillips is an energetic and entertaining story-teller. Aside from the thick glasses he wears, and the insulin shots he receives to combat his diabetes, his health is outstanding. In prison he worked out and played handball on a regular basis, and he has kept up a routine of playing golf nearly every day.

He has also kept his memories intact. To Phillips, the era of intense racial animosity between the NYPD and New York City's African American population is still vivid. He concedes that, in the 1960s, many cops treated black people with disdain, frequently calling them *nigger* to their face. Like many cops of his generation, who were the product of racially segregated upbringings, Phillips once viewed race as an issue of "us" versus "them," though today he denies that overt racial hostility was ever a driving factor in his career. "I never called anybody a nigger to their face," he says. "I never would have done that. I used that word as a reference with other cops and some whites, because that's the way I was brought up."

The NYPD's shooting war with the black liberation movement, he notes, was outside his realm of experience; by the time those events were unfolding, he was struggling for his survival, first as a Knapp Commission operative, later while facing double-murder charges.

Even if Phillips had been a racist during his years as a member of the

NYPD, his attitude was reconfigured after spending thirty-three years in the New York State penal system, where minorities make up approximately 70 percent of the population.

A sociable person by nature, Phillips likes to talk. His speech is flavored with street humor and casual profanities that reflect an adulthood spent in the male subcultures of police work and prison life. For instance, here is Phillips explaining how he tried to convince his criminal defense attorney, the legendary F. Lee Bailey, not to select a female as a juror at his first murder trial.

> I told [Bailey], "Don't put a woman on the jury. I gotta testify. Don't put a woman on the jury." He puts on a fuckin' ramrod German retired secretary. Looked like a fuckin' Nazi with a fuckin' swastika. I said, "Get that bitch off the jury. I'm gonna charm her? You're gonna charm her, loverboy? I'll tell you what—you ain't gonna charm her. Smooth as you think you are." He was a brilliant bastard, you know. So we finish the trial ten to two in favor of acquittal. Her and some fag that she sat next to. That trial lasted thirteen weeks. So they get friendly and so forth, her and the fag. They were the two holdouts. Hung jury.

Even now, nearly four decades later, Phillips remembers the precise moment at his second trial when the jury foreman pronounced him guilty.

> My knees buckled. I swear to Christ, they buckled like an old fuckin' horse. I thought, Holy fuckin' shit. Look at this. So now I try to get bail. What a fuckin' joke that was. I figured, if I got convicted, I would get bail while my case was under appeal. So I wasn't really worried about going to jail. And then they said, "No bail, you're going straight to prison." Holy fuck.

As a result of his live television appearance at the Knapp Commission hearings, which generated national news coverage, Phillips was perhaps the most publicly exposed corrupt cop in history. He entered prison a marked man.

[When] I got to Attica, I didn't hide. Went right into general population. When I walked out to the yard, every fuckin' head turned and looked at me: "What is this guy, out of his fuckin' mind?" Nobody came near me. I just sat with my back against the wall and watched TV. Then, little by little, I got a few friends. But it was a fuckin' nightmare. Came back to my cell every day, I'd close the door and say, "Whew, I made it through another day." But I knew that door was gonna open in the morning, and I was gonna have to go back out there.

In prison, even inmates who weren't hostile to Phillips knew he was radioactive, and they responded accordingly. Phillips remembers a day early in his incarceration at Attica when he learned the way it was going to be.

They had me work in the maintenance department. There was twelve of us working there, and there was this big hack [prison guard], really sweet guy, big, must have been six foot three, two hundred fifty or two hundred sixty pounds. He would pick us up in the morning and we would march down to the maintenance shop. So about the second day, he says, "Come here. I gotta tell you something. I gotta tell you how it is." He says, "You're on your own. I can't do nothin' for you." I says, "Did I ask you for anything? I don't ask nobody for nothin'. I know I'm on my own. You're a nice guy. I hear good things about you. Don't worry about me. I'll take care of myself." But he let me know right away that if anything happens, he's gonna look the other fuckin' way. If they take out a big knife and they're coming after me, he ain't gonna do nothing. And that's the first big reality check I had, right there.

Phillips was determined to do his time out in the open, not hiding away in protective custody or solitary confinement. It was exhausting, and required constant vigilance, but he knew he had to address potential confrontations immediately, or his position as an ex-cop surrounded by hardened criminals would put him in an impossibly vulnerable predicament.

A few guys got in my face, but [the hostility] was mostly behind my back. One time, there were three or four guys, breaking balls and so forth. I'd heard this was going on behind my back. So I picked out the leader of the group, and I says to the guy, "Can I talk to you?" I had two shanks. I says, "Look, I hear you're breaking my balls, and I don't appreciate it. All this backstabbing and other shit behind my back. I don't really give a fuck. You wanna come at me right now? You do what you gotta do. I got something for you, and I got something for me. 'Cause I'll stab the shit out of you and then put a shank in your hand, and I'll never do an extra day. So what do you guys want to do?" He says, "Oh, listen, it ain't that way." I said, "Oh, it ain't that way, huh? Well, you go fuck yourself. You and your friends stay at least ten fuckin' feet away from me, you son of a bitch."

Phillips's memory is filled with such episodes, especially from the first decade or so of his incarceration. Eventually, attitudes about Phillips within the prison system began to evolve. "The philosophy kind of changed," says Phillips. "The attitude was, 'Why do we give a fuck what he did to cops, or what happened to the cops? We don't like him because *he's* a cop, and he put people in jail.'"

His stock rose further, he recalls, after he studied law and became an invaluable jailhouse lawyer. "I helped eighty guys get out of prison," says Phillips. Of those, he claims, "at least fifteen percent were innocent. *Innocent.* Not that they got a new trial. They didn't do the crime." The other cases Phillips handled were reversed due to legal technicalities. "Legal Aid is atrocious," says the former cop. "Sloppy records. Briefs that read like they were written by a Chinaman in a dark alley. Terrible. Guy getting twenty-five to life gets an eight-page brief. I got a lot of cases reversed on ineffective counsel. I got three different reversals in three different courts in one day."

Asked whether he took on legal work on behalf of indigent inmates as a way to expiate the guilt from his life as a crooked cop, Phillips smiles. "I didn't do it to get saved," he says. "I did it for a job, to do something productive. Also, I guess it kind of protected me within the system. I could go into any prison in the state and I was welcomed like a soldier returning from the Philippines—that's the [kind of] welcoming party I got."

As Phillips was working on other cases, he was also working on his own.

Phillips's double murder conviction remains a head-scratcher. The evidence against him was limited: no fingerprints, no fibers, and the ballistics from the killer's gun did not match Phillips's service revolver. His conviction was based partly on eyewitness accounts from prostitutes who worked at the establishment of Jimmy Smith, the pimp who was murdered along with prostitute Sharon Stango. These witnesses said they'd seen Phillips now and then at Smith's midtown Manhattan bordello, and that he was there to extort money from Smith.

The most devastating witness against Phillips was Charles Gonzalez, the john who was also shot that night but survived. He identified Phillips as the shooter, proclaiming, "I'll never forget that face." Back in the early 1970s, before DNA evidence was available, such eyewitness testimony was virtually unimpeachable.

George Whitmore knew a thing or two about eyewitness testimony. Elba Borrero had been his accuser for a decade, seemingly unwavering in her belief that Whitmore had been her attacker, until it was shown that her memory was not nearly as steadfast in private as it had been when presented in court by prosecutors.

Bill Phillips was convicted primarily on the eyewitness testimony of one man: Charles Gonzalez.

At trial, Phillips's attorney had sought to cast doubt on Gonzalez's identification. At the moment when he'd supposedly seen Phillips, Gonzalez had been shot, was bleeding and barely conscious. How could he possibly have been so certain? The more Gonzalez was challenged, the more adamant he became that Phillips was the shooter. His testimony convinced the jury, and it was held up on appeal.

The closest Phillips came to seriously challenging his conviction came in 1979, when attorney William Kunstler agreed to file a petition on his behalf.

It was ironic that Kunstler, who had launched his career as a "radical" criminal defense lawyer by representing members of the Black Panther Party (including, for a time, Dhoruba Bin Wahad), was now seeking to defend one of the most notoriously corrupt cops in the history of the NYPD.

Kunstler gave credence to Phillips's contention that he had been framed for the double murder by people in the NYPD as payback for testifying against fellow officers. This theory, however, was not part of Kunstler's petition. Citing a federal statue, Kunstler pleaded that Phillips's conviction should be vacated for the simple reason that prosecutors were legally prohibited from using his Knapp Commission testimony against him in court. Phillips had been promised immunity for that testimony. The judge sidestepped the issue of immunity, however, ruling that Phillips's motion for dismissal on the grounds of immunized testimony had been filed too late. The conviction would stand.

Even now, after thirty-three years of incarceration and four years of freedom, Phillips pleads his innocence to anyone who will listen. He cites the fact that he was the one who told the Knapp investigators about his previous relationship with Jimmy Smith. He also notes that he himself insisted on showing his face on TV during the Knapp Commission hearings. "They offered me the opportunity to testify from behind a screen or wear a hood. I said no. I got nothin' to hide. You think I would have showed my face on national television if I knew there were witnesses out there who could identify me as the killer?" Even more important, Phillips is offended by the very notion that he would use violence as a means to collect money. "It was never my style. Never. I always believed in doing things the easy way. You got somebody by the balls, you don't need to twist his arm. You say, 'Here's the deal. We got you on this summons. You're gonna pay a big fine, or go to jail, unless you deal with us. So what you wanna do?' It was usually very easy. You don't have to beat anybody up. I'm gonna beat somebody up for money? What, are you crazy? In my whole career, where's the violence? Out of nowhere, I'm gonna go over and execute two people up close, in the most brutal fashion? And, besides, the shooter was left-handed, and I'm right-handed."

As he told me the story, in the living room of his apartment, Phillips hopped up and acted out the killing as it was described in a courtroom nearly four decades ago. He is still haunted by the details, still willing to break it down and make the legal case for his innocence.

There are many people—former prosecutors, retired cops, and senior citizens with long memories—who will never concede that Phillips might not be guilty. But his insistence on re-litigating his case is curious, to say the least. Having testified, as a condition of parole, that he committed the murders, he could easily let that version stand. In fact, by insisting now—in an interview for publication—that he lied to the parole board, Phillips could be jeopardizing his parole and risking a return to prison. As someone who was raised Catholic, Phillips has been given the chance the clear his conscious, to admit to his crimes and cleanse his soul as he prepares to meet his maker. Instead, he contends that "anyone who has ever taken a serious look at my case, aside from the prosecutors, knows I didn't do those murders."

One thing is clear: If Phillips did not do the killings for which he spent nearly a lifetime in prison, his case is one of the great injustices in the history of the New York jurisprudence. A dirty cop comes forward to testify against other dirty cops, only to be framed for a double homicide as payback for violating the Blue Wall of Silence? It's a violation of civil society almost too monstrous to contemplate. In fact, Phillips's conviction, fraught with open-ended legal questions and civil rights issues, was quickly forgotten. Few stepped forward to argue on behalf of Phillips, a notoriously dirty cop. His case fell between the cracks: Phillips was despised by "the system" for exposing a network of graft that included police officers, judges, and politicians. He was disliked by the political left and the counterculture as a symbol of police corruption. And he was loathed by the general public after detailing his own sleazy career as a dirty cop. No one was willing to take up the cause of Bill Phillips. And so he slinked off to prison, and the city and the public alike gladly forgot all about him and his historic role in exposing police corruption in New York City.

For Phillips, one key to understanding his situation came recently, after his release from prison. While working as a janitor at a Veterans Affairs hospital near where he lives, he was approached one day by a man roughly his age who looked familiar. "Hey," said the guy, "you're Bill Phillips, aren't you?"

"Yes," said Phillips.

"Do you remember me? My name is Ernie."

Phillips looked at the man, searched his memory bank. "Yeah. I remember you. You're from the Two-Five precinct. How you doing, Ernie?" At the same time Phillips remembered the face, he recalled that Ernie was one of the cops that was roped into the Knapp investigation. Phillips had named Ernie for taking money, and last he remembered, Ernie had been indicted.

"I'm doing good. Health is good. How are you making out? How'd you do in jail?"

"Well, it was pretty rough, you know. No fucking picnic, but I survived."

"Wow, yeah, I can imagine."

"No, Ernie, you probably can't imagine. But I appreciate you asking."

"Hey, Bill, one thing you should know. There ain't no hard feelings. You did what you had to do. We always thought that we could get caught. How we got caught was unexpected, but what're you gonna do?"

"That's nice, Ernie. Thanks."

"Another thing. Did you know what happened to all of us? The ones who got named? We all got our jobs back. Yeah. We went down to Florida, and in the interim we all got jobs as court officers down there. After you got convicted they called us back, about a year later, and reinstated us. But they wouldn't give the guys their back pay. So you know what I did? I held out and got my back pay. That's how it all played out."

Phillips pondered what Ernie was telling him.

"Anyway," said the old cop from long ago, "good luck to you. Hope to see you again."

"Thanks, Ernie. You're a good guy. Nice talking to you."

Ernie walked away, and Phillips was hit with a rush of emotion. What Ernie had just told him—that the cops who'd been indicted due to his Knapp testimony had all been reinstated—was the final piece of the puzzle. It reconfirmed what he'd always believed was a primary motive behind his conviction. "Nobody went to jail from the Knapp Commission hearings but me!" he says now. "And that was their plan. Their plan was to get me into jail and get me fuckin' killed."

Phillips takes some satisfaction in the fact that he thwarted their plans. "I'm the only cop who survived in general population all those years," he says. So, fuck them.

THE SAGA OF Bill Phillips is one of many dirty threads that had their origins in a time of violence and provisionary justice. Racial hostility was the dominant pattern, police corruption the active ingredient. Historical forces had come together to create a moral cesspool in which cops were assassinated simply for being cops, political activists were framed and unjustly imprisoned, and cops turned against cops as a corrupt police system was exposed and dragged into the light of day. Phillips had been a practitioner of this corruption. He'd attempted to do what he thought was right, and, much like Whitmore and Dhoruba, he had paid a heavy price.

After my long afternoon spent talking with Phillips, he drives me to the train station for my return to New York City. I ask him if he's been to the city since his release from prison.

"No," he says. "I have no real desire to go down there."

He is old now, his hair snow white, his skin pale—nearly translucent—from generations spent behind bars, hidden from the sun.

Not all of Bill Phillips's memories are pleasant, but he is content to be alive, to still be among the walking wounded from the era of the Savage City.

—T.J. English
January 2012

ACKNOWLEDGMENTS

THE EMOTIONAL CONTENT of this era in New York City history is still raw for those who lived through it. I owe a special debt of gratitude to those people on both sides of the divide who agreed to dredge up old and sometimes unpleasant or even traumatic memories. Their stories are now part of history. Many people were helpful in leading me to important sources or pieces of information; I am eternally grateful for their assistance.

Special thanks to Thomas Kelly, who first acquainted me with the Wylie-Hoffert murders; Dred-Scott Keyes of WBAI Radio; Jazz Hayden (the Mayor of Harlem); Judith Regan, who remains a supporter; Myron Beldock; Stephen J. Fearon; Dhoruba Bin Wahad; Robert Boyle; Tom Folsom; Bob Leuci; Sonny Grosso; Cleo Silvers; Shermika Williams, who transcribed many tapes; Kate O'Callaghan; Patrick Farrelly; George Whitmore; Judge Edwin Torres; Willie Rashbaum; Sean Gardiner; Graham Rayman; Carl Ginsburg; Joel Millman; Stacy Leigh; Roger Guenveur Smith, who told me Huey P. Newton stories; Chris Napolitano at *Playboy*; Steven Fishman; Len Levitt; Gerald Lefcourt; Randy Jurgensen; John M. Murtagh; Bill Phillips; and the great Harlem journalist Herb Boyd.

Putting this book together required an obsessive attention to detail, which—as always—can be a strain on personal relationships. I would like to thank those friends and family members who helped lighten the load and remained patient over the course of another long journey. Special thanks to Richard Stratton; Sophia Banda, who kept me strong; Ned Sublette, my literary compañero; the barmaids at the Distinguished Wakamba Cocktail Lounge; Tom Caldarola; Suzanne and Chris Damore; Maureen English; Margi English;

Mike English; Ed English; Philip Rotter; Dino Malcolm; Gh'ail Rhodes-Benjamin; Sandra Maria English; Peter Quinn; Ashley Davis; Ryan Schafer; Kevin Corrigan; and Matt Dillon.

My agents, Nat Sobel and Judith Weber, were invaluable in helping to shape this project at all stages of development. Lisa Gallagher, formerly of William Morrow, saw value in the subject matter immediately and was instrumental in getting things off the ground. Cal Morgan, my editor, brought good taste and a sharp eye to the proceedings; he guided *The Savage City* through the publishing process with a steady hand.

NOTES

The narrative of this book is based on primary sources: interviews with participants, archival documents, and unpublished manuscripts, as well as many of the books, newspaper and magazine articles, reports, transcripts, and law enforcement files listed throughout this section.

In instances where individuals were interviewed numerous times, they are usually listed by date of the first interview.

Abbreviations are used to designate the following institutions and agencies:

Papers of the National Association for the Advancement of Colored People (NAACP Papers)

New York City Municipal Archives (NYCMA)

New York Public Library (NYPL)

Schomburg Center for Research on Black Culture (SCRBC)

Paley Center for Media (PCM)

Vanderbilt University Television News Archives (Vanderbilt TVNA)

NYPD Bureau of Special Services (BOSS)

Organization of African American Unity (OAAU)

Revolutionary Action Movement (RAM)

Black Panther Party (BPP)

Federal Bureau of Investigation Counterintelligence Program (FBI COINTELPRO)

INTRODUCTION

xi **Safest Big City in America:** Mayor Michael Bloomberg of New York City began using this phrase in 2006 to characterize the city's declining crime rate. The term caught on primarily as a marketing tool to promote tourism.

xii   **Crime rates in NYC, 1963 to 1973**: Greenwood, Peter W., *Analysis of the Apprehension Activities of the New York City Police Department.*

xii   **Mechanical cotton picker:** Lemann, Nicholas, *The Promised Land*, pp. 3–6.

xii   **Sharecropping system:** Ibid., pp. 5–6, 11–25; Blackmon, Douglas A., *Slavery by Another Name*, pp. 90–91, 120–121.

xiii   **The black migration:** Lemann, *The Promised Land*, pp. 6–7; Biondi, Martha, *To Stand and Fight*, pp. 5–11, 28–31.

xiv   *My Father's Gun:* McDonald, Brian, *My Father's Gun*, pp. 14–27; interview with Brian McDonald (February 4, 2010).

xv   **The Lyons Law:** McDonald, *My Father's Gun*, p. 19.

xv   **McDonald's father:** Interview with Brian McDonald (February 4, 2010).

xvi   **Police brutality in NYC:** Biondi, *To Stand and Fight*, pp. 70–74.

xvi   **Forty-six unarmed African Americans killed by police:** Ibid., p. 60.

xvi   **"Lynching, Northern style":** Ibid.

xvi   **Harlem riot of 1943:** Ibid.; Jackson, Kenneth T. (ed.), *Encyclopedia of New York*, p. 124.

xvii   **Hinton Johnson incident:** Goldman, Peter Louis, *The Death and Life of Malcolm X*, pp. 56–49.

xix   **"A boiler that is allowed":** Cannato, Vincent J., *The Ungovernable City*, p. 166.

xx   **NYC crime statistics:** New York State Division of Criminal Justice Services, statistical analysis of seven major crime groups, 1963–1973.

1. BLOOD OF THE LAMB

3   **Martin Luther King Jr. stabbing incident:** "Dr. King, Negro Leader, Stabbed by Woman in a Store in Harlem," *New York Times*, September 21, 1958; "Martin Luther King Stabbed," *New York Daily News*, September 21, 1958; Branch, Taylor, *Parting the Waters*, pp. 243–245.

4   **New Yorkers depart for March on Washington, D.C.:** "Cars, Buses, Trains, and Planes Taking New Yorkers to Capital," *New York Times*, August 28, 1963; Petersen, Anna, "80,000 Lunches Made Here by Volunteers for Washington Marchers," *New York Times*, August 28, 1963; Hansen, Drew D., *The Dream*, pp. 25–27.

5   **The March on Washington:** "Gentle Army Occupies Capital; Politeness Is Order of the Day," *New York Times*, August 29, 1963; "Wagner Hails March; Cites Whites' Turnout," *New York Times*, August 29, 1963; Jones, Theodore, "Tired New Yorkers Head Home Full of Praise for Capital Rally," *New York Times*, August 29, 1963; "Rights Marchers Tell of Feelings," *New York*

Times, September 2, 1963; *Eyes on the Prize*, PBS documentary; Hansen, *The Dream*, pp. 1–64; Branch, *Parting the Waters*, pp. 833–864.

6–7 **"I have a dream" speech:** *Eyes on the Prize*, PBS documentary; Hansen, *The Dream*, entire book; Branch, *Parting the Waters*, pp. 846–887. Speech was broadcast in its entirety on Martin Luther King Jr. Day, January 19, 2010 (text version transcribed directly from audio by the author).

6 **The speech on television:** Adams, Val, "TV: Coverage of March," *New York Times*, August 29, 1963.

7 **"My name is Patricia Tolles":** Lefkowitz, Bernard, and Kenneth Gross, *The Victims*, p. 28; Raab, Selwyn, *Justice in the Back Room*, p. 14.

8 **Wylie-Hoffert crime scene:** Doyle, Patrick, and Sidney Kline, "2 Career Girls Found Savagely Slain," *Daily News*, August 29, 1963; "2 Girls Murdered in E. 88th St. Flat," *New York Times*, August 29, 1963; Lefkowitz and Gross, *The Victims*, pp. 29–37; Raab, *Justice in the Back Room*, pp. 14–15.

9 **Detective Lynch's notebook:** Lefkowitz and Gross, *The Victims*, pp. 34–35.

11 **"This is not the way humans should die":** Ibid., p. 37.

12 **"We don't even know":** Doyle and Kline, *Daily News*, August 29, 1963.

13 **George Whitmore background:** Interview with George Whitmore (April 3, 2009); interview with Gerald Whitmore (June 18, 2009); interview with Myron Beldock (January 27, 2009); interview with Selwyn Raab (April 22, 2009); Lefkowitz and Gross, *The Victims*, pp. 179–196.

14 **"The Negro is a sort of seventh son":** Du Bois, W. E. B., *The Souls of Black Folks*, p. 7.

14 **"I never did like big cities":** Lefkowitz and Gross, *The Victims*, p. 179.

14 **"I remember the night, that summer":** Ibid.

14 **"He was mean":** Ibid.

15 **"Sometimes you think they're all the same":** Ibid.

15 **Pig slaughter incident:** Ibid.; interview with George Whitmore (April 3, 2009).

15 **Sammy Davis Jr. in Wildwood:** Lefkowitz and Gross, *The Victims*, pp. 184–185.

16 **"I was a man who had one rule":** Ibid.; More on George Whitmore Sr. from: interview with George Whitmore (April 3, 2009); interview with Gerald Whitmore (June 18, 2009).

16 **Lieutenant Parker Johnson:** Lefkowitz and Gross, *The Victims*, pp. 193–194.

2. BUSINESS AS USUAL

18   **Detective Phillips and Wylie-Hoffert case:** Shecter, Leonard, with William Phillips, *On the Pad*, p. 384; Talese, Gay, "Air of Fear Grips Sedate East Side," *New York Times*, August 31, 1963.

19   **"Responded to a DOA with Kenny":** Shecter with Phillips, *On the Pad*, pp. 97–98.

19   **William R. Phillips Sr.:** Ibid.

20   **"There were many young cadets":** Ibid.

20   ·**Phillips's early career:** William Phillips, Knapp Commission testimony, October 18, 1971; Shecter with Phillips, *On the Pad*, pp. 50–75; Burton, Anthony, "How to Be a Corrupt Cop & Live to Tell," *Daily News*, October 20, 1970; interview with Mike Armstrong (August 12, 2009).

20   **"I jumped out":** Shecter with Phillips, *On the Pad*, pp. 83–84.

21   **"I told him I caught this guy":** Ibid.

21   **He comes back with ten dollars:** Ibid.

22   **"When you first get to a precinct":** Ibid.

24   **The prosecuter looked at Phillips:** Ibid.

24   **David Durk:** Lardner, James, *Crusader;* Lardner, James, and Thomas Repetto, *NYPD*, pp. 265–267, 272–274, 306–307; Levitt, Leonard, *NYPD Confidential*, pp. 34–35; Maas, Peter, *Serpico*, pp. 114, 189–93.

25   **Max and Philip Wylie:** Tomasson, Robert E., "In the Shadow of Brother," *New York Times*, September 23, 1975; Lefkowitz and Gross, *The Victims*, pp. 136–139

25   **Wylie-Hoffert investigation:** Cassidy, Joseph, and Henry Lee, "Seek an Ex-Admirer to Throw Some Light on Killing of 2 Girls," *Daily News*, 30, 1963; Bigart, Homer, "Killing of 2 Girls Yields No Clue; Police Question 500 in a Month," *New York Times*, September 27, 1963; Lefkowitz and Gross, *The Victims*, pp. 1–168; Raab, *Justice in the Back Room*, pp. 1–121.

26   **"There is a complete lack of physical evidence":** Bigart, *New York Times*, September 27, 1963.

26   **"The police, under intense pressure":** Ibid.

27   "Career Girls, Watch Your Step": Lefkowitz and Gross, *The Victims*, p. 135; ; Raab, *Justice in the Back Room*, p. 31.

27   **Heroin in Harlem:** Interview with Joseph "Jazz" Hayden (December 19, 2008); Brown, Claude, *Manchild in the Promised Land*, entire book; Cannato, *The Ungovernable City*, pp. 527, 534–535; Jackson, Kenneth T. (ed.), *Encyclopedia of New York City*, pp. 123–124; Haley, Alex, *Autobiography of Malcolm X*, pp. 155–156.

28   **"Around 1955, everybody wanted a slick bitch":** Brown, *Manchild in the Promised Land*, p. 193.

29　**JFK assassination:** The books, documentaries, and official investigations of the assassination are voluminous. A presentation of the racial climate surrounding events leading up to November 22, 1963, can be found in Branch, *Parting the Waters*, pp. 922–927.

29　**"We preach freedom around the world":** Branch, *Parting the Waters*, pp. 913–916; *Eyes on the Prize* (PBS documentary).

31　**"I know I should take into consideration":** Lefkowitz and Gross, *The Victims*, p. 191.

31　**Whitmore parting with mother:** Interview with George Whitmore (April 3, 2009); Lefkowitz and Gross, *The Victims*, p. 196.

3. THE BOWELS OF BROOKLYN

33　**Whitmore arrival in Brownsville:** Interview with George Whitmore (April 3, 2009); Lefkowitz and Gross, *The Victims*, pp. 197–199; Shapiro, *Whitmore*, pp. 9–11, 34–35.

33　**"By every number we have":** Connolly, Harold X., *A Ghetto Grows in Brooklyn*, p. 28; in addition, see Judge, Joseph B., "Brownsville: A Neighborhood in Trouble," *Dissent*, September/October 1966.

34　**Whitmore encounter with Patrolman Isola:** Interview with George Whitmore (April 3, 2009); interview with Jerome Leftow (February 17, 2009); interview with Myron Beldock; interview with Selwyn Raab; Lefkowitz and Gross, *The Victims*, pp. 211–213; Raab, *Justice in the Back Room*, pp. 37–40; Shapiro, *Whitmore*, pp. 2–6; Shapiro, Fred C., "Annals of Jurisprudence: The Whitmore Confession," *The New Yorker*, February 8, 1969.

36　**Seventy-third Precinct station house:** Viewed by author, June 2009. The building still stands, though it is vacant, boarded up, and has the look of a crumbling haunted house. A new Seventy-third Precinct station house opened in 1983, a few blocks from the old location.

37　**Details of Borrero identification of Whitmore:** Interview with George Whitmore (April 3, 2009); interview with Jerome Leftow (February 17, 2009); interview with Myron Beldock (January 27, 2009); interview with Selwyn Raab (April 22, 2009); Lefkowitz and Gross, *The Victims*, pp. 222–223; Shapiro, *Whitmore*, pp. 18–20; Raab, *Justice in the Back Room*, pp. 35–37; Shapiro, "Annals of Jurisprudence: The Whitmore Confession," *The New Yorker*, February 8, 1969.

43　**The "Third Degree":** McGill, T. O., "Third Degree in Police Parlance," *New York Times*, October 6, 1901.

45　**Details of Whitmore confession:** Interview with George Whitmore (April 3, 2009); interview with Jerome Leftow (February 17, 2009); interview with Selwyn Raab (April 22, 2009); interview with Myron Beldock (January 27, 2009); Roland, Charles, and Mel Juffe, "How Police Broke Wylie

Case: Step-by-Step Account," *Journal-American*, April 26, 1964; Lefkowitz and Gross, *The Victims*, pp. 215–249; Shapiro, *Whitmore*, pp. 14–68; Raab, *Justice in the Back Room*, pp. 41–53; Shapiro, "Annals of Jurisprudence: The Whitmore Confession," *The New Yorker*, February 8, 1969.

51   **Whitmore statement taken by ADA Koste:** Shapiro, *Whitmore*, pp. 52–58; Lefkowitz and Gross, *The Victims*, pp. 294–322; Raab, *Justice in the Back Room*, pp. 75–116 (Raab, in his book, publishes Whitmore's statement to Koste in its entirety).

52   **Reporters and photographers feast on Whitmore:** Shapiro, *Whitmore*, pp. 63–64.

55   **Whitmore appearance before Judge Comerford:** Interview with George Whitmore (April 3, 2009); interview with Jerome Leftow (February 17, 2009); interview with Selwyn Raab (April 22, 2009); Lefkowitz and Gross, *The Victims*, pp. 343–348. For a detailed profile of Judge James J. Comerford, see Trillin, Calvin, "American Chronicles: Democracy in Action," *The New Yorker*, March 21, 1988; *The Marcus-Nelson Murders*, Universal Studios/CBS Television movie. The scene of the Whitmore character before the arraignment judge in *The Marcus-Nelson Murders* is taken from actual transcripts of George Whitmore's appearance before Judge Comerford.

4. "GET THOSE NIGGERS"

58   **Bin Wahad reads newspaper accounts of Whitmore case:** Interview with Dhoruba Bin Wahad (September 16, 2008).

59   **Newspaper headlines:** Kanter, Nathan, and Henry Lee, "Confession: Stumbled into Killing Two," *Daily News*, April 26, 1964; Federici, William, and Lester Abelman, "Cops Had Questions, Say Only He Had the Answers," *Daily News*, April 26, 1964; *Journal American*; Buckley, Thomas, "Youth Is Accused in Wylie Slaying," *New York Times*, April 26, 1964.

60   **Bin Wahad upbringing in the Bronx:** Interview with Dhoruba Bin Wahad (September 16, 2008).

60   **"Back then, before heroin":** Ibid.

60   **Operation 42:** Freeman, Ira Henry, "Police Plan Nips Delinquency," *New York Times*, August 15, 1956.

61   **Youth gangs in NYC:** Bennett, Charles G., "$50,000 Allocated to Fight Teen-Age Gangs in Bronx," *New York Times*, May 13, 1955; Schumach, Murray, "Police Seek Curb on Youth Crime in a 5-Year Plan," *New York Times*, June 2, 1955; Knowles, Clayton, "Police Head Bars Pacts with Gangs," *New York Times*, August 16, 1956; Kihss, Peter, "4 Negro Areas Get Extra Police Units," *New York Times*, July 16, 1959.

61   **"The cops who used to patrol":** Interview with Dhoruba Bin Wahad (September 16, 2008).

61   **"A race riot could cause more destruction":** Kihss, *New York Times*, July 16, 1959.

61   **Jitterbugging and zip guns:** "19 in Teen Gangs Seized in Bronx," *New York Times*, November 10, 1957. A fictional but realistic depiction of early 1960s Bronx gang life can be found in *The Wanderers* (1973), the debut novel by Richard Price.

61   **"I lived not far from Yankee Stadium":** Interview with Dhoruba Bin Wahad (September 16, 2008).

61   **Bin Wahad family background:** Ibid.; Bin Wahad, Dhoruba, "The Future Past; A Biostory" (unpublished manuscript).

63   **Morris and McKinley housing projects:** Jackson, Kenneth T. (ed.), *Encyclopedia of New York*, pp. 568–569.

63   **Bin Wahad experiences in U.S. Army:** Interview with Dhoruba Bin Wahad (September 16, 2008).

64   **Bin Wahad shooting incident and arrest:** Ibid.; Richard Moore criminal rap sheet in FBI COINTELPRO file.

65   **"The racism that existed in the prison system":** Interview with Dhoruba Bin Wahad (September 16, 2008).

65   **Description of the Box:** Ibid.

66   **Writings of J. A. Rogers:** For a cogent analysis of the work of J. A. Rogers, see Sandoval, Valerie, "The Brand of History: A Historiographic Account of the Work of J. A. Rogers," *SCRBC Journal* 4 (Spring 1978).

66   **"We declare our right on this earth":** Breitman, George (ed.), *Malcolm X Speaks*, p. 175.

67   **Whitmore at Bellevue Hospital:** Interview with George Whitmore (April 3, 2009); interview with Jerome Leftow (February 17, 2009); Shapiro, *Whitmore*, pp. 80–85; Lefkowitz and Gross, *The Victims*, pp. 358–363; Raab, *Justice in the Back Room*, pp. 126–129.

67   **"I have never been in trouble in my life":** Lefkowitz and Gross, *The Victims*, p. 359.

68   **"I asked Whitmore, 'Were you beaten?'":** Interview with Jerome Leftow (February 17, 2009); Lefkowitz and Gross, *The Victims*, p. 349.

68   **Psychiatric assessment: "He is without guile":** Lefkowitz and Gross, *The Victims*, p. 360; Shapiro, *Whitmore*, p. 90; Raab, *Justice in the Back Room*, p. 127.

69   **Use of "truth serum":** Interview with Jerome Leftow (February 17, 2009); Lefkowitz and Gross, *The Victims*, pp. 361–362.

69   **"It broke every rule of self-incrimination":** Interview with Jerome Leftow (February 17, 2009).

69   **Civil Rights Act of 1964:** Branch, *Pillar of Fire*, pp. 358–359, 387–388.

70   "This past, the Negro's past": Baldwin, James, *The Fire Next Time*, p. 125.

70   **The riots of July 1964:** The most detailed account of the riots in Harlem and Brooklyn is in *Race Riots: New York 1964* by Fred C. Shapiro and James W. Sullivan; Montgomery, Paul L., and Francis X. Clines, "Thousands Riot in Harlem Area; Scores Are Hurt; Negroes Loot Stores, Taunt Whites—Police Shoot in Air to Control Crowd," *New York Times*, July 22, 1964; interview with Robert Leuci (February 12, 2009); interview with Joseph "Jazz" Hayden (December 19, 2008); Leuci, Robert, *All the Centurions*, pp. 59–63; Lardner and Reppetto, *NYPD*, pp. 253–255; "Who Pays for Riots," *Time*, August 7, 1964; "Gilligan on Duty, Precinct Secret," *New York Times*, November 12, 1964.

72   **William Epton:** A well-known Harlem activist who espoused a kind of street-corner communism, Epton would eventually be arrested, charged, and convicted for inciting the '64 riots and conspiring "to overthrow the New York State government." His lawyer claimed that he was being made into a scapegoat. Johnston, Richard J. H., "Jury Selected in Trial of Epton Resulting from Riots in Harlem," *New York Times*, November 27, 1965; Johnston, Richard J. H., "Plan for Revolt Is Laid to Epton," *New York Times*, December 1, 1965; Johnston, Richard J. H., "Epton Convicted on Riot Charges," *New York Times*, December 21, 1965; Roth, Jack, "Epton Gets Year in Anarchy Case; Harlem Leader Defends Views," *New York Times*, January 28, 1966.

73   **"The noise was incredible":** Interview with Robert Leuci (February 12, 2009); Leuci, *All the Centurions*, p. 61.

73   **Tactical Patrol Force (TPF):** Interview with Robert Leuci (February 12, 2009); Leuci, *All the Centurions*, pp. 67–68; Lardner and Reppetto, *NYPD*, pp. 254–255, 275; Lardner, *Crusader*, pp. 173–174, 181.

74   **"There were no social services in these neighborhoods":** Interview with Robert Leuci (February 12, 2009).

74   **"They hated us":** Ibid.

74   **"I walked in on a lot of beatings":** Ibid.

75   **Incident on 125th Street with Leuci and two Nation of Islam people:** Ibid.

75   **"A young man, barefoot, muscular":** Leuci, *All the Centurions*, p. 62.

76   **Mayor Wagner on television:** Shapiro and Sullivan, *Race Riots: New York 1964*, p. 158.

77   **"Sure, we make mistakes . . . You do in a war":** Benson, Barbara, "Why Harlem Riots; Indignities and Sadism at Hands of Police Charged," *New York Times*, July 22, 1964; Samuels, Gertrude, "Who Shall Judge a Policeman?:

Out of Negro Riots Have Come Persistent Charges of Police Brutality," *New York Times Magazine*, August 2, 1964.

77   **"I know there was more than one dead":** Interview with Robert Leuci (February 12, 2009).

5. GETTING FLOPPED

78   **Leftow's preparations for trial:** Interview with Jerome Leftow (February 17, 2009).

78   **Revelation that photo was not Janice Wylie:** Ibid.; interview with Selwyn Raab (April 22, 2009); Lefkowitz and Gross, *The Victims*, pp. 375–377; Shapiro, *Whitmore*, pp. 86–88; Raab, *Justice in the Back Room*, pp. 170–173; Zion, Sidney E., "The Suspect Confesses—But Who Believes Him?" *New York Times Magazine*, May 16, 1965; Shapiro, "Annals of Jurisprudence: The Whitmore Confession," *The New Yorker*, February 8, 1969.

79   **Whitmore alibi:** Interview with George Whitmore (April 3, 2009); Lefkowitz and Gross, *The Victims*, pp. 377–378; Shapiro, *Whitmore*, p. 95; Raab, *Justice in the Back Room*, pp. 171–172.

80   **ADA Glass meeting with Det. Bulger:** Cunningham, Barry, with Mike Pearl, *Mr. District Attorney*, pp. 95–98; Lefkowitz and Gross, *The Victims*, p. 368; Raab, *Justice in the Back Room*, p. 193; Shapiro, *Whitmore*, pp. 174–175.

82   **"If George were only being charged":** Interview with Jerome Leftow (February 17, 2009).

82   **Leftow meeting with ADA Koste and ADA Herman:** Interview with Jerome Leftow (February 17, 2009).

83   **"I guess you could say I was raised prejudiced":** Shecter with Phillips, *On the Pad*, p. 126.

84   **"I was about three or four years old":** Ibid.

84   **Police use of the term *mau mau*:** Burnham, James, "From a Cold War Notebook," *National Review*, October 29, 1964; McDonald, Brian, *My Father's Gun*, p. 16; interview with Brian McDonald (February 4, 2010); interview with Robert Leuci (February 12, 2009).

85   **Malcolm X on the Mau Mau Rebellion in Kenya:** Breitman (ed.), *Malcolm X Speaks*, pp. 106–107.

86   **Police as protectors against marauding Negro hordes:** The role of police as protectors against arriving waves of poor blacks from the South and impoverished Puerto Rican immigrants was touched upon by nearly every ex-cop I interviewed for this book. Most cops viewed the issue in terms of lawlessness and degradation of community standards. To blacks and Puerto Ricans, it seemed as though the police were racists. The police doubtless saw themselves as fulfilling their traditional role as protectors of property, in this case real

estate interests and property owners. Interview with Robert Leuci (February 12, 2009); interview with Brian McDonald; interview with Sonny Grosso (April 13, 2009); interview with Randy Jurgensen (February 12, 2010); interview with Robert Daley (January 21, 2010); interview with Eddie Ellis (May 15, 2009); interview with Joseph "Jazz" Hayden (December 19, 2008).

86   **Phillips and Kenny Keller:** Shecter with Phillips, *On the Pad*, p. 105.

87   **"[Madden] had all kinds of tricks up his sleeve":** Shecter with Phillips, *On the Pad*, p. 106.

87   **Phillips as "conditions man":** Ibid.

88   **Attitude of Phillips's wife:** Shecter with Phillips, *On the Pad*, p. 171.

88   **"We're working on a big swindle":** Shecter with Phillips, *On the Pad*, p. 154.

89   **"It's about eight o'clock in the morning":** Ibid.

89   **"Fun City":** The term "Fun City" was a public relations ploy devised to bolster the image of New York City. The term was embraced by, and became prevalent, during the early years of the Lindsay administration. As the city became more crime-ridden and decayed throughout the 1960s, the term was sometimes used derisively. Cannatto, *The Ungovernable City*, p. 146; *Fun City Revisited: The Lindsay Years*, PBS documentary.

90   **Phillips gets "flopped":** Ibid.; Knapp Commission Hearings testimony; Schultz, Ray, "Anatomy of a Murder Trial: The People v. William Phillips," *New York Times Magazine*, December 17, 1972; Daley, Robert, *Target Blue*, p. 402.

91   **"I was completely demoralized":** Shecter with Phillips, *On the Pad*, p. 174.

91   **Harlem as source of plunder for corrupt police:** Interview with Robert Leuci (February 12, 2009); interview with Edwin Torres (April 13, 2009); interview with Joseph "Jazz" Hayden (December 19, 2008); interview with Eddie Ellis (May 15, 2009); Shecter with Phillips, *On the Pad*, pp. 87, 176–186.

91   **"The first thing to do in a new precinct":** Shecter with Phillips, *On the Pad*, p. 177.

92   **"I got fucked all over the precinct":** Ibid.

92   **Officer Egbert Brown:** Ibid.

6. ON THE BUTTON

94   **"I knew I hadn't done nothin' wrong":** Interview with George Whitmore (April 3, 2009).

94   **Leftow preparations for Borrero trial:** Interview with Jerome Leftow (February 17, 2009).

96   **Borrero trial:** Interview with George Whitmore (April 4, 2009); interview with Jerome Leftow (February 17, 2009); interview with Selwyn Raab (April 22, 2009); Lefkowitz and Gross, *The Victims*, pp. 418–440; Shapiro, *Whitmore*, pp. 90–92, 94–103; Raab, *Justice in the Back Room*, pp. 131–144; Shapiro, "Annals of Jursiprudence: The Whitmore Confession," *The New Yorker*, February 8, 1969; *The Marcus-Nelson Murders*, Universal Studios/CBS Television movie.

101   **"I don't think I will be a free man soon":** Shapiro, *Whitmore*, pp. 100–101. Whitmore's correspondence with John Lawrence, who had briefly been an inmate at Bellevue Psychiatric Hospital while George was there, is detailed throughout *Whitmore*.

101   **Leftow summation:** Lefkowitz and Gross, *The Victims*, pp. 431–433; Raab, *Justice in the Back Room*, pp. 141–142.

102   **Lichtman summation ("on the button"):** Shapiro, *Whitmore*, p. 102; Lefkowitz and Gross, *The Victims*, pp. 433–435; Raab, *Justice in the Back Room*, p. 142; interview with Selwyn Raab (April 22, 2009).

102   **Whitmore found guilty:** McNamara, Joseph, "Career Girls' Slaying Suspect Convicted in B'klyn Rape Try," *Daily News*, November 19, 1964; interview with George Whitmore (April 3, 2009).

102   **"I was shocked":** Interview with Gerald Whitmore (June 18, 2009).

102   **"This helps to dispose of the police brutality charge":** Shapiro, *Whitmore*, p. 103; Lefkowitz and Gross, *The Victims*, p. 436; Raab, *Justice in the Back Room*, p. 143.

103   **Case of William Coleman:** Benjamin, Philip, "Confession Cases May Rise Sharply," *New York Times*, February 15, 1965.

103   **Selwyn Raab background:** Interview with Selwyn Raab (April 22, 2009); "The Original Kojak," *Time*, November 24, 1974.

103   **Raab investigation of Borrero jury:** Interview with Selwyn Raab (April 22, 2009); interview with Jerome Leftow (February 17, 2009).

103   **Existence of FBI lab report about the button:** Lefkowitz and Gross, *The Victims*, p. 441; Shapiro, *Whitmore*, pp. 107–108; Raab, *Justice in the Back Room*, p. 173; Shapiro, "Annals of Jurisprudence: The Whitmore Confession," *The New Yorker*, February 8, 1969.

105   **Raab's *Harper's* article killed by Hogan:** Interview with Selwyn Raab (April 22, 2009); Mayer, Martin, "'Hogan's Office' Is a Kind of Ministry of Justice," *New York Times*, July 23, 1967.

105   **Raab contacts Mrs. Birdine Whitmore:** Interview with Selwyn Raab (April 22, 2009).

105 **Mrs. Whitmore retains Miller and Kaplan:** Shapiro, *Whitmore*, pp. 105–106; Lefkowitz and Gross, *The Victims*, pp. 438–439; Raab, *Justice in the Back Room*, pp. 146–147.

106 **Attorney Stanley Reiben:** Lefkowitz and Gross, *The Victims*, pp. 437–447.

106 **Ricky Robles targeted as Wylie-Hoffert killer:** Ibid.; Jones, Theodore, "Police Doubted Whitmore Story," *New York Times*, November 9, 1965; "Two Lives for a Fix," *Time*, December 10, 1965.

108 **Lt. Thomas Cavanaugh background:** Van Gelder, Lawrence, "Thomas J. Cavanagh, Jr., 82, Who Inspired 'Kojak,' Dies," *New York Times*, August 4, 1996; Lefkowitz and Gross, *The Victims*, p. 486.

108 **Cavanaugh puts squeeze on Robles:** Lefkowitz and Gross, *The Victims*, pp. 486, 488–494; Shapiro, *Whitmore*, p. 115; Raab, *Justice in the Back Room*, pp. 191–192, 211–212.

109 **Robles confession:** Ibid.; Roth, Jack, "Wylie Case Arrest Is Based on Tapes," *New York Times*, January 29, 1965.

110 **NAACP involvement:** NAACP Papers, Whitmore file (SCRBC); "N.A.A.C.P. Seeks to Aid Whitmore in Rape Case," *New York Times*, January 9, 1965; Benjamin, Philip, "N.A.A.C.P. Presses Aid to Whitmore," *New York Times*, February 9, 1965; Kaplan, Samuel, "N.A.A.C.P. Seeking Reopening of Case," *New York Times*, February 13, 1965; "George Whitmore Jr.'s 'Confession,'" *The Crisis*, March 1965; Lefkowitz and Gross, *The Victims*, pp. 390–392; Shapiro, *Whitmore*, pp. 108–109, 118–119.

111 **Telegram to Gov. Rockefeller:** NAACP Papers, Whitmore file (SCRBC).

112 **Whitmore receives glasses at Sing Sing prison:** Interview with George Whitmore (April 3, 2009).

7. HARLEM NOCTURNE

113 **Malcolm X television interview:** CBS News, January 1965.

113 **Malcolm X split with Elijah Muhammad:** Haley, *Autobiography of Malcolm X*, pp. 290, 301–317; Breitman (ed.), *Malcolm X Speaks*, the chapter entitled "Declaration of Independence," pp. 18–22.

114 **Assassination of Malcolm X:** Breslin, Jimmy, "Malcolm X Slain by Gunmen as 400 in Ballroom Watch," *Herald Tribune*, February 22, 1965; Breitman, George, Herman Porter, and Baxter Smith, *The Assassination of Malcolm X*, entire book.

115 **Bin Wahad reaction to assassination:** Interview with Dhoruba Bin Wahad (September 16, 2008).

115 **Richard Moore becomes Dhoruba:** Ibid.

115   **Bin Wahad's readings in prison:** Ibid.

116   **"I definitely had a bad attitude":** Ibid.

116   **Bin Wahad before State Parole Board:** Ibid.

117   **Ossie Davis eulogy of Malcolm X:** The author listened to a recording of the eulogy at SCBR, January 21, 2010.

117   **Eddie Ellis background:** Interview with Eddie Ellis (May 15, 2009); Widener, Pam, "Eddie Ellis at Large," *Prison Life*, October 1996.

118   **Mosque Number Seven burned down:** "Muslim Mosque Burns in Harlem Blast Reported," *New York Times*, February 23, 1965; Kihss, Peter, "Mosque Fires Stir Fear of Vendetta in Malcolm Case," *New York Times*, February 24, 1965.

118   **"There was a lot of anger and frustration":** Interview with Eddie Ellis (May 15, 2009).

118   **Kitty Genovese murder:** Rosenthal, A. M., *Thirty-eight Witnesses*, entire book.

119   **"City in Crisis":** *New York Herald Tribune*, January 25, 1965. The series ran until spring, with articles under differing bylines. The subtitle of the series was "New York, Greatest City in the World—And Everything Is Wrong with It." For general mood of the city at the time, see also Lindsay, John, "Can New York Be Saved," *Saturday Evening Post*, October 9, 1965; Nichols, Mary Perot, "Is There a Chance for New York City?" *Village Voice*, October 28, 1965.

120   **"Something has gone out of the heart and soul of New York City":** Cannato, *The Ungovernable City*, p. 61; *Fun City Revisited: The Lindsay Years*, PBS documentary.

120   **"No problem facing New York City":** Ibid.

120   **"What is happening" (Buckley quote):** Cannato, *The Ungovernable City*, p. 62.

120   **Buckley announced candidacy:** Ibid.

120   **"Every time a judge and jury":** Breslin, Jimmy, and Dick Schaap, "The Lonely Crimes," *Herald Tribune*, October 25–29, 1965.

121   **"It's ten o'clock":** Cannato, *The Ungovernable City*, p. 163.

121   **Attitudes of cops toward Lindsay:** Interview with Sonny Grosso (May 13, 2009); interview with Randy Jurgensen (February 12, 2010); interview with Robert Daley (January 21, 2010); interview with Brian McDonald (February 4, 2010); interview with Michael Armstrong (August 12, 2009); Murphy, Patrick V., and Thomas Plate, *Commissioner*, p. 38.

121   **"It was just part of the job":** Shecter with Phillips, *On the Pad*, p. 212.

122   **"I've seen a guy brought in":** Ibid.

122 **"arms outstretched like Jesus Christ":** Interview with Robert Leuci (February 12, 2009).

122 **"I mean, I'm not a merciful guy":** Shecter with Phillips, *On the Pad*, p. 213

122 **The flake:** Ibid.; interview with Edwin Torres (April 13, 2009).

122 **Numbers racket in Harlem:** Grutzner, Charles, "Dimes Make Millions for Numbers Racket," *New York Times*, June 28, 1964; Powledge, Fred, "Pick a Number from 000 to 999," *New York Times Magazine*, December 6, 1964; Johnson, Thomas A., "Numbers Called Harlem's Balm," *New York Times*, March 1, 1971; Leuci, *The New Centurions*, p. 305. Writes Leuci: "A Harlem captain once told me that there were forty policy number drops in one Harlem division alone. To operate, they paid one hundred dollars a day, 365 days a year. Do the math. . . . The money was major, the backbone and heart of corruption in New York City. The pad went all the way up, right through police headquarters into the mayor's office."

123 **French Connection narcotics theft:** Blumenthal, Ralph, "Mobster Makes Offer on French Connection Case," *New York Times*, February 22, 2009; Leuci, *All the Centurions*, pp. 312–316, 318, 331; Lardner and Reppetto, *NYPD*, p. 269; Murphy and Plate, *Commissioner*, p. 116.

123 **Adam Clayton Powell Jr. accuses NYPD of corruption:** Grutzner, Charles, "Powell Is Called a Liar by Police," *New York Times*, February 20, 1965; "Powell Tells of Threats on Life Over Crime Expose," *New York Times*, March 4, 1965.

124 **Harry Gross gambling scandal:** Lardner and Plate, *NYPD*, pp. 224, 261–265, 276; Cunningham, Barry, with Mike Pearl, *Mr. District Attorney*, p. 163.

124 **Phillips connection to Freddy Clark:** Shecter with Phillips, *On the Pad*, pp. 222–224.

124 **"I go over to see Freddy for Christmas":** Ibid.

125 **Freddy Clark homicide:** Ibid.

125 **Phillips approaches Grosso with score:** Interview with Sonny Grosso (April 13, 2009).

126 **"Phillips was a good cop":** Interview with Edwin Torres (April 13, 2009).

126 **Phillips approaches Torres:** Ibid.

127 **Dick Gregory at Antioch Baptist Church:** "Negroes Blamed in Lag on Rights," *New York Times*, February 15, 1965; Shapiro, *Whitmore*, pp. 125–126.

127 **NAACP involvement with Coleman and Everett cases:** NAACP Papers, Whitmore file (SCRBC); Zion, Sidney, "Death Row Convict Lays Confession to Beating," *New York Times*, April 1, 1965.

128 **"The police have apparently" (NAACP statement):** Zion, Sidney E., "Inquiry Sought in Whitmore Case," *New York Times*, April 3, 1965.

129 **Whitmore accepted at Walt Disney School:** Interview with George Whitmore (April 3, 2009); Shapiro, "Annals of Jurisprudence: The Whitmore Confessions," *The New Yorker*, February 8, 1969; Lefkowitz and Gross, *The Victims*, pp. 189–190.

129 **Whitmore draws Malcolm X portraits at Sing Sing:** Interview with George Whitmore (April 3, 2009).

129 **Hearing before Judge Malbin:** Shapiro, *Whitmore*, pp. 131–132; Lefkowitz and Gross, *The Victims*, pp. 442–445; Shapiro, "Annals of Jurisprudence: The Whitmore Confessions," *The New Yorker*, February 8, 1969.

129 **Gerald Corbin affidavit:** Ibid.

130 **Judge Malbin questions juror:** Interview with Selwyn Raab (April 22, 2009); Shapiro, "Annals of Jurisprudence: The Whitmore Confessions," *The New Yorker*, February 8, 1969; Shapiro, *Whitmore*, pp. 211–212; Lefkowitz and Gross, *The Victims*, p. 444; Raab, *Justice in the Back Room*, pp. 193–194.

130 **Gerald Corbin testimony:** Ibid.

131 **Judge Malbin questions Lichtman:** Ibid.

132 **"The hearing revealed that prejudice and racial bias" (Judge Malbin ruling):** Ibid.

132 **Borrero conviction thrown out:** Ibid.

8. FATHERS AND SONS

133 **NAACP history:** Jonas, Gilbert, *Freedom's Sword*, entire book; Branch, *Parting the Waters*, pp. 49–53, 189, 190, 847–849; Branch, *Pillar of Fire*, pp. 271–274, 423–425; Biondi, *To Stand and Fight*, pp. 23–28, 112–113, 201.

133 **"To promote equality of rights" (NAACP charter):** NAACP official website.

135 **"I am positive that the police":** Roth, Jack, "'Confessions' Laid to Police," *New York Times*, January 28, 1965.

135 **"Call it what you want":** Ibid.

136 **Minnie Edmonds case (pretrial Hundley hearing):** Shapiro, *Whitmore*, pp. 137–146; Lefkowitz and Gross, *The Victims*, pp. 510–513.

137 **Whitmore at Hundley hearing:** Interview with George Whitmore (April 3, 2009).

138 **Minnie Edmonds trial:** Ibid.

141 **"Any person who claims to have deep feelings":** Haley, *Autobiography of Malcolm X*, p. 112. Also on effects of incarceration, see Vaught, Seneca, "Narrow Cells and Lost Keys: The Impact of Jails and Prisons on Black Protest, 1940–1972" (Ph.D. dissertation, Bowling Green State University, December 2006).

141 **Bin Wahad at Coxsackie, Comstock, and Green Haven prisons:** Interview with Dhoruba Bin Wahad (September 16, 2008).

142 **Bin Wahad encounter with his father at Green Haven prison:** Ibid.

142 **"The meeting was kind of routine":** Ibid.

143 **Background on Collins Moore:** Ibid.

144 **Bin Wahad sent to the Box:** Ibid.

145 **"This is the year of Whitmore":** Benjamin, Phillip, "Confessions Cases May Rise Sharply," *New York Times*, February 15, 1965; Shapiro, *Whitmore*, p. 165; Lefkowitz and Gross, *The Victims*, p. 526.

145 **Repeal of death penalty in New York State:** Apple, R.W., Jr., "Two Sides Testify on Death Penalty," *New York Times*, March 26, 1965; Shapiro, *Whitmore*, pp. 156–157; Lefkowitz and Gross, *The Victims*, p. 451; Raab, *Justice in the Back Room*, p. 180.

145 **Repeal of "Blue Ribbon" juries:** Schanberg, Sidney H., "Blue-Ribbon Jury Barred in State," *New York Times*, July 16, 1965.

146 **Wylie-Hoffert murder trial:** Interview with George Whitmore (April 3, 2009); Lefkowitz and Gross, *The Victims*, pp. 544–573; Raab, *Justice in the Back Room*, pp. 217–231; Shapiro, *Whitmore*, pp. 163–174.

147 **Whitmore on the stand:** Ibid.

151 **Posttrial press conference:** Shapiro, "Annals of Jurisprudence: The Whitmore Confessions," *The New Yorker*, February 8, 1969.

152 **Whitmore makes hooch in prison:** Interview with George Whitmore (April 3, 2009).

9. FEAR

153 **John Lindsay elected mayor:** Talmer, Jerry, "Battle for City Hall: The Story of John Lindsay," *New York Post*, October 25, 1965; "Lindsay's Astounding Victory," *New York Times*, November 3, 1965; Schumach, Murray, "The Oath Is Taken," *New York Times*, January 1, 1966; "New Mayor," op-ed, *New York Times*, January 1, 1966; Thimmesch, Nick, "The Fight for City Hall: Anatomy of a Victory," *New York Herald Tribune Magazine*, January 2, 1966.

154 **Civilian Complaint Review Board (CCRB):** "Lindsay Appoints Anticrime Panel," *New York Times*, November 27, 1966; Cannato, *The Ungovernable City*, pp. 155–188; Lardner and Reppetto, *NYPD*, pp. 256–258, 268–267, 322; Levitt, *NYPD Confidential*, pp. 98, 161–162; Alex, Nicholas, *New York City Cops Talk Back*, pp. 75–80, 115, 193, 206; Klein, Herbert, *The Police: Damned If They Do, Damned If They Don't*, pp. 20, 98–99.

154 **Vincent L. Broderick:** Madden, Richard L., "Lindsay Delaying on Head of Police," *New York Times*, November 28, 1965.

154 **"If you believe that a police officer":** Ibid.

155 **Howard Leary chosen as commissioner:** Cannato, *The Ungovernable City*, pp. 165, 470–471; Lardner and Reppetto, *NYPD*, pp. 257–258; Murphy and Plate, *Commissioner*, pp. 36–37.

155 **"I am sick and tired of giving in to minority groups":** Cannato, *The Ungovernable City*, p. 68.

156 **Incident at Joe's Place in Harlem:** "White Policeman Accused by CORE," *New York Times*, March 1, 1966; Montgomery, Paul L., "Police Transfer 3 in Harlem 'Disrobing' Incident," *New York Times*, March 2, 1968; Cannato, *The Ungovernable City*, pp. 335–337.

157 **CORE protest and press conference:** Robinson, Douglas, "CORE Vows 'to Escalate War' on 'Vicious Acts' by City Police," *New York Times*, March 3, 1966; Cannato, *The Ungovernable City*, p. 341.

159 **Lindsay pushes for new CCRB:** Cannato, *The Ungovernable City*, pp. 156–159, 167–170, 183–188; Lardner and Reppetto, *NYPD*, pp. 257–258.

159 **CCRB campaign:** Cannato, *The Ungovernable City*, pp. 168–169, 171–172; Cowan, Ruth, "The New York Civilian Complaint Review Board Referendum of November 1966: A Case Study of Mass Politics" (Ph.D. dissertation, New York University, 1970); Kheel, Theodore, "Facts and Myths About the Police Review Board," *New York World Journal Tribune*, October 23, 1966; Skolnick, Jerome, "Why Cops Behave the Way They Do," *New York World Journal Tribune*, October 23, 1966; McFadden, J. P., "Who Will Protect the Police?" *National Review*, April 5, 1966.

160 **"The only thing [it] didn't show":** Ibid.

160 **Roy Wilkins's response to PBA campaign:** Wilkins, Roy, "A Sly Campaign Against Negroes," *Amsterdam News*, October 15, 1966.

160 **CCRB complaints against Phillips:** Shecter with Phillips, *On the Pad*, p. 396.

161 **Phillips's "scores":** Ibid.

162 **"Money became just paper to me":** Ibid.

162 **"I sure had a fucking ball":** Ibid.

162 **Flies solo after six hours of instruction:** Ibid., p. 187.

163 **Meanwhile, a throng of onlookers gathered:** Ibid.

163 **Phillips lands plane on LIE:** Ibid.

163 **"She [was] really pissed off":** Ibid., p. 191.

163 **"I put a thousand dollars down":** Ibid.

163 **NYPD Flying Club:** Ibid., pp. 191–192; McDonald, *My Father's Gun*, pp. 236–238; Lardner and Reppetto, *NYPD*, p. 268.

164 **Incident with Officer Walter Jefferys:** Shecter with Phillips, *On the Pad*, pp. 197–200.

165 **"The job requires total commitment"**: Interview with Randy Jurgensen (February 12, 2010).

166 **Jurgensen career background:** Ibid.

166 **"Oh, yeah, I knew who Phillips was":** Ibid.

167 **Disputes between Whitmore attorneys:** Interview with George Whitmore (April 3, 2009); interview with Selwyn Raab (April 22, 2009); interview with Myron Beldock (January 27, 2009); Lefkowitz and Gross, *The Victims*, pp. 421, 423–424; Shapiro, *Whitmore*, pp. 217–221; Raab, *Justice in the Back Room*, pp. 234–235.

167 **"I thought they might kill each other":** Interview with George Whitmore (April 3, 2009).

167 **Second Borrero trial:** Interview with George Whitmore (April 3, 2009); interview with Selwyn Raab (April 22, 2009); Lefkowitz and Gross, *The Victims*, pp. 519–521, 522; Shapiro, *Whitmore*, pp. 128–136; Raab, *Justice in the Back Room*, pp. 258–260.

169 **"Your Honor, both Detectives" (ADA Schmier quote):** Lefkowitz and Gross, *The Victims*, p. 411; Shapiro, *Whitmore*, p. 193.

169 **"It is high time" (DA Koota quote):** Lefkowitz and Gross, *The Victims*, p. 522; Shapiro, *Whitmore*, p. 196. For a detailed profile of Aaron Koota, see Fleming, Thomas J., "Case of the Debatable Brooklyn D.A.," *New York Times Magazine*, March 19, 1967.

170 **The *Miranda* decision:** Graham, Fred P., "Curb on Police Questions Is Ruled Not Retroactive," *New York Times*, June 21, 1966; Shapiro, "Annals of Jurisprudence: The Whitmore Confessions," *The New Yorker*, February 8, 1969; Raab, *Justice in the Back Room*, pp. 243–249.

171 **Koota drops Edmonds indictment:** Shapiro, "Annals of Jurisprudence: The Whitmore Confessions," *The New Yorker*, February 8, 1969; Lefkowitz and Gross, *The Victims*, p. 519; Shapiro, *Whitmore*, p. 151; Raab, *Justice in the Back Room*, p. 259.

171 **Judge Barshay releases Whitmore on bail:** Anderson, David, "Whitmore Due to Go Free on Bail Today on Appeal After 2 Years in Jail," *New York Times*, July 13, 1966.

171 **R. Peter Straus posts bail:** "Whitmore Freed on Bail to Work for Jersey Town," *New York Times*, July 14, 1966; Shapiro, *Whitmore*, p. 209.

172 **Whitmore returns to Wildwood:** Interview with George Whitmore (April 3, 2009); Shapiro, *Whitmore*, pp. 211–212.

173 **SPONGE (Society for the Prevention of Niggers Getting Everything):** Cannato, *The Ungovernable City*, pp. 123–124.

173 **"Get the hell out of Bedford-Stuyvesant":** Cannato, *The Ungovernable City*, p. 136.

174 **Verbal attacks on Lindsay:** Ibid.

174 **Ernest Gallashaw incident:** Anderson, David, "Youth, 17, Wins Bail in Slaying of Boy, 11, During Racial Battle," *New York Times*, September 7, 1966; Cannato, *The Ungovernable City*, pp. 123–124, 604.

175 **"No more Whitmores":** Ibid.

175 **Gallashaw trial and verdict:** Gallashaw's attorney was Paul O'Dwyer, an Irish-born civil rights attorney and brother of former mayor William O'Dwyer. Reeves, Richard, "Gallashaw Free in Boy's Slaying," *New York Times*, October 14, 1966.

175 **New York Times poll:** Powledge, Fred, "Poll Shows Whites in City Resent Civil Rights Drive," *New York Times*, September 21, 1964.

175 **CCRB ballot measure vote:** Jacoby, Tamar, "The Uncivil History of the Civilian Review Board," *City Journal*, Winter 1993; Cannato, *The Ungovernable City*, p. 187.

10. BLACK POWER

179 **Bin Wahad released from prison:** Interview with Dhoruba Bin Wahad (September 16, 2008).

180 **"I'll never forget this shit":** Ibid.

180 **"It happened fast":** Ibid.

180 **Attempted robbery with Augustus Qualls et al.:** Ibid.

181 **"[The cops] didn't even say halt":** Ibid.

182 **Shakur brothers:** Ibid.; Balagoon, Kuwasi, et al., *Look for Me in the Whirlwind*, pp. 11, 24–25.

182 **Revolutionary Action Movement:** Ahmad, Muhammad, *We Will Return in the Whirlwind: Black Radical Organizations, 1960–1973*, pp. 95–166; Austin, Curtis J., *Up Against the Wall*, pp. 12, 30, 32–33.

182 **Republic of New Afrika:** Austin, *Up Against the Wall*, p. 253; Joseph, Peniel E., *Waiting 'Til the Midnight Hour: A Narrative History of Black Power in America*, pp. 55, 219.

182 **Speeches of Malcolm X:** Breitman, *Malcolm X Speaks*, entire book.

182 **"If we're going to talk about police brutality":** Ibid.

182 **"Recently, three students from Kenya":** Ibid.

183 **Eddie Ellis and others in the wake of Malcolm X assassination:** Interview with Eddie Ellis (May 15, 2009).

183 **"Lyndon Baines Johnson is bombing the hell out of Vietnam":** Joseph, *Waiting 'Til the Midnight Hour*, p. 145; Van Deburg, William, *New Day in Babylon*, p. 113.

184 **Stokely Carmichael background:** Carmichael, Stokely, *Black Power*, pp. 4–11; Joseph, *Waiting 'Til the Midnight Hour*, pp. 124–127; Van Deburg, *New Day in Babylon*, pp. 76–85.

184 **"The only way we going to stop them"**: Branch, Taylor, *At Canaan's Edge*, p. 333; Joseph, *Waiting 'Til the Midnight Hour*, p. 35.

184 **"Stokely had that intellectual brilliance"**: Interview with Eddie Ellis (May 15, 2009).

184 **"Voting rights was the issue"**: Ibid.

185 **"This country . . . knows what power is"**: Branch, *At Canaan's Edge*, p. 331; Joseph, *Waiting 'Til the Midnight Hour*, p. 163; Van Deburg, *New Day in Babylon*, p. 84; Lester, Julius, *Look Out, Whitey!*, p. 63.

185 **Use of term "black" instead of "negro"**: "Black Power and Black Pride," *Time*, December 1, 1967; Carmichael, *Black Power*, pp. 181–182; Lester, *Look Out, Whitey!*, pp. 11, 23–24; Cleaver, Eldridge, *Soul on Ice*, pp. 17–25.

185 **Lowndes County Freedom Organization**: Austin, *Up Against the Wall*, pp. 12–15; Branch, *Pillar of Fire*, pp. 23–25, 421, 511; Carmichael, *Black Power*, pp. 85, 87–88; Estes, Steve, *I Am a Man!*, pp. 31, 33–34; Joseph, *Waiting 'Til the Midnight Hour*, pp. 124, 128–130, 147, 164; Lester, *Look Out, Whitey!*, pp. 38–41; Van Deburg, *New Day in Babylon*, pp. 87–89.

185 **"We chose for the emblem a black panther"**: Carmichael, *Black Power*, p. 88; Austin, *Up Against the Wall*, p. 17; Pearson, Hugh, *Shadow of the Panther*, p. 142.

185 **Birth of Black Panther Party for Self Defense in Oakland**: Newton, Huey P., *Revolutionary Suicide*, pp. 115–172; Pearson, *Shadow of the Panther*, pp. 97, 107–112; Joseph, *Waiting 'Til the Midnight Hour*, pp. 175–178, 207–211; FBI COINTELPRO (confidential memo).

185–187 **Origins of black militancy in the United States**: The Black Panther Party was not the first black militant group in the United States. In Louisiana in the 1950s a group known as the Deacons for Self Defense advocated the carrying of arms, based around the concept of self-defense. In North Carolina, Robert F. Williams founded an organization that advocated direct confrontation with the KKK. He was expelled from the NAACP for his militancy and later hunted by the FBI. Williams was the first to tie the concept of armed self-defense to revolution. Together with his wife, Mabel, he established a radio program called *Radio Free Dixie* that was designed to be the voice of black militancy. In 1960, Williams, wanted by the FBI, fled to Cuba and became the first in what would be a long line of black militants who wound up fleeing American law enforcement and settling in Castro's Cuba. In 1962, Williams published *Negroes with Guns*, a book about his experiences taking on white supremacy, which Huey P. Newton and others in the black liberation movement cited as a formative work. Williams's example was the inspiration for the Revolutionary Action Movement (RAM), the most cohesive black militant organization before the Black Panther Party, with followers in the prison system and around the United States. Robert F. Williams died in Cuba in 1996.

185   **Black Panthers at capital building in Sacramento (May 2, 1967):** Newton, *Revolutionary Suicide*, pp. 153–159; Pearson, *Shadow of the Panther*, pp. 129–134, 140–141; Joseph, *Waiting 'Til the Midnight Hour*, pp. 169–170.

185   **New York City meeting among SNCC, RAM, and Huey Newton:** Interview with Eddie Ellis (May 15, 2009).

186   **"We were ready to stand and fight":** Ibid.

186   **"Open Letter to the Harlem Community":** Ibid.; FBI COINTELPRO file. Documents pertaining to the Black Panther Party in New York City first appear in 1968, though files of the NYPD's BOSS unit date as far back as the early 1960s, when they first penetrated the Nation of Islam and also Malcolm X's OAAU.

187   **OPERATION SHUT DOWN:** BOSS files (NYPD); FBI COINTELPRO file.

187   **"He still got drunk most every day":** Interview with George Whitmore (April 3, 2009).

187   **Aida de Jesus:** Ibid.; Shapiro, *Whitmore*, pp. 212, 225; Lefkowitz and Gross, *The Victims*, p. 498.

188   **Whitmore robbed in Brownsville:** Interview with George Whitmore (April 3, 2009).

189   **Gerald Whitmore and the Suicide Frenchmen:** Interview with Gerald Whitmore (June 18, 2009); interview with George Whitmore (April 3, 2009).

189   **George and Gerald confrontation with rivals:** Ibid.

189   **"I washed my hands of the whole thing":** Interview with George Whitmore (April 3, 2009).

190   **Gerald Whitmore arrest:** Interview with Gerald Whitmore (June 18, 2009); Perlmutter, Emanuel, "Brother of Whitmore Arrested in Slaying in a Brooklyn Brawl," *New York Times*, February 26, 1967; Anderson, F. David, "Gerald Whitmore Freed in Slaying," *New York Times*, March 4, 1967.

190   **"You know what you're being charged with?":** Ibid.

191   **George and Aida wedding (March 9, 1967):** Interview with George Whitmore (April 3, 2009); Shapiro, *Whitmore*, p. 215.

191   **George and Aida settle in Wildwood:** Ibid.

192   **"In view of the fact that the defendant's statements":** Shapiro, *Whitmore*, p. 211; Lefkowitz and Gross, *The Victims*, p. 554; Raab, *Justice in the Back Room*, p. 255.

192   **Whitmore replaces Reiben:** Interview with George Whitmore

(April 3, 2009); Shapiro, *Whitmore*, pp. 218–220; Lefkowitz and Gross, *The Victims*, p. 511; Raab, *Justice in the Back Room*, p. 255.

192 **Samuel Neuberger**: Ibid.

193 **Position of D.A. Aaron Koota**: Fleming, Thomas, "Case of the Debatable Brooklyn D.A.," *New York Times*, March 19, 1967.

193 **Third Borrero trial**: Interview with George Whitmore (April 3, 2009); interview with Selwyn Raab (April 22, 2009); Shapiro, "Annals of Jurisprudence: The Whitmore Confessions," *The New Yorker*, February 8, 1969; Shapiro, *Whitmore*, pp. 220–227; Lefkowitz and Gross, *The Victims*, pp. 554–560; Raab, *Justice in the Back Room*, p. 259.

194 **"I am restrained to say at the outset"**: Shapiro, *Whitmore*, p. 226; Lefkowitz and Gross, *The Victims*, p. 560.

194 **Judge Helfand decision**: "Whitmore Given 5-Year Sentence," *New York Times*, June 9, 1967; Shapiro, *Whitmore*, p. 225; Lefkowitz and Gross, *The Victims*, p. 559; Raab, *Justice in the Back Room*, p. 259; Shapiro, "Annals of Jurisprudence: The Whitmore Confessions," *The New Yorker*, February 8, 1969.

195 **"I would say from thirty-nine years of practicing in my borough"**: Lefkowitz and Gross, *The Victims*, p. 560; Shapiro, *Whitmore*, p. 227.

195 **"I thought that was it"**: Interview with George Whitmore (April 3, 2009).

11. "HOLY SHIT!"

196 **NYPD arrests of RAM**: Perlmutter, Emanuel, "16 Negroes Seized; Plot to Kill Wilkins and Young Charged," *New York Times*, June 22, 1967; "Mass Poison Plot Laid to Negroes," *New York Times*, September 28, 1967; Austin, *Up Against the Wall*, p. 62.

197 **The Harlem hate scare (Black Brotherhood)**: Griffin, Junius, "Anti-White Harlem Gang Reported to Number 400," *New York Times*, May 6, 1964; Breitman, *Malcolm X Speaks*, pp. 64–71.

198 **Urban riots in United States 1964–1967**: Rucker, Walter, and James Nathanial Upton (eds.), *Encyclopedia of American Race Riots*, pp. 238, 240–244; Rustin, Bayard, "A Negro Leader Defines a Way Out of the Exploding Ghetto," *New York Times Magazine*, August 13, 1967.

199 **Newark riot (July 1967)**: *Newark '67*, PBS documentary; Hayden, Tom, "A Special Supplement: The Occupation of Newark," *New York Review of Books*, August 24, 1967; Hayden, Tom, *Rebellion in Newark*, entire book.

199 **"The line between the jungle and the law"**: Hayden, "A Special Supplement: The Occupation of Newark," *New York Review of Books*, August 24, 1967.

200 **"They put us here because we're the toughest"**: Ibid.

200 **Killing of Jimmy Rutledge:** Hayden, *Rebellion in Newark*, pp. 33–34; *Newark '67* PBS documentary.

201 **Detroit riot 1967:** Rustin, "A Negro Leader Defines a Way Out of the Exploding Ghetto," *New York Times Magazine*, August 13, 1967; Rucker and Upton, *Encyclopedia of American Race Riots*, pp. 240–242.

201 **"My partner and me pulled up to 110th Street":** Shecter with Phillips, *On the Pad*, p. 208.

201 **East Harlem riot:** The riot described by Phillips is chronicled in Hamill, Pete, "El Barrio: Hot Night," *New York Post*, July 24, 1967, and "El Barrio: The Line," *New York Post*, July 25, 1967.

202 **"Our bosses told us, do nothing":** Ibid.

203 **"I came down the stairs":** Interview with Dhoruba Bin Wahad (September 16, 2009).

204 **Bin Wahad meets Iris Bull:** Ibid.

204 **Bin Wahad and Iris settle in East Village:** Ibid.

204 **Slugs jazz club:** Slugs became famous—or infamous—on a night in 1969 when trumpeter Lee Morgan was shot and killed on the bandstand by his wife.

204 **Further readings of Bin Wahad:** Interview with Dhoruba Bin Wahad (September 16, 2009).

205 **Cleaver article in *Ramparts*:** Cleaver, Eldridge, "The Courage to Kill," *Ramparts*, June 15, 1968; Cleaver, Eldridge, *Target Zero*, pp. 101–112.

207 **Bin Wahad attends "Rise on the Pentagon":** Interview with Dhoruba Bin Wahad (September 16, 2009). The march on the Pentagon was one of the seminal 1960s political events, chronicled in many histories of the era, most vividly in Norman Mailer's *Armies of the Night*, which won a Pulitzer Prize for literature.

207 **"One of the college students was talking":** Interview with Dhoruba Bin Wahad (September 16, 2009).

207 **Bin Wahad visits BPP office on Seventh Avenue and 141st St.:** Ibid.

208 **Dhoruba and Iris get married:** Ibid.

208 **Huey P. Newton shooting and arrest in Oakland:** Newton, *Revolutionary Suicide*, pp. 181–214; Austin, *Up Against the Wall*, pp. 49–56, 65–68; Ahmad, *We Will Return in the Whirlwind*, pp. 5–6; Heath, G. Louis, *Off the Pigs!*, pp. 37–38, 40–45; Hilliard, David, and Donald Weise (eds.), *The Huey P. Newton Reader*, pp. 212–228; Hilliard, *This Side of Glory*, pp. 175–178, 181; Joseph, *Waiting 'Til the Midnight Hour*, pp. 204, 206–207; Pearson, *Shadow of the Panther*, pp. 3, 7, 145–147, 220–221; Van Deburg, *New Day in Babylon*, pp. 113–116.

208 **"Free Huey" movement:** Ibid.

209   **Myron Beldock takes over Whitmore case:** Interview with Myron Beldock (January 27, 2009).

209   **"I'm sure Arthur used the word 'injustice'":** Ibid.

210   **Beldock background:** Ibid.; Glaberson, William, "A Foe of Injustice and Champion of Lost Causes," *New York Times*, September 21, 2004.

210   **"There was a basic prejudice to the system":** Ibid.

211   **"He was sweet tempered and pretty simple":** Ibid.

12. REVOLUTION

213   **Ellis plans for BPP based on Irish Republican Army model:** Interview with Eddie Ellis (May 15, 2009).

214   **Philosophical differences between SNCC and BPP:** Fraser, C. Gerald, "S.N.C.C. in Decline After 8 Years in Lead," *New York Times*, October 7, 1969; Ahmad, *We Will Return in the Whirlwind*, pp. 23, 27–28; Austin, *Up Against the Wall*, pp. 118, 129–132; Estes, *I Am a Man!*, pp. 87, 92; Heath, *Off the Pigs!*, pp. 16–18; Hilliard, *This Side of Glory*, pp. 146–148, 161; Joseph, *Waiting 'Til the Midnight Hour*, pp. 232–233, 236; Lester, *Look Out, Whitey!*, pp. 129–131; Pearson, *Shadow of the Panther*, pp. 142, 150–152, 158–164, 183; Wolfe, Tom, *Radical Chic and Mau-Mauing the Flak Catchers*, p. 78.

214   **Meeting with James Forman and BPP:** Fraser, "S.N.C.C. in Decline After 8 Years in Lead," *New York Times*, October 7, 1969; Hilliard, *This Side of Glory*, pp. 201–208.

215   **"You're either part of the solution or part of the problem":** This phrase was first put into use by Eldridge Cleaver and eventually became a kind of catchphrase for the Black Panther Party, used by many of the party's most notable speakers, including Dhoruba Bin Wahad.

215   **Origins and goals of COINTELPRO:** O'Reilly, Kenneth, *Racial Matters*, pp. 293–324; FBI COINTELPRO files; Churchill, Ward, and Jim Vander Wall, *The COINTELPRO Papers*, pp. 91–164.

215   **Eleven-page confidential memo:** The memo that was used to lay out the need for COINTELPRO was written by Assistant Director Mark Felt, who would later go on to achieve notoriety as Deep Throat, the secret Watergate source used by *Washington Post* journalists Bob Woodward and Carl Bernstein in their reporting on the scandal that would eventually bring down the Nixon administration.

216   **Black Agitator Index:** Interview with Robert Boyle (November 21, 2008).

216   **Bin Wahad reads *Soul on Ice:*** Interview with Dhoruba Bin Wahad (September 19, 2008).

217   **"The police do on the domestic level":** Cleaver, *Soul on Ice*, p. 122.

217   **Bin Wahad reaction to King assassination:** Interview with Dhoruba Bin Wahad (September 16, 2008).

218   **Bin Wahad visits BPP office in Brooklyn:** Ibid.

219   **Whitmore reaction to King assassination:** Interview with George Whitmore (April 3, 2009).

220   **Nationwide reaction to King assassination:** Branch, *At Canaan's Edge*, pp. 723–766; *American Experience: Eyes on the Prize*, PBS documentary.

220   **Lindsay response to King assassination:** Cannato, *The Ungovernable City*, pp. 210–215.

220   **Phillips shooting of Calvin McCoy:** "Burglar Suspect Killed in Harlem," *New York Times*, April 17, 1968; Shecter with Phillips, *On the Pad*, p. 194.

221   **"The guy is going like a raped ape":** Shecter with Phillips, *On the Pad*, p. 194.

222   **"A police officer is supposed to understand":** Ibid.

223   **BPP benefit at Fillmore East:** Interview with Dhoruba Bin Wahad (September 16, 2008); Sullivan, Dan, "Black Panther Benefit Is Held in East Village," *New York Times*, May 21, 1968.

224   **Oakland police shoot-out with Cleaver et al.:** Ahmad, *We Will Return in the Whirlwind*, pp. 16–17; Austin, *Up Against the Wall*, pp. 165–168; Pearson, *Shadow of the Panther*, pp. 154–156; Hilliard, *This Side of Glory*, pp. 181–185, 188, 191–192; Cleaver, *Target Zero*, pp. 85–96. In the wake of the shoot-out in Oakland that resulted in the death of Bobby Hutton, a group of prominent writers published an open letter in the *New York Review of Books* (May 9, 1968) denouncing the actions of the police. The letter was signed by, among many others, James Baldwin, Norman Mailer, Gloria Steinem, and Susan Sontag.

224   **"What We Want, What We Believe":** The BPP Ten-Point Program was as follows: 1. We want freedom. We want the power to determine the destiny of our Black Community. 2. We want full employment for our people. 3. We want to end the robbery by the white man of our Black Community. 4. We want decent housing, fit for shelter of human beings. 5. We want education for our people that exposes the true nature of this decadent American society. We want education that teaches us our true history and our role in the present-day society. 6. We want all black people to be exempt from military service. 7. We want an immediate end to POLICE BRUTALITY and MURDER of black people. 8. We want freedom for all black men held in federal, state, county and city prisons and jails. 9. We want all black people when brought to trial to be tried in court by a jury of their peer group or people from their black communities, as defined by the Constitution of the United States. 10. We want land, bread, housing, education, clothing, justice and peace.

And as our major political objective, a United Nations–supervised plebiscite to be held throughout the black colony in which only black colonial subjects will be allowed to participate, for the purpose of determining the will of black people as to their national identity. Source: *Black Panther*, vol. 3, no. 2, May 4, 1969.

224   **Influence of Frantz Fanon:** Both *Wretched of the Earth* and *Black Skin, White Masks* were essential texts for advocates of Black Power.

224   *The Battle of Algiers:* Directed by Gillo Pontecorvo, the movie depicts the successful guerrilla uprising in Algeria in the early 1960s. Nominated for an Academy Award for Best Foreign Language Film, the movie became an international phenomenon and de rigueur viewing for would-be revolutionaries around the globe.

Detective Randy Jurgensen remembers going to a screening of the movie with his partner, Sonny Grosso. Jurgensen and Grosso would eventually become part of a squad investigating BLA cases. *The Battle of Algiers* had been described to them as a black militant training film. "After seeing that movie," said Jurgensen, "I think for the first time we realized what we were up against. The movie opens with a revolutionary coming up behind a cop and putting a bullet through the back of his head. I said to Sonny, 'You still think this is about drugs? It ain't about drugs. We represent the system to these people, and they want to bring down the system. They're out to hunt and kill cops." Interview with Randy Jurgensen (February 12, 2010).

224   **BPP political education (PE) classes:** Weekly PE classes were an important social as well as educational tool for the BPP. Interview with Dhoruba Bin Wahad (September 16, 2008); interview with Cleo Silvers (March 26, 2009); interview with William "B.J." Johnson (January 23, 2010); Austin, *Up Against the Wall*, pp. 58–69, 89–99; Hilliard, *This Side of Glory*, pp. 133, 201–202.

224   **"Because of my studies in the joint":** Interview with Dhoruba Bin Wahad (September 16, 2008).

225   **"Some people joined the party to feed children":** Ibid.

226   **Sudden national growth of the BPP:** Caldwell, Earl, "Black Panthers Growing, But Their Troubles Rise," *New York Times*, December 7, 1968; Johnson, Thomas A., "Civil Rights Movement Facing Revolution Within a Revolution," *New York Times*, July 21, 1968; Stearn, Gerald Emanuel, "Rapping with the Panthers in White Suburbia," *New York Times Magazine*, March 8, 1970; "Review of Panther Growth and Harassment," *Black Panther*, January 4, 1968; Austin, *Up Against the Wall*, pp. 159–188, 273; Hilliard, *This Side of Glory*, pp. 150–175.

226   **Emergence of the *Black Panther* newspaper:** Hilliard, David (ed.), *The Black Panther: Intercommunal News Service, 1967–1980*. This book includes

numerous essays from a variety of writers within the Panther universe on the role and development of the newspaper.

227 **Use of the word *pig* to describe police:** Newton, *Revolutionary Suicide*, pp. 175–177. Newton takes full credit for instituting use of the term. In *The Revolutionary Art of Emory Douglas*, Amiri Baraka contributes an essay on the use of the word and the importance of Douglas's illustrations in communicating the message.

228 **Confrontation between BPP and NYPD on Nostrand Avenue:** Interview with Dhoruba Bin Wahad (September 16, 2009); interview with Gerald Lefcourt (January 25, 2010); McFadden, Robert D., "Police–Black Panther Scuffles Mark Brooklyn Street Rally," *New York Times*, August 2, 1968.

228 **"The Panther who had earlier stood":** Bin Wahad, "The Future Past" (unpublished manuscript).

228 **Incident at Brooklyn courthouse:** Interview with Dhoruba Bin Wahad (September 16, 2008); interview with Gerald Lefcourt (January 16, 2010).

229 **"A microphone was shoved in my face":** Interview with Dhoruba Bin Wahad (September 16, 2008).

230 **Shooting of police on Eastern Parkway:** Seedman, Albert, and Peter Hellman, *Chief*, pp. 371–373, 411; Daley, *Target Blue*, pp. 84–86.

13. "OFF THE PIGS!"

231 **Whitmore release from prison (June 15, 1968):** Interview with George Whitmore (April 3, 2009); interview with Myron Beldock (January 27, 2009).

231 **Whitmore borrows money from Shapiro:** Shapiro, *Whitmore*, p. 228.

232 **Whitmore employed by Nation of Islam:** Interview with George Whitmore (April 3, 2009).

234 **Opening of new BPP office:** Interview with Dhoruba Bin Wahad (September 16, 2008).

234 **"I think it was Lumumba who found the space":** Ibid.

235 **Ron Penniwell as liaison with West Coast Panthers:** Ibid.; Austin, *Up Against the Wall*, p. 274.

235 **Cleo Silvers's background:** Interview with Cleo Silvers (March 26, 2009).

236 **"The policies at the hospital were so misguided":** Ibid.

236 **"Somebody told me to go to the Panther office":** Ibid.

237 **"You can't sell the *Black Panther* newspaper":** Ibid.

237   **"To me, the PE classes were slow":** Ibid.

237   **"I became a green dog in karate":** Ibid.

238   **Statement by Joudon Ford:** Zion, Sidney E., "5 Black Panthers Held in Brooklyn," *New York Times*, September 13, 1968; Austin, *Up Against the Wall*, p. 274.

238   **Judge Furey responds to criticism by police spokesman:** Novitski, Joseph, "Judge Ouster Sought," *New York Times*, August 5, 1968.

239   **Formation of Law Enforcement Group (LEG):** Novitski, Joseph, "Brooklyn Police Set Up Group to Back 'Vigorous' Enforcement," *New York Times*, August 8, 1968; Spiegel, Irving, "P.B.A. Will Issue 'Get Tough' Advice," *New York Times*, August 12, 1968; Fox, Sylvan, "Many Police in City Leaning to the Right," *New York Times*, September 6, 1968; Grutzner, Charles, "Law Enforcement Group Is Creation of Protest," *New York Times*, September 7, 1968.

239   **"We're sick and tired of taking it on the chin":** Spiegel, "P.B.A. Will Issue 'Get Tough' Advice," *New York Times*, August 12, 1968.

239   **Kunstler becomes Panthers' attorney:** Interview with Gerald Lefcourt (January 25, 2010); Kunstler, William, *My Life as a Radical Lawyer*, pp. 58–59, 65–68, 183, 211; Burnham, David, "3 in Black Panther Party Win Hearing Over Bail," *New York Times*, August 24, 1968.

240   **Lefcourt at arraignment court:** Interview with Gerald Lefcourt (January 25, 2010).

240   **Beat-down by off-duty cops at Brooklyn courthouse:** Ibid.; interview with Dhoruba Bin Wahad (September 16, 2008); Burnham, David, "Off-Duty Police Here Join in Beating Black Panthers," *New York Times*, September 5, 1968; "Brutality, New York Style," *New York Times*, September 5, 1968.

241   **Meeting with Lindsay's Urban Task Force:** Interview with Gerald Lefcourt (January 25, 2010); Burnham, David, "Mayor and Leary Warn Policemen in Panther Melee," *New York Times*, September 6, 1968; Burnham, David, "Black Panthers Give Grievances," *New York Times*, September 7, 1968; Perlmutter, Emanuel, "N.A.A.C.P. Urges Inquiry on Police," *New York Times*, September 8, 1968; Fox, Sylvan, "Leary Says Police Reflect Community in a Swing to Right," *New York Times*, September 11, 1968; Burnham, David, "Panthers to Seek Voice Over Police," *New York Times*, September 11, 1968.

242   **Statement by John Birch Society:** Cannato, *The Ungovernable City*, pp. 166–167.

243   **Background on BOSS:** *Red Squad*, 1971 documentary; Churchill and Vander Wall, *The COINTELPRO Papers*, pp. 361, 363; Lardner and Reppetto, *NYPD*, pp. 189, 259.

243   **Infiltration of BPP by BOSS:** FBI COINTELPRO files; BOSS

files; O'Reilly, *Racial Matters*, p. 344; Kempton, Murray, *The Briar Patch*, pp. 34–35, 87, 110–111; Zimroth, Peter L., *Perversions of Justice*, pp. 47–52, 128–130, 201–203, 381–386; Austin, *Up Against the Wall*, pp. 284–286; interview with Dhoruba Bin Wahad (September 16, 2009); interview with Gerald Lefcourt (January 25, 2010).

244　**J. Edgar Hoover on BPP:** Hoover's public statement regarding the BPP set the tone for much of what followed.

245　**"The information we are receiving":** FBI COINTELPRO files.

245　**"If you accept the definition of a Negro":** Interview with Dhoruba Bin Wahad (September 16, 2008).

246　**Cleaver comes to NYC:** Fraser, Gerald C., "Cleaver Aims to Unite Black and White Radicals," *New York Times*, October 12, 1968; Austin, *Up Against the Wall*.

246　**Cleaver runs for president:** "Imprisoned Black Panther Enters Race for President," *New York Times*, May 14, 1968; "Cleaver Loses Appeal to Get on State Ballot," *New York Times*, October 18, 1968; Kifner, John, "Eldridge Cleaver, Black Panther Who Became G.O.P. Conservative, Is Dead at 62," *New York Times*, May 2, 1998.

246　**"Certain people . . . had an aura about them":** Interview with Dhoruba Bin Wahad (September 16, 2008).

246　**Cleaver press conference at Algonquin Hotel:** Fraser, "Cleaver Aims to Unite Black and White Radicals," *New York Times*, October 12, 1968.

247　**Joseph "Jazz" Hayden background:** Interview with Joseph "Jazz" Hayden (December 19, 2008).

248　**Shooting of two police officers (September 28, 1968):** "2 Policemen in a Car Are Injured in Unprovoked Harlem Shooting," *New York Times*, September 29, 1968; "Suspect, 26, Seized in Harlem Shooting of Two Policemen," *New York Times*, October 24, 1968.

248　**"You come outside in the morning":** Interview with Joseph "Jazz" Hayden (December 19, 2009).

249　**"You could start a nickel-and-dime crap game":** Ibid.

249　**"My uncle used to take me around":** Ibid.

250　**"Growing up in Harlem":** Ibid.

250　**"I observed them in the neighborhood":** Ibid.

251　**"My friend who was with me, he didn't hesitate":** Ibid.

252　**"They hunted me throughout Harlem":** Ibid.

253　**"I was hiding out with my girl":** Ibid.

253　**"I don't know how I survived that":** Ibid.

254　**"They shipped me off to prison":** Ibid.

14. WHITMORE'S LAST STAND

255 **Police attitudes toward the Panthers:** Interview with Sonny Grosso (April 13, 2009); interview with Randy Jurgensen (February 12, 2010); interview with Robert Daley (January 21, 2010); interview with Robert Leuci (February 12, 2009); interview with Gerald Lefcourt (January 25, 2010); "Police and Panthers at War," *Time*, December 12, 1969; Epstein, Edward Jay, "The Black Panthers and the Police: A Pattern of Genocide?" *The New Yorker*, February 13, 1971; Arnold, Martin, "Police and Panthers: Urban Conflict in Mutual Fear," *New York Times*, October 26, 1970; Alex, *New York Cops Talk Back*, pp. 101, 130; Daley, *Target Blue*, pp. 75–86, 170–183; Jurgensen, Randy, and Robert Cea, *Circle of Six*, pp. 44, 61, 87; Tanenbaum, Robert K., and Philip Rosenberg, *Badge of the Assassin*, pp. 15–21.

256 **"So I says, OK you son of a bitch":** Shecter with Phillips, *On the Pad*, pp. 241–242.

256 **"We make a meet for the next day":** Ibid.

257 **P.J. Clarke's Saloon:** For a time, P.J. Clarke's was a nexus of Manhattan nightlife. It has been used as a location for many movie shoots, most prominently *The Lost Weekend*, starring Ray Milland.

257 **Phillips's Triumph 250 sports car:** Shecter with Phillips, *On the Pad*, p. 18.

257 **Phillips scores off Jimmy Smith:** Ibid.

259 **Phillips's relationship with his father:** Ibid.

259 **"He got to be a pain in the ass":** Ibid.

259 **"He says, I don't want the surgery":** Ibid.

260 **Phillips visits father three or four times a day:** Ibid.

261 **Whitmore separates from Aida:** Interview with George Whitmore (April 3, 2009).

261 **Whitmore Sr. dies, house burns down:** Ibid.; Shapiro, *Whitmore*, p. 245; Lefkowitz and Gross, *The Victims*, p. 416.

261 **George and Nate's Excellent Adventure:** Interview with George Whitmore (April 3, 2009).

263 **Hearing before Judge Helfand:** Interview with Myron Beldock (January 27, 2009); interview with George Whitmore (April 3, 2009); Zion, Sidney E., "Whitmore Is on Trial Once Again on 5-Year-Old Rape Case," *New York Times*, March 28, 1969; "Whitmore Conviction Affirmed, But He Is Planning New Appeal," *New York Times*, July 29, 1970.

266 **Rockefeller report buried:** "Whitmore Report Cites Confession," *New York Times*, May 6, 1969; Lefkowitz and Gross, *The Victims*, pp. 507–509; interview with Myron Beldock (January 27, 2009); interview with Selwyn Raab (April 22, 2009).

266 **Nixon's law and order candidacy:** Perlstein, Ron, *Nixonland*, pp. 349–365.

266 **Cleaver jumps bail, settles in Algeria:** Caldwell, Earl, "A Federal Warrant Is Issued for Arrest of Eldridge Cleaver," *New York Times*, December 11, 1968; Austin, *Up Against the Wall*, pp. 187–188; Cleaver, *Target Zero*, pp. 49–54; Pearson, *Shadow of the Panther*, pp. 171, 229–230.

267 **Bombing incident at police station house:** Zimroth, *Perversions of Justice*, pp. 21–22, 146–148, 226.

268 **Shooting on Harlem River Drive (September 17, 1968):** This shooting constituted one of the criminal counts in the Panther Twenty-one case. Asbury, Edith Evans, "Panther Bullet Hit Belt, Witness Says," *New York Times*, January 13, 1971; Asbury, Edith Evans, "Policeman Denies Beating Panther," *New York Times*, May 13, 1970; Kennebeck, Edwin, *Juror Number Four*, pp. 21–22, 86, 111; Kempton, *The Briar Patch*, pp. 11–12, 18, 56, 201–203; Zimroth, *Perversion of Justice*, pp. 6–7, 104–105, 146, 234–235; Balagoon et al., *Look for Me in the Whirlwind*, pp. 81–82, 93.

269 *It's Time: Cadre News:* Interview with Dhoruba Bin Wahad (September 16, 2009). Vol. 1, no. 1 of *It's Time: Cadre News* was in the FBI COINTELPRO files I.

270 **Bin Wahad identified by COINTELPRO:** The first time Dhoruba Bin Wahad appears in a COINTELPRO report is when he was identified as being part of Eldridge Cleaver's security team at a public appearance in NYC in October 1968.

271 **Bin Wahad on Ralph White ("He was full of shit"):** Interview with Dhoruba Bin Wahad (September 16, 2009). Ralph White was a complex character. According to Gerald Lefcourt, who would cross-examine White on the witness stand, "He was conflicted. Whereas Gene Roberts blocked out his mixed feelings about being a cop and betrayer of his own people, Ralph White was torn up about it. I asked him on the stand, 'You spent all this time working with community groups, marching on behalf of social causes, advocating for poor and disenfranchised people in your community. And then you were an undercover police officer. So which is it? Who are you really? Where do you place your loyalties?' He took a deep breath and seemed like he was going to have a nervous breakdown when I asked these questions." Interview with Gerald Lefcourt (January 25, 2010). Ralph White's conflicted nature is also on display in *Red Squad* (1971), a documentary about BOSS in which he is interviewed.

271 **"We traveled like shadows":** Bin Wahad, "The Future Past" (unpublished manuscript).

272 **"The vast parking lot around the Pentagon":** Ibid.

273 **Account of Bin Wahad's arrest:** Interview with Dhoruba Bin

Wahad (September 16, 2009); Bin Wahad, "The Future Past" (unpublished manuscript); Kempton, *The Briar Patch*, pp. 16–17, 19; Zimroth, *Perversion of Justice*, pp. 156–159.

15. THE ROT WITHIN

275 **Robbery at Krown's Record Store:** Interview with George Whitmore (April 3, 2009); Whitmore State of New Jersey arrest report.

276 **Robbery at Allen's Delicatessen:** Ibid.

277 **Whitmore sentenced to jail in New Jersey:** Ibid.

277 **Panther Twenty-one indictment announced:** Zimroth, *Perversion of Justice*, pp. 21–35.

280 **Lindsay administration approached by Serpico and Durk:** Maas, *Serpico*, pp. 11–15, 280; Lardner, *Crusader*, pp. 213–216; Gelb, *City Room*, pp. 547–559; Cannato, *The Ungovernable City*, pp. 466–467, 469, 470; Shecter with Phillips, *On the Pad*, p. 189.

280 **Reporter David Burnham blows open police scandal:** Burnham, David, "Graft Paid to Police Here Said to Run into Millions," *New York Times*, April 25, 1970; Gelb, Arthur, *City Room*, pp. 554–555; Levitt, *NYPD Confidential*, pp. 1–3; Lardner and Reppetto, *NYPD*, p. 267.

281 **Lindsay appoints investigative commission:** Before the Knapp Commission came into being, Lindsay appointed an interim committee known as the Rankin Committee, which was comprised of Corporation Counsel J. Lee Rankin, D.A.s Hogan and Roberts, and Police Commissioner Howard Leary. After being in existence less than one month, the Rankin Committee reported in a letter to Lindsay that they had received 375 complaints in response to public pleas by the mayor for information and were unable to adequately investigate the claims. The committee also expressed concern about the wisdom of having allegations of police corruption investigated by officials who some segments of the public believed might conceivably be responsible for the conditions they were supposed to examine. It was in response to the Rankin Committee's recommendation that Lindsay issued an executive order appointing the Knapp Commission, with a total budget of $325,000 supplied mostly by federal grant.

282 **Phillips's response to formation of Knapp Commission:** Shecter with Phillips, *On the Pad*, p. 230.

282 **Pretrial conditions for Panther defendants:** One of the factors that turned the public against the prosecution in the early stages of the trial was the manner in which the defendants had their basic rights inhibited. One of the defendants, Lee Berry, was a Korean War veteran; his arrest had taken place at the Manhattan Veterans Hospital, where he was being treated for epilepsy. A special unit of arresting officers descended on the hospital and ordered

the supervising physician to discharge the patient as "a murderer, an arsonist, and a Black Panther." Berry was held in solitary confinement at the Tombs. He became ill but was denied treatment. He suffered numerous epileptic seizures while in custody and was eventually deemed too sick to stand trial with the other defendants. "Statement by the Central Committee of the Black Panther Party," *Black Panther*, April 27, 1969; *The Black Panther Party and the Case of the New York 21*, report by the Committee to Defend the Panther 21, 1969.

283 **Judge John M. Murtagh:** The recently concluded Chicago Eight conspiracy trial, which had been turned into a rowdy courtroom burlesque by Abbie Hoffman, Bobby Seale, and others, was rumored to be the reason D. A. Hogan assigned the Panther Twenty-one trial to Murtagh, who ran a tight ship and, logic suggested, could keep the defendants from turning the trial into a three-ring circus. Murtagh was only partly successful. His demeanor, according to a juror who would later write a book about the trial, was "humorless and rigid." Another author writing about the case noted that "[Murtagh] had an uncanny ability to appear biased even when he was ruling correctly." The defendants used the judge as a foil, referring to him in court variously as "pig," "faggot," "liar," "hanging racist," "fascist lackey," "grandee vulture," "dried up cracker in female robes," and "Hitler." According to Thomas Hughes, who served as a court clerk for Murtagh throughout the trial, the judge never wavered under the verbal onslaught. "Stoic would be a good word to describe John Murtagh," said Hughes. Interview with Thomas Hughes (May 13, 2010).

Murtagh was not a cardboard character; he was a complex man who had written two books, one about prostitution and the other about narcotics treatment, that were considered progressive in their day. Interview with John M. Murtagh Jr. (February 5, 2010); Van Gelder, Lawrence, "Panthers Cite Murtagh's Arrest in '51 on Neglect of Duty Charge," *New York Times*, March 3, 1970; Asbury, Edith Evans, "Fistfight Breaks Out at Panther Hearing," *New York Times*, February 4, 1970; Asbury, Edith Evans, "Panthers' Judge Acts on Turmoil," *New York Times*, February 5, 1970; Kempton, *The Briar Patch*, pp. 11–15, 88–89, 150; Kennebeck, *Juror Number Four*, pp. 8, 9–13, 47–48, 101, 150–175; Zimroth, *Perversion of Justice*, pp. 17, 100–103, 224–225, 229, 297–300.

283 **"I was referring to George Whitmore":** Interview with Dhoruba Bin Wahad (September 16, 2008).

284 **"Panther Twenty-one Manifesto":** Interview with Dhoruba Bin Wahad; interview with Gerald Lefcourt (January 25, 2009).

284 **Joseph A. Phillips:** Interview with Mike Armstrong (August 12, 2009); interview with Thomas Hughes (May 13, 2010). Hughes, Judge Murtagh's court clerk, also served as an assistant D.A. in Manhattan and knew

Joe Phillips, whom he described as having a knack for "rubbing people the wrong way"; Kempton, *The Briar Patch*, pp. 21–31, 75–80; Zimroth, *Perversion of Justice*, pp. 31–32, 36, 288–290, 292; Kennebeck, *Juror Number Four*, pp. 21–22, 89–112, 175.

284 **"a white Irish Catholic judge":** FBI COINTELPRO files (copy of report on the trial written by the Committee to Defend the Panther Twenty-one).

284 **Street protests outside the courtroom:** Interview with William "B.J." Johnson (January 23, 2010); interview with Cleo Silvers (March 26, 2009); Zimroth, *Perversion of Justice*, p. 97; Kempton, *The Briar Patch*, pp. 68–69, 112.

285 **Abbie Hoffman puts up money for Bin Wahad's bail:** Interview with Gerald Lefcourt (January 25, 2010); interview with Dhoruba Bin Wahad (September 16, 2008); FBI COINTELPRO files, confidential memo.

285 **Bin Wahad jailhouse meeting with David Hilliard:** Interview with Dhoruba Bin Wahad (September 16, 2008); Hilliard, *This Side of Glory*, pp. 228–230.

286 **"I was and still am a black nationalist":** Interview with Dhoruba Bin Wahad (September 16, 2008).

286 **Alex Rackley murder:** The murder of Alex Rackley was the beginning of a descent into violence that would eventually contribute to the destruction of the BPP. The trial also revealed just how riddled with informants the Panthers had become. Sheehy, Gail, "Black Against Black: The Agony of Panthermania," *New York*, November 16, 1970. Sheehy's two-part article on the New Haven trial was later published in book form as *Panthermania* (1971). "A Panther Admits He Killed Another," *New York Times*, January 17, 1970; Austin, *Up Against the Wall*, pp. 276, 289–293; Pearson, *Shadow of the Panther*, pp. 235–236.

287 **Additional support for BPP:** The Committee to Defend the Panther Twenty-one issued regular bulletins to generate publicity and solicit funds. Among their most notorious fund-raisers was a gathering of wealthy, mostly white Manhattanites at the Upper East Side duplex apartment of composer Leonard Bernstein, director of the New York Philharmonic. The party was famously lampooned by writer Tom Wolfe in an article in *New York* magazine that was later published in book form as *Radical Chic and Mau-mauing the Flak Catchers* (1970). Wrote Wolfe: "In the season of Radical chic . . . the very idea of [Black Panthers], these real revolutionaries, who actually put their lives on the line, runs through Lenny's duplex like a rogue hormone." Curtis, Charlotte, "The Bernsteins' Party for Black Panther Legal Defense Stirs Talk and More Parties," *New York Times*, January 24, 1970; "Upper East Side Story," *Time*, January 26, 1970.

288 **Bin Wahad released on bail:** Interview with Dhoruba Bin Wahad (September 16, 2008); interview with Gerald Lefcourt (January 25, 2010);

Asbury, Edith Evans, "Moore, Panther Leader, Freed on $100,000 Bail," *New York Times*, March 27, 1970.

288 **Bin Wahad travels nationwide:** Interview with Dhoruba Bin Wahad (September 16, 2008).

289 **Growing disillusionment with BPP Central Committee:** Interview with Dhoruba Bin Wahad (September 16, 2008); interview with Cleo Silvers (March 26, 2009); Austin, *Up Against the Wall*, pp. 286, 298–312.

289 **Thomas Jolly and Robert Bey as "knuckleheads":** Ibid.

289 **Huey Newton released from jail:** Fraser, C. Gerald, "Newton Expected to Set Up Headquarters in Harlem," *New York Times*, July 12, 1970; Newton, *Revolutionary Suicide*, pp. 295–316; Pearson, *Shadow of the Panther*, pp. 218–225; Austin, *Up Against the Wall*, p. 287.

290 **"When Huey and them founded the party":** Interview with Dhoruba Bin Wahad (September 16, 2008).

290 **Philosophical differences with Huey Newton:** Ibid.; interview with Cleo Silvers (March 26, 2009); interview with William "B.J." Johnson (January 23, 2009); Austin, *Up Against the Wall*, pp. 297–334.

290 **"These motherfuckers had no sense of history":** Ibid.

292 **New York sides with Cleaver faction:** Ibid.; "The Divided Panthers," *Time*, February 22, 1971.

292 **COINTELPRO fuels the split:** FBI COINTELPRO files, various memos; Churchill and Vander Wall, *The COINTELPRO Papers*, pp. 148–150; O'Reilly, *Racial Matters*, pp. 300–324, 329, 330.

292 **"To create friction":** FBI COINTELPRO memo.

293 **"Purpose of counterintelligence action":** FBI COINTELPRO (confidential Hoover memo).

293 **"Should reword this memo to convey":** FBI COINTELPRO (confidential Hoover memo).

293 **Fred Bennett murder:** Pearson, *Shadow of the Panther*, pp. 232–233; Austin, *Up Against the Wall*, p. 324; interview with Dhoruba Bin Wahad (September 16, 2008). Bin Wahad, who met Bennett on one of his trips to Panther headquarters in Oakland, cited the Bennett murder as having "raised the stakes" in the growing tension between the East Coast and Newton.

293 **"Increasing evidence points to rising dissention within BPP":** FBI COINTELPRO (confidential Hoover Airtel memo).

294 **BPP Central Staff Meeting in Queens:** Interview with Dhoruba Bin Wahad (September 16, 2008); FBI COINTELPRO files; Austin, *Up Against the Wall*, p. 317.

295 **Disagreements between Bin Wahad and Panther Twenty-one defendants:** Interview with Dhoruba Bin Wahad (September 16, 2008); interview with Gerald Lefcourt (January 25, 2010). Lefcourt, who was attorney of

record for both Dhoruba and Lumumba Shakur, noted that "Lumumba and the others were very upset with Dhoruba. In fact, they wanted to kick his ass. And it had nothing to do with any split between the East Coast and West Coast. The whole reason Dhoruba had been chosen as the one to be released on bail was because he was supposed to work every day on getting the others out of jail, to organize around the Panther Twenty-one and raise money. Lumumba felt Dhoruba was spending too much time womanizing and ego-tripping."

295 **Panther Twenty-one letter to the Weather Underground:** Interview with Dhoruba Bin Wahad (September 16, 2008); interview with Gerald Lefcourt (January 25, 2010); Austin, *Up Against the Wall*, p. 321; FBI COINTELPRO files.

295 **Bomb set off outside home of Judge Murtagh:** The bombing occurred early on the morning of February 21, 1970. Murtagh's son, John Jr., was eight years old at the time. Many years later, he described the event in a magazine article: "I still recall, as though it were a dream, thinking that someone was lifting and dropping my bed as the explosions jolted me awake, and I remember my mother pulling me from the tangle of sheets and running to the kitchen where my father stood. Through the large windows overlooking the yard, all we could see was the bright glow of flames below. We didn't leave our house for fear of who might be waiting outside. The same night, bombs were thrown at a police car in Manhattan and two military recruiting stations in Brooklyn. Sunlight, the next morning, revealed three sentences of blood-red graffiti on our sidewalk: FREE THE PANTHER 21; THE VIET CONG HAVE WON; KILL THE PIGS." Murtagh, John M., "Fire in the Night: The Weathermen Tried to Kill My Family," *City Journal*, April 30, 2008; interview with John M. Murtagh (February 5, 2010).

Six weeks after the firebombing at the Murtagh home, a mysterious blaze was ignited at the office building of the Panther Twenty-one defense team at Union Square West in Manhattan. Twenty-eight firemen were injured in the four-alarm blaze. A battalion chief characterized the fire as "highly suspicious." Attorney Lefcourt noted in the *New York Daily News* that his office had received numerous threats by mail and phone leading up to the fire; he suggested that papers crucial to the defense may have been damaged or destroyed in the fire, which resulted in yet more delays in a legal proceeding that would become the longest in city history. McCarthy, Philip, and McNamara, Joseph, "Panther Legal Offices Burn: 28 Are Injured," *Daily News*, April 13, 1970.

296 **"I told them not to publish it":** Interview with Dhoruba Bin Wahad (September 16, 2010).

296 **Newton expels the Panther Twenty-one:** Newton, Huey P.,

"On the Defection of Eldridge Cleaver from the Black Panther Party and the Defection of the Black Panther Party from the Black Community," *Black Panther*, April 17, 1971; Pearson, *Shadow of the Panther*, p. 220; Austin, *Up Against the Wall*, p. 310; Newton, *Revolutionary Suicide*, p. 327; FBI COINTELPRO files, various memos.

297 **Bin Wahad informed he is on Newton hit list:** Interview with Dhoruba Bin Wahad (September 16, 2008).

297 **Bin Wahad and others meet to discuss strategy:** Ibid. At this meeting, Afeni Shakur was five months pregnant with a child conceived by fellow Black Panther Billy Garland. The child would be born in East Harlem on June 16, 1971, and named Tupac Shakur, who would grow up to become a famous rapper and movie star, and eventually be shot dead as part of a war between East Coast and West Coast factions of the hip-hop industry.

297 **"This was some heavy shit":** Ibid.

298 **Bin Wahad and Cetewayo meet with Newton in New Haven:** Interview with Dhoruba Bin Wahad (September 16, 2009); Austin, *Up Against the Wall*, pp. 306–308; Hilliard, *This Side of Glory*, pp. 327–331. David Hilliard, who had been loyal to Newton since childhood, describes this meeting in *This Side of Glory* as the moment he knew Huey Newton was possibly losing his soul.

299 **Bin Wahad, Cetewayo, and Connie Matthews escape:** Interview with Dhoruba Bin Wahad (September 16, 2008); Austin, *Up Against the Wall*, pp. 311–313.

299 **Bin Wahad jumps bail:** Interview with Dhoruba bin Wahad (September 16, 2008); interview with Gerald Lefcourt (January 25, 2010); Asbury, Edith Evans, "2 Panther Defendants Are Missing," *New York Times*, February 23, 1971; Austin, *Up Against the Wall*, p. 320; Newton, *Revolutionary Suicide*, p. 327; FBI COINTELPRO files.

299 **Newton expels Bin Wahad et al.:** Interview with Dhoruba Bin Wahad (September 16, 2008); Newton, Huey P., "On the Defection of Eldridge Cleaver from the Black Panther Party and the Defections of the Black Panther Party from the Black Community," *Black Panther*, April 17, 1971; Asbury, Edith Evans, "Newton Denounces 2 Missing Panthers," *New York Times*, February 10, 1971; "Newton Assailed Action by Moore," *New York Times*, June 6, 1971; Austin, *Up Against the Wall*, pp. 320–321; Newton, *Revolutionary Suicide*, p. 327; Hilliard, *This Side of Glory*, p. 335; Pearson, *Shadow of the Panther*, p. 230.

299 **Robert Webb murder:** Austin, *Up Against the Wall*, pp. 313–314; FBI COINTELPRO files.

300 **"That crew who killed Webb":** Interview with Dhoruba Bin Wahad (September 16, 2008).

16. PANTHER JUSTICE

301   **NYPD concerns about BPP persist:** Asbury, Edith Evans, "Policeman Says Panther Shot at Him," *New York Times*, May 12, 1970; Faso, Frank, and Paul Meskill, "National Conspiracy to Kill Police Seen," *Daily News*, September 2, 1970.

301   **"It has been reported":** NYPD BOSS files.

302   **"This amendment would give control":** Black Panther file, Harlem branch (SCRBC); NYPD BOSS file.

303   **Marcy Housing Project "tribunal":** NYPD BOSS file.

304   **Phillips meets Xaviera Hollander:** Shecter with Phillips, *On the Pad*, pp. 22–30; Hollander, Xaviera, *The Happy Hooker*, pp. 286–292; Knapp Commission testimony, October 20, 1971.

305   **"Almost from the moment":** Hollander, *The Happy Hooker*, p. 1.

305   **Phillips and Hollander at P.J. Clarke's:** Ibid., p. 288; Shecter with Phillips, *On the Pad*, p. 22.

305   **Phillips and Officer O'Keefe:** Shecter with Phillips, *On the Pad*, pp. 29–31.

305   **Teddy Ratnoff:** Interview with Mike Armstrong (August 12, 2009); Markham, James M., "Uncovered Undercoverman Changes Jobs," *New York Times*, October 21, 1971; Shecter with Phillips, *On the Pad*, pp. 22–30; Hollander, *The Happy Hooker*, pp. 281–292. In her book, Hollander does not use Ratnoff's real name; she refers to him as "Abe the Bugger."

306   **Mike Armstrong:** Interview with Mike Armstrong (August 12, 2009).

307   **Armstrong meeting with Harlem editor:** Ibid.

307   **Armstrong meeting with ADA Phillips:** Ibid.

308   **Ratnoff goes to work for Knapp Commission:** Interview with Mike Armstrong (August 12, 2009); Shecter with Phillips, *On the Pad*, pp. 25–26; Markham, "Uncovered Undercoverman Changes Jobs," *New York Times*, October 21, 1971.

309   **Irwin Germaise:** Schultz, Ray, *New York Times*, October 17, 1972; Shecter with Phillips, *On the Pad*, pp. 36–41.

310   **"So we scrounged the money together ourselves":** Interview with Mike Armstrong (August 12, 2009).

310   **Germaise confronts Ratnoff:** Shecter with Phillips, *On the Pad*, pp. 40–41.

310   **Phillips and Germaise catch Ratnoff with wire:** Interview with Mike Armstrong (August 12, 2009); Shecter with Phillips, *On the Pad*, pp. 41–43. The dialogue among Phillips, Germaise, and Ratnoff is taken directly from the transcript of the wire recording in *The Knapp Commission Report on Police Corruption*.

312 **"I thought, shit, he's wired":** Shecter with Phillips, *On the Pad*, p. 43.

312 **Armstrong meeting with Phillips:** Interview with Mike Armstrong (August 12, 2009).

313 **Zyad Shakur press conference:** "Destroying the Panther Myth," *Time*, March 22, 1971; Knight, Michael, "Death Here Tied to Panther Feud," *New York Times*, March 10, 1971; Austin, *Up Against the Wall*, pp. 307–308.

314 **"The urban guerrilla must know":** Marighella, Carlos, *Mini-Manual of the Urban Guerrilla*, p. 6.

315 **Killing of Sam Napier:** Interview with Dhoruba Bin Wahad (September 16, 2008); interview with William "B.J." Johnson (January 23, 2010); interview with Gerald Lefcourt (January 25, 2010); Austin, *Up Against the Wall*, pp. 308–313.

316 **"After the Webb murder":** Interview with William "B.J." Johnson (January 23, 2010); Austin, *Up Against the Wall*, p. 314.

316 **Johnson and the Napier killing:** Ibid.

317 **"On the way out, I asked the sister":** Ibid.

318 **"The hit on the Queens distribution office":** Interview with Dhoruba Bin Wahad (September 16, 2008).

319 **"First, let it be understood":** Moore, Richard, "A Black Panther Speaks," *New York Times*, May 12, 1971.

319 **"These internal contradictions":** Ibid.

320 **Panther Twenty-one verdict:** "Panthers Acquitted," *Time*, May 24, 1971; Kennebeck, *Juror Number Four*, pp. 222–238; Zimroth, *Perversion of Justice*, pp. 363–404; Kempton, *The Briar Patch*, pp. 189–195; FBI COINTELPRO files, Airtel memo.

320 **COINTELPRO assessment of Panthers:** FBI COINTELPRO confidential memo.

321 **Shooting of Curry and Binetti outside home of D.A. Hogan:** O'Malley, Daniel, Patrick Doyle, and John Murphy, "2 Cops in Hogan's Guard Machine Gunned," *Daily News*, May 20, 1971; interview with Robert Daley (January 21, 2010); Tanenbaum and Rosenberg, *Badge of the Assassin*, pp. 15–17; Daley, *Target Blue*, pp. 75–86; Seedman and Hellman, *Chief*, pp. 257–270.

321 **Communiqué from BLA:** Ibid.

322 **Killing of Jones and Piagentini outside Harlem housing project:** Duddy, James, and Henry Stathos, "2 Cops Die in Harlem Ambush," *Daily News*, May 22, 1971; McCarthy, Phillip, and Henry Lee, "A Grim Hunt Seeks Out Cop Killers," *Daily News*, May 23, 1971; OPERATION NEWKILL files.

322 **BLA communiqué following Jones and Piagentini killing:** Ibid. The letter read, in part: "All power to the people. Revolutionary justice has been meted out once again by righteous brothers of the Black Liberation Army

with the death of two Gestapo pigs gunned down as so many of our brothers have been gun [*sic*] down in the past. But this time no racist class jury will acquit them. Revolutionary justice is ours. All Power to the people." OPERATION NEWKILL files.

322 **"We're in a war" (Kiernan statement):** *Passin' It On*, PBS documentary; Tanenbaum and Rosenberg, *Badge of the Assassin*, p. 15.

323 **Lindsay and Murphy encounter with officers outside station house:** Tanenbaum and Rosenberg, *Badge of the Assassin*, pp. 18–21.

324 **"There are those who call themselves your brothers":** "Why Kill Black Cops?" *Amsterdam News*, May 25, 1971.

325 **Whitmore meets Abby Mann:** Interview with George Whitmore (April 3, 2009); interview with Myron Beldock (January 27, 2009); interview with Selwyn Raab (April 22, 2009).

326 **Whitmore's growing disenchantment with his situation:** Interview with George Whitmore (April 3, 2009).

17. NEWKILL

327 **Attempted robbery at Triple-O social club:** Interview with Dhoruba Bin Wahad (September 16, 2008); interview with Robert Daley (January 21, 2010); Daley, *Target Blue*, pp. 81–86; Seedman and Hellman, *Chief*, pp. 442–444.

328 **Bin Wahad's time underground:** Interview with Dhoruba Bin Wahad (September 16, 2008).

328 **"The black underground":** *Passin' It On*, PBS documentary.

330 **"We were lucky to be taken alive":** Interview with Dhoruba Bin Wahad (September 16, 2008).

330 **Bin Wahad et al. arrested and held at Forty-eighth Precinct station house:** In the documentary *Passin' It On*, both Bin Wahad and Jamal Joseph allege that they were "tortured" while in custody, but there was never any evidence to back that up. In a photograph, Bin Wahad is seen being led from the station house with no visible signs of physical abuse.

330 **Police funerals:** The funeral in the Bronx for Waverly Jones was estimated to be one of the largest in NYPD history. The funeral for Joseph Piagentini was held in suburban Long Island, where the officer had lived with his wife, Diane, and two children. "Another Cop Mourned," *Daily News*, May 28, 1971; Tanenbaum and Rosenberg, *Badge of the Assassin*, p. 37.

331 **Largest NYPD manhunt in history:** Tanenbaum and Rosenberg, *Badge of the Assassin*, pp. 38–43; NYPD Task Force file memo.

Along with the official investigation, there began in the wake of the Jones and Piagentini shooting an unofficial enterprise. Detective Randy Jurgensen, who had been one of the first responders at the Jones and Piagentini murder scene, became part of a unit known as "Grosso's Groupettes," after lead detective Sonny Grosso. With the release of *The French Connection* (1970), in which actor Roy Scheider played Grosso, who served as technical adviser, the veteran cop was now a star in the department. He was given a squad of half a dozen cops and citywide jurisdiction to investigate cases involving the Black Liberation Army. Many on the force knew about the unit, but its existence was kept secret from the Lindsay administration, which was not yet willing to admit publicly that the BLA even existed. Interview with Randy Jurgensen (February 12, 2010); interview with Sonny Grosso (April 13, 2009).

331   **"Approximately 1000 DD-5's were submitted":** NYPD Task Force memo.

331   **Nixon meets with Hoover to discuss police shootings in NYC:** O'Reilly, *Racial Matters*, p. 321; Perlstein, *Nixonland*, p. 411. The *Daily News* ran a photo on page three of Nixon, Hoover, and Attorney General John Mitchell, under the headline "Discuss N.Y. Killings at White House," with the caption: "President Nixon is flanked by Attorney General John Mitchell and FBI Director J. Edgar Hoover at White House yesterday. Trio met to review federal efforts to help New York police track down slayers of Patrolman Waverly Jones and Joseph Piagentini." *Daily News*, May 27, 1971.

332   **Formation of OPERATION NEWKILL:** Interview with Robert Boyle (November 21, 2008); Churchill and Vander Wall, *The COINTELPRO Papers*, p. 158d; O'Reilly, *Racial Matters*, pp. 321–324; OPERATION NEWKILL files, various memos.

332   **"Due to the fact" (NEWKILL memo):** OPERATION NEWKILL files.

333   **Machine gun linked to Curry and Binetti shooting:** Ibid.; Daley, *Target Blue*, pp. 80–81; Seedman and Hellman, *Chief*, pp. 447–448; interview with Robert Boyle (November 21, 2008); McFadden, Robert D., "4 Seized in Bronx Holdup, Linked to Police Deaths," *New York Times*, June 6, 1971; Montgomery, Paul L., "Evidence Seen Growing in Police Shooting Here," *New York Times*, June 7, 1971; Van Gelder, Lawrence, "Roberts Links 2 Holdup Suspects to Police Shootings," *New York Times*, June 12, 1971.

334   **Pauline Joseph:** OPERATION NEWKILL files; Daley, *Target Blue*, pp. 81–85; Seedman and Hellman, *Chief*, pp. 448–449; interview with Dhoruba Bin Wahad (September 16, 2008); interview with Robert Boyle (November 21, 2008); interview with Robert Daley (January 21, 2010).

334   **757 Beck Street as headquarters for BLA cell:** Ibid.

337   **Bin Wahad indictments announced:** Darnton, John, "7 Panthers Indicted in Slaying of a Party Official in Corona," *New York Times*, July 30, 1971.

337   **Bin Wahad arraignment before Judge Riccobono:** "Black Panther Here Is Charged in the Shooting of 2 Policemen," *New York Times*, July 31, 1971.

338   **Robert Vickers incident:** OPERATION NEWKILL memo; Clark, Alfred E., "Members of Black Army Sought in Bronx Street-by-Street Hunt," *New York Times*, March 8, 1973.

338   **Twymon Myers:** Interview with Cleo Silvers (March 26, 2009); OPERATION NEWKILL memo.

338   **JoAnne Chesimard aka Assata Shakur:** OPERATION NEWKILL files; Daley, *Target Blue*, pp. 291–293; Seedman and Hellman, *Chief*, pp. 421, 424; Shakur, Assata, *Assata*, entire book.

339   **Phillips working undercover for Knapp investigators:** Interview with Mike Armstrong (August 12, 2009); Shecter with Phillips, *On the Pad*, pp. 233–286; *The Knapp Commission Report*, pp. 50–56.

339   **Phillips's use of word *nigger:*** Shecter with Phillips, *On the Pad*.

340   **Phillips's cover is blown:** Ibid.

340   **"How the fuck did I ever agree to do a thing like this?":** Ibid.

341   **Phillips's testimony at Knapp Commission hearings:** Interview with Mike Armstrong (August 12, 2009); Federici, William, and Paul Meskil, "Harlem Take Ran 70G Month: Payoff Cop Gives Knapp Lowdown," *Daily News*, October 20, 1971; Burton, Anthony, "How to Be a Corrupt Cop & Live to Tell," *Daily News*, October 20, 1971; Burnham, Davis, "Knapp Commission Hears of Police Bribes of Up to $1,500," *New York Times*, October 21, 1971; "Excerpts of Testimony by Patrolman Phillips on Graft-Taking," *New York Times*, October 20, 1971; "Excerpts from Testimony of Patrolman Phillips on System of Payoff to Police," *New York Times*, October 21, 1971; "A Glossary of Terms Relating to Corruption," *New York Times*, October 21, 1971; "Guarding the Guardians," *Time*, November 1, 1971; Shecter with Phillips, *On the Pad*, pp. 287–295; *The Knapp Commission Report*, pp. 40–41; *NBC News Report* (Vanderbilt TVNA), October 19, 20, 1971; *ABC News Report* (Vanderbilt TVNA), October 19, 20, 1971.

343   **"Thank God his dad's gone":** Clines, Francis X., "The Witness: Policeman's Son, a 'Decent Lad,' a Cool Grafter," *New York Times*, October 22, 1971.

344   **Commissioner Murphy response:** ABC Television statement (Vanderbilt TVNA), October 21, 1971; Pace, Eric, "Murphy Defends Honesty of the Average Policeman," *New York Times*, October 22, 1971; Daley, *Target Blue*, pp. 310–311; Lardner and Reppetto, *NYPD*, pp. 269–270, 271; Murphy and Plate, *Commissioner*, p. 178.

344   **Kiernan/PBA response:** Pace, Eric, "Inquiry Called 'Knapp

Circus': Leaders of Police Groups at Meeting Here Are Critical of the Corruption Panel," *New York Times*, October 23, 1971; Burnham, David, "Lindsay Defends Corruption Hearing: Tells P.B.A. Head the Inquiry Is in 'Best Interest' of Everyone on Force," *New York Times*, October 26, 1971.

344 **Totality of Knapp hearings (Droge, Logan, and Serpico):** "Knapp Unit's Head Defends Legality of Investigation," *New York Times*, October 24, 1971; "Knapp Urges Permanent Body on Police Corruption to Succeed His Panel," *New York Times*, October 25, 1971; "Knapp Witness to Tell of Lindsay Officials' Apathy," *New York Times*, October 30, 1971; Burnham, David, "Patrolman Says 'All But 2' of Colleagues Got Bribes," *New York Times*, October 23, 1971; "Cops as Pushers," *Time*, November 8, 1971.

346 **"The whole fucking Harlem stinks":** Shecter with Phillips, *On the Pad*, p. 168.

347 **"I didn't know what to say":** Ibid.

348 *New York Cops Talk Back:* This study by Nicholas Alex of police attitudes in the years of racial unrest and the Knapp Commission hearings is one of the most revealing documents of its time. Alex interviewed forty-seven white cops, who spoke freely and openly on condition of anonymity. The study was a follow-up to a previous book-length study by Alex of African American officers entitled *Black in Blue*.

349 **Foster and Laurie shooting:** Whelton, Clark, "The Blood on Avenue B," *Village Voice*, February 10, 1972; Kaufman, Michael T., "9 in Black 'Army' Are Hunted in Police Assassinations," *New York Times*, February 9, 1972; interview with Robert Daley (January 21, 2010); interview with Gerald Lefcourt (January 25, 2010); Silverman, Al, *Foster and Laurie*, pp. 3–44; Daley, *Target Blue*, pp. 412–415; Seedman and Hellman, *Chief*, pp. 482–485.

350 **"This is from the George Jackson Squad of the Black Liberation Army":** Daley, *Target Blue*, p. 417; Seedman and Hellman, *Chief*, p. 438; NEWKILL files contains a copy of the actual communiqué.

350 **"Too many policemen have been killed":** Kaufman, Michael T., "Murphy Asks for Federal Help in Hunt for Policeman's Killers," *New York Times*, February 18, 1972.

351 **Rise of "black army":** Arnold, Martin, "Murphy Suggests Roving Band May Have Killed 2 Policemen," *New York Times*, February 4, 1972; Kaufman, Michael T., "Evidence of 'Liberation Army' Said to Rise," *New York Times*, February 17, 1972.

351 **Murphy defends his position:** Gelsner, Lesley, "Murphy Defends Accusations of 9," *New York Times*, February 11, 1972.

351 **Injunction filed by Robert Bloom:** Kaufman, Michael T., "5 Seeking to Curb Police Publicity," *New York Times*, February 22, 1972; "A Justice

Refuses Motion to Dismiss Panthers' Charges," *New York Times*, February 23, 1972; Lubasch, Arnold H., "'Black Army' Link Allowed in Court," *New York Times*, February 29, 1972.

352 **Whitmore final appeal overturned:** Interview with Myron Beldock (January 27, 2009); interview with George Whitmore (April 3, 2009); "Whitmore Loses Bid for a Hearing," *New York Times*, February 29, 1972.

352 **Raab visits Whitmore at Green Haven:** Interview with Selwyn Raab (April 22, 2009).

18. LONG TIME COMIN'

355 **Raab and Beldock focus on Celeste Viruet:** Interview with Myron Beldock (January 27, 2009); interview with Selwyn Raab (April 22, 2009).

355 **"I'm not sure who came up with the idea first":** Interview with Myron Beldock (January 27, 2009).

355 **The hunt for Celeste Viruet:** Interview with Selwyn Raab (April 22, 2009); interview with Myron Beldock (January 27, 2009).

355 **Beldock, Raab, and crew travel to Puerto Rico:** Ibid.

356 **Encounter with hotel café busboy:** Ibid.

356 **Interview with Celeste Viruet:** Ibid.

359 **Frederick Douglass quote:** Bin Wahad often used another famous Douglass quote in his writing and as a guiding principle in his life: "Power concedes nothing without demand. It never has and never will."

359 **Napier murder trial in Queens:** Siegel, Max H., "Girl, 12, Describes Killing of a Black Panther Here," *New York Times*, March 25, 1972; McQuiston, John T., "Hung Jury Ends Panther 4 Trial," *New York Times*, June 15, 1972; interview with Dhoruba Bin Wahad (September 16, 2009).

359 **Bin Wahad pleads guilty to Napier charges:** McFadden, Robert D., "4 Black Panthers Plead Guilty to a Lesser Charge in Slaying," *New York Times*, May 22, 1973.

360 **Curry and Binetti attempted murder trial:** Fosburgh, Lacey, "A Black Panther on Trial Here in Attempt to Slay 2 Policemen," *New York Times*, November 4, 1972; Fosburgh, Lacey, "Patrolman Tells of 1971 Shooting," *New York Times*, November 7, 1972; Proctor, William, "Friends Link Moore to Gun, Cop Shooting," *Daily News*, November 10, 1972; Pearl, Mike, "Gun Is Key in Panther Case," *New York Post*, December 10, 1972; "Woman Faces New Grilling in Trial of Panther Moore," *New York Post*, November 11, 1972; Pearl, Mike, "Machinegun Trial: The Summations," *New York Post*, December 6, 1972; Pearl, Mike, "Machinegun Trial Going to Jurors," *New York Post*, December 7, 1972; "Moore Jury Still Out," *New York Post*, December 8, 1972; "Panther Jury Is Deadlocked," *Daily News*, December 9, 1972; McQuiston, John T., "Case on

2 Policemen Shot Here Ends in Mistrial," *New York Times*, December 10, 1972; "New Trial Set for Panther," *New York Post*, January 2, 1973; Proctor, William, "Panther Trial Opens," *Daily News*, January 3, 1973.

360 **"Here [were] two damaged white people" (juror Frank Treu):** *Passin' It On*, PBS documentary.

362 **"One of the other jurors says":** Ibid.

362 **Third Curry and Binetti trial:** Interview with Dhoruba Bin Wahad (September 16, 2008); Fosburgh, Lacey, "Panther Convicted of Attack on Police," *New York Times*, March 8, 1973.

362 **Bin Wahad sentencing:** Fosburgh, Lacey, "Panther Gets Life Term in Attack on 2 Policemen," *New York Times*, April 27, 1973.

363 **Grass eaters and meat eaters:** Interview with Mike Armstrong (August 12, 2009); *The Knapp Commission Report on Police Corruption*, p. 65; Levitt, *NYPD Confidential*, p. 8; Cannato, *The Ungovernable City*, p. 477.

366 **Phillips charged in double murder:** Kirkman, Edward, "Phillips Indicted in '68 Killing of Two," *Daily News*, March 21, 1972; Shecter with Phillips, *On the Pad*, pp. 301–325; interview with Mike Armstrong (August 12, 2009).

366 **"It was around three in the afternoon":** Shecter with Phillips, *On the Pad*, p. 304.

366 **Riot in front of Mosque Number Seven:** Interview with Randy Jurgensen (February 12, 2010); interview with Sonny Grosso (April 13, 2009); Jurgensen and Cea, *Circle of Six*, pp. 12–20; Grosso, Sonny, and John Devaney, *Murder at the Mosque*, pp. 6–7, 11, 12; Levitt, *NYPD Confidential*, pp. 12–13.

367 **"I thought I was shot":** Interview with Randy Jurgensen (February 12, 2010).

367 **Murder at the mosque:** The killing of Patrolman Phillip Cardillo was never solved and remains an open case.

368 **Phillips murder trial before Judge Murtagh:** Schultz, Ray, "The Anatomy of a Murder Trial: The People v. William Phillips," *New York Times Magazine*, December 17, 1972; Shecter with Phillips, *On the Pad*, pp. 332–362.

370 **Warden allows Whitmore to watch TV in hospital ward:** Interview with George Whitmore (April 3, 2009).

370 ***The Marcus-Nelson Murders:*** The movie begins with a disclaimer: "What you are about to see is a dramatization of one of the most controversial and bitterly debated police investigations preceding the Supreme Court's landmark *Miranda* decision of 1966. Name changes, compressions of time and composites of certain characters have been made to present this most significant story." The movie was viewed by the author at PCM.

The Marcus-Nelson Murders was generally praised for its realism and seriousness, though TV critic John J. O'Connor of the *New York Times* attacked the movie as "fiction covered with a layer of fact. . . . Mr. Mann's social indictment is highly questionable. The bad guys, policemen and prosecutors consumed with ambition, are either sadistic or slimy. . . . [Mann's] indictment is so broad that it disintegrates into a scenario for white hats and black hats. Without a strong measure of precision, old fashioned liberal 'guilt' isn't enough." O'Connor, John J., "C.B.S.'s 3-Hour Movie Examines Justice," *New York Times*, March 8, 1973.

371 **Whitmore's feelings about *The Marcus-Nelson Murders:*** Interview with George Whitmore (April 3, 2009).

372 **Airing of *The 51st State:*** The segment on the Whitmore case, approximately fifteen minutes in length, was devastating. Celeste Viruet is interviewed in shadows, using a translator. She notes that after giving the police her version of events—a version that contradicts that of Elba Borrero—she was never questioned again by investigators or prosecutors. *The 51st State* (episode no. 177), which aired January 1973, was viewed by the author at PCM.

372 **D.A. Gold reopens case:** Oelsner, Lesley, "Whitmore Rape-Robbery Case Reopened by District Attorney," *New York Times*, December 23, 1972.

372 **Beldock receives call from D.A.'s office:** Interview with Myron Beldock (January 27, 2009).

373 **"Selwyn was pretty certain it was going to be a dismissal":** Ibid.

373 **Riot at Green Haven prison:** Interview with George Whitmore (April 3, 2009); interview with Joseph "Jazz" Hayden; Darnton, John, "Clash Among Inmates Reported at Green Haven State Prison," *New York Times*, September 16, 1972; Darnton, John, "Security Is Tight at Green Haven," *New York Times*, September 17, 1972. According to some accounts, the riot was touched off by one inmate absconding with another inmate's pet bird. Jazz Hayden happened to be at Green Haven at the same time as Whitmore (though they didn't know each other). When the riot broke out, Hayden wound up in the middle of things; he was hit in the face and rushed to hospital with a broken jaw.

374 **Whitmore brought from Green Haven to NYC:** Interview with George Whitmore (April 3, 2009).

376 **Whitmore set free:** Interview with George Whitmore (April 3, 2009); interview with Myron Beldock (January 27, 2009); interview with Selwyn Raab (April 22, 2009); Ross, Edwin, and Marcia Kramer, "9-Year Legal Nightmare Ends; Whitmore Freed," *Daily News*, April 11, 1973; Oelsner, Lesley, "Whitmore Wins Freedom on Gold's New Evidence," *New York Times*, April 11, 1973; "Justice Uncoiled," *Time*, April 23, 1973.

376 **"I never expected to see the day":** Interview with George Whitmore (April 3, 2009).

EPILOGUE

379 **Lindsay runs for president:** Cannato, *The Ungovernable City*, pp. 501–515; *Fun City Revisited*, PBS documentary.

380 **Remnants of the BLA:** Interview with Sonny Grosso (April 13, 2009); interview with Randy Jurgensen (February 12, 2010); Clark, "Members of Black Army Sought in Bronx Street-by-Street Hunt," *New York Times*, March 8, 1973; Tanenbaum and Rosenberg, *Badge of the Assassin*, pp. 452–454; Muntaqim, Jalil, *On the Black Liberation Army*, pp. 2–18.

380 **Killing of Twymon Myers:** Interview with Sonny Grosso (April 13, 2009); interview with Randy Jurgensen (February 12, 2010); McQuiston, John T., "Fugitive Black Militant Is Killed in Bronx Shootout with Police," *New York Times*, November 15, 1973.

381 **Capture of Assata Shakur:** Kaufman, Michael T., "Woman Captured in Shoot-Out Called 'Soul' of Black Militants," *New York Times*, May 3, 1973; Gupte, Pranay, "Joanne Chesimard Pleads Not Guilty in Holdup Here," *New York Times*, July 21, 1973; Chambers, Marcia, "Mrs. Chesimard Wins Acquittal," *New York Times*, December 29, 1973.

382 **Phillips found guilty of double murder and attempted murder:** Clark, Alfred E., "Jury Convicts Phillips of 2 Brothel Murders in 1968," *New York Times*, November 22, 1974.

382 **"I could never, never spend the rest of my life in fucking jail":** Shecter with Phillips, *On the Pad*, p. 313.

382 **Phillips, the prison years:** Interview with Sean Gardiner (June 11, 2009); Gardiner, Sean, "Freeze Frame on a Bad Cop," *Village Voice*, August 8, 2006; Gray, Geoffrey, "Crooked Cop, Now Jailhouse Lawyer, Seeks Parole at 74," *New York Sun*, March 28, 2005; Gray, "Spitzer to Appeal Decision on Phillips Parole Hearing," *New York Sun*, April 5, 2005; Gray, "Time and Time Served," *New York Times*, February 5, 2007.

383 **Armstrong support of Phillips:** Mike Armstrong, former lead counsel for the Knapp Commission, has always contended that he does not believe Phillips committed the murders for which he was convicted, though Phillips believes Armstrong could have done more to advocate on his behalf. Interview with Mike Armstrong (August 12, 2009); interview with Geoffrey Gray (November 19, 2009); interview with Ido Mizrahy (November 19, 2009); Gardiner, "Freeze Frame on a Bad Cop," *Village Voice*, August 8, 2006.

383 **"Most of these guys were in diapers when I was testifying":** Gardiner, "Freeze Frame on a Bad Cop," *Village Voice*, August 8, 2006.

384 **Phillips before state parole board:** Transcript of Parole Board hearing, September 21, 1999, NY State Division of Parole.

385 **Phillips's 2007 parole hearing:** Transcript of hearing, September 19, 2007, NY State Parole Board.

385   **Phillips released from prison:** Gregorian, Dareh, "Freedom for '68 Slay Cop," *New York Post*, September 23, 2007; interview with Geoffrey Gray (November 19, 2009); interview with Ido Mizrahy (November 19, 2009); Lueck, Thomas J., "Officer Jailed for 32 Years Wins Parole," *New York Times*, September 23, 2007.

385   **Bin Wahad first hears of COINTELPRO:** Interview with Dhoruba Bin Wahad (September 16, 2008).

386   **Robert Boyle meets Bin Wahad in prison:** Interview with Robert Boyle (November 19, 2009); interview with Dhoruba Bin Wahad (September 16, 2008).

386   **Lawyers Boyle and Elizabeth Fink begin investigation:** Interview with Robert Boyle (November 19, 2009).

387   **U.S. government forced to release files on Bin Wahad:** Kifner, John, "Ex-Panther in Prison Says Evidence Was Concealed," *New York Times*, April 3, 1989; interview with Dhoruba Bin Wahad (September 16, 2009); interview with Robert Boyle (November 19, 2009).

387   **Judge McQuillan statement:** *People v. Bin Wahad*, statement of Justice Peter J. McQuillan, March 15, 1990.

388   **Bin Wahad charges reversed:** Sullivan, Ronald, "After 17 Years, Panther Conviction Is Upset," *New York Times*, March 16, 1990; Sullivan, Ronald, "Court Erupts as Judge Frees an Ex-Panther," *New York Times*, March 23, 1990; interview with Dhoruba Bin Wahad (September 16, 2008); interview with Robert Boyle (November 19, 2009).

388   **Bin Wahad lawsuit of state and federal governments:** Feur, Alan, "Defiant Ex-Panther Sues Defiant New York Police," *New York Times*, December 4, 2000; Weiser, Benjamin, "City Agrees to Settle Suit by Former Panther Leader," *New York Times*, December 8, 2000.

388   **Bin Wahad in Africa:** Interview with Dhoruba Bin Wahad (September 16, 2009); *Passin' It On*. On the DVD version of the film there is an interview "extra" with Bin Wahad in Ghana.

389   **"I don't know if I ever thought":** Interview with Dhoruba Bin Wahad (September 16, 2009).

389   **"I used to drive through Africa":** Ibid.

390   **"I got tired of everybody":** Interview with George Whitmore (April 3, 2009).

391   **Resolution of Whitmore's lawsuit:** Interview with Myron Beldock (January 27, 2009); interview with George Whitmore (April 3, 2009); Raab, Selwyn, "Judge Dismisses Whitmore's Suit Against the City," *New York Times*, April 16, 1979; "Court Ruling Allows Suit on False Charge," *New York Times*, February 27, 1981.

391   **Whitmore purchase of home:** Interview with George Whitmore (April 3, 2009).

391   **"One morning I woke up":** Ibid.

391   **Whitmore's "KKK problem":** Ibid.

392   **"Out on the ocean seemed to be the only place":** Ibid.

392   **Whitmore troubles with the law:** New Jersey police records, 1971–2007; interview with George Whitmore (April 3, 2009).

393   **Whitmore hit by car (2010):** Interview with George Whitmore (February 1, 2010).

393   **"I've had three heart attacks, been declared dead":** Ibid.

393   **New York City crime statistics:** Since the mid-1990s the city has seen the longest sustained period of declining crime rates in its recent history. Numerous civic and political figures have claimed credit for this phenomenon, and many have staked their careers on the city being safer and more secure. Although few would argue with the fact that the city is less crime-ridden today than it was thirty or forty years ago, in February 2010—in a survey conducted by a private research group—more than one hundred retired captains and high-ranking officers in the NYPD acknowledged that they knew that certain crime statistics were being manipulated for public consumption. Pressure to keep crime stats low led some precinct commanders to dispatch aides to crime scenes to persuade victims not to file complaints or to urge them to change their accounts in ways that could result in the downgrading of offenses to lower crimes. Retired members of the force reported that they were aware over the years of "ethically inappropriate" alterations of the numbers in the seven major crime categories, all of which helped create the illusion of a safer city. Rashbaum, William K., "Retired Officers Raise Questions on Crime Data," *New York Times*, February 7, 2010.

394   **Stop and frisk rate:** In 2010, a study by the Center for Constitutional Rights of NYPD "stop and frisk" data showed that blacks and Latinos were nine times more likely than whites to be stopped by police, but that once stopped, they were no more likely to be arrested, suggesting that they were not stopped because they were committing a crime but because of their ethnicity. The study came about as the result of a lawsuit filed by the New York Civil Liberties Union. Baker, Al, "New York Minorities More Likely to Be Frisked," *New York Times*, March 12, 2010; Rivera, Ray, Al Baker and Janet Roberts, "A Few Blocks, 4 Years, 52,000 Police Stops," *New York Times*, July 12, 2010; Rayman, Graham, a five-part series in *The Village Voice* that commenced with "The NYPD Tapes: Inside Bed-Stuy's 81st Precinct," May 5, 2010, and continued with "The Corroboration," August 25, 2010.

SOURCES

INTERVIEWS

Whenever possible, this book is based on firsthand accounts from people who lived through the events. Some of the interviews conducted were hours in length and ranged over numerous sessions, others short phone conversations to track down a specific piece of information. In the case of two interview subjects—George Whitmore and Dhoruba Bin Wahad—the interviews were extensive and involved follow-up conversations too numerous to list individually. Listed below are all interview subjects and the dates on which the major interviews occurred: Michael Armstrong (August 12, 2009); Myron Beldock (January 27, 2009); Dhoruba Bin Wahad (September 16 and 25, 2008; November 12, 2008; December 23, 2008; January 28, 2009; February 18, 2009; November 6, 2009; January 22, 2010); Robert Boyle (November 21, 2008); Robert Daley (January 21, 2010); Eddie Ellis (May 15, 2009); Sean Gardiner (June 6, 2009); Geoffrey Gray (November 19, 2009); Sonny Grosso (April 13, 2009); Joseph "Jazz" Hayden (December 19, 2008; January 23, 2009); Thomas Hughes (May 13, 2010); Randy Jurgensen (February 12, 2010); William "B.J." Johnson (January 23, 2010); Gerald Lefcourt (January 25, 2010); Jerome J. Leftow (February 17, 2009); Robert Leuci (February 12, 2009); Leonard Levitt (January 13, 2010); Brian McDonald (February 4, 2010); Ido Mizrahy (November 19, 2009); John M. Murtagh (February 5, 2010); William "Bill" Phillips (July 6, 20011); Selwyn Raab (April 22, 2009); Cleo Silvers (March 26, 2009); Edwin Torres (April 13, 2009); George Whitmore (April 3 and 5, 2009; June 18, 2009; September 21, 2009; December 1, 2009; February 1, 2010); Gerald Whitmore (June 18, 2009).

BOOKS

It is worth noting that three separate books were published about the Wylie-Hoffert murders and the legal travails of George Whitmore in the late 1960s. All three are excellent and come at the story from a slightly different angle. *Justice in the Back Room* (1967), by Selwyn Raab, frames the Whitmore story around the criminal justice issue of false or forced confessions; *Whitmore* (1968) by Fred Shapiro is a personal account of the life of George Whitmore (though Whitmore was only twenty-three years old when the book was published); and *The Victims* (1969) by Bernard Lefkowitz and Kenneth Gross focuses primarily on the police investigation into the Wylie-Hoffert murders and the ultimate conviction of Richard Robles. I cite all three as important sources for this book, though they are somewhat limited by the fact that they were published while the saga was still playing out in the courts and Whitmore's fate not yet determined.

Ahmad, Muhammad. *We Will Return in the Whirlwind: Black Radical Organizations, 1960–1975*. Chicago: Charles H. Kerr Co., 2007.

Alex, Nicholas. *New York Cops Talk Back: A Study of a Beleaguered Minority*. New York: John Wiley & Sons, 1976.

Austin, Curtis J. *Up Against the Wall: Violence in the Making and Unmaking of the Black Panther Party*. Fayetteville: University of Arkansas Press, 2008.

Balagoon, Kuwasi, et al. *Look for Me in the Whirlwind*. New York: Random House, 1971.

Baldwin, James. *The Fire Next Time*. New York: Dial Press, 1963.

———.*Notes of a Native Son*. Boston: Beacon Press, 1955.

Biondi, Martha. *To Stand and Fight: The Struggle for Civil Rights in Postwar New York City*. Cambridge, MA: Harvard University Press, 2003.

Blackmon, Douglas A. *Slavery by Another Name: The Re-Enslavement of Black Americans from the Civil War to World War II*. New York: Doubleday, 2008.

Branch, Taylor. *At Canaan's Edge: America in the King Years, 1965–68*. New York: Simon & Schuster, 2001.

———. *Pillar of Fire: America in the King Years, 1963–65*. New York: Simon & Schuster, 1998.

———. *Parting the Waters: America in the King Years, 1954–63*. New York: Simon & Schuster, 1988.

Breitman, George, Herman Porter, and Baxter Smith. *The Assassination of Malcolm X*. New York: Pathfinder, 1976.

Breitman, George (ed.). *Malcolm X Speaks*. New York: Grove Press, 1965.

Brown, Claude. *Manchild in the Promised Land*. New York: Macmillan, 1965.

Butterfield, Fox. *All God's Children: The Boskett Family and the American Tradition of Violence*. New York: Knopf, 1995.

Cannato, Vincent J. *The Ungovernable City: John Lindsay and His Struggle to Save New York City*. New York: Basic Books, 2001.

Carmichael, Stokely. *Black Power: The Politics of Liberation in America*. New York: Vintage, 1967.

Churchill, Ward, and Jim Vander Wall. *The COINTELPRO Papers: Documents from the FBI's Secret War Against Domestic Dissent*. Cambridge, MA: South End Press, 1990.

Cleaver, Eldridge. *Soul on Ice*. New York: McGraw-Hill, 1968.

———. *Target Zero: A Life Writing*. New York: Palgrave, 2007.

Conlon, Edward. *Blue Blood*. New York: Riverhead, 2004.

Connolly, Harold X. *A Ghetto Grows in Brooklyn*. New York: New York University Press, 1977.

Cunningham, Barry, and Mike Pearl. *Mr. District Attorney: The Story of Frank Hogan*. New York: Mason/Charter, 1977.

Daley, Robert. *Target Blue: An Insider's View of the N.Y.P.D.* New York: Delacorte Press, 1973.

Du Bois, W. E. B. *The Souls of Black Folk*. New York: New American Library, 1969.

Durant, Sam (ed.). *Black Panther: The Revolutionary Art of Emory Douglas*. New York: Rizzoli International Publications, 2007.

Ellison, Ralph. *Invisible Man*. New York: Random House, 1947.

Estes, Steve. *I Am a Man! Race, Manhood, and the Civil Rights Movement*. Chapel Hill, NC: University of North Carolina Press, 2005.

Fanon, Frantz. *The Wretched of the Earth*. New York: Grove Press, 1963.

Gelb, Arthur. *City Room*. New York: G. P. Putnam's Sons, 2003.

Goldman, Peter Louis. *The Death and Life of Malcolm X*. New York: Harper & Row, 1979.

Greenwood, Peter W. *An Analysis of Apprehension Activities of the New York City Police Department*. Washington, D.C.: Rand Institute, 1970.

Gregory, Dick. *Nigger: An Autobiography*. New York: E. P. Dutton, 1964.

Grosso, Sonny, and John Devaney. *Murder at the Harlem Mosque*. New York: Crown, 1977.

Haley, Alex. *Autobiography of Malcolm X*. New York: Grove Press, 1964.

Hansen, Drew D. *The Dream: Martin Luther King Jr. and the Speech That Inspired a Nation*. New York: HarperCollins, 2003.

Hayden, Tom. *Rebellion in Newark*. New York: Vintage Books, 1967.

Heath, G. Louis. *Off the Pigs! The History and Literature of the Black Panther Party*. Lenham, MD: Rowan & Littlefield, 1976.

Hilliard, David (ed.). *The Black Panther: Intercommunal News Service, 1967–1980*. New York: Atria Books, 2007.

Hilliard, David, and Fredrika Newton (eds.). *The Huey P. Newton Reader.* New York: Seven Stories Press, 2003.

Hilliard, David, with Lewis Cole. *This Side of Glory: The Autobiography of David Hilliard and the Story of the Black Panther Party.* Boston: Back Bay Books, 1993.

Hollander, Xaviera. *The Happy Hooker.* New York: Dell, 1972.

Jackson, Kenneth T. (ed.). *The Encyclopedia of New York City.* New Haven, CT: Yale University Press, 1995.

Johnson, Marilynn S. *Street Justice: A History of Police Violence in New York City.* Boston: Beacon Press, 2003.

Jonas, Gilbert. *Freedom's Sword: The NAACP and the Struggle Against Racism, 1909–1969.* New York: Routledge, 2004.

Joseph, Peniel E. *Waiting 'Til the Midnight Hour: A Narrative History of Black Power in America.* New York: Henry Holt, 2006.

Jurgensen, Randy, and Robert Cea. *Circle of Six: The True Story of New York's Most Notorious Cop Killer and the Cop Who Risked Everything to Catch Him.* New York: Disinformation Co., 2006.

Kempton, Murray. *The Briar Patch: The People of the State of New York v. Lumumba Shakur et al.* New York: E. P. Dutton, 1973.

Kennebeck, Edwin. *Juror Number Four: The Trial of Thirteen Black Panthers as Seen From the Jury Box.* New York: W. W. Norton, 1973

Klein, Herbert. *The Police: Damned If They Do, Damned If They Don't.* New York: Crown, 1968.

Kunstler, William. *My Life As a Radical Lawyer.* New York: Carol Publishing Co., 1994.

Lardner, James. *Crusader: The Hell-Raising Police Career of Detective David Durk.* New York: Random House, 1996.

Lardner, James, and Thomas Reppetto. *NYPD: A City and Its Police.* New York: Henry Holt, 2000.

Lefkowitz, Bernard, and Kenneth Gross. *The Victims: The Wylie-Hoffert Murder Case—and Its Strange Aftermath.* New York: G. P. Putnam's Sons, 1969.

Lemann, Nicholas. *The Promised Land: The Great Black Migration and How It Changed America.* New York: Vintage Books, 1992.

Lester, Julius. *Look Out, Whitey!: Black Power's Gon' Get Your Mama!* New York: Grove Press, 1969.

Levitt, Leonard. *NYPD Confidential: Power and Corruption in the Country's Greatest Police Force.* New York: Thomas Dunne Books, 2009.

Leuci, Robert. *All the Centurions: A New York City Cop Remembers His Years on the Street, 1961–1981.* New York: William Morrow, 2004.

Leyson, Burr W. *Fighting Crime: The New York Police Department in Action.* New York: E. P. Dutton, 1948.

Lindsay, John V. *The City.* New York: W. W. Norton, 1969.

Maas, Peter. *Serpico.* New York: Viking, 1973.

Marighella, Carlos. *Mini-Manual of the Urban Guerrilla.* Montreal: Abraham Guillen Press, 2002 (originally published in 1969).

McDonald, Brian. *My Father's Gun: One Family, Three Badges, One Hundred Years in the NYPD.* New York: Dutton, 1999.

Morris, Charles R. *The Cost of Good Intentions: New York City and the Liberal Experiment, 1960–1975.* New York: W. W. Norton, 1980.

Muntaqim, Jalil. *On the Black Liberation Army.* Montreal: Abraham Guillen Press, 2002 (first published in 1997).

Murphy, Patrick V., and Thomas Plate. *Commissioner: A View from the Top of American Law Enforcement.* New York: Simon & Schuster, 1977.

Newton, Huey P. *Revolutionary Suicide.* New York: Harcourt Brace Jovanovich, 1973.

O'Reilly, Kenneth. *Racial Matters: The FBI's Secret File on Black America, 1960–1972.* New York: Free Press, 1989.

Pearson, Hugh. *Shadow of the Panther: Huey Newton and the Price of Power in America.* New York: Perseus Books, 1994.

Perlstein, Rick. *Nixonland: The Rise of a President and the Fracturing of America.* New York: Scribner, 2008.

Raab, Selwyn. *Justice in the Back Room: The Explosive Story of Forced Confessions.* Cleveland: World Publishing, 1967.

Rosenthal, A. M. *Thirty-Eight Witnesses: The Kitty Genovese Case.* Brooklyn: Melville House, 2008.

Rucker, Walter, and James Nathanial Upton (eds.). *Encyclopedia of American Race Riots.* Westport, CT: Greenwood Press, 2006.

Seedman, Albert A., and Peter Hellman. *Chief!* New York: Arthur Fields Books, 1974.

Shakur, Assata. *Assata: An Autobiography.* Chicago: Lawrence Hill Books, 1987.

Shapiro, Fred C. *Whitmore.* Indianapolis: Bobbs-Merrill, 1969.

Shapiro, Fred C., and James W. Sullivan. *Race Riots: New York 1964.* New York: Thomas Y. Crowell Co., 1964.

Shecter, Leonard, with William Phillips. *On the Pad.* New York: G. P. Putnam's Sons, 1973.

Sheehy, Gail. *Panthermania: The Clash of Black Against Black in One American City.* New York: Harper & Row, 1971.

Silverman, Al. *Foster and Laurie.* New York: Little, Brown, 1974.

Tanenbaum, Robert K., and Philip Rosenberg. *Badge of the Assassin.* New York: Dutton, 1979.

Van Deburg, William. *New Day in Babylon: The Black Power Movement and American Culture, 1965–1975.* Chicago: University of Chicago Press, 1993.

Wolfe, Tom. *Radical Chic and Mau-Mauing the Flak Catchers.* New York: Farrar, Straus and Giroux, 1970.

Wright, Richard. *Native Son.* New York: Harper & Row, 1940.

Zimroth, Peter L. *Perversion of Justice: The Prosecution and Acquittal of the Panther 21.* New York: Viking, 1974.

PERIODICALS, ARTICLES, AND REPORTS

The newspaper and magazine articles used as source material for this book are cited individually in the chapter notes section. Most articles are drawn from the following publications: *New York Times, New York Daily News, New York Herald Tribune, New York Journal American, New York World Telegram & Sun, New York Post, Time, Newsweek, Muhammad Speaks, The Crisis, Liberator, Prison Life, City Journal, The East Village Other, Amsterdam News, Black Panther, The Militant, Ramparts, National Review,* and the *Village Voice.*

The findings of three governmental investigations informed the research and writing of this book. The U.S. Commission on Civil Disturbances (1968), which produced the Kerner Report, was formed by President Lyndon Johnson as a consequence of the riots in many U.S. cities between 1964 and 1968. Particularly in the wake of Martin Luther King Jr.'s assassination, the possibility of full-fledged racial insurrection in the country was looming on the horizon. To spearhead this commission Johnson turned to New York mayor John Lindsay, who was believed to have a good reputation with what was still commonly referred to as "the Negro community." The Kerner Report turned out to be one of the most lacerating critiques of the race problem in America. "Our nation is moving towards two societies, one black, one white—separate and unequal," stated the report. The Kerner Commission's conclusion that riots in the ghetto were the consequence of "white racism" was controversial. President Johnson's successor, Richard Nixon, used the report to formulate a countertheory that the "silent majority" who did not riot or engage in acts of civil disobedience were the true, neglected backbone of America.

Another source of information for this book was transcripts from U.S. congressional hearings into the activities of the Black Panther Party held in Washington, D.C., in 1970–71. Among others speaking before a congressional committee was FBI director J. Edgar Hoover. The hearings were primarily noteworthy for what they did not reveal and what would not be known publicly for the next five or six years: that the FBI had under way a covert counterintelligence investigation (COINTELPRO) into the lives of politically active African Americans that involved illegal wiretaps, unauthorized surveillance, harassment, and other violations of the U.S. Constitution.

One other report—the Knapp Commission Report on Police Corruption—was essential to the writing of this book and is cited where necessary in the text and also the chapter notes section.

DOCUMENTARIES, FEATURE FILMS, AND TELEVISON PROGRAMS

The Hate That Hate Produced (television documentary). Produced by and broadcast on CBS Television, 1959.

A Huey P. Newton Story (feature film). Director: Spike Lee. Written and performed by Roger Guenveur Smith, based on a one-man show by Roger Guenveur Smith. Produced by 40 Acres and a Mule, 1990.

Passin' It On (documentary). Director: John J. Valdez. Produced by the Independent Television Service. Broadcast on PBS Television, 1995.

Red Squad (documentary). Produced and directed by Pacific St. Film Archives: Howard Blatt, Steven Fischler, Francis Freedland, Joel Sucher. Pacific St. Film and Editing Co., 1971.

What We Believe, What We Want: The Black Panther Party Library (documentary). Presented by Roz Payne and Newsreel Films. A four-disc compilation that includes interviews with Panthers and former law enforcement agents, footage from key speeches and demonstrations, and three Newsreel documentary films: *Off the Pigs!*; *Mayday*; and *Repression*. AK Press Videos, 2006.

Revolution: Newark '67 (documentary). Producer/director: Marylou Tibaldo-Bongiorno. Broadcast on PBS Television, 2007.

The Battle of Algiers (feature film). Director: Gillo Pontecorvo. Produced and distributed in the United States by Allied Artists, 1967.

The Marcus-Nelson Murders (feature film for television). Executive producer and screenwriter: Abby Mann. Director: Joseph Sergeant. Produced by Universal Studio and broadcast on CBS Television, 1973.

American Experience: Malcolm X, Make It Plain (television documentary). Director: Orlando Bagwell. Produced by MPI Home Video and broadcast on PBS Television, 1994.

American Experience: Eyes on the Prize (documentary series). Director: Henry Hampton. Produced by PBS Home Video and broadcast on PBS Television, 1987.

Fun City Revisited: The Lindsay Years (documentary). Executive producer: Tom Casciato. Broadcast on PBS Television, 2010.

INSTITUTIONS

Archival research for this book took place at the following institutions: William Paley Center for Media (formerly known as the Museum of Television and Radio); the New York City Public Library (newspaper division); the New York City Municipal Archives; the Vanderbilt University Television News Archive, which can be accessed via their website; and the Schomburg Center for Research in Black Culture. The Schomburg Center has as part of its holdings the NAACP papers containing documents relevant to the Whitmore case, and also a file containing notes, minutes from meetings, strategy reports, and other documents from the Black Panther Party's influential Harlem branch.

COURT CASES

Many criminal proceedings involving key characters in this story are referenced throughout the book, and in some cases courtroom testimony is quoted from directly. The important cases are:

People v. Whitmore 1964 (Borrero assault and attempted rape trial I)

People v. Whitmore 1966 (Borrero II)

People v. Whitmore 1967 (Borrero III)

People v. Whitmore 1965 (Edmonds attempted rape and murder trial)

People v. Robles 1965 (Wylie-Hoffert double murder trial)

People v. Lumumba Shakur et al. 1969–71 (Panther Twenty-one conspiracy trial)

People v. Moore 1972 (Napier murder trial)

People v. Moore 1972 (Curry and Binetti attempted murder trial I)

People v. Moore 1973 (Curry and Binetti II)

People v. Moore 1973 (Curry and Binetti III)

People v. Phillips 1972 (Smith/Stango double murder and attempted murder trial I)

People v. Phillips 1974 (Smith/Stango II)

LAW ENFORCEMENT FILES AND DOCUMENTS

Formerly confidential FBI COINTELPRO files relating to the FBI's covert investigation of the Black Panther Party were perused as research for this book and are cited accordingly in the chapter notes. Also, NYPD Intelligence Division reports on the Black Power movement, including files of the Bureau of Special Services (BOSS), were essential, as were all files pertaining to OPERATION NEWKILL, the joint FBI-NYPD investigation that took place in 1971–72 after a series of shootings of police officers by members of the Black Liberation Army.

INDEX

as Whitmore supporter, 211
and Whitmore's arrest for gang fight, 190
Miranda decision, 170–71
Mississippi Freedom Democratic Party, 85
Mjuba (prisoner), 66, 67, 115
mock trials, Black Panthers, 303
Moore, Audrey Cyrus, 62–63, 141, 143, 179, 180
Moore, Collins, 62, 142–44, 179
Moore, Richard Earl. *See* Bin Wahad, Dhoruba al-Mujahid
Morris Houses (Bronx), 63
Morrisania housing projects (Bronx), 63, 179, 203
Moseley, Winston, 119
Mosque Number Seven (Harlem), 118, 232, 233, 366–67
Muhammad, Elijah, 113–14, 118, 232, 373
Muhammad Speaks newspaper, 67, 233
Murphy, Michael, 77
Murphy, Patrick V., 281–82, 323–24, 336, 344, 350, 351, 389
Murtaugh, John M., 283–84, 295, 299, 319, 321, 368, 369
Muslims
   and Mosque Number Seven, 366–67
   in prison, 66, 67, 115, 129, 373
   Whitmore's views about, 232, 233
   See also Nation of Islam
Myers, Twymon, 338, 380, 381

NAACP. *See* National Association for the Advancement of Colored People
NAACP Legal Defense Fund, 231, 276
Napier, Sam, 315, 316–19, 328, 333, 335, 337, 359–60
"narcotics eradication program" (BLA), 328
Nate (Whitmore's friend), 261–63, 275–76
Nation of Islam, 74–75, 113, 114, 115, 118, 232–34, 243, 366–67
National Association for the Advancement of Colored People (NAACP)
   Bin Wahad comments about, 319
   and Brooklyn Criminal Court incident, 242
   and Career Girls Murders, 127, 135
   and CCRB, 160
   and Evers murder, 30
   founding of, 133
   image of, 134
   King criticisms by, 134
   and Lindsay's reform initiatives, 160
   mission of, 133–34
   New York Black Panthers compared with, 213
   and police brutality, 128

pro bono legal activities of, 134
and Reiben-Miller disagreements, 167
tensions within, 133
and Whitmore case, 110–11, 112, 127, 128, 134–35, 145, 171, 172, 231
National Guard, 184, 199–200, 203, 220, 350
National Liberation Action (ALN), 314
National Review magazine, 85
National Urban League, 197
Negro: definition of, 245
Neuberger, Samuel, 192–93, 194, 195
New Haven, Connecticut: Black Panther rally in, 296–99
New Haven Railroad: "bombing" of, 278
New Jersey: Bin Wahad home in, 388
New Jersey Turnpike: Chesimard-police shootout on, 381
New Left, 246, 282
New York City
   Black Panthers in, 66–74, 204, 213–14, 225, 227–29, 246, 266–74, 287, 290, 291, 292, 296–97, 299–300, 301, 302, 314, 320, 321–22
   civil rights progress in, 69–70, 76, 393–94
   Cleaver's visit to, 246–47
   crime rate in, 393–94
   drugs in, 393
   effects of Newark riots on, 201
   elections in, 119–21
   image of, 394
   increase in crime in, 393
   in 1980s and 1990s, 393–94
   poverty in, 69–70, 74
   prevalence of drugs in, 27–28
   riots in, 70–77, 220–23
   segregation in, 82
   self-image of, 119
   Whitmore lawsuit against, 391
   See also specific person, topic or borough
New York Daily News, 12, 58, 59, 159, 163, 200, 255, 258, 278, 279, 280, 281, 318, 347
New York Herald Tribune, 30–31, 53, 58, 119, 120, 145, 151
New York magazine, 361
New York Police Department (NYPD)
   Alex interviews of, 348
   and Bin Wahad case, 386–87
   Bin Wahad civil lawsuit against, 388
   black liberation war with, 254, 314, 322–23, 332–33, 338–39, 347–48, 350–51, 360, 380–81, 388
   and Black Panthers, 226, 238–43, 266–74, 279–81, 301, 320, 360
   Buckley's influence on, 85

BOOKS BY T.J. ENGLISH

THE SAVAGE CITY
Race, Murder, and a Generation on the Edge

ISBN 978-0-06-182458-6 (paperback)

Through the stories of three desperate men—an innocent man wrongly accused of murder, a corrupt cop, and a militant Black Panther—T.J. English tells the story of race, violence, and urban chaos in 1960s New York City.

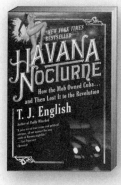

HAVANA NOCTURNE
How the Mob Owned Cuba . . . and Then Lost It to the Revolution

ISBN 978-0-06-171274-6 (paperback)

Havana Nocturne takes readers back to 1950s Cuba when it was a devil's playground for mob leaders, and shows how Fidel Castro trumped it all with the Cuban Revolution.

BORN TO KILL
The Rise and Fall of America's Bloodiest Asian Gang

ISBN 978-0-06-178238-1 (paperback)

T.J. English chronicles the gang of young Asian refugees—lost children of the Vietnam War—who laid the foundation for a terrifying underworld of violence and power in 1980s New York City.

PADDY WHACKED
The Untold Story of the Irish American Gangster

ISBN 978-0-06-059003-1 (paperback)

Paddy Whacked brings to life nearly two centuries of Irish American gangsterism, restoring the Irish American gangster to his rightful preeminent place in criminal history.